GRAND DUKE NIKOLAI NIKOLAEVICH

D1557066

Grand Duke

Nikolai Nikolaevich

SUPREME COMMANDER OF THE RUSSIAN ARMY

Paul Robinson

NIU Press / DeKalb, IL

© 2014, 2016 by Northern Illinois University Press

Published by the Northern Illinois University Press, DeKalb, Illinois 60115

First printing in paperback, 2016

all Rights Reserved

Design by Shaun Allshouse

Library of Congress Catalog[illegible] in-Publication Data

Robinson, Paul, 1966–

Grand Duke Nikolai Nikolaevich : Supreme Commander of the Russian Army /

Paul Robinson.

pages cm

ISBN 978-0-87580-734-8 (paper)

ISBN 978-0-87580-482-8 (cloth)

ISBN 978-1-60909-163-7 (e-book)

1. Nikolai Nikolaevich, Grand Duke of Russia, 1856–1929. 2. Generals—Russia—Biography. 3. World War, 1914–1918—Campaigns—Russia. 4. World War, 1914–1918—Campaigns—Eastern Front. 5. Nobility—Russia—Biography. I. Title.

DK254.N5R63 2014 940.4'1247092—dc23 [B] 2014002302

Table of Contents

Illustrations

List of Maps

List of Figures

Preface

The research for this book was made possible thanks to a generous grant, for which I am most grateful, from the Social Sciences and Humanities Research Council of Canada. Among other things, the grant enabled me to hire the services of several outstanding research assistants, to whom I wish to give special thanks: Irakli Gelukashvili, Alexandra Shirokova, Alfia Sorokina, and Andrea Beauvais. Other people to whom I owe a debt of gratitude are Alexandre and Christine Galitzine, both for sharing their personal archive and for their hospitality; François and Veronique Bouan du Chef du Bos for showing me around the Château de Choigny; Ginny and Luke Vania for accommodating me in Menlo Park; Sergei for arranging much of my travel in Russia; Pierre Bertrand for the maps; Adrian and Helen Taylor for looking after me during my travels in Europe and for finding me a copy of Prince Roman's memoirs; Richard Davies in Leeds for a boxful of Romanov-related books and for helping me with the quotations from Ivan and Vera Bunin; and of course Chione for her ceaseless support and editing.

Until the revolution of 1917, Russians used a different calendar from that of Western Europe. This meant that in the 19th century Russian dates were 12 days behind those of the West, and in the early 20th century, 13 days behind. To avoid any confusion, I give both dates; the old style first, the new style second in parentheses.

I have mainly followed the Library of Congress system for transliterating Russian words and names but with some adaptations (for instance *Pyotr*, not *Petr*), and making exceptions in cases where there is a widely recognized English alternative (thus *Wrangel*, not *Vrangel'*). For the names of tsars I have used the English equivalents—*Alexander* and *Nicholas*, not *Aleksandr* and *Nikolai*. In general, I have used the place names that Russians of the era would have recognized: thus *Lvov*, not *Lviv* or *Lemberg*. Again, I have made exceptions when there is a widely used English alternative—*Moscow*, not *Moskva*, etc.

Grand Duke Nikolai Nikolaevich

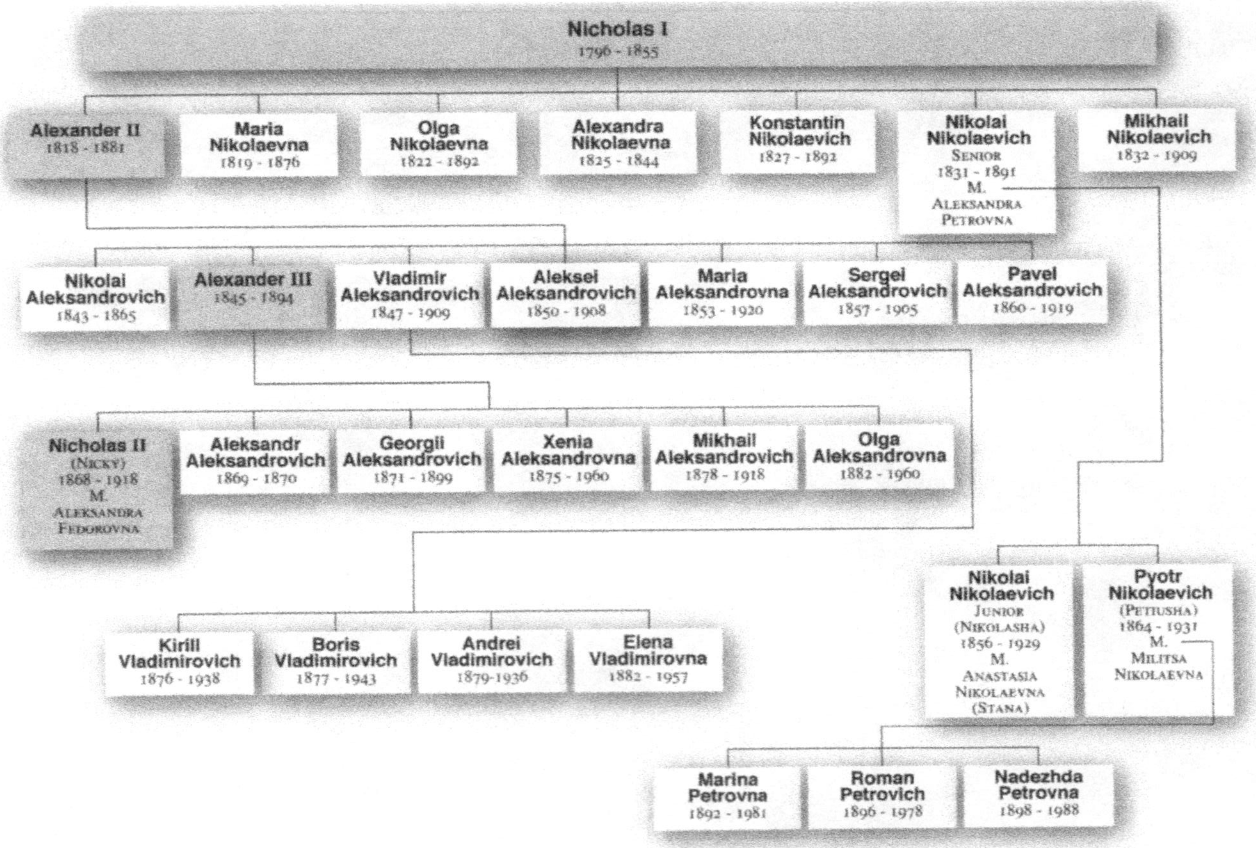
Nicholas I
1796 - 1855
Alexander II
1818 - 1881
Maria Nikolaevna
1819 - 1876
Olga Nikolaevna
1822 - 1892
Alexandra Nikolaevna
1825 - 1844
Konstantin Nikolaevich
1827 - 1892
Nikolai Nikolaevich
Senior
1831 - 1891
M.
Aleksandra Petrovna
Mikhail Nikolaevich
1832 - 1909
Nikolai Aleksandrovich
1843 - 1865
Alexander III
1845 - 1894
Vladimir Aleksandrovich
1847 - 1909
Aleksei Aleksandrovich
1850 - 1908
Maria Aleksandrovna
1853 - 1920
Sergei Aleksandrovich
1857 - 1905
Pavel Aleksandrovich
1860 - 1919
Nicholas II
(Nicky)
1868 - 1918
M.
Aleksandra Fedorovna
Aleksandr Aleksandrovich
1869 - 1870
Georgii Aleksandrovich
1871 - 1899
Xenia Aleksandrovna
1875 - 1960
Mikhail Aleksandrovich
1878 - 1918
Olga Aleksandrovna
1882 - 1960
Kirill Vladimirovich
1876 - 1938
Boris Vladimirovich
1877 - 1943
Andrei Vladimirovich
1879-1936
Elena Vladimirovna
1882 - 1957
Nikolai Nikolaevich
Junior
(Nikolasha)
1856 - 1929
M.
Anastasia Nikolaevna
(Stana)
Pyotr Nikolaevich
(Petiusha)
1864 - 1931
M.
Militsa Nikolaevna
Marina Petrovna
1892 - 1981
Roman Petrovich
1896 - 1978
Nadezhda Petrovna
1898 - 1988

Introduction

Six feet six inches tall, His Imperial Highness Grand Duke Nikolai Nikolaevich Romanov towered over those around him. Russians referred to him as "Big Nicholas," comparing him with "Little Nicholas," his first cousin once removed Tsar Nicholas II. The contrasting epithets reflected not just the two men's relative heights but also their moral stature. In the popular imagination, the Tsar was weak and indecisive, the Grand Duke strong and firm. To younger members of the Romanov family, he was *diadia groznyi*, "the terrible uncle," and in military circles before 1914 he was known as "the terror of the army."[1] During the First World War he acquired a remarkable popularity, which survived both the revolution and the subsequent civil war. "A legendary glory surrounded the personality of Grand Duke Nikolai Nikolaevich," wrote Russian historian Boris Kolonitskii in a recent study. "At the front servicemen literally worshipped [him]."[2]

From July 1914 to August 1915 the Grand Duke was Supreme Commander of the largest army in the world in the greatest war the world had ever seen. This was the culmination of a career that began when he was commissioned, at age 15, in 1872. In the following 40 years he served as Inspector General of Cavalry, Commander of the Guards and Petersburg Military District, and President of the Council of State Defense. The last of these appointments gave him responsibility for the defense and security policy of the entire Russian Empire. Displaced as Supreme Commander when the Tsar personally took charge of the army, he spent September 1915 to March 1917 as Viceroy of the Caucasus and Commander-in-Chief of the Caucasus Army. He was then briefly Supreme Commander again in March 1917.

The Grand Duke stood close to the center of political power. In 1889 he had become the commanding officer of the heir to the throne when the latter joined the cavalry as a junior officer. This established what was to become an extremely close relationship between the future Tsar Nicholas II and Grand Duke Nikolai Nikolaevich. Indeed, the Grand Duke, known to the Imperial family as "Nikolasha," was probably the person Nicholas II trusted more than anybody else and turned to for support in moments of crisis. In October 1905 Nicholas asked Nikolasha to assume the mantle of military dictator; instead, the Grand Duke persuaded Nicholas II to issue a Manifesto that promised the transformation of Russia's political system. The Grand Duke also had a role in introducing the Tsar and Tsarina to the infamous Rasputin.

Depictions of the Grand Duke tend to consist of either hagiographic praise by his admirers or vicious denunciations by his enemies. There is very little in between. This biography therefore aims to assess the Grand Duke in a more balanced fashion than has hitherto been the case.

In the eyes of many of the Grand Duke's contemporaries, he was a leader blessed with an extraordinarily strong will as well as considerable military talent. General A. A. Brusilov, who became famous for the so-called "Brusilov offensive" of 1916, remarked that the Grand Duke's appointment as Supreme Commander in 1914 "gave universal pleasure to the army, and, in my opinion, no better man could at that moment have been found for the post.... He was a man quite absorbed in his profession, who knew it both in theory and in practice.... His men trusted him as a leader, loved him, and feared him."[3] "He was a man on a grand scale, straight, and decisive,"[4] wrote General Iu. N. Danilov. Similarly, the British military attaché in Russia, General John Hanbury Williams, wrote in 1915 that "Throughout his Command the Grand Duke had shown himself a great soldier and at his dismissal he showed himself a very great gentleman."[5] Even the Grand Duke's enemies in the war showered him with praise. "The Grand Duke was really a great soldier and strategist," wrote the German general Erich von Ludendorff.[6]

On the other hand, General V. A. Sukhomlinov, who was the Russian Minister of War from 1909 to 1915, described the Grand Duke as "the evil genius" of the Russian monarchy.[7] General P. N. Shatilov, who observed him both in action, as Supreme Commander and as Viceroy of the Caucasus, and also later in exile, commented, "his image as a strong-willed and decisive commander did not correspond with his character"; on the contrary, his leadership was defined by "indecisiveness and the influence of others."[8] And the Russian émigré historian A. A. Kersnovskii claimed that the Grand Duke's strategic thinking "fluctuated like a weather vane in contradictory directions,"[9] while the Grand Duke himself was "a dilettante in strategy and an ignoramus in politics."[10]

The nature of Nikolai Nikolaevich's temperament caused as much dispute as evaluations of his professional abilities. Many considered him delightful. "The Grand Duke had a sunny charm, which won immediate allegiance, and he knew the secret of true friendship and companionship," wrote his adjutant's wife, Princess Julia Cantacuzen. "There existed a legend ... as to the Grand Duke's temper," she continued, "but in the ten or more years I knew him, it was certainly under perfect control."[11] "His servants loved him, his soldiers adored him, his officers honored him with absolute devotion, and he had warm frank friends and comrades, whom he treated as such, and who in return invariably trusted him," she asserted.[12] A British officer, Colonel Alfred Knox, similarly described the Grand Duke as "kindly and thoughtful."[13] And General G. O. von Raukh, who served under the Grand Duke for many years, remarked that his character was "polite, stable, and noble, but firm and definite." The stories of his rudeness, said Raukh, were "slander."[14]

Others, however, considered him "cruel and merciless."[15] The Grand Duke was "limited, uncultured, and wild," wrote A. A. Kireev in his diary. "The things you hear about him ... really, *une brute*!"[16] General N. A. Epanchin, who served as a corps commander in the First World War, agreed. "One can observe in his actions," he wrote, "an extreme irascibility, verging on fury, as well as a spiteful vengefulness."[17] Former Prime Minister Sergei Witte noted that Nikolai Nikolaevich "exercised considerable, and harmful, influence over the Emperor," and was mentally "unbalanced." "One cannot call the Grand Duke mad," Witte wrote, but "neither can one call him normal."[18]

In fact, Nikolai Nikolaevich was a more complex personality than either his supporters or detractors believed. He had undoubted military talent, and before 1914 was a zealous reformer of the Russian army, but his tenure as Supreme Commander ended in failure, for which his own deficiencies were in part to blame. He also lacked the will to power. In 1905, in 1917, and again during the 1920s, many of his countrymen regarded him as the man most able to save their country from chaos, the potential dictator they felt that Russia needed. It was a position the Grand Duke never wanted and rejected when it was offered. A traditional military man, he viewed his life as one of service to the state, not leadership of it. To misquote Rudyard Kipling, he was "the man who would not be king."

This book attempts to explain Nikolai Nikolaevich's popularity, which is something of a conundrum. The public enthusiasm for him raises important questions about the true state of public opinion in pre-revolutionary Russia, which perhaps was more patriotically inclined than historians have generally imagined. It is notable that when Nicholas II abdicated in March 1917, the Russian people repudiated neither the war nor even the Romanovs; one of the most popular men in Russia was in fact a Romanov, who represented war à l'outrance: Grand Duke Nikolai Nikolaevich.

The focus of exaggerated hopes for millions of Russians, Grand Duke Nikolai Nikolaevich was one of the foremost soldiers of his day. Despite this distinction, until now the only biography of him was one written by one of his former staff officers, General Danilov, in 1930.[19] Yet the character and actions of the man who led the Russian army in the First World War, and who had played a vital role in preparing it for war in the years beforehand, are of great significance. Using materials from archives in seven countries as well as a wealth of diaries and memoirs by the Grand Duke's contemporaries, this book evaluates his life and career. In the process, it includes a broader reassessment of issues such as bureaucratic politics and military reform in prewar Russia, the reasons for Russia's military defeats in 1914 and 1915, the causes of the Russian revolution, and the politics of the interwar Russian emigration.

CHAPTER 1

Education of a Soldier, 1856–1873

THE FAMILY INTO WHICH Nikolai Nikolaevich Romanov was born on 6 (18) November 1856, in the Winter Palace in Saint Petersburg was an unhappy one, although this would not become evident until some years later. The baby's father, Grand Duke Nikolai Nikolaevich Senior, and his mother, Grand Duchess Aleksandra Petrovna, greeted the arrival of their first child with joy.[1] On the day of his birth, the Emperor Alexander II hung cavalry insignia over the baby's crib[2] and formally enrolled him in His Majesty's Life Guards Hussar Regiment, as well as in the Life Guards Sapper Battalion and the Imperial Family's Fourth Rifle Battalion.[3] The young Grand Duke was thus a soldier from the very first day of his life, and in his heart he remained one until the day he died.

In this respect he was much like his father. A tall man with a "prominent, long thin nose,"[4] the older Grand Duke was a younger brother of Emperor Alexander II of Russia. Born on 21 July (2 August) 1831, he fought in the Crimean War,[5] and later became Supreme Commander of the Russian army during the war against Turkey in 1877 and 1878. His passions, which he passed on to his son, were the army, especially the cavalry, and country pursuits, in particular farming and hunting. One admirer, General N. A. Epanchin, described him in this way: "good, kind, sincere, courteous to the highest degree, he never offended anyone in his life, never did anybody any harm, he was a gentleman, a knight, in Russian a 'vitiaz' [knight/hero]."[6] Another witness gave this description of him: "A handsome man ... he was majestic, and attracted people to himself and was wholeheartedly loved by those close to him."[7] Others, though, were scathing in their criticism, especially of his professional military abilities. General M. D. Skobolev, a hero of the Russo-Turkish War of 1877–1878, told a British reporter that the Grand Duke "has about as much notion of conducting a campaign as I have of the differential calculus."[8] And when that war was over, persistent rumor had it that the Grand Duke had embezzled large sums of money while Supreme Commander, although a commission of inquiry subsequently found that he was merely guilty of exercising poor control over supplies.[9]

At the insistence of his parents, in February 1856 Nikolai Nikolaevich Senior, then aged 24, had married the 17-year-old Princess Aleksandra Petrovna Oldenburgskaia.[10] The Oldenburgskiis descended from kings of Norway, Sweden, and Denmark, and in the early 18th century had married into the Russian royal family. Duke Carl-Friedrich Holstein Oldenburg married Peter the Great's daughter Anna, who later became Empress of Russia. Their son subsequently became Emperor Peter III,[11] and their grandson Emperor Paul I. Paul I's daughter Ekaterina married back into the Oldenburgskii family in 1809 and her son was Aleksandra Petrovna's father, Pyotr Georgevich. Both Peter III and Paul I were notoriously unbalanced mentally. Some considered this an inherited family trait and ascribed Grand Duke Nikolai Nikolaevich Junior's excitable nature to his Oldenburg blood.[12]

The senior Grand Duke's bride, usually described as plain, extremely religious, and uninterested in appearances or high society, was hardly a fitting match for him. Although their first child was born just over nine months after their marriage, they had to wait seven years for the next one (Grand Duke Pyotr Nikolaevich, born in December 1863), and after that there were no more. Within about four years of his wedding, the senior Grand Duke began an affair with a ballerina, Ekaterina Gavrilovna Chislova, who bore him five illegitimate children. The relationship lasted the rest of the Grand Duke's life.

Despairing of happiness in her marriage, Aleksandra Petrovna eventually moved to Kiev and lived a separate life. She set up a hospital for the poor, founded the Pokrovskii Monastery in Kiev, and became a nun.[13] Prior to taking the veil, the Grand Duchess had suffered for many years from a leg ailment that left her unable to walk,[14] but, according to one story, the following occurred when she arrived at the monastery: "At four in the morning the nuns carried the immobile sick woman in their hands, but when they approached the gates, she stood up from her chair, went in and telegraphed the Emperor that God had performed a miracle and she 'had received her legs.'"[15]

Nikolai Nikolaevich Junior reportedly took his mother's side in the marital feud.[16] It would appear that in adulthood, the younger Grand Duke did not get on very well with his father.[17] Nevertheless, the surviving correspondence between father and son suggests a rather closer and warmer relationship in earlier years. Furthermore, Nikolai Nikolaevich Junior copied his father in most of his interests, above all his passions for the military, farming, and hunting. What he did take from his mother was a devout religiosity. As he admitted near the end of his life, "From the years of my childhood I acquired from my mother, the holy nun ANASTASIA [the name she took in the convent], the true Orthodox belief of the Russian people."[18]

All this lay in the future. Being a member of the Russian royal family meant frequent participation in ceremonies designed to display the wealth and power of the Romanov dynasty,[19] and shortly after his birth the young Grand Duke had his first public outing in the form of his baptism in the Winter Palace in Saint Petersburg. This was a full state occasion, attended by the Emperor and Empress, all of the Grand Dukes and Grand Duchesses, the Holy Synod of the Russian Orthodox Church, members of the State Council, ministers, ambassadors and their wives, generals and admirals, and members of the Imperial Court, carefully arranged in strict hierarchy. The Metropolitan of Novgorod and Saint Petersburg blessed the child with holy water, following which the guns of the Peter and Paul fortress on the other side of the Neva River fired 301 shots in salute, and the Emperor bestowed the order of Saint Andrew upon the infant Grand Duke.[20]

Within weeks, Nikolai Nikolaevich Junior fell seriously ill and came close to death. His doctors did not record the exact nature of the illness, which lasted from early February to early March 1857, but their notes leave no doubt as to its seriousness. On 6 (18) February, the doctor recorded that "the accumulation of gases in the stomach continues ... lots of phlegm in the chest." Thereafter, a dry cough "tortured the Grand Duke," until on 13 (25) February, the doctor recorded, "Today ... the condition of the Grand Duke is very serious.... Breathing 140. Pulse 140 to 160." This continued for another week, until by 23 February (12 March), the baby had begun to recover.[21] Given the rate of infant mortality in this era, this was a lucky escape.

We have little knowledge about the first five or six years of the Grand Duke's life. The next surviving record is a very formal little report he wrote, aged seven, to his father, on 22 April (4 May) 1864, in which he said, "I have the honor to report that the Emperor has seen fit to invite me to be with the Cossack brigade at the Imperial review taking place on 25 April, about which I most respectfully report to your Imperial Highness."[22]

Already by this age, the Grand Duke had acquired the nickname by which the rest of the royal family would know him all his life—Nikolasha (little Nicky). The name perhaps stuck because of its incongruousness—Nikolasha grew to be six and a half feet tall. In later years it also helped to distinguish him from Tsar Nicholas II, known as "Nicky." The Grand Duke happily adopted the nickname, often signing his personal letters simply "Nikolasha."

Like all members of the royal family, Nikolasha was educated at home.[23] Home was either the Nikolaevskii Palace in Saint Petersburg or another of his father's properties—the Znamenka Palace near Peterhof, or on occasion one of the senior Grand Duke's estates in the country, such as the one at Borisov in moder-day Belarus. Grand Duke Nikolai Nikolaevich Senior was

Grand Duke Nikolai Nikolaevich Junior aged four, 1861 (Private collection, France)

often away, and some of his son's letters to him during his absences have survived. They suggest an affectionate relationship between father and son and reveal an early interest in outdoor pursuits.

"Dear Papa," wrote the eight-year-old Nikolasha to his father on 17 (29) August 1865, "how are you? We miss you. Dear Papa, Mama and Petiusha [his brother Pyotr Nikolaevich] kiss you; it's boring at Znamenka since you left. We are all well, thanks to God. Goodbye dear Papa."[24] Four days later, he wrote again: "Dear Papa, what terrible weather we are having. Mama and Petiusha kiss you. How we miss taking those rides with you on horseback.... Goodbye, dear Papa. Your obedient son, Nikolai."[25] "Dear Papa," he wrote again on 24 August (5 September), "It is raining all the time here.... Two times we went for long walks. Vladimir Aleksandrovich went hunting with our hounds.... Uncle Misha kisses you.... Mama kisses you. Your obedient son, Nikolai."[26] And on 31 August (12 September), he wrote, "Dear Papa, all is well here. How are you? The weather here is now cold now hot. I will soon start studying three hours a day. We are going to Moscow and to my great pleasure will visit the zoo and especially the white bear. We are all, thanks to God, healthy.... Mama and Petiusha kiss you."[27]

On Christmas Day 1865, the nine-year-old Nikolasha presented a little poem to his father:

Almighty God
Full of grace
Hear my voice!
May God
Prolong the years
Of my much loved relative!
I have come to honor
My Papa with this greeting.
And may the Creator of men
And of happy days
Forgive his son.[28]

The religious tone reflected the attitudes of the era, but also perhaps maternal influence. Grand Duchess Aleksandra was said to have been a tender and loving parent, much concerned with the physical and moral development of her two sons. She insisted that they eat half a kilogram of fruit and vegetables a day and engage in regular physical exercise.[29] In an attempt to instill a degree of humility in her sons, she surrounded them with the children of ordinary servants.[30] This kind of exposure was not unheard of:

the sons and daughters of the Russian nobility were often brought up on estates where, isolated from other young people of the same age and social class, they mixed primarily with the servants. In some instances this practice forged a "feudal bond of affection" between master and servants, but the practice could also backfire, as "the servants were naturally afraid to discipline their master's children … [and] so tended to indulge them and let them have their way."[31] Certainly in the case of Nikolai Nikolaevich, close contact with servants does not seem to have produced the desired humility. The Grand Duke became notorious in later life for his harsh treatment of subordinates.

By the time he was 12, the young Grand Duke was spending a lot of time in the presence of the Emperor and Empress and enjoying the life at Court. "Dear Papa," he wrote on 18 (30) September 1869, "Thank you very much for your letter, which pleased me a lot.... I hope that your military maneuvers pleased you.… I, thank God, am well. I had a lot of fun at the balls, one time staying up to half past one, another time till three, and a third time till midnight. On the 29th we did a play, in which I participated.... It went very well and everybody was very happy." He noted that his mother was away from home (in what was by now a common refrain in their correspondence), but that he had just received four letters from her. He finished with with a reference to their frequent visits to the farm and time spent riding with the Emperor.[32]

Riding and dancing were not the only subjects occupying the young boy's time. There was also the serious matter of his academic education. Unfortunately, no record survives of what this consisted of or who taught him, but we can hazard a guess from what we know about the education of his peers. All Grand Dukes were tutored at home, in many cases by senior professors from Saint Petersburg's universities. Nikolai Nikolevich's cousins, the Grand Dukes Sergei Aleksandrovich, Konstantin Konstantinovich, and Dmitrii Konstantinovich, as well as the future Emperor Nicholas II, also received lessons from Konstantin Petrovich Pobedonostsev, a highly conservative believer in Russian autocracy, who instilled in his charges "an unquestioning belief in the inviolability of God, the Tsar and Russia."[33]

Nikolai Nikolaevich's education seems to have had a more military orientation than the average. His father's adjutants, many of whom went on to become generals, played an important role in his upbringing. Most important among these was Dmitrii Antonovich Skalon, a member of a distinguished military family that had produced numerous generals. Grand Duke Nikolai Nikolaevich Senior appointed Skalon as his son's main mentor, but it does not seem to have been a happy relationship. General V. A. Sukhomlinov, who was to become a bitter enemy of the younger Grand Duke, and is a far from reliable source, wrote many years later that "Skalon considered it his responsibility to struggle with all his might against the bad tendencies revealed in his ward. The insincerity, spitefulness and brutality of the young Grand Duke created a repulsive impression."[34] General G. O. von Raukh, although far more positively inclined to the Grand Duke than Sukhomlinov, did not altogether disagree. According to Raukh, as a young man Grand Duke Nikolai Nikolaevich Junior "was distinguished by a particular lack of self-restraint, harshness in his treatment of others, and arrogance, and in general lacked good humor. He himself ascribed many of these characteristics to the influence of his mentor General Skalon, whom he always remembered with disgust."[35]

Another tutor was General Ivan Fedorovich Tutolmin, a cavalry officer who had distinguished himself in the suppression of the Polish uprising of 1863–1864. In the later years of Nikolasha's youth Tutolmin arranged military soirées for him every Saturday with officers of the Petersburg garrison and the General Staff Academy; at these gatherings they discussed military subjects.[36]

The Grand Duke's education prepared him reasonably well to be a junior army officer, but it lacked any practical training in politics and statecraft because he was not expected to participate in the formation of state policy. The destiny laid out for him was that of a military officer, and law and politics were not on the curriculum at any of the military institutions where he trained. Once the Grand Duke rose to senior positions in which political understanding was necessary, this lack of knowledge became problematic.

The Grand Duke did at least see some of the continent beyond Russia. As a boy, he traveled occasionally to Western Europe, most often to France, where members of the Russian royal family regularly spent their holidays on the Riviera.[37] Nikolai Nikolaevich Junior became decidedly Francophile. He was fluent in French and spoke good German.[38] By contrast, he had only a "slight knowledge of English."[39]

In June 1871, at age 14, he took the next step in his education, entering the Nikolaevskii Engineering School.[40] He was, strictly speaking, too young for the school, which was meant for young men between 17 and 28 years of age who had already graduated from high school or its equivalent (such as a military cadet corps) and wished to be commissioned as officers in the Russian army.[41] However, Nikolasha was on an accelerated track for fast promotion.

Founded as part of a reform of the Russian army after the Crimean War, the military schools are considered by historians to have been "some of the most progressive sources of education in the empire."[42] Students at the Nikolaevskii Engineering School were subject to military regulations and discipline. At the end of two years of study they became commissioned officers. The general part of the curriculum included physical education, classes in the Russian language and Russian literature, and two foreign languages. The students were meant to master one of the languages fluently and acquire an elementary knowledge of the other. The practical part of the curriculum included fortifications, mining, military topography, construction, railways, and telegraphs. Cadets also had to learn horseback riding, dancing, fencing, and gymnastics. A summer camp enabled them to practice their skills in the field.[43]

There is no record of whether Nikolai Nikolaevich lived at the School with the other cadets, or whether he lived at home and merely attended classes. Given his status and relative youth, the latter seems more probable. Also, even though the program of the School was meant to last two years, he graduated after only one year, in yet another sign of his privileged status. At the end of May 1872, the Grand Duke left the School to join a training battalion, and a few weeks later, on 5 (17) July 1872, he received his commission and became a Second Lieutenant, at the youthful age of 15 1/2. His trajectory in life had already been set, as had his core beliefs and his character. His upbringing had provided little exposure to anything outside of the army, the Orthodox Church, and the royal family, and no reason to question any of those or his place within them. The motto of the Russian amy, "For Faith, Tsar, and Fatherland," encapsulated his beliefs well.

The Grand Duke's Orthodoxy rested on a belief in divine intervention, fate, miracles, and the importance of ritual. He had a fatalistic view of the world and regarded everything that happened as God's will. He believed in the miraculous powers of icons and the power of prayer to summon God to intervene on one's behalf, and he was susceptible to the claims of special powers from supposed "holy men." The social message of Christianity was decidedly secondary. Father Georgii Shavelskii, who during the First World War was chief chaplain of the Russian army and who in that capacity was at the Grand Duke's right hand for 12 months in 1914 and 1915, commented that the Grand Duke "believed strongly; religion with prayer was a necessity of his soul, of his style of life; he continually felt himself to be in God's hands. However, one must say that at times he was blindly religious.... For the Grand Duke the center of religion consisted of a supernatural, miraculous force, which one could summon to earth by prayer. The moral side of religion, demanding sacrifice, achievement, self-improvement—this side somehow faded into the background of his consciousness."[44]

The Grand Duke's religion converged with his belief in Tsarism. In the late 19th century, Russia remained an autocracy, in which the Tsar's powers were in theory absolute, reflecting the view that he was God's anointed ruler. Nikolai Nikolaevich fully accepted this view. As Shavelskii noted, "the Grand Duke grew up in an atmosphere of worship of the Sovereign."[45] The Grand Duke "was brought up in a strictly religious spirit, I would go further and say a religious-mystical ecstasy," agreed General Danilov. "His religion was closely connected to his understanding of the divine origin of Tsarist power in Russia and his inner conviction that, through his anointing, the Russian Tsar received some sort of special secret strength, placing him in terms of state reason in a position which was unattainable for others."[46]

In his youth and into his middle age Nikolai Nikolaevich was therefore a convinced supporter of the autocracy. General Raukh commented, "Grand Duke Nikolai Nikolaevich was the most loyal subject of all the subjects of the Sovereign Emperor Nicholas II; this was not blind worship of his Tsar, but a sense of loyalty carried to extremes; as a result one feeling dominated over everything else, that it was necessary to preserve the Tsar, to save the Tsar; Russia did not exist, he did not think about her—all his thoughts were concentrated on the Tsar alone, who *at that time* was *everything* for him."[47]

The Grand Duke held a correspondingly traditional view of military-civil relations and thought that soldiers should not only refrain from interfering in politics but also withhold their political views. Julia Cantacuzen, a granddaughter of American President Ulysses S. Grant who had married one of the Grand Duke's adjutants, commented that the Grand Duke "studiously avoided" politics "and demanded the same attitude from his court."[48]

The Grand Duke repeatedly proclaimed that he had no knowledge of civilian affairs, and "no opinions on these issues." "I don't understand civilian questions at all," he would say.[49] In this way, he was very like other Russian army officers of his time. As one historian has written, "What is most striking about the Imperial Russian Officer of the latter part of the nineteenth century is that he was apolitical."[50] This produced "immense political naivete."[51]

Nikolai Nikolaevich's cousin Grand Duke Aleksandr Mikhailovich recounted meeting him for the first time at a dinner in the Winter Palace. "All during dinner," he wrote, "Nikolasha kept such an erect position that I expected each moment to hear the bars of the National Anthem."[52] Like many military men, the Grand Duke exuded confidence, which he knew how to display even when suffering intense internal doubts. General Danilov recounted that on first meeting him, he was struck by "the thin, thoroughbred features of his face, his clear speech which articulated every word, and finally by his general self-confidence."[53]

However, various critics believed that observers confused loud words and a sharp temper with decisiveness. Shavelskii, for instance, considered that the Grand Duke's "decisiveness collapsed when serious danger began to threaten him." "In the face of great misfortunes he either fell into a panic or swam with the tide."[54] The émigré historian A. A. Kersnovskii concurred that "Impetuous and extraordinarily abrupt, the Grand Duke created the impression of a strong-willed man. But this impression was purely external. Not only did he lack a strong will, but he was all the time entirely in the power of those around him."[55] In the early 1920s exiled politician V. V. Musin-Pushkin would tell another Russian émigré, "I have known Nikolai Nikolaevich since childhood, and we call each other 'ty' [a sign of close friendship]. His character, and, as you call it, his strong-willed characteristics are well known to me. These strong-willed qualities are nothing other than extensive use of Grand Ducal irresponsibility. All his life he has been under the influence of others."[56]

Certainly the Grand Duke's external confidence hid an excitable nature. Danilov noticed the Grand Duke's "jerky movements and nervous, but always deeply sincere speech."[57] "Nervous movements," continued Danilov, "were the Grand Duke's constant companion."[58] Empress Aleksandra Fedorovna, who hated the Grand Duke, complained of "his loud voice & gesticulations."[59] His temper was notorious, although by his late middle age he seems to have learned to control it. The Grand Duke was reputed to be coarse and rude, not merely because he often lost his temper but also because he used parade ground language. His enemies told stories of vicious cruelty, including accounts of Nikolai Nikolaevich slicing off the head of one of his prized Borzoi dogs with a saber,[60] and beating the eyes out of the sockets of another with a riding crop.[61]

The sources for these stories are decidedly biased and unreliable, but the fact that the anecdotes circulated suggests that they had some resonance among the Grand Duke's contemporaries. However, despite this apparent reputation of the young Grand Duke as a spoiled, arrogant aristocrat with a violent temper, a wide circle of acquaintances knew him as considerate, polite, and charming. His royal upbringing had taught him how to be courteous. General Aleksandr Spiridovich, who was in charge of the personal security of Tsar Nicholas II, observed that Nikolai Nikolaevich "had manners which recalled the far distant epoch of the Emperor Alexander II."[62] A. F. Rediger, who first met the Grand Duke when he joined his training battalion after graduating from the Nikolaevskii Engineering School, and who subsequently became Minister of War, commented that the Grand Duke "had an explosive character, but I always saw him being impeccably polite with everybody."[63] As Julia Cantacuzen described it, the Grand Duke was "always full of understanding, ever helpful and generous to those in trouble, and as loyal to those below as to the Sovereign over him.... He had a trick of voice and manner and of smile, which made those around him feel individually flattered by what seemed to be his entire attention."[64]

Certainly, he was extremely faithful to those who won his favor. "The Grand Duke was firm in his sympathies and friendship," wrote Shavelskii. "If somebody, who had served under his leadership or with him, won his trust ... then the Grand Duke would remain his defender and protector forever."[65] The problem with this was that "having attached himself to somebody, he remained faithful to him to the end, and in particular was afraid of changing his closest assistants, closing his eyes to their sometimes serious defects."[66]

He extended this loyalty to both family and colleagues. According to Julia Cantacuzen, Nikolai Nikolaevich "brought up his younger brother and cared for the family of his morganatic half brothers and sisters. One of these sisters married our cousin Cantacuzen and I know that she was devoted to Nikolai Nikolaevich. They loved him a lot. His friends in the officers' club, to whom he was evidently also strongly attached, were captivated by him too."[67] Nikolasha's relationship with his brother, Pyotr Nikolaevich, was by all accounts extremely close. Because of the seven-year gap between them, the two brothers had little in common in their younger days, but once Pyotr Nikolaevich married and settled into the Znamenka palace outside Saint Petersburg, Nikolai Nikolaevich stayed regularly with him and the two became inseparable,[68] to the extent that during the First World War Nikolai Nikolaevich took his brother with him wherever he went. General Danilov commented that Pyotr Nikolaevich worshipped Nikolasha,[69] and Robert Rutherford McCormick, the editor and owner of the *Chicago Tribune*, who met both men in 1915, observed "the personal devotion of one brother to another."[70]

Just as observers differed in their views of Nikolai Nikolaevich's personality, so too did they vary in their opinions of his intelligence. Empress Mariia Fedorovna, wife of Emperor Alexander III and mother of Emperor Nicholas II, had a low opinion of him. "He suffers from an incurable sickness," she allegedly said, "he is stupid."[71] A. A. Kireev considered him "an idiot."[72] And General M. D. Bonch-Bruevich stated that Nikolai Nikolaevich was "not very bright," though he was cleverer than Nicholas II.[73]

Others were more positive. General Rediger wrote that the Grand Duke "was gifted with a lot of common sense, grasping the essence of every question extraordinarily quickly.... He possessed a huge memory."[74] Georgii Shavelskii similarly commented that "the Grand Duke's mind was shrewd and quick. The Grand Duke immediately grasped the thread of a conversation and the essence of the matter and then stated his opinion and decision, which was sometimes very original and always interesting and lively."[75] General A. A. Polivanov, Minister of War from June 1915 to March 1916, who later joined the Red Army and thus had no incentive to praise the Grand Duke in his memoirs, nevertheless wrote in them that Nikolai Nikolaevich possessed "correct strategic and tactical opinions, and an ability to quickly recognize the situation in maneuvers on the map."[76] And General Raukh wrote in his diary that "the Grand Duke is not intelligent, but you are often struck by his sober and correct view of things."[77]

As these more laudatory views came from people who knew the Grand Duke and his work much more closely than did his detractors, one can probably conclude that he was not the "idiot" that Kireev considered him to be. While he may not have been exceptionally intelligent, he was certainly bright enough by the standards of 19th-century military officers and more than capable of fulfilling the responsibilities of high command. Nevertheless, it appears that his mind was undisciplined and he was prone to impetuous decisions. After working under the Grand Duke for some years, Raukh realized that it was dangerous to brainstorm with him and throw out fresh ideas that had not been fully thought through: Nikolai Nikolaevich was liable to seize upon new ideas and demand that they be enacted,[78] and once he had made a decision, it could be difficult to persuade him to change his mind.

A second flaw cited by those who knew him was that he was not intellectually curious. This was a trait fairly typical of military officers of this period, particularly in the Russian army, whose "dominant mood was anti-intellectual."[79] Nikolai Nikolaevich was also a bit lazy. As General A. A. Brusilov, who actually thought quite highly of his abilities, put it: "As a member of the Imperial Family, his exalted position had disinclined him to hard work, especially in his youth."[80] Thus, wrote Shavelskii, "the Grand Duke was never capable of dirty, painstaking, prolonged work."[81] Rediger noted that Nikolai Nikolaevich "absolutely couldn't spend time reading things, as a result of which one had to report to him orally."[82] Overall, said Rediger, "the Grand Duke was a very strong personality: intelligent, dedicated entirely to affairs, a soldier in his soul, energetic, he just wasn't used to working, as a result of which he fell under the influence of those who were reporting to him."[83] Rediger concluded that the Grand Duke needed a strong right-hand man who could do his dirty work and who could also report honestly to him on all sides of an issue so that he could make an objective decision.[84] When he had subordinates who merely gave him one option to consider, he fell under their control.

Most of this remained to be discovered in 1872, when Nikolai Nikolaevich left the Nikolaevskii Engineering School to start his military career. What was clear was that the young Grand Duke had embraced his destiny as a soldier. His path in life was determined, and it would culminate with him at the head of an army of 6 million men.

CHAPTER 2

First Shots, 1873–1878

ON 27 APRIL (9 MAY) 1873, by now a 16-year-old second lieutenant, Nikolai Nikolaevich joined a cavalry training squadron.[1] Under normal circumstances, upon completion of the training period a young officer joined his regiment. Instead, in October 1873 the Grand Duke entered the Nikolaevskii General Staff Academy, becoming the first member of the Russian royal family to study there.

Entrance to the Academy was highly competitive. Between 1882 and 1906 it graduated only 1,792 officers.[2] Would-be staff officers took a preliminary examination at the headquarters of their local military district. If they passed this, they were then excused from duty for four months to study for the entrance examinations, which were held in August of every year. Subjects included "regulations for the branches of service and the economy of the regiments; tactical knowledge of all arms of the military; artillery from explosives to ballistics; fortifications ranging from permanent to temporary; mathematics up to trigonometry; military administration and the organization of the army; political history, both global and Russian, from the ancients to 1815; physical and political geography; and comprehensive examinations in the Russian, French, and German languages."[3] Of the approximately 1,500 officers who took the preliminary examination each year only about 150 won a place at the Academy.[4]

Whether the Grand Duke deserved to be among this elite is not clear. A short biography distributed many decades later by his personal office suggests that he did indeed take these entrance exams, since it claims that he passed them.[5] However, rumor had it that strings were pulled in his favor. Some 30 years after the event, the French military attaché in Saint Petersburg, Colonel Moulin, claimed that the Grand Duke "passed the examinations of the Staff Academy in front of a special commission (and a very indulgent one, of course)."[6] It seems likely that the Grand Duke had to meet at least some minimum standards, but very possibly not the same ones that applied for everybody else.

He clearly did not meet the normal entrance requirements. The Academy was for officers with at least four years' commissioned service, holding a rank of at least first lieutenant for officers of the Guard and captain for others.[7] Nikolai Nikolaevich had only been an officer for one year when he took the examinations and was only a second lieutenant. He was considerably younger and more junior than his classmates. It would appear that he did not take all of his classes at the Academy with the other students but studied at home and only attended some of the lectures and the examinations.[8]

The curriculum of the Academy lasted two years for all students, with an additional third year for those who had performed well enough. Students attended lectures from September to April and then participated in field exercises in the summer. Classes fell under three main headings: military art, which included tactics, strategy, and military history from ancient times through to the Franco-Prussian war of 1870–1871; geodesy, topography, and cartography; and military administration and military statistics, which included "the organization and equipping of troops, military economy and ... administration and supply of the army in wartime" and an analysis of the military capabilities of Russia's neighbors.[9] Students also had to take equestrian training and language classes in Russian, French, and German.[10]

Examinations at the end of each year determined whether students passed on to the next year. In the third year the surviving students had to pass two oral examinations, one on military history and the other on the art of war. They were expected "to make independent theoretical deductions supported by facts from recent wars, or to carry out comparative research about the theoretical and practical solutions of the given problem in other European armies."[11] Third-year students also had to write a research paper in which they resolved a specific strategic problem. For this they had to "study the topography and resources of a given locality,... independently draw up a plan of action,... and finally draft all the measures required to bring the chosen plan to fulfillment." This was considered the "most difficult, but also the most useful part of the studies of the additional year."[12]

Only 25 of Nikolai Nikolaevich's class managed to reach the third year.[13] Among them was the Grand Duke himself, whose final marks ranked him third in his cohort, as a result of which he was one of three officers awarded a silver medal and the inscription of his name on the marble wall of honor.[14] It is hard to tell whether this was merited. One of the other winners of a silver medal that year was A. F. Rediger, who commented that it was very unusual for three people to be so rewarded, as the medals were rarely given out and normally the maximum was two.[15] However, Rediger displayed no indignation about the Grand Duke's prize and did not suggest that it was undeserved. In any case, three years at the Staff Academy would certainly have left the Grand Duke very well prepared for life among the elite of the Russian army.

Nikolai Nikolaevich formally graduated from the Academy in April 1876 and was promoted to the rank of staff captain (he had become a first lieutenant shortly after starting at the Academy in November 1873).[16] By this time war was brewing in the Balkans, and soon it would draw in Russia and the young Grand Duke.

Revolts had broken out against Ottoman rule in Bosnia-Herzegovina in 1875 and in Bulgaria in 1876. The Ottoman Empire put down the Bulgarian revolt with great brutality, with the result that many in Christian Europe began to demand what nowadays would be termed a "humanitarian intervention." The European powers, including Russia, demanded that the Ottoman Empire reform its political system under European supervision and grant autonomy to Bosnia-Herzegovina.[17] To pressure the Ottoman Empire to accept these proposals, the Russians began a military buildup along the Russian border with Romania, threatening to move through Romania into Ottoman-held Bulgaria should the Ottoman Empire refuse their demands.

Emperor Alexander II gave Grand Duke Nikolai Nikolaevich Senior command of the Russian army as it prepared for war. The Grand Duke set up his headquarters in Kishinev, in modern-day Moldova, and on 18 (30) November, his 20-year-old son, newly promoted to the rank of full captain, was appointed a member of his staff. Nikolasha does not seem to have had a great deal to do in Kishinev and complained regularly of boredom. On 29 November (11 December) 1876, he wrote this to his brother:

> Dearest Petiusha! Dear brother!
>
> Many thanks for your letter. I was sincerely touched by it. It will mean a lot to me and be very nice if you will sometimes write to me. I myself particularly don't like writing, especially doing so often, so I ask you, dear brother, to write only when you want to, and only then will it be nice to receive your letters, which I will know you have written without any compulsion, because you want to. I am very happy that you enjoy riding on my horses, ride them whenever and as often as you want, the more you do so, the happier I will be. It is terribly boring in Kishinev.
>
> I am pleased that you have started to learn chess, which is the very best game. I advise you, my dear brother, to learn to play this game, but for God's sake never learn to play cards. After supper we will be playing chess. It is very enjoyable.
>
> May God preserve you.[18]

Two weeks later, on 12 (24) December, Nikolasha wrote again to his brother, this time with bad news: their father was seriously ill.[19] Six days later, Nikolai Nikolaevich sent another letter to his brother: "I sincerely thank you for your dear letters," he wrote, "every letter which I receive from you gives me great pleasure. It's terribly boring here, added to which Papa has been sick. We have lived through some very difficult days, as Papa was very *dangerously* ill, but now, thanks to God, Papa is noticeably beginning to improve, and his strength is returning."[20] On Christmas Day, Nikolasha received a telegram from Pyotr Nikolaevich, to which he replied, "It's terribly boring here. Our lives have been made even more boring because of Papa's illness. Papa's health is a lot better, but it's hard to say when he will get completely better. God grant that it be soon! I am exploiting the good weather to go riding for a few hours each day and often remember you."[21]

Presents from Pyotr arrived soon after, and Nikolasha sent another letter on 2 (14) January thanking him for them: "I thank you with all my heart for your dear presents and your letter. You gave me great pleasure and deeply touched me. The pipe is charming and the wallet *perfect*, just what I wanted.... It's terribly boring here.... I'm continuing to ride every day.... Today I'm going to greet the Guards on behalf of Papa on the occasion of the birthday of their commander Aleksei Aleksandrovich. Goodbye, dear Petiusha. With a warm embrace."[22]

"Have you been riding my horse?" he asked on 22 January (3 February), "I ride every day.... There is still nothing new for us in Kishinev.... Papa, thank God, is improving rapidly."[23] This was just as well, as war was approaching and the army needed its commander to be in good health. Meanwhile, Nikolasha's inactivity was coming to an end. According to his service record, in March 1877 he returned to Saint Petersburg as a courier to the Emperor and then traveled on to Germany, this time carrying the Emperor's greetings to the Kaiser.[24]

We have no information about when Nikolasha made it back to the army from Germany, but it was certainly by 10 (22) April, as on that date he met the Emperor at Zhmerinka in Ukraine. From there they traveled together to Tiraspol, where they joined Grand Duke Nikolai Nikolaevich Senior. On 12 (24) April, the Emperor addressed his troops and formally declared war on the Ottoman Empire.[25] The same day, troops of the Russian army began crossing the river Prut, which marked the boundary between Russia and Romania, and advanced south toward Bulgaria.

On 1 (13) May, Grand Duke Nikolai Nikolaevich Junior followed the army into Romania, after which his father sent him off to reconnoiter the river Danube,[26] which was the first large barrier standing in the way of the Rus-

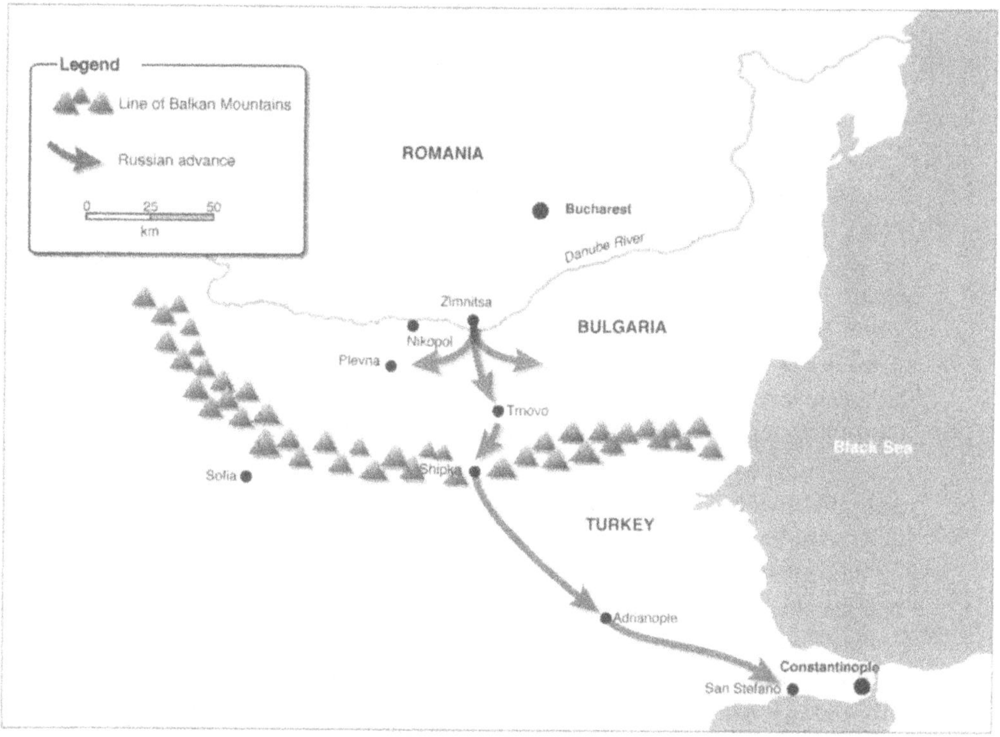

Map 1: The Russo-Turkish War, 1877–1878

sian army. By mid-June, the Russians were ready to force a crossing and chose to do so at Zimnitsa, opposite the town of Sistova. Around Sistova the southern bank of the Danube is steep, but two miles below the town there is a narrow depression. This provided a suitable location for a landing, for which reason the Ottoman army was defending it heavily with infantry and artillery.[27] It was here that the Russians attacked on the morning of 15 (27) June 1877 and that Grand Duke Nikolai Nikolaevich Junior received his first taste of combat.

The assault across the Danube began at about ne in the morning on 15 (27) June. The Ottoman troops were alert, and despite the cover of darkness the Russian pontoons soon came under fire. Nevertheless, most of the Russians made it to the far shore and began pushing the Ottoman forces back. The Russians then advanced up the heights behind Sistova, drove off the Ottomans, and captured the town. By the end of the day, 25,000 Russians were across the river and the southern bank was firmly in their hands.[28] Considering their task, Russian casualties were quite light, about 1,000 killed and wounded.[29] British war correspondent Archibald Forbes reported that "Among the slightly wounded was the young Grand Duke Nicholas Nicolaievitch,"[30] but if this was so, the wound must have been very slight as no other source makes any mention of it.

According to a popular account of the crossing of the Danube, Nikolai Nikolaevich urged his fellow soldiers not to duck when his boat came under heavy fire. "Lads!" he supposedly told them, "whether you bow to the bullets or not, those who are meant to live won't be touched, but those who are not meant to will receive no mercy."[31] There is no evidence to support this story, although it is entirely in keeping with the Grand Duke's fatalistic worldview. Another British war correspondent, Francis Stanley, reported that Nikolai Nikolaevich Junior did not cross the river until "victory was well assured,"[32] while yet another account states that he did not join in the main assault but helped supervise the embarking of the troops onto their pontoons, crossing only after most of the troops were already on the other side of the river.[33] He later went back to the Russian side of the Danube and met his father, who "embraced and kissed his son" and sent him off to report to the Emperor.[34] Nikolai Nikolaevich Junior was spotted by the correspondent of the London *Daily News*, who reported that "as we were passing the rear of the guns, the Grand Duke Nicholas the younger, son of the Commander-in-Chief, rode off from the battery to greet our general.... The young Grand Duke had been across the Danube and was in high spirits at the success of the enterprise."[35]

The Grand Duke's first combat mission had been a great success. On the following day, 16 (28) June, he received the cross of Saint George fourth class for "distinction in the battle during the crossing of the Danube at Zimnitsa and the seizure of the Sistova heights."[36]

From Sistova the Russians marched southeast toward the town of Biela, where they were blocked by a large Ottoman force. Rebuffed, they moved south to the town of Trnovo and set about securing their right flank by surrounding the Ottoman fortress of Nicopolos, which they took on 3 (15) July 1877. From there, they advanced southwest toward Plevna, but an attempt to seize that town on 8 (20) July failed. A large Ottoman army under Osman Pasha now occupied Plevna, and the Russian advance ground to a halt.[37]

To clear the way for an eventual advance to Constantinople, the Russians needed to secure the Bulgarian mountain passes that blocked the route south. To do this, at the beginning of July Grand Duke Nikolai Nikolaevich Senior dispatched an advance guard of about 5,800 infantry and 5,000 cavalry under General I. V. Gurko with instructions to reconnoiter the roads into the mountains, seize the passes, and if possible push forward and raise a revolt among the Bulgarian population.[38]

On 1 (13) July, as Gurko set out from Trnovo, two junior staff officers joined his detachment: Grand Duke Nikolai Nikolaevich Junior and Captain P. K. Gudim-Levkovich. According to one particularly hostile source, Gurko was not overly impressed with his new charges. Gudim-Levkovich turned up late, while Nikolai Nikolaevich managed to lead a column in the wrong direction due to some poor map-reading.[39] Whether this was true or not, the Grand Duke's assignment to the advance guard enabled him to experience one of the more dramatic episodes of the Russo-Turkish War.

Having set out from Trnovo, Gurko advanced rapidly southward to seize one of the key routes through the mountains, the Shipka Pass. His plan was for a force under General N. I. Sviatopolk-Mirskii to make a feint against the northern end of the pass, while he attacked it from the other side. On 5 (17) July, Sviatopolk-Mirskii split his troops into three columns and attacked the pass. The general led the central column, with Nikolai Nikolaevich accompanying him.[40] Reaching their destination required a long, tiring climb. Finally at about three in the afternoon, Sviatopolk-Mirskii and the Grand Duke reached a position from which they could see the Ottoman defenses. At that point, they came under fire from two lines of enemy trenches, a blockhouse and a redoubt. A firefight then ensued which lasted until seven in the evening, at which point the Russians retreated.[41]

The attack's failure did not matter, given that it was only a feint. The next day Gurko seized the Shipka Pass from the southern end. This was a crucial victory, not only because it cleared the way for an eventual advance toward Constantinople but also because it blocked the route of Ottoman reinforcements coming from the south who hoped to link up with Osman Pasha's force at Plevna. For his part in the capture of the Shipka Pass, Grand Duke Nikolai Nikolaevich Junior received a golden sword, inscribed with the words "For Bravery."[42]

At some point in August, Nikolasha rejoined his father outside Plevna. He was present during a four-day artillery battle from 26 to 29 August (7 to 11 September),[43] at the end of which the Russians attempted to storm the Ottoman defenses. The result was a catastrophic failure. Despite the great Russian advantage (84,000 Russian and Romanian troops facing only 36,000 Ottomans), the Russians were driven off with great losses, suffering over 15,000 casualties.[44] It was clear that Plevna could not be taken by storm. The Russians therefore settled on a new strategy—siege—gradually tightening the noose around Plevna until it was entirely cut off from outside, and then seeking to starve it into submission.

Throughout September and most of October, Grand Duke Nikolai Nikolaevich Junior remained with his father, who was besieging Plevna, and (according to his service record) participated in a three-day reconnaissance of the Ottoman defenses with his father in early September. Promoted on 10 (22) September to the rank of colonel at the youthful age of 20, he joined in another reconnaissance later in the month, this time with General E. I. Totleben, an expert in siege warfare, who had arrived to take command of the operations against Plevna.[45] In late October, as the siege of Plevna dragged on, his father, for reasons unknown, sent him to Saint Petersburg, where it seems he remained for several weeks before returning to duty in the Balkans in January 1878.

By this time, the military situation had shifted dramatically in Russia's favor. On 27 November (9 December) Osman Pasha had made a desperate attempt to break out of Plevna. This attempt having failed, Osman and his army surrendered.[46] Grand Duke Nikolai Nikolaevich Senior decided to waste no time in exploiting the situation and launched a winter campaign to bring the war to a rapid end. It was a stunning success. On 28 December 1877 (9 January 1878), the Russian army crushed the Ottomans at the battle of Shipka-Sheinovo, clearing the route to the Ottoman capital.[47] Constantinople now appeared to be within the Russians' grasp.

On 9 (21) January Nikolasha sent his brother birthday greetings from Bucharest.[48] Two days later he crossed through the Shipka Pass to join the army on the other side.[49] On 13 (25) January, he linked up with his father,[50] and on the next day father and son arrived at Adrianople.[51] Nine days later, a Prussian officer spotted Nikolasha attending a celebratory dinner for the officers of the Russian Eighth Army Corps. He was, wrote the Prussian some 15 years later, "a tall, handsome, and dignified young man, but even then as arrogant and distant as he still is."[52]

By 31 January (12 February), father and son were at San Stefano, just outside the walls of Constantinople. The Ottoman Empire was now at the Russians' mercy, and that same day it agreed to an armistice, bringing the fighting to an end. On 14 (26) March, both Grand Dukes sailed by yacht to Constantinople, where they met Sultan Abdul Hamid in the Dolmabahce Palace.[53] The next day, they toured Constantinople, but Grand Duke Nikolai Nikolaevich Junior had to cut the trip short, as he had fallen ill.[54] With this his first war had come to an end, and he returned to Russia.

It had been a positive start to the younger Grand Duke's military career. He had experienced combat and acquitted himself well, returning bedecked with medals and rewards. He had received not only the Saint George cross and his golden sword but also a Russian campaign medal and a host of other medals from Russia's friends and allies.[55] At only 21, the Grand Duke was already a highly decorated combat veteran. He had had what they call a "good war."

CHAPTER 3

Hunting and Riding, 1878–1895

AFTER THE RUSSO-TURKISH WAR, Grand Duke Nikolai Nikolaevich Junior settled into the life of a peacetime regimental officer. A portrait of him from around this time shows a young man with a thin moustache, a jutting chin, a high brow, gray-blue eyes, and a sharp nose. His slightly curly reddish-brown hair is parted down the middle.

On 14 (26) December 1878, the Grand Duke joined His Majesty's Life Guards Hussar Regiment, one of the most prestigious units in the Russian army. His service with the Hussars was quiet, and little documentation of it remains. In February 1879 he became a squadron commander, and in October 1879 he took over a battalion. In May 1884, he received an important promotion, becoming regimental commander.[1]

According to General Danilov, the Grand Duke was an attentive commander, who breakfasted several times a week in the mess to get to know his officers and who paid great attention to their personal development. Danilov recounted that in general Nikolai Nikolaevich was restrained in his behavior toward his officers, but he did sometimes lose his temper, especially during exercises. While he trusted and respected his officers, the Grand Duke was said to mercilessly punish those who did not fulfill their duties.[2]

In February 1885, the Grand Duke took two months' leave[3] and traveled to Paris. "I have moved to Rue Tronchet," he wrote to his brother on 22 February (6 March), "Count Tolstoy embraces you and Papa. Nikolasha."[4] On 20 March (1 April), Pyotr Nikolaevich was in Kiev visiting their mother. "Thanks for the telegram," Nikolai Nikolaevich telegraphed him from Paris, "I tenderly embrace you and Mama."[5]

By mid-April of that year, Nikolai Nikolaevich was back in Tsarskoe Selo, and in August he took the Hussars out on exercise as part of the annual military maneuvers of the Petersburg Military District held at Krasnoe Selo, near Saint Petersburg. Here he caught the eye of the French military attaché, Lieutenant Colonel de Sermet, when he revealed a new technique in controlling cavalry. De Sermet recorded the following observation:

Grand Duke Nikolai Nikolaevich Junior as a young man, 1880 (Private collection, France)

> Silent maneuvering is nothing new for us, but it is for Russia, where one changes formation with shouts as was fashionable in France before 1870. Grand Duke Nicholas the younger, who commands the Hussars regiment, presented his regiment changing formations silently, and at the signal of squadron commanders. This maneuver was a great success. It will perhaps be the start of a reform of command ... in the Russian cavalry.[6]

The 1885 exercises were the Grand Duke's public debut as a cavalry reformer; they provided early indications of the energy that would soon mark him out as one of the most prominent cavalry officers of his day. Silent maneuver was to become one of his trademarks, and in due course he would attempt to spread the practice throughout the Russian army.

On 31 August (11 September) 1885, the Grand Duke, aged just 28, was promoted to the rank of major general.[7] A month later he was once again in Paris, from where he telegraphed his father that he was "happy that you are pleased with the regiment."[8] In November 1885, he went on four months' sick leave.[9] The nature of the illness is unknown. It was not the last time that the Grand Duke would take a prolonged leave of this sort, so it is possible that he suffered from a serious, recurring condition. Unfortunately, we have no surviving records that can enlighten us on this point.

The next bit of information we have about the Grand Duke's activities is that he accompanied Emperor Alexander III on military maneuvers that took place in the Warsaw and Vilna military districts in August and September 1886, after which he joined the Emperor at the Imperial hunting lodge at Spala in Poland.[10] He then returned to Tsarskoe Selo, where he once again fell ill, reporting to his brother on 12 (24) November that "my health is better but weak."[11] A few weeks later he was in Paris. "I started my cure a few days ago," he wrote to his father on 1 (13) December, "Thank God, I feel well."[12]

Whatever the problem was, it seems to have evaporated fairly rapidly, for within a few weeks the Grand Duke, still in France, was out hunting again. "Thanks for your letter," he wrote to his brother from Paris on 26 December 1886 (7 January 1887). "I have just this minute got back from hunting on the Marne with the president. I killed 10 goats, 9 gray hares, 64 rabbits, and 130 pheasants. *A total of 216 animals.* Overall today we killed 509 animals. I have rarely shot as well as today."[13]

The Grand Duke remained in Paris until early March. In February he reported to his brother that he had received a letter from their mother,[14] whom he then appears to have visited in Kiev on his way home. "I am very pleased," he wrote to his brother before leaving Paris at the start of March, "that you have agreed to come and meet me at Vilna, so that we can go on together to Kiev.... Yesterday I went hunting.... Live a bit and you will see that nothing in the world is better than hunting. It is always comforting and keeps you healthy."[15]

Hunting was the Grand Duke's passion, and much of his personal correspondence consists of lists of the number and types of animals he killed. His interest in the sport began early in life; as a child he had kept his own pack of hounds on his father's Znamenka estate. Later, as a young man, he bred his own hunting dogs, primarily borzois, preferring dogs "distinguished by their ferociousness."[16] Finally, in 1887 he bought a country estate of his own, at Pershino in the Tula region south of Moscow.[17] Having done so, he immediately set about buying dogs to establish a hunt.[18]

Hunting was the most popular pastime of European royalty in this era, and the numbers of animals killed were truly extraordinary. In 1906, for instance, Kaiser Wilhelm II of Germany wrote to Emperor Nicholas II of Russia, "We had capital sport today. We killed 4,600 pheasants today and I brought down 1,001."[19] Archduke Franz Ferdinand of Austria-Hungary, whose murder in 1914 sparked the First World War, supposedly shot some 270,000 animals during his life, including 3,000 stags. According to Franz Ferdinand's biographer Gordon Brook-Shepherd, "For a party of six guns to shoot less than a thousand birds on a main day at any first-class estate would have been considered disappointing sport." The "all-time record" was "6,125 pheasant shot at Totmegyer in Hungary on 10 December 1909."[20] In the ten years before the First World War, the British royal estate at Sandringham witnessed the killing of "over one million head of game."[21]

The extravagance of royal hunting in European and Asian history has led some to view it in a political light rather than as a strictly recreational activity. Thomas Allsen writes, "The royal hunt served as an effective reaffirmation of a ruler's capacity to manage large-scale enterprises, that is to govern.... Such hunts, it is fair to say, were all about lavish expenditure of energy, and such expenditures are preeminently political acts."[22] In the same vein, Antony Taylor asserts that hunting "came to symbolize the vigour, vitality and ostentation of kings."[23] There may be something to this, but Russian imperial hunts in the late 19th and early 20th centuries were for the most part private affairs, limited to a small number of members of the royal family and close associates. In this sense they do not easily fit the same model. And while they could on occasion match the extravagance found elsewhere in Europe, they were generally modest by comparison. Certainly, the numbers of animals dispatched by Grand Duke Nikolai Nikolaevich could not compare to those slaughtered by Archduke Franz Ferdinand. Between 1887 and 1913 the Grand Duke and his guests killed 10,076 animals at Pershino.[24]

Reaching Pershino took a long journey by carriage from Tula. An American visitor described it in this way:

> For hours, we passed through a closely cultivated grain country, where the peasants were gathering the last vestiges of the crops, by methods in many instances not far removed from those employed in Egypt in the days of bondage, past flocks and [illegible]s, and droves of hobbled horses attended by barefooted boys and girls—through forest and open plain until the eye was delighted by the sight of the white walls of Monseigneur's mansion, nestled in the midst of an irregular hamlet of peasants' *izbas* [huts].[25]

Grand Duke Nikolai Nikolaevich renovated both the palace and the estate at Pershino and supervised the construction of new buildings for his hunt. Designed during the reign of Catherine the Great by an Italian architect, the green-roofed, white stone house stood on top of a small hill close to a river, in a park full of ancient lime trees. Nikolai Nikolaevich redecorated the inside of the house in a hunting motif. Pictures of dogs and hunting scenes hung on the walls, as did the Grand Duke's trophies: antlers as well as the heads of European bison, bears, wolves, lynxes, wild boar, elks, deer, and goats—all of which he had himself shot. Two big stuffed bears, standing with raised paws, guarded the corners of the main dining room, while stuffed wolves stood on the staircase landings. Paintings of the best dogs from the estate adorned the walls of the "club" room in the basement.[26] A dwarf, employed as the Grand Duke's "clown," was the caretaker.[27]

Elsewhere on the estate the Grand Duke set up two farms, "Otradnoe" and "Lesnoi." At Otradnoe, the Grand Duke bred Oxford sheep, a particularly large type of sheep developed in England in the early 1800s and bred mainly for meat, and Ardennes draft horses, a very old breed, supposedly dating back to Roman times. At Lesnoi, he focused on dairy products, using specially imported Swiss cattle.[28]

Hunting, though, was Pershino's main *raison d'être*, with the borzoi as the dog of choice. Tall and long-coated, borzois appear to have derived from a cross between Arabian greyhounds and more thickly coated Russian dogs. About two and half feet tall at the shoulders, they hunt by sight rather than scent, and "the practice was for the borzois—two together—to overtake the wolf, one at each side, catching him behind the ears, or at his throat, and bowl him over," whereupon the huntsman would "overpower the wolf, placing a wooden wedge faced with iron between his teeth, and tie him up."[29]

Favorites of Russian tsars and the nobility since at least the time of Ivan the Terrible in the 16th century, borzois suffered something of a decline following the emancipation of the serfs in 1861, which deprived many noblemen of the free manpower they had used in their kennels. This, combined with the mixing of borzois with other breeds, meant that by the mid-1870s "few Borzoi of the ancient type remained."[30] Grand Duke Nikolai Nikolaevich's hunt at Pershino was to play a major role in reviving the ancient breed.

The Pershino kennels accommodated about 365 dogs, of which around 150 to 160 were borzois. The Grand Duke took a close interest in the breeding of the dogs, deciding himself which males should be paired with which females,[31] while his hunt manager Dmitrii Valtsov scoured Russia and foreign lands for suitable new dogs to add to the pack. At first, according to Valtsov, "priority was given to fierce dogs, and sires were selected according to their ferociousness, as a result of which the beauty of their form suffered as did their correctness, which told upon their speed, without which victorious hunting of mother wolves is unthinkable—so in his new hunt the Grand Duke paid special attention above all to speed and pure breeding and then to the correctness of the sire's form."[32]

According to Valtsov, the result was dogs that were "completely perfect, in so far as perfection is possible on Earth."[33] "The heads of these dogs with their long brows," wrote Valtsov, "were exactly what was dreamt of by every hunter who sought the ideal of the ancient borzois, and thanks to this we created at the Pershino hunt those elegant heads from which one can immediately identify the Pershino origins of dogs from Pershino sires."[34] American visitor Joseph B. Thomas gushed in admiration that "it was nearly impossible for me to comprehend how these dogs could be so good, displaying everything that the ideal pictures had called for." "The size and evenness in type of the hounds were wonderful for any breed," wrote Thomas.[35]

The peak of the Pershino hunting season was normally from mid-September to mid-October.[36] On the day of a hunt, the Grand Duke would choose the location himself, and he and his guests would normally be ready to start around eight in the morning, at which point, wrote Valtsov, "The Grand Duke sits on his Kabardin horse, sounds the horn and the whole hunt moves off."[37] At midday the hunters would stop for lunch, after which the Grand Duke would again blow the horn and the hunters would resume the chase. According to Valtsov, "The Grand Duke himself was always in the center and the whole line would dress off from him.... the Grand Duke always led two dogs on a leash and behind him were two more dogs and an assistant groom, one of the groom's dogs being an English one. With these four dogs the Grand Duke would hunt the fleeing animal."[38] Valtsov described a typical day in October 1912:

> From eight in the morning the hunters began to collect in the large club room, in full hunting accoutrements, and while waiting for the Grand Duke carried on the normal pre-hunt conversations, about the weather, the ground, the pack of dogs, etc., until an official reported: "The Grand Duke has come downstairs and is getting dressed." Everybody rushes into the front room where the Grand Duke in his hunting clothes is putting on his hunting armour—a belt with a dagger, a leash, and a horn—and greets the guests, after which everybody rapidly puts on their cloaks for the road.[39]

On that October day, the weather was gloomy, and although the frost was gone, the ground was slippery. The hunters lined up, the horn sounded, "and the borzois happily strained on the leashes, knowing that now the hunting was starting.... The Grand Duke, taking two dogs on his leash, moved off into his normal position." A while later, "a first gray hare ran towards the Grand Duke, but noticing the dogs, turned around at high speed.... Another wanted to rush past the Grand Duke to the Brusovskii ravine, but the gray-haired one-year-old 'Varvar' and the two-year-old 'Krasotka' didn't let him run far and caught him before the ravine." By the end of the day, the hunters had killed two foxes, 29 gray hares, and seven white hares.[40] One of the Grand Duke's guests, N. Kravchenko, described another hunt:

> It was cold and a strong wind was blowing.... The Grand Duke, knowing all the locations around Pershino very well, himself arranged the guests and the borzoi handlers.... For a long time there was complete silence.... And there appeared the small dark silhouette of a dog.... It was a wolf.... Quickly the wolf disappeared in a small birch grove. But it appeared to me that he would come out again and this time on our side. And I wasn't mistaken. He appeared almost exactly where I expected him, and without hurrying went straight towards the Grand Duke, who was hidden on the edge of a young oak forest. I wasn't sure whether the Grand Duke noticed him, and how the wolf, shaking, turned around and went back. Already the beautiful black-coated dogs were chasing after him and after them raced the Grand Duke on his short roan horse.... One of them, a beautiful black-coated dog, suddenly leapt strongly forward and ate into the right side of the wolf's neck.... The wolf lay there, not stirring.... He didn't move, and, it seemed, showed no expression or perhaps complete indifference.... Eventually, the borzoi handler and his colleagues bound the wolf's feet and two men carried it off to the wagon.... The Grand Duke raised his silver horn and gave it voice. The clear sound of the call told us that the hunt was finished, and that somewhere, in a comfortable spot, a tasty lunch and some good wine were waiting for us.[41]

The acquisition of Pershino had given the Grand Duke a place that he could call his own. He now also had a mistress, a widowed merchant's daughter called Sofia Ivanovna Burenina. Just how the Grand Duke managed to strike up a liaison with her is not known, and unfortunately we also know very little about her other than that she was considerably older than he. In 1888, Nikolai Nikolaevich apparently attempted to persuade the Emperor to let him marry his socially inferior lover. On 22 January (3 February) 1888, court gossip Aleksandra Viktorovna Bogdanovich recorded in her diary,

> Grand Duke Nikolai Nikolaevich visited his father to ask his permission for his marriage to the merchant Burenina. His father, knowing the Tsar's objec-

> tions, told him to ask the Tsar. Nikolai Nikolaevich then went to Grand Duke Vladimir Aleksandrovich [brother of Emperor Alexander III] and told him what his father had said. Taking this as his father's consent, Vladimir Aleksandrovich told the Tsar, who initially declared his agreement. Nikolai Nikolaevich, happy, hurried back to tell his father, who shouted in a loud voice that this would never happen, but Nikolai Nikolaevich ran away from him, went to Tsarskoe Selo, had dinner, summoned all his friends and Burenina, and during dinner they exchanged rings. His father meanwhile hurried to the Tsar, who, having learnt the truth, was terribly indignant that he had been deceived, and withdrew his consent.[42]

A few days later, Bogdanovich recorded that "Dorofeeva Sh., who lives in Tsarskoe Selo, said that Grand Duke Nikolai Nikolaevich Junior is parading with Burenina....The other day her lamp fell over and the Grand Duke put it out and burnt himself badly. She was told this by Doctor Shepelev, who treated Grand Duke Nikolai Nikolaevich."[43]

General von Raukh, who worked closely with the Grand Duke for many years and got to know Burenina well, considered her to be a positive influence on the Grand Duke's character. "This was a woman who was not very well educated in a cultural sense," wrote Raukh, "but a surprisingly good woman, with a beautiful heart." In particular, she blunted some of the sharpness of Nikolasha's manner toward others, particularly those of lower rank. "Many times she said that all people were equal, that he himself was a person the same as everybody else." Raukh also noted that when he first met the Grand Duke around 1890, he sometimes displayed a lack of restraint, "and it was surprising how she immediately noticed this; she had only to say 'Nikolasha' and to call him over for him to calm down at once.... I know that he recognized the enormous benefit which she brought to him ... and I know that he valued her deeply."[44] Raukh held Burenina responsible for developing what he considered the Grand Duke's "polite, level and noble, but also firm and definite, character."[45]

In 1888, the Grand Duke had a busy summer of military exercises. In August and September he commanded a group of 30 cavalry squadrons in a mock battle against a similar force led by General A. P. Strukov. It was the first time that he had led such a large force, and he had to do it in front of his father, who was attending in the role of Inspector General of Cavalry. A. A. Mosolov, the future chief of the palace chancellery, observed the exercise and wrote:

> I have to admit that his Highness [Nikolai Nikolaevich Junior] coped very well with this not at all easy task, although he was a little nervous and often

> sent off his orderlies, of whom he had more than ten, for nothing. He would insist that they go at full gallop all the time, even when there was no need to hurry. When Nikolai Nikolaevich felt that the orderly was not galloping fast enough he would shout, "On! On!" with a very angry voice, whipping at the same time his entirely innocent horse.[46]

At the end of the exercises, Nikolasha traveled to Spala to hunt at the imperial hunting lodge.[47] In December he once again visited Paris, stopping off at Kiev on the way back in order to see his mother.[48] By now, he had been appointed Commander of the Second Brigade of the Second Guards Cavalry Division in October 1888, while simultaneously retaining command of the Life Guards Hussar Regiment.[49]

In 1889, the Grand Duke founded the Society for Encouraging the Field Qualities of Dogs and All Forms of Hunting,[50] of which he was president. Over time he also became patron of the Russian Society of Goat-breeding, President of the Imperial Military Society of Hunters, patron and President of the Society of Rifle Hunting, Racing and Horse Competitions in the Cavalry, President of the Society of Thoroughbred Dogs and Hunting Horses, and honorary President of the Society of Poultry Farming, among others.[51] In many cases he may have done little more than lend his name to the society's letterhead, but his decision to exclusively support military, hunting, and farming societies (he was not patron or president of any cultural or philanthropic organizations) reflects his lack of interests outside of the army and country life.

May 1889 marked an important turning point in the Grand Duke's life. That month, a new subaltern joined his regiment: Grand Duke Nikolai Aleksandrovich, the future Emperor Nicholas II.[52] Nikolasha and Nicky were to become extremely close. General von Raukh noted that "the special favor and quite exceptional trust which the Sovereign [Nicholas II] had in the Grand Duke ... had deep roots and developed out of their mutual relations from the time when the Heir to the throne served in the Life Guards Hussars, which the Grand Duke then commanded."[53]

Years later Nicky confessed to the Grand Duke, "You know, Nikolasha, I was very afraid of you when you were commander of the Life Guards Hussars and I was serving in that regiment."[54] Perhaps because he had once been Nikolasha's subordinate, Nicky never ceased to look up to him. One contemporary commented that Nikolai Nikolaevich was "the only member of our reigning house who can boast of being in possession of the absolute confidence of the Sovereign."[55] In return, Nikolasha was devoted to Nicky. He considered protecting him to be his most holy task. A. A. Kireev, who was certainly no fan of the Grand Duke, nevertheless grudgingly admitted, "One thing that is beyond doubt is the Grand Duke's dedication to the Sovereign. He would fall in battle for him."[56] French military attaché Colonel Moulin noted that relations between the two men were "very intimate and very affectionate."[57]

In August 1889, Nikolai Nikolaevich went on four months' leave. In December this was extended for another three months.[58] His service record does not give any indication of why he was absent for so long, or where he went. He traveled in Western Europe for at least part of the time; on 27 February (11 March) 1890, Nicky recorded in his diary that he had met Nikolasha, who had just returned from a trip to Spain.[59] What he had done there we do not know. Soon after, he resumed his regimental duties.

The Grand Duke was now taking on greater and greater military responsibilities. When the annual summer maneuvers of the Petersburg Military District came to an end in August 1890, he went south to Lublin in Poland to act as chief of cavalry for the exercises of the Warsaw Military District.[60] De Sermet's successor as French military attaché, Colonel Moulin, observed these exercises and was not impressed by the cavalry's performance. Reconnaissance was poor, he informed the French Minister of War, and there were "excessive tendencies to fight on foot."[61] Both of these habits (shoddy reconnaissance and a tendency to fight dismounted) were the subject of regular criticism by foreign observers in the years ahead. Moulin also criticized the Grand Duke's performance: "The Grand Duke Nikolai Nikolaevich Junior, a cavalryman full of enthusiasm, energy and zest," he wrote, "led his cavalry corps with the vigor of inexperience, and totally wore out his horses."[62]

By October, the Grand Duke was back with his brigade, but at the end of the year he finally relinquished command of both the brigade and the Life Guards Hussars, becoming instead commander of the Second Guards Cavalry Division.[63] He would hold this position for the next five years.

The Grand Duke began 1891 with 28 days' leave.[64] By this date, his father, Grand Duke Nikolai Nikolaevich Senior, was severely ill. The nature of the illness is unknown, but mouth cancer and syphilis have been suggested.[65] The older Grand Duke was also distraught at the death of his mistress, Ekaterina Chislova, in December 1889. Supposedly, in his final months he was "suffering from delusions" and "molested every woman he met, convinced that they were in love with him." After watching a ballet, he purportedly "became so aroused that he went backstage and tried to seduce everyone he saw."[66] On 13 (25) April 1891, he died in the Crimea.

On learning of his father's death, Nikolai Nikolaevich Junior traveled to the Crimea to bring the body back on a special train to Saint Petersburg for burial in the Peter and Paul fortress. Novelist Ivan Bunin, a future Nobel laureate, was in Orel when the train briefly stopped there, and years later, in his autobiographical novel *The Life of Arseniev*, he described Nikolai Nikolaevich Junior getting off the train:

> From the middle carriage of the train ... someone quickly appeared and stepped onto the red cloth spread out beforehand on the platform—a young giant with bright fair hair, in a red hussar's uniform, with sharp regular features and fine nostrils curved vigorously and as it were slightly contemptuously, with a rather too prominent chin; he struck me by his inhuman tallness, the length of his slender legs, the keenness of his regal eyes, but above all by his head, proudly and lightly thrown back, with short and waved bright fair hair, and a small pointed red beard curling firmly and beautifully.[67]

The senior Grand Duke left his sons huge debts. According to the ever-admiring Julia Cantacuzen, Nikolai Nikolaevich Junior "gave his younger brother the lion's share of their inheritance, and took on himself all the debts and obligations of the father's somewhat disorderly past and estates."[68] Pyotr Nikolaevich had married Princess Militsa Nikolaevna, the daughter of the ruler of Montenegro, in 1889, and so perhaps needed property more than his bachelor brother. Pyotr Nikolaevich received the Znamenka estate close to Peterhof, while Nikolai Nikolaevich took the Nikolaevskii Palace in Saint Petersburg, which he then sold to pay his father's debts.[69]

By August 1891, Nikolasha was on maneuvers once again at Krasnoe Selo. He caught the attention of Colonel Moulin, who noted that the Second Guards Cavalry Division was "vigorously led" by Grand Duke Nikolai Nikolaevich. "The cavalry generals leave a lot to be desired," wrote Moulin, "with the exception of Grand Duke Nikolai Nikolaevich Junior, who promises to be an excellent cavalry division commander."[70]

Moulin commented again on the Grand Duke's performance a year later, following the Krasnoe Selo maneuvers of July 1892, writing that

> The cavalry seems to want to reduce to a minimum the use of combat on foot... If the numerous efforts which were made to intervene in the combat of other arms generally failed and gave rise to some rather fantastic improbabilities, one should nevertheless be most grateful that they have completely broken with the previous tendencies to inaction. The old division commanders General Etter and Winter have gone, and have been replaced by young and vigorous chiefs: Grand Duke Nicholas and General Strukov. If at first they advertised with perhaps a little too much exaggeration their firm deter-

mination to make use of their cavalry, one must hope that they will be able to regulate their ardor and come to apply appropriately the well-placed spirit which motivates them.[71]

The picture of the Grand Duke that emerges from these descriptions is of an energetic but still somewhat inexperienced commander with a keen desire to reform the Russian cavalry. Personal circumstances would now intervene to delay the opportunity for him to accumulate more experience in high command.

At the start of August 1892, the Grand Duke attempted again to persuade the Emperor to let him marry Burenina. A handwritten note survives, written to Alexander III on 4 (16) August 1892 by the head of the Imperial Court, Count I. I. Vorontsov-Dashkov. "Your Majesty," Vorontsov-Dashkov wrote, "I will await your instructions to pass on to Nikolai Nikolaevich about Your Majesty's refusal of his marriage, in light of those changes in the Grand Duke's views about which you spoke today." On this the Emperor had scribbled, "You can tell him. He didn't say anything to me today about a wedding."[72] Another letter, apparently from Vorontsov-Dashkov to Nikolai Nikolaevich, then says, "His Majesty, in light of Your Imperial Highness's declarations of completely different desires to those which you said at first, and seeing that Your Imperial Highness wishes to marry not in order to calm your conscience by legalizing your relations, but in order to live openly with the person in question, will no longer agree to your marriage."[73]

It would appear from this that the Emperor may initially have agreed to the request, but once again withdrew his approval. Nineteenth-century Romanovs engaged in numerous scandalous love affairs. Grand Duke Nikolai Nikolaevich Senior's ballerina was one example, as was Emperor Alexander II's long term relationship with his mistress, Ekaterina Dolgorukova. The latter, according to historian Richard Wortman, "appeared as the central episode of an orgy of self-indulgence and self-enrichment carried on by members of the imperial house."[74] When Alexander III acceded to the throne in 1881, he brought with him a more conservative view of marriage and family, "in opposition to his father's frivolity and fickleness."[75]

Court gossip Aleksandra Bogdanovich claimed in her diary that in this instance Burenina had visited Nikolai Nikolaevich's mother in Kiev and persuaded her to write to the Tsar asking his permission for the Grand Duke to marry. Alexander agreed on condition that Burenina had no official position and that he would ignore the marriage. When Nikolai Nikolaevich objected, the Emperor "lost his temper and refused to let him marry." In a reference to Burenina's humble origins the Emperor supposedly complained that his family "had married into every European court (*evropeiskii dvor*), but not yet the merchants' courtyard (*gostinnyi dvor*)."[76]

Whatever the real circumstances of the Tsar's refusal, it hit Nikolai Nikolaevich hard. He took two months' leave and then, in mid-November, went on leave for another four months,[77] leaving Saint Petersburg for Pershino on 14 (26) November. On 5 (17) December he wrote to Nicky from Pershino with dramatic news:

> Dear Nicky ... I'm writing to you from the countryside, where the doctor has locked me up for the next four months in view of the fact that, quite unexpectedly for me, he found in me the beginnings of a dangerous heart illness—and the main condition of a successful cure is complete rest, for which he locked me up here.... Without treatment, he predicts a very serious outcome and very quickly.... I was at the regimental holiday but alas I could not even drink a glass of wine to your health, as it is strictly forbidden. There are no words with which I can express to you (and indeed I don't need to, as, thank God, you know it well) how *sincerely* upset everybody was that once again you were not at the holiday.... I ask you to believe *with all your heart* my feeling of unlimited devotion to you.[78]

For a while the Grand Duke's military career appeared to be at an end. Colonel Moulin reported to Paris on 31 December 1892 (11 January 1893) with the following: "A rumor is circulating that the Grand Duke Nicholas Junior, commander of the 2nd Guards Cavalry Division, intends to quit his divisional command."[79] If so, Nikolai Nikolaevich soon changed his mind. On 22 February (6 March) 1893, Moulin reported,

> The impending return of Grand Duke Nicholas Junior to the command of his division is being announced after several months away in one of his estates in Tula in a sort of disgrace or sulk following a morganatic union. He had moreover a grave illness which required treatment. Everyone here is deploring in advance the loss which the cavalry would suffer if he were to quit the service. There is an almost unanimous belief that, apart from a bit of experience, which he still has to acquire, he is, after General Gurko, the only commander in Russia who truly understands the cavalry spirit.[80]

Moulin was right. Four days later, the Grand Duke received a promotion to lieutenant general, and although he took another two months' leave in March and April, he resumed his military duties.[81] In the decade that followed he would lead the charge to reform the Russian cavalry and imbue it with the "cavalry spirit" of which Moulin spoke.

CHAPTER 4

Inspector General: Reforming the Cavalry, 1895–1904

THE SECOND HALF of the 19th century was a period of fierce debate about the future of the cavalry. Many felt that the development of modern firearms meant that cavalry charging with drawn sabers against well-prepared infantry had little chance of victory. There was general agreement, moreover, that cavalry had performed poorly in the European wars of the mid-19th century—the Crimean War, the Austro-Prussian War, and the Franco-Prussian War.[1] Thus a British officer commented in 1873 that "the days of the cavalry had passed away."[2]

In contrast to the wars in Europe, the American Civil War of 1861–1865 had seen cavalry play an important role, but even in this case cavalry had proved its value mainly through raiding and reconnaissance rather than mounted combat. Some in Russia therefore argued that the cavalry should be converted to mounted infantry.[3]

Accordingly, in 1882 the Russian army turned all its non-Guards line cavalry regiments (Hussars and Uhlans) into Dragoons.[4] This change strengthened the Russian cavalry trait so deplored by foreign observers: the tendency to dismount and fight on foot. Complaints followed that the Russian cavalry now lacked the traditional "cavalry spirit" and horsemanship required for aggressive combat on horseback, yet neither was the cavalry very good at tasks such as reconnaissance.[5] By the 1890s many felt that some type of counter-reform was necessary, and under the leadership of Grand Duke Nikolai Nikolaevich, this took the form of a reinvigoration of the cavalry as an independent arm trained to fight primarily on horseback.

The Grand Duke was part of a wide movement.[6] Across Europe in the 1880s and 1890s, writes British historian Gervase Phillips, "ambitious and reforming cavalry officers argued that cavalry ... could use a combination of mounted charges and dismounted fire from their new carbines, backed by machine-guns and horse artillery, to overcome infantry, or to clash with like-minded enemy cavalry."[7]

Historians have generally viewed this idea as reactionary and unrealistic.

"Progress," writes Gerard J. De Groot, "reduced the cavalry to little more than handsome men on fine horses," while "very few cavalrymen were prepared to accept the inevitable decline of their arm. They correctly perceived progress as a threat to their existence, and therefore actively resisted its implications."[8] The impotence of cavalry on the Western Front for most of the First World War is an important factor in this assessment, but the same negative perception has carried over to studies of Russia, where there was far more scope for the use of cavalry than there was in Western Europe, and where shock tactics often did prove successful during the Civil War of 1917–1921.[9] Thus historian Stephen Brown writes of the "conservative prejudice of the [Russian] cavalry," claiming, "changes to the traditional organisation, armament, and tactics of the cavalry were resisted by the cavalrymen" largely for social reasons, as aristocratic officers considered fighting on foot to be incompatible with their elite status.[10] Another historian, John Steinberg, agrees. The Russian cavalry, he writes, was "the most anachronistic branch of the military service."[11]

A number of revisionist analyses appearing in recent years have evaluated the cavalry counter-reformers' actions in a far more positive light.[12] According to Gervase Phillips, for instance, cavalry has "served as a convenient scapegoat" for military failure. In reality, he continues, "Although less talented as self-publicists than many of their critics, cavalrymen were often more astute as commentators on the impact of technological and tactical developments on the battlefield."[13]

Alexis Wrangel has noted that during the First World War, the Russian cavalry made "as many as 400 cavalry charges," which resulted in the capture of 170 enemy guns and the defeat "of one entire enemy army" (the Austrian Seventh Army at Gorodenko in April 1915). Thus, although mounted attacks were hardly a daily occurrence, they clearly retained their usefulness.[14] A study of the Australian cavalry by historian Jean Bou is illuminating in this regard. Trained before the First World War to rely entirely on rifles, the Australian Light Horse discovered during combat in Palestine in 1917 and 1918 that "while firepower was undoubtedly vital, the exclusive use of the rifle had not provided the tactical flexibility that mounted troops needed in this campaign."[15] As a result, the Australians equipped their troops with swords, with which they carried out a number of successful charges, indicating "the continued tactical utility of sensibly executed shock tactics carried out under the right circumstances."[16] As Bou notes:

> In mobile warfare in open country, the effects of firepower were diffused and cavalry had scope to employ not just fire tactics but also their traditional weapons using modern methods. In Palestine cavalrymen noted that artillery

> generally had little effect on them, provided they could move rapidly and in extended formations. Much the same thing was noted of machine-gun fire, and widely circulated tactical advice actually advocated galloping at any machine-guns that suddenly opened fire on mounted cavalry.[17]

This did not mean that cavalry should opt for "hell-for-leather close order cavalry charges"; but a combination of "relatively dispersed formations ... concealed approaches ..., comprehensive use of fire and manoeuvre, and the judicious use of shock tactics"[18] could be successful on the modern battlefield. Success required the adoption of what Gervase Phillips refers to as the "hybrid concept,"[19] which gave both swords and rifles to the cavalry, allowing them to fight either on horseback or on foot.

This "hybrid" approach resembles what Grand Duke Nikolai Nikolaevich sought to create in Russia. It would be wrong, therefore, to regard his efforts to revitalize the cavalry as necessarily indicating a lack of understanding of the nature of contemporary warfare. In fact, the Grand Duke and his like-minded colleagues in other European countries, while recognizing the occasional utility of cavalry charges, also acknowledged that they would be more difficult in the modern age. In response, they endeavored to train their cavalrymen to move faster, to make better use of ground to approach the enemy unseen, and to take better care of their horses.

Moreover, there was a not entirely unfounded fear that the focus on dismounted action and reconnaissance would diminish the "cavalry spirit" and made troops less aggressive.[20] This point mattered because roles such as reconnaissance and screening required aggressive action. Count Gustav Wrangel of the Austro-Hungarian army argued that to carry out successful reconnaissance, friendly cavalry would first have to defeat the enemy's cavalry, and such duels would "without doubt, be in favor of that one who is imbued with the greater offensive spirit. Cavalry which seeks its salvation in the rifle easily loses the impulse to charge home on the enemy."[21]

Re-creating the "cavalry spirit" in Russia was to be a long and difficult process. In the 1893 summer maneuvers at Krasnoe Selo, Grand Duke Nikolai Nikolaevich caught the eye of both French and British observers. In a report to Paris, French attaché Colonel Moulin commented, "Among the division commanders, General Grippenberg for the infantry and Grand Duke Nicholas Junior for the cavalry are those who seem to possess the most military qualities."[22] That said, the exercise did not go entirely well. According to a report produced by the Intelligence Division of the British War Office:

On the 12th August [31 July], the Grand Duke Nicholas Nicolaevich ordered his cavalry division (2,400 strong, with 18 horse artillery guns) to advance westward in a single column. Wishing to save as much time as possible, he selected a forest road, which considerably shortened the distance to be traversed. The guns were placed towards the head of the column. During the passage of a narrow defile, a gun was upset and blocked the road, thereby delaying the advance for some 45 minutes. The result was that the Grand Duke was prevented from reaching and occupying the ground which he had intended to search, and he had to be content with a position not nearly so suitable and too restricted.[23]

The British observer was much more positive about the Grand Duke's performance later in the exercise, writing,

After the manoeuvres had been concluded there was a cavalry and horse artillery day at Krasnoe Selo on 17 [5] August against a "marked" enemy; the Grand Duke Nicholas was in command of 48 squadrons and 30 horse artillery guns. He kept his force rapidly on the move for some 90 minutes; there was no shouting or excitement.... The force was very well handled ... and there is no doubt as to the ability of the Grand Duke in moving large bodies of cavalry.[24]

In October 1893 Nikolai Nikolaevich was appointed to chair a commission reviewing the cavalry regulations.[25] This was a very significant appointment as it gave him the opportunity to shape the future direction of tactics and training. He expounded his views on these matters to a French exchange officer, Captain Deville, who met him at Krasnoe Selo during the 1894 summer maneuvers. The Grand Duke, wrote Deville to the Minister of War in Paris,

Treated me with a consideration which was disproportionate to the modesty of my situation. The Grand Duke wanted me to see the division that he commands on the exercise area, and assigned me his own aide-de-camp, giving me in excellent French all the explanations that he deemed necessary.

In the first place, one of the things that struck me most keenly was Grand Duke Nicholas' worth as head of cavalry. And please believe me, Minister, that in this purely military assessment I can lay aside the gratitude induced in me by His Highness's generosity and champagne, and that I will try to judge only the soldier, leaving where they belong the grand nobleman and the kind dinner host.

> The Grand Duke is a man 37 to 38 years old, who rides a horse remarkably well, very tall, very vigorous, with a profound grasp of everything to do with the cavalry. There is no doubt among senior officers that he is, as a cavalryman, the best at conducting maneuvers in Russia and a true leader of men.[26]

Deville wrote that he had spent a great deal of time with Nikolai Nikolaevich, who had shared with the French exchange officer his ideas on tactics. As Deville noted, "The Grand Duke is an absolute partisan of the cavalry's complete independence. He does not consider beneficial, for his arm, the tendency of certain writers today to combine its action with that of the infantry and the artillery and to check the supposedly adventurous temper of large masses of cavalry. He seemed very fixed in this opinion."[27]

While commanding troops on maneuver, wrote Deville, the Grand Duke showed that "he is in total control of himself and of his troops." While he sometimes used trumpets, he preferred "silent maneuver using signals, in which all soldiers are well trained. At the start there were a few mistakes; the Grand Duke reacted with great severity, and during the entire maneuver there was perfect order, everyone in his correct place and the alignments and the pace very correct."[28]

Deville was much taken with what he considered the "quasi-equality outside working hours." "During maneuvers, the troops were criticized, sometimes quite energetically," Deville wrote. "But, after the exercise, the Grand Duke, sitting on the drinks wagon of a kvas and vodka seller, laughed and joked with the youngest sub-lieutenant, bringing as much good grace as he had previously shown harshness when correcting faults."[29]

Once the summer exercises at Krasnoe Selo were over, the Grand Duke went to Pershino for the autumn hunting there and then joined Emperor Alexander III to hunt at Spala in Poland.[30] After this the Emperor traveled down to the Crimea. This was to be his final journey. A month later, on 20 October (1 November) 1894, Alexander III died. Given that he was only 49 years old, this was an unexpected blow, especially to his unprepared son, the 26-year-old Grand Duke Nikolai Aleksandrovich, who now ascended the throne as Tsar Nicholas II.

Three weeks later, on 14 (26) November 1894, Nicholas hastily married his longtime sweetheart, Princess Alix Viktoria Helena Luise Beatrice of Hesse and by Rhine, who took the Russian names Aleksandra Fedorovna. On the same day, as an early sign of his favor, Nicholas appointed Grand Duke Nikolai Nikolaevich to the honorary rank of general-adjutant.[31] Several months later, on 6 (18) May 1895, the new Tsar then appointed the Grand Duke to the post of Inspector General of Cavalry.[32] The Inspector

General was responsible for the training and doctrine of all cavalry units in the Empire as well as for matters such as the supply of horses. To this end he reviewed and updated the cavalry regulations, inspected cavalry units on exercise, and supervised the breeding of remounts. This new post gave Nikolasha, now aged 38, Russia-wide responsibility, and with it the opportunity to spread his ideas to all the cavalry regiments of the Empire.

In an early demonstration of his style as inspector general, in autumn 1895 the Grand Duke reviewed cavalry maneuvers in the Warsaw military district. At the end of these, district commander General Shuvalov assembled the generals who had commanded the troops and passed on the Grand Duke's observations. According to the French consul in Warsaw, Monsieur Boyard, these observations included "criticisms formulated in quite lively terms." "In military circles," reported Bozard, "nobody is hiding the fact that the somewhat severe criticisms made by the Grand Duke Nicholas were directed primarily at the command," above all, at Shuvalov himself.[33]

This set what was to become the pattern of Nikolai Nikolaevich's tenure as Inspector General of Cavalry, with him descending on units in barracks or on exercise, carrying out an inspection, and then issuing ferocious denunciations of the incompetence he believed he had witnessed. The Grand Duke became notorious for losing his temper and berating commanders in savage terms. Colonel A. A. Ignatiev, who in the First World War would be the Russian military attaché in Paris, commented, "the entire cavalry from general to soldier called Nikolai Nikolaevich 'the sly one,'" a Russian phrase for the devil.[34] The Grand Duke's "sarcastic sentences," he said, "seemed even more poisonous due to being whistled through his teeth," as he shouted hysterically, "'I'll show you how to do it!' 'I'll teach you how to command,' or simply, 'Get off the field!'"[35]

P. A. Polovtsov, an officer in the Grodno Hussars, wrote in his memoirs,

> [The Grand Duke] used to come nearly every year on a tour of inspection, and when he was there everyone's nerves, from the most important cavalry general's down to those of the most inconspicuous private, were strained to the utmost. Even the horses seemed to understand that the Grand Duke had arrived. Nobody wanted to experience the sad and shameful fate of a certain cavalry regiment which passed only once at a slow pace in front of the Grand Duke and received the curt order to return to their quarters because His Imperial Highness was so disgusted that he did not wish to see them any more.[36]

General von Raukh, who served with the Grand Duke during his period as Inspector General of Cavalry, as well as later, stated that he was present at all the reviews the Grand Duke undertook between 1895 and 1901 and that the stories about his lack of restraint were exaggerated. Many times, wrote Raukh, the Grand Duke saw that his instructions were not being carried out, "and, as the French say, he took his gloves off and called things by their proper names—people didn't like this, and they weren't used to it, but there was never anything out of place, or undeserved about it."[37]

Others disagreed. Polovtsov, for instance, recounted the harrowing experience of his own regiment:

> After our division had finished its manoeuvres, he called up all the commanding officers and expressed his criticisms in a very sarcastic way. His exceptionally tall figure on his big Irish hunter towered over the others, his riding-stick was beating nervously on his top-boot (always a bad sign), and he said a lot of unpleasant things, not missing a single detail. He concluded by saying that the whole of the manoeuvre was an accumulation of mistakes, that even at the end the division could not assemble decently, that the Hussars of Grodno could not find their place in the formation and galloped all over the field with their tongues out, like mad dogs. After this speech, the Grand Duke coldly saluted and rode away.[38]

The Russian army took issues of honor seriously, and insults of any sort were liable to result in a challenge to a duel.[39] Consequently, officers tended to avoid making offensive statements to one another. The Grand Duke's sharpness was unusual. His status meant that challenging him was out of the question, but in this instance, shamed by his dressing-down, the colonel of the Grodno Hussars assembled his officers, told them that the Grand Duke had insulted the regiment and that he intended to resign his position as commanding officer. The next morning, three other colonels, three brigadier-generals, and the divisional commander followed suit. Faced with this gesture of protest, the Grand Duke suddenly warned the Grodno Hussars that he would visit their barracks. According to Polovtsov:

> Precisely at three, the Grand Duke arrived, and stopped at the drill ground. We all came up to greet him. He said that he wanted to see how quickly one of our squadrons could turn out. He looked at his watch and asked for the second squadron. The squadron turned out in an incredibly short time (something like six or seven minutes, I think), and galloped up to the Grand Duke in perfect order. He thanked the officers and the men, and then said that he felt thirsty, so he was taken to the garden.
>
> When we were all seated, a glass of champagne was offered to His Imperial Highness, but he found it too small and asked for something larger. A huge

> silver goblet containing exactly a bottle of champagne was brought, filled to the brim. The Grand Duke, holding it in his hand, addressed us, saying, "Gentlemen, yesterday I was a bit nervous, and in criticising the manoeuvres I used language to which your colonel took offence. I did not wish to offend him or the regiment. For him, as a cavalry officer, I have always had the greatest esteem, and as for your regiment, I consider it as one of the best units in the Russian army. So I hope yesterday is forgotten, and I raise this cup to the prosperity of the glorious Hussars of Grodno and to the health of their distinguished colonel." The Grand Duke drained the huge tankard to the very last drop as if it had been a liqueur glass.... The band and the singers were called in, and when he [the Grand Duke] left, and we accompanied him to his carriage, he drove away in the best of spirits, followed by our loud cheers.[40]

In 1896, less than a year into his tenure as inspector general, the Grand Duke issued new cavalry regulations. These made almost no reference to other arms, such as infantry and artillery, apparently on the assumption that the cavalry would act independently. They also stressed offensive action and speed. "Attack," they said, "must be carried out energetically [and] suddenly.... The success of an attack on infantry demands rapid movement."[41]

The new regulations were largely the work of the Grand Duke's chief of staff, General Fyodor Fyodorovich Palitsyn. General Rediger opined that the Grand Duke "blindly trusted Palitsyn,"[42] but that Palitsyn was exactly the sort of strong chief of staff the Grand Duke needed.[43] In a similar vein, A. A. Ignatiev commented, "This pair, consisting of the strong-willed but unbalanced Nikolai Nikolaevich, and the comically calm, but educated and cunning Fedia Palitsyn, satisfied the requirement that a commander combine both will and intelligence."[44]

The Grand Duke's reforms met resistance from an early stage. In May 1896, he traveled to Moscow to attend the coronation of Nicholas II. While there, he also attended a meeting of district commanders chaired by Field Marshal Gurko, under whom he had served during the Russo-Turkish War. The purpose of the meeting was to discuss a proposal to remove Cossack regiments from cavalry divisions. The Grand Duke wished to make the cavalry move faster, but the Cossacks, due to the inferior quality of their mounts, could not keep up with regular cavalry at full gallop. He therefore felt that they should operate separately. At the Moscow meeting, the military district commanders unanimously opposed the change. The Grand Duke supposedly "defended his proposal with extreme irritation ... and struck the table with his fist." In response, Gurko reprimanded him and declared the meeting closed.[45]

This was not the last time that the military district commanders stood in the Grand Duke's way. While the Inspector General of Cavalry was specifically responsible for cavalry training and tactics, the commanders of the districts into which the Russian army was administratively divided were generally responsible for training all the units in their area, including the cavalry. This created an overlap of responsibilities. Years later the Grand Duke would complain that "in my time as Inspector General of Cavalry I more than once observed how commanders did not fulfill and did not want to fulfill my instructions."[46] Palitsyn concurred, commenting, "As chief of staff of the Inspector General of Cavalry I observed the incessant struggle which his Most August Inspector General of Cavalry had to wage with the commanders of the military districts."[47]

The Grand Duke's struggle to introduce silent maneuvering illustrates how difficult it was to enact change in the cavalry. After attending a maneuver in 1898, for instance, Nikolai Nikolaevich complained that "instead of silent movement behind the commander, one could hear prolonged commands by regimental commanders, which were then repeated by their subordinates."[48] In 1899 he wrote, "The movement of units in silence behind their commanders still hasn't caught on, and, unfortunately, regimental commanders primarily use loud commands."[49] And in 1903 he again drew attention to the requirement that "commands not be shouted out, and that movement ... be carried out not according to commands but to simple movements behind the commander. A lot of commands are still being given out."[50]

The Grand Duke's post-exercise reports reveal a strong eye for detail and some pronounced and normally quite sensible views about cavalry tactics. While he felt that cavalry could successfully defeat enemy infantry on its own, he was well aware that this was only possible if commanders acted rapidly, made the best possible use of terrain, and kept firm control over their forces. Thus in 1899 he criticized commanders for failing to use favorable terrain and for making frontal attacks.[51] He declared his belief that "In contemporary conditions of battle, large units can achieve serious victory against infantry which is yet not fully disordered," but at the same time he made it clear that "the suddenness of cavalry units' appearance is the main guarantee of their success against infantry," an observation he made again later.[52]

Reforming the cavalry required training a new generation of officers in the new spirit and tactics. For this reason, in 1896 the Grand Duke turned his attention to the Officers' Cavalry School, through which all officers in the cavalry were required to pass. Henceforth the School paid a great deal of attention to improving riding skills. There was a feeling that officers had grown fat and lazy. Having been spared the rigors of work in the field, they preferred the quiet life of barracks and the parade ground. The new curriculum at the Officers' Cavalry School sought to shake this out of them with vigorous physical exercise on horseback. This included hunting with dogs on long-distance courses over rough terrain. Hunting was common in European armies, and some English regiments even went so far as to take their hounds with them when posted to India,[53] but its inclusion as a formal part of the military curriculum was unusual, if not unique. One suspects that the Grand Duke's personal interest in hunting was a factor, although some observers considered the practice beneficial. Colonel Ignatiev, for instance, noted that "The severe demands of the cavalry school played a useful role. Gradually cavalry commanders began to consist more and more of real cavalrymen and less and less of people inclined to peace and obesity."[54]

Critics, however, felt that any benefits of the new curriculum at the Officers' Cavalry School were offset by a decreased focus on the broader aspects of officers' education. General F. A. Keller, who in the First World War commanded the Tenth Cavalry Division and then the Third Cavalry Corps, delivered this indictment: "[The Officers' Cavalry School] causes our national cavalry harm." He considered the School's leaders "[specialists] only in jumping and riding, ignorant of and unwilling to consider the needs of combat units," and he complained that the School had forgotten "that it was educating not riding masters but combat officers."[55]

Still, from what he wrote after the 1896 maneuvers, it appears that Colonel Moulin felt the Grand Duke was moving in the right direction :

> One cannot dispute that the influence of the new Inspector General is excellent. He has reanimated a corpse, despite the groans about his severity and his toughness, even on generals commanding divisions. Certainly, the Grand Duke Nicholas has character faults and fads which are not justified. But he has an iron will, and is breathtakingly busy. He rushes from one end of Russia to the other for inspections, there is not a troop of cavalry which doesn't feel threatened by his unexpected arrival.... There is a cavalry spirit which is developing, in a word there is hope.[56]

The Grand Duke was keen to learn from other countries, and in 1897 he visited France, Austria-Hungary, and Germany to observe their cavalry in action.[57] He also received the heads of states of all these countries in Russia. First, in April 1897, Emperor Franz-Joseph of Austria-Hungary came to Saint Petersburg. Grand Duke Nikolai Nikolaevich led the parade in the Emperor's honor. Grand Duke Gavriil Konstantinovich described the scene:

> The parade finished with a cavalry attack.... At the end of the Field of Mars all the cavalry at the parade was laid out, that is to say two divisions.... At the command of Grand Duke Nikolai Nikolaevich, the entire mass of cavalry rushed in a gallop towards the Emperors. Nikolai Nikolaevich galloped in front of the centre of all this mass.... He stopped several paces from the Emperors and commanded "Stop! Eyes right!" All the galloping mass of cavalry stopped in one instant in front of the Emperors. Nikolai Nikolaevich turned his face to them and commanded, "Sabers away, lances down, obey!" Sabers flashed in the sun. "Officers," Nikolai Nikolaevich's voice rang out again. The officers lowered their weapons, and saluted, and trumpets played the Guards march. Nikolai Nikolaevich turned around with lowered saber to face the Emperors. The Austrian Emperor then approached Nikolai Nikolaevich and shook his hand.[58]

The second visitor was German Emperor Wilhelm II. As Nicholas II noted in his diary, Kaiser Wilhelm was delighted over being appointed an admiral in the Russian fleet, and he "began to shower honors right and left," even bestowing "regiments upon uncles Misha, Kostya, and Nikolasha."[59] Nikolai Nikolaevich became honorary colonel of a regiment from Mecklenburg.

Finally, after participating in maneuvers in the Warsaw and Vilnius military districts, at the end of August, the Grand Duke took part in a parade for President Felix Fauré of France while the latter attended the annual exercises at Krasnoe Selo.[60] The next three years brought some important changes in the Grand Duke's personal life. One change was that, for reasons unknown, he ended his long-term relationship with Sofia Burenina and installed a new mistress in her place, the actress Mariia Aleksandrovna Pototskaia. Born in 1861, Pototskaia had joined the Aleksandrinskii Theater in Saint Petersburg in 1893 "to play the roles of ingénues and young heroines."[61] She received mixed reviews. Theater critic A. R. Kugel wrote, "she cannot be considered either an extremely experienced or extraordinarily subtle actress." She was, according to a modern art historian, "a mediocre actress ... capable of repeating familiar things meticulously, but incapable of new roles."[62] Nevertheless, a less demanding observer, Grand Duke Gavriil Konstantinovich, described her as "a beautiful and interesting woman and a wonderful artist."[63]

Nikolasha and Pototskaia lived together in a palace on Italianskaia Street in Saint Petersburg, on the corner of Mikhailovskaia Square (now known as Arts Square), which the Grand Duke had bought in 1896. Here the Grand Duke built up a large collection of weapons, porcelain, and glass. His nephew, Prince Roman Petrovich, commented that

> Uncle Nikolasha was a passionate collector of objects for which there was no common denominator. Besides his interest in begonias, he collected English hunting etchings, Russian pictures showing the construction of private houses, jewelry made of green chrysotile, tobacco cans from the beginning of the 19th century, and much more. But most of all he was interested in porcelain. Even in his youth he had gathered porcelain, and over the years he acquired a collection which was not only immensely valuable, but also quite comprehensive. My uncle owned a collection of Russian faience and foreign porcelain, with many beautiful examples of Sèvres porcelain and porcelain from Saxony and Berlin.[64]

The palace, which is nowadays the home of the Music and Comedy Theater, was fabulously decorated. Nikolasha commissioned architect A. S. Khrenov to redesign the facades and interior. The latter featured an ornate gala staircase, a Golden Foyer, a Yellow Drawing Room, White and Green Halls, and a Buffet-Grotto.[65] Invited by the Grand Duke to dinner, the ballerina Lydia Kyasht described it as "a store-house of art treasures. I became so fascinated in looking at them that I forgot the time and was late in taking my call at the theatre." "As for the Grand Duke," Kyasht continued,

> I found him a delightful and entertaining host. He insisted on my eating plenty of the delicious food he had provided, and declared ballet dancers worked so hard they needed sustaining with plenty of nourishment. He did not give me any wine to drink, and for that I liked him. Delicious soda drinks were prepared instead for me. The thing that struck me most about my host was his immense height, and in fun I complained that he entirely dwarfed me. He immediately retaliated by jumping on a chair, and demonstrating how he could transform himself into a giant if he so wished. Some people called him serious minded, but I found him full of fun both then and when we met again on future occasions.[66]

In April 1900, the Grand Duke's mother died in Kiev.[67] There is almost no personal correspondence surviving from this period of the Grand Duke's life, and we do not even know whether he traveled to Kiev for her funeral, but he did not take any official leave. In May 1900 he was back in Saint Petersburg for the annual May military parade. Julia Cantacuzen described this in typically gushing terms:

> Heading the cavalry, rode a man [Grand Duke Nikolai Nikolaevich] for whom a ripple of enthusiastic comment ran through the lines of spectators. Straight as an arrow, he sat on his enormous charger, a splendid bay; and

> from the crown of his round, white furred cap, to the toe of his high-arched boots, he was every inch the smart and well-groomed soldier; but he looked more than that, as one absorbed details. His head was small and classic, with luminous piercing eyes and eagle nose, chiseled finely; and while a small, gray, close-clipped mustache and beard covered his mouth and chin, one felt the strength and power in them, which pervaded the man's whole appearance.[68]

In December 1900, the Grand Duke received a promotion to general of cavalry,[69] the most senior rank in the army except for field marshal. Aged 43, he was now at the top of his profession. He remained active as Inspector General of Cavalry, and in 1901 he carried out further reforms. Previously, it had been the responsibility of each regiment to find its own horses. The Grand Duke now centralized the process through the creation of special remount commissions, which he inspected in 1902.[70]

Many of the army's horses came from the Don Steppe in southern Russia, where they were bred on privately owned horse farms. By 1900 this source was under threat. The Russian government wished to give more land to peasants, so it resolved to eliminate private horse breeding and open the Don Steppe to colonization and intensive agriculture. Nikolai Nikolaevich attempted to create a new source of mounts by establishing horse breeding in the Astrakhan and Kirgiz steppes. But as he admitted some years later, "all my instructions and demands had no success."[71] The reasons for this failure are not known.

The year 1902 saw the Grand Duke acquire two new properties. The first of these was the estate of Bezzabotnoe ("Carefree") near Saint Petersburg. Here the Grand Duke further developed his passion for farming, in particular breeding a special type of gray goat noted for its milk.[72] The second property was Chaïr in the Crimea (the name derived from a Tatar word meaning "mountain garden"). The Russian royal family regularly visited the Crimea during the winter, and Grand Duke Pyotr Nikolaevich had previously built himself a palace near Yalta known as Diulber. Pyotr Nikolaevich was a great admirer of the Orient, and had hired architect Nikolai Krasnov to design Diulber in Moorish style.[73] Nikolai Nikolaevich in turn asked Krasnov to build his Crimean house. Its most notable feature was the rose garden, which years later, in Soviet times, became famous in a popular song that ran, "In the park of Chaïr the roses blossom." According to one visitor,

> The palace was intimate, consisting of two stories, and was oriented towards the sea, but the large dining hall opened through a Venetian window over Ai-Petri [a peak in the Crimean mountains]. There was a good orchard, a cyprus wood, a small and picturesque garden, and a magnificent rose garden, which,

> by the variety of its roses, rivaled Livadia and Massancha and was the object of its proprietor's constant attention. The property descended in a terrace and finished with a little platform overhanging the sea. Below, picturesque fragments of rocks and heaps of stones suffered the assaults of the agitated sea. Stuffed cormorants received visits from their living counterparts.[74]

From 1902 onward the Grand Duke would regularly visit Chaïr as well as Pershino, although his work continued to occupy most of his time. In May 1902, he led a parade at Krasnoe Selo for the new President of France, Emil Loubet,[75] and in September he attended maneuvers near Kursk, south of Moscow, then traveled to Bulgaria to participate in the celebrations of the 25th anniversary of the liberation of Bulgaria in the Russo-Turkish War.

On his return he received a new appointment that put him at the heart of Russian war planning. In November 1902, the Tsar named him commander-designate of the Russian North West Front in the event of war. Simultaneously, the Tsar made the Minister of War, General A. N. Kuropatkin, commander-designate of the South West Front. Russian war plans in this era assumed that the enemy would probably be Germany or Austria-Hungary or both. The Grand Duke would command the forces fighting Germany, while Kuropatkin would lead those fighting Austria-Hungary.

The central problem facing Russian planners was what to do about Poland, which stuck out in a huge salient, flanked by German East Prussia to the north and Austro-Hungarian Galicia to the south. Deploying large numbers of troops to Poland at the start of a war was dangerous, as they might be cut off by a pincer attack from north and south, but mobilizing the army further to the east meant abandoning Poland, an option many considered politically unacceptable.

Kuropatkin and the Grand Duke did not see eye to eye on this issue. On learning that he was to be commander-designate of the North West Front, the Grand Duke met Kuropatkin on 19 (30) November 1902. After the meeting, Kuropatkin wrote in his diary that he worried the Grand Duke had already decided on his plan and that it did not involve defending Poland. "I fear," wrote Kuropatkin, "that his decision will be unfavorable for us, to surrender the forward theater without a fight."[76]

The Grand Duke was by now starting to make his influence felt at the highest levels of the Russian military. In March 1903 he wrote to the Emperor proposing that Russia split the administration of the army. At that time, one person, the Minister of War, was responsible for both war planning and administrative issues. Many felt that this was too much, and that strategic planning suffered as a result. The Grand Duke proposed the following:

> Russia's military power, its vast dimensions, the variety of the political and military significance of its borders, make it difficult to combine in one person the complicated and difficult work of executing measures to develop and perfect all the resources of the state.... Supreme power, having given the broad direction of policy, should have two independent organs: a war ministry as an administrative institution ... and a general staff, the supreme power for using military resources in time of war.[77]

The first of these, wrote the Grand Duke, should be under the Minister of War; the second should be under a new position of Chief of the General Staff. The Minister of War should keep control of all the institutions of the Ministry, but the Chief of the General Staff should control the officers of the General Staff, military communications, military-topographical matters, and the General Staff Academy.[78] As we shall see in the next chapter, this idea would form the basis of a reform carried out in 1905.

In June 1903 Nikolasha accompanied the Tsar and other members of the royal family to the town of Sarov in the Nizhnii Novgorod region northeast of Moscow to witness the canonization of Serafim of Sarov, an 18th-century Russian hermit whose deeds were much admired by Nicholas II and his wife. The canonization reflected the firm belief of many in the royal family in the miraculous powers of holy men, a belief fostered particularly by Nikolasha's sister-in-law, Grand Duchess Militsa Nikolaevna. She and her sister, Anastasia Nikolaevna (nicknamed Stana), were daughters of Prince Nikola, the ruler of Montenegro. In 1889 Militsa had married Grand Duke Pyotr Nikolaevich, while Stana married Georgii, the Duke of Leuchtenburg. A third sister, Elena, married the King of Italy. Militsa and Stana were known as the "black sisters" on account both of their Montenegrin roots and of the evil influence they were believed to have on Empress Aleksandra Fedorovna, whose closest confidantes they were. Militsa was the older and more outgoing of the two, "a very clever woman, smart, ambitious, and prone to intrigue," according to General von Raukh. Stana, by contrast, "preferred to keep quiet."[79] Militsa was fascinated with oriental religion, wrote several works of theology, and supposedly "exercised a great moral and religious influence" on the Empress.[80] According to Baroness Sophie Buxhoeveden:

> The sisters were devoted to each other and had delightfully warm and attractive manners. The Empress soon became really intimate with them,... [and] saw them nearly every day.... The Grand Duchesses awakened in the Empress a real interest in theological questions.... Through her friendship with the Grand Duchesses Militza and Stana, [the Empress] became inter-

> ested in mystical questions, she developed a belief in the existence of people in the world, who, by their saintly lives can become links between humanity and God.[81]

In 1901 Militsa and Stana had introduced the Tsar and his wife to a supposed holy man from France, Philippe Nizier-Vachod, whom they called simply "Monsieur Philippe." The Empress hoped that, after four daughters, Philippe's powers would help her finally bear her husband a son and heir. The Emperor and Empress visited Monsieur Philippe at Grand Duke Pyotr Nikolaevich's palace at Znamenka on more than one occasion,[82] and although there is no record of whether Nikolasha attended these sessions, it seems likely.

Nikolasha dabbled in spiritualism, including table turning. When Raukh asked him whether this was true, he admitted it, although somewhat bashfully, claiming not to believe in it and to have tried it only to get proof that it was trickery.[83] Spiritualism and séances were extremely popular across Europe and North America in the second half of the 19th century, and even well-educated people believed in ghosts, fairies, and other supernatural phenomena. Nikolai Nikolaevich's interest in these matters was not out of the ordinary.[84] In any case he seems to have lost interest after a short time. In July 1902 Empress Aleksandra Fedorovna wrote to her sister Ella: "About Nikolasha—I said that in bygone days spiritualism interested him, [but] he has dropped it long ago."[85]

Belief in miracles was common not only among members of the Russian royal family but also among the Russian population. According to historian Leonid Heretz, traditional Orthodoxy saw the causes of events as lying "not in the realm of the material and the observable, but rather in the sphere of the spiritual or, for lack of a better term, the 'supernatural.'" Fate determined everything, and people believed in the "omnipresence of supernatural forces and the relative powerlessness of man." Large calamities were due to the judgment of God, and "general well-being was dependent on general adherence to God's laws, understood primarily as ritual observance."[86]

The canonization of Serafim of Sarov provided Nikolasha and other Romanovs with an opportunity to associate themselves publicly with Russian folk religion and, as Richard Wortman says, demonstrate "the union of tsar and people" as they gathered together with tens of thousands of ordinary worshippers to celebrate the new saint.[87] Nicholas II recorded in his diary on 18 (31) July 1903, that "At the hottest time of the day, Uncle Sergei, Nikolasha, Petiusha, Yuri and I set off for the hermitage by foot, along the Sarovka.... At 6.30 the service began.... It was a very solemn moment when the glorification began and then the kissing of the casket. We left the church at this time, having stood for three hours." The next day he wrote, "We heard of many people being cured today and yesterday. Another cure happened in the cathedral, while the holy relics were being carried round the altar. God is miraculous through his saints."[88]

After the celebrations at Sarov, Nikolasha returned to the task of planning for war. In August 1903 he surveyed the Vilna military district, one of the key areas he would be responsible for defending in the event of a war with Germany.[89] In September he inspected exercises in the Warsaw military district. As was so often the case, the Grand Duke was critical of what he saw, writing to Nicholas II on 26 September (9 October) 1903, that "The maneuver undoubtedly did a lot of good, as it made it possible to point out many deficiencies. Thanks to my critique, commanders took away much which was instructive for their education in the field."[90]

The Grand Duke next continued his inspection of the Western border and then once again met with Kuropatkin to consider their plans for the defense of the Empire. According to Kuropatkin, the Grand Duke told him he had come to the conclusion that it was necessary to fortify the town of Grodno in Belorussia, which controlled the route into Lithuania. The Minister of War considered such measures to be a mistake.[91] This disagreement would be the start of a debate—which would later become very significant—about the role of fortresses in the defense of the Western frontier.

The Grand Duke and Kuropatkin never reached agreement. On 27 January (4 February) 1904, the Japanese attacked the Russian fleet in Port Arthur and war broke out between Russia and Japan. Both the Grand Duke and Kuropatkin were natural candidates to take command of the troops in the Far East. According to General Rediger, Nicholas II initially wanted Nikolai Nikolaevich to take command of the army but changed his mind because he felt that Kuropatkin was more popular.[92] Others told a different story. According to General Danilov, for instance, the Tsar simply wanted to keep the Grand Duke close by him.[93] Whatever the truth, the Tsar did not appoint Nikolai Nikolaevich, who spent the war safely in Saint Petersburg. Instead, Kuropatkin got the job and headed off to the Far East to lead the struggle against Japan.

Observers were generally critical of what they saw of the Russian cavalry's performance during the war, despite the ten years it had spent under the Grand Duke's aegis. Their criticisms ran along predictable lines: it was insufficiently aggressive, prone to inaction, poor at reconnaissance, and overly fond of fighting on foot.[94]

To some extent these criticisms were fair, but as one modern British historian points out, foreign officers' observations "[may] have been influenced by their own continuing arguments more than any objective analysis."[95] Furthermore, the overwhelming majority of the Russian cavalry in the Far East consisted of irregular Cossack units. The war did not provide a very good testing ground for the Grand Duke's reforms. That said, the experience does suggest that his reform agenda had not completely succeeded.

More generally, opinions about the Grand Duke's time as inspector general vary. Supporters claimed, "In the ten years between 1895 and 1905, the Russian cavalry was again put in its old and glorious place.... Its inspector general could look back at all this with a feeling of complete satisfaction and justified pride."[96] Even future Minister of War General Sukhomlinov, who loathed the Grand Duke, reluctantly admitted, "in educating our cavalry he did a very great deal. With his strong personal initiative he woke up the Russian cavalry."[97]

These positive comments came from cavalrymen who appreciated the return of the traditional "cavalry spirit," but questions remain as to whether this was the correct direction in which to take the Russian cavalry. "Grand Duke Nikolai Nikolaevich prepared the cavalry excellently as an *independent arm*," writes historian Maksim Os'kin, "but modern war requires close cooperation with infantry and artillery.... This was not done."[98]

The one criticism of the Grand Duke as a cavalry leader that is certainly incorrect is that he suffered from the traditional Romanov affliction of "paradomania." Perhaps because he was so good at organizing parades, one of the foremost historians of the late Imperial Russian army, Bruce Menning, has described him as "a pedant whose main concern was 'appearance and order in formation' and for whom field exercises were secondary."[99] This is very far from the truth. Grand Duke Nikolai Nikolaevich was a serious soldier who put a great deal of emphasis on field training and determinedly enforced high standards among his officers. As Sukhomlinov noted, he "brought the cavalry out of vegetation in the manège into the field."[100]

The Grand Duke had been an energetic inspector general. Greater challenges now lay ahead. In 1905, revolution struck Russia, and the Tsar called on Nikolasha to rescue him in his hour of need.

CHAPTER 5

The October Manifesto, 1905

BY JANUARY 1904, the 47-year-old Grand Duke Nikolai Nikolaevich was one of the most important people in Russia, not merely because of his increasingly central role in strategic military planning but also because of his personal closeness to Nicholas II. He was a regular dinner and evening companion to the Emperor and his wife, as were his brother, Pyotr Nikolaevich, Pyotr's wife, Militsa, and Militsa's sister, Stana. On 25 January (7 February) 1904, for instance, the Emperor recorded in his diary, "Nikolasha and Stana dined with us and sat with us for a long time."[1] Similarly, he wrote on 27 January (9 February), "Nikolasha and Stana came to see us after dinner,"[2] and on 30 January (12 February) he noted, "Nikolasha and Stana spent the evening with us."[3]

These diary entries reveal something else of importance: Nikolasha was spending a lot of time with Stana. Judging by the Emperor's diary, the Grand Duke rarely visited the Emperor alone. He was nearly always in the company of his brother, Militsa, Stana, or some combination of them. Nikolasha and Stana would soon be romantically entangled.

An occasional companion during the visits was Nicholas II's military secretary, Prince Vladimir Orlov. The owner of the source of the popular Narzan mineral water, Orlov was said to be "so obese that, when sitting, he was unable to see his own knees."[4] Tall thin Nikolasha and short fat Orlov made an improbable pair, but the two were to become close political allies.[5] Orlov would be the Grand Duke's eyes and ears at Court in the years to come, a role that would earn him the enmity of the Empress, who denounced him as "fat Orlov, who is N's [Nikolasha's] colossal friend."[6]

The Grand Duke visited the Emperor throughout the winter and spring of 1904.[7] In July 1904, Nikolai and Pyotr Nikolaevich went to Pershino, and on their return to Saint Petersburg the brothers, with Militsa and Stana in tow, once again spent an evening with the Emperor.[8] In August, the Grand Duke accompanied the Emperor on a visit to the Don region.[9]

By this time, the political situation in Russia was becoming unstable. Rapid population growth had worsened the economic plight of the peasantry,[10] while industrialization had created a small but growing working class that was becoming politically radicalized. The Tsars had failed to undertake meaningful political reforms, refusing to integrate either the liberal middle classes or the more radical workers and peasants into the political system.

The war with Japan exacerbated the situation. When in August 1904 the Japanese defeated the Russian army at the battle of Liaoyang,[11] many in Russia held the government responsible and demanded drastic reform of the country's political institutions.[12] This was particularly true of the more democratically inclined sections of the nobility and the middle classes, many of whom were involved in the zemstva, organs of local self-government first instituted in the 1860s.

Uncertain how to react to the growing political opposition, the government vacillated, creating an image of weakness and thereby encouraging resistance. After revolutionary terrorists assassinated the Minister of the Interior, Viacheslav Konstantinovich von Plehve, on 15 (28) July 1904, Nicholas II endeavored to appease the liberal democrats by appointing as von Plehve's successor Prince Pyotr Sviatopolk-Mirskii, who was known to support concessions to the zemstva. The appointment backfired, as zemstva members interpreted it as a further sign of weakness and exploited it to expand their efforts to force radical political change.[13] On 6 (19) November, zemstva leaders held a national congress and issued resolutions demanding an elected legislature and freedom of the press and of association. In short, they demanded nothing less than an abolition of the autocracy.[14]

Soon afterward the unrest spread to the poorer elements of the population. A strike by workers at the Putilov factory in Saint Petersburg was copied at other plants, and on 9 (22) January 1905, about 150,000 workers marched to the Winter Palace to present a petition for better working conditions and political reform. The Saint Petersburg city authorities responded with brutal violence, shooting at the marchers and attacking them with cavalry. Perhaps 1,000 people were killed or wounded in the events of what became known as "Bloody Sunday." The result was outrage across Russia, manifested in strikes, peasant uprisings, and mutinies in the armed forces. Russia teetered on the brink of revolution.

Meanwhile the news from the war got worse. In early 1905, the Japanese army won a clear victory over its Russian opponents at the Battle of Mukden. Shortly afterward, on 28 February (13 March), the Tsar summoned Nikolasha to the Imperial Palace at Tsarskoe Selo to discuss what should be done about the situation in the Far East.

The Grand Duke used the meeting as an opportunity to revive the proposal he had made two years previously to split the Ministry of War, as well as to put forward a fresh suggestion for a new administrative organ to supervise the making of national defense policy. The Tsar, Nikolasha, and a group of other senior military and civil officials agreed that Kuropatkin should be replaced as commander in the Far East.[15] The meeting also focused on the general situation, which those present viewed pessimistically. Nikolai Nikolaevich declared that "the whole course of the campaign gives one no right to hope that it will go any better in the future."[16] He then put forward his proposal to create a new body, the Council of State Defense, which would coordinate all parts of the government involved in national security policy.[17] Once the meeting broke up, work on creating this Council began.

The Tsar had not yet given up all hope of victory against Japan. Two days after the meeting, he instructed Nikolasha to chair a commission tasked with investigating what resources were available to continue the struggle.[18] A little over two weeks later, the Grand Duke reported back that he considered the war a lost cause. The Siberian railway could only transport half of what the army needed, and the army's morale was low. Continuing the war would require time to establish new bases, but the Grand Duke wrote,

> The whole progress of the campaign gives little hope that this can be accomplished, and the current situation and the condition of the army make me doubt that we have found the resources and that the enemy would give us the time we need... All of this, combined with the unnaturally sad domestic situation, brings me to the grave conclusion that we must prepare the ground on which the war can be ended, for, given our current position and the sum total of all the facts, we cannot count on brilliant successes.[19]

Following the commission's report, the Grand Duke's priority was enacting his proposed reforms in military administration. The ideas for these reforms had circulated within the Russian military for many years,[20] but the experience of the Russo-Japanese War gave them new impetus. The Ministry of War contained within it a body known as the "Main Staff," which was responsible for many issues, including not just operational planning but also administrative matters.[21] There was a widespread feeling within the army that the lack of a senior officer who concentrated solely on strategic planning was a major deficiency.[22]

Not everybody was in favor of the changes. When asked by the Tsar to give his opinion, the commander of the Kiev Military District, General Sukhomlinov, objected that the changes would divide authority and that no single person would bear full responsibility for all military policy.[23] Sukhomlinov's opposition won him the Grand Duke's lasting enmity. From this moment on, relations between the two men would become extremely hostile.

Sukhomlinov's arguments did not prevail, and the project went ahead. As a first step, in May 1905 the Grand Duke chaired a series of six meetings of senior officers to discuss the reform of military institutions. Those present resolved that the work of the Main Staff should be split into two parts: a Main Directorate of the General Staff would now handle issues related to the preparation for war, and a Main Staff would deal with administrative issues. Every arm of service would now have its own inspectorate general. Most of those present, including the Grand Duke, also agreed that the new Chief of the General Staff should be subordinate directly to the Emperor, not to the Minister of War. The reasoning behind the latter change was that "the main deficiency of the current structure of military governance is the absence of an authoritative figure specially occupied with preparing for war and responsible for this preparation."[24]

Meanwhile, the Grand Duke chaired another series of seven meetings to draw up regulations guiding the work of the proposed new Council of State Defense. At the second of these, on 9 (22) May 1905, he expressed the following view: "The responsibilities of the Council should consist primarily of coordinating the actions of all ministries in preparing for war, in eliminating disagreements between institutions on these matters, and overseeing the execution of Imperial orders."[25] The Grand Duke thus saw the Council's role from the beginning as being one of coordination rather than control, and the role of its President as being to run a collective council in which institutions could get together to resolve disputes, rather than serving as a sort of military dictator issuing orders to those institutions. This is certainly how he ran the Council as long as he was its President.

Nevertheless, he was adamant that the President must be informed of any government institution's actions that affected defense planning. This included the Foreign Ministry. Thus on 10 (23) May, the Grand Duke commented that "coordination of the actions in the sphere of foreign policy with those in the area of preparations for war is extraordinarily important. Policy without force is a soap bubble. Every political combination must rest on real force. The President of the Council must be fully informed of foreign policy, in order that he can report to the SOVEREIGN EMPEROR in a timely fashion about the extent of our preparedness for war."[26]

The result of all these meetings was the creation of a new Council of State Defense, whose members included the Naval and War Ministers, the Chief of the General Staff, the Chief of the Naval Staff, the Inspectors General of the various arms, and other generals and admirals as nominated by the Emperor. The Council was empowered to discuss all matters of military management, oversee the execution of its decisions, and discuss proposals put forward by the War and Naval Ministries. The President of the Council had the right to report directly to the Emperor. If it could fulfill its mandate to create agreement among the ministries, the Council had the potential to become the central body in national security policymaking. This was certainly the aim. However, the new Council lacked executive power. Its decisions remained subject to the Emperor's approval, and while the President of the Council had the right to report to the Emperor, the Minister of War and the Navy Minister retained this right also, and it was accorded to the new Chief of the General Staff as well. This meant that if any of the three were unhappy with the decisions of the Council they could simply bypass them.

This was exactly what happened. The creation of the Council of State Defense was part of a general movement in the aftermath of the Russo-Japanese War to develop what historian David McDonald refers to as "United Government," another part of which was the establishment of Russia's first Council of Ministers. The problem, as McDonald notes, was that united government "worked only when [Tsar] Nicholas respected it," and in practice he always saw it as a threat.[27] The Russian Emperor never liked surrendering his independence and found that the existence of a body dedicated to ensuring agreement among ministries restricted his own freedom of action. Nor was he alone in disliking united government. Many in the bureaucracy felt that it created a wall between themselves and the Emperor and thereby threatened their parochial interests. As a result, they sought to undermine it.

It would take some time for these problems to become obvious. In the meantime, on 8 (21) June 1905, Nicholas II issued an order establishing the Council of State Defense and appointing Grand Duke Nikolai Nikolaevich as its President. Two weeks later, the Emperor released the Grand Duke from his post as Inspector General of Cavalry. The 48-year-old Grand Duke now became, after the Tsar, the foremost military official in the land.

By this time the political situation inside Russia had deteriorated further. On 14 (27) June 1905, the sailors of the battleship *Potemkin* mutinied.[28] Thousands of industrial workers were on strike, and in the countryside peasants were encroaching on the property of large landowners and burning down manor houses.[29] Lacking a large rural police force, the government had to use the army to quell these disorders, but this was creating discontent among soldiers.

Under the circumstances, Nicholas II came to the belated conclusion that the war against Japan must be brought to a close. In late June 1905 he took advantage of an offer to mediate by US President Theodore Roosevelt and dispatched former Finance Minister Sergei Witte to the United States to negotiate a peace settlement. Before leaving, Witte met Grand Duke Nikolai Nikolaevich, who briefed him on the military situation in the Far East. According to Witte, the Grand Duke "would not offer any opinion on whether or not peace should be negotiated or under what conditions it should be made, except to say that under no circumstances should we cede a square inch of our soil.... In his usual precise way, and in considerable detail, he told me that the army could not endure another defeat of the magnitude of the ones at Liaoyang and Mukden." Continuing the war, said the Grand Duke, would "probably entail the loss of up to 250,000 dead or wounded, and would probably cost a billion rubles."[30]

Witte successfully negotiated a peace settlement that resulted in the Treaty of Portsmouth between Russia and Japan, signed on 23 August (5 September) 1905. This obliged Russia to withdraw from Manchuria and to cede the southern half of the island of Sakhalin to Japan. Russia had lost the war.

While Witte was in the United States negotiating peace, Nicholas II sought to strengthen Russia's weak international position by striking a deal with the German Emperor, Wilhelm II. On (11) 24 July, the Emperors of Russia and Germany met on Nicholas's yacht off the Finnish coast and there signed a short mutual defense pact, known as the Treaty of Bjorkö, committing each side to come to the aid of the other, if either was attacked, and also obliging the Russians to inform the French and to propose to them that they join the pact. On learning of the treaty, both Witte and Russia's Foreign Minister, Count V. N. Lamsdorf, neither of whom had been warned in advance, were furious. In their eyes, it was inconceivable that France would accept the invitation to join the new Russo-German pact, and the result of the Bjorkö treaty would be the destruction of Russia's alliance with France, which most in the Russian government considered essential to their nation's security.

On his return to Russia, Witte enlisted the help of Grand Duke Nikolai Nikolaevich to get the Emperor to rescind the Treaty of Bjorkö. According to Witte, the Grand Duke "accepted the argument that the treaty would put the Emperor in a dishonorable position and he would not have agreed to it had he understood the implications.... The Grand Duke promised to help." A few days later, the Emperor summoned Witte, Lamsdorf, and Nikolasha to his palace at Peterhof, where the three "explained to His Majesty why the treaty should be annulled."[31] The Emperor agreed to inform the Germans that the treaty would not come into effect unless France accepted it. This guaranteed that it remained a dead letter. The brief pact with Germany came to an end, while the Franco-Russian alliance persevered.

In July 1905 the Council of State Defense began its work, meeting on 18 (31) July to discuss reinforcing the Turkestan Military District in Russian-controlled Central Asia. The Foreign Ministry feared that the British might exploit the current Russian weakness by invading Central Asia from India via Afghanistan and had asked the Ministry of War to prepare a plan to reinforce the region. The Ministry of War had done this, but the Ministry of Finance was unwilling to provide the necessary funding. The Emperor had therefore referred the matter to the Council.

This first Council meeting revealed early disagreements between General Rediger, the Minister of War, and the new Chief of the General Staff, General Palitsyn. The latter felt that the plans to reinforce Turkestan were unnecessary. A British attack through Afghanistan was, he said, unlikely as it would be "pointless." By contrast, Rediger argued that the Turkestan Military District needed forces that could be mobilized into "a solid armed force capable of successful battle on a broad front." At present, Rediger complained, there were enough forces to advance a little way into Afghanistan and seize Herat, but no more.[32]

That the Russian Ministry of War should be contemplating invading Afghanistan so soon after losing a war against Japan rather beggared belief, even if this was merely contingency planning. After hearing the arguments, Grand Duke Nikolai Nikolaevich intervened to restore a degree of sanity. "In Turkestan," he said, "the aim right now should be defending our borders. Thoughts about advancing on Herat should not be taken into consideration." The question, the Grand Duke continued, should be what forces were needed for purely defensive purposes. The best way to strengthen the defenses of Central Asia was not to deploy additional troops there but to build a railway from Tomsk to Tashkent. The Grand Duke argued that Russia might need to fight on any of its frontiers, and to be able to do so, it should not place troops directly on those frontiers but, rather, should "[keep] a strong and well-equipped army in the centre of the country, which would be connected with the borderlands by a well-developed rail network," border regions having only those forces needed until rail-borne reinforcements arrived. The Grand Duke won this argument. The Council voted unanimously to support his position.[33]

The Council of State Defense met again on 1 (14) September to discuss the promotion system for senior officers, and the Grand Duke and War Minister Rediger again found themselves on opposite sides of the argument.

In 1899 the Russian army had introduced a system of age requirements for officers, with upper limits for every rank. The purpose of this was to keep the army young and the quality of the officer corps high, by eliminating officers who failed to get promoted before they reached the upper age limit for their rank. As the army could not afford to lose officers during wartime, it had suspended the age restrictions for the duration of the war against Japan. The question that now arose was whether to reinstate them or abolish them. Opinion within the Council of State Defense was almost evenly divided. Having heard the arguments for and against, Grand Duke Nikolai Nikolaevich declared that he had argued against the age limits when they were originally proposed. Practice had shown that they were harmful, and if commanders carried out proper appraisals of subordinates, there would be no need for them. The real problem was that the appraisal system was "completely unsatisfactory," he said. Given the need to eliminate the large complement of overage officers that had accumulated during the war against Japan, it would make sense to reinstitute the age limits until demobilization was complete, as this would enable the army to get rid of the excess officers, but as soon as that was done the system should be abolished. The Grand Duke won the argument, but only just, with the Council voting by seven votes to five to do as he suggested.[34]

There were yet more disagreements when the Council met again on 22 September (5 October) to discuss proposals that Rediger had put forward to change the system by which officers were appointed to command positions. Rediger proposed the creation of regimental commissions responsible for promotion decisions. These would consist of members of the same regiment as the officer being evaluated and would be chaired by the regimental commander. The suggestion provoked sharp responses. Nikolai Nikolaevich lent his voice to those who opposed it, saying that Rediger's proposed system was not the best way of choosing senior officers. Rather, the best results would come from "the establishment of strict responsibility of commanders for painstakingly checking the accuracy of the appraisals which are given to them."[35]

Given the lack of agreement on the issue, the meeting resolved to consult more widely and to ask military district commanders to call special meetings to discuss the matter. The Council then established its own position. Five of those present, including Rediger and Grand Duke Pyotr Nikolaevich, voted that regimental commissions were in principle desirable. Five, including Grand Duke Nikolai Nikolaevich, voted against this position.[36] The issue was put off until the results of the wider consultation could be known.

The Grand Duke's tolerance of dissenting views on this issue was in keeping with the manner in which he would run the Council over the next two and a half years. He permitted free exchanges of views and did not attempt to force his own opinions upon the group. According to Rediger, the Grand Duke would greet Council members in the room next to his office, where there was a "big, wide table, covered in a green cloth."[37] Sitting at the end of the table nearest his office, Nikolai Nikolaevich would introduce the question to be discussed but would not at first state his own opinion. This had the advantage of not suppressing any dissenting voices, but it did reduce his ability to influence the direction of the debate. As Rediger states, "At meetings under his chairmanship, the Grand Duke told everybody to state their opinion freely and it was possible to argue with him as much as you liked. Whenever somebody felt shy about opposing his point of view, he would say, laughing, 'Please, speak, I know that you don't agree with me, but each one of us must speak his mind.'"[38] Minutes of the meetings of the Council of State Defense confirm this. The atmosphere was one of open discussion, and although Nikolai Nikolaevich would sometimes express firm views on a subject, he would wait until everybody else had spoken before doing so. He seems to have been genuinely interested in hearing everybody's opinion.

This style of command contrasted strongly with his previous brusqueness and forcefulness. It fitted, however, with his preference for listening rather than talking. As Grand Duke Aleksandr Mikhailovich described him, "he talked and listened, listened more than he talked, it being his traditional habit to leave a visitor impressed by his ability to keep his own counsel."[39] Furthermore, chairing the Council of State Defense was not the same as commanding cavalry. The Council members were not subordinates but peers, and the President's task was to coordinate the various organs of state defense, not to command them. He had no authority to tell members what to think or say or to make decisions on their behalf, and he needed their expertise on matters outside his area of competence. This required openness in debate.

At the end of September 1905, Nikolai Nikolaevich went to Pershino for the autumn hunting. Leaving the capital at a time of national emergency seems in retrospect rash and irresponsible. However, at the time there was no obvious reason to expect a sudden crisis. In fact, the situation had improved over the previous two months, with fewer eruptions in the cities and the countryside.[40] When the situation suddenly took a turn for the worse, it came as a surprise to everyone, including the revolutionary leaders.[41]

The spark for the sudden breakdown in order was a strike by Moscow printers that began in late September. Further unrest soon ignited and spread rapidly to other workers and other cities. Before long these local events gave rise to a general strike across the country, and law and order began to break down.

By mid-October it was obvious that the government could not regain control with half-measures. It had to either make significant political concessions or use overwhelming force. The choice was a stark one between reform and dictatorship. The Tsar's advisors were split between the two options.

Hardliners, such as the Minister of the Imperial Court, Baron V. B. Fredericks, were determined to defend the Tsar's absolute powers and opposed any concessions that undermined them.[42] Others, such as Sergei Witte, War Minister Rediger, and the Deputy Minister of the Interior D. F. Trepov, believed that the army was not in a fit state to restore order by force alone. Witte in particular felt that a military dictatorship was not a feasible option.[43] He urged the Tsar to make political concessions.

The Tsar was unable to make up his mind. In any case, if he chose to install a military dictatorship, he would need a dictator. The obvious choice was Grand Duke Nikolai Nikolaevich.

In Pershino, the Grand Duke suddenly received a telegram from the Emperor. It was short and to the point. "Come. Nicholas," it said.[44] On reading it, the Grand Duke left immediately for Saint Petersburg.

Getting there was not easy, as most of the railways were not working, while the cross-country routes were clogged with seasonal mud. First the Grand Duke rode with a small retinue some 60 kilometers from Pershino to the town of Serpukhov in the Moscow region. There, the local authorities managed to get a locomotive and a single wagon, which took the Grand Duke to within about ten kilometers of Moscow, at which point he transferred to a horse-drawn troika, which took him into the city. From there he took a specially arranged two-wagon train on to Saint Petersburg.[45]

Upon his arrival in the capital on the morning of 15 (28) October, the Grand Duke went straight to see the Emperor. Joining him were Witte and the director of His Majesty's Chancellery for the Receipt of Petitions, General Adjutant O. B. Richter. The day before, the Emperor had asked Witte to prepare a draft manifesto promising political reform. The Emperor received the four men at 11 o'clock in the morning, and Witte proceeded to lay out the options—issuing a manifesto promising a constitution or establishing a military dictatorship with the Grand Duke as dictator. According to Witte, "As I read, the Grand Duke asked many questions, to which I replied in detail, adding my opinion that while a constitution would not guarantee immediate calm, given the bloody war we had been through and the disorders we were experiencing, it would restore calm more quickly than would a dictatorship."[46] The meeting adjourned without a decision, and the Grand Duke set off to consult others to determine what he should do. General von Raukh, who spoke to him shortly afterward, wrote that the Grand Duke's overwhelming consideration was "to save the Tsar."[47] As Raukh put it:

> He told me that having arrived in Petersburg, he first of all set himself the task of finding out the true state of affairs in Russia and for this purpose

> turned to D. F. Trepov, who painted an extremely grave picture of the whole situation, from which he concluded that the Tsar was in very serious danger, which meant that he had to think above all about how to save him. Then he went to Count Witte, and had a long conversation with him, during which the latter showed that the only way out of the situation was to grant liberal reforms (i.e., a constitution), and in addition declared that *he would carry out the reforms and pacification of the country himself.* Still unconvinced by these arguments, he then met representatives of the right, Goremykin, Baron Budberg, and Count Aleksei Pavlovich Ignatiev, who rejected Witte's plan and the need for liberal reforms, but at the same time *none of them agreed* to take power into their own hands and to take responsibility.[48]

If Raukh is to be believed, it was this final point that swung the Grand Duke in Witte's favor: Witte was willing to take responsibility for seeing through his policies, whereas the supporters of dictatorship were not. These were not, though, the only people with whom Nikolasha met. On 16 (29) October, he also had a meeting with a representative of what might be called the "loyalist" trade unions, M. A. Ushakov. Ever the source of scurrilous rumors, A. A. Kireev reported,

> Nikolai Nikolaevich lost that empty head which God gave him. He met a delegate of the revolution and held negotiations with him.... The delegate [i.e., Ushakov], a severe man, frightened the Grand Duke. He explained to the Grand Duke that the Tsar must answer with his life for the terrible consequences of the Japanese war. Crossing himself, the Grand Duke began to swear that the Tsar was not to blame for the war. "You're Orthodox, you believe in God," he said. "Yes, I believe," replied the revolutionary, "But the cross is yours." And the Grand Duke began to cross himself.[49]

Ushakov's own account was rather less dramatic. The Grand Duke asked him what the workers wanted. In reply Ushakov said that although the workers were for the most part loyal, they wanted a constitution, and Witte was the only man capable of carrying out the required reforms.[50] The discussion with Ushakov seems to have helped convince the Grand Duke that he must support Witte's proposal. Certainly, he did not wish to become dictator. As a military man he was disinclined to playing any role in politics, and those whom he had consulted had not given him much confidence that a dictatorship could succeed.

The Tsar was still undecided, and some of his entourage continued to hope that they could persuade Nikolai Nikolaevich to accept the mantle of dictator. On 17 (30) October, Nicholas II invited the Grand Duke to lunch at Peterhof. Before meeting the Emperor, Nikolasha visited Baron Fredericks. It appears to have been an extremely emotional meeting. According to Kireev, who, it must be said, is never a very reliable source, the Grand Duke "ran to Fredericks, ran like a madman around his room with tears in his eyes.... 'We must, must save the Sovereign,' he repeated, 'Are you willing to sacrifice your life for this?' 'Of course.' 'Well, we must save the Tsar, save him,' he repeated, running in tears about the room."[51] Similarly, General Mosolov wrote that Fredericks later gave this account of the Grand Duke's reaction to being told he should be nominated as dictator: "Unnaturally agitated, the Grand Duke pulled out his revolver and shouted: 'If the Sovereign does not accept Witte's program and wants to nominate me dictator, I will shoot myself in front of his eyes with this very revolver. We must go to the Sovereign. I came to you to tell you what I have just said. Support Witte come what may. We must do this for our own sake and for Russia's.'"[52]

After leaving Fredericks, the Grand Duke went to see the Tsar and recommended that he support Witte. The Tsar accepted the Grand Duke's recommendation, summoned Witte to Peterhof, and signed the Manifesto.[53]

That evening the Grand Duke returned to Petersburg. He seemed, according to one witness, to be "happy and pleased." Referring to events of 17 (30) October 1888, when a train carrying Emperor Alexander III had crashed at Borki in Ukraine, resulting in the death of 23 people but not injuring any members of the Imperial family, he told Witte, "Today is the 17th anniversary of the day when the dynasty was saved at Borki. It seems to me today that the dynasty has been saved from no less a danger as a result of the historical action which has just taken place."[54] The Grand Duke was right to be pleased, as his decision to turn down the role of military dictator was wise. He had no experience of civil affairs and was unqualified to wield political power. It is a point in his favor that he was aware of his own limitations.

The Manifesto that he had persuaded the Tsar to sign fundamentally altered Russia's system of government. Previously, the powers of the Tsar were in theory absolute. This was no longer the case, for the Manifesto provided for a new elected assembly, the Duma, whose consent would be required for any legislation. The Manifesto also guaranteed important individual rights, such as freedom of conscience, speech, assembly, and association. In short, the Manifesto meant that the Tsar ceased to be an absolute ruler, and for the first time Russia had, at least to some limited extent, institutions of constitutional democracy.

Grand Duke Nikolai Nikolaevich had not suddenly become a liberal democrat. He explained his actions as being driven above all by necessity. According to General Danilov, he said, "I supported him [Witte] only because I considered him the only person capable of carrying out reforms. At that minute the situation was such that, apart from him, there was nobody else suitable, and reforms were necessary."[55] Similarly, Raukh wrote, "His decision was not the result of Count Witte's influence, for he was absolutely not one of the latter's supporters .... but his own deduction from the situation in Russia, as being the *only* possibly way out in his opinion and the only method of *saving the Tsar*."[56]

His enemies did not see it this way. The more reactionary elements of the Imperial Court never forgave Nikolai Nikolaevich for what they saw as a betrayal. October 1905 marked the beginning of a serious break in relations between the Grand Duke and the Court. Perhaps most importantly, Empress Aleksandra Fedorovna, a firm believer in Tsarist absolutism, blamed Nikolasha for the creation of the new constitutional order, which limited her husband's powers. As she wrote to Nicholas II ten years later, writing as always in imperfect English, "We are not ready for a constitutional government, N's fault and Wittes it was that the Duma exists, & it has caused you more worry than joy."[57] Relations between Nikolasha and Empress Aleksandra never recovered, and the arrival on the scene a little later of Grigorii Rasputin deepened the rift still further.

CHAPTER 6

Restoring Order, 1905–1906

ON 19 OCTOBER (1 November) 1905, two days after signing the Manifesto, Nicholas II recorded in his diary that he lunched with Nikolasha and the "black sisters," Militsa and Stana.[1] The diary makes it clear that they and Grand Duke Pyotr Nikolaevich continued to be regular visitors throughout the next few months. This was especially true of Militsa and Stana, who remained the Empress's closest confidantes. At some point in late October 1905, the two Montenegrin sisters told the Empress of a new holy man. This was the infamous Grigorii Rasputin.[2] According to Militsa's son, Prince Roman Petrovich:

> When Archimandrite Theophan [Inspector of the Saint Petersburg Theological Seminary] learnt that Uncle Nikolasha intended to visit the Valaemskii Monastery, he arranged a meeting with Rasputin in the house on Italianskaia Street where my uncle lived. Uncle Nikolasha found Rasputin's stories and pilgrimages very remarkable, and the man made an excellent impression on him. He knew that my mother [Militsa] was very interested in the history of the monastery, and advised her to invite Rasputin.[3]

Militsa met Rasputin and on 1 (14) November 1905 introduced him to Nicholas and Aleksandra. Nikolai Nikolaevich thus played a pivotal role in bringing Rasputin to the Imperial couple's attention.

Rasputin's almost hypnotic powers attracted zealous followers (including the Emperor and Empress) who were convinced that he had mystical healing powers. On 30 July (12 August) 1904, the royal couple had finally celebrated the birth of a son and heir, the Tsarevich Aleksei, but unfortunately the boy suffered from hemophilia and came close to dying on several occasions. The Empress came to believe that Rasputin had the power to heal her son. She therefore brooked no criticism of the "holy man," and before long a serious rift had formed between Aleksandra Fedorovna and "the black sisters." This falling out further undermined her relations with Nikolasha.

In the meantime, Nikolasha had received another important appointment. On 26 October (8 November), the Emperor named him Commander of the Guards and of the Petersburg Military District. Nicholas II clearly felt the need for a more dynamic leader in the Russian capital, and a few days later wrote to his mother to say, "God grant that Nikolasha does well. I am convinced he will try everything possible—he is such a good soldier at heart and so energetic—let's hope he will be less abrupt in his manners with his subordinates than he used to be."[4]

Nikolasha moved immediately to replace the District's most senior officers with others more amenable to him. He appointed General M. A. Gazemkampf as his Deputy Commander, General A. V. Brilevich as his Chief of Staff, and General G. O. von Raukh as his Quartermaster (a title that in the Russian army described the officer responsible for operational planning). According to the Minister of War at the time, General Rediger, Gazenkampf "was a very useful person for the Grand Duke, knowledgeable, hard working, possessing a huge memory," but he was also liable to change his mind whenever the Grand Duke contradicted him.[5] Gazenkampf, Brilevich, and Raukh "hated one another," claimed Rediger. Raukh proved to be the strongest personality and gradually became the most influential.[6]

The new team faced an immediate crisis. On 26 October (8 November), the very day that the Grand Duke and his staff learned of their new assignments, sailors in the Kronstadt garrison mutinied, seized weapons from the arsenals, rioted through the streets of the town of Kronstadt, attacked their officers, and destroyed the officers' quarters.[7] Located on Kotlin Island in the Gulf of Finland, a short distance from Saint Petersburg, Kronstadt and its fortresses protected the Russian Baltic fleet and the approaches to the Russian capital. Its proximity to Saint Petersburg made the mutiny there extremely dangerous.

The Commandant of the Rifle School in Saint Petersburg, Major General Ragozin, cobbled together an improvised force consisting of two companies of soldiers studying at the school and two machine-gun companies. Grand Duke Nikolai Nikolaevich asked the Naval Ministry to provide barges to transport this force to Kronstadt.[8] The detachment sailed across to Kotlin Island the next morning and rapidly restored order. The Grand Duke's first crisis as Commander of Petersburg Military District had been successfully dealt with. A little later he issued an order thanking the troops: "I declare my gratitude to Major General Ragozin for the initiative he displayed and the rapid formation of the detachment, I thank with all my heart all the officers for their commendable zeal, and to the other ranks I declare my heartfelt 'Thank You.'"[9]

Unfortunately, relations between the Grand Duke and the navy went downhill within days. On 27 October (9 November), the Grand Duke gave Raukh a message to pass on to the Chief of the Naval Staff, Admiral A. A. Virenius. The message instructed Virenius not to send the naval squadron at Sveaborg fortress, outside Helsinki, back to Kronstadt. The next day, Raukh informed the Naval Minister, Admiral Birilev, of the message. The Sveaborg squadron sailed back to Kronstadt anyway, and Birilev, according to Raukh, denied ever knowing about the Grand Duke's instruction.[10] Nikolai Nikolaevich was furious. "I am on the verge of giving a report saying that I am laying down all responsibility for restoring order in Kronstadt," he wrote to Raukh. "The restoration of order is possible only if the sailors, with Birilev at the head of them, fulfill all my instructions unconditionally, and as a guarantee Birilev must not issue any orders or undertake anything without my permission."[11]

Ensuring that the armed forces remained loyal was a vital concern. To this end, on 11 (24) November, the Grand Duke chaired a meeting of the Council of State Defense to consider measures to "improve the allowances and way of life of lower ranks." General Rediger put forward proposals to increase soldiers' salaries and improve their food and overall conditions by, for instance, providing bedding, soap, and other essentials. Nikolai Nikolaevich fully supported Rediger's proposals. All the proposed measures were, he said, "urgent." The Council approved the proposals in full.[12]

Declarations that conditions were to improve were one thing; implementation was another. Improvements depended upon funds that were not always available. A year after the Council's decision, in November 1906, the Petersburg Military District issued an order to its units announcing that new scales of rations were being introduced but that these would cost more than the sums being provided to units. In light of the lack of funds to pay for the initiative, Grand Duke Nikolai Nikolaevich instructed commanders to abide by the new scales only if possible, although he also instructed them to "incline toward the improvement of soldiers' food and increasing its variety." He further expressed the hope that "commanders of all levels will invest their heart into this important matter and will approach this problem not purely from a formal standpoint, but with the aim of genuinely improving soldiers' conditions, without exceeding existing monetary allowances."[13]

In any case, the causes of the mutinies in the army went beyond poor living conditions and included political agitation among soldiers by revolutionary groups. On 19 November (2 December) 1905, the Grand Duke met Sergei Witte, who had become president of the newly created Council of Ministers (in effect becoming Russia's first prime minister), and spoke to him about the "danger of the influence of propaganda."[14]

In the aftermath of the October Manifesto, Russia went almost overnight from having a strictly censored press to having almost total press freedom. The result was an explosion of revolutionary publications. The staff of the Petersburg Military District decided to counter the revolutionary agitation by buying a newspaper and turning it secretly into their own organ for spreading pro-government propaganda among the troops. They settled on the newspaper *Golos Rossii* (*Voice of Russia*), which was published in a workers' district of Saint Petersburg. The Tsar personally gave Grand Duke Nikolai Nikolaevich 100,000 rubles in cash to finance the scheme, which the Grand Duke passed on to Raukh. The revamped newspaper was issued daily and distributed free to all units in the garrison under the pretense that it was an independent publication.[15]

Such measures could not produce instant results. In the meantime, disturbances continued, especially in the fleet. Particularly troublesome were the crews of the Eighth, Fourteenth, and Eighteenth Flotillas, which were based in the naval barracks in Saint Petersburg. The Grand Duke decided to remove these crews to Kronstadt. When, however, the officers of the Fourteenth Flotilla ordered the crew to assemble on the morning of 24 November (7 December) 1905, the sailors refused. Faced with this mutiny, Nikolai Nikolaevich sent the Life Guards Cavalry Regiment to arrest the ringleaders and force the remaining sailors onto the barges that had been readied to take them to Kronstadt. As the Grand Duke informed the Emperor, he had given an order to the cavalry that "In the event of disobedience, and especially of aggressive actions, they should compel them with force of arms."[16] The action had the desired effect. Once the army had surrounded their barracks, the sailors backed down and agreed to go to Kronstadt. No violence was necessary, the mutiny came to an end, and a potentially destabilizing element was removed from the capital.

To improve morale and discipline, the Grand Duke arranged a series of reviews of units before the Emperor. These took place at the Emperor's palace at Tsarskoe Selo on the units' regimental holidays, many of which fell late in November and December. The night beforehand, the unit would hold an officers' dinner with the Emperor and the Grand Duke in attendance.[17] This probably did more to raise officer morale than it did to elevate spirits among the other ranks, but anything that deflected the troops' focus away from suppressing revolution and back toward normal garrison life probably served a useful purpose.

One of these parades was for the Finland Regiment, which celebrated its hundredth anniversary in December 1905. A painting of the occasion, which now hangs in the Hermitage in Saint Petersburg, shows the Emperor and a party of senior officers marching behind an aged priest in blue-and-gold robes, reviewing the officers of the regiment in the manège at Tsarskoe Selo. The Emperor, in a blue uniform with gold epaulettes, with the light blue sash of the Order of Saint Andrew over his shoulder, is carrying his infant son, wrapped up in a white ermine cloak. Nikolasha is several feet behind. Now 49 years old, he stands as straight as ever, but his short hair has mostly gone gray, and he has a short pointy gray beard and a curly moustache. His chin and his pinkish nose jut purposefully forward, and his gray-blue eyes stare fixedly at the scene in front of him. The painting speaks of imperial tradition and power. There is no hint of the revolution brewing throughout the country.[18]

Maintaining an appearance of normality was an important part of the Grand Duke's plan for keeping order in the capital. He was opposed, therefore, to declaring martial law in Saint Petersburg, saying, "I find that martial law has been completely debased in recent times, for it has been introduced everywhere, but the measures called for by it are in practice not implemented. As a result, it only frightens and constrains peaceful inhabitants and doesn't frighten our enemies at all."[19]

Normal life for the Grand Duke himself meant, besides his work, spending time at his club, where he was a regular visitor, speaking with colleagues, playing cards, or watching billiards.[20] At the height of the revolutionary activity, he had to limit his visits, both because of the pressure of work and because of security concerns.[21] Terrorists attempted to kill him on several occasions, but he found the resulting security irksome. Eventually, he did agree to reduce his visits to the club and theaters, but only on condition that his guards make their security measures as discreet as possible, so that he would not notice them.[22] According to Julia Cantacuzen, the Grand Duke did not like the secret police (the Okhrana) or the uniformed security police known as the Corps of Gendarmes. He even issued an order banning the gift of regimental buttons to officers of the Guards who left their regiments to join either the Okhrana or Gendarmes.[23] He also strongly objected to the Gendarmes running agents inside military units to spy on soldiers.[24]

On 28 November (11 December), the Grand Duke summoned the commanders of all the units in the Petersburg Military District to his palace for a pep talk. He urged them "to pay particular attention to discipline and the state of morale in their units, and demanded that officers be especially close to their soldiers in order to win their trust, and that they talk with soldiers to explain events to them."[25] The Grand Duke also warned his commanders against taking the law into their own hands, as had happened when several officers threatened the editor of the newspaper *Rus'*, to whose political stance they objected. This, he said, created "a bad impression in the mass of society which was well disposed to the army." He concluded, "I believe that everything will turn out well, because I believe in you and your units.... I ask you to trust me as you trusted my father, and to believe that I will be able to lead you when it is necessary."[26] His speech, wrote Raukh, "was pronounced with great élan, great sincerity, and it was wonderful to see what a strong impression it had on all those present."[27] When the Grand Duke finished, the response was "a common cry: We believe, and Hurrah. It was very triumphant."

Word of the meeting reached the Tsar, who was delighted by what he heard and wrote to his mother, "Not long ago he [Nikolasha] held a reception of commanding officers and addressed them in a fiery speech on loyalty and fidelity to their oath, delivered so impressively that it moved his audience to tears. Their cheers were heard in the streets outside. I was told this by several people who were there!"[28]

Some of these officers would soon see action, as it was necessary to send troops from Saint Petersburg to quell troubles elsewhere in the country, especially in the Baltic region, the southern parts of which saw some of the highest rates of violence in the entire Russian Empire in 1905. The government had already declared martial law in the province of Kurland on 6 (19) August, and now on 22 November (5 December) followed up with a similar declaration of martial law in Lithuania. Martial law was extended into other parts of the Baltic region later in December.[29] In this corner of the Empire, revolutionary violence had taken on a nationalist tinge, directed against the German-speaking nobility who owned much of the land in the region.[30] Peasants had driven the landlords from their estates, deposed local authorities, and established their own governments.[31]

On 30 November (13 December), Nikolasha and General V. V. Sollogub, the Governor General of the Baltic, finalized a plan to send punitive detachments to the Baltic, the most important of which was a group of troops under Major General A. A. Orlov in the northern Baltic region.[32] Nikolai Nikolaevich selected Orlov, whom he knew well, because of his "energy,"[33] but initially he considered Orlov's actions "insufficiently tough." With the Grand Duke's approval Raukh wrote to Orlov demanding more decisive action: "Nobody on high is going to condemn you for excessive severity but, rather, for a lack of it. You must exploit the mood of society, which is outraged by the armed actions of the revolutionaries and so will justify every kind of extreme response; this mood will soon pass, only terror can stop terror."[34] Orlov reacted as desired, unleashing what one historian calls "an unspeakable reign of terror," killing some 1,170 people.[35] By January 1906, the army had largely restored order in the Baltic region. Although the Grand

Duke was prepared to make political concessions when necessary, he had no qualms about using brutality to restore order.

New crises continued to erupt. In early December 1905 socialists declared an uprising in Moscow, distributed arms to workers, and set up barricades. Within a few days, the rebels had seized large parts of the city and most of the railway stations, although the Kremlin remained under government control. Lacking confidence in the loyalty of his troops, the Governor General of Moscow, Admiral Dubasov, withdrew most of them from the streets and requested reinforcements from Saint Petersburg.[36] Nikolai Nikolaevich was reluctant to provide them and initially refused.[37] The Grand Duke told Witte that his primary task was to protect Petersburg and the surrounding area where the Emperor and his family lived, and that if he sent troops to Moscow he would have insufficient soldiers in the capital.[38] The Tsar overruled him and insisted that the troops be sent.[39] The Grand Duke therefore dispatched the Semenovskii Guards Regiment, commanded by Major General G. A. Min, to Moscow. It arrived on 15 (28) December, and three days later joined in the final attack against the rebels with relish. Ordered by Dubasov to "exterminate the gangs of insurgents,"[40] Min told his troops, "Act without mercy, there will be no arrests." After shelling the rebel stronghold in the Presnaia district, the Guards broke into the district and "wreaked bloody vengeance."[41] By 19 December (1 January), the uprising was over, and the Semenovskii Regiment returned to Saint Petersburg.

The Grand Duke's reluctance to send troops to Moscow marked a growing divergence of views between him and Prime Minister Witte. The latter was attempting to split the revolutionary forces by holding talks with their more liberal wing. The attempt failed, in part because the liberals felt that they had the upper hand and saw no need to work with the government. In the Grand Duke's eyes, this tactic merely discredited the government. "This unsteadiness," wrote Raukh, "the vagueness of Witte's policy, quickly led to the Grand Duke losing faith in him, and already in December the Grand Duke and D. F. Trepov, then Court Commandant, came to the mutual conclusion that they should apply all their resources to ensuring that Count Witte should not be allowed to open the State Duma, in other words to obtain his dismissal before the Duma."[42]

Witte, meanwhile, had come to the conclusion that the Grand Duke was a reactionary and a supporter of the "Black Hundreds,"[43] the term given to those on the extreme right wing who opposed the October Manifesto and wished to return to the old autocratic order. Viciously anti-Semitic, the Black Hundreds incited pogroms against Jews, whom they held responsible for the revolution. Foremost among the Black Hundred groups was the

Union of the Russian People, led by Aleksandr Dubrovin, a doctor living in Saint Petersburg. Witte's suspicions that Nikolasha had reactionary political leanings increased when he learned of a meeting the Grand Duke had had with Dubrovin in December 1905.

Raukh later claimed that the meeting was his own idea. He had met Dubrovin and come away with a "good impression."[44] He was, nevertheless, alarmed when Dubrovin admitted that activists in his party were planning to kidnap Witte. Dubrovin said that he lacked the authority to stop them, and that the only person whom they would listen to was Grand Duke Nikolai Nikolaevich.[45] When Raukh reported this, the Grand Duke agreed to meet Dubrovin and two other members of his party.[46]

According to Raukh, after a meeting of about half an hour on 16 (29) December, "when the Grand Duke left, they [Dubrovin and his colleagues] told me that they were delighted with His Highness's words and that in no event would they carry out any acts without his permission.... The essence of the Grand Duke's words consisted of showing the inappropriateness of any acts, and [the Grand Duke] concluded by promising that if circumstances changed and real danger threatened the Emperor, he would appeal to them for help."[47] After this, claimed Raukh, neither he nor the Grand Duke ever had any contact with the Union of the Russian People again. The Grand Duke, he wrote later, "never had any contact with any political parties, for he was firmly of the point of view that a military man must stand aside from all political parties."[48]

Around this time, the Grand Duke proposed a plan to the Emperor to reopen the Trans-Siberian Railway, much of which had been seized by troops who had mutinied on their way back from the war in the Far East. The Emperor described the plan in a letter to his mother as "an excellent idea." It involved pushing a detachment of troops under the command of General A. N. Meller-Zakomelskii eastward along the railway as far as Irkutsk, while simultaneously sending another detachment under General P. K. von Rennenkampf westward from Kharbin. As the Emperor told his mother, "Their object would be to re-establish order at the stations along the line, and in the towns, to arrest all agitators and to punish them with exemplary severity."[49]

Meller-Zakomelskii set out on 1 (14) January 1906, and Rennenkampf eight days later. The two acted with great ruthlessness. Meller-Zakomelskii "achieved his success by shooting or hanging dozens of people, flogging hundreds, and arresting thousands."[50] His and Rennenkampf's troops fired on trains containing mutinous soldiers, forced the soldiers off the trains, beat them, and then sent the mutineers on their way to their final destination. By February 1906, the government had regained complete control of the Trans-Siberian Railway.[51]

At the start of 1906, the situation in Russia seemed to be slowly improving, and the need for political concessions had somewhat subsided. On 3 (16) January, the Grand Duke met the Tsar at his palace at Tsarskoe Selo. That morning the conservative newspaper *Novoe Vremia* had contained an article about a proposal to confiscate state and private land and redistribute it to peasants. On the train to Tsarskoe Selo, Nikolai Nikolaevich discussed the article with Raukh, and the two agreed that the idea was a bad one. Neither the state nor large-scale private landowners had sufficient land to satisfy the demands of the many millions of peasants, they felt, besides which the idea challenged the principle of private property. Nikolai Nikolaevich said he would discuss the matter during his meeting with the Tsar. That evening Raukh received a brief letter from the Grand Duke on the matter: "I gave my report," the Grand Duke wrote, "You can be completely calm—Nothing of the sort will happen. On the contrary, they will issue an order not to exploit the hopeless position of many ruined landowners and not to harm the price of land, but to pay the true price to landowners who wish to sell their land. Thank God, with God's help, Russia and the Tsar will be saved. Your Nikolai."[52]

On 28 January (10 February) 1906, the Grand Duke attended a meeting to discuss how the army could best be deployed for internal security. Also present were Interior Minister P. N. Durnovo, the War Minister, General Rediger, the Deputy War Minister, General Polivanov, and the Chief of the General Staff, General Palitsyn. The meeting took place at Witte's insistence. Expecting further violent incidents in the countryside in the summer, Witte and Durnovo argued that the army should be scattered around the provinces in small garrisons, under the control of the local civil authorities, to prevent disorder and crush it when it broke out. General Rediger strongly objected. The plan would in effect turn the army into a police force. Grand Duke Nikolai Nikolaevich also disliked it and suggested a compromise. Giving the civilian authorities control of the army would be dangerous, he argued. Nevertheless, the army needed to be prepared for the eventuality that the police might require its help. The best way of ensuring that the army could provide this help would be to use the existing military district organizations and to divide the country into regions, each with its own commander. Within these districts the troops should be concentrated in large groups (rather than dispersed, as Witte had proposed). Provincial governors who needed assistance could turn to the regional military commander, while the concentration of forces under that commander would ensure that troops could rapidly strengthen threatened points.[53]

The Grand Duke's proposal won the meeting's support and provided the basis for an agreement when the group met again a month later on 1 (14) March. It was then agreed that troops would remain under the commanders of the military districts. These districts would be divided into regions, with a military commander appointed for all the troops in each region. Troops would not be split up into formations smaller than a regiment, independent battalion, or battery.[54] Through this compromise, Witte and Durnovo got additional troops for internal security, but the army maintained its control over them and ensured that they were kept in reasonably large formations.

In the meantime, the Council of State Defense had renewed its work after a pause of several months. Following the discussions in the Council the previous summer, the Ministry of War had prepared two options for the defense of Turkestan. Opening a meeting of the Council on 4 (17) February 1906, Nikolai Nikolaevich noted that the political situation was very different from the last time the Council had discussed the issue, especially because of the end of the war with Japan. He therefore invited debate on the ministry's proposals.

Most of those present [illegible] that offensive action was out of the question, but that they must be ready to parry a blow at any time. For this reason, General Palitsyn maintained that they should keep units in the Turkestan Military District at full readiness. This would mean keeping the existing number of battalions, each with the wartime complement of five companies. Rediger, meanwhile, insisted that finding money for Turkestan was extremely difficult, and it would have to come out of the budget of the rest of the army. They should, he said, avoid any offensive ideas, such as seizing Herat in Afghanistan, and instead focus on intelligence and railway construction.[55]

In response, Grand Duke Nikolai Nikolaevich laid out his strategic concept. Finance was important, he said, but money alone should not decide matters of state. In all issues, he maintained, one should start with a theoretical discussion and then move on to discuss what could be done in practice.[56]

The Grand Duke proceeded to explain what he considered the theoretical ideal in this instance. Based on the assumption that Russia had three possible enemies in the East—Japan, China, and the British Empire in India—he told the Council this:

> Remembering that preparing for the worst is the sole guarantee of success, we have no right to take into account just one enemy, but must consider all three. Because of this, there should be no suggestion of aggressive actions on our side. Our policy in the Far East should be demonstrably peaceful, but with a powerful fist behind it, and we should build all our proposals on the

> idea that, if we are dragged into war, we will be ready on a large front not only to parry the blow directed against us but also to seize the initiative in our own hands by going onto the offensive. All decisions concerning the preparation and grouping of our forces should derive from these ideas, following the well-known principle: if you want peace, prepare for war.[57]

The members of the Council agreed unanimously with this analysis, although Rediger expressed doubts that a Russian offensive against Afghanistan would deter others from attacking Russia. The Grand Duke agreed with Rediger on that point but countered that they must be equally unsure of the impact if Russia suffered a first blow without responding. "We must," he said, "seize the moral initiative in our own hands ... and for this must be in a position of suitable readiness for going onto the offensive."[58]

A few days later, the Council of State Defense turned to the question of the Far East. The meeting began with a report from Foreign Minister Lamsdorf, who noted that Russia needed to strengthen its defenses in that area. The Grand Duke then asked Council members for their opinions. A long discussion followed, focusing mainly on the relative merits of concentrating forces in the Usuriisk or Zabaikal regions.

The Usuriisk region bordered on the Pacific Ocean and contained Russia's principal far eastern city, Vladivostok. At the time, the Trans-Siberian Railway was not finished; there was a gap between Lake Baikal and Usuriisk. The last leg of the rail journey to Vladivostok had to be made through China along the Trans-Manchurian Railway via Kharbin. This made the defense of Russia's Pacific shoreline immensely difficult. Japanese naval superiority would allow Japan to land substantial forces anywhere along the coast, while the Chinese could cut reinforcements from Russia along the railway. Until the Trans-Siberian Railway was completed, these factors gave the Russians only three options: one (a very expensive option), place as many forces in Usuriisk in peacetime as would be needed to defend it successfully in time of war; two, concentrate forces in Zabaikalsk and gamble on being able to use these to reinforce the Pacific coast; or three, admit that there was no way Usuriisk could be defended and so leave only as many troops there as were needed for internal security.

Most of those on the Council favored the second option, but the Grand Duke supported the third. In the event of war, Russia would be doomed to defeat in Usuriisk, he said. It would be best to leave the region only lightly defended. Territory would be lost, but at least the army would survive, "the living force, the troops will remain untouched."[59] The Grand Duke also suggested that the fortress in Vladivostok should be abandoned. Like many of

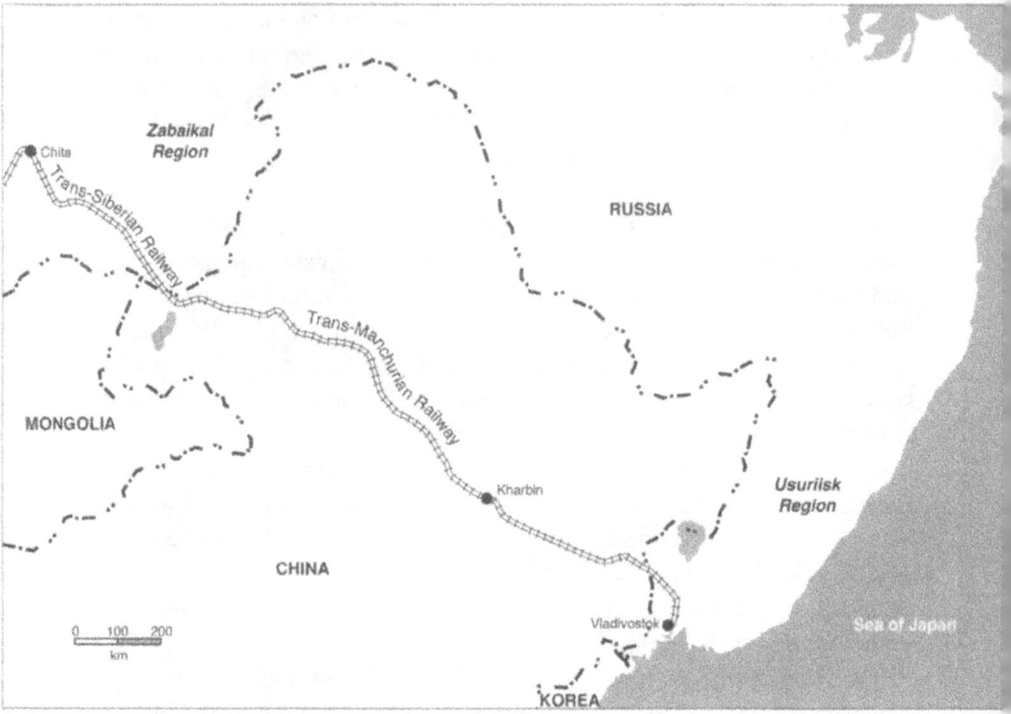

Map 2: The Far East

Russia's fortresses, its defenses were obsolete, and upgrading it would be very expensive. "Vladivostok as a fortress cannot have a powerful impact on the successful outcome of the campaign, and so the large expenditures required to improve it are not needed," said the Grand Duke.

This was probably a correct assessment. Even if Vladivostok were upgraded, Japanese naval superiority would probably mean that any forces in it would find themselves surrounded and have to surrender before they even had a chance to influence the campaign. But other members of the Council did not agree. The Grand Duke asked them to vote on whether Vladivostok was needed as a fortress. Eight of those present voted yes and also said that it should be strengthened and turned into the "strongpoint" of the defense of Usuriisk. Only the Grand Duke voted in favor of eliminating the fortress. He was also on his own when the Council voted on how many troops should be kept in Usuriisk. Whereas he voted to limit the number of troops to those needed for internal security, his colleagues preferred to keep a large amount of forces there.[60]

In this case, as during the initial debate about Turkestan in July 1905, the Grand Duke's standpoint was probably more realistic than that of his colleagues. His isolation on this issue also reveals that the Council of State Defense was certainly not a rubber stamp for his opinions. Its members did not feel in any way obliged to follow his lead, nor did he attempt to make them do so.

On 15 (28) February 1906, the Council of State Defense returned yet again to the issue of Turkestan. The Ministry of War argued against keeping units in Turkestan permanently at their wartime complement of five companies. Grand Duke Nikolai Nikolaevich disagreed. As he often did, he stressed the psychological impact of offensive action. In the event of war in Central Asia, a rapid blow against Afghanistan could influence England and Japan. "At present," he said, "our credit in the East is undermined and we need at the first instance to raise it, and for this to rely on real strength or, to put it another way, on the military preparedness of our troops. The East understands this well, and we must do everything to prepare for and guarantee our initial success." The majority of the Council agreed with the Grand Duke and voted to maintain battalions in Turkestan at wartime strength.[61] This represented a defeat for the Ministry of War, which started to become very frustrated with the Council.

The next significant meetings the Grand Duke attended were those of a special council called by the Emperor to draft the new Fundamental Laws, which would govern the country. According to Raukh, when Nicholas II asked Nikolasha to join the council, he agreed to do so but at the same time made the following clear: "he has no knowledge of civilian issues, doesn't understand them, and so will not intervene in them, for they don't concern him; he will sit in the meetings, because the Sovereign wants him to, but will not state his opinions."[62] Raukh noted that, as far as the Grand Duke's political opinions were concerned:

> Having spoken for and recognized the necessity of granting the Manifesto, the Grand Duke was and remained convinced that the Manifesto was appropriate and necessary for the country's development and that because of this it was the government's duty to observe it strictly and bring it into life; he also thought that the scale of the rights granted corresponded to requirements and so there should be no talk about expanding them.... He understood nothing about civilian questions. He always regarded state issues very broadly; his opinion was often impractical and unrealistic, i.e., it was difficult to enact it when it clashed with reality, but his views and personal opinions were never small-minded or fake. I will say that his thoughts were sometimes naive but always honest and straight.[63]

The council to discuss the Fundamental Laws met several times in April at Tsarskoe Selo. Those attending included the Emperor; Grand Dukes Nikolai Nikolaevich, Mikhail Aleksandrovich, and Vladimir Aleksandrovich; and various ministers and members of the State Council. Nikolai Nikolaevich did not say much at the meetings, but contrary to what he may have told Raukh he was not entirely silent either. At the first meeting on 7 (20) April, he spoke out twice. The first time was during a debate about who should have the right to amend the Fundamental Laws. Some believed that as the Manifesto said no laws could be passed without the support of the Duma and State Council, this should apply to the Fundamental Laws also. Others felt that the Tsar should retain the right to amend them himself. This was a matter of considerable importance. If the Tsar had the power to amend the Fundamental Laws by himself, the new constitutional order was something the Tsar could abolish whenever he wanted and so was not strictly speaking a constitutional order at all. Nikolai Nikolaevich's view on the matter was, as he said, that "the fundamental laws should say only that the Duma cannot change the fundamental laws." That said, the Emperor alone should have the authority to change those parts of the fundamental laws that concerned the royal family. "We must," he said, "state in the fundamental laws that the institution of the royal family can be changed solely by the Sovereign Emperor."[64]

The second issue on which Nikolai Nikolaevich spoke out was the status of Finland. Witte had expressed his dislike of a statement in the draft laws that Finland was part of Russia; he believed this statement could cause problems. Nikolai Nikolaevich agreed, noting that Finland was "a volcano." "Without doubt one can expect a worsening of the situation. It is better to reject any reactionary amendment which will make things worse."[65]

On 9 (22) April, the council discussed possibly the most important issue of all: whether the Fundamental Laws should contain a statement that the Tsar's powers were "unlimited." Nikolai Nikolaevich spoke only very briefly but decisively, saying simply, "with the Manifesto of 17 October Your Imperial Majesty already struck out the word 'unlimited.'"[66] With this short statement, the Grand Duke admitted that the days of absolute monarchy were over. This view prevailed, and the Fundamental Laws avoided any mention of the Tsar's unlimited power.

In the third and fourth meetings on 11 (24) April, Nikolai Nikolaevich's main concern was with Article 13, which concerned the governance of the armed forces. The draft article stated that the Emperor was responsible for the management, disposition, and training of the military. In the Grand Duke's eyes this was too specific, indeed "dangerous." He was adamant, he said, that the Duma should not concern itself with any matters concerning military institutions. The wording of the draft created the possibility that the Duma could claim the right to intervene in military matters which were not specifically listed as being the Emperor's responsibility. Rather than having a list of competencies, it would be better to have a simple statement that the Emperor would be responsible for all issues concerning the defense of the realm. The Emperor agreed.[67]

Finally, the Grand Duke intervened in a debate about citizens' rights. In line with his earlier discussion with the Emperor about the confiscation of land, he stressed the need to include a firm statement in the Fundamental Laws about the inviolability of property rights. This resolution, he said, "must be worded in a very clear and decisive manner."[68]

Following nationwide elections in March 1906, the Duma assembled for its official opening in Saint Petersburg on 26 April (9 May). This event sparked great hopes (that a new era in Russia's political development was beginning), and fears (that the Duma's actions would only produce continued conflict). Opposition parties dominated the chamber, particularly the liberal Constitutional Democratic Party (known because of its Russian initials "K. D." as the Kadet party). Believing that political momentum was in their favor, they pushed for further reform, demanding that the Tsar appoint a government supported by the majority of the Duma. This demand, in effect, amounted to the creation of a parliamentary form of government. The Tsar refused.

By this time, the Tsar had dismissed Witte as chairman of the Council of Ministers, having lost faith in him following his failure to produce a victory for pro-regime forces in the Duma elections. His replacement was I. L. Goremykin, a loyal but decidedly conservative functionary who regarded the Duma with contempt. The combination of Goremykin as Prime Minister and an opposition majority in the Duma eliminated any chance that government and Duma might cooperate. Within days, the two were deadlocked, and the Council of Ministers rapidly came to the opinion that the Duma should be dissolved.[69]

The tension between government and Duma worried Nikolai Nikolaevich, who was concerned that it would result in trouble among Saint Petersburg's workers. General Raukh claimed that he suggested to the Grand Duke that ministers hold a secret meeting with Kadet party leaders to determine what their real position was. Raukh wrote that the Grand Duke liked the idea ("He grabbed onto it, as his impetuously impressionable character often did") and that he proposed it to the Tsar, who approved it.[70] Raukh may have been exaggerating the role that he and the Grand Duke played in this matter, since the Council of Ministers had already been carrying on secret negotiations with the Kadets. Regardless, the new Foreign and Interior Ministers, A. P. Izvolskii and P. A. Stolypin, did secretly meet with Kadet leader P. N. Miliukov. They came away convinced that the Kadets were determined to form a government entirely by themselves and implement their entire election manifesto, with what the ministers believed would be catastrophic results.[71] The secret talks did nothing to resolve the political impasse.

Crises, meanwhile, kept erupting. The next was a mutiny by the First Battalion of the Preobrazhenskii Guards Regiment. In June 1906, units of the Petersburg Military District went to Krasnoe Selo for the start of their summer maneuvers. Nikolai Nikolaevich's predecessor, Grand Duke Vladimir Aleksandrovich, had sent the troops by train from Saint Petersburg to Krasnoe Selo, a distance of about 25 kilometers. Nikolasha, however, considered this inappropriate and ordered that the soldiers should march.[72] This caused some discontent, which increased when the soldiers of the First Battalion of the Preobrazhenskii Guards Regiment were then ordered to march from Krasnoe Selo to the Imperial palace at Peterhof, where they were scheduled to carry out guard duties. After arriving at Peterhof, on 10 (23) June, members of two companies assembled to present a list of demands, saying that if these were not satisfied they would refuse to carry out their orders.[73] The petition included demands for "full issue of bed linen, money to buy gear, the release of the soldiers who had been arrested, freedom to discuss their needs"; it also included the statement, "We express our solidarity with the demands of the Duma deputies on allotting land to the peasants." At this point the petition had crossed into political territory.[74]

Senior officers, including the Regimental Commander, Major General Gadon, and the Divisional Commander, Major General Ozerov, chose to negotiate. Ozerov spoke to the officers of the battalion and told them to get the soldiers to write their demands down without fear of reprisal. But this attempt at letting off steam only encouraged the unit's extremist elements in their growing insolence toward their superiors.[75]

At this point, Grand Duke Nikolai Nikolaevich decided to intervene to restore order, so he sent a detachment of troops under General Orlov to Peterhof to surround the battalion and arrest the ringleaders. Orlov rapidly achieved this objective, rounding up the main mutineers without any opposition.

According to Raukh, on the day after the mutiny ended, Generals Palitsyn and Rediger visited Nikolai Nikolaevich at Krasnoe Selo, and the Grand Duke showed them a letter, which he had received from the Tsar. The Tsar's letter suggested disbanding the battalion. Palitsyn agreed and said that they should expel the entire battalion from the regiment and exile it to a remote location where it would gradually die out as the conscripts finished their terms of service. Raukh suggested an empty barracks at Medved in Novgorod province as a suitable location. The Grand Duke accepted the proposal and said that he would make this recommendation to the Tsar.[76]

A harsh, and utterly unprecedented, Imperial order then expelled the entire battalion, including all its officers, from the ranks of the Guards. It was reformed into a "special battalion" and sent to Medved to wither away. The Tsar allowed no exceptions to the punishment. When the Grand Duke asked him whether a Captain Maksimov, who had been abroad at the time of the mutiny, should be expelled from the Guards with the other officers, the Tsar insisted that he should.[77] The incident reinforced Nikolai Nikolaevich's image as a strong-willed leader, though it also earned him some enemies among those who were appalled that he could treat the premier infantry regiment in the land with such harshness. If Raukh is to be believed, however, the idea was the Emperor's, not the Grand Duke's.

The mutiny of the Preobrazhenskii Guards Regiment was not the last one of 1906, but although mutinies, strikes, and peasant uprisings continued throughout the rest of the year, none were quite as dramatic. A degree of peace began to return to the land. For Grand Duke Nikolai Nikolaevich, this meant that he could at last turn to the tasks of reforming the army and training it for war.

CHAPTER 7

The Council of State Defense, 1906–1907

THE SUMMER OF 1906 saw continuing turmoil in Russia, and despite his view that military officers should stay out of politics, Grand Duke Nikolai Nikolaevich found himself playing on occasion a decidedly political role.

By the start of July 1906, the Tsar's ministers had resolved to petition the sovereign to dissolve the Duma. War Minister Rediger informed Nikolai Nikolaevich of this decision on 2 (15) July, following which the Grand Duke summoned General Raukh and told him to speak to the Prime Minister, I. L. Goremykin, and ask him and Interior Minister P. A. Stolypin to visit him at his palace to explain the government's action. On the evening of 4 (17) July, the Grand Duke had dinner at the yacht club, and then went to his palace with Raukh. At eight o'clock, Goremykin and Stolypin arrived, and the Grand Duke asked them why they had decided to dissolve the Duma. Stolypin gave the explanation. The conflict between the government and Duma, he said, had "reached extreme limits, a crisis is close, and the quicker it is resolved the better." There were only two ways out of the current difficulty: allow the Kadet party to form a government or dissolve the Duma. The former option would mean the enactment of the Kadets' entire program of reform. In that case, said Stolypin, the country as a whole would shift dramatically to the left at which point, "The Kadets will soon understand that power is slipping out of their hands." The parties of the far left would then throw out the Kadets, and anarchy would result. The only way to avoid this scenario, Stolypin argued, was to dissolve the Duma.[1]

According to Raukh, having heard this, the Grand Duke asked a few questions, primarily about security measures, after which Goremykin and Stolypin left. The Grand Duke and Raukh then went back to the club. There, Raukh asked to speak in private with the Grand Duke and, he claimed, told him that dissolving the Duma would be unpopular and something would have to be done to assuage public opinion. Raukh suggested dismissing Goremykin and replacing him with Stolypin. If Raukh's account is accurate, then in making this suggestion he was clearly stepping over the normal boundaries of civil-military relations. But according to Raukh, the Grand Duke did not object. Instead, after thinking for a while, he merely told Raukh to telephone his brother, Grand Duke Pyotr Nikolaevich, and ask him to come to Krasnoe Selo. Nikolai Nikolaevich and Raukh then themselves left Saint Petersburg for Krasnoe Selo to participate in the summer exercises.[2]

A little later, Pyotr Nikolaevich arrived at Krasnoe Selo, where he had a long meeting with his brother. Afterward, Nikolai Nikolaevich revealed what had happened. According to Raukh, "It turned out that he decided to use the influence which Grand Duchess Militsa Nikolaevna, Grand Duke Pyotr Nikolaevich's wife, then had." Pyotr Nikolaevich had spoken with Militsa, who then spoke with the Tsar and Tsarina and persuaded them to replace Goremykin with Stolypin.[3] If this is true, and we only have Raukh's word for it, it was fairly remarkable. Not only had Nikolai Nikolaevich entered firmly into the realm of politics but he had relied on the personal leverage of Grand Duchess Militsa to achieve a change of great state importance. At any rate, Stolypin did replace Goremykin, and on 8 (21) July announced that the Duma had been dissolved.

This brief foray into politics notwithstanding, Nikolai Nikolaevich's main concern was reforming and training the army. The Council of State Defense also began to take up more of his time. Many of the issues now coming before the Council were very contentious, especially those concerning the navy. One such issue was a proposal to create a flotilla on the Amur River, which marked Russia's border with China. The flotilla could help protect communications with the Far East along the Amur until the rail link with the Far East was completed. The Council had approved the idea of the flotilla in principle when discussing the defense of the Far East in February 1906. Both the Naval Ministry and the Ministry of War (which had responsibility solely for the army) agreed that the flotilla was necessary, but the former argued that as the flotilla could not operate independently of land forces, the land forces should control it, and so the Ministry of War should pay for it, whereas the latter said that it was a naval matter and so the Naval Ministry should pay.[4]

After discussing the matter at length, the Council divided clearly between its army and navy members. Army members said the navy should control and pay for the flotilla, while the navy members said that the army should. As the army outnumbered the navy in the Council, the army won, and the Council determined that the navy should take responsibility for the flotilla.[5]

The Council was also divided on the issue of promotion commissions. A consultation with the commanders of the military districts had revealed that they were opposed to the creation of regimental and divisional commissions for evaluating officers. War Minister Rediger disagreed, however, and remained convinced of the benefits of such commissions at the level of combat units.[6] The subject therefore returned to the Council of State Defense for further discussion on 20 July (2 August) 1906.

Grand Duke Nikolai Nikolaevich supported the district commanders. "In our army irresponsibility reigns and always has reigned," he argued. "During all my service, punishment for official misdeeds has been so rare, that one can say that there has hardly been any at all. The essence of the problem is not this or that system, but the fact that there is no responsibility." To address this problem, unit commanders should be responsible for all their subordinates, and so they alone should appraise them. By contrast, "a committee is irresponsible and because of this should not be assigned the business of appraisal," he said.

The Council came to a compromise; the army would create commissions at divisional, corps, and district levels, but these were to be of a purely advisory capacity, with final responsibility remaining with commanders.[7]

On the same day as this meeting, units of the Petersburg Military District commenced their summer maneuvers on the exercise grounds at Krasnoe Selo.[8] Many troops were still needed for security duties and the maneuvers were on a smaller scale than normal. Still, the Grand Duke was determined to use the opportunity to provide some serious military training, and he set three objectives for the summer maneuvers: "to test new tactical concepts discerned from the recent experiences of the Russo-Japanese War"; "to provide some practical training for conducting night operations"; and "to give troops the opportunity to experience the character of contemporary war" by practicing combined-arms operations.[9]

On 1 (14) August, the troops paraded in front of the Emperor. Once this formality was out of the way, the more serious training began. The one report we have of it is provided by Colonel Moulin, whose view of what he saw, and Nikolai Nikolaevich's role in it, was generally very positive. Moulin felt that the Grand Duke, who was overall director of the maneuvers, was obsessed with the cavalry and would not leave it alone. As a result, "he demands that it intervene in combat, and each time it is then put out of action for a while because it is exposed to fire which decimates it."[10] Nevertheless, Moulin felt that

> As director of the maneuvers, Nicholas Nikolaevich is extremely active, extremely attentive to every detail. He doesn't hesitate to move in order to see everything. He dispatches his numerous aides-de-camp in all directions, seeking information, making himself aware of every movement.... He is the

spirit, the moving force, the regulator of the entire maneuver. One could not ask for a director of maneuvers to throw more of his heart and soul into his business. The zeal and activity of the Grand Duke is a stimulant for everybody.... Nicholas Nikolaevich sometimes loses his temper. But one feels that he is keeping a check on himself, and making a veritable effort to remain calm and courteous....

Although the execution leaves something to be desired, and despite the numerous faults and old errors which coexist with the interesting innovations resulting from the experience of the war, there are grounds for hoping that if the Grand Duke, closely advised as he is by General Palitsyn, continues to direct his subordinates with the ardor which he has just exhibited in his debut, four or five years from now the troops of the Guard and the Petersburg Military District will be far superior in their tactical training than they were before the war.[11]

Moulin also had the chance to observe the post-exercise debriefing the Grand Duke gave his senior officers in the presence of the Emperor. According to Moulin, the Grand Duke asked the senior commanders to explain how they had understood their mission, what they had based their decisions on, and what incidents had been contrary to or had disrupted the communication of their orders. "All these points," wrote Moulin, "were the object of a precise, sharp, and profound enquiry directed by the Grand Duke." Nikolai Nikolaevich then summed up for the Emperor, paying particular attention to the use of cavalry, reconnaissance, the transmission of orders and reports, and the losses produced by enemy fire. His comments were "simple, wise, and practical, bearing the imprint of a man who knows his profession," wrote Moulin.[12]

After the summer exercises, in September the Grand Duke went on leave to Pershino, returning to the capital around 8 (21) October.[13] There then followed a flurry of activity in the Council of State Defense. In the first instance, on 19 October (1 November), the Council of State Defense returned to the issue of the Amur River Flotilla. The Naval Minister, Admiral Birilev, announced that he would have to ask the Council of Ministers for additional credits to fund the flotilla but added that the ministers would probably not grant them. As a result, the project would be delayed for years. This provoked an outburst from the Grand Duke. "I have come to the opinion," he said, "that at present some sort of oppression is lying on all representatives of military and naval institutions, reflecting badly on their actions. This happens mainly because nobody is sure that he will be given the money which is necessary for this or that undertaking. It seems to everybody that they are not carrying out a living productive work but, rather, some sort of academic labor, which will never be completed due to the complete lack of guarantee that the necessary resources will be granted." He was convinced, he continued, that they needed to lay out the facts and their position in response to several key questions: What was the situation of the Russian armed forces compared to before the Japanese war? What did they need to do, and what expenditures on the armed forces were necessary to ensure that those forces were not weaker than their enemy's? And what must they do to ensure that the armed forces could resist an incursion across their borders? All the members of the Council agreed with the Grand Duke's statement.[14]

In essence what the Grand Duke was demanding was some basic strategic thinking that would answer the fundamental questions facing Russia, so that its military requirements could be drawn up and an appropriate budget to meet those requirements could be determined also. In the absence of such a strategy, any discussions of military policy would be rudderless.

Strategic planning was not the Grand Duke's responsibility. Rather, it was the task of the Chief of the General Staff and of the Chief of the Naval Staff. These men could not, however, simply impose their solutions on the rest of the defense establishment. They required the consent and cooperation of the Naval and War Ministries, funding from the Finance Ministry, the agreement of the Council of State Defense, and so on. Perhaps, if the threats to Russia had been singular and clear and if the national finances had been in good shape, agreement among these various bodies would have been possible. As it was, institutions were more concerned with protecting their own share of the pie than with reaching agreement on broad national objectives.

The effect of the lack of an overarching defense plan became clear when the Council of State Defense met on 26 October (8 November) and 10 (23) November to discuss plans put forward by the navy to rebuild the Baltic Fleet, which had been largely destroyed at the Battle of Tsushima in May 1905 during the Russo-Japanese War.

Admiral Birilev, the Naval Minister, began by stating that, in the absence of a current war plan, he was not presenting a complete shipbuilding program, merely a partial one, starting with the construction of two new battleships. His justifications included prestige, defense requirements, and supporting defense industries. "Russia cannot exist as a great power without a fleet," Birilev said, adding that if the battleships were not built, 30,000 workers in Saint Petersburg would lose their jobs.[15]

Grand Duke Nikolai Nikolaevich immediately picked up on this last point and asked whether it was actually true that Saint Petersburg's factories would go out of business without the battleship contracts. He asked Finance Minister V. N. Kokovtsov to answer this question. Kokovtsov replied that if the sole purpose of building battleships was to keep factory workers employed, it was a mistake. From an economic point of view it was better to close the factories. The question was really a different one: if they closed the factories now but then decided later that they needed to build more ships, would they have to spend even more money reconstructing the factories?[16]

Nikolai Nikolaevich responded to Kokovtsov, saying that his words made it clear that "from an economic point of view the question of unemployment was not of serious importance," but on the other hand it was impermissible to stop the factories from working, and so they should be given shipbuilding work. But this did not mean that they had to build battleships. It was not clear that such ships were needed or were suitable to the military tasks the fleet would be given.

A discussion then followed in which even the naval officers present were divided. Nikolai Nikolaevich summarized the debate by concluding that the factories should serve the fleet, and not vice versa. Only when the purpose of the Baltic Fleet had been determined could the Council decide whether to support the Naval Ministry's request.[17] The meeting ended without agreement.

When the Council of State Defense returned to the subject on 10 (23) November, it discussed what the roles of the Baltic fleet should be and what ships were appropriate for it. Again, opinions differed sharply. Some of those present felt that Russia must compete for control of the Baltic Sea against potential enemies, a role that required battleships. Others felt that a more appropriate task for the fleet was coastal defense, which implied much smaller vessels.

Having heard the various opinions, Grand Duke Nikolai Nikolaevich concluded that "the majority of naval members of the council are having difficulty in saying definitely that we must build two battleships immediately." Again, he complained about the lack of broader strategic direction. If naval and army institutions could present the Council with a jointly agreed-upon plan to defend the Baltic coastline, then the question of the battleships could be discussed in relation to this plan, and the Council could come to a logical decision. In its absence, however, the proposal to build two battleships "is so impractical that it is extremely difficult at present to give a definite answer." The Grand Duke therefore asked Council members whether they felt that they could decide the issue in the absence of a complete shipbuilding program. Eighteen members of the Council said no, while only two (Admirals Birilev and Dikov) said yes.[18] This decision amounted to a rejection of the navy's proposal.

Next on the agenda was the question of fortresses. This was to become one of the most controversial issues in Russian defense policy in the years that followed, especially with regard to the chain of fortresses in Poland. During the 19th century Russia had built a series of seven fortresses in Poland, at Kovno, Zegrze, Osovets, Novogeorgievsk, Warsaw, Ivangorod, and Brest-Litovsk. Their purpose was to cover the area further east in which the mass of the Russian army would mobilize and so buy time for the mobilization to be completed unhindered.[19] By 1906, advances in artillery technology meant that the Polish fortresses were obsolete. This was true also of other fortresses in Russia, such as those at Vladivostok in the Far East, Libava (modern-day Liepaja) on the Baltic coast, and Ochakov on the Black Sea coast. If the fortresses were to continue to fulfill their assigned role, they would need major upgrades. Faced with this problem, many officers in the Russian army, including Grand Duke Nikolai Nikolaevich, were to speak out in favor of demolishing some or all of these fortresses, but others demanded that large sums of money be spent on rebuilding them.

In September 1905, Grand Duke Pyotr Nikolaevich, who was now Inspector General of Engineers, had sent his brother a memorandum about the fortresses. The total cost of bringing all of those in Poland up to the necessary standard would be 200 million rubles, he wrote, but if one added fortresses elsewhere in Russia, the total would be some 300 million. Pyotr Nikolaevich requested that the Council of State Defense review the fortresses' significance and list the priorities among them, so that resources could be directed accordingly.[20]

This set in motion a process that would continue for several years. Initially, Grand Duke Nikolai Nikolaevich passed on Pyotr Nikolaevich's memorandum to the Ministry of War and replied that he would put the issue to the Council of State Defense once he had heard the views of the minister, the Chief of the General Staff, and the Inspector General of Artillery.[21] After much delay, in May 1906 the Chief of the General Staff, General Palitsyn, finally produced a list of priorities. The most important fortresses, said Palitsyn, were Brest-Litovsk, Vyborg (in Finland near Saint Petersburg), Kronstadt, and especially Novogeorgievsk, which he said was "*the key* to the possession of the Warsaw fortified region." The second most important fortresses, Palitsyn continued, were Warsaw, Vladivostok, Kars (on the Turkish border), Kushka (in Turkestan), and Ochakov. Third-ranked fortresses were Libava, Kovno, Zegrze, Osovets, Ivangorod, and Sevastopol (in the Crimea). All others were in the fourth rank.[22]

Palitsyn's rankings did not please the Grand Duke Nikolai Nikolaevich. He felt that they were divorced from any wider strategic plan. The Council of State Defense, he replied, could only determine the priorities among the fortresses "when the military-political importance of each of the probable theaters of war is determined, the tasks and aims of our operations in each of the theaters are clarified, and depending on this the significance of each of our fortresses is precisely defined also."[23] Palitsyn disagreed. The significance of each of the fortresses was very clear, he replied: "there is no doubt about the importance of the fortresses."[24]

The Council of State Defense finally got around to the matter on 18 November (1 December) 1906. Nikolai Nikolaevich began the meeting by presenting Palitsyn's list, after which a debate followed. The Deputy Minister of War, General Polivanov, said that the condition of the fortresses was worse than imagined, and given the amounts required to put them in order, "one can conclude that Russia will never be in a position to do so." Nikolai Nikolaevich agreed. He noted that it was better to have a few well-built fortresses than a large number of obsolete ones, but "nobody has given any information about the comparative significance of the fortresses, and so artillery institutions could not undertake any rational measures to arm them." Palitsyn had given the Council of State Defense a proposal without explaining the guiding principles behind it. Without these guidelines, such a complex issue could not be decided.[25]

In response to this clear rebuke, Palitsyn replied that since the fortresses were fixed objects, they should form the basis of the mobilization plan, rather than be determined by that plan.[26] Nikolai Nikolaevich objected. Although he "agreed with the opinion stated by General Polivanov," he argued that discussing Palitsyn's proposal properly required that they examine "all the facts which can shed light on this issue from all sides." "This is possible only by clarifying the mobilization plan," and on that basis determining which fortresses should be kept and which ones eliminated. The Chief of the General Staff needed first to tell the Council what the mobilization plan was, and until he did so, the Council could not discuss the matter. The Grand Duke's argument formed the basis for the Council's decision not to endorse Palitsyn's list but, rather, to review the matter in more depth.[27]

The issue came up again a few days later. At a meeting on 27 November (10 December), the Council of State Defense resolved that the Chief of the General Staff should define the significance of each fortress in the general defense plan and present this plan to the Council.[28] It then moved on to discuss once again the fortress at Vladivostok. Following the previous meeting at which it had been resolved to rebuild and strengthen the fortress, the Ministry of War had established a commission to determine what needed to be done. The commission had now reported back with the news that upgrading the Vladivostok fortress would cost the extremely large sum of 182 million rubles. In light of this new information, General Rediger told the

Council of State Defense that the issue needed to be reconsidered. This in turn necessitated yet another discussion of the general plan of defense for the Far East.[29] In essence, despite the earlier decision, the entire subject returned to square one.

During the debate that followed, Generals Polivanov and Palitsyn argued that Vladivostok fortress should be strengthened as much as financially possible. Grand Duke Nikolai Nikolaevich disagreed, and repeated his earlier doubts about the value of fortresses:

> The defense of the region should rest above all upon the living force. The presence of several fortified points in the Priamur region ... would give the troops the opportunity to act in more favorable conditions and more safely than would Vladivostok alone, however powerful it might be. Being easily cut off by the Japanese, Vladivostok cannot exert a great influence on the defense of the region, and spending 200 million rubles on strengthening it will not bring the same benefit as spending the same sum on strengthening other points.[30]

The Grand Duke concluded that the Chief of the General Staff should work out a general plan for the defense of the Far East, including an explanation of Vladivostok's role in it; simultaneously, action could begin on rectifying deficiencies in the fortress using existing resources. The Council concurred with the Grand Duke's conclusions.[31]

This was typical of the Council's work. It would make a decision, but that decision would rarely hold for long. Instead the matter would come back for further discussion once the decision proved unworkable for financial or other reasons. At this point, it would become clear that there was no strategic plan that could be used as the basis for making a rational decision. The naval and general staffs proved incapable of producing such plans, but the Council was insistent that it was their responsibility. The result was paralysis.

The next issue to pit the army against the navy was the fate of the coastal fortress at Libava, a naval base in Latvia. On 30 November (13 December) 1906, the Council of State Defense debated whether to preserve the fortress or demolish it and turn Libava into a purely commercial port. A naval captain by the name of Stahl said that given the navy's weakness after the Japanese war, Libava was no longer any use as a naval base. His superiors, Admirals Birilev, von Niedermuller, and Virenius disagreed. Grand Duke Nikolai Nikolaevich supported Shtal. Building the Libava fortress had been a "mistake," he said. Given that the money required to strengthen the fortress was not available, the port should become entirely commercial. The Grand Duke did not prevail. The Council voted by ten votes to nine to keep the Libava fortress.[32]

The debate about Libava gave Admiral Birilev at least one minor victory over Grand Duke Nikolai Nikolaevich. He would lose the next round. At the end of November and during the beginning of December, the Council of State Defense held a series of meetings to determine command relations between naval and ground forces in combined coastal defense operations. The Russo-Japanese War had shown the importance of this matter, but it remained difficult to secure agreement as to who should be in charge of whom when naval and ground forces worked together. At the November and December meetings Admiral Birilev argued again and again against subordinating naval forces to army commanders. Again and again, he lost the argument.[33]

This appears to have been the last straw for Birilev. A few weeks later, in January 1907, he tendered his resignation to the Emperor, telling others that the reason for his departure was "the malign influence exerted by Grand Duke Nikolai Nikolaevich,"[34] whom "he could not get on with."[35]

By the time of these discussions, the Grand Duke's private life was about to undergo a significant change. His relationship with Mariia Pototskaia had ended several months earlier, and he was by now courting Stana.[36] According to Lydia Kyasht, Pototskaia was devastated by the breakup and "was so desperate that she took to drugs in a vain attempt to forget her grief and stifle the pangs of memory."[37] Nikolasha did, however, make generous financial provision for her, giving her his palace on Italianskaia Street.

Stana was still married to the Duke of Leuchtenburg. Nevertheless, rumors began to circulate in late October 1906 that Nikolasha planned to marry her.[38] Some regarded the prospect with horror. A. A. Kireev, never a friend of the Grand Duke, wrote in his diary on 6 (19) November, "I can't believe my ears! On the order of the 'spirits' ... *for the good* of Russia Nikolai Nikolaevich must marry Stana Nicolaevna, but S. N. is the wife of Georgii Leikhtenbergskii. But so what! Nous avons changé tout cela! [We have changed all that!]"[39] A couple of weeks later, Kireev wrote down another rumor: "Stana Nikolaevna has convinced Nik. Nik. and the Tsar that the soul of the celebrated Philippe replaced her own soul after his death??? and became her new soul," he wrote.[40]

Nikolasha's cousin Grand Duke Konstantin Konstantinovich peddled similar stories in his own diary. "According to Andrusha [Grand Duke Andrei Vladimirovich]," he wrote, "Nikolasha is declaring that he hasn't lifted a finger to bring about his marriage, that it was inspired from above, that it would have been impossible without Philippe's influence from beyond the grave."[41] Stana, however, first had to get a divorce, and the couple then had to get permission from the Church to marry, something that was not guaranteed given that they were already brother- and sister-in-law. It would take some months before a wedding would be possible.

Meanwhile, the beginning of 1907 brought some changes in the Grand Duke's staff. On 1 (14) January, General Raukh, previously the Quartermaster of the Petersburg Military District, replaced General Brilevich as the district's Chief of Staff. This cemented his position as the Grand Duke's right-hand man. On 1 (14) February, Aleksandra Bogdanovich recorded in her diary, "I understood from [Colonels] Vannovskii and Vivian that the nickname 'Moltke' belongs not to Palitsyn, as I had heard earlier, but to Raukh, who is now all powerful with Grand Duke Nikolai Nikolaevich, while Palitsyn's relations with him are not what they were." [Moltke was a reference to the great German general Helmuth von Moltke the Elder, who as Chief of the Prussian General Staff during the Franco-Prussian War was not strictly speaking in command of Prussia's armies but was, as it were, the "power behind the throne."][42]

In late January 1907, the Council of State Defense met again to discuss reports made by the Commanders of the Vilna, Kiev, Warsaw, and Turkestan Military Districts. A second set of meetings to discuss these reports took place in April 1908. The report from the Warsaw Military District emphasized the problems with the district's fortresses. These were outdated, said the report, and the few available resources should be concentrated on just a few of them, particularly Novogeorgievsk and Brest-Litovsk. "One should not be distracted by the number of fortresses, ignoring their quality," the report finished, using words that Grand Duke Nikolai Nikolaevich underlined in his copy.[43]

An oft-repeated claim has it that Nikolai Nikolaevich led a faction of the Russian army devoted to keeping Russia's chain of fortresses at the expense of the maneuver army. This claim has had such an influence on analyses of Russia's performance in the First World War that it deserves further scrutiny.

The claim originated in Norman Stone's 1975 book *The Eastern Front*, where the author attempted to explain why during the First World War the Russian army had chosen not to retreat from Poland when facing a large German offensive in the summer of 1915. The reason, he argued, was to be found in prewar debates about fortresses. According to Stone, when General Sukhomlinov, by then Minister of War, had proposed dismantling Russia's fortresses in Poland in 1909, Nikolai Nikolaevich and his supporters thwarted his proposal and insisted that the fortresses must be repaired at great cost. Having invested his reputation in these fortresses, the Grand Duke then did not want to abandon them when they were threatened in the German summer offensive of 1915 and so chose to stand and fight rather than withdraw and surrender them to the enemy.[44]

Other historians have pointed out some serious flaws in Stone's thesis. William Fuller, for instance, has pointed out that many of those associated with the Grand Duke "actually *agreed* with Sukhomlinov on the inutility of the fortresses,"[45] while Allan Wildman has noted that the Grand Duke's right-hand man in operational planning during the First World War, General Danilov, was in fact "the architect of the dismantling of the fortresses."[46]

The evidence above would suggest that Stone's thesis is indeed entirely wrong. It is true that Grand Duke Nikolai Nikolaevich did believe that fortresses had a role to play in modern war. As we have seen, in 1903 he had proposed building a new fortress at Grodno. In an ideal world, he probably would have liked to have rebuilt Russia's fortresses in Poland. But, as his interventions in the debates of the Council of State Defense show, he was very much aware that Russia did not have the resources to spare for such a rebuilding program. Indeed, the minutes of the Council show that he was firmly of the view that when funds were short, they ought to go to what he called the "living force" (in other words, the maneuver army), and not to the fortresses. In short, he was far from being a die-hard supporter of fortresses, and it makes no sense to claim that his actions during the First World War were dictated by his alleged prewar determination to rebuild them.

Fortresses were not the only sensitive subject tackled in the report from the Vilna Military District to the Council of State Defense. The report also contains the following pronouncements:

> From time immemorial Jews have been an evil for our army, and their negative qualities are now being fully revealed: almost total avoidance of conscription, production of panic during battle and dissatisfaction in time of peace, sowing discord and criminally aiding and abetting the infiltration of malicious persons into the army.... Economically our army is not only completely dependent but completely in the hands of the Jews.... The army's dependence on the Jews is a great evil, and decisive and permanent, not temporary, measures must be taken to liberate the army from such bondage.[47]

Perhaps because the numbers of Jews in the army had risen from about 1,500 in the Vilna Military District in 1890 to around 5,000 by 1906, anti-Semitic army officers were convinced that there were far too many of them.[48] Those present at the meeting of the Council of State Defense that discussed this report proposed various measures to deal with the alleged problem: the army could free itself from Jews by prohibiting them from joining the army; or, if that was unacceptable, Jews could be allowed to buy their way out of conscription. Grand Duke Nikolai Nikolaevich objected to these proposals. He told the meeting,

> Jews are undoubtedly an undesirable element in our armed forces; as well as their unattractive moral cast of mind, they are weak, cowardly, and completely void of a sense of duty. Nevertheless, replacing their personal military obligations with financial ones would be a great injustice to the core population of the Empire [i.e., Russians] and also to the other nationalities within it. The Jew will gladly pay money for his blood; but at the same time, with particular greed, he will suck the money back from the population in which he lives. Better not to give him this new source of income, and to make him carry out his military obligations on the same basis as others. One can say that the Jew is undesirable for military service; but it is not completely just to consider him a useless, even harmful, element.... There are too few of him in the general mass of troops to be harmful.... If you use Jews almost exclusively as musicians, buglers, drummers, tailors, cobblers, saddlers, painters, and joiners, you can even get a great deal of benefit from them.[49]

The Grand Duke's arguments held sway. The Council of State Defense concluded unanimously that freeing Jews from military service would be unfair to other nationalities. At the same time, the Council expressed a desire that Jews should as much as possible be employed in non-combat positions.[50]

In February and March 1907, the Grand Duke and the Council of State Defense returned to the issue of the Far East. In November 1906, the Council had instructed General Palitsyn to produce a plan for the defense of the Far East. Palitsyn now presented that plan, and the Council met seven times to debate it. Palitsyn said that although the Council had previously decided that the main concentration of Russian forces should be in the Zabaikal region, studies by the general staff had indicated that it was impossible to concentrate large amounts of troops there. He had therefore decided that the concentration should be pushed further east into Manchuria. Military practicalities meant that there was no option but to infringe Chinese neutrality.

A fierce debate then followed. Some of those present supported Palitsyn's proposals, but others objected to them. Nikolai Nikolaevich was in the latter camp. Palitsyn's plan would only work if the Chinese agreed, he said, and there was no guarantee of this best-case scenario. The best option, he said, would be to prepare bases in Zabaikal and then move forward along the Amur River. This argument won the day.[51]

The meeting then turned to the perennial matter of the Vladivostok fortress. Once more, the Grand Duke stated his belief that the fortress should be eliminated. This time he won the support of General Rediger. The rest of the Council, however, continued to believe that the fortress should be kept.[52]

In late March 1907, Grand Duke Nikolai Nikolaevich received some good news. His marriage to Stana had been approved, her divorce having come through in November 1906. On 22 March (4 April), Emperor Nicholas II wrote to his mother,

> Some time ago the Metropolitan, Antonius, came to see me about certain matters. I took this opportunity to ask him for his opinion of the marriage of Nikolasha and Stana and whether he thought it permissible. He said he would put the question to other members of the Holy Synod and would let me have their opinion. In a week's time he brought the answer which was that, as marriages in similar circumstances were freely admitted by the bishops of various dioceses, they had no objection, provided the wedding was a modest one and took place somewhere not too near Petersburg. I must say I was delighted with this answer which I sent on to Nikolasha there and then together with my consent to his marriage. Thus this rather difficult and delicate matter which affects Nikolasha's and especially Stana's position so much is at last settled. You would hardly know him now, so happy is he and so lightly does he bear the burden of his service. And *I* am in such *need* of him![53]

The Dowager Empress was not impressed. "I do not attempt to hide from you," she replied to her son, "the fact that the news of the proposed marriage surprised me very much, especially after what you had said before. What worries me is that it all reflects upon *you*: as things are now it would seem better to avoid anything that could rise to criticism. But since it is all settled there is no use in discussing it further."[54]

The wedding was arranged for April in the Crimea. Before then, however, the Grand Duke still had to attend another meeting of the Council of State Defense to discuss the development of the navy. Undeterred by its defeat in the Council the previous year, the navy produced several options for a naval rebuilding program and presented them to the Emperor. Nicholas II selected option four: building one new naval squadron in the Baltic Sea and refitting the existing vessels of the Black Sea Fleet. This became the basis of what became known as the "small program," which would cost 870 million rubles over ten years, a considerable sum of money. The Emperor passed this plan on to the Council of State Defense for review. The Council met on 9 (22) April to discuss it. Army members were distinctly hostile. Grand Duke Nikolai Nikolaevich also opposed the program. Once again, he insisted that it could not be approved until a general defense plan had been produced. The Council rejected the small program and supported the Grand Duke's position that approval must wait until the general defense plan was ready.[55]

This done, the Grand Duke headed south to the Crimea for his wedding. At 50, he was somewhat old to be marrying for the first time, but he was certainly in love and overjoyed by the prospect. Stana was 38 and had two children from her previous marriage to the Duke of Leuchtenburg: a son, Sergei, and a daughter, Elena, now aged 17 and 15 respectively. The Duke had spent much of his time abroad, where he had a string of mistresses. Her second marriage was to be far more successful.

After arriving in the Crimea, Nikolai Nikolaevich wrote to a friend, Olga Ivanovna Chertkova, to thank her for her wedding present and express his joy at his pending nuptials. Your present, he told her, "touched me to the depths of my soul. Accept my thanks with all my heart." "The Crimea," he continued, "is a perfect delight!! The weather is wonderful—everything is blossoming ... the house on the seashore is delightful.... In one word—heaven.... In such conditions—unavoidable happiness. For a long time, I sought it—and when I had lost all hope of finding it, unexpectedly I have received it."[56]

The wedding took place on 29 April in the chapel of the Livadia Palace. According to a report in the *New York Times*, "The bride, who was unattended, was gowned in satin and wore a costly diamond tiara," while "a guard of honor, commanded by Colonel Dundadze, commandant of the Yalta garrison, attended and presented arms." Guests included Grand Duke Pyotr Nikolaevich and Grand Duchess Militsa Nikolaevna, Prince Dolgorukii, representing the Emperor, and representatives from Montenegro, Italy, and the German and Austrian regiments of which Nikolai Nikolaevich was honorary colonel.[57]

The royal family stayed away. The Emperor's sister, Grand Duchess Ksenia, recorded in her diary on 29 April (12 May), "The wedding of Nikolasha and Stana takes place today in Livadia. They even found somewhere to get married! Sandro [her husband, Grand Duke Aleksandr Mikhailovich] absolutely refused to send a telegram!"[58] The next day she wrote, "Yesterday's wedding took place in the little Livadia church, and was attended by a large number of guests and officials, afterwards there was a huge lunch. Mama is beside herself—and so upset she had to take tranquillizing drops."[59]

Despite the hostility within the royal family, the marriage of Nikolasha and Stana was to prove a happy one. Some time later, Stana would tell Julia Cantacuzen, "When any one has been as unhappy as I, she is glad to have a home with a kind husband, and to be quiet."[60]

CHAPTER 8

Fall from Favor, 1907–1908

NIKOLAI NIKOLAEVICH'S MARRIAGE brought him great personal joy, but the year that followed was professionally difficult and saw him fall from Imperial favor.

After the wedding, the Grand Duke remained in the Crimea until the end of May 1907, then returned to Saint Petersburg. There he found waiting for him a letter from War Minister Rediger complaining that the Council of State Defense was too stuck in abstractions and divorced from reality. Nikolai Nikolaevich replied that he agreed entirely.[1] It would appear that the Grand Duke was losing faith in his own creation.

The remarkably contentious relationship between the army and the navy contributed to the ineffectiveness of the Council of State Defense, whose members fiercely defended their own narrow interests. Another problem was the fact that discontented senior officers could appeal directly to the Emperor to overturn decisions they did not like. This was especially true of the navy, of which Nicholas II was fond. General A. F. von den Brinken, who succeeded General von Raukh as Chief of Staff of the Petersburg Military District in 1908, commented, "There is nothing we can do. The Sovereign, always such a good and gentle person, whenever anybody attempts to say anything against the navy, becomes literally savage, bangs his fist on the table and doesn't want to hear anything. It was like that with Grand Duke Nikolai Nikolaevich. It's some sort of hypnosis, and, because of it, the naval command can do anything it wants."[2]

After the Council of State Defense had rejected the proposed small shipbuilding program in April 1907, the new Naval Minister, Admiral Dikov, bypassed the Council and persuaded Nicholas II to support the proposal anyway. On 9 (22) June 1907, the Tsar gave the program his formal approval.[3] This action by the Tsar considerably undermined the Council's credibility.

The army, meanwhile, was coping with a shortage of funds and a chaotic structure. Infantry companies came in 11 different types, ranging in troop numbers from 100 to 300 men; regiments had varying numbers of battalions; and artillery brigades had anywhere from two to nine batteries.[4] In

November 1906, Grand Duke Nikolai Nikolaevich had issued a request for proposals to rectify this situation.[5] By summer 1907, almost nothing had been done. As the Grand Duke explained to the Council of State Defense on 25 July (7 August) 1907, the fundamental problem was a lack of money, and he urged the Council to accept the need for cuts. He suggested that the Council create a commission under the Deputy Commander of the Petersburg Military District, General Gazemkampf, to draw up proposals for reform. The Council agreed.[6] The commission would report later in the year.

Meanwhile, Nikolai Nikolaevich sought to bring new blood into the Guards and the Petersburg military district by appointing officers who had distinguished themselves in the war against Japan and who could teach the lessons learned in that war. To this end, he selected officers based on merit rather than social background. In 1906, for instance, the Grand Duke appointed General P. A. Lechitskii to be Commander of the First Guards Infantry Division. Lechitskii's appointment was particularly notable because he had never previously served in the Guards. The son of a priest, he had spent most of his career in line regiments in Siberia before fighting in the Russo-Japanese War. Another appointee was General L. V. Lesh, who like Lechitskii had served in Siberian infantry regiments and distinguished himself in the Russo-Japanese War. The Grand Duke named him commander of the Guards Rifle Division in June 1908.

The Grand Duke also invited junior officers from line regiments to apply to join the Guards. This was not very successful, in part because the high cost of being a Guards officer made it very difficult to attract many volunteers,[7] but one man who did benefit from this policy was Captain A. P. Kutepov, the son of a forestry official who had previously served with the Eighty-Fifth Vyborg Regiment and won the Order of Saint Vladimir in the Russo-Japanese War.[8] Kutepov joined the Preobrazhenskii Guards Regiment. Later he rose to the rank of general during the Russian Civil War, and in exile in the 1920s he became one of the Grand Duke's closest associates. The Grand Duke's efforts to bring men such as Kutepov, Lechitskii, and Lesh into the Guards belies a widely held theory that he led a faction of aristocratic cavalrymen in the Russian army and that this faction acted in opposition to the faction of lowly born infantrymen led by General Sukhomlinov.[9]

The Grand Duke took the business of training his troops seriously and did not allow either the revolution or shortages of funding to undermine his determination to carry out practical, realistic training all year round. Unlike many other commanders, for instance, he required troops to go on exercises in winter as well as summer.[10] His orders placed particular emphasis on developing shooting skills, with both officers and other ranks being made to participate in regular competitions.[11] The Grand Duke also emphasized physical fitness. He established a commission to promote the moral and physical development of lower ranks, provided funds for sports,[12] and ordered that units organize fencing and gymnastics competitions.[13]

In July and August 1907, the troops of the Guards and of the Petersburg Military District went on their annual summer maneuvers. According to Raukh, the Grand Duke "paid particular attention to improving shooting in the infantry and especially the cavalry.... Then he paid great attention to the matter of fortifications and the use of terrain, which the Japanese had taught us a lot about; then, artillery fire from concealed positions and firing over the heads of the troops." The Grand Duke organized an entire exercise involving such overhead fire, designed to provide a more realistic battlefield experience. "Finally," wrote Raukh, "The Grand Duke paid great attention to the training and general education of commanders," summoning them all for detailed post-exercise debriefings, at which he would "draw everybody into the conversation and mutual discussion."[14]

Contemporary observers held Nikolai Nikolaevich in high regard as a trainer of soldiers.[15] General N. N. Golovin (who at the time was a colonel on the Grand Duke's staff) wrote, "The Grand Duke Nikolai Nikolaevich rendered great services to Russia during the pre-war period.... If our first-line troops were of the high standards we have claimed for them above, Russia was chiefly indebted for this to the G. O. C. Saint Petersburg District."[16]

The maneuvers of summer 1907 also gave the Grand Duke a chance to strengthen Russia's alliance with France by hosting the French Chief of Staff, General Brun, during the exercises at Krasnoe Selo. Brun's trip, which took place from 16 (19) to 21 July (3 August), was a great success. According to a French diplomatic report, "The reception by Grand Duke Nicholas and the military authorities was most warm," and "the relations between the two Staffs are now established on the best possible foundations."[17]

After the summer maneuvers were over, Nikolai Nikolaevich enjoyed a relatively quiet period, with a hiatus in the meetings of the Council of State Defense until late in the year. The Council did not reassemble until 28 November (11 December), when it held the first of a series of meetings to discuss the role of the army's Inspectors General.

As Grand Duke Nikolai Nikolaevich had discovered in his time as Inspector General of Cavalry, there was considerable overlap between the duties of the Inspectors General of the various arms (cavalry, infantry, artillery, and engineers) and those of the commanders of the military districts. This resulted in confusion and conflict. The Emperor therefore asked the Council of State Defense to evaluate what the duties of the Inspectors General should be.

In the Council meeting that followed, the main point of contention was whether the Inspectors General should be subordinate to the Emperor or the Minister of War. Nikolai Nikolaevich, however, felt that the real issue was the relationship of Inspectors General to the district commanders. The Council needed above all to determine which was senior in the hierarchy, he said. If it did so, the other matters would become easier to resolve.[18] Having been an Inspector General for ten years, and serving now as Commander of the Petersburg Military District, he spoke from experience in saying, "I am fully convinced that Inspectors General must always be higher than district commanders." "In my time as Inspector General of Cavalry," he continued, "I more than once observed how commanders did not execute and did not want to execute my instructions." The regulations should make the power of the Inspectors General very clear, he concluded, so that this would no longer happen.[19] Nevertheless, when the issue went to a vote, the Council compromised, giving the Inspectors General and the district commanders equal seniority.[20]

Nikolai Nikolaevich rounded off the year with a long memorandum to the Tsar on 25 December (7 January), in which he laid out in detail his views on reforming the army. Gazemkampf's commission on army reorganization had now concluded its work, producing a report based on proposals put forward by General Palitsyn and General M. V. Alekseev. Historians consider that this constituted a call "for fundamental transformation" of the army,[21] but the Grand Duke found its conclusions insufficiently bold.

The army's position was so critical, the Grand Duke told the Tsar, that the current proposals did not go far enough. The Ministry of War and the Council of State Defense had to be reformed, he said, by reunifying management of the army under the Ministry. Russia's reserve forces also needed radical change. There was, wrote the Grand Duke, general agreement that the initial battles of a future war would be decisive and that it would be necessary to maximize the number of forces available for those first battles. He suggested that Russia abolish its existing reserve forces and replace them with a system of "hidden cadres."[22] These would consist of troops who in peacetime trained with the regular army but once war began formed the cadres of new reserve units.[23]

The Grand Duke also offered his views on the structure of military units. All infantry corps should have two divisions, he wrote, and all infantry divisions should have three infantry brigades and an artillery brigade, with six squadrons of Cossacks added in time of war. The existing system of military districts should be reviewed and probably abolished. Instead, Russia should be divided up into corps areas, and all units should belong to a corps.

Cavalry too required a complete reorganization. Cossack units should all be grouped into Cossack divisions, which would then be disbanded when war broke out, with the Cossack squadrons parceled out to infantry corps and divisions. Other cavalry divisions should be organized into four-regiment divisions, which would act as the army-level cavalry. Also, there were not enough machine guns. Each infantry battalion should have two. The size of field artillery batteries should be reduced from eight guns to four. Heavy artillery, meanwhile, needed to be entirely renewed, so that it could be on a par with the mobile siege batteries possessed by the Germans. Armies and corps should have the latest communications equipment. The railways needed to be developed further, and the army should recognize that "automobiles are fated to play a not unimportant role in future war." Officer training had to be improved, as did the soldiers' barracks.[24] The Grand Duke then moved on to the question of fortresses:

> Given the insufficiency of the living force, one must find something else to help defend the state: fortresses. But one must be very, very careful with this question. Fortresses give great assistance only when their number does not exceed the urgent need for them by one iota. Any excess in this matter is harmful, because fortresses fix and suck out the living force—the army. One must always remember that the state can wage war successfully only if it has a living force that is correctly organized, equipped with all it needs, instilled with the correct military spirit, and possessing sufficiently high quality commanders, for only such an army can undertake active operations in the broad sense of the word. By contrast, fortresses alone, even with good garrisons, cannot guarantee the state's security, because in fortresses the living force will be paralyzed.[25]

Whether to upgrade the fortresses was a financial question, the Grand Duke said, "But we must decide the most important thing: which is more important—the living force or the fortresses? If there is not money for both, then whichever is recognized as the most important should be perfected and raised to the necessary height, but that which is recognized as less important, we should only maintain as it is, improving it only to the degree that it is urgently necessary and possible."[26] The implications were clear: the "living force" was more important than the fortresses, and so the fortresses should not receive substantial resources.

The Grand Duke's memorandum was a radical call for sweeping changes to the Russian army's structure, organization, and priorities. It gives the lie to an oft-repeated suggestion that Nikolai Nikolaevich headed a reactionary clique within the army dedicated to opposing reform.

The proposals were, in fact, far too radical for the Grand Duke's peers in the army and government. At the end of March 1908, the Council of State Defense met to consider the ideas and decided that they were too "burdensome" and that "the state lacked the resources for a fundamental reorganization of the armed forces."[27]

In the longer term, though, the Grand Duke's ideas formed the basis for change. Once General Sukhomlinov became Minister of War in 1909, he introduced many of them, such as the proposal to replace the existing reserve brigades with "hidden cadres."[28] Despite their personal animosity, Sukhomlinov and Grand Duke Nikolai Nikolaevich were not far apart in their views of what the Russian army needed.

The initial failure of the Grand Duke's reform plan coincided with a loss of Imperial favor, caused in part by Rasputin. Although Nikolasha, Militsa, and Stana had been responsible for introducing the Emperor and Empress to Rasputin, at some point they turned against him. The reason is not clear. One account has it that Rasputin had publicly expressed his opposition to Stana's marriage to Nikolasha,[29] while another states that he had insulted Father John of Kronstadt, one of the most revered religious leaders in Russia, whom Nikolasha and his wife and sister-in-law greatly admired.[30] Militsa's son, Prince Roman Petrovich, told a slightly different story. According to him, the split came one evening when Rasputin visited Znamenka, began talking about the Empress, and asked Militsa and Pyotr Nikolaevich to go with him to visit her. When they said that they saw no reason to do so, "Rasputin railed about the importance of his mission as a preacher. He spouted a host of religious arguments so strange that my mother interrupted him and said that his views sounded quite heretical. These words annoyed Rasputin and he accused my mother of being biased against popular beliefs and not understanding them." Rasputin then spoke about Saint Serafim of Sarov in a "rude and unfriendly way." Pyotr Nikolaevich expelled him from the palace and told him that he was no longer welcome.[31]

Whatever occurred, it pushed Nikolasha, his brother, and their wives firmly into the anti-Rasputin camp. For the Empress, this was unforgivable. The Montenegrin sisters, once her firmest friends, now became, along with Nikolasha, her most bitter enemies. Years later she wrote to her husband, "Would to God N [Nikolasha] was another man & had not turned against a man of Gods [Rasputin]."[32] In his turn, the Grand Duke regretted the role that his family had played in introducing Rasputin to the royal couple. "Imagine my horror," he told Chaplain Georgii Shavelskii during the First World War, "Rasputin got to the Tsar through my house."[33]

By the beginning of 1908, Nikolasha's tenure as President of the Council of State Defense was almost at an end. On 28 January (10 February), the Council met to discuss recent instability in the Balkans and the prospect of war with the Ottoman Empire. It resolved that given the extreme weakness of the army, Russia should avoid any measures that might complicate the political situation. Furthermore, its members agreed it was unlikely that Russia would fight a war against the Ottoman Empire alone, and so in the event of war, there should be a general and not a partial mobilization of the Russian armed forces.[34]

Prime Minister Stolypin objected to this conclusion. The plan for a general mobilization, he said, assumed a war against Germany and Austria-Hungary and if enacted would see the dispatch of large numbers of troops to the west of Russia, where they would have to be quartered, fed, and otherwise supplied at great expense. Stolypin argued that Russia should limit itself to a partial mobilization if it fought a war against the Ottoman Empire, and he asked Grand Duke Nikolai Nikolaevich to review the Council decision.[35]

The Grand Duke summoned the Council of State Defense to reconsider the matter at a meeting on 25 February (9 March) 1908. Both Prime Minister Stolypin and Foreign Minister Izvolskii attended. Nikolai Nikolaevich began by asking those present whether war against the Ottoman Empire required a partial or a general mobilization. The Deputy Minister of War, General Polivanov, responded that he could not foresee a war with the Ottomans alone: he therefore supported general mobilization. Izvolskii, however, warned that a general mobilization could provoke Germany and Austria-Hungary and should therefore be avoided. Conflict in the Balkans might cause other powers to step in, he said.

Having heard the various opinions, Nikolai Nikolaevich admitted that although he had previously supported a general mobilization, Izvolskii's warnings that this could provoke counter-measures from Austria-Hungary and Germany had convinced him not to. He now supported a partial mobilization instead. But if there was to be a war, Russia must act decisively, he argued. "We absolutely do not intend to fight Turkey," he said. Nevertheless, if there was a war, "Once war is declared, we must smash Turkey, come what may, our victory must be complete and the object of the war must be Constantinople." That said, he concluded, "If a war with Austria-Hungary and Germany begins simultaneously with that with Turkey, then we will not fight seriously against Turkey, as we must turn all our forces against the strongest and most dangerous enemy."[36] Stolypin lent his support to what the Grand Duke had said. The Council then reversed its previous decision and voted to order only a partial mobilization in the event of war with the Ottoman Empire.[37]

This was to be the last significant meeting of the Council of State Defense under the Grand Duke's chairmanship. By now, discontent with the military system established in 1905 had become widespread. At the start of March 1908, the military district commanders met in Saint Petersburg to discuss reorganizing the army. They unanimously told Grand Duke Nikolai Nikolaevich that the division of the Ministry of War since 1905 had proved harmful and that management of the army should be reunited in a single institution. The Grand Duke promised to report this conclusion to the Emperor.[38]

This he did soon after, writing to the Emperor and informing him also that he believed that the Council of State Defense had outlived its usefulness and that he offered to resign as its President.[39] While it would take several weeks before the Emperor accepted his resignation, the Grand Duke never attended any more Council meetings.

Another blow to the Grand Duke's prestige came on 27 May (9 June) 1908, when, in a speech in the Duma, the leader of the Octobrist Party, A. I. Guchkov, denounced the Council of State Defense and the role played by various Romanovs in Russian defense policy. The Octobrists were constitutional monarchists and stood roughly in the center of the Russian political spectrum. Although they favored a move toward a more liberal order, they were generally loyal to the political system as established by the Manifesto of October 1905. Their leader was one of the more colorful figures of the era. Guchkov had fought numerous duels and joined the Boer Army to fight the British in the Second South African War of 1899–1902. A fierce Russian patriot, he used his position as Chairman of the Duma's defense committee to argue for increased defense spending and military reform. He was also politically ambitious. He wished to expand the Duma's control over military affairs, and for this reason he supported Rediger's notion that the Ministry of War should reunite all army affairs under its own management. Guchkov's logic here was simple: the Minister of War was obliged to report to the Duma and answer its questions; the Council of State Defense and the Inspectors General were not. Abolishing them would enhance the Duma's power, and therefore also his own.[40]

In his speech of 27 May (9 June), Guchkov blasted the Council as "an obstacle to reform and to all improvement in our state defense."[41] He also denounced the presence of Grand Dukes in high positions in the army. "To place such men in charge of responsible and important branches of our military establishment," said Guchkov, "is abnormal." "We are," he concluded, "entitled to address ourselves to this small number of irresponsible persons and to demand of them the renunciation of material advantages and the self-esteem which are attached to the posts occupied by them."[42]

The speech infuriated Grand Duke Nikolai Nikolaevich, who was also angry that War Minister Rediger had failed to denounce it. In fact, as Rediger wrote in his memoirs, he "entirely agreed" with Guchkov. Visiting Nikolai Nikolaevich, Rediger "found him politely cold and extremely reserved—he was obviously angry with me."[43] The Grand Duke then wrote to the Tsar what was in effect a letter of resignation. "I accuse nobody," he began, before pointing out that neither the Minister of War nor the Chairman of the Council of Ministers had refuted Guchkov's speech. On the one hand, "the speeches of Duma deputies are not at all important for us military men. Only the word of the Sovereign has any value for us." On the other hand, "the impression that Guchkov's speech has produced in Russia is visible," and as it had not been refuted, one had to take that impression into consideration. The fact that the people who could have responded had not done so, and had not been dismissed as a result, would appear to indicate that, as Nikolai Nikolaevich put it, "the monarch recognizes that Guchkov's words are justified. If that is so, we Grand Dukes must ask to resign our posts." The only conclusion to which the Grand Duke could come was the following: "The prestige of the Grand Dukes is shaken, Russia cannot have any more confidence in them."[44] He therefore proposed that authority for defense matters be re-unified under the authority of the Minister of War and suggested that the Tsar issue an order relieving him of the presidency of the Council while expressing his gratitude for his labors.[45] Nikolai Nikolaevich himself then drafted the order in question for the Emperor, who issued it almost unchanged soon thereafter. "Your Highness," it said,

> On 27 October 1905 I confided in you the command of the Guards and the Petersburg Military District. You expressed to me your concerns about the difficulties which could arise from combining this post with that of President of the Council of State Defense. While recognizing that your observations were well founded, I nevertheless ordered you to execute my will, as I considered your nomination to the new post to be necessary. On 25 December 1907, you submitted to me your report on the faults which you had noticed in the statute of the Council of State Defense, as well as on the reorganization of the Ministry of War. Your report coincides with my point of view as far as the second point is concerned. As a result I examined it very carefully. I have ordered the Ministry of War to present a draft of reforms.... And because of my decision to revise the statutes of the Council of State Defense and to reorganize the Ministry of War, I can now free you from the presidency of the Council of State Defense.... For the fruitful and always cheerful labor you have carried out in the role of President of the Council of State Defense, I declare my special and cordial gratitude.[46]

With this, Nikolai Nikolaevich ceased to play a role in the higher administration of national defense. In December 1908, his enemy General Sukhomlinov replaced Palitsyn as Chief of the General Staff. In March 1909, Sukhomlinov took over from Rediger as Minister of War. In this capacity, he rapidly undid the reforms of 1905, bringing the General Staff back under the control of the Ministry and in August 1909 persuading the Council of Ministers to abolish the Council of State Defense. A new regime now took control of the Russian army, led by a general personally hostile to Grand Duke Nikolai Nikolaevich.

The Grand Duke remained Commander of the Guards and Petersburg Military District, but he had little to show for the two and a half years he had spent heading the Council of State Defense. The extent to which he was to blame for the Council's failure is disputable. On the one hand, in what was to be a characteristic element of his leadership style both during the First World War and later when he attempted to unify quarrelling Russian émigrés in the 1920s, he seemed to expect others to be able to come to an agreement by themselves; he apparently viewed his own role as that of an enabler of debate and an arbiter in the event of stalemate. He did not take charge. On the other hand, he often showed sound judgment. On matters such as the defense of the Far East, the future of Russia's fortresses, and the naval rebuilding plan, his positions were eminently sensible, as was his insistence on the requirement that fundamental strategic issues be decided before questions such as the structure and deployment of troops were considered.

Above all, what the Grand Duke's tenure as President of the Council of State Defense shows most clearly is that he was not the barrier to reform that Guchkov claimed he was. Guchkov's attack on the Grand Dukes was an act of political theater rather than an accurate statement of fact. Unfortunately, the claim has gone unchallenged, and the prevailing view remains, as John Steinberg says, that "The Romanovs rigidly resisted and suppressed ideas, schemes, and undertakings that challenged the status quo."[47] This certainly was not true of the three Grand Dukes who sat on the Council of State Defense. Grand Duke Pyotr Nikolaevich, who was Inspector General of Engineers, had much less experience than his brother, having left active service quite young due to poor health,[48] but he was conscientious, and despite some differences of opinion General Rediger considered him "honest, good, and intelligent."[49] Contemporaries also generally thought quite highly of the Inspector General of Artillery, Grand Duke Sergei Mikhailovich. Rediger, for instance, considered him "the most outstanding artillerist in our army,"[50] and General A. S. Lukomskii wrote that Sergei Mikhailovich displayed "great knowledge and energy" in the role of Inspector General.[51]

As for Nikolai Nikolaevich, as his energetic activity as Inspector General of Cavalry and Commander of the Petersburg Military District demonstrated, he was a serious military officer determined to raise standards. And as his memorandum to the Tsar on military reform proved, he was more radically minded than many of those around him.

The failure of the Council of State Defense was thus not a product of the allegedly reactionary nature of the Grand Dukes. Rather, the problem was that, as one historian notes, the Council represented "interest group politics run amok."[52] Meant to coordinate the work of the various agencies involved in national security, it instead merely accentuated the differences between them, as each fought for its own preferred projects and resisted compromise.[53] More fundamentally, as the Grand Duke repeatedly pointed out, decisions on specific issues were extremely difficult and made little sense in the absence of a fully developed strategic plan of state defense. Such a plan never appeared: creating one was the responsibility of the General Staff and the Naval Staff, but they seemed to be incapable of producing it. As a result, decisionmakers were left without any guidance as to defense priorities.

Grand Duke Nikolai Nikolaevich's efforts to reform the Russian army at the highest level had failed. Nevertheless, as Commander of the Guards and Petersburg Military District he remained committed to reform. He exercised his troops in a manner that was realistic and that accorded with the lessons of recent military experience. Having lost his post as President of the Council of State Defense, he could now concentrate on training his soldiers for war.

CHAPTER 9

The Calm before the Storm, 1908–1913

ON 3 (16) APRIL 1908, Grand Duke Nikolai Nikolaevich issued a long set of instructions for the forthcoming summer maneuvers. These instructions reflected a contemporary understanding of the lessons from the recent Russo-Japanese War. The Japanese had been on the offensive throughout almost all the war, whereas the Russians remained on the defensive. Observers believed that the Russian army's passivity had contributed to its defeat and that this showed that, despite the strength of defensive positions at the tactical level, the offensive was superior strategically. Nevertheless, the same observers recognized the value of entrenchments for tactical defenses at the same time as they stressed the need to disperse attacking units to overcome such defenses. The feeling was that armies needed to "loosen up the rigid structure of units on the attack," ending the previous system of tight control by commanders and instead "encouraging both soldiers and junior officers to show initiative on the battlefield."[1] All of these ideas appeared in the Grand Duke's exercise instructions for 1908.

The maneuvers of 1907, recalled the Grand Duke, had "showed that the troops had forgotten much of what they had learned the year before." In particular, "use of terrain, studied thoroughly in 1906, was once again completely unsatisfactory. Only after I issued several instructions did people remember the methods they had learnt and did things once again go right. I won't allow every camp to repeat over and over things which have been studied and mastered the year before."

The Grand Duke emphasized a number of points he wanted soldiers to work on during the 1908 exercises: initiative and independent action, aggression and attack, reconnaissance, communications, and entrenchments.[2] The first of these reflected what would be a noticeable feature of the Grand Duke's command style in later years: a tendency to delegate authority. In effect, the Grand Duke favored what in modern Western armies is called "mission command," or sometimes (using the German word) *Auftragstaktik*. Many officers throughout Europe shared his point of view. Indeed, "the basic principle of decentralized command had become firmly established in the

Prussian army by the middle of the nineteenth century."[3] In Russia, though, rigid command systems remained more common. In the aftermath of the Russo-Japanese War, senior officers such as Grand Duke Nikolai Nikolaevich sought to change this method of leadership into something more akin to the Prussian model.

Mission command requires that officers give their subordinates a mission and then leave it to them to determine how to execute it. This reflects a belief that, in the chaotic conditions of war, those closer to the action have a better knowledge of the situation and are better placed to decide what to do than their superiors. Putting *Auftragstaktik* into practice requires encouraging initiative among all soldiers, whatever their rank. In his order of 3 (16) April 1908, Grand Duke Nikolai Nikolaevich wrote,

> The characteristics of contemporary battle, with its particularly complicated conditions, bring to the forefront the individual development of every rifleman and the work of unit commanders and of small military units.... Consequently, one must above all focus all one's strength on training each individual soldier, and on developing initiative in commanders of all levels, including non-commissioned officers.
>
> It is necessary to encourage every display of intelligent initiative, every attempt to take action in the spirit of the general objective. Mistakes are forgivable. Only inaction and passivity should be mercilessly punished.... A clear understanding of their rights and obligations, a clear understanding of the given task, together with a deeply inculcated habit of initiative, of striving to advance, will give [commanders] the necessary independence, will produce a strong will and free them from fear of responsibility.
>
> It is impossible to foresee all the chances of battle. Only the commander who has learned to act at his own risk, without instructions from above, can turn the situation to his own benefit.
>
> At the decisive moment of battle, the future winner and the future loser are materially very closely matched and almost identically confused. The advantage belongs to he who has a strong will, who is not afraid of responsibility, and who at that moment is capable of taking a risk.
>
> Without risk and a strong will, there is no success.[4]

Like most of his contemporaries, Nikolai Nikolaevich believed firmly in the merit of the attack over the defense. When defense was necessary, it should be conducted aggressively. "I must draw attention to a characteristic inherent in many, namely, passivity, especially in defense," the Grand Duke wrote. He continued,

> Passivity in defense is the most dangerous tendency in military affairs. In all situations our will prevails over that of our enemy when we undertake energetic actions.... Passive opposition is a prelude for retreat, and at best can only hold the enemy back for a short time. Passivity is usually the inevitable consequence of fear of responsibility.... One must not forget that defense is a necessary, temporary evil, which one must strive to avoid by energetic and decisive actions.[5]

Having outlined his fundamental philosophy, the Grand Duke then touched on individual aspects of warfare. The first was reconnaissance. This, he wrote, "needed a lot of work." Reports tended to arrive late. Cavalry needed to carry out reconnaissance at greater distances. Furthermore, reconnaissance alone was not enough; the information gathered needed to be relayed to commanders in good time. This linked to another concern: communications. These needed improvement, especially between infantry and artillery.

Finally, the Grand Duke ordered that in the coming maneuvers leaders pay particular attention to training troops in entrenchment. Both infantry and artillery should practice digging themselves in without waiting for the support of engineers, and every position they occupied should be immediately protected with fortifications.[6] The Grand Duke considered this matter significant enough to issue a second order about it on 16 (29) July. In this he ordered all commanders to draft a fortification plan every time that their units moved into a new location.[7]

The summer maneuvers at Krasnoe Selo began in late July and continued through into mid-August. On completion of the maneuvers on 4 (17) August, the Emperor sent Nikolasha an official letter of thanks. "The impression I gained while present at the Krasnoe Selo camp," wrote the Tsar, "once again confirmed the expertise and persistence with which you are leading the troops of your district.... I express my deep gratitude for your productive, energetic work."[8]

This mended a rift. The Tsar had confirmed the Grand Duke's resignation from his position as President of the Council of State Defense on 26 July (8 August) in the middle of the maneuvers.[9] The French ambassador in Saint Petersburg, Vice Admiral Charles Philippe Touchard, wrote to the Minister of Foreign Affairs in Paris, Stephen Pichon, that relations between the Emperor and the Grand Duke were cold when the former visited the latter at Krasnoe Selo.[10] General Polivanov similarly commented in his diary on 5 (18) July about "the cold attitude of the Emperor and the Empress toward Grand Duke Nikolai Nikolaevich."[11] And A. A. Kireev wrote on 5 (18) August that "A black cat has run between the Tsar and Tsaritsa on the one hand and Grand Duke Nikolai Nikolaevich on the other."[12]

The Tsar's thanks for the Krasnoe Selo maneuvers apparently did much to restore relations. Admiral Touchard observed to Minister Pichon that "Grand Duke Nicholas' unhappiness has receded in the face of the affectionate statements of esteem which the Emperor issued" following the maneuvers.[13] While the enmity between the Grand Duke and the Empress was to prove permanent, the bond with the Emperor was soon firm again.

On 21 August (3 September) 1908, the Grand Duke issued a long order giving his comments on the summer maneuvers, then left on leave. In October, he issued a further order with an attachment providing even more detailed comments by his Chief of Staff, General von den Brinken (who had replaced Raukh in June).[14] Both made it clear that, despite the Emperor's praise, they were not entirely happy with the performance of their troops.

The quality of shooting was much higher than it had been the year before, but it still needed work in some units, and the Grand Duke stated that he considered this a matter of primary importance for commanders to work on over the winter. Furthermore, he added, "Shooting in the cavalry must also be improved." In his time as Inspector General of Cavalry, Nikolai Nikolaevich had emphasized mounted operations, but now he argued, "The combat conditions of contemporary theaters of war more and more demand that cavalry be able to fight on foot and repel the enemy with fire.... The advantage will lie with the side which knows how to use firearms best."[15]

The cavalry also needed to pay more attention to reconnaissance, he said. "When troops are halted, reconnaissance takes place, and with rare exceptions, it is good, but as soon as units begin to maneuver, and during battle, reconnaissance comes to an almost complete stop." The artillery needed to practice acting in conjunction with infantry and cavalry, "for only in this way can one achieve the coordination of all three arms." In the same vein, he noted, "The experience of the last camp showed that engineering troops are insufficiently merged with other arms."

To rectify these problems, the Grand Duke ordered commanders to start winter exercises in October, with troops out in the field at least once a week for one or two days. Commanders were also to encourage shooting and gymnastics. Finally, wrote the Grand Duke, "I demand that at every opportunity training should take place outdoors, and that this time be used to examine the barracks."[16]

On 29 October (11 November), the Grand Duke issued another order emphasizing the need for initiative and independence. "It is impossible to command large units, one can only manage them," he wrote, "and this requires outstanding tactical preparation of all subordinate units, down to platoon level inclusively."[17]

To this order, General von den Brinken added more specific criticisms in a detailed annex. "Cavalry," he complained, "seems not to consider reconnaissance a matter of the first importance." Senior commanders were too involved with trivial matters that their subordinates should have been handling, and the commanders' orders were stifling initiative. Communications were poor, especially between different arms (infantry and artillery in particular). Artillery reconnaissance was inadequate, and the artillery spent too much time firing on the enemy's artillery and too little time supporting its own infantry.[18]

Despite the Grand Duke's call for initiative and risk-taking, von den Brinken observed that the exercises revealed "A tendency to passive action, a lack of initiative.... At the recent camp, passivity, and the tendency to defensive actions, continued to be revealed on almost the previous scale." Another deficiency was that commanders tended to use reserves in little packets to support their line, rather than concentrating them to use en masse. "The Most August Commander-in-Chief ordered me to remind you once again, that the main purpose of reserves is not to give support but to strike a *decisive blow*," wrote von den Brinken.[19]

These instructions for, and comments on, the 1908 summer exercises provide the most detailed picture we have of the Grand Duke's tactical ideas and his attempts to introduce them into the Petersburg Military District. They show him to have been keen to modernize the way in which the Russian army fought.

On 6 (19) December 1908, the Grand Duke visited the Emperor,[20] and later that day he wrote a letter to his wife. "I have not written to you for so long, my Angel, and I am so used to speaking to you in French, that it is somehow *uncomfortable* to write in Russian," he said.[21] The next day, he wrote again, calling Stana "My Divine Salvation, Gift of God," an expression he would use repeatedly in French and Russian in other letters. Although he had some problems sleeping, in general, he wrote, "everything is all right and good." "God preserve you," he concluded.[22]

Stana spent much of her time at Chaïr in the Crimea. Having given his palace on Italianskaia Street to Mariia Pototskaia, the Grand Duke lacked a home in Saint Petersburg. He therefore commissioned A. S. Khrenov, who had renovated his previous palace, to build him a new one, which was erected on the northern bank of the Neva at 2 Petrovskaia Naberezhnaia, sandwiched between the Peter and Paul Fortress and the "Little House of Peter the Great," a small wooden cabin built for Peter in 1703.

The new palace, wrote Prince Roman Petrovich, was ugly on the outside but beautiful within. "From the large bright hall," he wrote, "an imposing marble staircase led up to a level where the official rooms, the dining room, and reception hall were located.... An exceptionally crafted bronze railing artfully framed the stairs." On either side of the main doors were niches containing tea sets that had belonged to Empresses Elizabeth and Catherine II. The Grand Duke's collections of porcelain and crystal were on display on shelves in the main dining room. "Uncle Nikolasha was not particularly interested in art and had no views about music," wrote Roman Petrovich, "but he had a fine artistic sense for furnishings, and really understood the different styles. My uncle's favorite was Empire style, and he furnished the rooms of the palace in this style."[23]

In addition to a new house, in 1909 the Grand Duke acquired a new member of his household, Boris Zakharevich Malama, who became his personal doctor. Malama had studied medicine in Kiev and then served as an army doctor during the Russo-Japanese War, winning the Orders of Saint Anne and of Saint Stanislav.[24] Malama would henceforth accompany the Grand Duke almost everywhere he went and would follow him into exile in 1919.

Another development in 1909 was the appointment of V. A. Sukhomlinov as Minister of War. The two men had been at odds ever since Sukhomlinov had opposed the Grand Duke's reform plans in 1905. "My relations with Grand Duke Nikolai Nikolaevich were always very cold," Sukhomlinov wrote. "Instinctively, I could not stand his callous, spiteful, inhuman attitude to everyone around him.... [He was] my deadly enemy ... who with all his strength tried to destroy me."[25] Similarly, the Grand Duke wrote some years later, "Sukhomlinov was my main enemy."[26]

Almost immediately after his appointment, Sukhomlinov proposed a plan to eliminate Russia's fortresses in Poland. This plan was aligned with his desire to reorganize Russia's defenses to mobilize further to the rear. It also echoed the war plans the Grand Duke had made as prospective commander of the North West Front in 1903. Mobilizing deeper inside the Empire would end the need for fortresses to cover the concentration areas in Poland: it would save millions of rubles that could be spent instead on the rest of the army.

In April 1909, Sukhomlinov presented this plan to the Emperor. Many years later, the Grand Duke wrote that he had opposed it. "I considered it an unpardonable mistake to tear down our fortifications," he said, "My conscience is clear.... Had my word been listened to ... the war would have turned out differently.... Sukhomlinov alone was to blame."[27] However, at the time, General Polivanov recorded in his diary that on receiving Sukhomlinov's plan the Tsar gave it to the Grand Duke for comment, and the latter endorsed it.[28] This is not implausible. The Grand Duke had hardly been a supporter of the fortresses when chairing the Council of State Defense, and although the antipathy between the Grand Duke and Sukhomlinov was deep, it reflected personal dislike more than serious differences about the future of the army.

Similarly, the wider significance of the two men's mutual dislike has been greatly exaggerated. While each had his supporters, it would be wrong to view the Russian army as split into rigid factions aligned with either the Grand Duke or Sukhomlinov, as has been proposed by Norman Stone.[29] Many important officers in the army did not fit into either a Grand Ducal or a Sukhomlinovite faction, while others managed to serve both men equally loyally.

A case in point was a group of officers known as the "Young Turks," which emerged around this time. The group subsequently became closely associated with Grand Duke Nikolai Nikolaevich and was allegedly persecuted by Sukhomlinov. The group acquired its name because it included younger, up-and-coming staff officers dedicated to reforming the Russian army.[30] Many of them were members of the "Society of Zealots of Military Knowledge," established in 1894, whose journal became a forum for discussions of military reform.[31] Grand Duke Nikolai Nikolaevich became the society's honorary president,[32] thereby giving his support and encouragement to its activities.

The Grand Duke was far from being the Young Turks' only sponsor, however.[33] Indeed, Sukhomlinov knew of the Young Turks' meetings and did nothing to stop them, and one of the group's most notable members, A. S. Lukomskii, later headed Sukhomlinov's office during the First World War. It would be quite wrong to view the Young Turks as the Grand Duke's "faction." There were many divisions within the Russian army prior to the First World War, due to both doctrinal and personal differences, but the idea that the army was split into rigid groupings is wide of the mark.

At the end of June 1909, the Grand Duke accompanied the Emperor to a celebration of the two hundredth anniversary of the Battle of Poltava, at which the army of Peter the Great had defeated the Swedes under King Charles XII.[34] Once the celebrations were over, Nikolai Nikolaevich returned to Saint Petersburg for the 1909 summer maneuvers. Beyond that, the rest of 1909 passed quietly. In November, the Grand Duke traveled south to the Crimea, where he held a dinner at Chaïr, with the Emperor in attendance, for officers of His Majesty's Life Guards Hussars.[35] By this point, the Grand Duke seemed to be once again firmly back in his sovereign's good books. In January 1910, the two dined at a German soirée at which they wore the uniforms of the German regiments of which they were honorary colonels.[36] While Germany and Austria-Hungary were considered Russia's most likely enemies in case of war, that war was not considered an imminent prospect.

The next major event in the Grand Duke's life was a trip to Montenegro in August 1910, to celebrate the fiftieth anniversary of the reign of his father-in-law, Prince Nikola, who at this point elevated himself from Prince to King of Montenegro. The Emperor dispatched Nikolai Nikolaevich to the Montenegrin capital, Cetinje, to represent Russia at the official celebrations and also to inform Nikola that he had been appointed a field marshal in the Russian army. The trip served a diplomatic purpose in strengthening Russia's position in the Balkans.

On his return, the Grand Duke sent the Emperor a long letter detailing his experiences. "Dear Nicky," he began, and recounted that his group had set off by boat on 18 (31) August. Eventually, they reached the port of Antivari (modern-day Bar), where they anchored opposite the palace of the heir to the throne, Prince Danilo, and then landed. "Everyone was pleased to see Your representative on Montenegrin soil," the Grand Duke told the Tsar.

After lunch in Prince Danilo's palace, the Grand Duke and his entourage drove to Cetinje. "The beauty of the road is indescribable," the Grand Duke wrote. "The Caucasus is undoubtedly mighty, but there is nothing like this there. It is indescribable, it grips you, enchants you, caresses you—it delights!! We climbed to 1,200 metres above sea level. A pass, then down, in volcanic chaos toward Lake Scutari. What a beautiful lake! Once again a big climb, then down *again* to a lake in the valley," and onward down to the winter residence of the royal family, before climbing again to Cetinje.

In the Montenegrin capital, Nikolai Nikolaevich attended a dinner in King Nikola's honor at which he raised a toast to his father-in-law, telling him,

> In appointing you Field Marshal of the Russian army, my Most August Sovereign wishes to once again strengthen the bonds of friendship linking our two brotherly peoples and to pay tribute to Your Majesty's military prowess and to the military glory of Montenegro. Greeting Your Majesty on these momentous days for Montenegro, the Sovereign leader of Russia greets through you all the Montenegrin people, sending it his wishes of peace and prosperity under Your Royal Majesty's wise leadership.[37]

Nikolai Nikolaevich was smitten by his wife's homeland. "The country is so enchanting in every respect," he wrote, "that it was absolutely necessary to go out more to see things." Once the official ceremonies were over, the Grand Duke went to see the Bay of Catarro. Finally, on the eve of his de-

Nicholas II and Grand Duke Nikolai Nikolaevich on maneuvers, c.1910 (Imperial War Museum, Q052794)

parture, he traveled by car to the Ostrog monastery. Built in a vertical cliff face in the 18th century, the monastery was a popular place of pilgrimage. "The majesty of the view," wrote the Grand Duke, "corresponded to the spiritual grandeur which one felt long before one got there." Stating that he found Montenegro "so wonderfully good ... that leaving was very difficult," and asking permission to remain a few days before leaving for Pershino, he signed off, "With a feeling of particularly boundless love, Your loyal subject, Nikolasha."[38]

In November 1910, the Grand Duke went abroad again, this time to Hungary, where he went hunting. En route he sent a letter to Stana from Warsaw: "I am kissing you by correspondence, My divine salvation, gift of God," he wrote. "I love you. Your own heart will tell you how much I love you."[39] A few days later he wrote again from the village of Pusztaszer: "My divine salvation, gift of God,... During the hunt I received a telegram that you had not got any news from me. Every day since my departure I have sent you telegrams and letters.... I am very upset that you have been worried by this." He had not slept well, he said, but the hunting had been good. That day they had killed 2,300 animals.[40] The next day, "The hunt was marvelous," and they killed 3,150 more.[41]

From Hungary, Nikolai Nikolaevich traveled back to Saint Petersburg, where he immediately clashed with Sukhomlinov. The Minister of War had arranged a war game for senior officers who would command armies in the event of war against Germany or Austria-Hungary. Sukhomlinov aimed to use the occasion as a sort of examination for senior commanders, to determine who was up to the task of commanding an army.[42] Nikolai Nikolaevich, who as Commander of Petersburg Military District was scheduled to command the Sixth Army in the event of war, refused to participate in such a test and persuaded the Tsar to cancel the war game at the last minute. Sukhomlinov believed that the Grand Duke was afraid of looking bad,[43] but General Polivanov wrote in his diary that the military district commanders objected to the exercise, considering it badly arranged, and at a lunch with the Grand Duke persuaded him to ask the Tsar to cancel it.[44] Whatever the true reason, the event did nothing to improve the Grand Duke's relations with the Minister of War.

Sukhomlinov's war game having been successfully sabotaged, the Grand Duke visited Poland in mid-December for further hunting at Skernevitse. From there he wrote to Stana on 13 (26) December 1910 that they had been told that it was an exceptional year for hunting: they could expect to kill 10,000 animals in five days.[45] In the event, the weather was terrible and the hunting poor. Still, wrote the Grand Duke, "I shot *very* well."[46]

In May 1911, Nikolai Nikolaevich went to Moscow to attend the unveiling of a statue of Emperor Alexander III.[47] A few weeks later, in June, Nicholas II issued an official order thanking the 54-year-old Grand Duke for 40 years of service in the Russian army.[48] Further thanks followed the 1911 summer maneuvers.[49] The Grand Duke then went on his usual autumn vacation.

While away Nikolai Nikolaevich learned that Prime Minister Pyotr Stolypin had been shot in Kiev on 1 (14) September (Stolypin died four days later). Nikolai Nikolaevich wrote immediately to the Tsar to offer his support. "It is true that the price is high," he wrote,

> But the Lord works in mysterious ways. He knows better than we what to do. Believe firmly that everything is for the best. The fact itself, as well as the circumstances in which it was carried out, will eventually create in Your loyal subjects an understanding that the discord shaking the foundations of the Russian state must at last be ended. This should give you confidence that all your undertakings in this spirit will find willing executors, which will guarantee the success of the struggle. I strongly hope that YOUR IMPERIAL MAJESTY will not forget that I will be happy to lay down my life if You need it. May God preserve you.... Of course, my first instinct was to come to you, but remembering the telegram I received from you in Pershino in 1905, "Come, Nicholas," I am waiting.[50]

The Grand Duke, it seems, was hoping for a call that would bring him back into the Emperor's innermost circle. He returned in due course to Saint Petersburg and then followed the Imperial family to the Crimea in November, attending there the 16th birthday party of the Tsar's oldest daughter, Grand Duchess Olga Nikolaevna,[51] but the call did not come.

In February 1912, the French government invited Nikolai Nikolaevich to visit France to see the French Army on maneuvers. The Grand Duke accepted the invitation happily. Colonel Matton, the French military attaché in Saint Petersburg, wrote that the head of the Grand Duke's royal court, General Rostovtsov, had told him that Nikolai Nikolaevich was "absolutely delighted." On receiving the invitation, "in his joy he exclaimed noisily and bursting out laughing, 'I would love to see the expression on Basil's face!' He [Rostovtsov] added that Basil is the Emperor of Germany! And as a corrective, thinking that perhaps he had gone too far, my interlocutor added that the Grand Duke doesn't hate the Germans; 'he doesn't like them or hate them,' he said."[52]

The Grand Duke stated that he wished to make the visit in May, and before long he and the French had agreed on an itinerary.[53] However, in late March the Grand Duke fell ill, suffering from fever and a "dry pleurisy," a form of inflammation of the lungs.[54] He traveled down to the Crimea, where he hoped that his health would improve in time to go to France in May. This did not happen. On 8 (21) April, Ambassador Louis telegraphed French Prime Minister Raymond Poincaré to say that the Grand Duke's health would not permit him to make the trip. The Grand Duke asked whether it would be possible to come instead in the autumn.[55]

By June, Nikolasha was well enough to return to Saint Petersburg to participate in several ceremonial events, such as parades to celebrate the 25th anniversary of the Tsar's enrolment in the Preobrazhenskii Guards Regiment,[56] and to greet Kaiser Wilhelm II of Germany, who arrived in Russia on 21 June (4 July).[57] A short while later, Colonel Matton had lunch with the Grand Duke and Stana. By now, the Grand Duke had reached agreement with the French to reschedule his visit to France for September, when he would be able to watch the late summer exercises. "Throughout the entire length of the meal," wrote Matton to the French Minister of War, "the Grand Duke Nicholas did nothing but speak of his future trip to France. He is enchanted by coming to our big maneuvers and manifested his joy loudly. He went so far as to tell me that he didn't regret having been ill, as this had forced him to put off his trip to the time of maneuvers which particularly interested him, and, if necessary, he would voluntarily fall sick again to get this result." The Grand Duke expressed various desires: to see a combat between cavalry divisions ("he reckons that each division should have a battalion of cyclists," wrote Matton); to visit the fortresses in the east of France; and to talk to somebody who knew about Ardennes horses, which his father had introduced into Russia and which particularly interested him.[58]

Soon after this, the Russian summer maneuvers began. Further cementing the Franco-Russian alliance, French Prime Minister Raymond Poincaré attended the maneuvers and dined at Krasnoe Selo with his Russian counterpart, V. N. Kokovtsov, and Grand Duke Nikolai Nikolaevich.[59] Among the soldiers at the maneuvers was a newly commissioned officer in the Blue Cuirassier cavalry regiment, Prince Vladimir Sergeevich Trubetskoi. "One could sense," wrote Trubetskoi in his memoirs, "that from the moment Nikolai Nikolaevich appeared on the field, all the commanders, and especially the major ones, became deeply agitated, because Nikolai Nikolaevich was considered the terror of the Guards with full justification." According to Trubetksoi:

> The Grand Duke looked very striking on horseback.... The look in his eyes was intent, predatory, seeming to see all and forgive nothing. His movements were assured and unconstrained, his voice was incisive, loud, a bit guttural, accustomed

> to giving commands, and shouting out words with a sort of half-contemptuous carelessness. Nikolai Nikolaevich was a guardsman from head to toe, a guardsman to the marrow of his bones.... Everybody trembled before him.[60]

Once the maneuvers at Krasnoe Selo were over, just one ceremonial duty was left for the summer: a review of troops on 26 August (8 September) to celebrate the one hundredth anniversary of the Battle of Borodino.[61] The next day, the Grand Duke left Moscow to go to France, arriving in Paris two days later. Accompanying him were Stana, Doctor Malama, a retinue of eight generals, his equerry Captain Baron de Wolff, and his adjutant Colonel Cantacuzen.[62]

The highlight of the trip proved to be a visit to the French maneuvers taking place in the region of Nancy in French Lorraine. While the Grand Duke's visit was purely military, rather than diplomatic, the choice of Nancy, close to German-occupied Lorraine, had symbolic significance. Certainly the visit revealed the Grand Ducal couple's love of France. According to Colonel de Laguiche, who replaced Matton as the French military attaché in Saint Petersburg:

> During the Grand Duke's trip to Nancy, the Grand Duchess went to the French frontier and got a young girl to fetch a bit of earth and a thistle [the symbol of Lorraine] from the annexed territory [i.e., that part of Lorraine conquered by the Germans in 1870–71].... At the moment when the train was leaving for its return to Russia, the Grand Duchess let me see that she had kept these souvenirs. She did more. Upon her return to Russia, the thistle was put in water, bloomed, and produced seeds. The seeds were collected, planted, and tended by the Grand Duchess herself until they had germinated; then they were entrusted to a gardener with the words, "These are plants which people destroy everywhere. If anything happens to any of them, you will not remain in my service for one minute." The earth in which the seeds were sown was the earth of Lorraine, "so that they should feel at home," mixed with Russian earth, so that "they should learn also to love Russia and to cement forever the Franco-Russian union."[63]

The Grand Duchess told Laguiche that the thistles would be sent to six French officers the moment that their country was reunited (i.e., when Lorraine was recaptured from the Germans).

The earth and thistle were not the only souvenirs the Grand Duke and his wife took back with them to Russia. They also went home with a French tricolor, which the Grand Duke subsequently took with him to his headquarters during the First World War, and then to the Caucasus when he became Viceroy of the Caucasus in August 1915.[64]

While Nikolai Nikolaevich was in France, another visitor mysteriously appeared in Paris. This was Stana's brother, Prince Danilo. The Russian Foreign Ministry informed the Grand Duke of Danilo's presence,[65] but the two apparently did not meet. It is not known why Danilo was in Paris, but it seems likely he had a serious purpose, for Montenegro was preparing to go to war.

Montenegro coveted parts of northern Albania, which at that time was still under Ottoman control. On 25 September (8 October) 1912, Montenegro declared war on the Ottoman Empire, starting what became known as the First Balkan War. Montenegrin forces seized the Albanian town of Scutari the next day. Shortly afterward, Serbia, Bulgaria, and Greece declared war as well. Together these countries rapidly routed the Ottomans.

Their victory created fears that the war would spread. Austria-Hungary did not want Serbia to become too powerful and objected to Greek, Serbian, and Montenegrin plans to partition Albania.[66] Germany, Austria-Hungary, and Italy, who together made up the Triple Alliance, made it clear that they would not permit the Montenegrins to keep Scutari and insisted that it be included in the territory of a new, independent, Albanian state. This put Russia in a bind. Either it risked war with the Triple Alliance or it abandoned its ally Montenegro.

On 9 (22) November 1912, General Sukhomlinov proposed that the Russian army mobilize the troops of the Kiev, Warsaw, and Odessa Military Districts, so that Russia could be ready in case of war with Austria-Hungary. This was a dangerous proposal, as it could very well provoke a military response from the Austro-Hungarians and Germans.

At the height of the tensions, Grand Duke Nikolai Nikolaevich and his wife dined with the new French military attaché, Colonel Pierre Adolphe Henri Victurnien Marquis de Laguiche, comte de Sivignon. According to Laguiche, during dinner Stana displayed "an extreme ardor, and predicted great events."[67] She was "as passionate as ever, blowing on the fire as much as she could." Throughout dinner, she did most of the talking, telling Laguiche that the Albanian Alps belonged rightly to Montenegro, as did parts of the Sandzak of Novi-Pazar in Serbia. "As for Bosnia and Herzegovina, they were dependencies of Montenegro by their history and origin, and they would return to the breast of the motherland," although that, said Stana, "will be the business of another war." Throughout all this, Nikolai Nikolaevich merely "nodded approval" and let his wife do the talking.[68]

The belligerent attitude in Grand Duke Nikolai Nikolaevich's household created a strong impression that the Grand Duke himself believed that Russia should support its Balkan allies.[69] He has been described as one of the "most intransigent members" of the "war party," who was "among those most active in pressing Nicholas II to intervene militarily on Serbia's behalf" in 1912 and 1913.[70] In fact, the Grand Duke was far too much of a soldier to be part of any political "party," however informal, and while we have clear evidence of his wife and sister-in-law trying to influence Russian foreign policy in the Balkans, there is no record that the Grand Duke himself did the same. We also have no way of telling how closely his own views coincided with those of Stana and Militsa. On the one hand, Colonel Laguiche considered that Stana had "little influence" on her husband but that he was "completely under the control" of her equally belligerent sister, Militsa.[71] On the other hand, General Danilov later wrote that the Grand Duke did not share either Montenegrin sister's position: he was, said Danilov, neutral regarding Montenegrin claims.[72] Certainly, though, some of the more nationalistic elements in Russia believed that the Grand Duke was on their side. Thus, wrote Foreign Minister S. D. Sazonov, in early 1913, "there were public demonstrations in favor of the Grand Duke Nikolai Nikolaevich" and in support of Montenegro, Serbia, and Bulgaria.[73] The Grand Duke's name became increasingly associated with Panslavism and a strong defense of Russia's interests.

The Grand Duke's association with these causes made no difference to Russia's foreign policy, over which Nikolai Nikolaevich had little or no influence at this stage of his life. The Grand Duke had no official position linking him to foreign affairs, and it was not his area of expertise. There were many others on whom the Tsar relied for policy advice, including Prime Minister Kokovtsov and Foreign Minister Sazonov, both of whom opposed taking any action to support Montenegro.[74] Heeding their advice, the Tsar rejected Sukomlinov's proposal for a partial mobilization of the Russian army and, instead, accepted a peace settlement that included the creation of an independent Albania. The crisis was, at least temporarily, resolved.

The war scare having passed, in early 1913 the Russian royal family embarked on a long series of celebrations to commemorate the three hundredth anniversary of the Romanov dynasty. These began with a service in Kazan Cathedral in Saint Petersburg in February, an event Grand Duke Nikolai Nikolaevich would certainly have attended. The Grand Duke does not seem to have then accompanied the Imperial couple on a tour along the Volga River,[75] but he did rejoin them in Moscow in May for a celebration in the Kremlin.

That summer, General Joffre came to Russia to observe the maneuvers of the Petersburg Military District. Nikolai Nikolaevich took responsibility for arranging the General's itinerary while at Krasnoe Selo,[76] and he invited Madame Joffre to stay with him and Stana in Saint Petersburg while her husband watched the exercises.[77] The Grand Duke himself led a parade in

Joffre's honor.[78] The Frenchman was not particularly impressed by the maneuvers,[79] but he was pleased by the assurances he received about the help Russia would give France in time of war.

French and Russian planners were fully aware that in the event of war, Germany would first turn nearly all of its might against France in the hope of knocking it out of the war quickly before Russia could finish mobilizing. The French wanted guarantees from the Russians that they would attack Germany at the earliest opportunity in order to pull German troops away from France. Joffre pressed this point upon the Grand Duke. "I took advantage of the situation," he wrote, "to insist to him several times about the necessity I saw of speeding the Russian mobilization and starting an offensive as soon as possible.... The Grand Duke assured me that we would be satisfied: he fully understood the need for the Russian army to take a rapid offensive."[80]

The possibility of war remained strong due to continuing problems in the Balkans. Bulgaria, Serbia, and Greece had fallen out over the division of Macedonia, and in June 1913 Bulgaria declared war on its former allies, thus starting the Second Balkan War. Bulgaria was soon defeated and in August 1913 agreed to peace terms that gave most of Macedonia to Serbia and Greece. Next, claiming that they needed to defend themselves against Albanian bandits, Serbia and Montenegro sent troops into Albania and occupied swathes of Albanian territory along their frontiers. On 5 (18) October, Austria-Hungary sent them an ultimatum, ordering them both to withdraw their troops from Albania within eight days. The Serbs and Montenegrins conceded, averting another war, but many in both Austria-Hungary and Serbia were now itching for a fight.

Although one modern Russian historian has claimed that Nikolai Nikolaevich took a belligerent stance during the tensions of October 1913,[81] there is insufficient evidence to substantiate this claim. In November, the Grand Duke held a dinner in the Crimea for officers of the Life Guards Hussars Regiment,[82] then returned to Saint Petersburg. It was the last Christmas that he would ever spend in the Russian capital.

CHAPTER 10

Supreme Commander, Summer 1914

AS 1914 OPENED, Nikolai Nikolaevich, now aged 57, was in good health and spirits. A Russian diplomat, Andrei Kalmykov, noted that "In his fifties, the grand duke preserved the sprightly vivacity of youth." "The uniform he chose to wear," wrote Kalmykov, "accentuated his height. The vertical plume of his shako, his lean face, his short cavalry jacket—which looked even shorter on him—his long legs in tight breeches and small narrow boots, all gave him the appearance of a man of one dimension."[1] His hair was now gray, but he remained thin and fit, and his posture was as straight as ever. In pictures of military parades, he towers over those around him.

Nikolasha's energy seemed unabated. He was no longer, however, at the center of military and political power. Sukhomlinov continued to maintain a firm grip on the military bureaucracy, and in March 1914 he appointed General N. N. Ianushkevich to the post of Chief of the General Staff. A former professor of military administration at the General Staff Academy, Ianushkevich was undoubtedly Sukhomlinov's protégé, a fact he himself acknowledged, writing to Sukhomlinov some time later that "For my career over the past 6–7 years I am exceptionally indebted to the goodness you have shown me."[2] Ianushkevich's lack of experience in matters of strategy led to severe criticisms of his appointment. According to Colonel Laguiche, this was especially true "among supporters of Grand Duke Nicholas. The bad mood which I have noticed in the latter for some time must come from that."[3] Despite this, the Grand Duke and Ianushkevich were to develop a very close relationship once the First World War broke out. The fact that Ianushkevich owed his position to Sukhomlinov proved not to be a barrier to winning the Grand Duke's trust.

In April 1914, the Grand Duke went on leave until early June. Shortly afterward, on 15 (28) June 1914, a Bosnian terrorist, Gavrilo Princip, murdered the heir to the Austro-Hungarian throne, Archduke Franz Ferdinand, in Sarajevo.

Grand Duke Nikolai Nikolaevich was at his Bezzabotnoe estate when news of the assassination arrived. His nephew Prince Roman Petrovich noted that when Stana brought up the political situation during dinner, the Grand Duke "immediately changed the subject."[4] His main concern at the time was not the threat of war but the summer maneuvers at Krasnoe Selo, scheduled to start on 11 (24) July. A second concern was yet another French visitor, President Raymond Poincaré, whom the Grand Duke was due to host in his capacity as Commander of the Petersburg Military District.

Poincaré arrived in Saint Petersburg on 7 (20) July 1914, and on 9 (22) July the Grand Duke organized a dinner for him at Krasnoe Selo. It would be the occasion for an ostentatious show of Franco-Russian solidarity and a fervent display of belligerence from the Grand Duke's wife and sister-in-law. King Nikola had telegraphed them, they said, to warn that "We shall have war by the end of the month." Stana arranged for the dinner table to be decorated with Lorraine thistles she had grown from the one she had brought back in 1912, and she and Militsa accosted the French ambassador, Maurice Paléologue, and showed him a box containing some of the earth she had had collected in German-occupied Lorraine. "There's going to be war," the sisters supposedly told Paléologue. "There'll be nothing left of Austria.... You're going to get back Alsace and Lorraine.... Our armies will meet in Berlin.... Germany will be destroyed."[5]

The next day, the Grand Duke's troops held a parade for Poincaré at Krasnoe Selo. It was, wrote Paléologue, "A magnificent pageant of might and majesty. The infantry marched past to the strains of the *Marche de la Sambre et Meuse* and the *Marche Lorraine*." That evening, the French hosted a farewell dinner aboard the vessel *France*.[6] No sooner had they departed than the Austro-Hungarian government issued an ultimatum to Serbia, couched in terms designed to be impossible to accept and so to provide Austria-Hungary with the excuse it wanted to take revenge on Serbia for its role in the Archduke's murder.

The Russian Council of Ministers, now under the chairmanship of a new Prime Minister, I. L. Goremykin, met the following day to discuss Russia's response. Foreign Minister Sergei Sazonov opened the debate by framing the issue in terms of Russia's honor. Germany, he said, "has looked upon our concessions as so many proofs of our weakness."[7] The time had come when Russia had to take a stand or lose all credibility as a major power.[8]

Next to speak was the Agriculture Minister, A. V. Krivoshein, a man who enjoyed great respect among his colleagues. Making concessions could not guarantee peace, he argued. Russia had to use "stronger language." This argument, said Finance Minister P. L. Bark, "made a profound impression on us."[9]

The Council resolved to lend its support to Serbia and to ask the Tsar for permission to mobilize the Odessa, Kiev, Kazan, and Moscow Military Districts.[10]

Having learned of the Council of Ministers' decision, Nicholas II called another meeting of the Council, to take place in Krasnoe Selo on the following day, 12 (25) July. Nikolai Nikolaevich, despite having no ministerial position, attended the meeting at the Tsar's request and remained silent throughout. Whether the Grand Duke and the Tsar talked beforehand we do not know. General Sukhomlinov was convinced that the Grand Duke and Sazonov had joined forces before the session to convince the Tsar of the need to mobilize the army,[11] but he produced no evidence to support this assertion.

All in all, it seems unlikely that Nikolai Nikolaevich proffered an opinion on the matter because he considered such political questions beyond his competence as a soldier.[12] But any conclusions about the Grand Duke's role in the start of the First World War will have to remain within the realm of speculation.

The Council of Ministers session the Grand Duke attended was short. It merely confirmed the previous day's decision to carry out a partial mobilization of the army. After the meeting, the Tsar and the Grand Duke attended a ballet performance at the Krasnoe Selo theater. According to Julia Cantacuzen,

> The bell rang and interrupted comment, and we entered to find our places, and to stand near them until the Emperor came in, followed by his court and the functionaries of the camp on duty; at their head the Grand Duke Nicolas Nicolaiovitch, commander of the Imperial Guard and of the camp. Amid a great noise of spurs and sabers, the Sovereign having seated himself, with the Grand Duke on his left, the whole house did likewise.... It would be difficult to find two faces more completely contrasted than those of the two Nicholas Romanoffs—our Emperor and his second cousin. The latter, in the small, stocky form beside him, evidently saw not only the person of a revered Sovereign, but also the embodiment of ideals of which he had made a second religion. As I looked at the two, the childish, charming appeal for sympathy with his pleasure, expressed in the eyes and smile of the younger man, and the answering gleam of devotion and respect in the proud old face, struck me forcibly.[13]

War was not yet inevitable, but the Russian General Staff now began to have doubts about the viability of the decision to order a partial mobilization. General Danilov, the Quartermaster General, who had been out of the capital, arrived back on 13 (26) July. He called a meeting of staff officers and argued that a partial mobilization was highly undesirable.[14] Should Russia carry one out, and then discover that it was at war not just with Austria-Hungary but also with Germany, it would need to escalate to a general mobilization, but at that point the entire schedule would have been disrupted by the prior partial one. The result would be chaos. At Danilov's urging, General Ianushkevich therefore agreed to prepare not one but two orders: one for a partial mobilization and another for a complete mobilization.[15] The military planners had begun to take over decision-making from the political leaders.

On 15 (28) July, Austria-Hungary declared war on Serbia. At this point, Ianushkevich pressed Foreign Minister Sazonov to change his position and support a general mobilization.[16] This was the fateful moment at which Austria-Hungary's war against Serbia turned into a conflict engulfing most of Europe. The Russian Council of Ministers met again to consider Ianushkevich's request and gave it their approval, recommending to the Tsar that he order a general mobilization. The Tsar initially agreed then changed his mind and ordered a partial one instead. Nicholas still hoped to avoid war, but his diplomats and generals now believed that it was inevitable and that Russia must act to protect itself. Sazonov and Ianushkevich tackled the Tsar and persuaded him to change his mind back again. On the evening of 17 (30) July, Nicholas II ordered Ianushkevich to issue the order for a general mobilization of the Russian army.[17]

The Tsar believed strongly that a ruler's place was at the head of his troops and regretted not having led his army during the Russo-Japanese War. On 18 (31) July, he told the Council of Ministers that he wished to take command of the army. The ministers were horrified. The Tsar was needed in the capital to deal with administrative matters, they argued. It was best for him to appoint somebody else.[18] Nicholas reluctantly agreed.

The next day, 19 July (1 August), Germany declared war on Russia. Two days later, it declared war on France. The First World War had begun.

Having abandoned his plan to take command himself, Nicholas II needed to find a replacement. In his hour of need, he turned to the man whom he had always trusted above all others—Grand Duke Nikolai Nikolaevich. On 18 (31) July the Grand Duke had received an order appointing him to the command of the Sixth Army, but the next day, the Tsar summoned him and informed him that he was instead appointing him Supreme Commander of the armed forces.[19]

Nikolai Nikolaevich accepted the appointment immediately, although he requested that he be allowed to take General Palitsyn as his Chief of Staff and General Alekseev as his Quartermaster General. The Tsar rejected this request and insisted that the Grand Duke accept Generals Ianushkevich and Danilov in those positions.[20] The Tsar's decision made some sense, in that the latter two generals already occupied the posts of Chief of the General

Staff and Quartermaster General and so would provide continuity between peace and war. With hindsight, however, the Tsar's choice of staff was a poor one, especially, as we shall see, in the case of Ianushkevich. The Grand Duke later described his reaction to his own appointment:

> Words cannot express what I felt at that moment. Everything connected with this appointment shot faster than lightning through my heart, and left in me an indescribable, indelible, and over-exuberant feeling. I replied that His Majesty's will had always been sacred, and always will be sacred. I possessed no right to refuse. I recognized my immense responsibility to the Fatherland, but it was my duty to point out that I felt unprepared and very unsure of what I could do but accomplish this task with confidence and a happy hand. I had no knowledge of the mobilization plan. I would have to immediately carry out a plan I had not designed, in accordance with the strategic concentration of troops. Despite my explanation, His Majesty the Tsar was fully convinced that I would not disappoint his trust.... For my part, I asked His Majesty the Tsar to promise on his honor and conscience that whatever might happen—the loss of Saint Petersburg, Moscow, the Urals, even Siberia, he would conclude no peace. His Majesty the Tsar gave me his solemn promise on this. Thus ended our conversation, and I took my leave.[21]

The next day, 20 July (2 August) 1914, the elite of Russia assembled under the massive chandeliers of the Nicholas Hall, the largest room in the Winter Palace, for a prayer service and to hear the Tsar issue a Manifesto announcing Russia's entry into the war. Prince Roman Petrovich met Nikolai Nikolaevich at Znamenka before leaving for the Winter Palace. He found the Grand Duke standing on the steps outside the palace holding a bundle of German medals, which he proceeded to throw into some nearby bushes. It turned out that his valet, when laying out his uniform that morning, had attached to it the medals the Grand Duke had received from Germany. Furious, Nikolasha shouted to his valet, "Burn the Mecklenburg uniforms," and then left for Saint Petersburg.[22]

On his arrival the Grand Duke found some five to six thousand people, including members of the Royal family, senior military officers, court officials, ministers, and members of the Duma and State Council, crammed into the Nicholas Hall. Together they sang a Te Deum. During the service, the Grand Duke knelt at the Emperor's side. He was, wrote the Finance Minister Pyotr Bark, "visibly extremely nervous."[23] Julia Cantacuzen, who was present, described the scene in adulatory terms:

> Nicholas, the grand duke, knelt by him [the Emperor], even thus towering with his shoulders above the multitude. His head thrown back, his silvered hair catching the light of sun and candles, eyes flashing, nostrils distended, and his mouth drawn into a straight hard line, his whole figure showed the same training and power to command himself and others, as when I had first seen him nearly fifteen years before; and his look of exaltation was that of a crusader, ready to do or die in a great cause. Every one spoke of him afterwards, both as he had looked when kneeling before us, and as when he rose and stood a moment facing the crowd, and then departed, following the Sovereigns from the great hall. He drew all eyes, and held them, and he left the men somewhat surprised at the special cheers they had spontaneously given him.[24]

Once the service was over, the Emperor went out on the balcony of the Winter Palace and read the Manifesto to the vast crowd that had assembled on the square beneath. Next, he re-entered the palace, and according to another witness:

> Grand Duke Nikolai sought to extract their Majesties from the crowd which surrounded them, and they created with great difficulty a passage into the interior apartments. Now, everybody turned toward the Grand Duke Nikolai Nikolaevich. We already saw him as Supreme Commander, and called on him to lead our armies to victory. Officers surrounded him, and in the midst of incessant hurrahs carried him on their arms.[25]

"One seemed to *feel* him in the room, where his immense height put him head and shoulders above the tallest of the guard officers," wrote Julia Cantacuzen, "He stood as straight as an arrow, and walked with the graceful elastic stride of one in good training.... We turned to him with gratitude ... and as he realized the sentiment expressed, his appreciation showed in his flashing looks, and in the sudden beauty of his rare smile."[26]

The rapturous reception swept the Grand Duke along with it. He sought out the French ambassador and, according to Paléologue, "hurled himself upon me with his usual impetuosity and embraced me till I was half crushed."[27] The Grand Duke then extracted himself from the crowd and followed the Imperial couple into the interior apartments of the palace.

Georgii Shavelskii, the head chaplain of the Russian army, met the Grand Duke for lunch a few days later. "The Grand Duke arrived joyous, radiant," wrote Shavelskii:

> The lunch was extraordinarily lively. It was clear that everybody was experiencing great pleasure at the Grand Duke's appointment to a high post, and nobody wanted to think about the horrors of war, and about the experiences which awaited them. The Grand Duke himself was undoubtedly pleased with the appointment. The honor which had fallen on him to lead our army in a great war flattered him; and he was pleased by the attention which the Emperor had shown him in making this appointment, something which he always greatly valued. Furthermore, the Grand Duke was undoubtedly a supporter of war against the Germans, which he considered inevitable and necessary for Russia.[28]

It did not take long for the realities of war to make themselves known. While the Grand Duke was enjoying the adulation of the crowd in the Winter Palace, the German Army crossed the frontier of the Russian Empire and invaded Poland, occupying the border town of Kalisz. Shortly afterward, believing that they had been attacked by local inhabitants, German troops "reduced the centre of Kalisz to ash and rubble, slaughtered many of its inhabitants, and caused others to flee in panic and terror."[29] According to the British military attaché at the time, Colonel Alfred Knox: "When he [the Grand Duke] spoke of the alleged barbarities committed by the Germans at Chenstokhov and Kalish, he became excited and gesticulated vehemently."[30] For Nikolai Nikolaevich, the German actions were proof of German barbarity and underlined the justness of the Russian cause. The Grand Duke had no doubt that Germany was responsible for the war. "The war was brought on by the Germans at the instigation of the Kaiser, and not by the allies," he said a while later. "The Kaiser intended war and felt that the right moment had arrived.... Russians had no wish to go to war had not the Germans taken steps which they were bound to recognize as a possible danger to them."[31] This belief sustained him throughout the months that followed.

The Grand Duke had played no role in the preparation of Russia's latest plans for war. General Danilov briefed him on them, and the Grand Duke accepted them without demur.[32] In particular, he agreed with the idea that Russia should invade German East Prussia as early as possible in order to draw German troops away from France. On 23 July (5 August), he met Ambassador Paléologue and reassured him on this account: "God and Joan of Arc are with us!" he reportedly told the Frenchman. "We shall win."

The Grand Duke seemed to be carried away with enthusiasm. "I shall order the offensive as soon as the operation is feasible," he assured Paléologue.[33] As their conversation came to an end, Nikolai Nikolaevich asked the Frenchman "to convey to General Joffre my heartiest compliments and the assurance of my unshakeable confidence in victory. Tell him that side by side with my own Commander-in-Chief's flag I shall carry the flag he gave me when I was at the French maneuvers two years ago." And then shaking Paléologue's hand, he led him to the door and finished, "And now, into God's hands!"[34]

In these early days of the war, the Grand Duke's primary consideration was how to help the French. It became clear very soon that, as expected, Germany was concentrating the vast majority of its army against France, in the hope of knocking it quickly out of the war. It was vital that the Russians put pressure on Germany in order to give at least some relief to the French. The best way to do this would be to attack East Prussia. This strategy, if successful, would have the additional benefit of eliminating the threat to Poland's northern flank. With this thought in mind, the former Chief of the General Staff, General Ia. G. Zhilinskii, had promised his French counterpart back in 1911 that Russia would launch an offensive against Germany on the 15th day after mobilization began.[35] Since Russian mobilization would take many more than 15 days to complete, this meant that Russia's armies would be only half ready when they invaded Germany.

Making promises in peacetime is one thing, but keeping them in wartime is quite another. When considering their options in the years before 1914, Russian war planners could not agree on whether to concentrate their forces against Germany or Austria-Hungary in the event that Russia found itself fighting both of them. The result was what Bruce Menning calls "a dangerous strategic compromise."[36] This was a war plan known as Plan 19A, which stated that Austria-Hungary should be Russia's point of main effort, without, however, precluding the possibility of an offensive against German East Prussia.[37]

Plan 19A stated that operations against East Prussia should not be ruled out, but a Supreme Commander who felt that such an offensive was unwise could have refrained from ordering it. Grand Duke Nikolai Nikolaevich was not such a man. Not only had the excitement of the war instilled an undue optimism in him, but he was also naturally inclined toward offensive operations and seizing the initiative. Perhaps more important, he was convinced of the imperative need to assist France early in the war. The Grand Duke made his choice: he would come to France's assistance. "The Supreme Commander of the Russian army," wrote Laguiche (now promoted to brigadier general) to the French Minister of War, "wanted to respond to France's desires and remain faithful to the undertakings he made to our ambassador to not lose 'a quarter of a second.'" "History will condemn me," the Grand Duke told Laguiche, "but I have given the order to march."[38]

On 24 July (6 August), General Ianushkevich issued an order to General Zhilinskii, now commanding the North West Front facing Germany, telling him that "The Grand Duke finds that we must prepare for an energetic onslaught at the first opportunity in order to relieve the position of the French."[39] The next day, Ianushkevich telegraphed Zhilinskii again. "In light of the direction of the main German forces against France, and the need to support our ally," he wrote, the Grand Duke ordered the First Guards Corps and the First Corps to move to Warsaw to form a new army (eventually called the Ninth Army).[40] Their objective was in part to protect the Polish capital from the German forces, which had already advanced into western Poland, but more importantly to be the advance guard of a new force that would advance westward into Silesia and then on toward Berlin.[41] The plan, Nikolai Nikolaevich told the Tsar, was now first to clear Russia's flanks by means of attacks against East Prussia in the north and Galicia in the south, and then once this was done to use this new force in central Poland to launch a decisive strike into the heart of Germany.[42] This constituted a significant change to Plan 19A, weakening the forces available for the attack on East Prussia and creating an entirely new axis of operations. It was a further reflection of the excessive optimism gripping the Russian high command.

On 28 July (10 August), Ianushkevich telegraphed Zhilinskii and again emphasized the need to help France:

> Paying attention to the fact that Germany first declared war against us, and that France, as our ally, considered it its duty to immediately support us, we must, because of the same allied obligations, support the French, in light also of the fact that the Germans are preparing their main blow against them. This support should be expressed in the form of a most rapid offensive by us against the German forces left in East Prussia.... The Supreme Commander thinks that the armies of the North West Front must prepare to undertake a calm and systematic offensive in the immediate future.[43]

The First Army, located on the eastern edge of East Prussia, should start the offensive, wrote Ianushkevich. The Second Army in northern Poland would then strike the southern frontier of East Prussia. The two armies were to keep in close contact with one another, and their aim should be to encircle the Germans. The Grand Duke believed that the offensive could start on the 14th day of mobilization, Ianushkevich concluded.[44]

Two days later, the Grand Duke issued similar instructions to his troops facing Austria-Hungary, with Ianushkevich sending the following order to General Alekseev, now Chief of Staff of the South West Front:

> The Supreme Commander recognizes that it is necessary for the armies of the South West Front to finish their preparations to fulfill the offensive tasks given to them in the Imperial instructions of 1912 [i.e., Plan 19A]. This is necessary because France is asking us to support it not only with the armies of the North West Front but also those of the South West Front.... In light of this, the Supreme Commander has ordered you to finish your preparations so that, making the sign of the cross, you start a calm, but decisive, offensive.[45]

As yet, the Grand Duke had not met many of the men who would make up his staff. They assembled for the first time for a church service on the morning of 31 July (13 August). The next day they set out for Supreme Headquarters. Before doing so, the Grand Duke issued one final directive, one of potentially great political significance. This was a Manifesto to the Polish people, issued over the Grand Duke's signature on 1 (14) August 1914 and designed to win the support of the Poles for the Russian war effort. "Poles!" it read:

> The hour has struck for the realization of the hallowed ambitions of your fathers and ancestors.
>
> One hundred and fifty years ago the live body of Poland was torn to pieces, but her spirit did not die. It has lived on in the hope that the hour will come for the resurrection of the Polish nation and its fraternal reconciliation with Great Russia.
>
> The Russian troops are bringing you the good news of this reconciliation.
>
> Let the frontiers which have severed the people of Poland be wiped out, and may Poland be reunited under the scepter of the Russian Tsar.
>
> Under this scepter Poland will be reborn, autonomous, free in her faith and tongue.
>
> Russia awaits from you only a similar respect for the rights of those nationalities with whom history has bound you.
>
> With open heart and brotherly, outstretched hand, Mighty Russia comes forward to meet you. She believes that the sword which routed the foe at Grunwald [the scene of a battle in 1410 in which the Poles defeated the Teutonic Knights] has not rusted.
>
> From the shores of the Pacific Ocean to the northern seas Russian hosts are moving forward.
>
> The dawn of a new life is rising for you.
>
> May the sign of the Cross—the symbol of the suffering and resurrection of nations—gleam in this dawn.
>
> Supreme Commander, General-Adjutant, Nikolai.[46]

The key points were the promises of autonomy and the reunification of Poland "under the scepter of the Russian Tsar." The first represented a significant political concession to Polish nationalism, while the second amounted to a statement of expansionist war aims including the annexation of the German- and Austrian-held parts of Poland. In this way, the Manifesto served a number of purposes: it laid out Russian territorial claims; it sought to preserve the loyalty of Poles already living within the Russian Empire and to win the support of those elsewhere; and it preempted any attempt by Russia's enemies to win the Poles to their side with promises of Polish independence.[47]

Although it bore his name, the Manifesto was not solely the Grand Duke's work. Its origins are unclear, though the idea very possibly originated with Foreign Minister Sazonov, who produced the first draft with the assistance of Prince Grigorii Trubetskoi, an official in the Foreign Ministry.[48] Thereafter, Sazonov, the Tsar, Grand Duke Nikolai Nikolaevich, and Generals Sukhomlinov and Ianushkevich all seem to have had a hand in writing the final version.[49] Crucially, although the Tsar had certainly approved the Manifesto,[50] he did not add his own signature to it, instead allowing it to go out under the Grand Duke's name. This was an unfortunate lapse, as it created the impression that the Manifesto might not actually have Imperial approval but, rather, be the Grand Duke's personal initiative. It left some room for back-tracking, and with that for doubts among Poles about the Russian government's sincerity. Thus although Poles initially greeted the Manifesto "with enthusiasm,"[51] in time this faded. As the British consul in Warsaw, H. Montgomery Grove, noted in late 1914, "nobody seems to believe in the sincerity of the Grand Duke—they have had ample experience of Russian promises on many occasions."[52] Consequently, beyond staking out Russia's war aims, the Manifesto did not have the positive impact its drafters had hoped for. Within the Russian Empire, Poles were generally loyal to the Tsar, but outside of that part of Poland controlled by Russia before the war, they remained for the most part rather hostile toward their supposed liberators.

With the proclamation of the Polish Manifesto, the Grand Duke's work in Saint Petersburg was done. It was time for him to move to the army's Supreme Headquarters, which was located in Baranovichi, in what is nowadays Belarus. On the evening of 1 (14) August, he attended a service at the church at Znamenka. "When Uncle Nikolasha came into the church," wrote Prince Roman Petrovich, "he went immediately to the iconostasis to kiss the holy image, and then stood in the middle of the church.... The priest handed him a flag, the standard of the Supreme Commander, which his father had flown during his command in the Russo-Turkish War.... Uncle Nikolasha took the flag, kneeling. Then he handed it to his adjutant and ran with hasty steps from the church."[53]

From there, the Grand Duke went to the Peterhof train station. It was, wrote Danilov, "a wonderful, completely summery evening."[54] The Grand Duke, wrote another observer, was in a "very good mood.... It was impossible to look at his imposing figure, full of fire, energy, and iron will, without admiration." At 11 pm, "Smoothly, with no whistles, the train quietly departed,"[55] and Nikolai Nikolaevich set off for war.

CHAPTER 11

Stavka

AS THE GRAND DUKE'S TRAIN headed south, heavy fighting was already under way in Belgium, Alsace, and Serbia, and Russian troops had clashed with their Austro-Hungarian enemies along the frontier. But despite the urgency of the military situation, the train carrying Nikolai Nikolaevich and his staff traveled slowly. The Grand Duke had ordered it to avoid the main lines so as not to disrupt the troop trains carrying soldiers to the front.[1] According to the British military attaché, Colonel Alfred Knox, who would soon be replaced by a more senior officer, Major General John Hanbury Williams, "the meals on the train are well cooked but simple. We lunch at 12.30—three courses—and dine at 7.30: soup, joint, and sweet, a glass of vodka, claret or madeira." The Grand Duke "spoke of sport, and said that he was determined to go to England for shooting after the war.... After lunch he took Laguiche, Yanushkevich and Danilov with him to discuss military matters." Later, wrote Knox, "He told me how he hated the Germans because one could never trust them; that this war had been forced upon us and we must crush Germany once and for all to enable the nations to live in peace; the German Empire must cease to exist and be divided up into a group of states."[2]

En route, the Grand Duke's train stopped for him to hold a meeting with the Commander of the North West Front, General Zhilinskii. There is no record of what the two men said, although one presumes that they discussed Zhilinskii's forthcoming offensive into East Prussia. This halt, on top of the indirect route taken, meant that it was not until the morning of 3 (16) August, two and half days after setting out, that the Grand Duke completed his 1,000 kilometer journey and reached the Supreme Headquarters, known in Russian as "Stavka," in Baranovichi.

Baranovichi was a town of some 25,000 to 30,000 people, with a substantial Jewish population. According to a French visitor, the houses were "wooden and low" and the inhabitants were "almost all poor."[3] Grand Duke Kirill Vladimirovich, who was on the naval staff at Stavka, considered it "a desolate and God-forsaken place."[4] French ambassador Maurice Paléologue agreed, calling it "a miserable little country town."[5]

The Russians had chosen Baranovichi because it was roughly in the middle of the front and at the junction of three railway lines, putting it in a good central position from which to communicate with the armies to the north and south. From there the Supreme Commander could quickly travel by train to meet his front-line commanders, receive updates from them, and pass on his instructions.

Stavka consisted for the most part of two trains, in which the staff both worked and lived. The first train contained the coach in which Grand Dukes Nikolai and Pyotr Nikolaevich lived. Attached to this were a restaurant car, in which the staff had its meals, a coach that served as the Chief of Staff's office, and two more coaches for the foreign military attachés and members of the Supreme Commander's personal staff. The rest of Stavka was in the other train, close by.

The trains sat on sidings in a sparse pine and birch forest, which visitors inevitably considered delightful. The Tsar wrote in his diary that Stavka was in a "charming wood [in which] the ground is sandy and not at all damp.... It is difficult to believe that a great war is waging not far from this place; everything seems so peaceful and quiet."[6] A British officer, Captain (later Major) the Lord Glyn, who was part of a delegation that visited in spring 1915, agreed, commenting in a letter home that Stavka was located in "a wonderful wood of fir and birch—so quiet and so removed from all these horrors."[7] And similarly, a French visitor, General Paul Pau, commented, "The impression one gets from a stay at Stavka is of the calm, the tranquility of spirit, the confidence, which animates everyone there. No noise; the most perfect order reigns everywhere."[8]

The Grand Duke's train was situated next to the one permanent building, which prior to the war had been the office of the military railway brigade. Quartermaster General Danilov took over this building and made it the operational planning center. It was, according to another of Stavka's senior officers, General P. K. Kondzerovskii, "the pulse and center of all of Stavka's life, on which depended the mood of the Grand Duke and those around him."[9]

Next to the operations center was a small fenced-off garden, with garden chairs and tables, in which the Grand Duke and his brother liked to sit when the weather was good. It was, wrote Kondzerovskii, "the Grand Duke's favorite spot."[10]

The Grand Duke's own carriage was, according to a British visitor, Bernard Pares, "spacious and comfortable but simply appointed."[11] French ambassador Maurice Paléologue described a "roon and comfortable apartment spread with bearskins and eastern rugs.... His bedroom gets its light from four windows on one side of the carriage and is very simply furnished, but the walls are completely covered with icons: there must be at least two hundred of them!"[12] General Felix Iusupov (not to be confused with his son, also called Felix, who would become famous as one of Rasputin's assassins) similarly noted that the Grand Duke's bedroom "was entirely adorned with icons, all gifts from close friends."[13]

Despite Stavka's central location, communications with the front were very difficult. Initially, Stavka's sole communication device was a single Hughes apparatus,[14] a type of telegraph machine on which operators used a keyboard to type out messages and hold a slow conversation with the person at the other end of the line. Matters later improved, but the situation was never very good. The lack of communications put Stavka at a severe disadvantage: it had great difficulty in finding out exactly what was happening at the front, and even more difficulty in transmitting detailed and timely instructions to commanders.

Accentuating this problem was Stavka's small size. The Grand Duke had a staff of just 60 men to help him run the 6-million-strong Russian army.[15] By way of contrast, the General Headquarters of the British Expeditionary Force in France had a staff of about a thousand men by the end of the war.[16] Stavka's size was insufficient for it to provide the Grand Duke with anything but the most general information about the situation at the front or for him to give anything more than the broadest instructions to his subordinates. He had little choice but to delegate a great deal of responsibility to those beneath him.

At the start of the war, the Russian army consisted of two main groupings—the North West Front under General Ia. G. Zhilinskii, and the South West Front under General N. Iu. Ivanov. The former's primary initial objective was to conquer East Prussia; the latter's was to defeat the Austro-Hungarian armies in Galicia.

A former cavalryman, Zhilinskii had observed the Spanish-American War in Cuba as an attaché to the Spanish Army in 1898, and then he had served on the staff of Admiral E. I. Alekseev, the Viceroy for the Far East, during the Russo-Japanese War. He had had little contact with Grand Duke Nikolai Nikolaevich during his career and was much less in his confidence than was General Ivanov, an artilleryman who had distinguished himself as a corps commander in the Russo-Japanese War and who had won the Grand Duke's trust due to his performance as Governor of Kronstadt from 1906 to 1908. Unfortunately, Ivanov and Quartermaster General Danilov did not get on well,[17] and relations between the headquarters of the South West Front and Stavka became inc: ingly tense as the war went on.

The military staff at Stavka consisted of four departments: the Quartermaster's department, headed by General Danilov, which was in charge of operations; the Orderly General's department, led by General Kondzerovskii, which dealt with personnel matters; the Communications department under General S. A. Ronzhin; and the Naval department under Admiral D. V. Neniukov.[18]

There were also a number of personnel at Stavka who were at the Grand Duke's personal disposal for whatever tasks he chose to assign. These included his brother, Grand Duke Pyotr Nikolaevich, Generals B. M. Petrovo-Solovovo and D. B. Golitsyn (the Master of the Imperial Hunt), and several adjutants.[19]

A small number of civilians worked at Stavka: representatives from the Russian Foreign Ministry under Prince N. A. Kudashev and members of a Civil Affairs Office under Prince N. L. Obolenskii. The latter group was necessary because the Supreme Commander had immense civil powers in the areas immediately behind the front. The Ministry of War had been in the process of revising the Statute of Field Administration (the regulation governing this issue) when war broke out; as a result the Ministry had to rush the updated version through very rapidly in July 1914. The revised Statute stated that civilian officials were to execute the Supreme Commander's orders throughout the "theater of military operations." In this zone, the Supreme Commander could "issue and enforce compulsory decrees, peremptorily dismiss civil officials, establish maximum prices, set internal tariffs, effect requisitions, and regulate military censorship."[20] As the "theater of military operations" covered a large part of Russia's western provinces, including the Baltic region, Finland, Poland, Belorussia, and much of Ukraine,[21] Nikolai Nikolaevich became, in effect, the head of a parallel government ruling a large section of the Russian Empire.

The final group at Stavka consisted of the military attachés sent by Russia's allies: for France, General de Laguiche; for Britain, General Hanbury Williams; for Belgium, General de Ryckel; for Serbia, Colonel Lontkievich; for Montenegro, General Martinovic; and for Japan, General Oba, later replaced by General Nakajima.[22] Hanbury Williams rather resented Laguiche's preferential access to the Grand Duke. Laguiche "plays the part of confidential adviser and wants me to play the monkey when chestnuts have to be pulled out of the fire," he complained. "The other allied officers all dislike and resent his methods."[23] Nevertheless, Hanbury Williams showed an appreciation of Laguiche when he described him in a letter to the British Minister of War, Lord Kitchener: "an excellent fellow, but a born attaché—having done Berlin, Vienna, etc. and has got the trade in his bones—hangs about and asks questions of every one he sees."[24]

An infantry officer who had fought with distinction in Sudan and South Africa, Hanbury Williams had a distant family connection to Russia through an ancestor who had been a British envoy to the court of Catherine the Great in the late 18th century. General Kondzerovskii considered him to be "dry and reserved, but without the impertinent arrogance and standoffishness that are characteristic of Englishmen."[25]

While Hanbury Williams seems to have enjoyed his time in Russia, the same could not be said of his Belgian colleague, Lieutenant General Louis-Désiré-Hubert baron de Ryckel. De Ryckel had attended a crucial meeting at which the King of the Belgians had decided to reject a German demand to allow the *Kaiserliche Armee* to pass through Belgium unopposed. For his role in persuading the King to fight, the Russians regarded de Ryckel as a "hero."[26] De Ryckel, according to Kondzerovskii, "didn't look much like a soldier.... He loved to eat and drink, was very good-natured and sweet. He loved laughing, and then it was impossible to look at him without laughing oneself, as his large stomach literally bounced."[27] De Ryckel felt neglected by his own government. When the Grand Duke asked him about a Belgian military mission that was visiting Russia, he had to admit complete ignorance, as also a while later when Nikolai Nikolaevich thanked him for the arrival in Russia of a Belgian armored car unit. "My situation here has been difficult," he wrote to the Belgian Minister of War.[28]

We know less of the other attachés. Lontkievich was the youngest and spoke excellent Russian.[29] Oba was a veteran of the Russo-Japanese War who had participated in the siege of Port Arthur.[30] His presence was a sign of how much Russo-Japanese relations had recovered after the end of the war in 1905.

The five men at Stavka who were closest to Grand Duke Nikolai Nikolaevich were his brother Pyotr, Generals Ianushkevich and Danilov, Laguiche, and the head chaplain of the Russian army, Father Georgii Shavelskii.

Grand Duke Pyotr Nikolaevich appears to have had no discernible official duties beyond occasionally greeting foreign dignitaries. His primary role seems to have been to lend moral support to his brother, who described him as his "valerian drops,"[31] and his "guardian angel."[32] According to General Kondzerovskii, "The difficult days at the front, in times of failure, were very hard for the Grand Duke [Nikolai Nikolaevich]. On these days, his younger brother never left his side, calmed him, cheered him up, and I would say replaced his tender, loving wife."[33] An American visitor, Robert Rutherford McCormick, once watched Nikolai Nikolaevich exit his coach and walk toward a chair in the sun. Pyotr Nikolaevich picked up his brother's walking stick and moved the chair into the shade. "I do not recount this as a remarkable thing for a Grand Duke to do, not being familiar with their habits," wrote McCormick, but, "I call attention to the devotion of one brother to another."[34]

Pyotr Nikolaevich's son, Prince Roman Petrovich, described another incident that aptly summarizes his father's role at Stavka. "One evening," wrote the Prince,

> My uncle came suddenly into the part of the train where my father lived, and without saying a word, he vigorously and intimately embraced him. Because my father felt the tremendous emotional impulse of his brother, he asked him to sit with him and tried to calm him. After a brief silence, Uncle Nikolasha told him with tears in his eyes that he had just signed an order for an offensive on the front against a huge enemy force. He knew that such an order would burden his conscience with many lives. My uncle suffered so terribly under this responsibility that my father advised him to seek relief from his anguish in prayer. When my uncle heard my father's words, he threw himself on his knees and prayed for a very, very long time.[35]

Ever since the First World War, Chief of Staff Ianushkevich has received an almost universally bad press, becoming in essence the "fall guy" for Stavka's many failures. Much of this criticism is justified, but at the same time one suspects that his bad reputation also owes something to efforts by others to deflect blame for Russia's defeats away from themselves and the Grand Duke.

Aged 46, Ianushkevich's expertise was in military administration, which he had taught at the General Staff Academy. He had little knowledge of operational matters and was poorly qualified to hold the position of Chief of Staff of an army at war. One thing which can be said in his favor was that he was fully aware of this. He almost entirely abdicated responsibility for operational planning to Danilov and focused on the administrative side of his work. Even so, he felt out of his depth, writing to Sukhomlinov,

> You know better than anybody that I don't consider myself a Moltke, that I never asked for this position.... The best thing ... would be to relieve me of my post. Then ... my conscience would be clear.... I don't want to cause the Grand Duke to be blamed for not firing me. I don't want to harm him or the cause.... I know that the Grand Duke is enormously good to me and my leaving will surprise and distress him, but this is a matter of the success of a historic war and I don't want to be the reason it goes badly.[36]

Sukhomlinov rejected Ianushkevich's numerous requests to resign. Meanwhile, the Grand Duke seemed unaware of Ianushkevich's deficiencies and developed great confidence in him. "The C.G.S. [Chief of the General Staff] is in absolute touch and confidence with the Gd Duke," Hanbury Williams noted in a letter to Lord Kitchener,[37] expressing an opinion echoed by the Foreign Ministry's representative at Stavka, Prince Kudashev, who wrote that "The Grand Duke trusts Ianushkevich unconditionally."[38]

Ianushkevich was undoubtedly intelligent, and Stanley Washburn, correspondent for *The Times*, wrote, "[he] impressed me as one of the ablest soldiers intellectually that I have ever met. Keen, shrewd, restrained, and well-poised, he strikes one as quite the ideal of a strategist and organizer."[39] Alfred Knox, however, considered that he "gave the impression rather of a courtier than of a soldier,"[40] and Robert Rutherford McCormick wrote, "Of the most polished manners, sitting at his desk upon which were photographs of his wife and children, he made a different figure from the prevalent military idea presented by the equestrian statue."[41]

Ianushkevich tightly controlled access to the Grand Duke. Visitors could not see the Supreme Commander without first telling Ianushkevich what they planned to say, and the Chief of Staff then briefed the Grand Duke on what to expect at the meeting. As a result, the Grand Duke never received an oral report without having first heard Ianushkevich's version of it. Finance Minister Pyotr Bark was astonished to find that this screening applied even to Ministers, and that he had to report to Ianushkevich before he spoke to the Grand Duke.[42] General Ivanov also objected to this style of command. "You would think that the Grand Duke would speak to us," Ivanov complained to Chaplain Shavelskii, "listen to our reports, our thoughts and proposals, consult with us. Not a bit of it. This hasn't happened. He sends the Chief of Staff to us, and he himself sits in his wagon. We speak with General Ianushkevich. And how he then reports to the Grand Duke, what he passes on, whether he does pass it on, or perhaps adds something of his own, we do not know."[43] General Hanbury Williams commented, "The Grand Duke had no knowledge nor opinions other than those supplied by Yanouchkevitch."[44] This was an exaggeration, but the accusation was not an entirely unfounded.

Ianushkevich distrusted Danilov, who in return disliked Ianushkevich. Danilov felt that the Chief of Staff had a "cruel and undisciplined character,"[45] while Ianushkevich complained that Danilov "considers everybody, without exception, an idiot." "He is extremely ambitious, in love with power, and cannot stand contrary opinions." Ianushkevich avoided entering the operations department except for the daily morning briefings. "I can't bear any more than that," he said.[46]

Known as "Black Danilov" to distinguish him from the red-haired chief of supply of the North West Front, General N. A. Danilov ("Red Danilov"), and from the Commander of the Kronstadt fortress, Major General A. V. Danilov ("White Danilov"), the Quartermaster General of the Russian army had both admirers and detractors. Together they paint a picture of an intelligent and hardworking but rather somber and stubborn man. Colonel Knox considered him "the hardest worker and the strongest brain in the staff.... He was a stern, silent man, a great disciplinarian and an exacting chief."[47] Chaplain Shavelskii commented that he was "honest, assiduous, extraordinarily hardworking ... but he seemed to me slow-witted ... narrow, sometimes naive," and "more stubborn than was necessary."[48] To Admiral Bubnov, a member of the naval staff at Stavka, Danilov seemed "strict and demanding." "Possessing a strong character, bordering on stubbornness, he was not distinguished by the breadth of his views."[49] Another colleague, General Kondzerovskii, considered him "extremely imperious and proud, with a very high opinion of himself."[50]

In addition to consulting Ianushkevich and Danilov, the Grand Duke spoke regularly with Laguiche. Ambassador Paléologue noted the "affectionate confidence which the Grand Duke Nicholas displays toward General de la Guiche."[51] In August 1915 General Hanbury Williams wrote this in a memorandum:

> When I first came here [Stavka] a year ago, I was in an awkward position. I was the only allied representative except Laguiche, who was "ami de la maison" [a friend of the house] and very much in the councils of the Grand Duke, with whom he had been to France in addition to having been Military Attaché of the allied Power of France for 3 years at St Petersburg. It was gradually conveyed to me by one means or another that Laguiche was the "doyen" and that Genl. Joffre was the person to whom the Grand Duke looked for communication regarding the action and cooperation of the Allies in France and Belgium. And that I was to look to Laguiche for information etc. as to the position here. He had frequent interviews with the Grand Duke and the C. G. S. and conveyed to me only such information as he chose, which was evidently very little. Wherever I went I was forcibly reminded that the British Representative took a back seat—and that the Army looked upon Laguiche as *the* man who mattered.[52]

The Grand Duke's reliance on Laguiche reflected the priority the Supreme Commander gave to the alliance with France. As he had promised Paléologue, Nikolai Nikolaevich took the French flag he had received in France to Stavka and flew it there. This was one of just two flags the Grand Duke had brought with him, the other being the Supreme Commander's standard, which his father had taken on campaign in the Russo-Turkish War.[53]

The final person at Stavka on whom the Grand Duke relied was Chaplain Shavelskii. A thin-faced priest with a receding hairline, shoulder-length black hair, an untidy pointy beard, and small oval glasses,[54] Shavelskii was, along with Ianushkevich, the only man who always dined at the Grand Duke's table.[55] "He has a grand air, does Father George," wrote a French observer, "with his long black robe, and around his neck the orange and black ribbon of Saint George, the cross detached and stuck on his chest. His eyes, behind the golden glasses, are lively, deep, and attractive."[56] The Grand Duke kept Shavelskii continually at his side. During his 1915 visit to Stavka, General Pau observed that Shavelskii's influence was "very high," that he had "great moral authority," and that at Stavka, after the Grand Duke, he was "the personality most in view: the Emperor and the Grand Duke Nicholas show him the highest deference."[57]

The Grand Duke himself, now 57, was beginning to show his age. Although most of the time he retained his old military bearing, photographs and newsreels of this time show him occasionally stooping and sometimes using a cane. He was not able to exercise much, and during the first few months of the war put on weight,[58] with the result that in December 1914 he decided to go on a diet.[59]

The Grand Duke invariably charmed foreign visitors to Stavka. Colonel Knox, for instance, noted how "in August 1914, he [Nikolai Nikolaevich] told him [Knox] to be sure to bring his pipe with him, so that he might smoke it after dinner while the Russians smoked their national cigarettes." This, commented Knox, showed how the Grand Duke "was kindly and thoughtful."[60] Similarly, Robert Rutherford McCormick recorded that "Upon the day of my arrival I was pouring Narzan water into a glass half full of claret when I heard a deep voice say, 'Ce n'est pas bien que vous faites là' [That's not a good thing you're doing there].... Upon looking up I was told that Narzan water and claret mixed badly. This instance will give you an idea of the Grand Duke's personal care for his guests."[61] These little gestures seemed to make a great impression on visitors.

The Grand Duke's care extended to the staff at Stavka. His infamous bad temper was largely absent during his time as Supreme Commander. Witnesses record only a few instances of the Grand Duke losing his cool. McCormick, for instance, noted, "Once I saw him in a fury. It was the day I came to say goodbye. He had just heard of a seventeen-year-old sister of mercy who had been assaulted by an entire raiding detachment and who was suffering from peritonitis and syphilis. His aids [sic], while sharing his feelings, were awed by their intensity."[62]

Both Danilov and Shavelskii wrote that they could only remember one occasion on which the Grand Duke lost his temper at Stavka. The object of his anger was his adjutant Major Derfelden, who had fallen asleep and failed to report to him as required. "You don't know how to serve. I'll teach you how to serve," the Grand Duke shouted. However, within a few moments, he had apparently forgiven the adjutant and offered him a cigarette.[63] "The Grand Duke's treatment of the members of his staff," wrote Shavelskii, "was always unpretentious, cordial, caring."[64]

As Supreme Commander, therefore, Nikolai Nikolaevich was far from the fierce short-tempered officer of former times. Some attributed this to the influence of his wife, although he may simply have mellowed with age. Whatever the cause, it meant that the Grand Duke was rather more forgiving than he would have been in the past. While he did occasionally dismiss generals, he did so much less frequently than some of his counterparts who led foreign armies.[65] The image of the stern unforgiving commander owes more to the Grand Duke's prewar reputation than to anything he did during the First World War.

Holding himself in check cannot have been easy for a man as emotional as Nikolai Nikolaevich. While the Grand Duke did not have to face the terrors of combat, his position entailed considerable emotional tension. To cope with this, he kept a strict routine. Life at Stavka followed the same orderly pattern every day. Nikolai Nikolaevich got up quite late, at about nine o'clock in the morning, prayed, consulted his doctor, and met one of his adjutants, who delivered any telegrams received during the night. He then had breakfast and at ten o'clock went to General Danilov's office for a two-hour briefing on military operations. At 12 o'clock there was lunch, after which the Grand Duke worked some more until four o'clock. Then there was tea, which he took in his own carriage. At six o'clock every day he would write a letter to his wife. Dinner was at seven thirty.[66] If necessary, General Danilov would brief the Grand Duke again in the evening.[67]

Apart from attending Danilov's briefings on operational matters, the Grand Duke's work involved making decisions on civil affairs in the areas under the army's control, meeting the endless array of visitors who paraded through Stavka, and signing orders, most of them of an administrative nature. He also occasionally left Stavka to hold meetings with the front commanders. The general impression was of quiet routine rather than of energy. Thus Hanbury Williams commented, "Here at General Headquarters the attitude is one of perfect calm and patience (one would sometimes like to put a little ginger into it)."[68]

The food at Stavka was good, although as General Kondzerovskii noted, the menus were "more French than Russian. Russian dishes such as borshch, shchi etc., were rare."[69] Finance Minister Bark commented that "The Grand Duke kept an excellent table and there was great variety in the menu."[70] General Hanbury Williams described dinner on 23 September (6 October) 1914, as "the usual zakouska to begin with, followed by a very simple dinner, soup, fish, roast beef and Yorkshire pudding, soufflé and fruit, with kvass and light wines."[71] On the occasion of a visit by General Pau the menu was "hors d'oeuvre of smoked fish and red caviar, two main courses, fruits, raspberry ice cream, Madeira, Bordeaux, and mineral water."[72]

A partition divided the dining car in the Grand Duke's train into two sections. The first section contained four small four-man tables. The first of these was the Grand Duke's table, at which the Grand Duke always sat with General Ianushkevich and Chaplain Shavelskii, along with a distinguished visitor, if one was present, and if not, with another member of the staff on a rotating basis. The next table was reserved for Grand Duke Pyotr Nikolaevich, Laguiche, Hanbury Williams, and General Golitsyn. At the third sat Danilov and the Japanese and Belgian attachés, and at the fourth the Montenegrin and Serbian representatives. Beyond the partition were six more tables for other members of the staff.[73]

Before meals, the officers would stand and await the occupants of the main tables. Here is how McCormick described the scene: "The Commander-in-Chief enters, followed by the Grand Duke Peter, the Chief of Staff, and guests in order of rank. The chaplain blesses the chief, and the chief blesses the chaplain's hand. Then he walks through the car, shaking hands with all those whom he sees for the first time that morning."[74] Talk about work was strictly forbidden, but events at the front inevitably affected the mood. "When things were going well at the front," wrote Admiral Bubnov, "the Grand Duke took a lively part in the conversation and made witty jokes. But when the situation at the front left something to be desired, the Grand Duke was gloomy and lunch passed by quickly in silence."[75]

The conversation at the Grand Duke's table was more often in French than in Russian. To Shavelskii, the Grand Duke talked about "market-gardening, horticulture, fishing, cooking" and other agricultural matters.[76] With others he often talked about sport or what they would do after the war. According to Hanbury Williams, the Grand Duke's conversation showed "his great sense of humor, the good stories he would tell, his delight in talking over questions of sport and so on, and his unfailing hospitality and enjoyment of a good dinner in good company, followed by the enormous cigar over which he would chaff us who were his neighbors at table, and laugh at the plans which we proposed for the days of peace, when we hoped to meet under other circumstances."[77]

Another important part of the Grand Duke's life at Stavka was regular church services. These took place in the small wooden garrison church every Sunday as well as on religious holidays and other special occasions, such as after major victories. The Grand Duke attended every service, standing throughout.[78] According to General Danilov, these services "had an extraordinarily beneficial effect" upon the Grand Duke, and after attending church he always had "a joyful smile and softened expression on his face."[79]

Apart from the meals, there was little by way of entertainment at Stavka. A nearby cinema showed films twice a week, but the Grand Duke rarely attended.[80] Although he sometimes went out for short walks or car rides, most of the time he stayed in his train. Shavelskii commented that "the Grand Duke sat whole days and nights in his wagon, like a prisoner in solitary confinement."[81]

Remarkably, the Grand Duke never visited the front lines or went anywhere close to them. Hanbury Williams believed that he was blocked by General Ianushkevich, who "is either afraid of the G. D.'s skin, or his own responsibility."[82] Laguiche, on the other hand, believed that the reason was that the Grand Duke "did not want to overexcite the Emperor's sensitivity and jealousy of the adoration shown to the Commander in Chief. He once replied to this effect when a General begged him to visit the front on account of the effect which his popularity could produce there: 'Ah, don't speak to me of my popularity! Let's hope that it doesn't become the death of me!'"[83]

Admiral Bubnov supported this theory, writing that the Grand Duke was afraid that visits to the front would arouse suspicion that he was seeking popularity among the troops.[84] Shavelskii, however, put forward a far more prosaic explanation for the Grand Duke's behavior. He claimed that Ianushkevich had spoken to the Grand Duke about visiting the front, but the latter had categorically refused. He did not want to miss the daily letter he received from his wife, which he would do if he left Stavka. "This," wrote Shavelskii, "was too great a deprivation for him."[85]

The fact that the Grand Duke avoided the front meant that he never had to face directly the human realities of the war he was managing. Meanwhile, Stavka's isolation affected the Grand Duke's style of command. In particular, it accentuated his preference for delegating responsibility and granting maximum initiative to subordinate commanders.

Commandant Langlois, a French officer who visited Stavka on several occasions, noted after one of his trips, "the Grand Duke, despite his very authoritarian character, endeavors not to encroach at all on the initiative of front commanders; these have, for instance, complete freedom to make any modifications they want to the composition of their armies without asking the slightest permission, only having to report the change in the order of battle once it is done."[86] General Danilov confirmed this: "The staff of the Supreme Commander carefully avoided interfering in the details of how operations were carried out and overloading lower-level staffs with superfluous orders.... Interference of higher-level staffs in the work of lower levels normally creates a tense atmosphere."[87] "The Supreme Commander had very responsible, but at the same very limited functions, in general consisting of issuing instructions to fronts of more or less general tasks and regulating relations between them," Danilov wrote.[88]

The Grand Duke thus mostly left front commanders to determine for themselves what to do. While he did sometimes issue firm and categorical instructions, many of his communications to his generals were closer to being suggestions than orders. Grand Duke Andrei Vladimirovich, who worked on the staff of the North West Front, complained that instructions from Stavka took the form of "The Grand Duke suggests, but, however, and nevertheless it is desirable, but if it's possible, then perhaps."[89]

When he did meet the Front Commanders, the Grand Duke tended to give in to their requests and demands, feeling that they knew better than he did what the real situation was. On other occasions, when the staffs of the Fronts met with senior personnel from Stavka for joint conferences, he sat to one side, believing it best that the staffs reach a mutual decision amongst themselves, which he could then approve. Alternatively, he would have Ianushkevich speak for him. The Commander of the Guards Corps, General V. M. Bezobrazov, noted this tendency when he wrote, "the Grand Duke avoids speaking about real business and sends one to Ianushkevich."[90] For a man reputed to possess an iron will, the Grand Duke turned out to have an oddly detached style of command.

This style was not something peculiar to him. The great German general Helmuth von Moltke the Elder, for instance, "believed that commanders should be given the freedom to fight their own battles guided by general directives rather than detailed orders."[91] The British military historian J. F. C. Fuller complained that "Moltke brought his armies to starting points and then abdicated his command and unleashed them. He never issued an order [at the battle of Sedan in 1870] except for a few suggestions to General Blumenthal."[92] Similarly, though less successfully, the commander of the Austro-Hungarian army in the First World War, General Conrad, had "long-held convictions regarding the decentralization of decision-making" and his staff complained that he "allowed too much initiative" to subordinates.[93] According to one of his biographers, the British Commander-in-Chief Douglas Haig's principle of command was, "after laying down the broad outlines of strategy, to leave all levels of execution to his subordinate generals, and to be largely guided by them." Haig supposedly had "an exaggerated respect for the 'man on the spot.'"[94] And Marshal Ferdinand Foch, who became Supreme Commander on the Western Front in 1918, maintained a very small staff, and many of his instructions, according to Elizabeth Greenhalgh, "were pious hopes rather than practical orders."[95]

The tendency to delegate reflected the difficulty of commanding enormous armies over vast areas in an era of limited communications. However, the Grand Duke sometimes took it to extremes. Front commanders did not exactly ignore Stavka, but they were prone to drag their heels when instructions did not suit them. Coordination between the fronts was poor and, quite naturally, the Fronts tended to be interested only in their own area of operations and to be reluctant to help one another; and the Supreme Commander seemed unwilling to challenge Front commanders when their plans contradicted his. The result was a lack of "grip."

Perhaps because of this, some historians have referred to Grand Duke Nikolai Nikolaevich as a "figurehead" who did little more than sign the papers put in front of him by his subordinates.[96] This goes too far. Admiral Bubnov noted that the Grand Duke "was informed of all details of military operations and in practice, not just nominally, commanded them."[97] The Grand Duke could not devolve all responsibility. In the realm of operational planning, his Front commanders did not always agree on priorities. Nor did Quartermaster General Danilov always agree with the Front commanders. Faced with differing proposals from the Fronts, all claiming priority on the same limited set of resources, the Grand Duke had to adjudicate between them. He also had to make decisions on civil issues. Certain of his preferences undoubtedly made themselves felt. His Francophilia, for instance, was unquestionably important, especially in determining Russia's actions in the early weeks of the war. So too was his preference for offensive action, although it must be noted that in this he was hardly unique. While the Grand Duke was never the firm decisive commander of the public imagination, he was never entirely a figurehead.

On 3 (16) August 1914, the day that the Grand Duke arrived at Stavka, he already had an important decision to make. The First Army of the Russian North West Front, led by General P. K. Rennenkampf, had crossed the German border into East Prussia. The Second Army of General A. V. Samsonov was approaching East Prussia from the south. General Zhilinskii had requested on 30 July (12) August that the Second Army march further to the left in a more northwesterly direction. This maneuver ran the risk of separating the First and Second Armies but offered the advantage of making it harder for the Germans to escape encirclement by putting Russian forces deeper into their rear. On arrival at Stavka, Ianushkevich sent the Grand Duke's answer: "The Supreme Commander fully approves the decisions you have taken," wrote Ianushkevich to Zhilinskii, "especially your intention to carry out a deeper turning movement from the west, and expresses a deep confidence that your decisions will be inflexibly and energetically executed."[98]

That evening, the Grand Duke summoned his staff for their first dinner at Stavka. Before sitting down in the dining car, wrote one witness, General A. A. Samoilo, the Grand Duke "spoke with satisfaction about what a magnificent picture Russia now presented, covered with military personnel, hurrying from all sides toward the Austrian and German borders. On the happy faces of the Supreme Commander himself and of his Chief of Staff Ianushkevich and the military officers around them, one could not notice the slightest trace of the colossal responsibility they had for the millions whose fate was entrusted to them."[99]

Swept up in the excitement of the war, the Grand Duke and his staff anticipated a rapid victory. It would not be long before they would be disabused of this expectation.

CHAPTER 12

Opening Salvoes, August 1914

AS THE ARMIES OF RUSSIA, Germany, and Austria-Hungary marched to war in August 1914, railways and geography had a profound effect on their movements.

Railways gave Germany and Austria-Hungary a great advantage, especially Germany, whose railways' capacity was vastly superior to Russia's. The Germans could move an entire army from one part of the Eastern Front to another, or from the Western Front to the Eastern, in just a few days. By contrast, Russian rail movement was limited and slow. The Germans were able to shift forces rapidly around the front, keeping the Russians off balance and plugging any gaps that appeared when the Russians were on the offensive. The Germans' advantage in railways was a major factor in their victories in 1914 and 1915, and one about which the Russians could do very little.

Geographically, the most obvious feature of the Eastern Front was the Polish salient, which stuck out westward between German East Prussia to the north and Austro-Hungarian Galicia to the south and was bisected by the Vistula River and its tributaries, the Bug, Narev, and Bobr. To win the war, the Russian army would need to advance deep into either Germany or Austria-Hungary—or both. Breaking through to the heart of Austria or Hungary would be difficult, as the route was blocked by the Carpathian Mountains at the southern end of the front, on the western edge of Galicia. From a geographical point of view, the route into Germany via Poland was considerably easier, but it was also militarily dangerous as long as East Prussia and Galicia remained under enemy control and able to threaten the extended Russian flanks. Initially, therefore, the Russians needed to secure those flanks by invading and conquering East Prussia and Galicia. This was the purpose of the campaigns of August 1914.

The Russian plan for the invasion of East Prussia was for the First Army under General Rennenkampf to attack first, crossing into the German province through its eastern frontier. If things went its way, the First Army would engage and hold the German forces in place, while the Second Army under General Samsonov would advance from northern Poland, cross over

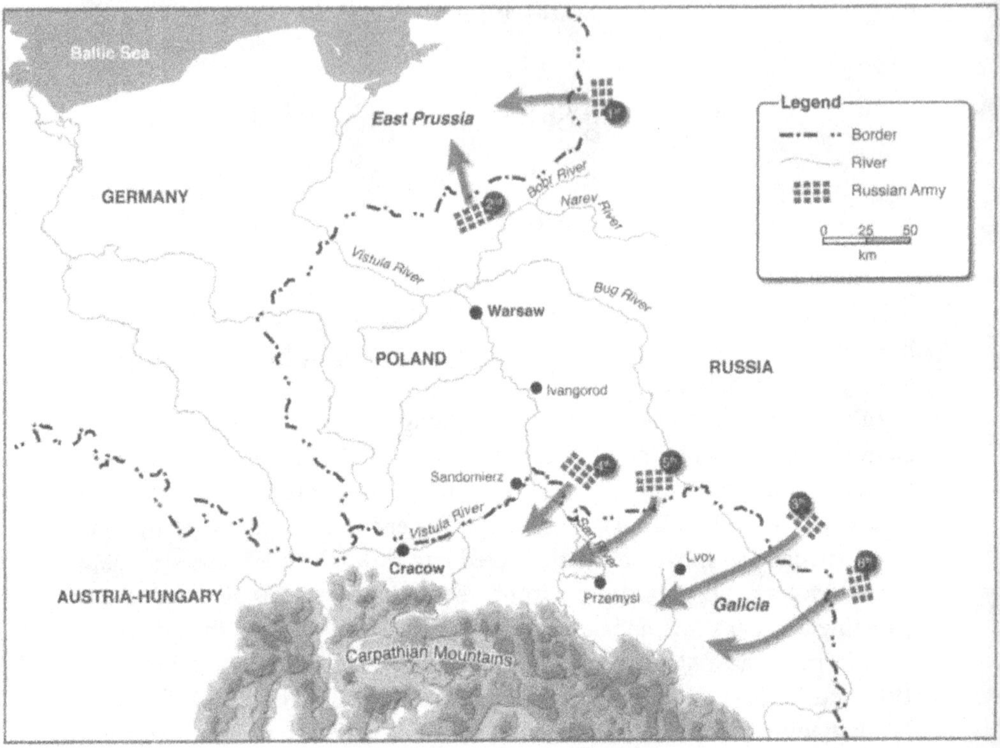

Map 3: The Eastern Front, August 1914

the southern border of East Prussia, and cut off the German retreat. However, concern that the Germans might not stand and fight against Rennenkampf but might instead flee rapidly to the west, so avoiding encirclement, prompted a decision to shift Samsonov's line of advance to the left. Doing so widened the gap between the First and Second Armies, a vulnerability the Germans were soon able to exploit.

Because the Russians chose to begin their offensive as early as possible, neither of the two Russian armies had completed its mobilization before it began its advance. The First and Second Armies had only about 75 percent of their full complement of infantry and only 60 percent of their cavalry.[1] The former crossed the German border with only six and a half under-strength infantry divisions, and the latter with even fewer. Against these 12 divisions were eight and a half German divisions.[2] This meant that the Russians did enjoy numerical superiority, but not by much. Meanwhile, the terrain was difficult, communications were poor, the lack of cavalry severely hampered reconnaissance, and the Germans—while having fewer men—actually had a two-to-one advantage in terms of heavy artillery.[3] The situation was not nearly as favorable to the Russians as Stavka imagined.

At first, though, the invasion of East Prussia went well. On 4 (17) August, the German commander, General Hermann von François, attacked Rennenkampf's army at Stalluponen near the German-Russian border. After an inconclusive battle there, François withdrew a short distance to the town of Gumbinnen. Then on 6 (19) August, Russian cavalry clashed with the Germans at nearby Kauschen and captured a German artillery battery.

Poor communications meant that once he had launched the offensive, these initial battles were completely out of the Grand Duke's control. According to Danilov, Stavka received "only fragmentary and incomplete" news about them. The lack of information disturbed the Grand Duke. On 6 (19) August, Ianushkevich telegraphed Rennenkampf, complaining that "The complete absence of news for two days from the army staff about your situation compels me, on the Supreme Commander's orders, to ask you to immediately telephone to communicate the events which have taken place during this time. The Grand Duke is sending you his adjutant Colonel Kotsebu."[4]

The Grand Duke was also concerned with the situation of the South West Front, as the Front commander, General Ivanov, wished to delay his attack until he had received all his troops.[5] Wanting Ivanov to start as soon as possible, the Grand Duke left Baranovichi by train on the night of 5 (18) August and traveled to the headquarters of the South West Front at Rovno, arriving there at nine the following morning. Once there he urged Ivanov to start operations against the Austro-Hungarians; he then returned to Stavka.[6]

Before leaving for Rovno, on 4 (17) August the Grand Duke had issued a proclamation to the minority nationalities of the Austro-Hungarian Empire, calling on them to support Russia. It read as follows:

> The Vienna government declared war on Russia for the reason that Russia, true to her historic traditions, would not abandon defenseless Serbia or permit her subjugation.
>
> Peoples of Austria-Hungary!
>
> Entering on Austro-Hungarian territory at the head of the Russian forces, I hereby declare to you in the name of the GREAT EMPEROR of RUSSIA, that Russia, which has already repeatedly shed her blood for the release of peoples from a foreign yoke, seeks only re-establishment of right and justice. To you also, peoples of Austria-Hungary, she is now bringing freedom and the realization of your national aspirations.

> The Austro-Hungarian government, for centuries past, has sown discord and hostility between you because its power over you has been based solely on your differences.
>
> Russia, on the contrary, seeks only that each of you shall develop and prosper, preserving the priceless inheritance of your Fathers—your language and Faith—and that, united with kindred brothers, you may live in peace and concord with your neighbors, duly respecting their individuality.
>
> Convinced that you will assist with all your strength toward the attainment of this aim, I call upon you to meet the Russian forces as true friends and champions of your best ideals.
>
> Nikolai.[7]

The proclamation made it clear that the Russians hoped to exploit national divisions within the Austro-Hungarian Empire to their own benefit and had in mind the destruction of the Austro-Hungarian Empire and its fragmentation into smaller nations. From the very beginning of the war, the Russians were pursuing decidedly absolutist goals.

On 5 (18) August, the Grand Duke issued a second proclamation, this time directed at the Russian inhabitants of Galicia, inciting them to rebellion and making it clear that Russia intended to annex Galicia to its empire:

> Brothers!
>
> Divine Justice is being meted out. Patiently and with Christian submissiveness the Russian people have suffered under a foreign yoke, but neither flattery nor oppression have been able to destroy their hopes of freedom.
>
> Like the impetuous current which rends rocks asunder so that it may mingle with the sea, there is no force which can arrest the Russian people in their outburst for unity.
>
> No longer will Rus be in bondage. Having cast off the yoke, may the heritage of Holy Vladimir, the land of [12th-century Ukrainian prince] Yaroslav Osmomysl, and of the [13th-century Ukrainian rulers] Princes Daniel and Roman, raise the banners of a single, mighty and united Russia.
>
> May Providence consummate the hallowed task of the founders of the Russian land.
>
> May the Lord help his anointed, the Emperor Nicholas Aleksandrovich of All the Russias, to complete the work of the Great Prince Ivan Kalita [ruler of Moscow from 1325 to 1340].
>
> And you! Long suffering and kindred Rus! Rise and meet the Russian hosts!
>
> Russian brothers who are being freed! You will find a place within the bosom of Mother Russia. Do not insult people whatever their nationality, and

do not seek your happiness in the persecution of foreigners as the Swabians have done, but turn your sword on the foe, and your hearts toward God, with a prayer for Russia and the Russian Tsar.

Nikolai.[8]

For the moment, the most intense fighting was in East Prussia. On 7 (20) August, the German Eighth Army, which defended East Prussia, launched an attack on the Russian First Army at Gumbinnen with most of its mobile forces. The attack was a dismal failure, and at the end of the day the Germans abandoned the battlefield.

On the next day, Samsonov's Second Army finally entered East Prussia. The Grand Duke was concerned about Samsonov's flank and the possibility that German forces that had entered western Poland would advance toward Warsaw. He was therefore extremely upset to hear that troops of the Guards Corps had moved out of Warsaw.[9] On 8 (21) August, Ianushkevich telegraphed the commander of the North West Front, Zhilinskii, to tell him that the Grand Duke wished to draw his attention "to the absolute impermissibility of allowing the enemy in any circumstance to surge, even temporarily, toward Warsaw." Zhilinskii was not to move the Guards Corps out of the Warsaw region, where it would remain as the Grand Duke's strategic reserve.[10] He was, however, allowed to use the First Corps to support the Second Army's operations.[11] This strengthened the Second Army's position, although rather belatedly.

Nikolai Nikolaevich continued to demand that his armies move rapidly.[12] Unfortunately, the Grand Duke's army commanders failed to share his sense of urgency. After his victory at Gumbinnen, the First Army's commander, General Rennenkampf, ordered two days' rest for his troops.[13] This pause was decisive, for it allowed the German Eighth Army to withdraw out of contact with the Russian First Army, and to redeploy to strike Samsonov's troops.

The Grand Duke was unaware of this problem, for Stavka continued to receive almost no information about Zhilinskii's front. On 10 (23) August, Ianushkevich complained to Sukhomlinov that "For three days we have not received *any news*."[14] As far as the Grand Duke knew, Rennenkampf was still advancing after his triumph at Gumbinnen. The Grand Duke wrote to the Tsar, informing him of "the complete victory of our glorious First Army" and requesting that the Tsar grant Rennenkampf an appropriate medal or reward.[15] The next day, he wrote again to say, "I don't dare to insist, but I very much request this, as, first of all, he deserves it, and second, the First Army will take such recognition as a reward from the monarch to it."[16]

Meanwhile, the situation on the South West Front was very fluid. The Russians had expected the Austro-Hungarians to deploy most of their troops further to the southeast than they actually did and so had concentrated large forces to meet an Austro-Hungarian attack that did not actually take place. In turn this meant that the Russians were weaker on their own right, where the main Austro-Hungarian blow was actually aimed. Since both sides on the South West Front had strong left flanks and weak right flanks, the battle pivoted in a clockwise direction as both sides advanced on their left and withdrew on their right.

The Russian Fourth Army absorbed the initial Austro-Hungarian assault, which began on 7 (20) August. To the Fourth Army's southeast lay the Fifth Army, and then the Third and Eighth Armies. Success depended on holding the Austro-Hungarian attack against the Fourth and Fifth Armies and then having the Third and Eighth Armies drive forward as fast as possible to relieve the pressure and turn the enemy's flank.

On 10 (23) and 11 (24) August 1914, the Austro-Hungarian left flank struck the Russian Fourth Army near the town of Krasnik and drove it back with heavy casualties.[17] Suddenly, the right wing of the Russian South West Front was looking vulnerable. The Grand Duke's response was immediate. First, he urged the Third and Eighth Armies to advance more speedily.[18] On 10 (23) August, Ianushkevich informed Ivanov that the Grand Duke "has ordered you to pass on his inflexible will that the attack of these armies must be carried out with greater energy and speed than in the first days of the offensive."[19] Second, the Grand Duke released the Eighth Cavalry Division and the Third Caucasian Corps, which were part of the reserve he had been assembling near Warsaw, and sent them south to Ivangorod to support the South West Front.[20] Soon afterward, Nikolai Nikolaevich also provided the Guards Corps and the Eighteenth Corps, creating a new Ninth Army on the far right of the South West Front. This meant abandoning the plan to build up an army in central Poland to strike toward Berlin, but it created a powerful force able to hit the advancing Austro-Hungarians in the flank.

It would take time for the Russian reinforcements to arrive and halt the Austro-Hungarians. In the meantime, the Grand Duke remained unsatisfied with the speed of the Third and Eighth Armies' advance. On 12 (25) August he traveled once again to Rovno to see General Ivanov and to prompt him to move faster. He also replaced some of the commanders who had performed poorly in the first two weeks of the war, most notably the commander of the Fourth Army, General Zaltsa.[21] The Grand Duke further ordered the Fifth Army to take "decisive action" in support of the Fourth Army,[22] which involved swinging it round from its southern direction of advance toward the west in order to hit the right wing of the Austro-Hungarians as they attacked the Fourth Army.

Having given his orders, the Grand Duke headed north to meet Zhilinskii and discuss the situation of the North West Front. By this point, Rennenkampf's First Army had entirely lost touch with the Germans. Rennenkampf believed that they had withdrawn toward Konigsberg, and the Grand Duke reported this to the Tsar on 12 (25) August.[23] Again the Grand Duke pressed his front commander on the need to move rapidly,[24] but Zhilinskii convinced him that the battle was going according to plan. The First and Second Armies were advancing "unceasingly," the Grand Duke told the Tsar on 13 (26) August,[25] adding a day later, "Everything at the front is going well, thank God."[26]

This was far from the truth. While Rennenkampf advanced toward Konigsberg, the German Eighth Army had moved in an entirely different direction, embarking on trains and moving southwest to attack Samsonov's Second Army, which had been advancing slowly northward across the center of East Prussia. On 14 (27) August, one day after Zhilinskii had assured the Grand Duke that all was well, the Germans struck.

Initially, the German attack hit the Second Army's left flank near the town of Soldau. The next day the Germans struck the right flank as well. By 16 (29) August, the Germans had surrounded large parts of the Second Army and its troops began to surrender en masse. Facing catastrophe, Samsonov shot himself. Within a short while, the Germans captured 100,000 Russians and 400 guns.[27] While parts of the Second Army escaped, the Russian attempt to capture East Prussia had ended in failure, with enormous losses.

In Galicia, meanwhile, the Third Army had made some good progress, defeating the Austro-Hungarians along the Zlota Lipa River in a battle fought from 13 (26) to 15 (28) August.[28] At this point, the Third Army's commander, General N. V. Ruzskii, ordered a pause in order to carry out reconnaissance in the direction of the Galician capital, Lvov.[29] The Grand Duke immediately countermanded the order. Ianushkevich telegraphed Ivanov on 17 (30) August:

> The Supreme Commander categorically orders the immediate development of the most energetic actions by the Third and Eighth armies. General Ruzskii's halt, whatever its reasons, is entirely inadmissible, as it gives the enemy a breathing space, and will allow him to transfer forces from Lvov to the north. With a rapid onslaught, General Ruzskii must hold the enemy before him by the throat, developing turning movements with his right flank to the north of Lvov. In the forthcoming decisive days on the Austrian front, the Grand Duke orders all armies to exert extremely intensive efforts.[30]

This intervention had the desired effect: the Third and Eighth Armies renewed their offensive and drove the Austro-Hungarians back from their next defensive line along the Gnila Lipa River, opening the way toward Lvov. On the South West Front, the tables were beginning to turn in Russia's favor.

On 18 (31) August, Grand Duke Nikolai Nikolaevich finally learned of the disaster that had befallen Samsonov and his army. At 2:20 pm, the Grand Duke sent a brief message to the Tsar speaking of "very worrisome news" and saying that he was awaiting further information.[31] At 5:10 pm he confirmed that Samsonov was dead.[32] To Laguiche, the Grand Duke put on a brave face. "We are happy to make such sacrifices for our allies," he told the Frenchman.[33]

Despite the Grand Duke's bravado, the defeat shook him badly. Ianushkevich noted in a letter to Sukhomlinov that "The Grand Duke holds himself in check, and for most people appears almost carefree. But speaking with him, I know what an incredible effort he has to make to do this."[34] "Pray," the Grand Duke told Chaplain Shavelskii, who recorded that the Supreme Commander was clearly "very disturbed."[35]

According to Shavelskii, the Grand Duke was also very worried by what the Tsar's reaction to the defeat would be.[36] At 7:37 pm on 18 (31) August, the Grand Duke sent the Tsar a long telegram giving full details of the defeat and adding,

> The reasons for the 2nd Army's catastrophe are: the lack of communications between its corps and the involuntary loss of the telegraph link between the late commander of the 2nd Army and his staff.... In addition, I have reason to believe that the staff of the front hid some information about the situation at the front from me, hoping to correct it. Nevertheless, YOUR MAJESTY, I myself take full responsibility.[37]

With this, the Grand Duke managed to simultaneously claim to take responsibility for the defeat and yet blame it on his subordinates. It is strange, therefore, that he did nothing to change the front's staff or leadership at this stage. Despite his doubts about Zhilinskii's reliability, he continued to accept reassurances that matters were under control. This would contribute to another defeat shortly afterward in the First Battle of the Masurian Lakes.

The Grand Duke was now concerned that the Germans, having defeated Samsonov, would swing eastward and attack the Russian First Army. To guard against this, he ordered Rennenkampf to withdraw to a line further to the east and to defend this "come what may," with "total stubbornness."[38]

On 20 August (2 September), the Grand Duke traveled north again to meet General Zhilinskii at his headquarters at Belostok. As the Grand Duke later told the Tsar, his concern at this point was "preserving the First Army in order to cover the route to Petrograd [as Saint Petersburg had been renamed after the war broke out]." It was for this reason that he had ordered the First Army to withdraw to a line further east. He suspected, however, that the North West Front had not followed his orders.

Zhilinskii met the Grand Duke at the train station and informed him that the North West Front was no longer capable of mounting offensive operations. This convinced Nikolai Nikolaevich that the point of main effort should now be against the Austro-Hungarians in order to win a decisive victory in Galicia.[39] The meeting also confirmed the Grand Duke's suspicions that Zhilinskii was not carrying out his instructions to withdraw the First Army to the east. In an order of 18 (31) August, the Grand Duke had told the First Army to occupy a line running between the towns of Angerburg and Insterburg, but instead it had taken up positions further west, along a line from Angerburg to Allenburg. Despite this, the Grand Duke concluded that the meeting "gave me some hope that everything would now go better."[40]

The North West Front remained a source of concern, but on the South West Front, the Russian armies continued to advance. On 20 August (2 September), the Grand Duke wrote to the Tsar that the Third Army was approaching Lvov and the enemy was retreating "in complete disorder."[41] The next day Lvov fell to the Russians, and Nikolai Nikolaevich asked the Tsar to award Crosses of Saint George third and fourth class to General Ruzskii and fourth class to the commander of the Eighth Army, General A. A. Brusilov.[42]

From this point on, the situation on the South West Front was sufficiently good that further major interventions by the Grand Duke were not necessary. For ten days, fighting raged across the South West Front as the Russians advanced and the Austro-Hungarians desperately tried to counter-attack. On 29 August (11 September), the Austro-Hungarian commander, General Conrad, ordered his armies to retreat.[43] The Russians pursued for another two weeks until finally halting their Galician offensive on 12 (25) September.[44] Galicia was now firmly under Russian control.

In the north, by contrast, things went from bad to worse. The Grand Duke issued a "categorical instruction" to the Quartermaster of the North West Front, General N. A. Oranovskii, to "take all measures to secure the flanks of the First Army,"[45] to protect against a possible German attack. He also ordered the creation of a new Tenth Army to cover the area between the First and Second Armies.[46]

The Germans were preparing a major offensive against the First Army. In the aftermath of their defeat at Gumbinnen some weeks earlier, the Germans had briefly panicked and, fearing the loss of East Prussia, had dispatched two additional corps to the province from the Western Front. On the positive side, this partially justified the Russian offensive, as it meant that it had succeeded in pulling some German forces away from France. On the negative side, these two corps were now available to join those already in East Prussia to attack the First Army.

The Germans amassed over 200 battalions and 1,000 guns for the attack, giving them a small but definite advantage of numbers. The offensive began on 25 August (7 September) and developed into what became known as the First Battle of the Masurian Lakes. The next day Ianushkevich telephoned Zhilinskii and informed him that "The Grand Duke gives you complete freedom to lead the North West Front."[47] This was fairly typical of the Grand Duke's command style and of his preference for devolving initiative, but considering the past failure of the North West Front and the Grand Duke's developing suspicions that Zhilinskii was not following his instructions, it is hard to explain.

On 28 August (10 September), as the German attacks continued, the Grand Duke once more visited Zhilinskii at Belostok. He came away convinced that "command of the North West Front was seriously broken."[48] The next day, in light of the "worrying situation," he asked the Tsar to delay a planned trip to Stavka,[49] and the day after he informed the Sovereign that "the news about General Rennenkampf is more and more worrying and inspires in me the most serious fears."[50]

Consolation came, if only briefly, on 30 August 1914, when the icon of the Apparition of the Mother of God to Saint Sergei of Radonezh (one of Russia's most revered saints) arrived at Stavka, having been sent there by the Tsar from its home in the monastery at Sergeev Posad near Moscow. The Grand Duke attended a service in celebration at the Stavka church, and he issued this order to the Army announcing the icon's arrival:

> This holy icon has accompanied the Russian army in all its major wars, and OUR SUPREME LEADER THE SOVEREIGN EMPEROR has given us a new sign of His love for the army, since I am sure that the recognition of Russian warriors that this holy icon is among us will give us new strength in the struggle with the enemy and still more faith in the help of God.
>
> I believe that God will not abandon us and will give our arms and those of our allies final and complete victory. I am sure that every last one of you, valiant Russian warriors, shares this confidence.
>
> God is with us.
>
> General Adjutant Nikolai.[51]

According to Chaplain Shavelskii, "The Supreme Commander rejoiced, convinced that the arrival of the holy icon would bring good fortune to the front, that we would undoubtedly receive the help of the Mother of God."[52] In a seemingly miraculous coincidence, no sooner did the staff return to their work than the Grand Duke received good news from the South West Front—28,000 enemy prisoners had been taken. Two hours later, Stavka received another telegram—the French had defeated the Germans on the Marne and stopped their drive toward Paris. "It was remarkable," wrote Shavelskii, "that after the holy icon's arrival at Stavka, on all the holidays of the Virgin (1 October, 22 October, 21 November, etc.), Stavka invariably received good news from the front."[53] Faith in such miracles sustained the Russians' morale.

Later that day, the Grand Duke visited a hospital train full of wounded soldiers that had halted at Baranovichi. He passed through the train, speaking to soldiers, and handing out crosses of Saint George to those he considered the most deserving. The visit over, the Grand Duke ordered that he be told every time that a hospital train passed through, and at first he made a habit of visiting them all. Eventually, though, the number of casualties and of hospital trains became so large that this became impractical.[54] This was as close as the Grand Duke ever got to witnessing the human cost of the war.

By now, the situation in East Prussia was critical, with Rennenkampf in full retreat before the German offensive. Losses were terrible. In addition to reporting the good news from the South West Front, Nikolai Nikolaevich penned a report to the Tsar explaining the causes of the First Army's defeat. After the catastrophe suffered by the Second Army, he had, he said, ordered the First Army to withdraw to a new line, but his "categorical instructions," repeated several times, had not been carried out.[55] The Grand Duke thus put the blame squarely on Zhilinskii's shoulders. To some extent this was fair, but the Grand Duke had suspected that Zhilinskii was not following orders and yet had done nothing about it.

The next day, Zhilinskii informed the Grand Duke that he had relieved Rennenkampf of his command and replaced him with General Epanchin. In the early afternoon, the Grand Duke commented to the Tsar that Zhilinskii's message had created a "dispiriting impression on him." "I am inclined to think that Zhilinskii has lost his head," he continued, "and in general is incapable of leading operations." [56]

The Grand Duke now at last dismissed Zhilinskii and appointed Ruzskii as the new Commander of the North West Front. The front's situation was becoming more and more serious, Nikolai Nikolaevich told the Tsar, and he had sent Ianushkevich to check on Rennenkampf.[57] Finally, he admitted, "I completely recognize that I have been unable to insist on the execution of my demands. Therefore, I lay down my guilty life in front of Your Majesty."[58]

Soon afterward, Ianushkevich returned from visiting Rennenkampf. The Commander of the First Army seemed in good form and told Ianushkevich that, despite heavy losses, all his corps had successfully extracted themselves from the battle.[59] Reassured, the Grand Duke decided that Rennenkampf could keep his job. Zhilinskii remained the focus of the Grand Duke's wrath. Ianushkevich spoke to Zhilinskii's Quartermaster, General Oranovskii, who explained that he had several times told the Commander of the North West Front about the Grand Duke's instructions, but that "General Zhilinskii always replied that it was too early to withdraw."[60] "More and more General Zhilinskii's guilt is becoming clear," the Grand Duke wrote to the Tsar on 2 (15) September.[61]

With the First Army's retreat, the troops of the North West Front were back to where they had started operations a month before, with the front line now lying along the Russian-German border. The soldiers of the South West Front, by contrast, had advanced deep into enemy territory. Grand Duke Nikolai Nikolaevich deserves some credit for the victory in Galicia. Once it became clear that the Austro-Hungarians threatened the Russian Fourth Army with defeat, the Grand Duke moved very rapidly to reinforce the right flank of the South West Front with the units he had been assembling to form a strategic reserve to strike into Germany. This meant abandoning his initial plan, but he did so without delay, stabilizing the situation on the right and laying the ground for a later counter-attack. At the same time, his continual pushing of the Third and Eighth Armies had some effect in making them move forward faster. In particular, his intervention on 17 (30) August to override Ruzskii's order to his troops to pause helped the Russians keep the initiative in their hands. Throughout this period, the Grand Duke ran backward and forward between the two fronts, displaying an energy that surpassed anything he showed later in the war. On the South West Front, it seems to have had a positive effect.

The Grand Duke's performance with regard to the North West Front was less impressive. Here, two issues stand out: the first is whether the offensive into East Prussia should have taken place at all; the second is how the offensive was handled once it was started.

As far as the first of these is concerned, there can be no doubt that the final decision to invade East Prussia, and to do so at the earliest opportunity, was the Grand Duke's.[62] The Grand Duke admitted as much in a letter to the Tsar: "My guiding objective was the following: I looked at our actions in East Prussia as a forced act, proving our desire to fulfill our allied obligations regarding France, drawing forces from the West to the East and so helping the success of our allies."[63] The Grand Duke's concerns for France were genuine.

General Laguiche noted his "constant thought to respond to our desires" and added, "it is touching to see his preoccupation in this regard": whenever good news arrived, the Grand Duke would joyfully exclaim, "General Joffre will be happy!"[64]

On the one hand, this strategy led to the mauling of two Russian armies with no territorial gains in compensation. On the other hand, in terms of the objective set for it—drawing German forces from the West to the East—it did achieve its aim, as the Germans diverted two corps from France to East Prussia. Erich von Ludendorff, who played a major role in the battles in East Prussia, and who from 1916 was Quartermaster General of the German Army, remarked that the transfer of these two corps had had "fatal results,"[65] weakening the German attack on France at a crucial moment. In the strategic context of August 1914, the decision to invade East Prussia was not an unreasonable one.

The handling of the operation is another matter. Inherent flaws in the plan and the general situation—including the weakness of the two Russian armies, the lack of cavalry for reconnaissance, the geographical difficulties posed by the East Prussian terrain, and the German advantage in railways—perhaps all meant that the operation was doomed from the start. Still, the Russians did make serious mistakes that contributed to the extent of the disaster.

Most of these mistakes were the fault of the commanders of the North West Front and First and Second Armies rather than of Stavka and the Grand Duke. The latter had almost no control over the flow of the battle once it had started. For days the Grand Duke went without any news at all. That said, he could have exercised more control over those operations than he did. Nikolai Nikolaevich's admission to the Tsar about having been "unable to insist on" the execution of his orders, combined with the free hand he gave to Zhilinskii after knowing that the latter had not carried out his orders—and his optimism after Samsonov's defeat that "everything would now go better" and Zhilinskii would now at last fulfill his instructions—all point to a failure of leadership on the Grand Duke's part, whether or not his complaints about Zhilinskii were correct.

The defeats in East Prussia severely dented the Grand Duke's hopes for a speedy triumph. Still, in September 1914 the situation on the Eastern Front did not look too bad from the Russian point of view. The Russian army had now fully mobilized, Galicia was firmly under Russian control, and the vast bulk of the German Army was stuck in France, having failed to achieve its objectives. There was reason to believe that Russia now held the initiative and could exploit it to decisive effect. With this in mind, Stavka began planning what was to become one of the largest and most ambitious operations of the First World War, the Warsaw-Ivangorod Operation.

CHAPTER 13

The Warsaw-Ivangorod Operation, September–October 1914

THE DEFEAT IN EAST PRUSSIA did not dent Nikolai Nikolaevich's enthusiasm for offensive operations. On 4 (17) September, General Laguiche reported to Ambassador Paléologue, "the Grand Duke has no intention of slowing down by engaging in sieges nor of advancing toward Vienna.... He will redirect all his forces against Germany and above all against East Prussia or (in the most favorable case) simultaneously against East Prussia *and* the regions to the west of the Vistula. But they will march with caution because they realize that they advanced too precipitously at the start."[1]

The Grand Duke's belief that a second offensive against East Prussia was possible rested on an understanding that the bulk of Rennenkampf's First Army had escaped unscathed. He was soon disabused of this notion. On 3 (16) September, the new commander of the North West Front, General Ruzskii, visited the Grand Duke at Stavka, after which he left for the front headquarters at Belostok. From there, three days later, he telegraphed the Grand Duke to tell him that the First Army's losses were "very great," and that he could not rely on the army to undertake active operations.[2] There was, the Grand Duke told the Tsar, a big difference between this news and what Rennenkampf had told him.[3]

Alarmed, on 6 (19) September, the Grand Duke took the train up to Belostok, where he found Ruzskii in "a very good mood." The two men agreed to take urgent measures to bring the First Army back up to strength, including ordering every regiment in the Sixth Army in the region of Petrograd to send one battalion to the First Army.[4] Nevertheless, it was obvious that the North West Front was not in a position to immediately undertake a major offensive. Furthermore, the Russian army was already encountering what would soon become a chronic problem: a shortage of ammunition. On 8 (21) September, Nikolai Nikolaevich telegraphed the Tsar to tell him that "For two weeks there has been a shortage of artillery shells, as a result of which I have requested that deliveries be speeded up." The Grand Duke asked the Tsar to order the expedited deliveries.[5]

The Russians' greatest deficiency was in heavy artillery. When the Austro-Hungarians had retreated in August 1914, they had left behind a large garrison in the fortress of Przemysl, which was now well behind the Russian front line and surrounded by Russian troops. The Russians' shortage of heavy artillery meant that a direct assault on Przemysl would be unlikely to succeed, and the Grand Duke had no desire to become bogged down in a long siege. On 8 (21) September, he telegraphed General Ivanov with this message:

> A siege of Przemysl is not part of my plans. I consider that you should limit yourself to screening it. Our lack of heavy artillery means that we cannot count on a successful outcome of a siege. You must find the enemy's living force and smash it. If it turns out that the enemy's main forces have withdrawn behind the Carpathians, you should cork up the exits from the mountains and with the rest of your forces move in a northwesterly direction toward Cracow and Poznan.[6]

This telegram shows that the Grand Duke was now thinking in terms of a strike by the South West Front into the German province of Silesia, with the front's left flank resting on the Carpathians.

A major German redeployment meant that this plan never got off the ground. On 1 (14) September 1914, the Chief of the German General Staff, General Helmuth von Moltke the Younger, ordered the Eighth Army in East Prussia to dispatch two corps to the area of Cracow to support the Austro-Hungarians. Three days later, he ordered the Eighth Army to send additional forces to Cracow and Upper Silesia, creating a new Ninth Army. This was to link up with the Austro-Hungarians and launch a counter-offensive against the Russian South West Front. The transfer of the German forces began the same day.[7]

For once, Russian intelligence detected German movements in good time, learning of the buildup in the area of Cracow almost as soon as it began. On 9 (22) September, the Grand Duke went by train to Kholm, where he met both Ruzskii and Ivanov and discussed how the two fronts could coordinate their actions against this new German threat. Ivanov agreed to redeploy the Fourth Army, consisting of three corps, to Ivangorod, to cover a possible German advance in that direction.[8] The Grand Duke also dispatched a cavalry corps under General A.V. Novikov to southwest Poland to reconnoiter and determine the exact strength and intention of the German force and to provide a covering force to slow any German attack and win time for the

South West Front to redeploy further to the rear.[9] With this, the Warsaw-Ivangorod operation began.

Rather than being the product of a single master plan, the operation evolved, somewhat confusingly, in response to two distinct objectives: the first was to parry the expected German blow from Cracow; and the second was to launch an attack from the Vistula into Silesia.

On 12 (25) September, the Fourth Army began its move north to take up positions near Ivangorod. On the same day, Ianushkevich telegraphed Ivanov, asking him for suggestions on how to strengthen his right flank.[10] Ivanov wrote back saying that he could turn his front northward, leaving just eight corps in Galicia and sending ten corps to Ivangorod.[11] To discuss this further, Grand Duke Nikolai Nikolaevich returned to Kholm the next day, 13 (26) September. The Grand Duke ordered Ivanov to send not just the Fourth Army but also the Ninth Army to Ivangorod. The armies would move up the right (i.e., eastern) bank of the Vistula, and then once in place cross over to the left (i.e., western) bank and advance westward.[12] This marked a considerable expansion of the scale of the operation. Several hundred thousand men were now to change direction, march a considerable distance, and reposition themselves to launch a major counter-offensive. Coordinating such a maneuver was a considerable logistical challenge. Unsurprisingly, it did not go entirely smoothly.

Before long the Grand Duke's ambitions for the redeployment of his armies grew even more grandiose, with the objective changing from merely parrying the expected blow from the direction of Cracow to driving the German army back and then invading Germany itself. On 15 (28) September, Ianushkevich instructed the commanders of the North West and South West Fronts that "The Supreme Commander sets the general task of both fronts as being to prepare for the largest possible offensive from the middle Vistula in the direction of the upper Oder for a deep penetration into Germany." To this end, the South West Front was ordered to "energetically strive" to transfer "at least ten corps and even better three armies to the left bank of the Vistula."[13]

While the Grand Duke was issuing this order, the Germans were at last beginning their move, advancing out of their concentration area near Cracow toward Sandomierz. According to General Ludendorff the German move was meant merely to support an attack due to start a few days later by the Austro-Hungarian Army, which was "to seek a decision south of the Vistula, relieve Przemysl and cross the River San."[14] This meant that to achieve its objective, the German Ninth Army needed to engage the Russians and pull them away from Galicia. In this sense, the German plan succeeded even

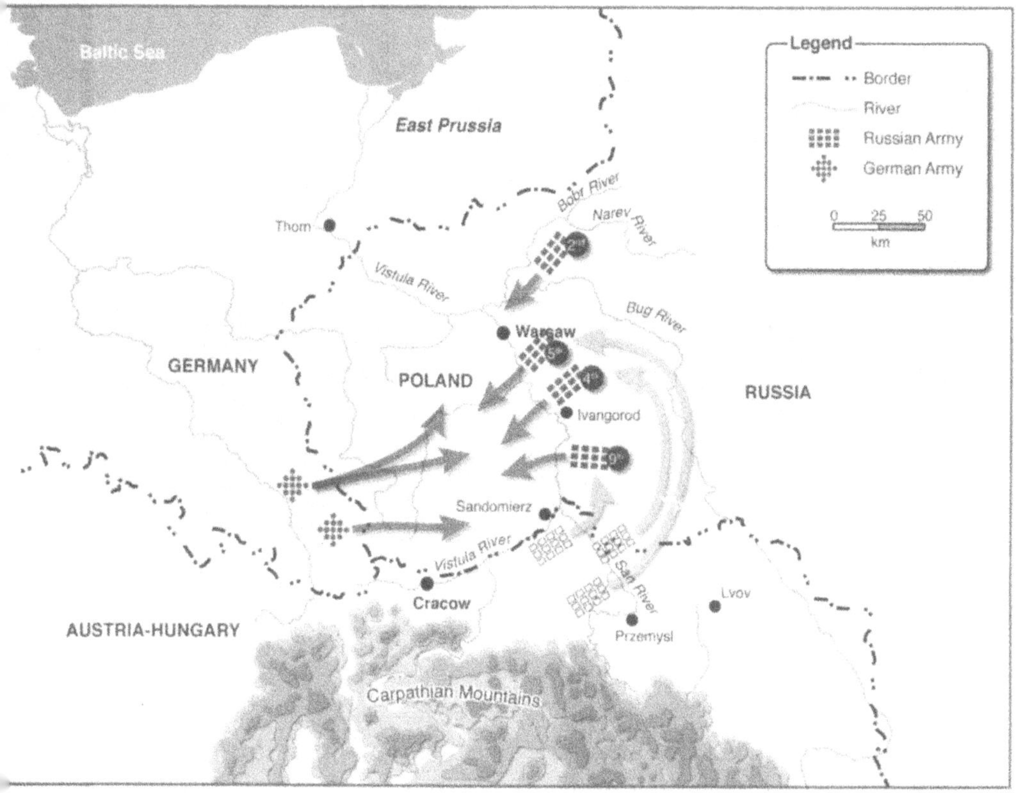

Map 4: The Warsaw-Ivangorod Operation

before it started, because the Russian South West Front had already begun to move north to new positions. However, the German command thought that it would confront large Russian forces in southern Poland heading toward Cracow. Instead, the Germans found themselves advancing into empty space, facing only the covering force of Novikov's cavalry corps. Their lines of communication became overextended, while the Russians won time to amass a significant force of several armies to counter-attack en masse. The Germans in effect found themselves advancing into a trap.

Closing the trap required the largest possible Russian force. For this reason, on 16 (29) September, the Grand Duke asked Ruzskii to send troops from the North West Front to join those from the South West Front now assembling on the Vistula.[15] With this, the plan underwent another change. As it stood, the South West Front was to send two armies to the Vistula. The first of these, the Fourth Army, had begun its move on 12 (25) September. The second,

Grand Duke Nikolai Nikolaevich and General Ianushkevich (in car) and Nicholas II (on foot receiving salute), 1914 or 1915 (Library of Congress)

Ninth Army, started out on 15 (28) September. The Grand Duke had already suggested to Ivanov that he send a third army, and to confirm this he went yet again to Kholm on 18 September (1 October). At this meeting he and Ivanov decided to send the Fifth Army northward also. The army began its move the next day, on 19 September 9 (2 October).[16] In addition, the Grand Duke now instructed the North West Front to send the Second Army, which had been reconstituted following its defeat in East Prussia the previous month. Thus Ianushkevich telegraphed Ivanov and Ruzskii that "For the achievement of the general task of a deep penetration into Germany along the upper Oder, the Supreme Commander sets as the immediate objective the defeat of the enemy's forces which are attacking on the left bank of the Vistula, by developing a strong blow against his left flank." For this purpose, the Grand Duke ordered the Second Army to concentrate "rapidly" in the region of Warsaw, from where it could hit the Germans' left. Furthermore, in order to ensure that the entire operation would be under the control of a single person, the Grand Duke assigned responsibility for all forces deployed on the Vistula to Ivanov.[17] This put the Second Army also under Ivanov's command.

The plan for the Warsaw-Ivangorod operation now took its final form. It was extremely ambitious, involving the movement of four armies parallel to the front over considerable distances. Maneuver on such a scale was to be extremely rare during the First World War. It was difficult to coordinate, and risky. Nevertheless, the Grand Duke had great hopes. "In the coming days," he wrote to the Tsar on 18 September (1 October), "I foresee the start of a new and probably prolonged period of battles on the left bank of the Vistula against large German and Austrian forces, the outcome of which will be of decisive importance."[18]

Three days later, the Tsar honored the Grand Duke with a visit to Stavka. This was to be the first of many. Far from finding such visits an imposition, Nikolai Nikolaevich seems to have derived great cheer from them,[19] seeing them as signs of the Tsar's continuing goodwill. The Grand Duke's elevation to the post of Supreme Commander does not seem to have changed in any way his relationship with the Tsar. Julia Cantacuzen commented that her husband had noted how, in the Tsar's presence, the Grand Duke "stood aside on all occasions, even from his own place of supreme command, how he handed reports to the Emperor, putting the latter into his own place, while he remained merely in attendance."[20] Father Shavelskii similarly wrote:

> Other Grand Dukes ... during their conversations with the Emperor behaved familiarly, simply, standing at ease, addressing the Emperor as "ty" [the familiar form of address]. Grand Duke Nikolai Nikolaevich never forgot that it was the Emperor standing before him; he stood at attention while he spoke with him. Although the Emperor always called him "ty" or "Nikolasha," I never once heard Grand Duke Nikolai Nikolaevich call the Emperor "ty." His form of address was always, "Your Majesty"; his reply, "Yes, Your Majesty." And yet he was the Emperor's uncle, who was 15 years older, and who had been his commanding officer, and of whom the Emperor had at that time been very afraid.[21]

"For me he is the Emperor," the Grand Duke told Shavelskii, "I was brought up to honor and love the Emperor. Furthermore, I love him as a person."[22]

On 24 September (7 October), the Emperor summoned Nikolai Nikolaevich to his dining car. According to Shavelskii, "Within a few minutes he [the Grand Duke] returned, excited, with tears in his eyes; on his neck hung the order of Saint George third class. He went straight to the Chief of Staff and said, 'Go to the Emperor; he is calling for you.' Everyone went up to congratulate the Grand Duke. I heard his words, 'This reward isn't mine, it is the army's.'"[23]

The Grand Duke then issued an order to the troops of the Russian army, using typically flamboyant language:

> I accept this high MONARCHICAL favor as an expression of HIS special goodwill and gratitude for the whole series of heroic achievements and victories gained by you. I am indebted to you, TSARIST warriors, miraculous heroes, for this great reward, and I address you with all my heart and soul with words of my fervent, heartfelt gratitude. The high honor given to us by the TSAR's visit and by the blessing of our SOVEREIGN, will strengthen us for further self-sacrificing service of TSAR and MOTHERLAND, not sparing our bodies to our last drops of blood.
>
> I firmly believe and trust that God will help us in this difficult deed.
>
> God is with us.
>
> Nikolai, General-Adjutant.[24]

Several days later, on 20 September (3 October), the German Ninth Army finally reached the Vistula near Ivangorod and Sandomierz. It was now in something of a bind, as its way forward was blocked by the Russian Fourth and Ninth Armies on the Vistula's right bank (the Fifth Army had only just started its move). The Germans could not expect to cross the Vistula successfully in the face of such opposition, but retreating the way they had come would mean abandoning the Austro-Hungarians whose offensive into Galicia had now started. Lacking any other good options, the Germans swung north and started to march toward Warsaw.

This put the Polish capital in serious danger. Nikolai Nikolaevich had ordered the North West Front to send the Second Army to Warsaw to strike at the German left flank, but Ruzskii had dragged his heels, claiming that the situation on his front made the transfer premature. Despite repeated promptings from the Grand Duke, the Russian Second Corps, which Ruzskii had originally promised would be ready to move by 17 (30) September, did not board trains for Warsaw until 23 September (6 October), almost a week late. The Fourth Corps, due to be detached from the First Army to join the Second Army in Warsaw, was even slower. On 24 September (7 October), Ianushkevich expressed frustration that the First Army's commander, General Rennenkampf, could "decide on an instruction directly contrary to the orders of the Supreme Commander." Troops of the Fourth Corps began to arrive in Warsaw only on 27 September (10 October).[25]

By this time, the Germans had begun their swing toward Warsaw, while Austro-Hungarian forces had reached the river San and relieved the besieged fortress of Przemysl. As the German Ninth Army clashed with the Russian Second Army outside Warsaw, it was time for the Russian Fourth, Fifth, and Ninth Armies to enter the battle by crossing to the left bank of the Vistula. The Fourth Army was first off the mark, Ivanov having ordered it to cross the Vistula on 27 September (10 October). The crossing failed. Two days later, elements of the Third Caucasian Corps managed to get a foothold on the left bank, but their position was extremely tenuous and could not be developed further. The Russian plan had ground to a halt. The only consolation was that Austro-Hungarian attempts to cross the river San failed equally badly, dashing Austro-Hungarian hopes of recapturing Galicia.

Demoralized by his failure, General Ivanov asked the Grand Duke to come to Kholm. On the night of 28 September (11 October), Nikolai Nikolaevich did so, holding a meeting with Ivanov the next morning. The Grand Duke found the commander of the South West Front in a depressed and worried mood. He ordered Ivanov to move the Fifth Army up toward Warsaw to combine with the Second Army, and to speed up its movement.

Given the Fourth Army's failure, the success of the operation now depended largely on the outcome of the Second Army's planned offensive from the direction of Warsaw. This meant that it was desirable to put the best possible commander in charge of the Second Army. The Grand Duke proposed appointing Ivanov's Chief of Staff, General Alekseev. Ivanov, though, said that he would only part with Alekseev if he received Danilov as his new Chief of Staff in return. The Grand Duke refused.[26] Ivanov in turn asked whether it would be possible to swap the commanders of the Second and Tenth Armies, Generals Sheideman and Sivers, feeling that he would be more confident if Sivers was in command of the Second Army during the battle for Warsaw. The Grand Duke agreed in principle but first asked Ianushkevich to find out whether Ruzskii had any objections. Ruzskii did. Swapping the army commanders would be "harmful," he claimed.[27] As a result, the change did not go ahead.

The incident reveals again the Grand Duke's strange weakness in the face of his front commanders. He allowed Ivanov to overrule him regarding Alekseev's appointment as commander of the Second Army. He then initially agreed to Ivanov's request to swap Sheideman and Sivers, because, as Ianushkevich wrote, "the Supreme Commander will go to any lengths just to guarantee Nikolai Iudovich's [Ivanov's] spiritual calm and give him confidence in success."[28] However, he then insisted on consulting Ruzskii and, in effect, gave him a veto. It is almost as if the Grand Duke felt that keeping his front commanders happy was more important than telling them what to do and making the appointments that he felt most appropriate.

The Grand Duke's meeting with Ivanov convinced him that Ivanov was demoralized and in no mood to lead the operation successfully.[29] On his return to Stavka, therefore, the Grand Duke reversed his previous decision to put the whole operation in the hands of the South West Front and instead divided responsibility for it between the two fronts.

To this end, on 30 September (13 October), Ianushkevich telegraphed Ivanov and Ruzskii, telling them that the plan remained to defeat the enemy on the left bank of the Vistula by means of a strong blow to his left flank. The Grand Duke, said Ianushkevich, assigned responsibility for this to the North West Front, which was to collect the strongest force possible. For this purpose, the North West Front was to take command of both the Second and Fifth Armies. The South West Front's task, meanwhile, was to draw as many of the enemy as possible on to itself in order to make the North West Front's task easier.[30]

The front commanders continued to delay, however. By 3 (16) October, the Grand Duke was growing impatient and demanded that the front commanders inform him when they would be ready to start the general offensive.[31] The next day he ordered them to start operations on 5 (18) October and "to pass on to their troops his instruction to carry out the forthcoming offensive urgently and stubbornly."[32]

"We must foresee that at first this offensive will develop slowly, with stubborn battles," the Grand Duke told the Tsar.[33] But he was confident of success. "The most energetic measures have been taken to obtain numerical superiority over the enemy," he wrote to Lord Kitchener, adding, "the current situation all along our front is such that one can with a certain tranquility envisage future events which will have as their aim the deep penetration of our armies into Germany."[34]

At this point the South West Front put a spanner in the works. Having confirmed with Stavka that it would begin its attack at one in the afternoon on 4 (17) October, it then sent another telegram three hours later saying that it was not ready! "The Supreme Commander," Ianushkevich told Ivanov, "greatly regrets that you did not manage to clarify the situation earlier."[35] This was as close to a rebuke as the Grand Duke ever issued in his tenure as Supreme Commander.

The North West Front's offensive finally got under way in full strength on 7 (20) October, with the Second and Fifth Armies striking the German left. "The Supreme Commander," Ianushkevich telegraphed Ruzskii that morning, "expects that the offensive which will start today, in accordance with your directive, will not slacken, but will develop with iron energy."[36] The decisive moment in the campaign had arrived.

The attack by the Second and Fifth Armies got off to a good start, and the Germans began to fall back. It was now vital that the Russians not repeat Rennenkampf's mistake in August 1914 and allow the retreating Germans to slip away. If they could keep up with the enemy, they had a chance to inflict major damage upon him. Fully aware of this, Grand Duke Nikolai

Nikolaevich demanded a rapid pursuit. On 9 (22) October, the Fourth and Ninth Armies began belatedly crossing over to the left bank of the Vistula. The Grand Duke was concerned that poor roads and the destruction of bridges by the retreating Germans were delaying the Second Army in its pursuit of the enemy.[37] Ianushkevich informed Ivanov and Ruzskii that the Grand Duke ordered them to "continue the most energetic offensive" and to take "energetic measures" to determine the enemy's line of retreat so as not to lose contact.[38]

Instead of pursuing energetically, however, General Ruzskii now asked for permission to stop his advance. Although the Russian Second and Fifth Armies had pushed forward, Ruzskii believed that the Germans wished to resume their advance toward Warsaw. A meeting engagement between the two sides was possible, he informed Ianushkevich on 13 (26) October. Ruzskii requested that the Second and Fifth Armies be allowed to halt in their current positions until the Fourth and Ninth Armies had had an opportunity to advance.[39] In response, Ianushkevich told Ruzskii, "The Grand Duke does not constrain you in any of your decisions, leaving you free to act according to circumstances. From my own point of view, I consider it my duty to mention to you the significance which His Highness gives to keeping Warsaw in our hands."[40]

The Grand Duke's decision to give carte blanche to Ruzskii in the midst of a battle over which he might have been expected to keep the tightest control was rather odd, though entirely in keeping with his style of command. Ruzskii's request to halt, and the Grand Duke's concerns over the safety of Warsaw, were in fact unnecessary, as the Germans had by now had enough. It was clear, wrote Ludendorff, that "If the Ninth Army stood where it was it would ultimately be surrounded and defeated." On 14 (27) October, therefore, the German Command gave the Ninth Army the order to withdraw.[41] The Russians were victorious.

The Grand Duke was delighted with this success. The next day, 15 (28) October, he wrote to the Tsar, telling him, "Yesterday's immense success at the front was an unexpected gift of the Lord God.... God helped us to smash them along the whole front and force them to retreat. I assign special significance to this success, and with God's help it must certainly have some influence on the Germans.... I hope that God will grant yesterday's great success to influence the Galician theater also."[42] The Grand Duke expressed similar sentiments to General Hanbury Williams. "I am sure that the Russians have gained confidence by the defeat of the Germans outside Warsaw," the Briton wrote to Kitchener. "They do not 'buck' at all about their victories, but simply say 'Grace à dieu nous avons fait bien.' [Thanks to God we have done well.]"[43]

"On the entire front on the left bank of the Vistula the enemy's forces are in full retreat," the Grand Duke told the Tsar on 16 (29) October.[44] The next day, Ianushkevich informed Ruzskii, "The Supreme Commander gives you permission, in the event that you find the situation appropriate for this, to move the corps of the 2 and 5 armies to the front of Lenchitsa, Lodz, Volborzh, and Sendov."[45] There was no indication of what Ruzskii should do if he did not consider this appropriate. At the same time, though, Ianushkevich gave rather more categorical instructions to the South West Front, whose armies were moving more slowly than desired. "Fourth and Fifth armies should urgently strive to reach their designated front as quickly as possible," Ianushkevich said.[46]

The South West Front's slow progress was in part due to the fact that Ivanov believed that before pressing forward too far in southern Poland, he first needed to protect his flank further south and drive the Austro-Hungarians back from the San. The Grand Duke concurred with his front commander, as was so often the case. "The Supreme Commander fully shares your thought about the need to achieve success on the San and push forward the Third Army to the west prior to developing the offensive operation on the left bank of the Vistula,"[47] Ianushkevich informed Ivanov on 19 October (1 November). This was not necessarily a good decision. Although the desire to protect the flanks was understandable, the offensive on the left bank of the Vistula constituted the Russian army's point of main effort at this time. The priority was to prevent the Germans from slipping away, which required rapid pursuit. Holding back to wait until success was achieved along the San detracted from that objective.

Stavka's instructions at this point were confusing and seemingly contradictory. Having apparently agreed to allow the South West Front to halt on the left bank while it focused on securing its flank, on the next day, 20 October (2 November), Ianushkevich informed Ruzskii that "The Supreme Commander, having given General Adjutant Ivanov the order that the armies of the South West Front should start an energetic offensive, finds it necessary that the armies of the North West Front should support this offensive in the most decisive fashion."[48] "Frankly speaking," Ivanov complained, "it is impossible to detect in Stavka's instructions either an exact task or a fixed objective."[49]

In part this may have been because the objective was changing. The Grand Duke was now thinking further ahead, turning his attention from pursuing the retreating Germans to planning a new operation to advance into Germany. On 20 October (2 November), Ianushkevich telegraphed Ruzskii and Ivanov to inform them that "the final aim, toward the achievement of which all our efforts must be exerted, is an invasion of Germany.... Securing the flanks of the forthcoming operation is so important that the Supreme Commander does not consider it possible to advance the corps of the Second and Fifth armies any further forward until more decisive results have been achieved in East Prussia and on the river San." The Grand Duke instructed the North West Front to throw the Germans back behind the Masurian Lakes in East Prussia and told the South West Front to seize the passes through the Carpathian Mountains and attempt to send cavalry out of them into the Hungarian plain. "The Supreme Commander," wrote Ianushkevich, "considers it necessary to carry this out with complete stubbornness and urgency, bearing in mind that every delay in fulfilling these tasks will result in disadvantageous delays in the operation on the left bank of the Vistula."[50]

This in essence marked the end of the Warsaw-Ivangorod operation and the start of a new phase of the war in which the Russian High Command hoped to use the territory it had recaptured in western Poland as a base from which it could invade Germany.

Two elements had been crucial to the success of the Warsaw-Ivangorod Operation: the choice of the Vistula as the line on which to concentrate and the assembly of a particularly large offensive force—four armies. The two were connected. By deploying along the Vistula, the Russians forced the Germans to advance deep into Poland, an inevitably slow process that gained the Russian army time to amass a sufficiently large body of troops to not merely halt the German advance but throw it back in a decisive fashion. The plan as it eventually developed was bold, but taking the risk had proven to be justified.

General Palitsyn, who spent this period at Stavka, considered that the Grand Duke deserved the credit for the operation's success, writing in his diary that when the Grand Duke decided to redeploy his armies and counter-attack the Germans on the left bank of the Vistula, "I saw great moral courage and greatness of soul."[51] "This decision of the Grand Duke," wrote Palitsyn, "was his decision, and nobody can take away from him the greatness of it."[52]

Indeed the Grand Duke deserves credit for the speed with which he reacted and the ambition of his response. The manner in which he handled the operation once it began was rather weaker. The movement of the Russian armies was slower than desired, in part due to good logistical reasons but in part also due to a not always completely cooperative attitude from Front and Army commanders. The slow buildup of the Second Army around Warsaw was a case in point, as was the sudden announcement by the South West Front that it was not ready to join the planned general offensive on 5 (18) October, despite having previously said that it was. In one sense, this was not the Grand Duke's fault: if the Front and Army commanders had failed to ready their troops in time, he could hardly instantaneously make them ready from his position far away in Stavka. However, he proved excessively tolerant of his subordinates' tardiness, doing no more than deliver two mild rebukes to Ivanov and Rennenkampf via Ianushkevich.

As he had during the battles in East Prussia in August 1914, the Grand Duke allowed a great deal of latitude to his Front commanders, as evidenced by his message to Ruzskii giving him a free hand to do as he wished during the pursuit of the Germans, even stopping the pursuit in order to defend against what proved to be an imaginary German attack on Warsaw. Similarly, Nikolai Nikolaevich's reaction to Ivanov's request to change the Commander of the Second Army showed an apparent unwillingness to confront his generals and take a decision himself. This perhaps explains some of the confusing and contradictory instructions given during the pursuit of the Germans. General Danilov later hinted at the problem in a comment about the Grand Duke's decision to take the Second and Fifth Armies away from South West Front and give them to North West Front, so splitting control of the operation. The Grand Duke made this decision, Danilov wrote, because he "recognized that it was necessary to stop being merely an observer of the directives he had given and instead to take the leadership of operations into his own hands."[53] The Grand Duke's leadership at this stage does speak of a flexible mind, willing to adapt plans to changing circumstances, but it raises the question of why he was acting "merely as an observer" of an operation which he himself considered to be of great significance.

Looking back at the Warsaw-Ivangorod operation, General Danilov called it "one of the most successful strategic combinations.... We gained an undoubtedly very large victory over our opponents."[54] It was, he wrote, "the best example of Russian strategic art, carried out under the leadership of Grand Duke Nikolai Nikolaevich."[55] This perhaps makes rather too much of the victory. The repeated delays and inconsistent pursuit meant that the German Ninth Army escaped from the Russians' clutches. The Russian victory was not as complete as it might have been.

The Germans would soon come looking for revenge. If the Warsaw-Ivangorod operation was one of the largest battles of the war, the one that followed—the Battle of Lodz—was one of the most confusing.

CHAPTER 14

The Battle of Lodz, November 1914

VISITING STAVKA ON 12 (25) October 1914, Prince Vladimir Orlov commented, "The general feeling here is that everything is going well, morale is wonderful, and the soldiers are fighting heroically."[1] On 26 October (8 November) 1914, Russian reconnaissance units reached the town of Kalicsz on the Polish-German border.[2] Further south, Russian forces for a second time encircled the Austro-Hungarian fortress of Przemysl, cutting off over 100,000 Austro-Hungarian troops inside the fortress. Grand Duke Nikolai Nikolaevich was now determined to press forward with an invasion of Silesia in eastern Germany, and Ianushkevich informed General Ruzskii that the Grand Duke gave him complete freedom to adjust his lines as he wished in order to establish the best possible starting point for the attack.[3]

Despite the fact that a large-scale offensive into Germany required lengthy preparation, the Grand Duke was keen to start as rapidly as possible, especially as there was some evidence that German reinforcements were arriving from the Western Front. Presciently, on 28 October (10 November), Ianushkevich warned Ruzskii and Ivanov that "losing contact with the Germans ... is extremely unfavorable for us, as, using his railways, our enemy can easily change the grouping of his forces, creating a favorable situation for himself in his preferred direction."[4] Ianushkevich instructed the North West and South West Fronts to start their attacks on 30 October (11 November) or "in any event no later than 31 October." The final objective of the operation, Ianushkevich told Ruzskii and Ivanov, was "a deep penetration into Germany." The Grand Duke ordered the four armies now located on the left bank of the Vistula to attack the enemy to their front; the two armies in the center were to defeat the Germans at Chenstokhov; the army on the right was to strike the enemy on the front near Kalicsz; and the army on the left was to advance toward Cracow in order to protect the left flank of the operation.[5]

The plan was somewhat unrealistic, especially given the speed with which the Grand Duke wished it to take place. An advance into Germany required enormous logistical support: railways had to be repaired in western Poland, and ammunition and other supplies had to be stockpiled in sufficient quantities to support several weeks of operations. Even if this was done and the Russians did manage to penetrate into Silesia, they would find themselves in a highly industrialized region with a well-developed rail network which the German army could use to transfer large numbers of troops from elsewhere to counter-attack. This would most likely stop any Russian offensive before it got very far. Observing the planning at Stavka, General Palitsyn predicted in his diary that the attack would fail: "it is not at all provided for and not prepared," he wrote, adding that the Grand Duke's staff was inadequate.[6] The plan to invade Silesia was based on "a fatal overestimation of success," Palitsyn concluded.[7] He did not record whether he passed these warnings on.

The Grand Duke, meanwhile, was increasingly worried by unconfirmed reports of new German units arriving on the Russian front and the possibility that the Germans might use these troops to preempt the Russian offensive. Russian intelligence had detected German forces assembling to the north of Kalicsz in the area of Thorn, from where they could strike into northwest Poland. This news strengthened Nikolai Nikolaevich's desire to start his offensive as soon as possible, before the Germans could launch their own attack. On 30 October (12 November), however, he received some bad news. The Commander of the Fourth Army, General Evert, suddenly announced that his army would not be ready to attack for over a week due to "exhaustion of its dry rations." The Grand Duke was not pleased. "His Highness," wrote Ianushkevich to Ivanov, "asks you to bear in mind the immense disadvantageousness of a delay of the general offensive, solely because of the Fourth Army's lack of preparedness.... The Supreme Commander asks you to explain."[8]

The Grand Duke was not, in any case, inclined to delay for long beyond the original 31 October start date for the offensive, and for once he expressed his opinion forcibly to Ivanov. "The accumulation of Germans north of Kalicsz obliges us to consider the possibility that they may start an offensive and then seize the initiative, which I cannot allow," the Grand Duke telegraphed Ivanov later on 30 October (12 November), unusually sending the message directly and in his own name rather than through Ianushkevich. "The only means of us retaining the initiative is to go on the offensive no later than 1 November," the Grand Duke said, "therefore, I order you to do everything so that the Fourth Army goes onto the offensive no later than the first."[9]

The Grand Duke's concerns about German plans were entirely correct. Anticipating that the Russians planned to invade Silesia, the Germans had decided to prevent them by launching an offensive, and they had used their railways to redeploy their forces, building up a large concentration of troops in the region of Thorn. Their aim was, in Ludendorff's words, to strike an "overwhelming and annihilating blow" against the Russian right flank.[10] To ensure success, the Germans sent further reinforcements from the Western Front, and they chose as their point of main effort the dividing line between the Russian First and Second Armies. On 29 October (11 November), they struck.

Nikolai Nikolaevich's instructions to his Fronts on 30 October (12 November) came too late, for the German offensive had already begun. The fact that Stavka was not aware of this reveals again the communications problems bedeviling the Russian army in 1914. The North West Front did not at first consider the German attacks to be significant,[11] and it took several days for the Russian High Command to realize that they constituted a major offensive.

Still unaware of what was happening, on 31 October (13 November) Ianushkevich instructed Ruzskii that the Grand Duke gave him the right to choose the exact moment at which his offensive should start.[12] The next day,

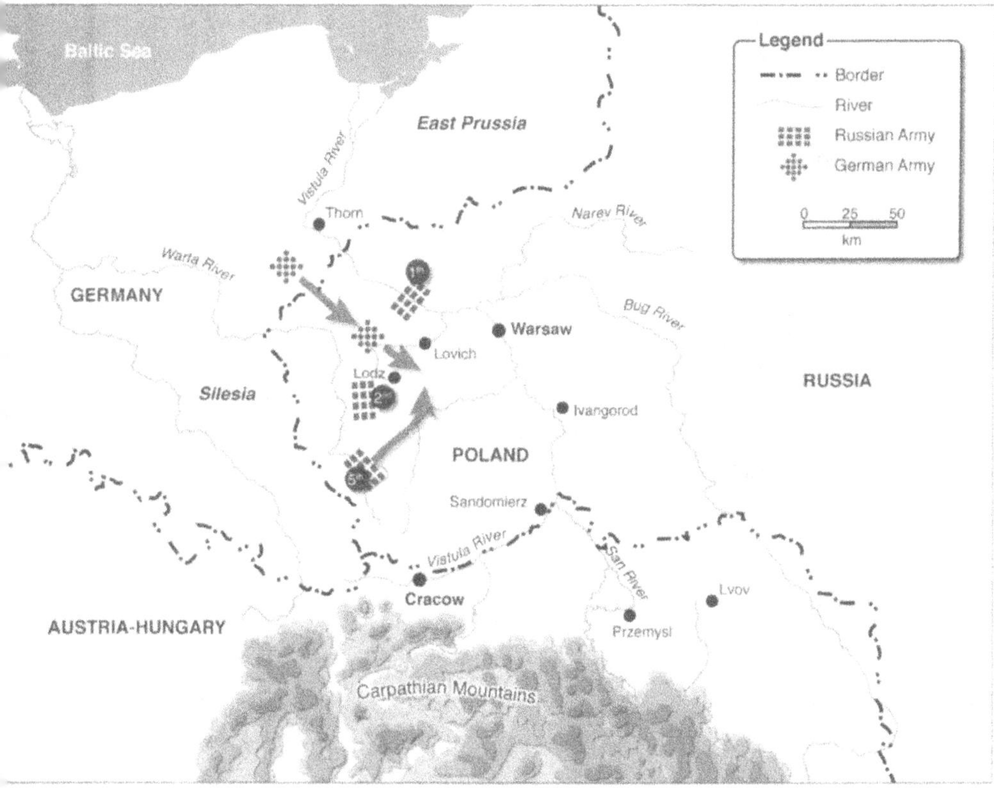

Map 5: The Battle of Lodz

the German assaults drove a wedge between the left flank of the Russian First Army and the right flank of the Second Army. By 2 (15) November, it was clear that the situation was not what the Russians had imagined it to be.

Despite this, the Grand Duke continued to hope that he might be able to launch his planned attack. On 4 (17) November, General Hanbury Williams reported that the Grand Duke was "in good spirits," despite "some retiring" on the Russian right flank.[13] The same day, the Grand Duke wrote to the Tsar telling him that the North West Front would start its offensive the next day. He had yet to realize how serious the situation had become. Thus on 5 (18) November, the Grand Duke telegraphed Ruzskii with this message:

> Pass on from me to all army commanders, and through them to all remaining commanders, that I consider our strategic position good. The hour has come when everybody must exert all their strength so that our going over to a general offensive is crowned with success. Our side has overwhelming strength, and the main thing is that God is with us. Remembering this, making the sign of the cross, bravely and in concert, giving each other full support, forward against the enemy for the glory of Tsar and motherland. General Adjutant Nikolai.[14]

The optimistic message hid a growing dissatisfaction with the course of events. The gap between the First and Second Armies was getting larger, creating the danger that the Germans might penetrate deep into the Russian rear. The Grand Duke was particularly displeased with the performances of the commander of the First Army, General Rennenkampf, and the commander of the Fifth Siberian Corps, General Sidorin. The result was an unusually severe telegram from Ianushkevich to Ruzskii: "The Supreme Commander is extremely distressed with the instructions of some senior commanders over the past few days, some of which are hard to explain," such as "the inexplicably rapid withdrawal of General Sidorin which has created a crisis in our operation between the Varta and the Vistula," and "the incomprehensible instructions of General Adjutant Rennenkampf to abandon Plotsk with its crossing." "The Grand Duke," continued Ianushkevich, "being extremely distressed by these facts and restraining himself from declaring his unhappiness directly to the above mentioned generals has ordered me to ask Your Excellency nevertheless to let them know about it."[15]

Ianushkevich's message points to a sense of growing crisis. In compensation for this, there was at least good news from the South West Front. Having thrown the Austro-Hungarians back from the river San, the Russians had advanced into the Carpathian Mountains and taken one of the key passes, the Uzhok Pass. "Our strategic situation remains quite good," the Grand Duke reassured the Tsar on 6 (19) November.[16]

Before long, his tone would change. Two days later, on 8 (21) November, following reports from Ruzskii that the Germans had penetrated deep into the Russians' positions, the Grand Duke finally admitted to the Tsar that General Ruzskii "considers the situation serious." "Communications with the staff of the Second and Fifth armies," the Grand Duke wrote, "are being maintained only by radio.... From all the information I have received from General Ruzskii I cannot paint for myself even an approximate picture of the situation of the left bank of the Vistula."[17]

The Grand Duke now beseeched General Ivanov to come to the help of the North West Front, although he did so in his typical manner, using terms that were far more of a suggestion than an order, and using Ianushkevich as the conduit:

> It would be extremely desirable from the general point of view if you found it possible to send one corps from the Fourth Army through Petrokov toward Bendkov for a joint offensive to Koliushki with the column of the Fifth Army attacking Pushin Rzgov. The Supreme Commander asks you to consider this question, and if there is any possibility of supporting the North West Front without stopping your action against the Chenstokhov group to carry out the suggestion above.[18]

The next day, 9 (22) November, the Grand Duke was slightly more optimistic. "Although news about the course of the battle is very meager," he told the Tsar, "our forces in general are holding their positions."[19]

The optimism was unjustified. German forces had broken through the Russian lines north of the city of Lodz and penetrated into the Russian rear. Fearing that the Russian Second Army was in danger of being surrounded, Ruzskii telephoned Ianushkevich to inform him that he intended to withdraw from Lodz.[20] The Grand Duke, according to Danilov, disagreed with Ruzskii's analysis of the situation. However, Danilov continued, "It was obvious that he [the Grand Duke] had to take into account the conclusions of the responsible leader of the operation" (i.e., Ruzskii), and the Grand Duke therefore approved Ruzskii's withdrawal plan.[21] In light of this, Ianushkevich telegraphed Ivanov to approve a withdrawal by the South West Front as well. "The situation on the left bank of the Vistula in the armies of the North West Front is such," wrote Ianushkevich, "that it is extremely difficult to give any definite instructions."[22] "Over the past few days some confusion has been reigning in the staff," the Foreign Ministry's chief representative at Stavka,

Prince Kudashev, wrote to Foreign Minister Sazonov the same day.[23]

In fact, retreat was unnecessary. The Germans had advanced too far, and a counter-attack by units of the Russian Fifth Army on 10 (23) November succeeded in surrounding the advance elements of the German army northeast of Lodz, cutting off the German Twenty-Fifth Reserve Corps and the Third Guards Division, a force some 60,000 strong, from the rest of the German army. All of a sudden it was the Germans who were facing disaster.

Grand Duke Nikolai Nikolaevich now canceled his approval of Ruzskii's and Ivanov's withdrawal plans.[24] The German attacks had failed, he told the Tsar: "We have firmly held our position."[25] Stavka was now convinced that it was on the brink of a major victory and ordered special trains to come to Lodz to take away the expected haul of German prisoners.[26]

Russian hopes were to be cruelly dashed. On the night of 10–11 (23–24) November, the 60,000 encircled Germans escaped, breaking out westward and successfully making their way back to their own lines. Victory had slipped out of the Russians' grasp. The Grand Duke's only comment in his daily report to the Tsar was that the enemy was continuing to withdraw.[27]

The fighting in northwest Poland now settled down into a prolonged battle of attrition. The Germans attempted to push forward once again, but their momentum had been broken and their progress was slow. Further south, while the fighting had been waging around Lodz, the Russian South West Front had been advancing toward Cracow and Chenstokhov in line with the original plan for an attack on Silesia. On 15 (28) November, the Grand Duke approved a proposal from the South West Front for most of its force to halt in their current positions.[28] Further large-scale offensives were out of the question until the army had had time to recuperate.

On 16 (29) November, the Grand Duke traveled with Ianushkevich and Danilov to the headquarters of the North West Front in the town of Sedlets to hold a conference with Ruzskii and Ivanov. Danilov gave the two Front commanders a report in which he stated that the Russian army was running out of reserves. It was necessary to abandon the idea of invading Silesia. Nevertheless, Danilov argued that North West Front should attack in East Prussia to protect its right flank, while the South West Front should continue in the direction of Cracow.[29] This was too much for the Front commanders, who reported that the condition of their armies was even worse than Danilov had imagined. The Grand Duke told the Tsar that Ruzskii described the situation on his front as "extremely risky," the "complement of our forces extremely weakened." In light of this, Nikolai Nikolaevich sided with the Front commanders and rejected Danilov's proposals for attacks in East Prussia and the Cracow region. Instead he ordered the North West Front to withdraw to a shorter line. This obliged the South West Front to withdraw as well, to avoid creating a gap between the two Fronts.[30]

The Grand Duke had by now finally had enough of General Rennenkampf, whom he condemned for his slow response to the initial German attack toward Lodz and for allowing the encircled Germans to escape on the night of 10–11 (23–24) November. Nikolai Nikolaevich fired him as commander of the First Army. Rennenkampf later demanded an official inquiry into his performance in order to clear his name, but the Grand Duke would have none of it. Such an inquiry was "extremely undesirable," Nikolai Nikolaevich told the Tsar.[31]

Although the Grand Duke had agreed to a withdrawal of both the North West and South West Fronts, he almost immediately started backtracking. It was clear that he did not really want to withdraw and, if he had to, did not want to do it too rapidly. On his return to Stavka from the meeting at Sedlets, the Grand Duke personally telegraphed Ivanov to tell him that

> A premature withdrawal of all the corps of the front entrusted to you ... could immediately worsen the situation, which on your front is rather favorable. I therefore categorically order you ... in no event to carry out a general withdrawal of your forces, but to withdraw gradually, starting with the right flank, and only so far as is required by the actual situation. It is necessary to bear in mind that you have in front of you an enemy whose morale has been undermined by a whole series of failures and whose ability to maneuver is probably limited.[32]

Ivanov replied that his armies would "maintain their dispositions to continue action against the Austrians." This in turn prompted another message from the Grand Duke to Ivanov, telling him, "I can only exchange kisses with you with all my heart for your last telegram. God thank you.... I am confident that you will fulfill that wonderful directive which you gave to your heroic armies."[33]

Russian intelligence now revealed the arrival of three new German corps on the Russian front. Over the next few days, the Germans renewed their attacks in northwest Poland, aiming to advance toward the town of Lovich,[34] while also striking southeast out of East Prussia toward Prasnysh. The pressure on the North West Front was growing inexorably.

In the midst of this, on 19 November (2 December), the Tsar arrived at Stavka for another visit. "I arrived exactly at 12.30," the Tsar wrote to his wife. "N. met me at the big station behind the wood. He looks well and calm, though he has lived through terrible moments."[35]

The continued German pressure and the transfer of extra German troops from the Western Front persuaded the Grand Duke to appeal to France for support, and he asked General Laguiche to go to Petrograd to send a message to Joffre. "The Grand Duke," Laguiche told Joffre, "not desiring to withdraw to fortified positions and wishing to continue his movement forward, which corresponds to our interests, would be happy if the French army could support it in its current situation by taking the offensive with the least delay possible."[36] Laguiche told the British ambassador to Russia, George Buchanan, that while Ianushkevich favored a withdrawal to gain time to resupply the army, the Grand Duke "would like if possible to continue to advance. His decision would no doubt be influenced by the reply which he received from the French commander-in-chief."[37] Joffre replied that he was due to launch an offensive imminently. In fact, he did not begin until 5 (18) December,[38] which was not soon enough to help the Russians. Even if it had been sufficiently successful to persuade the Germans to bring some troops back to the Western Front, the French offensive could not have had that effect immediately. As it was, it seems to have had no impact at all.

On 22 November (5 December), the Grand Duke agreed to a further withdrawal by the North West Front.[39] Three days later the Russians abandoned Lodz, which the Germans immediately occupied. Although the Grand Duke had hoped to avoid a general withdrawal in western Poland, it was becoming increasingly clear that refraining from such a withdrawal would not be possible.

The Russian army was now in a precarious position, in great part because the first few months of the war had largely exhausted its stocks of rifle and artillery ammunition. Industrial production could not come close to making up the shortfall. Shortages of rifles and footwear left the troops woefully ill-equipped. The situation, Ianushkevich told Sukhomlinov, was "tragic."[40]

In late November, the Grand Duke took a few small steps to address some of the worst problems. He sent one of his adjutants, Colonel A. P. Kotsebu, to investigate the shortage of rifles in the Fourth and Ninth Armies,[41] and he instructed the head of the state stud farm, Prince Shcherbatov, to investigate the supply and condition of the army's horses. He also issued an order complaining of chaos on the railways and giving supply officers 15 days to sort out the problems; this deadline came and went with no obvious effect.[42]

On 29 November (12 December), the Grand Duke received a visit from the Chairman of the Duma, M. V. Rodzianko, and the two men discussed the supply issue. According to Rodzianko, the Grand Duke asked him to use his influence to organize the supply of footwear for the army as soon as possible. Rodzianko suggested that the best way of meeting the army's needs was to work with public organizations such as the zemstva, which could be done by calling a conference of provincial zemstvo chairmen and organizing the provision of supplies through them. "The Grand Duke entirely agreed with my proposal," Rodzianko claimed later.[43]

This marked the beginning of an important shift in the Grand Duke's political outlook. In an effort to better supply the army, he began to bypass central government institutions such as the Ministry of War and started looking for support from elements of civil society who promised that they could meet the army's needs. These included bodies such as the All-Russian Union of Zemstva and the All-Russian Union of Towns, which had been established by local officials at the start of the war and which mobilized local resources to organize medical and other supplies for the army. Their members were for the most part people of a liberal political persuasion, who believed that the central government was incompetent and needed replacing by a government responsible to the Duma. While the Grand Duke remained committed to Tsarist autocracy, he became increasingly sympathetic to these people's point of view and more and more inclined to believe that the authorities in Petrograd should make some concessions to the liberal opposition. Although the Grand Duke had always had very decided views on the need to separate military and political matters, his frustration at the central government's inability to provide supplies for the army pushed him slowly into meddling in political affairs.

Rodzianko and the Grand Duke also talked about the malign forces in the Court that in their view were undermining Russia's war effort, in particular Rasputin, who was well-known to be opposed to the war. Rumors were by now circulating through Russia that Rasputin had asked to come to Stavka and the Grand Duke had replied that, if he did, he would hang him. Rodzianko asked the Grand Duke if this was true and later reported as follows in his memoirs: "The Grand Duke laughed and said, 'Well not exactly.' It was clear from his answer that something of the sort had actually taken place."[44] In addition, wrote Rodzianko, "The Grand Duke complained of the fatal influence of the Empress Alexandra Fedorovna. He said frankly that she was a hindrance to everyone. When at Stavka the Emperor agreed to everything, but on rejoining her he altered all his decisions. The Grand Duke realized that the Empress hated him and desired his dismissal."[45]

Rodzianko was not the only person with whom the Grand Duke discussed his dislike of the Empress. The Grand Duke also regularly denounced her to Shavelskii, telling him repeatedly, "Put her in a monastery, and everything will be different, and the Emperor will be different. She is leading everybody to destruction."[46]

As the war progressed, a popular mythology developed that blamed Russia's military problems on a pro-German cabal within the Court that wished to make peace with Germany on terms unfavorable to Russia. The Russian aristocracy and the Russian army were well stocked with people of German origin, exemplified by generals with names such as Rennenkampf, Plehve, and von Raukh. Many Russians were deeply suspicious of the influence wielded by such "Germans" and believed that the German-born Empress, allied with Rasputin, was the key figure in a "German party" conspiring to undermine Russia's interests. Nikolai Nikolaevich's dislike of the Empress and Rasputin was common knowledge, and the Grand Duke became the symbol of struggle against not only the external enemy but also the "German within."

Russian censors found numerous examples of this attitude in letters written by ordinary Russians.[47] Rumors circulated from almost the first days of the war that the Grand Duke had intervened to prevent the Tsar from signing a separate peace with Germany. Some also saw Nikolai Nikolaevich's dismissal of General Rennenkampf as part of a general purge of German officers in the army.[48] Before the war, the Grand Duke had been well-known in the army but little liked. Now his popularity received an enormous boost.

This was in spite of the lack of visible success at the front. By the end of November 1914, the focus of fighting on the North West Front had shifted largely to the area of Prasnysh, northwest of Warsaw, where the lines ebbed to and fro without either side being able to gain a decisive advantage. To discuss what to do, on 30 November the Grand Duke went to Brest-Litovsk for another conference with Ivanov and Ruzskii.

This time, the Grand Duke told the Tsar, both Front commanders said that due to "the extremely weak complement of their armies," the lack of officers and replacements, "the significant shortage of rifles," "a severe shortage of artillery shells," "an insufficient supply of boots," and a lack of warm clothing, they wished to withdraw further so as to shorten their lines to build up reserves and be able to resupply their troops. In light of the general situation, the Grand Duke concluded, "I was forced to approve the decisions of both commanders."[49]

The Grand Duke's line that he was "forced" to do what his commanders wished was one that he would use again on other occasions, and it indicates the slightly unbalanced relationship that existed between him and them. Furthermore, having gone to Brest-Litovsk, the Grand Duke did not actually attend the meeting there but, instead, let his senior officers debate among themselves what to do; he then had Ianushkevich brief him on their conclusions.[50] This was not the only time that the Grand Duke did this: his habit was to wait nearby while the generals conducted their discussions, then make a decision once Ianushkevich had reported to him. It was a rather strange way of conducting business.

On 1 (14) December, the units of the South West Front began to withdraw to positions further to the east.[51] The North West Front had also pulled back, although it still kept a foothold on the left bank of the Vistula, blocking the route to Warsaw. With this, the Battle of Lodz came to an end.

Tactically, the battle was a bloody draw. The Germans had gained some ground, but not any of great significance. Nevertheless, from a strategic point of view, the Battle of Lodz was far more of a German success than a Russian one, as it thwarted the Russian plan to invade Silesia and took the initiative on the Eastern Front out of the Russians' hands. Russian losses of men and equipment were considerable, with the Second and Fifth Armies alone losing 100,000 men between them,[52] while supplies of ammunition had become critically low. In the aftermath of the battle, Russian offensive power was severely diminished.

Throughout, Grand Duke Nikolai Nikolaevich had exercised very little control over events, operating at times almost entirely blind. When he did intervene forcibly, it was primarily to prevent his Front commanders from withdrawing. The Grand Duke displayed a marked preference for offensive action and an extreme reluctance to cede territory on the left bank of the Vistula. This remained the pattern of his future behavior. The Grand Duke stood for war à l'outrance. Whatever happened, he would fight. Still, the fact that he did eventually agree to withdraw in this case showed that he was not completely inflexible.

The battles of November 1914 left the Russian army in a state of exhaustion. Recovering its offensive ability required a prolonged period of comparative rest, during which it could receive reinforcements and supplies. Russia's enemies had other plans.

CHAPTER 15

Winter, December 1914–January 1915

DECEMBER 1914 FOUND THE RUSSIAN army in Poland holding the line at a series of rivers on the left bank of the Vistula—the Bzura, the Ravka (a tributary of the Bzura), the Pilitsa, and the Nida. The decision to halt at this line rather than further to the east had been the Grand Duke's. Visiting Stavka in December, General Hanbury Williams's predecessor as British military attaché, Colonel Knox, reported that General Ianushkevich had told him that he had advised the Grand Duke to withdraw behind the Vistula but that the Supreme Commander had insisted on holding positions further forward.[1] In line with this decision, Ianushkevich told Generals Ruzskii and Ivanov that the Grand Duke considered it "necessary to hold the armies of the North West Front along the line of the rivers Bzura and Ravka which they now occupy."[2]

On 5 (18) December, the Grand Duke handed out crosses of Saint Vladimir to the Allied military attachés.[3] The Grand Duke, wrote Colonel Knox in his diary, "was as nice as ever, but seemed much worn and worried."[4] Among Nikolai Nikolaevich's concerns was the army's continuing supply problem. Early that day he issued an order describing his displeasure with the state of the army's supplies and blaming incompetent officers. "I have reached the conclusion," the Grand Duke wrote, "that rear and supply services from the fronts of the army down to individual units are not at the level which is desired and possible." Reports suggested that there were in fact sufficient reserves of supplies in the rear, but that these were not reaching the front. As a result, "units often either do not receive bread or receive it in an inedible form, and are not supplied in time with a sufficient quantity of boots and warm clothing, horses do not receive forage, although millions of pounds of it have been purchased, etc." "Unfortunately," wrote the Grand Duke,

> I see that not all commanders are up to the mark. Wherever the command cares for its men and is strictly exacting of representatives of the supply service, affairs are excellent. But where the opposite is the case there are examples of disturbingly criminal inaction by the authorities. Military quartermasters

Map 6: The Bzura-Pilitsa-Nida River Line

often display no initiative and wait for instructions. Those in charge of artillery supply care neither for the even and careful expenditure of combat supplies nor for the collection of weapons on battlefields. One must not forget that there are moments in battle when all the attention of combat commanders is involuntarily directed forward, and to wait at that time for directions and instructions on matters of material supply is straightforwardly criminal. On the other hand, I consider all commanders guilty who, recognizing that such

> colleagues are unsuitable, leave them to carry out their responsibilities despite their clearly harmful attitude.... I categorically demand that commanders take the most energetic and draconian measures to check the reasons for the delay of supplies which are at the fronts' disposal but have not reached the troops.... To restore order it is necessary to instill strict responsibility, put those guilty on trial, and not to limit oneself, as has been the case in the past, to transferring them to a new post or dismissing them from the service.... I ask all senior commanders to free Me from the need to use the full scope of the powers entrusted to Me by the Emperor to punish the guilty.... Nevertheless, if it is necessary, I will do so without any indulgence.[5]

As the First World War progressed, stories began to circulate among the troops of the Russian army portraying the Grand Duke as a friend of the ordinary soldier and a hard taskmaster of senior officers. Popular rumors claimed that "he tore the epaulettes off cowardly commanders with his own hands, arrested thieving quartermasters, personally shot traitors, and beat officers who were sitting behind the lines in restaurants with a whip."[6] Most if not all of these stories were baseless. Nevertheless, the rumors played well with the troops, among whom the Grand Duke became extremely popular, despite the fact that almost none of them ever saw him. As one soldier wrote in a letter in early 1915: "You will not be surprised that all is well set up here. This is all due to the Grand Duke, who has become for us a second Suvorov [a great Russian general from the time of the Napoleonic Wars]. We believe in him and put our lives in his hands."[7]

On 5 (18) December, the Germans launched a large-scale offensive along a 200-kilometer front against the Russian defenses on the Bzura-Ravka-Pilitsa-Nida line. Twenty-five German divisions faced 33 Russian ones. In accordance with the Grand Duke's instructions, the Russians fought where they stood. The resulting battles included none of the grand maneuvers of the previous months. Instead what followed was a series of frontal assaults, each of which descended into a prolonged battle of attrition. Writing in the 1930s, the Russian émigré historian A. A. Kersnovskii assessed that the Russian strategy had lacked vision. Instead of standing where they were, and being ground down by the enemy, the Russians should have attempted to maneuver, creating a strong reserve and then counter-attacking, he wrote.[8] This tactic had worked during the Warsaw-Ivangorod Operation, but at that point the Russians had been stronger while the Germans had been substantially weaker. It was also not obvious that fighting the Germans further to the rear would give the Russians any particular advantage over fighting them where they were, while doing so would expose Warsaw to capture. In any case, the Grand Duke was not one to withdraw unnecessarily, and in a sense he was justified: despite their losses the Russians held their ground, and the German advance made no progress. The cost, though, was high. Russian casualties eventually amounted to some 200,000 men,[9] and the army was prevented from taking the pause in operations that it needed to recuperate.

Rumors about the Grand Duke's state of mind now spread around the diplomatic community. In December 1914, the British ambassador to Russia, George Buchanan, heard from his French counterpart, Paléologue, that "Grand Duke Nicholas was in such a state of depression that he spent most of his time on his knees before his icons, declaring that God had abandoned him." The story was, Buchanan said, "pure invention,"[10] but this did not prevent him from pressing the British attaché at Stavka, General Hanbury Williams, for an update on the Grand Duke's health. In response, on 9 (22) December, Hanbury Williams noted that "The Grand Duke was on a diet for a bit but nothing else. He is perfectly fit and as keen as ever and [I] should not think has the slightest idea of resigning.... He is a man who shows his feelings ... but he is quite cheerful and only last night was telling me of some good work that had been done against the Austrians."[11] "The Grand Duke seems very well and in good spirits,"[12] Hanbury Williams added two days later, commenting again on 13 (26) December, "the Grand Duke seems very well and cheery."[13]

The day of this latter remark, the Tsar arrived at Stavka for a visit.[14] On the next day, news arrived of trouble in the Caucasus. On 16 (29) October, the Ottoman Empire had entered the war on the side of Russia's enemies. In December the Ottoman army invaded the Caucasus, advancing toward the town of Sarykamysh in Russian-controlled Armenia and inducing panic in the Russian defenders. The commander of the Russian Caucasus army, General A. Z. Myshlaevskii, ordered a general withdrawal, abandoned his army, and fled to the Caucasian capital, Tiflis.

Concerned, the Grand Duke summoned General Hanbury Williams for an interview. Nikolai Nikolaevich told the Briton that he regarded the Caucasus as a secondary theater, and although he considered the situation "very serious" he would not pull troops away from fighting the Germans and Austro-Hungarians to reinforce it. He wished to know if the British could find some way of striking the Ottoman Empire to persuade it to draw troops away from the Caucasus. Hanbury Williams replied that the British army lacked the means to do so and asked whether a naval demonstration might suffice. According to Hanbury Williams, once he heard this suggestion, the Grand Duke "jumped at it gladly," and the attaché rushed off to Petrograd to send a telegram to England passing on the Grand Duke's request.[15]

When Lord Kitchener received Hanbury Williams' message, he forwarded it to the First Lord of the Admiralty, Winston Churchill, who asked the Admiralty to prepare a proposal to force the Dardanelles strait with battleships. A few days later the British War Council accepted the resulting proposal.[16] In due course this developed into what became the ill-fated British campaign at Gallipoli.

In late December, good news arrived from the front. In the south, the Russian Third Army had attacked the Austro-Hungarians in the Carpathian Mountains and made good progress in the area of the Uzhok Pass. On 20 December (2 January), the Grand Duke wrote to the Tsar to report that the Third Army had taken over 22,000 Austro-Hungarian prisoners.[17] A few days later, there was even better news. In the Caucasus, the Ottoman army had advanced too far too fast in harsh winter conditions and worn itself out. The Russian Caucasus Army, now led by General N. N. Iudenich, counterattacked in the region of Sarykamysh and routed the enemy, driving them back over the border into the Ottoman Empire. "I am ineffably happy to greet YOUR MAJESTY with the full and decisive victory granted by the Lord God to the heroic Caucasus Army," the Grand Duke wrote to the Tsar.[18] The Russian victory rendered moot the Grand Duke's request to the British for help. Nevertheless, British planning for an assault on the Dardanelles had built up a momentum of its own and continued, notwithstanding the elimination of its original rationale.

While the victories in the Carpathians and the Caucasus provided some reassurance to the Grand Duke, the situation in Poland remained tense. Although there were several days of quiet in mid-December, on 23 December (5 January) the Grand Duke reported to the Tsar that the Germans had conducted strong attacks on the left bank of the Vistula in the region of the village of Borzhimov. The Grand Duke ordered the commandant of the Ivangorod fortress, General Shvarts, to supervise the preparation of new defensive positions to the rear,[19] in case a further withdrawal should be necessary, but he remained adamant that this should be avoided if at all possible. On 25 December (7 January), Ianushkevich telegraphed the following to Ruzskii: "The Supreme Commander asks Your Excellency to instill in the armies subordinate to you ... the basic thought that the forces located on the left bank of the Vistula should not permit any possibility of a withdrawal."[20] The next day, the Grand Duke told the Tsar, "I have again instructed the Commander of the armies of the North West Front on the necessity of holding the positions occupied by us come what may."[21]

As 1914 came to an end, the German attacks in Poland ground to a halt and the situation at the front stabilized, but the Grand Duke remained frustrated with the state of his supplies and so sought change in the administration of the army. As a first step, he asked Ianushkevich to broach with Sukhomlinov the idea of circumventing the Inspectorate General of Artillery, headed by Grand Duke Sergei Mikhailovich, and of creating a new organization for artillery supply that would be subordinate to the Supreme Commander.[22] Also, it would appear that during the Tsar's last visit to Stavka, the Grand Duke and his main ally at Court, Prince Vladimir Orlov, had discussed replacing the unpopular Interior Minister, N. A. Maklakov, with somebody more amenable to liberal public opinion. On 30 December (12 January), Orlov wrote to the Grand Duke to tell him that he had put the idea to the Tsar, who had approved it. Maklakov would be replaced in January, he said.[23] In fact, this did not happen. Similarly, nothing came of the Grand Duke's suggestion for a change in the administration of artillery supply. But the fact that the Grand Duke was now pushing for such changes was an indication of how the demands of war were encouraging him to reassess his traditional view of the necessity of separating military and political power.

New Year's Day brought the Grand Duke a present from the British government—a message informing him that King George V had appointed him a Grand Commander of the Order of the Bath. According to Hanbury Williams, "His Imperial Highness was much gratified at this mark of the King's pleasure and particularly touched with the arrival of this welcome news on the first day of the Russian New Year."[24] A couple of days later, the Grand Duke also received news that the French army had awarded him its top honor, the Médaille Militaire.[25]

A French visitor to Stavka, Commandant Jacques Langlois, was impressed by the fact that the disappointments of 1914 had not reduced the Grand Duke's desire to take the battle to the enemy. "The Grand Duke preserves an excellent moral and physical health," wrote Langlois, "despite allowing *no* distractions and being absorbed solely in thinking of military operations.... He remains merry and full of zeal; his forward energy and offensive spirit are not for a moment diminished."[26] The Grand Duke's "offensive desires are intact and only the execution has been deferred," Langlois told Joffre.[27]

The Grand Duke's shows of optimism for the benefit of his allies did not blind him to the fact that the condition of the Russian army left much to be desired. On 1 (14) January 1915, he issued an order condemning the poor training received by the army's recruits, which, he wrote, "was far from the appropriate level." The reasons, he said, were an insufficient number of training personnel, a lack of rifles, and finally, "an incorrect organization of training in many reserve battalions. They demand beautiful bearing, marching, and rifle handling from lower ranks, but the most important things—

shooting, service in the field, the actions of the rifleman in battle, the bayonet attack—remain in the background. Such an organization of business is straightforwardly criminal.... I suggest that the relevant commanders take the strictest measures to organize this most important matter correctly."[28]

The next day, 2 (15) January, the Grand Duke summoned the Foreign Ministry's representative at Stavka, Prince Kudashev, to discuss Italy and Romania, both of which remained neutral. The Grand Duke, Kudashev recorded, had some doubts about the value of both countries as potential allies. An Italian or Romanian declaration of war would benefit Russia, the Grand Duke felt, only if it resulted in Austria-Hungary withdrawing troops from the Russian front; otherwise, it could be harmful.[29] On the whole, though, the Grand Duke regarded the entry of both Romania and Italy into the war on Russia's side as desirable. In the coming months attempts to bring this about would have an important influence on Russian strategy. In particular, the desire to persuade Romania and Italy to join the war would encourage the Grand Duke to focus the Russian army's offensive efforts against Austria-Hungary rather than Germany. This went against the desires of both General Danilov and General Ruzskii, who favored yet another attack into East Prussia.

At the start of January 1915, Danilov wrote a memorandum outlining the army's options. In this he reasserted his belief that Germany was the main enemy. A deep incursion into Germany could not succeed, he wrote, unless East Prussia was first conquered. The focus of Russian operations should, therefore, be East Prussia.[30]

Having read Danilov's memo, Grand Duke Nikolai Nikolaevich asked to be told Ruzskii's opinions of it. On 4 (17) January, Danilov visited Ruzskii at his headquarters in Sedlets, and the two generals reached agreement that the North West Front should prepare an offensive into East Prussia. For this purpose, a new army, the Twelfth Army, should be created.[31] Hearing this, the Grand Duke concurred. The following day, 5 (18) January, he approved the creation of the new Twelfth Army and of the appointment of General Plehve as its commander.[32]

Following this, on 8 (21) January, the Grand Duke visited General Ruzskii in the town of Teuszcz just east of Warsaw. There, the Grand Duke inspected troops of the Fourth Siberian Corps, which had just arrived in Poland from the Far East. It was, wrote General Hanbury Williams, "one of the coldest days we have had this winter.... We motored off to the grounds, an open plain of ploughed fields, walked around the ranks, and the Grand Duke addressed the men."[33] After lunch with Ruzskii and his staff, the Grand Duke returned to Stavka.

On arrival back at Stavka, the Grand Duke learned of British plans for a naval attack on the Dardanelles. On 11 (24) December, he discussed the matter with Hanbury Williams. "The Grand Duke," wrote the British attaché, "laid great emphasis on the importance to the Allied cause of action against Turkey, as the crippling of that country would, of course, have the most telling effect in the Balkans. He would not promise support, either naval or military, but would naturally use every endeavour, should the opportunity present itself, to strengthen the hands of the Allies."[34] In a reply he prepared for Kitchener, the Grand Duke commented that, even if Russia brought all its naval forces in the Black Sea together, they would only be equal to those of the Ottoman Empire. A naval operation had "little hope of success," and Russia could not spare the troops for a landing on Ottoman soil without significantly weakening the main theater of operations. For these reasons, the Grand Duke concluded, "we cannot give any help to the allied fleets, however strong our desire to do so."[35]

Two events now forced the Grand Duke to reconsider his decision to focus Russian efforts in early 1915 on East Prussia. The first was a series of Austro-Hungarian offensives in the Carpathian Mountains. The second was a German offensive in East Prussia.

The first of these was a product of the obsession of the Grand Duke's Austro-Hungarian counterpart, General Conrad, with relieving the besieged fortress of Przemysl. The garrison of Przemysl was running low on supplies and could not hold out much longer. Conrad elected to relieve the fortress by advancing toward Przemysl by the shortest possible route—straight across the Carpathian Mountains. The passes were covered in snow, temperatures were well below zero, and the Austro-Hungarians had to bring men and supplies up narrow roads along which some vital equipment, such as heavy artillery, could not travel. A more inauspicious setting for an offensive could probably not have been found on the whole Eastern Front.

The first Austro-Hungarian attack began on 10 (23) January 1915. Initially, it had some success, including the recapture of the crucial Uzhok Pass. Disturbed by the Austro-Hungarian advance, the commander of the Russian South West Front, General Ivanov, requested that Stavka send him reinforcements. Grand Duke Nikolai Nikolaevich agreed, and on 13 (26) January, he ordered General Ruzskii to send the Twenty-Second Corps to the South West Front. Further transfers of troops followed.[36] The Austro-Hungarian offensive thus weakened the North West Front at a time when it was meant to be preparing an attack of its own against East Prussia. The transfer of troops also turned out to be unnecessary. In the midst of terrible blizzards, the Austro-Hungarian attack halted, and the Russians counter-attacked. Although fighting continued for some time, the effort to relieve Przemysl failed.[37]

Meanwhile, the Germans were preparing a surprise in East Prussia. The Grand Duke's daily telegrams to the Tsar make it clear that Stavka was at least partially aware that the German army was deploying additional troops in northern Poland and East Prussia. On 13 (26) January, for instance, the Grand Duke told the Tsar that German activity in these areas was increasing. "Evidently," he wrote, "the enemy is expecting our offensive in this region, or is himself preparing some decisive action."[38]

This was an accurate prediction, but the Grand Duke did nothing about it—indeed, as we have seen, on the very same day he approved the sending of a corps from the North West Front to the Carpathians. Information about enemy movements was contradictory, and the Grand Duke did not fully appreciate the significance of the German moves. On 15 (28) January, he reported that there was some change in enemy activity in the area of Gumbinnen in East Prussia,[39] but on 17 (30) January he wrote that reconnaissance had not revealed any strengthening of the enemy north of the Vistula. What had been spotted was the arrival of a large number of troop trains on the Vistula's left bank.[40] This suggested an attack there, and indeed this began the next day, on 18 (31) January, with an attack on the line of the Ravka River.[41] For several days the Germans attempted to break through the Russian lines, and to prevent them, the Russian North West Front sent in reinforcements. This fitted the German plans, for the attack on the left bank was a diversion; the main attack would come soon after in East Prussia.

On 22 January (4 February) Nicholas II arrived at Stavka for another visit. It was "a clear, frosty day," according to General Spiridovich, who accompanied the Emperor. "Around was deep snow.... The mood at Stavka was calm."[42] "I have found Nikolasha's staff here in very good spirits," the Emperor wrote to his wife on 24 January (6 February).[43] The next day he wrote to her again, saying,

> I visited Nikolasha and inspected his new railway carriage, a very comfortable and practical one, but the heat in it is such that one cannot endure it half-an-hour. We discussed thoroughly several important questions and, to my joy, came to an entire agreement on all those we touched upon. I must say, that when he is alone and in good humor he is sound—I mean to say, he judges correctly. Everybody has noticed a great change in him since the beginning of the war. Life in this isolated place, which he calls his "hermitage," and the sense of crushing responsibility which rests upon his shoulders, must have made a deep impression upon his soul.[44]

The Emperor also recorded that he was delighted to see General Ivanov, who came to Stavka on 23 January (5 February).[45] Ivanov pressed the Grand Duke to send more reinforcements to the South West Front and to permit him to launch an offensive of his own. Speaking to the Grand Duke face-to-face rather than, as had often been the case before, through Ianushkevich, Ivanov explained that the situation of his troops in the Carpathian Mountains was very difficult, due to the lack of proper accommodation and the harsh winter conditions. The army needed to descend from the mountains, which meant that it needed to push the Austro-Hungarians back onto the Hungarian plain. Doing this was impossible, however, without additional men. The Grand Duke found Ivanov's argument convincing, although, according to Danilov, he felt that it would be better to attack with the South West Front's right flank around the side of the Carpathians rather than go directly through them as Ivanov was proposing. Despite this one proviso, he agreed to let South West Front have additional resources.[46] Thus, having originally succumbed to Danilov's and Ruzskii's preference for an attack on East Prussia, the Grand Duke now found himself agreeing to an attack in the south. Once again he had proved to be malleable in the face of pressure from his Front commanders.

The Emperor left Stavka on 26 January (8 February). Before he departed, the Grand Duke had one request for him—could he invite his wife to visit him at Stavka? The Emperor gave his permission, and on 28 January (10 February), the Grand Duke telegraphed Stana to come. Soon, however, he had to cancel the invitation,[47] for a new crisis had enveloped the Russian army. Undetected by the Russians, the German army had redeployed four corps from the Western Front to East Prussia. On 25 January (7 February), they struck the Russian Tenth Army, which occupied the easternmost part of East Prussia. The Tenth Army was soon forced to retreat. On 28 January (10 February), Ivanov asked the Grand Duke to send him the Fifteenth Army Corps, which had been reconstituted after being destroyed in August 1914 and was now in reserve at Gomel. The Grand Duke refused the request: as many troops as possible were needed in the north to parry the German blow.[48]

On the same day, Nikolai Nikolaevich traveled to Gomel to review the Fifteenth Army Corps for himself. The temperature was "about 20 below zero," General Hanbury Williams noted. "After the inspection the Grand Duke made the usual address to the troops and called 3 cheers for the Emperor."[49] "I passed on the words of YOUR MAJESTY," the Grand Duke told the Tsar in a telegram later that day. "Triumphantly, everyone unanimously, from the heart, promised to justify the trust of their adored Sovereign Supreme

Leader and to prove themselves in battle not only as fine lads but as ready with YOUR blessing and with the help of God to carry out heroic achievements. I am enraptured by the corps in every respect."[50] General Laguiche, who was also present, recorded the event in detail:

> This visit has given birth in the Grand Duke to a feeling of profound satisfaction and of great confidence in Russia's resources. Without doubt he knew that the 15th Corps was reconstituted.... He certainly did not expect the result which was achieved.... The attitude of the men was perfect; "A regiment of the Guard," cried the Grand Duke, as he passed along the front of the first rank. Evidently, the clothing and equipment were entirely new from top to bottom; there was nothing astonishing in that, but the human material was superb. Tall men well turned out, holding themselves perfectly under arms and responding loudly and intelligibly, in a satisfying manner, to the questions which the Grand Duke asked them. The movements were well coordinated, executed crisply; there was no fidgeting in the formations listening to the Grand Duke's words. The general impression was one of troops well in hand, already used to discipline.... The Grand Duke ... seemed to me truly satisfied beyond his expectations.[51]

The boost that the review provided to the Grand Duke's morale did not last long. The Tenth Army was continuing to retreat in East Prussia, and by the end of January 1915 the situation in East Prussia had become critical, as the Germans sought to encircle the Tenth Army by pressing on both of its flanks. On 3 (16) February, the Grand Duke told the Tsar that the Tenth Army had been unable to withdraw in a satisfactory manner: "The headlong retreats of Generals Epanchin on the right wing and Leontovich with the cavalry," wrote the Grand Duke, "have allowed the enemy ... to penetrate deep into the rear of the army and come out on the path of the center of the army's retreat."[52] While most of the Tenth Army managed to get away, the Twentieth Corps found itself surrounded in the Augustow forests located on the Russian–East Prussian border.

Despite the setback in East Prussia, on 2 (15) February the Grand Duke ordered General Ruzskii to send one division south to the Carpathians. He also made it clear yet again that the North West Front must not withdraw on the left bank of the Vistula. "The Grand Duke," Ianushkevich informed Ruzskii, "draws your attention to the fact that even if everything is not perfect with us, our opponent is in the same position, with his units significantly reduced in size and without officers, as is clear from the information provided by the staff of your front. In the Supreme Commander's opinion, all these facts bear witness to the fact that we can and should hold our positions on the left bank of the Vistula."[53]

Two days after issuing this order, on 4 (17) February the Grand Duke went to Sedlets for another meeting with Ruzskii and Ivanov. Once again, he did not actually attend the main discussions but left his senior officers alone to talk about the issues among themselves. The debate revealed sharp divisions between the North West and South West Fronts. Ruzskii insisted that he needed to redeploy large numbers of troops from the left to the right bank of the Vistula, which would mean that it would become impossible to hold his current positions on the left bank. He argued that he should withdraw from these to new positions in the rear. Ivanov protested, saying that this would have a negative impact on morale and would adversely affect his right flank, forcing him to make radical changes to his dispositions. The meeting broke up without agreement.

Briefed on these discussions, the Grand Duke took Ivanov's side. He gave instructions that the North West Front could shift troops from the left to the right bank of the Vistula, but it was to hold its positions on the left bank regardless. His instructions confirmed the Grand Duke's consistent view on this matter.[54]

By 10 (23) February, the resistance of Twentieth Corps in the Augustow forests had come to an end, and the remnants of the corps had surrendered. The original German plan had been for a double envelopment, which would result in the destruction of the entire Tenth Army. As was nearly always the case, such a double envelopment proved impossible to achieve. In this case, the Russian left flank held firm, and only the right flank collapsed, leading to the destruction of Twentieth Corps in the center. Still, what became known as the Second Battle of the Masurian Lakes ended with a clear German victory. Russian losses amounted to 56,000 men and 185 guns.[55]

This significantly altered the strategic situation, putting an end to Russian plans for an offensive to conquer East Prussia. Whereas previously the bulk of the German forces had been on the left bank of the Vistula, now they were on the right, moving southward out of East Prussia toward Warsaw, and also threatening to advance eastward out of East Prussia into the Baltic region and toward Petrograd. Further south, the Austro-Hungarians were preparing a second offensive in the Carpathians in another attempt to relieve Przemysl. The main threats to the Russian line therefore lay on the extreme left and right flanks, rather than in the center as before.

The Grand Duke remained absolutely determined to hold on to the left bank of the Vistula, but in recognition of the changed situation he asked his Front commanders to denude the left bank of as many troops as possible and switch them to the right bank and to the Carpathians.[56] On 10 (23) January, Ianushkevich telegraphed Ruzskii and Ivanov to tell them that they should weaken the left bank "to an extreme degree" and concentrate their forces on their flanks. Having said that, he added that it was necessary to "preserve in our hands as large a bridgehead as possible on the left bank of the Vistula for the possible development of our future offensive actions." The positions on the left bank, Ianushkevich concluded, could only be abandoned with the express permission of the Supreme Commander.[57]

Grand Duke Nikolai Nikolaevich remained calm throughout the winter battles, hiding any inner turmoil he might have been suffering from outside observers, all of whom reported his good spirits and his desire to resume the offensive as soon as it was feasible. The most evident feature of his leadership of military operations in this period was his determination not to surrender further ground on the left bank of the Vistula, which was required as a bridgehead for possible future offensive operations against Germany. It was clear that General Ruzskii considered his position there exposed and wished to withdraw. He held his ground only at the Grand Duke's insistence and repeated instructions. Whether the Grand Duke's decision to hold the left bank was wise is debatable, but his determination to do so revealed some of the strength of mind for which he was famous.

The battles of December 1914 and January 1915 left the Russian army severely weakened. Soon, albeit briefly, the tide of war would turn once again in Russia's favor.

CHAPTER 16

Behind the Lines

ACCOMPANYING GRAND DUKE Nikolai Nikolaevich on his review of Fifteenth Army Corps in Gomel on 28 January (10 February) 1915, General Hanbury Williams noticed that "One old Drum Major covered with medals had 38 years service. The old boy proceeded to his place in the corner of the square where the Grand Duke embraced him.... The whole turn out was excellent."[1] Chaplain Shavelskii noticed the drum major also. The Grand Duke's speech to the troops "made a huge impression," he wrote. "And now, when he had barely finished speaking, an old drummer standing on the right flank, without being given any command, struck his drum with all his might. A loud 'hurrah' rang out, drowning out the drum. The Grand Duke, with tears in his eyes, threw himself at the drummer, embraced him and kissed him. It was a surprisingly touching picture."[2]

Doctor Malama had noticed something that the others had not. "The Grand Duke's been caught out!" he whispered to Shavelskii, "The drummer's a Jew. The Grand Duke probably doesn't know this." On their way back to Stavka, Shavelskii pointed this out to Nikolai Nikolaevich. "You know he's a Jew," he said. "So what, he's served in the regiment a long time," the Grand Duke replied, but then abruptly changed the topic. "It was obvious," Shavelskii wrote, "that he somewhat regretted his act."[3]

Just three days beforehand, on 25 January (7 February), Ianushkevich had sent army commanders a message, of which the Grand Duke must have been aware, authorizing them to expel "all Jews and suspect individuals" from the entire theater of military operations. Army commanders responded "energetically," and a wave of expulsions followed.[4] Shavelskii believed that the incident with the drummer indicated the Grand Duke's "ability to change his opinions and convictions when life gave him reason to do so,"[5] but there is no indication that the encounter actually softened Nikolai Nikolaevich's attitude toward Jews.

The expulsion of Jews from the areas immediately behind the front lines was merely one of a series of oppressive measures ordered by Stavka during Nikolai Nikolaevich's tenure as Supreme Commander. The Russian army targeted not only Jews but also citizens of hostile countries who were living within Russia's borders and the descendants of Germans who had come to Russia in the 18th century and established agricultural colonies. The conquest of Galicia also led to efforts to russify the province by suppressing the Ukrainian language and forcibly converting Uniate Christians to Russian Orthodoxy.

After the war these policies slipped off the historical radar, overshadowed as they were by the dramatic events of the Russian revolution and civil war and later by the Second World War. Only in the past 15 years have a series of historians such as Peter Gatrell,[6] Eric Lohr,[7] and others revealed the sheer scale of the Russian army's repressive actions.

In the process of rediscovering this history, historians have paid relatively little attention to the role played by Grand Duke Nikolai Nikolaevich in these wartime repressions. The tendency of both the Grand Duke's contemporaries and modern historians was and has been to blame them on General Ianushkevich. Gatrell, for instance, repeats a description of Ianushkevich as a "diabolical sadist" and comments that "Ianushkevich took the lead in singling out Jews for special treatment."[8] Lohr, meanwhile, writes that "Stavka commander Nikolai Nikolaevich Ianushkevich ordered that both army and civilian officials should most vigilantly root out spying among enemy subjects, Russian-subject Germans, and Jews," adding that Ianushkevich was "a major force in the campaigns against spying and enemy aliens."[9] Similarly, historian Peter Holquist has claimed that Stavka's policies were the direct result of Ianushkevich's personality, and that with another Chief of Staff the army might have behaved very differently.[10]

Ianushkevich was indeed largely to blame for what happened, but this is not the whole picture. The Chief of Staff did not have a particularly endearing personality, but one of his more positive characteristics was a willingness to take full responsibility for anything Stavka did. Early in the war Ianushkevich expressed a firm view that the Grand Duke was not somebody who could be held accountable for his decisions and that since somebody had to be accountable, it should be the Chief of Staff—in other words, himself.[11] In this way, Ianushkevich deliberately shielded the Supreme Commander from criticism, ensuring that blame for anything that went wrong would fall upon him and not his superior. These actions by Ianushkevich help to explain both Nikolai Nikolaevich's extreme loyalty toward his Chief of Staff and the Grand Duke's continued popularity despite the disasters the Russian army suffered in 1915.

The 1914 Statute of Field Administration gave the Supreme Commander almost dictatorial powers in the areas directly behind the front lines. From an early stage in the war, these powers embroiled the Grand Duke in political controversy. A case in point was Galicia once it fell under Russian control in the campaign of August 1914. On 19 August (1 September) 1914, the Grand Duke confirmed provisional regulations for the Russian administration of Galicia,[12] and shortly afterward he appointed Count G. A. Bobrinskii as Galicia's Governor General.[13] In the months to come, the governance of Galicia would prove to be a great source of tension among Stavka, the South West Front, the Council of Ministers in Petrograd, and the authorities of the Russian Orthodox Church.

In particular, Nikolai Nikolaevich was soon in conflict with the Russian Orthodox Church regarding the treatment of the Uniate Church and its members. The Uniate Church in Ukraine recognized the authority of the Catholic Pope in Rome, while retaining its own distinct rites and traditions, which were similar to those of Eastern Orthodoxy. Now that the conquest of Galicia had brought large numbers of Uniates under Russian control, some Orthodox leaders wished to exploit the opportunity to unify the Uniate and Orthodox Churches. This was to be done by removing Uniate priests, especially the most senior among them, and converting Uniates to Orthodoxy. As a first step, at the end of August 1914, the Russian Ministry of the Interior ordered General Ianushkevich to arrest the Uniate Metropolitan Archbishop of Lvov, Andrei Sheptitskii.[14] Shortly afterward, General Brusilov, commanding the Russian Eighth Army, deported Sheptitskii to Kiev.[15]

These measures caused considerable concern at Stavka. The Grand Duke was especially perturbed by newspaper reports of Orthodox priests forcibly converting Uniate believers to Orthodoxy. On 13 (26) September, he told Ianushkevich that the army should protect the religious rights of the Galician population. "Political disloyalty should not be identified with religious differences," the Grand Duke said.[16] The next day, on 14 (27) September, he telegraphed the Tsar asking him to stop all activities to unify the Uniate and Orthodox Churches in Galicia.[17] These activities, the Grand Duke told the Tsar, "could result in strong disturbances among the population in the rear of the army."[18]

The Grand Duke also held a meeting with Nikolai Bazili, one of the Foreign Ministry's representatives at Stavka, whom Ianushkevich had sent to Galicia to investigate the governance of the captured province. Bazili reported that the repressive measures of the Russian authorities were alienating the local population, and the Grand Duke therefore wrote to the President of the Council of Ministers, I. L. Goremykin, to request a change in policy.[19]

The message to Goremykin had no discernible outcome, but the Grand Duke's request to the Tsar did, bringing a quick response from the Tsar in the form of a telegram to Count Bobrinskii. The Tsar ordered that Bobrinskii should approve Uniate requests to join the Orthodox Church only if they were entirely voluntary and came from the Uniates themselves.[20]

The Tsar's intervention constituted a victory for the Grand Duke, but it was to be short-lived. Before long, efforts to convert Uniates recommenced at an even faster pace, and the Grand Duke was forced to fight the battle against them once again. The Tsarist state was far from monolithic, and different parts of it often pursued agendas that were entirely at odds with those of the other parts.

In this case, the Orthodox Church was able to pursue its agenda despite the Supreme Commander's opposition. Consequently, the Grand Duke developed a very hostile relationship with some Church leaders. Most notably he clashed with Metropolitan Evlogii, who had been appointed Archbishop of Galicia, and with V. K. Sabler, the Procurator of the Holy Synod (in effect the government minister in charge of the Russian Orthodox Church). Evlogii visited Stavka in late October or early November 1914. The Grand Duke's attitude to him during his visit was, according to Chaplain Shavelskii, "reserved."[21] Sabler in turn visited Stavka in January 1915, and he and the Grand Duke discussed church policy in occupied Galicia.[22] According to Shavelskii, Sabler's reception at Stavka was "rather ungracious. He was invited to lunch and supper, but not seated next to the Grand Duke, like other respected ministers, but at a different table. And both at lunch and at supper the Supreme Commander addressed not a single word to him.... He left Stavka dissatisfied."[23]

Shortly after this, in February 1915 Shavelskii visited Lvov, and on his return to Stavka he briefed the Grand Duke about the efforts of the Orthodox Church to convert Galician Uniates. Having heard the chaplain's report, the Grand Duke "helplessly shrugged his shoulders," according to Shavelskii. Referring to his earlier appeal to the Tsar to prevent conversion efforts, the Grand Duke replied, "What can I do? You know that I asked the Sovereign. The Sovereign promised. I fully understand that nothing but harm comes from these reunification attempts. Let us wait a while more."[24] In effect, the Grand Duke simply gave up the struggle. He was not inclined to push the Emperor hard when he did not get what he wanted from him.

According to General Danilov, the Grand Duke's failure to prevent the conversion of Uniates showed that he was "practically powerless to establish in conquered enemy territory that order which he considered just and expedient," especially in matters of religion.[25] This excuses the Grand Duke a little too much. He could have pushed the matter further. Faced with the Tsar's indifference, he chose not to. Furthermore, although he continued to oppose religious oppression in Galicia, other measures of russification won his support. For instance, on 5 (18) November 1914, General Ivanov requested that the Grand Duke approve a set of regulations governing education in Galicia. These subordinated the schools to Count Bobrinskii, set up an inspectorate under his control,[26] and promoted the Russian language at the expense of others. The Grand Duke approved the regulations, issuing an order on 24 November (7 December) to that effect.[27]

The Grand Duke also proved to be a zealous persecutor of Galicia's Jewish community. In his report to the Grand Duke, Bazili had not only complained about the attacks on the Uniates but had also urged action against the Jews. Such action, Bazili explained, would win Russia the support of local Ukrainians, who were generally anti-Semitic. Jews, Bazili claimed, "sabotaged the efforts of the Russian administration by withdrawing coinage from circulation and jacking up prices."[28] The Jews must be given a "warning," the Grand Duke wrote in the margin of Bazili's report.[29]

This was not an isolated incident. Anti-Semitism in the Russian army ran deep. From the beginning of the war the Russian army targeted Jews for persecution wherever they found them, not only in Galicia. Almost within days of the outbreak of the war, Russian soldiers were accusing Jews of spying for the enemy and were expelling them from their homes and beating, robbing, and killing them.[30]

At first these actions were spontaneous rather than products of a deliberate policy promulgated by Stavka, but the Russian High Command did nothing to stop them. Indeed, many of the staff at Stavka thoroughly approved.[31] As noted earlier, historians have almost universally cast General Ianushkevich as the primary villain in this regard, but the Grand Duke had the power to stop Ianushkevich and never did. Insofar as an organization's ethical climate derives from its leaders, Grand Duke Nikolai Nikolaevich must take the blame not merely for his own acts but for the wider abuses committed by his army. He did not set the tone at the start, but he acquiesced and thereby in effect gave official support to these abuses.

He also occasionally took an active role in persecutions. For instance, in late November 1914, as the Battle of Lodz ground to a close, the Grand Duke issued an order giving formal approval to the practice of taking and, on occasion, executing Jewish hostages.[32] Several more anti-Jewish instructions followed in the months to come. In April 1915, for instance, the Grand Duke received the report of a senior legal official whom he had sent to investigate the court system in Galicia and was disturbed to find that Jews were continuing to occupy posts in the Galician courts. "The Supreme Commander has ordered the immediate dismissal of these people from their posts," Ianushkevich wrote on 16 (29) April.[33] Ianushkevich also wrote to Count Bobrinskii, telling him that because Jews might also be occupying other official positions in Galicia the Grand Duke wished him to investigate all institutions to determine if this was the case. Jews were to be dismissed from all government jobs.[34]

Jews were not Stavka's only target. Another issue bothered the Grand Duke: what to do with enemy citizens living within Russia. In August 1914, the Ministry of Internal Affairs had decreed that all male Austro-Hungarian and German citizens aged between 18 and 45 who were capable of bearing arms should be arrested.[35] This was not enough for Nikolai Nikolaevich. On 3 (16) October, he sent a telegram to Prime Minister Goremykin with this message:

> Improbably horrifying atrocities carried out by German and to some extent Austrian troops are being confirmed more and more often. German atrocities are committed not just against our wounded but also against peaceful civilians. They spare neither old women nor children. There is mass robbery. In light of this, I consider it necessary to ask you to urgently take the most decisive and severe measures across the whole extent of Russia regarding the subjects of the states who are fighting against us, without regard to their social position, putting them on the same footing as prisoners of war. Failure to take such measures could arouse a just feeling of indignation.
>
> General-Adjutant Nikolai.[36]

This would mark the start of an increasingly severe campaign of repression against people of Austro-Hungarian or German origin. The campaign eventually spread even to those who were subjects of the Russian Empire.

On 8 (21) October, Ianushkevich telegraphed Goremykin saying that the Grand Duke wished to know what decision the government had made in response to his message of 3 (16) October, as he had not yet received a reply.[37] The Grand Duke was apparently annoyed at the Prime Minister's failure to respond, crossly telling Ianushkevich in the presence of others, "Ivan Loginovich [Goremykin] considers me a little boy, has washed his hands of me, and has not even replied to me."[38]

The same day, Ianushkevich also wrote that the Grand Duke had been following stories in the press regarding suspicious behavior by Russian subjects of German origin and regarding Germans and Austro-Hungarians fictitiously transferring ownership of their enterprises in Russia to Russian nationals while continuing to control them from abroad. The Grand Duke, wrote Ianushkevich, "is of the opinion that the facts communicated in the newspapers require immediate investigation, and in the event that they are confirmed, decisive measures must be taken to stop them."[39]

On 11 (24) October, the Grand Duke finally got a reply to his letter to Goremykin. The Council of Ministers had discussed his request but had decided that rounding up and deporting large numbers of enemy citizens would cost a great deal of money and use up police resources better dedicated to other matters.[40] This did not deter the Grand Duke, who simply bypassed the civil authorities, ordering military commanders to keep all enemy citizens who had not yet been arrested under close observation.[41] Failure to do so, wrote Ianushkevich to the Governor of Odessa, General Ebelov, on 12 (25) October, would result in court-martial.[42]

In November 1914, Nikolai Nikolaevich received the minutes of two meetings held by the Council of Ministers to discuss what action to take against enemy citizens living in Russia. He read them attentively and was not happy with what he saw.

The Council had determined that measures taken against enemy citizens should be limited to the area of military operations, and not implemented throughout the entire Empire. On 3 (16) November, General Ianushkevich wrote to Prime Minister Goremykin to tell him that the Grand Duke disagreed. The Grand Duke, he said, believed that the measures should apply throughout the entire territory of the Empire, and that all enemy citizens should be expelled from the country rather than merely deported to remote locations within it.

As for businesses owned by enemy citizens, the Supreme Commander did not believe that these should all be closed down or confiscated, Ianushkevich wrote, but he did believe that it was necessary to "deprive these people of the powerful position which ownership of industrial enterprises creates for them in the surrounding localities and which could be used to harm Russia." The Council should announce that it would close any enterprises whose owners refused to hand over management before a designated date. The Grand Duke also supported the confiscation of foreign-owned factories that were fulfilling military orders.[43]

This was not the last of Nikolai Nikolaevich's interventions in this area. On 20 December (2 January), Ianushkevich wrote to the commander of the Russian Sixth Army, General K. P. van der Flit, that the Grand Duke wished to avoid any disruptions to the life of the Imperial family, and so ordered him to deport all enemy subjects aged between 17 and 60 from the coastal zone around Petrograd.[44] Examples such as this show that Grand Duke Nikolai Nikolaevich was no mere observer of measures taken against enemy citizens but a prime mover of them.

At the end of 1914, the Grand Duke turned his gaze from enemy citizens and Jews to people of sometimes quite distant German origin who were actually Russian subjects. On 26 December (8 January), Ianushkevich telegraphed the Chief of Staff of the North West Front, General Oranovskii, to inform him that "According to information which we have received, German colonists living on the right bank of the Vistula have been sending signals to the Germans. The Supreme Commander has ordered that those making these signals should be hanged at the place of their crime without carrying out any investigation and that all German colonists should be expelled from the region of the Vistula in the shortest possible time."[45]

Further repression of the descendants of German colonists followed in the months to come. On 12 (25) June, Ianushkevich wrote to the Commander of the Kiev Military District to protest that he had not yet expelled all German colonists from his district. As the enemy was approaching, German colonies could be "a ready base for a German attack," Ianushkevich said. Consequently, he added, the Grand Duke "has ordered that German colonists be expelled in the shortest possible time."[46] A similar order went out to the Odessa Military District.[47]

The Grand Duke's obsession with German spies, as well as Ianushkevich's habit of controlling the flow of information to him, was clearly revealed in an incident in late 1914 that pitted Nikolai Nikolaevich against the Ministry of Foreign Affairs. The Ministry had arranged an exchange of German and Russian consuls via Spanish diplomats. The Russian police had previously arrested the former German consul in Kovno as a spy and imprisoned him in the Peter and Paul Fortress in Petrograd, and the Grand Duke was annoyed to find that the Ministry of Foreign Affairs had included that same consul on the list of those to be exchanged. He wrote to Foreign Minister Sazonov to object and received a reply that, according to Vladimir Orlov, "was very disrespectful," to the extent that Ianushkevich hid it from the Grand Duke, as "it would have left the Grand Duke no option but to fly off to Petrograd and smack Sergei Dmitrevich [Sazonov] in the face with a stick."[48]

Fear of spies was not a uniquely Russian phenomenon. It was widespread throughout Europe both before and during the First World War. During the war, all belligerents interned enemy citizens en masse lest they engage in espionage. The Russians, however, took spy mania to extremes not seen elsewhere.[49]

General Danilov cast the blame for the Russian military's spy mania entirely onto Ianushkevich, complaining that the Chief of Staff "burned with a righteous hatred of any possibility of treachery and espionage."[50] Blaming Ianushkevich lets the Grand Duke off the hook too easily, although it should be said that as Commander of the Petersburg Military District, Nikolai

Nikolaevich refused to read anonymous denunciations.[51] As Supreme Commander, the Grand Duke would pass any denunciations on to General Dzhunkovskii, the Deputy Minister of the Interior, who would reassure him that most of them were nonsense.[52] On this subject Dzhunkovskii wrote, "All such non-military matters, in which he [the Grand Duke] considered himself not competent, worried him more than military failures."

In one case, Dzhunkovskii intervened with the Grand Duke to prevent the arrest (on Ianushkevich's orders) of a Frenchman, Monsieur Goujon, who managed a factory in Moscow. Ianushkevich had sent a telegram to the Governor of Moscow, General Iusupov, ordering him to arrest Goujon on suspicion of espionage, but after Dzhunkovskii protested to the Grand Duke that Goujon was innocent, the Grand Duke revoked the order.[53]

On the one hand this case illustrates how Ianushkevich and not the Grand Duke was the initiator of most accusations of espionage. On the other hand, it also shows that Nikolai Nikolaevich was not just a foil for his Chief of Staff and was perfectly capable of overruling him. When he did not, he was culpable for the arrests of innocent people. While unsupported accusations from those outside the army had little effect on the Grand Duke, he seems to have had an unquestioning attitude toward accusations made by his own military intelligence agencies, whose accuracy he took largely for granted, despite the often dubious nature of their reports.

As President of the Council of State Defense he had often said that the safest path was to prepare for the worst. As Supreme Commander he shared the "better safe than sorry" attitude of many of his colleagues. Early in the war he therefore issued a decree allowing for the use of military field courts-martial for anybody in the theater of military operations accused of espionage.[54] These courts dispensed with much of the normal trial procedure and were meant to be used only in situations where guilt was deemed to be so clear that normal due process was superfluous. In practice, they allowed military commanders to try and execute suspected spies very rapidly without proper consideration of the evidence. This laid the ground for some serious miscarriages of justice in which Grand Duke Nikolai Nikolaevich took a very active role.

On 8 (21) February 1915, the Grand Duke wrote to the Tsar to complain about Russia's ambassador to Romania, S. A. Poklevskii-Kozell, who had been accused of treason. The Grand Duke had just learned that the Tsar had dismissed the accusations against Poklevskii-Kozell, and he told the Tsar, "I have in my hands other facts which confirm the crime.... As long as Kozel-Poklevskii [sic] remains in Bucharest, Romania will not enter the war.... Only a vigorously led enquiry can shed light on this. It is extremely important that Kozel-Poklevskii's behavior be explained."[55]

Russian military intelligence suspected Poklevskii-Kozell of sabotaging Russian efforts to persuade Romania to join the war on Russia's side. The intelligence department of the Russian South West Front sent an agent, I. L. Kurtz, to Bucharest to investigate, and Kurtz sent back reports supposedly confirming Poklevskii-Kozell's guilt. M. K. Lemke, who worked at Stavka, considered Kurtz "untalented and corrupt"[56] and found his report decidedly untrustworthy, but the Grand Duke believed the charges. In this case, as in others, he lacked discernment when presented with accusations of espionage.

The next target of the Grand Duke's anti-espionage zeal was an officer in the Gendarme Corps, Lieutenant Colonel S. A. Miasoedov, who was arrested by the Russian police on 18 February (3 March) 1915, on charges of spying for Germany. A Russian army officer, Lieutenant I. P. Kolakovskii, had come forward claiming that he had been captured by the Germans, recruited as a spy, and then sent back to Russia with instructions to assassinate Grand Duke Nikolai Nikolaevich. Kolakovskii claimed that he had been told that Miasoedov was also a German spy. Miasoedov was accused of providing the Germans with information that had enabled them to defeat the Russian Tenth Army during the Second Battle of the Masurian Lakes.

Learning of this, the Grand Duke insisted that Miasoedov be tried before a field court-martial. Military lawyers informed him that a field court-martial was not possible in this case, as Miasoedov was only under investigation and not guilty beyond all doubt. Nevertheless, Nikolai Nikolaevich found a way to ensure that Miasoedov would not be able to defend himself properly. As he told Grand Duke Andrei Vladimirovich:

> I began to think and then asked my lawyers the following question: You say that you can only send to a field court-martial somebody who has been caught while committing the crime: so! Will there be a moment in the investigation process at which the suspected crime becomes an established fact? Yes, there will be such a moment. That means, I said, that at that moment he will no longer be under arrest in a state of suspicion but in the state of completion of the crime. Yes! That means that when the investigation process is finished and the accusation of espionage is proven, we can hand him over to the court. And so, I ordered them to tell me immediately when the fact of espionage was established. As soon as they told me this, I gave the order to hand him over to a field court-martial.[57]

This ensured Miasoedov's conviction, despite the flimsy evidence against him. Within days, a field court-martial found Miasoedov guilty and sentenced him to death. He was executed five and a half hours later.

This was not the end of the matter. The Grand Duke also ordered the arrest and trial of several of Miasoedov's associates. Three of them, all Jews, were convicted and hanged. Some, however, were acquitted, a result with which the Grand Duke was, according to one account, "extremely dissatisfied." The Grand Duke ordered their retrial, and four more were executed.[58]

A common explanation of the manner in which the Russian army treated Miasoedov is that he provided a useful scapegoat for its defeat in the Augustow forests.[59] Historian William C. Fuller, for instance, casts doubt on whether the Grand Duke and Ianushkevich believed in Miasoedov's guilt and suggests that they "arranged the condemnation of Miasoedov despite knowing that nothing had been proved against him." Miasoedov served as a convenient scapegoat for the Grand Duke, Fuller claims, since the former's conviction and execution "provided [the Grand Duke] with a permanent, ironclad excuse that absolved him of any responsibility regardless of the disasters that occurred at the front."[60] Peter Gatrell extends this line of argument further to encompass Stavka's targeting of minorities such as Jews and German colonists. "The army went out of its way … to target vulnerable minorities in an attempt to find scapegoats for military failure," he writes.[61]

While there may be something to the scapegoat hypothesis, less cynical motivations were probably much more important. The Grand Duke's negative attitude toward Miasoedov inclined him to believe the charges of espionage, which, contrary to Fuller's claims, the Grand Duke and his staff seem to have genuinely thought were true. Furthermore, if Miasoedov was meant to be a scapegoat, the Grand Duke and Ianushkevich certainly never held him up as the cause of any military defeats. Indeed, the Grand Duke already had somebody to blame for the disaster in East Prussia—General Epanchin, whom he fired as commander of the Third Army Corps, accusing him of withdrawing without permission and so exposing the flank of the Twentieth Corps, which was then surrounded.[62]

More generally, rather than blaming enemy spies for their defeats, the Grand Duke and Ianushkevich consistently pointed in another direction—at the shortage of ammunition, especially artillery shells. On 24 February (9 March), for instance, the Grand Duke complained to the Tsar that on the North West Front there were only 140 shells per gun. "I predict," he wrote, "that in several days there will be no shells at all.... If our enemies do not cease their operations ... our position will be hopeless.... The losses from the lack of shells are great, but the spirit is cheerful."[63] Again and again, both the Grand Duke and Ianushkevich would argue that this shortage of ammunition and the enemy's abundance of it were the primary cause of their problems. Thus the Grand Duke told the Tsar in May 1915 that the enemy's success was "due only to the expenditure of a colossal amount of artillery shells."[64]

It would appear that both the Supreme Commander and his Chief of Staff sincerely believed in their spy hunts. The two men did their country great harm. The news of Miasoedov's conviction and execution reverberated throughout Russia. Many Russians saw the treason affair as evidence that enemy agents were close to the center of power, particularly because Miasoedov was known to be an acquaintance of War Minister Sukhomlinov. Dissatisfaction with the War Ministry's inability to provide the army with the weapons and ammunition it needed was already generating stories that Sukhomlinov was incompetent; now some began to speculate that he was actively sabotaging Russia's war efforts. Sukhomlinov wrote to Ianushkevich on 10 (23) March to tell him that the affair "has created a completely impossible atmosphere in Petrograd; unpleasantness, gossip, and slanders have acquired improbable dimensions."[65]

The Miasoedov episode damaged the legitimacy of the regime and so helped bring the revolution of 1917 a little closer. In all of his efforts to make the areas behind the front lines secure, Grand Duke Nikolai Nikolaevich in fact achieved the opposite. However much General Ianushkevich was at fault for this, the Grand Duke clearly shared the blame.

CHAPTER 17

The Carpathian Offensive, February–April 1915

BY FEBRUARY 1915, the First World War was locked in stalemate. In an effort to break the deadlock, the belligerent powers sought to persuade neutral nations, particularly Italy, Romania, and Bulgaria, to join the war on their side. Consequently, Russia and its allies shifted their gaze toward the Balkans and considered how they might influence the course of events there to their advantage. To coordinate their efforts, Britain and France sent military missions to Russia to discuss joint action.

The first to arrive was that of the British, led by General Sir Arthur Paget, which arrived at Stavka on 8 (21) February. The next day, Paget summarized his initial meeting with Nikolai Nikolaevich in a letter to Lord Kitchener:

> After dinner we met in conference, the Grand Duke, C of S [Chief of Staff—Ianushkevich], & [Captain] Glyn [Paget's adjutant]. The Grand Duke begged me to speak to him in the most open manner as one soldier to another and to hold nothing back. I gave him a summary of my messages to you and my opinion of the situation in the Balkan states and I told him that you had entertained the idea of actually supporting Serbia. In two words—he was in complete agreement with you and fully endorsed my views.[1]

"The Grand Duke has given us, ever since our arrival, every facility to see everything we desired & all secret papers," Paget reported a few days later, adding,

> The Grand Duke has again impressed upon me that it is of vital importance to her [Russia] that some move should be made by England or France to relieve the pressure, which under the circumstances can only cause the existing line to fall further back. The Grand Duke strongly favors Ragusa as a base, a landing there would certainly draw off a large force from the Carpathians & would probably induce Italy to move. Such action would probably bring in Romania whose present policy is causing the staff here some worry.[2]

Captain Glyn found Stavka charming, "so quiet and removed from all these horrors," but in a couple of letters home he was very unforthcoming. "We have seen much but I cannot write," he said.[3] He did, however, provide a hint of some of the discussions with Grand Duke Nikolai Nikolaevich. "There is much to see and to do and each day we have sent wires back to K [Kitchener] to say what the Grand Duke wants from us in the form of arms etc."[4] The Grand Duke's efforts to get weapons from the French having failed, he was now pinning his hopes on the British.

At the front, meanwhile, the Germans had changed directions after driving the Russians out of East Prussia. They had turned in a south and southeasterly direction, advancing into northern Poland, with some troops moving directly toward Warsaw via the town of Prasnysh and others attacking Russian positions along the Bobr and Narev Rivers. The German advance did not go as well as that in East Prussia. On 11 (24) February, the Germans captured Prasnysh, but two days later a Russian counter-attack drove them back out. The Grand Duke informed the Tsar that they had captured 2,600 prisoners.[5]

On 14 (27) February, in an effort to relieve Przemysl, the Austro-Hungarian army began another offensive in the Carpathians. It proved even less successful than the previous one.[6] After some initial progress it soon stalled, and by 17 February (2 March) Nikolai Nikolaevich was able to report to the Tsar that the latest Austro-Hungarian effort to reach Przemysl had failed.[7]

The defeat of the Austro-Hungarian offensive combined with the Russian victory at Prasnysh meant that the situation at the front now became much more stable. The Germans continued to assault Russian positions along the Bobr River, but the Russian lines held firm. By 16 February (1 March) the Russians were in a position to take the offensive themselves, pushing the Germans back toward East Prussia. The Grand Duke instructed Ruzskii to limit his attacks to "strong but short blows" and to pursue the Germans only as far as the border.[8]

The Grand Duke had by now decided to focus his efforts on the south. Ianushkevich told Ruzskii that the Grand Duke warned him, "The current military and political situation, especially because of developing events in the Balkan peninsula, powerfully demand that we develop further our offensive actions against Austria-Hungary in Galicia and Bukovina. This circumstance requires the strengthening at the first opportunity of the forces of the South West Front at the expense of the North West Front by no less than one corps." The Grand Duke asked that Ruzskii identify which divisions he could send to the South West Front.[9]

This marked an important shift in the Grand Duke's thinking. The priority was now to inflict a defeat on Austria-Hungary in order to encourage Italy and Romania to enter the war on Russia's side.

As the focus of their attention moved toward the Balkans, the Grand Duke and his staff reappraised their attitude toward the British attack on the Dardanelles, which if successful would have a significant effect on the political situation in the Balkans. For that reason, it now fitted in well with Russian strategic thinking.

British and French ships began a preliminary bombardment of Ottoman fortresses in the Dardanelles on 6 (19) February. In light of this, the Grand Duke reversed his previous opposition to Russian participation in the operation. On 1 (14) February, he had written to Prime Minister Goremykin that Russia could not join in any attack on the Dardanelles until after Germany had been defeated.[10] Now, though, on 17 February (2 March), Ianushkevich informed General Hanbury Williams that the Russians planned to commit an infantry corps and the entire Black Sea Fleet to the Allied operation.[11] The Grand Duke telegraphed Foreign Minister Sazonov and asked him to get the agreement of the Bulgarian government for the Russian fleet to use the port of Burgas. This was, he said, "necessary to ensure the success of our operation to seize the Bosphorus."[12]

Late February brought the Grand Duke some cheer. Once the battle in East Prussia was over, the Grand Duke renewed his invitation to his wife to come to see him in Stavka, and she arrived there on 19 February (4 March) for a one-day visit. While there, Stana met General Hanbury Williams and told him how glad she was to see him, at which point, Hanbury Williams wrote, "the Grand Duke suddenly put his arms around me and said to her 'Mais oui! Et nous sommes tous enchantés de ce cher Général!' [But yes! We are all enchanted by this dear General!] I blushed a khaki blush and retired."[13] The Grand Duke was delighted by his wife's visit and immediately after her departure wrote to thank the Emperor for giving him permission to invite her, saying that he would be very pleased if the Emperor came to Stavka at the end of February, and adding,

> Filled with the greatest gratitude for the great kindness and happiness given to me by Your Majesty, I am hurrying to tell you this.... The meeting with my dearly beloved wife has given me great moral strength.... I am always very pleased at your arrival and presence at Stavka, and will now be particularly happy as there are many questions of a political character, in view of the forcing of the Dardanelles, about which I consider it to be of the utmost importance that I give you my personal report. Loyal to Your Imperial Majesty to the last drop of my blood, Nikolai.[14]

Before the Emperor came to Stavka, the Grand Duke had another visitor, General Paul Pau, who was leading a mission from the French army.

After arriving at Baranovichi station on 21 February (6 March), General Pau reviewed a group of Russian soldiers, then visited Grand Duke Nikolai Nikolaevich in his train. The Frenchman gave the Grand Duke his Médaille Militaire, then returned to his own train carriage. A short while later, the Grand Duke visited him. Here is one French account of the event:

> He arrives in a car, jumps lightly, and with one bound climbs the four steps of the wagon, throwing behind him his coat, which a Cossack catches on the fly.... The interview over, the Grand Duke reappears and puts on his coat again with unusual ease and chic. Dressed in this coat, a sort of long gray coat, bordered and lined with white Astrakhan, wearing a classic papakha [a Caucasian fur hat], he really looks like a great lord. With a gesture and a smile, he permits us to photograph him, jumps in his car, and departs at full speed.[15]

The next morning the French contingent attended church with the Grand Duke and his staff, following which they discussed the situation at the front. Finally, in the afternoon, the Grand Duke and General Pau had "a long secret discussion" about the "coordination of Russian operations with those of France and Britain, combined operations in the Dardanelles, and the need for a combined Franco-Anglo-Russian action on the Danube, either through Serbia or through Ragusa," from which "the two chiefs departed with a preoccupied air."[16] The French then left to visit the headquarters of the South West Front at Kholm.

The situation on the South West Front was by now better. The Russian Eighth Army under General Brusilov was driving the Austro-Hungarians back in the Carpathian Mountains. The North West Front was also attacking, attempting to push the Germans back in the areas of Prasnysh and the Augustow forests. These attacks were limited in scale, but the initiative was passing back into Russian hands. Lack of resources meant, however, that a more general offensive along the front was not possible. The Grand Duke had by now definitely decided that the South West Front should have priority, and so on 1 (14) March he ordered the North West Front to cease its offensive operations.[17]

General Pau returned to Stavka on 1 (14) March, as did the Tsar, the latter staying this time for ten days. The next day, the Tsar dined with the Grand Duke and General Pau. "N. is in good humor and as always demands rifles and ammunition," the Tsar wrote to his wife.[18] Pau and his mission eventually departed (this time for good) on 4 (17) March, but before they did, more Frenchmen arrived—Ambassador Paléologue and Commandant Langlois. In contrast to every other observer, who found the Grand Duke in good spirits, Paléologue (a notoriously inaccurate source of information[19]) reported the following:

> I found him pale and emaciated, with a drawn face. With his habitual openness and decisiveness, he told me: "I am going to speak to you of grave matters. It is not the Grand Duke Nicholas who is speaking to you, but the Russian general officially addressing the French ambassador. In this capacity, I am obliged to tell you that the immediate cooperation of Italy and Romania is an urgent necessity, of unspeakable value. I repeat and underline, *of unspeakable value*. Do not interpret this as a cry of distress. I remain convinced that with God's aid we will win. But without the immediate cooperation of Italy and Romania the war will be prolonged for months with terrible risks."[20]

Their official discussion over, the Grand Duke offered Paléologue a cigarette and asked him questions about France. "I can't find words to express my admiration for France," he supposedly told the ambassador.[21]

Later, the Grand Duke spoke also to Langlois about Italy and Romania, telling him that he "attached a special price to Italy and Romania's entry into the war."[22] Evidently aware that his discussion with Paléologue had created a depressing impression on the French ambassador, the Grand Duke assured Langlois that he "had not issued a cry of distress" and that "he would never have spoken thus if he had not been asked for his opinion."[23]

Langlois had a different take than Paléologue: "I have not found that the Grand Duke has changed; he seemed to me still as ardent, still as confident in final success.... He particularly insisted on his *confidence* in the glorious end of the war for the Allied armies." Officers in the Russian army, wrote Langlois, had total faith in the Grand Duke: "They believe in him as they believe in God."[24]

On 6 (19) March, Ianushkevich issued orders for the South West Front to take the offensive against Austria-Hungary, instructing Ivanov and Ruzskii that

> The Supreme Commander's aim is that the entire North West Front will carry out operations of a purely defensive character, and he assigns the most important task of the future campaign to the South West Front. The general idea in this is to act energetically, beginning with the left flank of the South West Front, advancing approximately in the direction of Budapest and further with a wide sweeping movement of the whole line Cracow-Poznan-Thorn.... This direction and the character of these actions have been chosen because they provide us with an opportunity to link up with the Romanian army, in the event that it joins us.[25]

In this way, the strategic indecision that had plagued Stavka for the past few months, as to whether to concentrate against Germany or Austria-Hungary, was finally resolved, with the choice being the latter. The decision was definitely the Grand Duke's. Quartermaster General Danilov recorded that he himself "was not a supporter of it.... I remained convinced of the need to direct our main effort against Germany."[26] The Grand Duke thus overruled his own chief of operational planning. As Ianushkevich's telegram made clear, the Grand Duke's logic was political—he hoped that victory against Austria-Hungary would encourage Romanian entry into the war. The discussions the Grand Duke had had with Generals Paget and Pau and with Ambassador Paléologue and Commandant Langlois, combined with the news of the British bombardment of the Dardanelles, undoubtedly played into this decision: the Allies would make a concerted, joint effort to influence events in the Balkans in their favor.

General Ruzskii, the commander of the North West Front, did not like the new policy favoring the South West Front and asked to be able to withdraw his troops from the left bank of the Vistula. This brought a sharp reply from Stavka. On 4 (17) March Ianushkevich telegraphed Ruzskii to inform him, "The Supreme Commander again confirms his inflexible will regarding the unconditional necessity that the armies of your front on the left bank of the Vistula hold the bridgeheads they now occupy."[27] The North West Front would have to hold the line.

The Grand Duke's firm attitude toward Ruzskii contrasted strikingly with the latitude he gave to General Ivanov and the South West Front. Ivanov's instructions were to start his offensive with his left flank, attacking the Austro-Hungarians in Bukovina. This would shorten the Russian line. Instead, Ivanov elected to attack the Austro-Hungarian center, in an effort to break directly through the Carpathian Mountains into Hungary. According to Danilov, the view in Stavka was that "to be successful, the executor of the plan has to be the one who creates it," and that the Grand Duke had either to let Ivanov carry out the operation in his own way or take control of the armies himself.[28] Rather than do the latter, the Grand Duke gave way.

The Russian offensive in the Carpathians began on 7 (20) March. Two days later, at 1100hrs on 9 (22) March 1915, great news reached Stavka—Przemysl had surrendered. The Russians captured some 130,000 prisoners and over 1,000 pieces of artillery. The Grand Duke was elated. "Just at this very minute," the Tsar wrote to his wife that morning, "Nicolasha came running into my carriage, out of breath and with tears in his eyes, and told me of the fall of Przemysl."[29] General Dzhunkovskii, who was at Stavka at the time, met Grand Duke Nikolai Nikolaevich shortly afterward. "He received me joyfully, excited," wrote Dzhunkovskii, "he embraced me and kissed me. It was wonderful to see his radiant face, how it shone."[30]

"The celebration in Stavka on the occasion of the fall of Przemysl was great," Chaplain Shavelskii wrote.[31] The Grand Duke and the Tsar drank champagne together,[32] and at two that afternoon there was a celebratory service in the Stavka church. The Tsar then awarded the Grand Duke another medal—the Cross of Saint George second class. The Grand Duke announced this award in an order to his troops:

> Today, on the day of the fall of Przemysl, the SOVEREIGN EMPEROR has made me happy by awarding me the order of Saint George second class. I accept this high MONARCHICAL reward with a blessing and ineffable gratitude, as an expression of special gratitude to you wonderful heroes for your uncountable heroic deeds.
>
> I pray to God that he will send us his blessing to bring the war to a successful conclusion.
>
> I express the firm belief that you, remembering that God is with us, will gladden with your heroic hearts our adored Supreme Leader.
>
> Accept from me my sincere heartfelt gratitude.
>
> This order is to be read in all companies, squadrons, batteries, and teams.
>
> Nikolai, Adjutant General.[33]

The capture of Przemysl gave an added boost to the Grand Duke's popularity. On 12 (25) March, a congress of zemstvo leaders awarded him the title of "Glorious Epic Hero" (*Slavnyi Bylinnyi Bogatyr'*).[34] One Russian general did not, however, join in the general celebration. On 12 (25) March, General Ruzskii informed the Grand Duke that he wished to resign as commander of the North West Front on grounds of ill health.[35] The Grand Duke accepted the resignation and appointed General Alekseev in his place.[36]

The victory at Przemysl transformed the situation on the Eastern Front in Russia's favor. That said, the Austro-Hungarians were far from finished, and while the Russian Third Army got off to a good start in the Carpathians, Brusilov's Eighth Army ran into "particularly heavy resistance," as the Grand Duke told the Tsar. On 19 March (1 April), he commented also that the Austro-Hungarians were transferring troops from the left bank of the Vistula to the Carpathians. "Evidently," he wrote, "our offensive in the Carpathians has seriously worried the high command of our opponents."[37]

On 22 March (4 April), Foreign Minister Sazonov telegraphed Stavka to ask the Grand Duke his opinion regarding the negotiations then underway to persuade Italy to join the war. Italy wanted territory along the Dalmatian coast. While some of this would in theory come from Austria-Hungary, the Italian demands clashed with the interests of two of Russia's allies—Serbia and Montenegro. Sazonov wanted to know if the Grand Duke considered it expedient to sacrifice their interests in order to win over Italy. The next day, Ianushkevich replied that the Grand Duke did not. Indeed, he believed that Montenegro must gain control of the port of Cattaro, which was one of the main naval bases of the Austro-Hungarian Empire, while Serbia should win access to the Mediterranean Sea. In reply, Sazonov said that the main issue under discussion was Italy's desire to annex the peninsula of Sabioncello near Ragusa (Dubrovnik). The Grand Duke in turn responded that "some concessions were necessary" but these "should not be taken to extreme" and opposed giving Italy Sabioncello. Similarly, a few weeks later, he insisted that Romania should be told that its demands were "extreme and unacceptable."[38] However keen he was to get Italy and Romania to join the war, he was not willing to accede to absolutely any demands that they might make.

On 24 March (6 April), the Grand Duke ordered General Alekseev to designate one corps out of those in the North West Front to send south to reinforce the operation in the Carpathian Mountains.[39] Alekseev chose the Third Caucasian Corps, and the Grand Duke ordered it to join the South West Front.[40] General V. M. Dragomirov, the Chief of Staff of the South West Front, announced that the Front intended to deploy the corps in the area of Kamenets-Podolsk near the far southern end of the front line. This brought a sharp rebuke from the Grand Duke. He wished to reinforce success on the main line of operations, not send troops to a secondary theater. "I definitely do not permit sending Third Caucasian Corps to Kamenets-Podolsk," he told Ivanov, "and I order you to send it to the Carpathians, in the region of our active operations, to develop our offensive and bring it to a successful conclusion."[41]

The Russian advance in the Carpathians had not yet gone so far as to allow the Russians to get through the mountains and descend into the plains of Hungary, but they were close. The German high command could not afford to let its ally collapse. It therefore decided to reinforce the Eastern Front prior to launching a counter-offensive.

This action did not go unnoticed. From 25 March (7 April) onward, the Grand Duke's daily updates to the Tsar made regular mention of German movements. On 25 March (7 April), Nikolai Nikolaevich reported that a German division previously on the left bank of the Vistula had appeared in the Carpathians. There was information, he told the Tsar, that the Germans were regrouping on the Western Front and would be sending cavalry and possibly even infantry units to the east.[42] On 26 March (8 April), the Grand

Duke wrote that there was as yet no sign of the Prussian Guards cavalry or other units believed to have been sent from Belgium, adding, "As the Germans have in the past few days significantly strengthened their forces in Alsace, the purpose of the forces sent eastward from Belgium has still not been explained."[43]

On 28 March (10 April), General Ivanov ordered a temporary halt to offensive operations in the Carpathians. As the Grand Duke explained to the Tsar, "Our forces need to be brought up to full strength and resupplied." In addition, the Grand Duke noted that "An undoubtedly fundamental regrouping is taking place among the German forces in the Carpathians; new units are perhaps being brought up. News is arriving of the appearance of groups of German officers in areas in which previously only Austrians operated. Information from France speaks of the transfer from the Western Front to the east of three German cavalry divisions and, perhaps, the Fifth Field and Forty-First Reserve Corps."[44]

On 30 March (12 April), the Grand Duke noted a further regrouping of German forces in the Carpathians.[45] At Stavka, suspicions were growing that something was afoot and the most likely explanation of the German moves was that they were planning an attack against the Russian Third Army, which occupied the right of the Russian position in the Carpathian Mountains. To counter such an attack, Stavka needed to create reserves. All spare units had already been assigned to the Fronts; the Grand Duke had no significant reserves at his own disposal. Therefore on 30 March (12 April), Ianushkevich wrote to Alekseev, telling him it was important that the Grand Duke have at least one corps as a reserve. The purpose of German redeployments was not yet clear, said Ianushkevich, but there was evidence of a "probable blow by the Germans against the center of the Third Army" to hit the Russian right flank in the Carpathians. This, said Ianushkevich, "could be successful," given that the Third Army occupied an extended front. He concluded that the Grand Duke considered it "extremely necessary" to quickly form a reserve, to which end Alekseev should provide him with one corps.[46]

Alekseev, however, was not inclined to send any troops apart from the Third Caucasian Corps, which had already left to join the South West Front. Here, the Grand Duke's lack of forcefulness manifested itself with fatal consequences. Stavka's assessment of German plans had been entirely right: the Germans were planning an attack, and although it would not take place for some time yet, when it did, it would happen exactly where Ianushkevich had predicted. In late March, the Grand Duke still had time to do something about it by building up a reserve, but having decided that this was necessary, he failed to follow through and insist that Alekseev provide the troops he asked for. As a result, when the attack came, the Russians lacked sufficient reserves to counter it decisively and could only send in reinforcements in small packets. The Grand Duke's failure to prepare for the German blow, despite having warning of it, was perhaps the greatest mistake he made during his time in command.

In early April, the Grand Duke received another visitor, this time an American, Robert Rutherford McCormick. Known almost universally in later life as "The Colonel" (his rank in the army after the United States joined the war in 1917), McCormick was the publisher and editor of one of America's foremost newspapers, the *Chicago Tribune*, and one of the most influential men in America.

Both Nikolai Nikolaevich and Pyotr Nikolaevich made a strong impression on McCormick, who was in any case inclined to support the Russian cause in the war. Pyotr Nikolaevich, he commented, "may be compared to Aaron bearing up the arms of Moses," while of Nikolai Nikolaevich he wrote, "His pictures show a stern face, and stern it is in repose; but my recollection will be of a man in a laughing exchange with his brother, a smiling conversation with one of his guests."[47] Shortly before leaving, he said goodbye to Nikolai Nikolaevich, who "was kind enough to invite me to return again at any time." McCormick then asked Ianushkevich if he could return the next year, "to which he replied," McCormick wrote, "in all seriousness, 'Certainly, or if you prefer it, the year after.'"[48] By spring 1915, any illusions that the war would be a short one had been dispelled.

On 5 (18) April, the Tsar made yet another trip to Stavka. The same day, he and Nikolai Nikolaevich decided that he should visit occupied Galicia. Later this would prove to be a very controversial decision, for Russia would lose control of Galicia not long after the Tsar went there, making his trip seem in retrospect to have been prematurely triumphant. Everybody then tried to blame everybody else for persuading the Tsar to go there. In particular, the Grand Duke's supporters claimed that the idea originated among members of the Court,[49] while his enemies argued that the idea was the Grand Duke's.[50]

The evidence suggests that the latter group was right.[51] The most compelling evidence comes from the Tsar himself. On 5 (18) March, he wrote to his wife, "I had a long conversation with N.; then the usual Report, and to church. He suggested that I should go as soon as possible to Przemysl and Lvov, as later it would be necessary to take certain measures in Galicia."[52]

The trip to Galicia began almost immediately, on 8 (22) April. The Grand Duke traveled ahead of the Tsar and the following day met him at the railway station at the town of Brody on the prewar Russian-Austro-Hungarian border. From there the Tsar and the Grand Duke drove together by car to

Lvov, stopping en route to observe some of the battlefields of the previous August.[53] In due course, they arrived at Lvov, where they attended a church service, presided over by Metropolitan Evlogii.

In advance of the trip to Galicia, Nikolai Nikolaevich had dispatched Georgii Shavelskii to Lvov to speak to Evlogii, telling him to instruct the Metropolitan to avoid touching on political issues during his speech of welcome. Evlogii protested, asking that he at least be able to address the Tsar as "sovereign master of this land." Shavelskii told him not to: the outcome of the war was uncertain, and they could not say for sure who would be master of Galicia. Despite this, when the time for the church service came, Evlogii delivered "a long, political speech,"[54] saying that the Galician people viewed the Tsar as a liberator, and speaking of the joy of seeing Russian eagles flying over the Carpathians.[55] The Grand Duke was furious. He stood there listening, according to Shavelskii, "agitated, biting his lips, shifting from foot to foot, at times looking at me in a strange way."[56]

After spending the night in Lvov, on 10 (23) April the Tsar and the Grand Duke went to the town of Sambor, where they met the commander of the Eighth Army, General Brusilov. From there, the party moved on to review troops of the Third Caucasian Corps, and after that they traveled to Przemysl, where they spent the night. The next day the Tsar and the Grand Duke inspected the captured Austro-Hungarian fortress and then returned by car to Lvov. The morning after, they went back by train to Brody, and the trip was over. The Grand Duke, according to Shavelskii, had been very afraid that somebody would try to assassinate the Tsar during the visit. "Thank God," he said when they finally left Lvov.[57]

The trip to Galicia marked the apogee of the Grand Duke's term as Supreme Commander of the Russian army. Never again in the First World War would Russian troops be so far inside enemy territory, or seemingly so well placed to achieve final victory. In tune with the celebratory mood, at Brody the Tsar gave the Grand Duke another award—a diamond-studded sword inscribed with the words, *na osvobozhdenie Chervonnoi Rusi* ("for the liberation of Red Russia," i.e., Galicia).[58] The inscription was premature. The Germans were massing on the Eastern Front, and within days they would strike a terrible blow.

CHAPTER 18

The Battle of Gorlice-Tarnow, May–June 1915

THE RUSSIAN OFFENSIVE in the Carpathian Mountains severely damaged the Austro-Hungarian army, to the point that it created a serious fear in Germany that Austria-Hungary might not survive much longer. In April 1915, the German High Command reluctantly concluded that it must come to the aid of its ally. The chief of the German general staff, General Erich von Falkenhayn, decided to transfer an entire army—the Eleventh Army under General August von Mackensen—to the Eastern Front in order to launch a major offensive against the Russians at the northern end of the Carpathian Mountains near the towns of Gorlice and Tarnow. The location of this attack was well chosen. A breakthrough at Gorlice could threaten the rear of the entire Russian line in the Carpathians by cutting off the entrances to the mountain passes. To escape encirclement, the Russians would have to abandon their hard won gains in the Carpathians without a fight.

To distract the Russians, on 14 (27) April German cavalry launched a raid deep into the Russian rear, striking north out of East Prussia into the Baltic region. The attack caused the Russian defense some considerable difficulty but failed to divert Stavka's attention from the Carpathians. On 15 (28) April, the Grand Duke informed the Tsar that "A large concentration of enemy forces in the Carpathians in the region of Gorlice is evident,"[1] adding the next day that the attacks in the Baltic region had the character merely of a "reconnaissance in force," whereas "the concentration of new German units is being more and more clearly revealed in the region of Gorlice, where units of three corps which had been considered to be in the west have been identified."[2] The next day, 17 (30) April, the Grand Duke told the Tsar, "The demonstrations of the Germans to the north of the Narev have had no success. The concentration of German-Austrian forces on the Western Galician Front continues."[3]

The Grand Duke's telegrams reveal that he had advance warning of the German attack, but he did not seem to realize the extent of the danger and

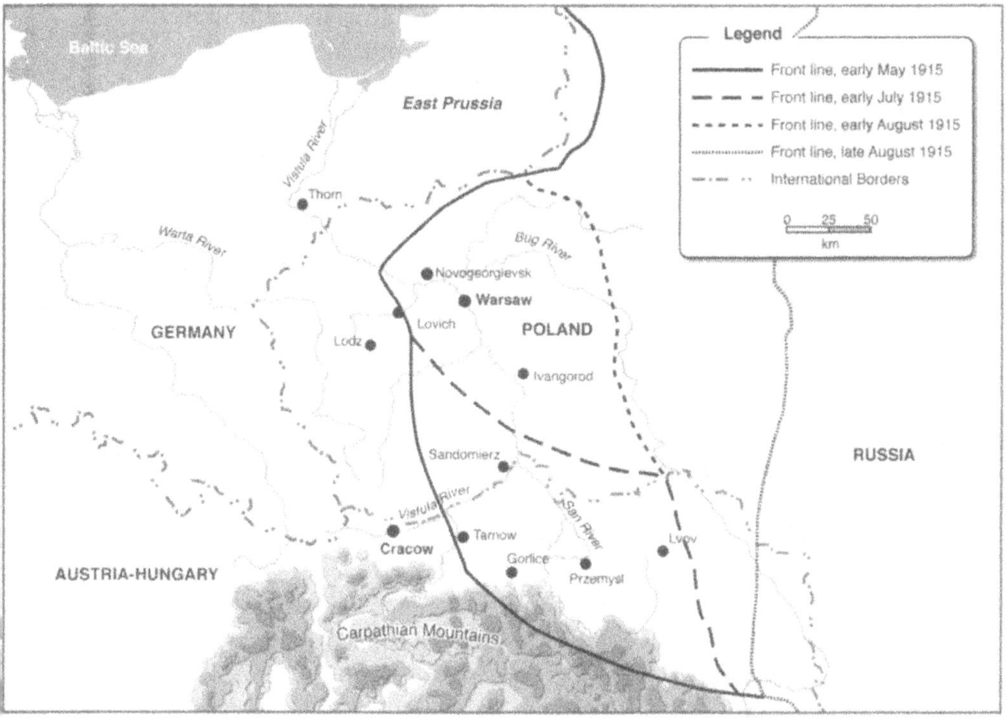

Map 7: The Battle of Gorlice-Tarnow and the Great Retreat

did not take any large scale counter-measures. When the attack came, the Russian army was ill placed to meet it.

The main blow of the German offensive fell on the Russian Third Army, which was spread thinly over a very long front. On 18 April (1 May), the German Eleventh Army began a bombardment of the Third Army's positions. The next day, the German infantry began its assault on a 50-mile front between Gorlice and Tarnow.[4] The Third Army's defenses lacked depth, and most of its troops had been located in the forward lines. Once these had been swept aside, there was little in reserve to halt the German advance. The Army's situation rapidly became critical.

Nikolai Nikolaevich's response was slow and indecisive. On 20 April (3 May), he instructed the North West Front to send one division to the Third Army's assistance and suggested to Ivanov that he detach the Thirty-Third Corps from the Ninth Army (which was located on the far south of the

Russian line) and send it to Gorlice to aid the Third Army.[5] However, when Ivanov protested that this would endanger an attack he planned to undertake with the Ninth Army, the Grand Duke withdrew his suggestion,[6] thus allowing Ivanov once again to divert him from his chosen course.

The third day of the German offensive, 21 April (4 May), found the Grand Duke relatively confident that his army could halt the enemy advance. "In Galicia," he wrote to the Tsar, "the enemy is not displaying any energy. On the front of the main enemy attack, the gaps which appeared in our lines have been filled."[7]

By the following day the complacent mood had vanished. There was a large hole in the Russian line, necessitating a retreat at least as far as the line of the Visloka River, which lay a short way to the east of the current positions. The headquarters of the South West Front requested permission to withdraw even further to the river San. The Grand Duke rejected the request. Ianushkevich informed Ivanov that the Supreme Commander "categorically ordered that he would not permit a withdrawal by the Third Army further east than the line of the lower Visloka."[8]

The following day, 23 April (6 May), the Grand Duke repeated his instruction; the line of the lower Visloka was to be "the limit of permissible retreat."[9] He confirmed this message after traveling to Kholm to discuss the situation in person with General Ivanov. There, the Grand Duke confirmed his "inflexible will that the line of the lower Visloka constitutes the limit of the Third Army's permissible retreat." He also instructed Ivanov to form a reserve from units of the Eighth Army and told the North West Front to send two divisions to the South West Front. Another division was dispatched from Odessa.[10] The lack of a large army-wide reserve now became painfully obvious. Despite the huge size of the Russian army, the Grand Duke was reduced to sending a division here and a division there. A few divisions were not sufficient to halt the German advance, especially when they arrived in dribs and drabs rather than en masse.

The only significant reserve at the Grand Duke's disposal was the Fifth Caucasian Corps in Odessa. On 25 April (8 May), he ordered this to move to Lvov.[11] Fortunately, the Germans had not proven able to keep pace with the withdrawing Russians. The Third Army was able to extricate itself from the fighting and retreat unhindered behind the Visloka, where it awaited the next German attack. On 26 April (9 May), the Grand Duke again repeated his instructions to Ivanov to hold firm on that line, personally telegraphing him to make his point clear. "I categorically order you not to withdraw without my specific instructions," he told Ivanov. "In general, I ask you to give up the idea of withdrawal."[12]

The Grand Duke's instructions rested on wishful thinking. On 27 April

(10 May), the Third Army counter-attacked. The attack failed.[13] The Chief of Staff of the South West Front, General Dragomirov, telephoned Ianushkevich in a panic. "Our strategic situation is completely hopeless," Dragomirov announced. "Whether we will hold the San, God knows."[14]

Faced by this report, Grand Duke Nikolai Nikolaevich reluctantly reversed his position: the Third Army could withdraw from the Visloka as far as the river San. "The circumstances which forced the commander of the South West Front to take this extreme decision were so categorical," the Grand Duke told the Tsar, "that I was forced to give it my approval. I have not lost hope that with the withdrawal to the line of the San and Vistula it will be possible not only to hold but also, with God's help, to pass to the offensive."[15]

The Grand Duke telegraphed Generals Ivanov and Alekseev to give them his new instructions:

> At present I establish the main task of the armies of the South West Front as being to exert all their strength to defend that part of Galicia which has been conquered by us, for which purpose the extreme eastern boundary of the defensive line are the rivers San and Dnestr, which must be defended actively, preserving for ourselves full freedom to again pass to a decisive offensive against our enemy at the first favorable opportunity. I ask the Commander of the armies of the South West Front to bear in mind the sacrifices borne by our valiant troops in conquering Galicia, and so make him responsible for ensuring that, unless absolutely required, we do not surrender unnecessary territory to the enemy.[16]

The Third Army now withdrew behind the river San, while the rest of the South West Front also moved back in order to stay in line, pulling back out of the Carpathians into Galicia, pursued by the Austro-Hungarian army. The Germans and Austro-Hungarians had now set themselves a new objective—crossing the San and recapturing Przemysl. To meet this threat, on 2 (15) May, Ianushkevich informed Ivanov that the Third, Fourth, Eighth, and Eleventh Armies were to hold their current positions. The Grand Duke, said Ianushkevich, ordered that heavy artillery should be taken out of the fortresses of Brest-Litovsk and Przemysl and moved to the front line. "The Supreme Commander counts on all these measures being carried out quickly and urgently," Ianushkevich concluded.[17]

The Grand Duke, meanwhile, was trying to do something to address the army's shortage of ammunition. At the start of May, he met a British officer, Colonel W. Ellershaw, whom Lord Kitchener had sent to Russia to determine Russia's needs and see what Britain could do to help.[18] On the Grand Duke's behalf, Ianushkevich told Ellershaw that he gave Kitchener "a free hand" to sign contracts for weapons and ammunition on Russia's behalf.[19] Ellershaw then returned to Britain with a letter from Ianushkevich, approved by Grand Duke Nikolai Nikolaevich, repeating this statement.[20]

The hopes that Stavka placed in the British proved unjustified. The ammunition failed to materialize. Thus the Russian Foreign Ministry's representative at Stavka, Prince Kudashev, wrote a little while later, "Ianushkevich is terribly indignant with Kitchener, finding that he is not fulfilling his role in good conscience."[21]

Also in early May, the Grand Duke received a visit from the Chairman of the Duma, Rodzianko, who reported, "The atmosphere at Stavka was depressing."[22] According to Rodzianko, the Grand Duke had pleaded with the Tsar to instruct the head of the Department of Industry, V. P Litvinov-Falinskii, to determine what more private industry could do to help the war effort. The Tsar had agreed but then changed his mind. According to Rodzianko, Nikolai Nikolaevich blamed the Minister of the Interior, Maklakov, for the Tsar's reversal. Maklakov regarded private industrialists' demands to be given a greater role in war production as a ploy to gain political power. "My position in general is very difficult," the Grand Duke supposedly told Rodzianko. "The Emperor is being influenced against me."[23]

Meanwhile, the situation at the front was continuing to deteriorate. On 3 (16) May, the Germans assaulted the Russian positions along the San. Unusually, the Grand Duke now skipped a link in the chain of command and contacted the commander of the Third Army, General Radko Dmitriev, directly by telegram. "It is time to stop and to fortify the positions which the forces entrusted you to occupy on the San," the Grand Duke told him. "I hold you responsible for the defense of the San. In accordance with the instructions given to you by General Adjutant Ivanov, your forces must occupy a position on the left bank of the San which will not oblige us to abandon Przemysl."[24] The Grand Duke also telegraphed Ivanov, telling him,

> I demand that all resources be exhausted before deciding on abandoning Przemysl. It is difficult to hold existing positions with passive defense, maneuver is needed, as is support from neighboring armies, on whose front the enemy is significantly weakened and is acting sluggishly. Do you consider it possible to create a maneuver group of the largest possible strength out of the complement of the Eighth Army and to strike the flank of the enemy with these forces from the direction of Przemysl?... The continuous tendency of the commander of the Third Army to retreat, which you justly do not share, demands that you exert the strongest influence on General Dmitriev, and if necessary that you replace him with another person of your choice.[25]

"The mood of the commander of the Third Army is, unfortunately, not firm enough," the Grand Duke told the Tsar.[26] He had more confidence in the commander of the Eighth Army, General Brusilov, to whom he telegraphed directly on 4 (17) May, "Being accustomed to, and always confident of, your energetic actions, I am convinced that you, in accordance with General Adjutant Ivanov's directive, will not only hold Przemysl, the possession of which I consider more than important, but will also, through a stubborn defense of your right flank and active operations on the rest of your front, consolidate the general situation."[27]

The bad news from the front was by now inducing a political crisis. Many Russians held their government responsible for the army's defeats. Within the Council of Ministers some of the more politically moderate members of the government felt that change was necessary, and that to appease public opinion it was necessary to dismiss the more reactionary of their colleagues, such as Interior Minister Maklakov. On 4 (17) May, the Agriculture Minister, A. V. Krivoshein, came to Stavka and urged Grand Duke Nikolai Nikolaevich to support this plan.[28] This meant persuading the Tsar, who arrived at Stavka for a week-long visit the next day, 5 (18) May. As soon as the Tsar appeared, the Grand Duke and Ianushkevich went to his train carriage to brief him on the situation at the front.[29] The Tsar recorded his impressions in a letter to his wife. The only positive point was that "N. is very pleased with Gen. Alekseev," the commander of the North West Front. Otherwise he had this to say:

> When I arrived, a mood of depression and despondency reigned here. In a half hour's talk, N. has clearly explained the whole state of affairs. Ivanov's chief of staff, poor General Dragomirov, went off his head, and he began to tell people right and left that it was necessary to retreat to Kiev.... Since January, N. had given them all strict orders to fortify their positions in the rear. This was not done.... Poor N., while telling me this, wept in my private room, and even asked me whether I thought of replacing him by a more capable man. He was not at all excited; I felt that he was saying exactly what he thought. He kept on thanking me for staying here, because my presence here supported him personally.[30]

While the Tsar was at Stavka, the Grand Duke summoned Rodzianko for another talk about war production. This time, Rodzianko brought with him Litvinov-Falinskii as well as two of Russia's leading industrialists, A. I. Putilov and A. I. Vyshnegradskii. Rodzianko was now pushing for the creation of a "special council" to coordinate war production, consisting of representatives of the government and of industry and other organizations, such as the zemstva. Along with Litvinov-Falinsksii, Putilov, and Vyshnegradskii, Rodzianko pressed this idea on Grand Duke Nikolai Nikolaevich and also urged him to use his influence to persuade the Tsar to dismiss his more unpopular ministers.[31] As yet, the Grand Duke did not act, but it seems that he found Rodzianko's arguments attractive. Bit by bit, Nikolai Nikolaevich was moving toward a major intervention in domestic politics.

Immediate measures were needed to stabilize the situation at the front. To this end, on 6 (19) May the Grand Duke instructed General Alekseev to send a corps from the North West Front to the South West Front.[32] The German and Austro-Hungarian armies had crossed the San and were approaching Przemysl. The Grand Duke had to decide whether to try to hold on to Przemysl or to abandon it without a fight. "In principle," the Grand Duke wrote later, he had decided on the night of 7 (20) May "to regard Przemysl not as a fortress, but as a sector of a position prepared in good time, the holding of which was expedient from a military point of view only while it facilitated our maneuvering in the region of the San."[33] In theory this meant that the Grand Duke accepted that the Russians should abandon Przemysl if holding it did not assist the operations of the armies around it.

This idea fitted with the Grand Duke's overall view of the utility of fortresses. General Hanbury Williams noted, "In considering the question of holding or abandoning fortresses, the Grand Duke expressed himself as a firm supporter of the doctrine that fortresses by themselves constituted a danger and a weakness, and he was anxious to abandon all such as were involved."[34] This position in turn coincided with the views the Grand Duke had expressed while Chairman of the Council of State Defense. However, while he may have felt that holding onto Przemysl did not make sense militarily, he took a very different view politically. Thus, he told the Tsar, "considerations of the impression which the abandonment of this point would have on society made us exhaust ourselves in an effort to keep it."[35]

On 10 (23) May, the Grand Duke ordered the North West Front to hold its ground, despite having had to send large numbers of troops to support the South West Front. Ianushkevich informed Alekseev that the Grand Duke considered it "very desirable" that the North West Front retain its positions along the Vistula and Narev Rivers and that it should withdraw "only as a last resort."[36] This fitted the general pattern of the Grand Duke's orders in the summer of 1915: repeated calls to hold firm, followed eventually by a reluctant agreement to permit withdrawal.

Observers differed in their opinions of the Grand Duke's morale at this time. The Tsar had commented on the air of despondency at Stavka, with Nikolai Nikolaevich weeping and asking about being replaced. General Laguiche, in contrast, recorded on 10 (23) May that "From the point of view of morale, there is nothing to fault; I have indicated the firmness and tenacity of Grand Duke Nicholas, who always thinks of renewing the offensive as soon as the supply of artillery munitions permits it."[37] Two days later, Laguiche commented that the situation at the front seemed better and that the Grand Duke was "confident and in control of himself."[38]

Unfortunately for the Russians, Laguiche was wrong in believing that the situation had improved. On 11 (24) May, the Germans and Austro-Hungarians began a major attack toward Przemysl and soon made significant progress. On 12 (25) May, Chaplain Shavelskii found the Grand Duke "not only upset, but outright depressed."[39] Shavelskii had just returned from a visit to the headquarters of the South West Front at Kholm. There he had found General Ivanov in a bitter mood. "It was not at all easy to listen to Nikolai Iudovich [Ivanov]," wrote Shavelskii. Ivanov complained that Stavka "does not listen to him, ignores his requests, slights him with sharp refusals." Above all, Ivanov complained about the Grand Duke's attitude to him: "The Grand Duke doesn't cherish me, doesn't value me. Whatever I ask, he refuses; whatever I advise, he does the opposite," Ivanov said, adding a complaint that the Grand Duke didn't speak to him in person but instead made him talk to Ianushkevich.[40]

On his return to Stavka, Shavelskii passed Ivanov's comments on to the Grand Duke. "The Grand Duke listened to me completely calmly," Shavelskii wrote, "even though he could see a lot which was offensive in General Ivanov's complaints." Then according to Shavelskii, the Grand Duke replied,

> Ah, that Nikolai Iudovich! Nothing satisfies him, nothing pleases him. I've never paid him any attention, not spoken with him? I've embraced him and kissed him. It's too little, he's always unhappy, offended..... You take any regiment from his front to help the Northern front, where it has always been harder, because our enemy there is the Germans, and it's a terrible insult to him. And he's always asking and asking: send me new units, send reinforcements, send rifles, guns, shells, uniforms; he asks when it's necessary and when it's not, and always for huge quantities, which we don't have.... And you refuse him, you cut down his demand, and once again it's a bloody insult. And it's like that with everything.[41]

Shavelskii then protested that Ivanov was perhaps partially correct. "Take for instance, his complaint about the way the military conferences with the

Commanders in Chief of the Fronts are conducted," said the chaplain. "You don't attend them. The Chief of Staff meets the Commanders in Chief and reports the results of the conference to you. The Commanders in Chief might well be offended that you don't favor them with your presence and personal conversation." Shavelskii then apologized for being so outspoken, to which the Grand Duke replied, "No, I am very grateful, be open with me."[42]

On 13 (26) May, a day after this conversation, the Grand Duke wrote a telegram to the Tsar reporting further enemy advances near Przemysl. Nikolai Nikolaevich put the blame firmly on the shortage of supplies. "Our forces will continue to stubbornly defend the approaches to Przemysl," the Grand Duke told the Tsar. "According to the evidence of all commanders, our losses result primarily from the enemy's superiority in the number of artillery batteries, especially heavy ones, and in the provision of firearms ammunition."[43]

Over the next few days fierce fighting continued along the San front. On 15 (28) May, the Grand Duke informed the Tsar, "As before, the position remains serious,"[44] but on 17 (30) May he was slightly more confident, reporting, "our position has got a little better."[45] That day, he also wrote to the Tsar regarding possible Russian participation in the British operation in the Dardanelles. The German attack at Gorlice-Tarnow had forced the Grand Duke to send the Fifth Caucasian Corps, which had been earmarked for the Dardanelles, to Galicia, but he still wished to find a way of helping the British, who had landed at Gallipoli on 12 (25) April. "Considering the participation of our forces in the operations of the allied expeditionary detachment in the Dardanelles to be extremely desirable," he told the Tsar on 17 (30) May, "I have ordered the speedy preparation and concentration of the Fortieth Siberian Regiment in Vladivostok."[46] Two days later, he gave the Tsar his reasons for this decision: "Sending this detachment," he wrote, "will have an undoubted moral significance in the sense of our participating in the capture of Constantinople at the same time as our allies."[47] The Allies, however, were not impressed with the offer of troops from Vladivostok and turned it down.[48] Russian troops never did go to the Dardanelles, and the only Russian contribution to the operation was a cruiser, the *Askold*, which sailed to the Mediterranean from the Far East and eventually joined the Allied fleet.[49]

On the night of 17 (30) May, Nikolai Nikolaevich went by train to Kholm to meet General Ivanov, arriving there the next morning. Perhaps bearing in mind Ivanov's complaints, the Grand Duke immediately summoned him to the train to discuss matters in person.[50] The Grand Duke told the Tsar that they talked about the future tasks of the South West Front, but beyond this he provided no details,[51] and there is no record of any specific decisions. The meeting over, the Grand Duke returned to Stavka.

By now the situation around Przemysl had deteriorated. On 20 May (2 June), General Brusilov determined that he could no longer hold the fortress, and he abandoned Przemysl to the enemy. By the afternoon of 21 May (3 June), it was entirely in German hands.[52] The Grand Duke informed the Tsar that his senior commanders had told him that the defeat was due "solely to the [enemy's] overwhelming superiority in both number and power of artillery, not to their skill in using it, and also to their abundant supply of firearms ammunition." Losses were heavy, the Grand Duke reported, but all the Russian artillery and supplies in Przemysl had been successfully evacuated.[53]

Nikolai Nikolaevich now issued new instructions. The army was to defend a line running from the Narev and Bobr Rivers in the north, down along the Vistula, and then along the rivers San, Dnestr, and Prut.[54] The Grand Duke's main concern was that the Germans might exploit their success in the south to launch a strike further north toward Warsaw.[55] With this in mind, on 23 May (5 May) Ianushkevich instructed Ivanov to send two divisions to the North West Front, whose commander General Alekseev had telephoned the Grand Duke asking for permission to withdraw that part of his army located north of the Narev back to the line of the river. This would shorten the line and allow the army to release troops from the front line to form a strong reserve. Hearing Alekseev's proposal, General Palitsyn commented in his diary that it had merit, but that the current positions were powerfully fortified, and so stronger than the line of the Narev, and that a withdrawal could create panic in Warsaw.[56] Nikolai Nikolaevich evidently agreed. Ianushkevich replied to Alekseev that the Grand Duke had asked him to tell him, "our move to new positions will inevitably result in an attempt by the enemy to attack us, which will inevitably lead to losses of men and of rifles and to significant expenditure of ammunition, which is extremely undesirable at the present time.... The line of the Narev is the last boundary to which we can permit withdrawal without fundamentally breaking the entire strategic position." Having said this, Ianushkevich finished by telling Alekseev that the Grand Duke nevertheless granted him permission to make the final decision on this matter himself. The Grand Duke would not object if he withdrew to the Narev, he said, on condition that in this case he constructed a second line of fortifications behind the Bobr and Narev Rivers.[57]

On 25 May (7 June), the Grand Duke wrote two long messages to the Tsar—the first in the form of a report and the second as a telegram. In both, he laid the blame for his recent defeats on shortages of weapons and ammunition.

In his report, the Grand Duke commented that the South West Front had received considerable reinforcements but, "In the absence of ammunition, these significant reinforcements not only haven't enabled us to throw back the enemy ... but also do not even give us the right to consider that the South West Front's position has got any better." There was evidence, the Grand Duke continued, that Germany was planning to send 10 to 12 extra divisions from the Western Front to Poland to strike Warsaw. However, he had no spare troops to give the North West Front, added to which, "There are no rifles for the replacements, and what rifles there are, are just a drop in the ocean. The quality of replacements in the sense of their training is beneath all criticism." "In such conditions," the Grand Duke wrote, "no strategy is suitable. We cannot seize the initiative back into our hands. We can only limit ourselves to parrying the blows." The Grand Duke then concluded,

> Painfully and hurtfully, thanks to the lack of the necessary amount of shells, bullets, and rifles, our truly super-heroic, valiant troops are suffering unprecedented losses but the results of their efforts do not compensate for these losses. I raised the question of the lack of bullets back at the end of August. Since then I have repeatedly asked for extra measures. Now it is clear: measures were not taken in time, and those which were taken had a peace-time character, not corresponding at all to the demands and circumstances of war.... Until we receive the necessary quantity of ammunition and rifles it is impossible to count on any success.[58]

In his telegram to the Tsar, the Grand Duke added to this bleak prognosis. He had, he said, received a message from General Ivanov saying that the enemy "was able to overcome the firmness and stubbornness of our valiant troops ... not because of the skill of their maneuvers, nor due to the fighting qualities of their soldiers, but only by the superiority of artillery fire," which the Russians had been unable to counter due to the lack of guns and bullets. The army was short 300,000 rifles and could not expect to rectify this situation soon.

Despite this, the Grand Duke continued, "I consider it necessary to use all our strength, resources, and means not to allow the enemy to quickly develop operations on the South West Front, counting on exhausting his colossal reserves of ammunition due to his need to take every position by means of a significant expenditure of shells." There was some evidence, the Grand Duke claimed, that the quality of enemy shells was declining, with many of those made in 1915 failing to explode. There was also some evidence from France that German artillery fire was getting weaker due to a shortage of ammunition. The enemy's success was "due only to expenditures of a colossal amount of artillery shells," and there was, the Grand Duke concluded, reason to believe that eventually the Germans would run out.[59]

The Grand Duke's latest strategy, therefore, was simply to stand his ground and force the enemy to fight every inch of the way, exhausting his supplies. This was far removed from the grand maneuvers of the early months of the war, and it indicated that the Grand Duke now recognized that attrition and not maneuver would decide the war. He had almost certainly recognized this fact earlier than most. It demanded a significant change in approach to military strategy, but the Grand Duke's plan was not very subtle. It almost literally reduced the Russian infantry to cannon fodder, their role being little more than to make the enemy use up his shells. It also rested on an overly optimistic assumption of how long it would take before the Germans and Austro-Hungarians ran out of supplies, and it assumed that the Russians could outlast their enemies in a war of attrition. The scale of Russian losses was now so great that this was far from certain. On 26 May (8 June), the Grand Duke reported to the Tsar that the South West Front alone had lost 300,000 men between 15 (28) April and 15 (28) May.[60] If this rate of losses continued, the Russians might well crack first.

This was especially true given the fragile nature of public opinion in Russia. On 28 May (10 June), anti-German riots broke out in Moscow. Mobs vandalized shops bearing German names, as well as the houses of people believed to be German or of German origin.[61] Some of the rioters alleged treason by German sympathizers in high places, including Empress Aleksandra Fedorovna, while others demanded that the Tsar abdicate and that Grand Duke Nikolai Nikolaevich take his place on the throne.[62]

Paradoxically, the worse the situation at the front became, the more popular the Grand Duke became. Commandant Langlois noted "the absolute adoration of Grand Duke Nicholas, who for the people is the veritable incarnation of their hatred of the Germans."[63] In a study of patriotic culture in First World War Russia, Hubertus Jahn has noted that "Patriotic imagery reveals that Russians had a pretty clear idea against whom they were fighting in the war, but not for whom and for what."[64] While the average Russian may not have been particularly loyal to notions such as "Tsar" and "Motherland," he undoubtedly disliked the Germans intensely and wished to see them defeated. Grand Duke Nikolai Nikolaevich embodied this negative patriotism. Writing shortly after the Grand Duke's dismissal as Supreme Commander in August 1915, Commandant Langlois provided a fair summary of the causes of Nikolai Nikolaevich's popularity, commenting that

> The Grand Duke incarnated all the military qualities; everybody had confidence in him, despite the defeats. In their faith in him, the most obscure peasant, the least informed person, every last soldier, were absolutely convinced that the reverses were not the Grand Duke's fault, but solely due to the lack of material resources at his disposal.... Everybody knew perfectly well the Grand Duke's feelings toward Germany, everybody knew that he and his wife, the Grand Duchess, were animated by a spirit of wild hatred [of Germany].... The Grand Duke truly incarnated the Russian idea, the orthodox idea, the loyalist idea, raised against Germanophile ideas. For all these reasons, in Russia the Grand Duke truly became the idol of the army and of the people.[65]

The Grand Duke was, says a modern Russian historian, what we would nowadays call a "Teflon commander."[66] Russians blamed everybody for the defeats except him. He himself seems to have derived at least some pleasure from his popularity. According to Commandant Langlois, the Grand Duke "saw the hand of God in the fact that he, little loved by the troops under his command in time of peace, had become extremely popular since the start of the war."[67]

By the end of May 1915, the Grand Duke had come to the view that the problems with supply were due to the incompetence of government ministers, including his old enemy, Minister of War General Sukhomlinov. On 29 May, he spoke to General Laguiche about the munitions question, following a trip by the Frenchman to Petrograd to investigate the issue. "The Grand Duke's openness was astonishing," Laguiche reported. "I remain surprised by his understanding of the current circumstances. He made me speak to him with complete candor, naming the persons whose role has been more than detrimental.... The Grand Duke was absolutely insistent in that regard."[68]

On the same day, Nikolai Nikolaevich spoke also to Hanbury Williams. Unlike Laguiche, the Briton felt that the Grand Duke was "very sketchy on anything approaching detail, and indeed on the question generally." Hanbury Williams considered the experience rather frustrating. "To be quite frank with you," he told Kitchener, "he is not much use on these occasions—his name counts & he 'matters' a lot in one way, but he don't 'run this show' much really."[69]

In the meantime, the German and Austro-Hungarian armies continued their advance, pushing eastward from Przemysl deeper into Galicia. Russian efforts to halt them proved fruitless. Despite this, Commandant Langlois, making his third visit to Stavka at the beginning of June 1915, found Grand Duke Nikolai Nikolaevich in a positive mood. Langlois reported on the close relations that existed between the Grand Duke and General Ianushkevich. Between them, he wrote, "reigns an intimacy which is quite remarkable for two men of such opposite natures." In addition, he noted the following:

> As always, the Grand Duke Nicholas displays an uncommon energy and inextinguishable morale. His offensive spirit has not yet been disavowed, not for a single instant; even if the circumstances force him to retreat, they do not crush him at all and he thinks only of the moment when the material conditions will permit him to advance again. His physical health remains equally perfect.... In a word, Grand Duke Nicholas very much gives the impression of a LEADER, in the most elevated sense of the word.[70]

On 4 (17) June, Nikolai Nikolaevich traveled to Kholm for a conference of the two Front commanders and other senior officers. As always he did not attend the conference, although he told the Tsar that he had made several important decisions while there.[71] According to General Palitsyn, Ivanov expressed a wish to retreat further, but Alekseev opposed this.[72] The officers at the meeting agreed that the army should "temporarily go on the defensive," with the main tasks being "firmly holding in our hands the center part of the forward theater and the roads leading to the south and to the north from East Prussia and Galicia into Russia."[73] The German advances in Galicia, combined with the continued presence of large German forces in East Prussia, meant that Poland was now threatened from both north and south, and vulnerable to a pincer operation. Withdrawal from the left bank of the Vistula was an obvious option. The meeting of 4 (17) June ruled this out. Nikolai Nikolaevich confirmed the decision. The army would fight to defend Poland.

This decision fitted in with all the others the Grand Duke had taken since the Germans began their attack at Gorlice-Tarnow. Again and again, he ordered his armies to stand firm, to hold the line they occupied, and not to retreat. In this way, he stamped his character firmly on the conduct of military operations. Whether he was wise to act in this way is hard to determine. His motives were in large part political—he wished to avoid the adverse effect that retreat would have on public opinion. The Grand Duke, Danilov later commented, "clung firmly to the opinion that we should not yield a single inch of Russian land to the enemy unless the surrender of this land was undoubtedly called for by military necessity."[74] But in the end the Grand Duke had to retreat each time anyway, and so the adverse effect was not avoided. All he managed to do was delay the inevitable by a short while, at a great cost in men and equipment.

The Grand Duke's strategy was understandable but definitely unsuccessful. On 7 (20) June, the Grand Duke had to admit that it was no longer possible to hold Lvov, and he gave Ivanov permission to evacuate it.[75] The following day, the enemy occupied the city. Within a few days, the whole of Galicia was in Austro-Hungarian hands. The battle for Poland would begin soon after.

CHAPTER 19

The Great Retreat, July–August 1915

ON 2 (15) JUNE 1915, Prince Vladimir Orlov wrote to General Ianushkevich:

> We are living through a very dangerous time. The terrible cloud of revolution is approaching.... Everyone is demanding the dismissal of [Interior Minister] Maklakov, [War Minister] Sukhomlinov, [Justice Minister] Shcheglovitov, [Procurator of the Holy Synod] Sabler, and [Trade and Industry Minister] Shakhovskoi.... Reason says that we must throw them a bone. We must dismiss Maklakov and Shcheglovitov, that alone will bring calm.... For now, I think that the Grand Duke [Nikolai Nikolaevich] does not need to intervene in this matter ... but if we don't succeed, then we will have the Grand Duke in reserve.[1]

Orlov's fears of the "cloud of revolution" were fully justified. The military defeats of May and June 1915 had heightened dissatisfaction with the Russian government. Liberal groups were demanding political change as the only way to see the war through to a successful conclusion. Orlov's aim was to appease them by firing some of the ministers who were considered the most reactionary. His reference to the Grand Duke suggests that he felt confident that the latter was of the same mind. This was indeed the case, and the Grand Duke now brought himself out of "reserve" and moved decisively to effect a change in government.

An opportunity arose when Nicholas II came to Stavka on 11 (24) June for one of his regular visits. As soon as the Tsar arrived, the Grand Duke went to his train to see him and requested that Sukhomlinov be dismissed.[2] "When I arrived," the Tsar wrote to his wife, "I found N. grave, but quite calm.... I asked him whom he would recommend in Sukhomlinov's place. He answered—Polivanov."[3] The Tsar accepted the Grand Duke's recommendation and agreed to dismiss Sukhomlinov and appoint Polivanov in his place. The Grand Duke was delighted. Seeing Chaplain Shavelskii walking past his wagon, he tapped on the window and summoned him in. "Congratulations on a great victory," he said, "Sukhomlinov is dismissed!" "And Sabler?" Shavelskii replied. "Wait, wait, Sabler will be too," the Grand Duke said.[4]

Next, Nikolai Nikolaevich proposed to the Tsar that he hold a joint meeting of the Council of Ministers and the Army High Command in order to coordinate their actions.[5] The Tsar agreed and ordered most of his ministers to come immediately to Stavka. Two ministers—Sabler and Shcheglovitov—were pointedly not invited. It was clear that their dismissal was now just a matter of time.

The ministers arrived the following day, 13 (26) June, and the next morning the Tsar dismissed Shcheglovitov and Sabler from their posts, replacing them with A. A. Khvostov and A. D. Samarin as Minister of Justice and Procurator of the Holy Synod respectively. The latter appointment particularly pleased the Grand Duke. According to Shavelskii, when the Grand Duke heard of it, "he quickly leapt from his place, ran to an icon of the Mother of God which hung in the corner of the wagon, and, crossing himself, kissed it. Then, just as quickly, he unexpectedly lay down on the ground and kicked his legs in the air. 'I want to somersault with joy,' he said laughing." The Grand Duke then got up again, grabbed his sword, and ran to see the Tsar. His conversation with the Tsar was not entirely satisfactory, however. Emboldened, the Grand Duke raised the subject of Rasputin, but the Tsar simply pretended not to understand what he was saying. "You can work with the Emperor," the Grand Duke told Shavelskii, "he understands and agrees with intelligent arguments. But She [the Empress].... It's all her fault. There is only one way out. Lock her up in a monastery, then everything will turn out well."[6]

On the afternoon of 14 (27) June, the Council of Ministers met under a tent set up near the trains at Stavka. Also present were the Tsar, Grand Duke Nikolai Nikolaevich, General Ianushkevich, and General Iusupov. The meeting reached agreement that in order to encourage political unity in the country the Duma should be recalled by the end of August. In addition, the meeting endorsed Rodzianko's proposal to create a special council to oversee war production. The result was the Special Council for National Defense, consisting of representatives of various ministries, the Duma, the unions of zemstva and towns, and the War Industry Committees.[7] The event was a political victory for the Grand Duke. New ministers were in place, a hand of friendship had been extended to the liberal opposition, and efforts were being made to unify government and society for a successful conclusion of the war.

Unfortunately for Russia, in the long term none of these measures had any significant effect. Nicholas II soon reversed course, while the special council proved too unwieldy to be a useful tool for improving war production. The meeting of 14 (27) June was, in retrospect, the peak of the Grand Duke's political influence. But his intervention engendered resentment in some circles and accentuated fears that his growing popularity was undermining the Emperor's authority. The Empress was particularly unhappy with the Grand Duke's new prominence in Russian politics. On 17 (20) June she wrote,

> Oh I do not like N. having anything to do with these big sittings wh[ich] concern interior questions, he understands our country so little & imposes upon the ministers by his loud voice & gesticulations. I can go wild at times at his false position.... He has no right to meddle in other affairs & one ought to set ones fault to right & give him only all the military things.... Nobody knows who is the Emperor now.... It is as tho' N. settles all, names the choices & changes—it makes me utterly wretched.[8]

Complaints about Nikolasha became a common theme in the Empress's correspondence. She particularly disliked the choice of Samarin as Procurator of the Holy Synod, as Samarin used his authority to purge Rasputin's supporters from positions in the Orthodox Church. "That's Dzhukonskys work and Samarin's excited on through Nikolasha by the black women [Militsa and Stana]," she wrote to her husband, "I cried so awfully when I heard they had forced you to name him at the Headquarters & I wrote to you in my misery, knowing Nikolasha proposed him because he was my enemy & Gregory's [Rasputin's] & through that yours."[9] "M. [Militsa] and S. [Stana] spread horrors about me," she wrote a little later, "and that I was going to be shut up in a Convent."[10]

The Empress would soon have the pleasure of seeing the Grand Duke fall from grace. On the Eastern Front events were about to unfold that would lead the Tsar to replace him as Supreme Commander.

The middle of June 1915 had brought a brief respite to the Russian army while the Germans and Austro-Hungarians halted to bring up supplies and reinforcements and to reorient their armies for the next stage of their offensive. Despite the recent defeats, the Grand Duke continued to express the view that the Russian army would be able to hold onto Warsaw should the Germans attack in that direction.[11] This confidence soon received a sharp shock. On 21 June (4 July), Nikolai Nikolaevich received an alarming telegram from General Alekseev. According to a letter by the Tsar to his wife, "[the telegram] said that the Germans had broken through our lines and were penetrating far into the rear. N. left immediately in his train."[12] The Grand Duke rushed up to the headquarters of the North West Front at Sedlets to consult with Alekseev.

On arrival, he discovered that the situation was not as bad as it had been made out to be: a Russian counter-attack had successfully closed the breach in the lines. The Grand Duke telegraphed the Tsar to tell him that "on the whole, the situation had not changed for the worse."[13]

Generals Ianushkevich and Danilov had accompanied the Grand Duke to Sedlets and held a meeting on 22 June (5 July) with Alekseev and his Chief of Staff, General A. A. Gulevich, to determine future options. The Grand Duke, as usual, sat outside the meeting, and while waiting for it to end talked to General Palitsyn. According to Palitsyn, the Grand Duke was especially concerned about the fortress of Novogeorgievsk, west of Warsaw. Theoretically, Russian control of this fortress, which sat astride the roads, railway, and rivers leading to Warsaw, would make it difficult for any enemy to seize the Polish capital from the west. If, however, the Russians abandoned Warsaw and the line of the Vistula, then holding onto Novogeorgievsk would be superfluous and the fortress would find itself surrounded by the enemy. Palitsyn recorded this in his diary:

> While the senior officers met, I sat with His Highness and we chatted. The main theme of our conversation was our holding on to Poland and all that flowed out of that. I stated my arguments, which did not correspond to the decision of 5 June [to defend Poland].... Grand Duke Nikolai Nikolaevich was very worried about Novogeorgievsk. To defend it, or to abandon it? And he twice asked me this question. I could not give an exact reply, for I was not certain myself.... Novogeorgievsk had lost its importance. But how to throw away what in the national consciousness was a stronghold?[14]

The minutes of the meeting at Sedlets indicate that those present decided to recommend that Alekseev be given the right to determine for himself whether to defend the Vistula and Narev Rivers or to withdraw, with the proviso that he was to withdraw only in the event of extreme necessity. The army should also prepare to evacuate the fortress of Ivangorod. As for Novogeorgievsk, it had "lost its significance" and would be "unable to hinder the enemy's actions." The meeting did not, however, make a decision on whether to try to hold it. First, those present agreed, they needed to find out whether evacuating Novogeorgievsk was in practice possible.[15] In summary, the group concluded that they would continue to try to hold onto Warsaw but would not do so if this meant putting the army as a whole at risk and that Alekseev, as the commander on the spot, should be the person to decide if this was the case.

The Grand Duke confirmed nearly all the conclusions of the meeting in a personal telegram to Alekseev later on 22 June (5 July).[16] In this way, he gave

Alekseev the choice of whether to defend Warsaw, handing over responsibility for a crucial military and political matter. This reflected the immense faith the Grand Duke had in Alekseev, who was, Shavelskii noted, the only general the Grand Duke called by the familiar form of address, "ty," rather than the more formal "vy."[17]

The one conclusion of the 22 June (5 July) meeting that the Grand Duke refused to accept was the one about Novogeorgievsk. Instead, he "ordered the Commander of the North West Front to review this in detail, after which he was to present the issue to the Supreme Commander."[18]

To this end, Alekseev sent Palitsyn to Novogeorgievsk to see whether an evacuation of the fortress was practicable. According to Palitsyn, Alekseev said that at that point he was in favor of abandoning the fortress. Palitsyn reported that they would need 200 trains to remove the materiel at Novogeorgievsk. These trains could perhaps be found, but the lack of rail lines and loading facilities meant that the Russians could not manage more than seven or eight trains a day, which meant that evacuating the fortress in a short period of time was impossible. Having reported this, Palitsyn decided that Alekseev had not really wanted to evacuate after all and had sent him to investigate because he knew what the answer was going to be and wanted some reassurance that he was doing the right thing.[19] Whatever the truth, the result was that Alekseev decided not to abandon the fortress but instead to garrison it and to attempt to hold on to it, even if it was surrounded.

The decision to defend Novogeorgievsk turned out to be a very poor one. It had nothing to do with prewar debates about whether to keep the fortress or dismantle it, and the final decision appears to have been the product of both political considerations and an unwillingness by all concerned to adopt a definite course of action. Everyone seemed to have severe doubts that holding onto the fortress was wise, but no one was willing to act on them. The Grand Duke accepted that Alekseev should have the final say on whether to hold the line of the Vistula River, but he then pulled back somewhat from that position when he demanded that Alekseev review the Novogeorgievsk situation and report to him. Alekseev then passed responsibility onto Palitsyn, who, as he admitted, did not know what to do and felt that he was being used to provide justification for what Alekseev wanted to do anyway. The result was a form of paralysis, which meant that the Russians ended up deciding by default to defend the fortress, because they could not reach a decision to abandon it early enough to enable them to do so. Grand Duke Nikolai Nikolaevich must take a large part of the blame for this situation.

Novogeorgievsk notwithstanding, the meeting of 23 June (6 July) marked an important turning point in Russian strategy. As Ianushkevich noted in a message of 26 June (9 July), "in the coming months the preservation of the living force has top priority in preference to holding on to territory, and even more to capturing it from the enemy."[20]

While retreating from Galicia, the Russian army had engaged in a scorched-earth policy, destroying or removing anything that might be of use to the enemy. This had led to a series of complaints of unnecessary destruction of private property. On 26 June (9 July), the Grand Duke issued an order demanding an end to such excesses:

> It has come to my attention that during the cleansing of some areas of the theater of military operations military units and also some individuals belonging to the military have allowed themselves to carry out various forms of violence, destroying buildings, forests, and woods. Taking into account the fact that such events radically contradict the instructions and orders given out at various times on this subject, I order the undeviating and immediate taking of measures to halt this attitude toward the local population and its property, allowing the destruction of local inhabitants' property only when the military situation and general military objectives require it.[21]

Those guilty of committing such crimes should be punished immediately, the Grand Duke ordered, with punishments ranging up to the death penalty.

On the same day, Nikolai Nikolaevich issued a second order, stating, "During the retreat of our armies from Galicia ... various baseless rumors began to be widely spread, among both the lower ranks and the civilian population, about the discovery of treason." The purpose of these rumors was to undermine troops' faith in their leadership, the Grand Duke asserted. "I warn that I will view any clandestine accusation against people who are completely innocent or simply have a non-Russian name and are honestly serving Tsar and Motherland, as an impermissible attempt to sow discord in the ranks of our valiant army." Anybody who spread untrue rumors was to be punished with the full severity of the law.[22]

The two orders represented an attempt to restore discipline, but neither the scorched-earth policy nor the spy mania had come out of nowhere. They were at least in part the product of the permissive environment that Stavka had encouraged. To prevent supplies falling into the hands of the enemy, Ianushkevich had "ordered crops and surplus food supplies systematically destroyed."[23] As for spy mania, the Grand Duke himself had been guilty of the very crime he now condemned—accusing innocent people of espionage. Belatedly, it seems, he had come to realize the dangers of his policies, although the orders of 26 June (9 July) served merely to cast the blame onto others.

In any case, the June orders do not seem to have been very effective. On 6 (19) July, the Archbishop of Warsaw wrote to the Grand Duke to complain, "your orders ... are not being carried out, and the region is still being destroyed with complete mercilessness."[24] The Grand Duke's reply was not altogether reassuring. "Measures are being taken to check this," he wrote to the Archbishop. "Many complaints are not confirmed. I have again ordered that whatever could be of help to the enemy in battle must be destroyed, and I consider any indulgence in this matter unfounded."[25]

By late June, the Germans were finally ready to begin their next major move, aiming to strike central Poland from the south and from the north. The main attack was to come in the south from Mackensen's Eleventh Army, which had used the previous few weeks to reorient itself from its previous eastward line of march to face northward. Meanwhile, German forces in East Prussia were to attack toward the Narev River, to threaten Warsaw from behind.

By 29 June, the Germans' intent was becoming clear to Stavka. On that day, Grand Duke Nikolai Nikolaevich wrote to the Tsar to tell him that the bulk of the German forces in Galicia had been redeployed to the area south of Kholm and would probably attack toward that town.[26] A few days later, on 2 (15) July, he reported that captured enemy soldiers had said that an offensive toward Kholm was imminent,[27] and then on 3 (16) July, he told the Tsar that they must expect an attack in that direction soon.[28] This proved accurate, for the German Eleventh Army began its offensive on the same day.[29] "In general," the Grand Duke reported to the Tsar on 4 (17) July, "the enemy has evidently decided to exert all his strength in order to put us in a difficult position on the left bank of the Vistula by means of attacks on the lower Narev and in the direction of Kholm."[30]

Fortunately for the Russians, German progress was relatively slow. The Russian defenses on the Narev held firm, while rain delayed the German advance in the south. This meant that German hopes of achieving a double envelopment, cutting off the Russians on the left bank of the Vistula with pincers from north and south, proved over-ambitious. Nevertheless, the German attacks were sufficiently threatening that holding onto the left bank and Warsaw was becoming an increasingly risky option for the Russians.

Alekseev now requested that the Grand Duke come to Sedlets again to speak to him. This the Grand Duke did on 6 (19) July. On his arrival, Alekseev reported to him in person, telling him that the Germans were collecting significant forces on the line of the Narev and Bobr Rivers, and that if they broke through that line it would be necessary to abandon Warsaw. The Grand Duke agreed with Alekseev and gave him permission to leave Warsaw and redraw his line when he felt it necessary.[31] In those circumstances, a garrison would be left in Novogeorgievsk as "a strong fortress to be invested by the enemy."[32]

General Palitsyn recorded in his diary that Grand Duke Pyotr Nikolaevich had told him that "The Supreme Commander's mood is good—he is relying on Alekseev. More than anyone else. There is only one issue, how to extract the army and save it."[33] Nikolai Nikolaevich himself praised Alekseev in a telegram to the Tsar:

> Our views are at one. We look at and evaluate the situation identically—the results of the heroic battles directly conform to the lack of shells, cartridges, and rifles.... Without these shortages, the result of the battles would have been entirely different. It is my holy duty to bear witness to the fact that the army is fulfilling its duty with supreme selflessness—there are a mass of heroic deeds. Now, as always, in all respects I come away with the most pleasing feeling about General Alekseev.[34]

Alekseev did not as yet consider the situation so desperate as to require the abandonment of Warsaw, so for now the Russians continued to hold onto the left bank of the Vistula. The Grand Duke meanwhile hoped for divine intervention. On 8 (21) July, he issued a message to the army:

> Today, on the day of the celebration of the icon of the Mother of God of Kazan, in accordance with the will of the SOVEREIGN EMPEROR and the order of the Most Holy Synod, prayers have ascended to the Holy Virgin that She will obtain victories for the Russian army from the Lord.
>
> I deeply believe that the prayer of the Tsar, in union with His people, will be heard by the Lord God.
>
> All Russia has united and merged its strength to supply the army with all it needs for successful struggle with the enemy.
>
> Remember, heroic army and fleet, entrusted to me by the Sovereign will of the Supreme Leader: the Tsar and all Russia with him are helping you with prayer and labor; filled with this knowledge, we will display our gratitude with courage and new deeds.
>
> God and his omnipotent help are with us, and we believe. This is the guarantee of victory.
>
> Nikolai.[35]

Despite the Grand Duke's prayers, divine help was not forthcoming. On 10 (23) July, German forces gained a foothold across the Narev River from which they could threaten Warsaw's line of communication with Russia.[36] The Grand Duke told the Tsar on 12 (25) July that it might be necessary to evacuate Russian troops from the left bank of the Vistula, "so as not to leave them in a very unfavorable strategic position."[37]

On 15 (28) July, the Grand Duke went yet again to Sedlets, this time to discuss the area in and around Riga, where, as Alekseev told him, the situation was not so threatening as to require a radical regrouping of forces. The North West Front should reinforce the Baltic region with just one infantry division and some cavalry, Alekseev said. General Danilov disagreed and felt that stronger reinforcements were needed. He argued that it would be wise to withdraw from Warsaw and the Vistula to a shorter line further east. The Grand Duke sided with Alekseev and ordered the South West Front to send one cavalry division to the north. He also reconfirmed Alekseev's right to determine for himself when it would be necessary to withdraw.[38]

The Grand Duke's "confidence in General Alekseev is great," General Laguiche reported after the meeting.[39] Nikolai Nikolaevich confirmed this in a telegram to the Tsar: "I took away from the journey to Sedlets on 15 July the conviction that General Alekseev is leading the forces entrusted to him with great calm and firmness," he wrote.[40]

Alekseev could not halt the German advance. On 16 (29) July, the Germans crossed onto the right bank of the Vistula south of Ivangorod, putting those Russian forces that remained on the left bank at risk of being cut off.[41] On 18 (31) July, the Austro-Hungarians captured Lublin, and the next day Kholm.[42] Further to the north, the Germans slowly expanded their bridgehead across the Narev.[43] The noose was closing around the Russians on the left bank of the Vistula. On 22 July (4 August), Alekseev abandoned Warsaw to the enemy, who occupied it the same day. The armies of the North West Front escaped encirclement and withdrew in good order, but the effort to hold the capital of Poland had failed.

On 23 July (6 August), General Hanbury Williams recorded this in his diary: "Warsaw has fallen ... the Grand Duke is undismayed."[44] A day later, Nikolai Nikolaevich visited the headquarters of the South West Front, now located at Rovno, to meet General Ivanov. The Grand Duke told Ivanov that he should withdraw his right flank only if it was under "real pressure" but approved Ivanov's suggestion to fortify the rear as far as the Dnepr River in Ukraine.[45] The possibility of a very long retreat was now a distinct possibility. The army was still fighting hard and withdrawing in good order, but its fighting strength was much reduced.

The Grand Duke's main concern was now that the Germans might advance in the northern sector of the front line toward Petrograd.[46] On 27 July

(9 August) the Grand Duke ordered General Ivanov to send two divisions to the area of Vilna to protect against this threat.[47] He instructed Alekseev on no account to allow these divisions to be blockaded in the fortress at nearby Kovno, and he "categorically ordered" him to "use them only to strengthen the position on the roads to the north of Kovno."[48]

Despite the gravity of the situation, the Grand Duke continued to put on a brave face. On 29 July (11 August), General Laguiche reported the following:

> During our conversation, the Grand Duke insisted at length on his absolute conviction of the happy outcome of the war. With his always mystical spirit, he found proof of divine protection in the fact that these last four months which have been so painful have only brought Russians closer together and given them confidence. His morale is higher than you can imagine.[49]

The Grand Duke, said Laguiche, was carrying out a regrouping of his armies, a move designed to create a reserve that could be used to regain the initiative. "The offensive still remains the dominant idea," Laguiche concluded.[50]

It is hard to tell the extent to which the Grand Duke's confidence was real and not just for show. In contrast to the happy picture painted by Laguiche, Julia Cantacuzen wrote that Stana told her that she "feared her husband would have a complete nervous breakdown." "He is in despair," Stana allegedly said.[51]

Although he hid it well, there can be little doubt that the strains of defeat were playing on the Grand Duke's nerves. On 31 July (13 August), for instance, he attended a ceremony to lay the foundation stone of a side chapel in the main church in Baranovichi. According to Shavelskii:

> When the moment came to lay the foundation stone, I took a four-cornered slab, made out of cement rather than stone. But no sooner had I lifted it than it disintegrated into little pieces.... The Grand Duke's face suddenly changed. He left the church looking gloomy, and returned home gloomy. "The Grand Duke is very upset, he considers the story with the stone a bad omen," Doctor Malama told me.[52]

As the situation worsened, Russians looked for people to blame. The favorite targets of members of the Council of Ministers were Generals Ianushkevich and Danilov. Already in mid-June, Agriculture Minister Krivoshein had attempted to persuade the Grand Duke to dismiss the two men, a suggestion the Grand Duke did not take kindly.[53] On 24 July (6 August), a meeting of the Council of Ministers heard a series of attacks on Ianushkevich and Danilov,[54] following which Krivoshein decided to try again to persuade Nikolai Nikolaevich to get rid of them. This brought a sharp response from the Grand Duke, who on 1 (14) August sent a message to Krivoshein, telling him that "replacing these people would bring nothing but harm, since the reason for the failures is not these people but the lack of shells, rifles, cartridges, and the lack, and untimely arrival, of reinforcements and their poor training." The Emperor had appointed Ianushkevich and Danilov, the Grand Duke said, and so only he could replace them. As for his own future, the Grand Duke concluded, "Things could have turned out differently, namely, my removal could have been considered the guarantee of success. In that case, I would have joyfully surrendered my post.... And so, one word from the Emperor is enough, but only His word."[55]

The Grand Duke's loyalty to Ianushkevich and Danilov in part reflected his view of his own relationship with the Tsar—as the Tsar had appointed them, he had no right to change them. It also reflected the more general loyalty the Grand Duke showed throughout his life to those he felt close to. "Due to his nobility and pride, the Grand Duke will not blame his staff," Palitsyn wrote on 4 (17) August. "[He believes that] the cause of all the evils is the shortage of military supplies."[56]

While the Grand Duke retained his confidence in Ianushkevich and Danilov, the man whose abilities he valued the most was Alekseev. On 2 (15) August, the Grand Duke traveled again to Alekseev's headquarters, this time to discuss the idea of creating a new Northern Front, which would have responsibility for defending the Baltic region. According to General M. D. Bonch-Bruevich, at the meeting that followed, Alekseev offered to resign because of the recent defeats, but the Grand Duke "in a conciliatory mood, embraced the general and assured him that he himself, as Supreme Commander-in-Chief, was answerable for what went on at the front." Alekseev's "note of repentance," Bonch-Bruevich noted, "brought the Grand Duke into a state of complete mollification."[57]

On 4 (17) August, another disaster befell the Russian army. The commandant of the Kovno fortress, General Grigoriev, abandoned his post and fled. A short while later, the fortress surrendered to the Germans. The Grand Duke ordered that Grigoriev be arrested and tried by field court-martial.[58] Shavelskii found the Grand Duke weeping in his carriage. "Father, it's awful," the Grand Duke told him. "Kovno has been surrendered without a fight. The commandant has abandoned the fortress and run away somewhere. The fortress troops have fled. The army is retreating. What more can one do in such a situation? It's awful, awful."[59]

Even worse news followed shortly. When withdrawing from the left bank of the Vistula, Alekseev had left a substantial garrison in the fortress of Novogeorgievsk. For the first time on the Eastern Front, the Germans brought up special heavy siege artillery previously only used in the west. With this they rapidly bombarded Novogeorgievsk into submission. On 6 (19) August, after only a few days' resistance, the 80,000-strong garrison surrendered to the Germans. The decision to hold onto Novogeorgievsk had proved to be a costly mistake.

The Tsar now came to a fateful decision—he would dismiss Grand Duke Nikolai Nikolaevich as Supreme Commander and take command of the army himself. Nicholas II had always felt that his correct place was at the head of his troops. The defeats of summer 1915 convinced him that the time had come to act. On 6 (19) August, he wrote a personal letter to Nikolai Nikolaevich informing him of his decision to take his place. "Dear Nikolasha," the letter read,

> Now that a year of war has passed and the enemy occupies a large expanse of our land, I have decided to take supreme command of the army.... I select General Alekseev as my chief of staff. I appoint you Viceroy of the Caucasus and commander-in-chief of the Caucasus Army.... I am confident that you will accept this important appointment as visible proof that my feelings toward you have not changed in the slightest and that you will enjoy my full trust. Give Generals Ianushkevich and Danilov my thanks for their service.... Knowing how much you value Prince Orlov, I place him at your disposal and think that he will be your assistant in civilian affairs. I thank you from all my heart for your efforts, and all the torments and sufferings which you have experienced during the year of war because of the heavy responsibility lying on your shoulders. If there were any mistakes ... then I sincerely forgive them.... I embrace you and Pyotr. With sincere affection. Nicky.[60]

It took some time for the Grand Duke to receive the letter. The Tsar instructed General Polivanov to deliver it, but Stavka was in the process of moving and so delivery was delayed. The front had moved so far to the east that it was approaching Baranovichi. Stavka was no longer safe and needed to move. Its new location was the town of Mogilev in eastern Belorussia. The Grand Duke left Baranovichi on 7 (20) August and arrived in Mogilev the following day. There he set himself up in the house of the provincial governor on a small rise running down to the banks of the river Dnepr. Stavka would remain in Mogilev until the revolution of 1917.

General Polivanov arrived in Mogilev on the evening of 9 (22) August, bearing the Tsar's letter. He went straight to the governor's house, where he informed the Grand Duke that the Tsar had decided to replace him. On hearing this, Nikolai Nikolaevich "crossed himself with a broad gesture." He seemed pleased, however, at the news that he was being appointed Viceroy of the Caucasus, and asked whether he could take General Ianushkevich with him, to which Polivanov gave a positive reply.[61]

On his return to Petrograd, Polivanov told his colleagues in the Council of Ministers that the Grand Duke

> was very pleased with his appointment to the Caucasus, which he sees as a quite honorable solution for himself.... I must add that the Grand Duke impressed me as a man whose nerves are shot and who is completely worn out. I do not refer to the moral aspect, but in the purely physical sense, his departure from Headquarters will be an enormous relief to him.[62]

A few days later, in a conversation with Shavelskii and General Alekseev, the Grand Duke blamed the Empress and Rasputin for his dismissal, telling them, according to Shavelskii,

> As you both know, I did not lift a finger for my popularity. It grew against my will and desire, it grew among the troops and the people. This worried, excited and angered the Empress, who greatly feared that my glory, if you can call the people's love for me that, would eclipse that of her husband. To this one must add the matter of Rasputin. Knowing my hatred of him, Rasputin exerted all his strength to rouse the imperial family against me. Now he is openly boasting, "I sank the Supreme Commander...." I want to warn you not to take any steps on my behalf. No good will come of it, and you will only harm yourselves.[63]

When General Polivanov informed the Council of Ministers of the Tsar's decision on 6 (19) August, the ministers were aghast. "The popularity of the Grand Duke is still great, and he serves as a symbol around which our last hopes are united. The army also, though furious at its commanders and staffs, considers Nikolai Nikolaevich its real leader," said Krivoshein. "There can be no doubt that the Emperor's decision will be interpreted as the result of influence of the notorious Rasputin," said Interior Minister Shcherbatov. "One must not forget that the Grand Duke has the favor of the deputies [of the Duma] because of his attitude toward public organizations and representatives." The ministers deputized Polivanov to try and get the Tsar to change his mind.[64] The Tsar refused.

On 14 (27) August, Laguiche found the Grand Duke "admirably calm, tenacious" and "very touched" by a telegram he had received from General Joffre and the French Minister of War, Alexandre Millerand.[65] The Grand Duke was, however, keen to speed up the change of command. On 14 (27) August, he wrote to Polivanov,

> I reported to the Emperor that after I received his letter, I put all the forces which are being regrouped at the disposal of General Alekseev, and I will not interfere in his orders.... I do not consider that I have the moral right to give orders now that General Alekseev has been chosen as chief of staff. I cannot have any faith in myself. I can give orders again to everyone, but, for all my desire, I do not have the strength to do so usefully now that I am no longer trusted. This state of transition must not continue for long.... I am sure that you agree with me. Report this to the Emperor. I consider that the Emperor's arrival at Stavka is urgently needed.[66]

Although it had not been officially confirmed, news of the Grand Duke's impending departure had leaked out and become widely known in the country. In Moscow, a group of liberal politicians met at the house of industrialist and Duma deputy A. I. Konovalov and passed a resolution calling for a new government "possessing the confidence of the country." The Moscow city council then followed suit, passing a similar resolution and sending a greeting to Grand Duke Nikolai Nikolaevich.[67]

The Council of Ministers was alarmed. Moscow was, Polivanov told his ministerial colleagues, "announcing to all of Russia its unshakeable confidence in the Supreme Commander the Grand Duke.... We must draw the attention of His Majesty to this, and beg him to postpone the change in command." Krivoshein proposed a compromise: the Tsar would take over as Supreme Commander, but the Grand Duke would remain at Stavka as his assistant. Polivanov supported Krivoshein's proposal. "According to the news reaching the War Ministry," he said, "the dismissal of the Grand Duke is being discussed in the trenches, and the soldiers are saying that their last defender, a man who can control the generals and officers, is being taken away from them."[68]

The Council of Ministers discussed the matter a second time on 21 August (3 September). Prime Minister Goremykin argued that it was impossible for the Tsar to change his mind. The majority of the ministers disagreed. Eight of them signed a collective letter protesting the Grand Duke's dismissal and requesting to resign, saying,

> We dare once again to tell You, Sovereign, that the decision you have taken, according to our most thoughtful consideration, threatens Russia, You, and Your dynasty with the direst consequences.... Finding ourselves in such circumstances, we are losing our faith in the possibility of serving You and the Motherland with any consciousness of utility.[69]

Such outright collective opposition to the Tsar by his ministers was unprecedented in Russian history. But the Tsar refused to yield. "I have acted as my conscience told me to," the Tsar told Grand Duke Dmitrii Pavlovich.[70]

On 18 (31) August, the Grand Duke dined with General Bezobrazov. "The general mood of the staff is tense and all clam up," the general recorded in his diary, adding, "The Grand Duke is nice to me."[71] Three days later, the Grand Duke had dinner with General Palitsyn, who also noted his impressions in his diary. "The Grand Duke tries to be cheerful," wrote Palitsyn, "and says that he thanks God that this enormous responsibility has been taken from him and he is happy. I don't believe it."[72]

On 23 August (5 September), the Tsar finally arrived at Stavka to take command and the same day issued an official letter thanking Grand Duke Nikolai Nikolaevich for his services as Supreme Commander.[73] The Grand Duke in turn issued a final order to his troops:

> Today, valiant Army and Fleet, the Sovereign Supreme Leader Emperor has become your chief. Bowing before your heroism for over a year of war, I send you My sincere, heartfelt, fervent thanks. I firmly believe that, knowing that the Tsar to whom you have sworn oaths is leading you, you will accomplish new, unprecedented deeds, and will help your Anointed achieve victory. General-Adjutant Nikolai.[74]

The Grand Duke and Alekseev met the Tsar at the railway station at Mogilev and took him to Stavka. They then went to church to celebrate the Tsar's arrival.[75] The Tsar described events in a letter to his wife:

> N. came in with a kind, brave smile, and asked simply when I would order him to go. I answered in the same manner that he could remain for two days; then we discussed the questions concerned with military operations, some of the generals and so forth, and that was all. The following day at lunch and dinner he was very talkative and in a very good mood, such as we have not seen him for many months.... N. repeated to me that he was going from here quite calmly, knowing that I had such help in Alekseev. We spoke a good deal about

> the Caucasus. He is fond of it, and interested in the people and in the beautiful country, but he begs not to be left there for long after the end of the war. He has immediately put on a beautiful old Circassian sword, a present which [Prince G. D.] Shervashidze gave him several years ago, and will wear it all the time. He intends to stay in Pershino for twelve days, and then go straight to Tiflis to meet the old count V. [Vorontsov-Dashkov, the outgoing Viceroy of the Caucasus] at Rostov-on-Don. The whole collection of black women [Militsa and Stana] will join him at Kiev at his place, and they will all go together.[76]

On 24 August (6 September), the Grand Duke said goodbye to Hanbury Williams and Laguiche. To both he expressed his great confidence in Alekseev. Hanbury Williams wrote to Kitchener that the Grand Duke "asked me to tell you personally and privately that he had known Gen. Alexieff for many years, longer than he had known Yanuchkevitz and Danilof, and that he had a very high opinion of his capability and was sure that you could place the utmost confidence in him."[77] The Grand Duke similarly told Laguiche, "You can have the same confidence in General Alekseev's work as in mine. We have known each other for a long time, we have often worked together; our frame of mind is the same; our views identical; he is a trooper and we understand one another without having to spell things out."[78]

The next day, 25 August (7 September) 1915, the Grand Duke at last left Stavka. At two in the afternoon, he assembled his former staff and said goodbye. He was, according to General Kondzerovskii, "very agitated, thanked everybody for their service, and said that we now had the great honor of serving His Majesty and he hoped that we would be even more diligent and assiduous."[79] At six in the evening, the Grand Duke boarded his train at Mogilev station. "The Grand Duke, standing at attention by the window of his wagon, saluted the Emperor," General Spiridovich wrote. "The Emperor, with a slight smile, replied."[80] The Grand Duke's train pulled out of the station. A new chapter in his life was about to begin.

CHAPTER 20

Victory in the Caucasus, September 1915–April 1916

GRAND DUKE NIKOLAI NIKOLAEVICH, now aged 58, initially had some doubts about his appointment as Viceroy of the Caucasus. According to his nephew, Prince Roman Petrovich, he felt "unprepared" for it.[1] "Military affairs did not frighten me," Nikolai Nikolaevich wrote later, but "Civilian matters, which were quite complicated, made me nervous. I had never dealt with civil matters, and in more than 40 years of military service had never come into contact with them." Still, "The Caucasus lured me," he wrote, "and I was happy about the prospect of getting there. I was quite clear about the many difficulties which were to come to me as Viceroy because of the many ethnic groups. But I am very attached to the Oriental and so was confident of coping with the people."[2]

Before going to the Caucasus, the Grand Duke traveled to Pershino, where he spent several weeks' leave on his estate. There he was joined by his wife, Stana, as well as by his brother, Pyotr Nikolaevich, his sister-in-law Militsa, and his nephew Roman. At first, he spent a few days receiving official visitors from Petrograd and the Caucasus. He then took time off and hunted almost every day until the eve of his departure. On the day he departed, he inspected the estate, gave instructions for its management, and went to church, before driving to Tula railway station where he met General Ianushkevich and Prince Vladimir Orlov. The Grand Duke, his family, Ianushkevich, and Orlov then left by train for the Caucasus.[3]

En route, they stopped at Rostov-on-Don where Nikolai Nikolaevich's train pulled up next to that of the outgoing Viceroy of the Caucasus, Count Vorontsov-Dashkov. The Grand Duke later recorded, "My special train stopped right next to the Count's train. As soon as we stopped, the very old count came into my wagon in his full dress uniform. After a fairly long conversation, he went back to his train. Immediately after, I paid him a so-called return visit, and we had a detailed and interesting conversation." What exactly the two men spoke about is unknown. According to Prince Roman

Petrovich, as soon as the Grand Duke's train left Rostov, Nikolai Nikolaevich changed out of his army summer uniform and put on a long Caucasian cloak, known as a *cherkeska*. This would be his preferred dress from that moment on until the end of his life, and it symbolically marked his new association with the Caucasus.[4]

From Rostov, the Grand Duke's train headed over to the eastern side of the Caucasus, stopping eventually at Baladjari near Baku in Azerbaijan. Here the governor of Baku presented a delegation of oil barons and members of local social organizations. Observing members of the press, the Grand Duke gave a speech of thanks in the station waiting room. Later, the Grand Duke wrote, "This was the first time in my life that I, as a representative of the Tsar, had to make an official speech to civilians and representatives of the press. And this was without any preparation—knowing that every word I said as the newly appointed Viceroy would be analyzed and was of political importance."[5]

From Baladjari, the train traveled westward across the Caucasus, and at 11 in the morning on 23 September (6 October) 1915, pulled into the main station in the Caucasian capital Tiflis (Tbilisi). Nikolai Nikolaevich alighted from his train, inspected an honor guard of Cossacks, and then greeted a delegation from the town council, headed by the Mayor of Tiflis, Aleksandr Khatisov. The Grand Duke and Khatisov spoke briefly, then Nikolai Nikolaevich quickly crossed through the main station hall and out into the bright sunlight beyond. Here a white Arabian horse was waiting for him. He rode out of the station square accompanied by an escort of Cossacks in bright red *cherkeskas*. His family and staff followed in cars.[6]

From the station, the Grand Duke rode toward the Saint Aleksandr Nevskii Military Cathedral. Schools were closed for the day, and the children were out in the streets to greet him.[7] According to the British consul in Tiflis, P. Stevens, "the Grand Duke proceeded through very crowded streets gaily decorated with bunting, lined with troops and school children."[8] The Grand Duke, according to another report, "rode his horse effectively, continually avoiding the scattered flowers and the flags which children were waving."[9] Cathedral bells rang out to greet him, and clergymen met him outside the cathedral and accompanied him inside for a short religious service.

This service was originally meant to mark the end of the day's ceremonies, according to the plan drawn up by Count Vorontsov-Dashkov for his successor's arrival. Grand Duke Nikolai Nikolaevich changed the plan and added several more stops to the day's events. After finishing the service at the Military Cathedral, he drove to the Sioni Cathedral of the Georgian Orthodox Church, where the Georgian Exarch greeted him and another short service followed. He went next to the Vank Cathedral of the Armenian Apostolic Church, where the Armenian Patriarch met him. Then he moved on to the Shiite mosque and after that the Sunni one. Finally, he went to the Viceroy's palace and the day's ceremonies were over.[10] The addition of the Georgian, Armenian, and Muslim religious sites was highly symbolic. It indicated the Grand Duke's determination to show that he intended to treat all the ethnic and religious groups of the Caucasus equally. This intention on his part was to be an important element of his policies throughout his time as Viceroy.

Grand Duke Nikolai Nikolaevich now issued his first statement as Viceroy of the Caucasus:

> I have today arrived at Tiflis.... I greet all nationalities inhabiting the Caucasus.
>
> I pray the Almighty to bestow His Blessings on me and to help me in serving the Lord Emperor during my administration of the affairs of the Caucasus which His Imperial Majesty has been pleased to entrust to me.
>
> The fundamental principle which for the benefit of the country shall mark the inception of this administration shall be a belief in the sincere feelings of loyalty of all the peoples to the Lord Emperor, and their love for Russia with which the Caucasus forms an inseparable whole.
>
> Animated by fidelity to the service of the Tsar, boundless love for Russia, and a desire to bring benefit to the best of my ability to the country, I enter upon the labors before me fully anticipating that the hour will come when, fortified with the confidence of the country and an ardent longing of all the races of the Caucasus to amicably work with me toward a state of general benevolence, together with them I shall delight in the moral and intellectual prosperity of the country, its development, the expansion of its countless natural resources and its general welfare.
>
> Nikolai, General Adjutant[11]

The Grand Duke's message, and in particular his greeting to "all nationalities," was well received.[12] The Georgian newspaper *Tanamedrové Azri* commented that many in the Caucasus remembered the Grand Duke's manifesto to the Poles and considered him a friend of the Empire's minority nationalities. "According to some," said the newspaper, "with the change of Viceroy, a new epoch is commencing in the political life of the Caucasus."[13]

As Viceroy the Grand Duke was responsible for the civil administration of the Caucasus. He was also Commander-in-Chief of the Caucasus Army. The Army, however, already had a highly competent commander, General N. N. Iudenich. Shortly after his arrival at Tiflis, the Grand Duke traveled to Iudenich's headquarters in the fortress of Kars. There, the Grand Duke insisted that Iudenich should remain in direct command of the army, while he (the Grand Duke) would concentrate on the civilian aspects of his position.[14] The army staff was split into two: an operational staff under Iudenich at Kars and a staff responsible for rear areas and supply based in Tiflis and run by the Army Chief of Staff, General L. M. Bolkhovitinov.[15]

This created a dual power structure, with the Caucasus army having both a commander-in-chief and a commander. As the latter, Iudenich had no control over his army's supply system. Indeed, there was no army-level supply as such: each corps was responsible for its own area of operations. And while Iudenich was notionally free to plan and determine the army's operations, major decisions still needed the Grand Duke's approval. General P. N. Shatilov, who served on Iudenich's staff, wrote, "I saw clear interference by the Commander-in-Chief in operational matters. This interference always had a restraining character, and only made it more difficult for General Iudenich to manifest his will."[16] According to Shatilov, relations between Iudenich and the Grand Duke, and between both men's staffs, were often cold.[17] This was perhaps an inevitable complication of the confusion of responsibilities.

General Palitsyn, who had accompanied the Grand Duke to the Caucasus as his personal military advisor, was scathing about the division of power. "There is no master in the sense that I understand it," he wrote. "In essence there is one army, two chiefs, one chief of staff, a head of the military district, and an army without rear institutions."[18] There was, he added, "no unity" in operational and supply matters, no clear division of responsibilities.[19] This was, Palitsyn considered, "a curious situation."[20]

After visiting Iudenich at Kars, Grand Duke Nikolai Nikolaevich returned to Tiflis. He lived and worked in the Viceroy's palace in the center of the town and soon established a firm routine. In the mornings, he dealt with military matters, generally meeting some or all of his closest military advisors—Generals Bolkhovitinov, Ianushkevich, and Palitsyn—in his study. At precisely 12:30, "so punctually that many of the staff set their watches by him" according to Prince Roman Petrovich, Nikolai Nikolaevich would leave his study, enter the billiards room next door, stride down the hall, and drink a glass of vodka before going into the dining room to eat. As many as 30 people might be present for lunch, with the Grand Duke and Stana seated at the center of the table. When the meal was over, Nikolai Nikolaevich would return to his study and spend the afternoon working on civilian affairs, often meeting with Prince Orlov or other officials. In the evening, if work permitted, he liked to spend time with his family.[21]

Also living in the palace were Stana; Stana's daughter from her first marriage, Princess Elena; Grand Duke Pyotr Nikolaevich and Militsa; and Pyotr Nikolaevich and Militsa's children, Prince Roman and Princesses Marina and Nadezhda. Nikolai Nikolaevich's study, which was located over the private entrance into the palace, was large. A post-revolutionary inventory of the palace lists it as containing 11 armchairs and 25 sets of antlers, brought down from the Grand Duke's home in Petrograd. Some effort had been made to redecorate in the Grand Duke's taste, with beaver pelts scattered around the palace and pictures of the Crimea and of the house at Chaïr hung on the walls of the corridors.[22]

Nikolai Nikolaevich also had the use of a country home in Kojori, 20 kilometers to the southwest of Tiflis.[23] Given the pressures of his work, he spent most of his time in Tiflis, but he did manage to get out and about a little more than he had done from Stavka, regularly visiting the Black Sea Fleet in the port of Batum and making several visits to see military units and the scenes of recent battles along the front in Eastern Anatolia, a hundred or so kilometers to the southwest.

One such visit early in the Grand Duke's time in the Caucasus was to the First Caucasian Cavalry Division, commanded by General N. N. Baratov. After the Grand Duke had reviewed the troops, the divisional staff invited him to dinner. In Caucasian tradition, every feast had a president, a sort of master of ceremonies known as a "tulumbash" or "tamada," who was not the most senior person present but, rather, the one who ran the feast, organized the toasts, made jokes, and fined those who misbehaved. On this occasion, the tulumbash was Baratov, and Grand Duke Nikolai Nikolaevich found himself in trouble. According to one of those present, A. G. Emelianov:

> The Grand Duke didn't know Caucasian customs, or perhaps did know but didn't want to abide by them. Without the tulumbash's permission nobody can make a toast to those present. The Grand Duke rose and began to speak.
>
> "Forgive me, Your Highness," General Baratov interrupted him, "You are fined."
>
> Twinkles appeared in the Grand Duke's eyes, and everybody around him fell silent.
>
> "What do you mean fined? By whom and what for?" the Grand Duke asked.
>
> Baratov replied: "According to Caucasian custom, *nobody* can speak without the tamada's permission. Those who have broken the law are fined. Would Your Highness mind draining this punishment goblet?"
>
> The vessel was fairly large and the Grand Duke managed to drink it to the bottom.... The Grand Duke was pleased with the turn of events, and both at the front and in Tiflis praised Baratov's deed in defending Caucasian tradition.[24]

The Grand Duke left the cavalry division with a good impression of Baratov. A short time later he would put him in charge of an expedition that arose out of his first major decision as Viceroy of the Caucasus, an invasion of Persia.

Persia was neutral, but the British had occupied the oil fields in the south of the country, while a small Russian force was present in the far north in Persian Azerbaijan.[25] Germany, meanwhile, was working hard to bring Persia into the war on its side, recruiting supporters, especially in the Gendarme Corps, and forming armed groups with the purpose of launching a coup d'état. In Isfahan a pro-German group murdered the Russian vice-consul in May 1915 and several months later made an attempt on the life of the British consul-general. By autumn 1915, the situation in Isfahan was so dangerous that the Europeans in the city (except for the Austro-Hungarians and Germans) had to flee.[26]

In summer 1915, German agents spread out from Isfahan, recruiting armed bands and paying their members in gold. In Shiraz, German supporters attacked and imprisoned the British consul and the rest of the British colony. The Russian and British consuls in Kermanshah fled in the face of an Ottoman incursion. By October 1915, Persia seemed to be slipping into enemy hands.[27]

To prevent this from happening, in October 1915 Nikolai Nikolaevich ordered the sending of an expeditionary corps of 14,000 men under General Baratov to Qazvin in northern Persia. The logic of the order was akin to an early 20th-century version of the domino theory: Russian prestige in the Muslim world had suffered because of events in Persia; if nothing was done to rectify this, unrest might spread to neighboring Muslim countries, especially Afghanistan, where the Emir had just received a German envoy, Oskar von Niedermayer.[28] Were Afghanistan to become an ally of Germany, this might in turn threaten Russian-controlled Central Asia and the British Empire in India.

The purpose of the Persian expedition was above all else to restore Russian prestige. From this derived various limits on operations—in particular, a need to treat the local population with restraint. On 23 October (5 November), the Grand Duke informed the Ministry of Foreign Affairs:

> The significance of the corps consists of raising our prestige in Persia.... The attitude to the Persian civilian population must be very benevolent and, as a true guarantee of this, troops must pay the population for everything that they acquire at prices which are satisfactory to the population.... As far as the further tasks of the expeditionary corps are concerned, they will depend on the situation once the troops have finally concentrated at Qazvin.[29]

The Grand Duke repeated these instructions on the next day to Baratov, telling him, "Until the Persians declare war on us, the task of the forces now concentrated in Persia consists of raising the prestige of Russia's name. The attitude to the Persian population must be very friendly."[30] The Grand Duke also emphasized the issue of prestige in a letter to General Alekseev, writing that "Without doubt energetic actions are needed to raise and establish our prestige in Persia, otherwise what is now happening in Persia will spread to Afghanistan. Only by such actions can we hope to hold onto Afghanistan."[31]

Baratov's corps sailed across the Caspian Sea and landed at the northern Persian port of Enzeli on 28 October (10 November).[32] Two weeks later, on 12 (25) November, Persian gendarmes in the town of Hamadan mutinied. The next day, the Grand Duke ordered Baratov to march on Hamadan to suppress the mutiny,[33] adding that he gave Baratov the freedom to determine the size of the force and the time of its move, "as you know the situation far better."[34] Baratov's objectives, the Grand Duke told Iudenich, were to return the Russian consul to Hamadan and disarm the mutineers. Similar missions to Kermanshah and Qom were to be undertaken at a later stage.[35]

The Grand Duke was keen to coordinate the actions of the expeditionary corps with those of the British army, which was at that point advancing through Mesopotamia (Iraq). On 23 November (6 December), he summoned the British military representative in the Caucasus, Major Marsh, to a meeting and asked him to keep him continually informed of British operations.[36] The Grand Duke remained very loyal to Russia's allies, taking with him to the Caucasus the French flag that Joffre had given him in 1912.[37] On 26 November (9 December), he attended a meeting of members of the Order of Saint George and sent a telegram to General Laguiche at Stavka, telling him, "At the traditional dinner on the holiday of Saint George, the knights of the Order of Saint George of the Caucasus Army and I raise our glasses in honor of the allied armies and to the glory of their heroic chief and soldiers. I ask you to pass on our sentiments to the representatives of the allied armies."[38]

As the civil authority in the Caucasus, the Grand Duke decided to introduce the system of zemstva, which provided a form of local self-government in much of the rest of the Russian Empire but which did not yet exist in the Caucasus. This was not a new idea, but Vorontsov-Dashkov had never gone beyond agreeing to it in principle. The Grand Duke wanted to move more speedily. On 20 November (3 December), he wrote to Agriculture Minister Krivoshein that, having acquainted himself with the region, he believed that "it is necessary to work out very rapidly the legislation which has already been agreed in principle about introducing zemstva into the Caucasus." This

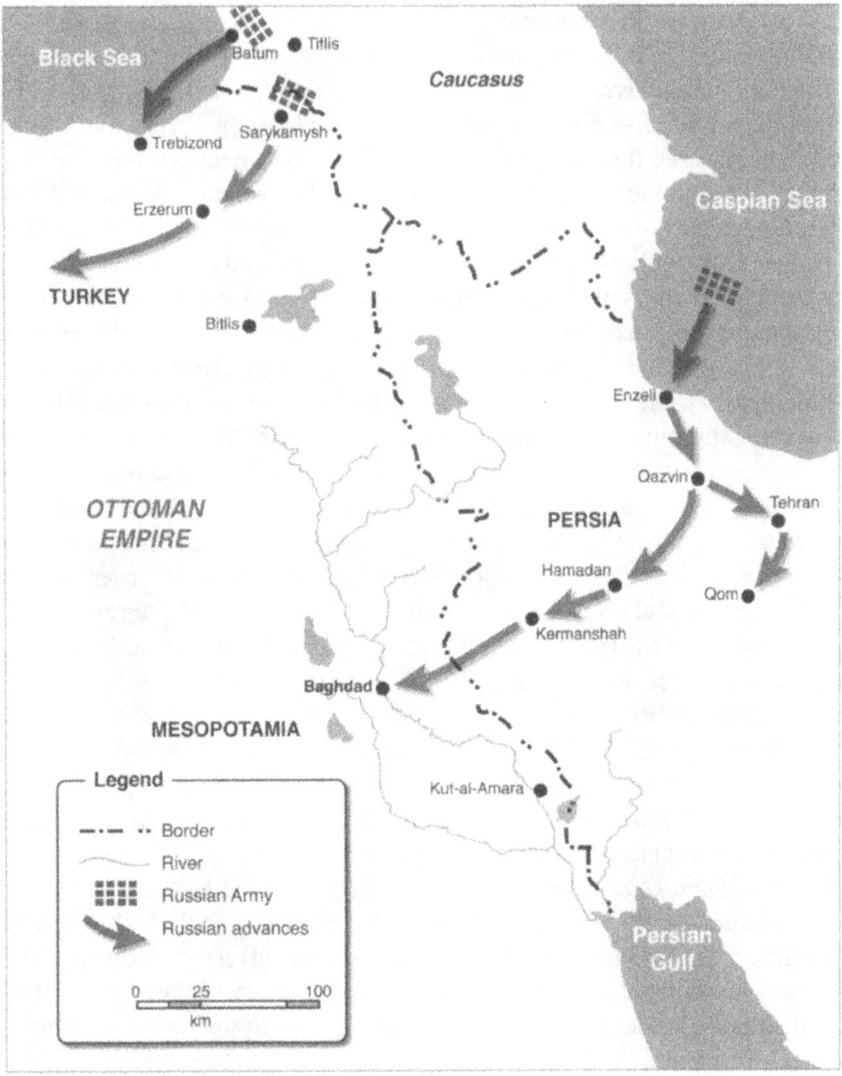

Map 8: The Caucasian and Persian Fronts, 1915–1917

Grand Duke Nikolai Nikolaevich and members of the Order of Saint George, Tiflis (*Novoe Vremia*, 23 January 1916)

was complicated by the region's ethnic disparity as well as the varying levels of economic development in different areas and among different groups. The Grand Duke asked Krivoshein to recommend somebody who had the necessary skills and knowledge to accelerate the process.[39]

The other major shift in policy under the Grand Duke was a more even-handed approach to the nationalities question in the Caucasus than that of his predecessor. Historian Andreas Kappeler has noted that the policies the Russian Imperial state adopted toward minority nationalities tended to be "illogical and inconsistent."[40] At times, the state cooperated with them and gave them space to maintain their own culture; at other times, it chose to suppress or even assimilate them. This was as true of the Caucasus as any other part of the Empire. In that area, by the late 19th century Armenians had a fairly well-developed sense of national identity. Consequently, the Russian state became increasingly suspicious of them as potential separatists, and later as revolutionaries, and in response attempted to russify them. The governor of the Caucasus in the mid-1880s, Prince A. M. Dondukov-Korsakov, first closed all Armenian schools and then, after reopening them, put their teachers under strict surveillance.[41] Subsequently, "a wholesale attack was launched against all educational and charitable institutions of the Armenians,"[42] culminating in a 1903 decision to expropriate all the land owned by the Armenian Church.[43]

The arrival of Vorontsov-Dashkov as Viceroy in 1905 put an end to this repressive policy, and Vorontsov soon developed a reputation for favoring the Armenians.[44] Believing that previous policies had proven counterproductive and had alienated the Armenian people, he restored the land confiscated from the Armenian Church and eliminated the requirement that Armenian schools teach pupils in Russian.[45] Once the First World War began, he sought to use Armenians' hostility toward the Ottoman Empire to mobilize them as allies. Even before the Ottomans had declared war on Russia, Vorontsov requested permission from Foreign Minister Sazonov to arm Ottoman Armenians in order to provoke an uprising.[46] He also permitted the formation of several Armenian volunteer regiments.[47]

In contrast to his generous attitude toward Armenians, Vorontsov harbored a decidedly negative view of Muslims and seems to have seen them as a potential fifth column. Thus after an uprising by Muslim Adzharians, he ordered the deportation of 10,000 Muslims from the frontier zone, while the Russian army massacred tens of thousands more.[48] After setting up a relief committee for refugees, his wife, Countess Vorontsova-Dashkova, rejected a request from Azeris that the committee provide aid for them too. According to Mayor Khatisov, she told them, "I know no Tatar [i.e., Muslim] refugees; I only know Tatar traitors."[49]

Grand Duke Nikolai Nikolaevich had very different opinions. "There is no Armenian question, any more than there is a Iakut question," he supposedly said (the Iakuts were a people in the north of Siberia).[50] The Armenian units created by Vorontsov had been accused of committing atrocities against Muslims, thereby alienating the latter, with negative consequences for the Russian war effort.[51] In December 1915 these units were disbanded. This move did not imply a return to the repressive anti-Armenian policies of the period prior to 1905, but it was the start of what was to be a far more pro-Muslim policy than that of Vorontsov-Dashkov. The Grand Duke's stance fitted with the traditional tendency of Russian statesmen to view Islam as a primarily religious matter of no great political significance,[52] and thus to regard Muslims as loyal subjects of the Tsar.

On 2 (15) December 1915, Baratov's troops took Hamadan in Persia.[53]

From there they advanced on the Muslim holy city of Qom. At Foreign Minister Sazonov's request, the Grand Duke instructed Baratov to be very careful to avoid doing anything that could lead to accusations that Russian troops were insulting Islam.[54] Two days later, on 7 (20) December, Baratov's troops entered Qom.[55]

Nikolai Nikolaevich celebrated what was Christmas Day according to the Western calendar, 12 (25) December, by holding a reception for members of a British ambulance unit that was serving in the Caucasus. The Grand Duke as usual won over his visitors with his charm. One of the Britons, Sarah Broom Macnaughtan, described the event in a letter to a friend:

> Yesterday (Christmas Day) we were invited to breakfast with Grand Duke Nicholas. A Court function in Russia is the most royal that you can imagine—no half measures about it! The Grand Duke is an adorably handsome man, quite extraordinarily and obviously a Grand Duke. He measures 6 feet 5 inches, and is worshipped by every soldier in the Army.... In the middle of the déjeuner the Grand Duke got up, and everyone else did the same, and they toasted us! The Grand Duke made a speech about our "gallantry," etc., etc., and everyone raised glasses and bowed to one. Nothing in a play could have been more of a real fine sort of scene. And certainly S. Macnaughtan in her wildest dreams hadn't thought of anything so wonderful as being toasted in Russia by the Imperial Staff.[56]

While the Russians were advancing in Persia, the situation on the main Caucasian Front against the Ottoman Empire had been stable since the Grand Duke took up the post of Viceroy, with Russia enjoying a slight advantage on the main front line, then located between Sarykamysh and Erzerum in eastern Turkey. This was about to change.

Bulgaria had entered the war on the side of Russia's enemies in October 1915, and the British had evacuated Gallipoli in December. Together, these events had freed up large numbers of Ottoman troops in western Turkey that could now move east to combat Russia. With this in mind, General Iudenich wished to launch a preemptive attack before the enemy's reinforcements could arrive. In late December, Iudenich traveled to Tiflis to ask the Grand Duke for permission. Nikolai Nikolaevich was initially reluctant, but he eventually agreed.[57] By 27 December (9 January), Iudenich was ready and telegraphed the Grand Duke to ask whether he could start the attack. According to Palitsyn, "The Grand Duke hesitated." Palitsyn and Bolkhovitinov insisted that the offensive should go ahead, and the Grand Duke conceded: Iudenich could begin his attack.[58]

The Russian offensive began the next day, 28 December (10 January). Despite the winter conditions, it was a great success. After six days of fighting, the Ottoman army abandoned its positions and withdrew, having lost some 25,000 men, compared with 10,000 men for the Russians.[59] The Ottoman troops fell back on the fortress of Erzerum, the most powerful strongpoint on the entire front. The Russians pursued, and on 6 (19) January 1916, the Chief of Staff of the First Caucasian Army Corps, Major General V. G. Lastochkin, telegraphed to ask for permission to storm Erzerum on the run with the forward elements of the corps before the enemy could organize his defenses. Grand Duke Nikolai Nikolaevich refused. "The decision was correct," Palitsyn claimed later. Being so far away, the Grand Duke could not on the basis of a single telegram order an assault on a major fortress, Palitsyn wrote.[60]

Operations now paused for a short while, as Iudenich brought the mass of the Caucasus Army up to Erzerum. Iudenich was convinced that the Ottoman forces had been so severely weakened by his offensive that they would not be able to defend the fortress effectively. He asked for permission to mount a full-scale assault on Erzerum.

Reconstructing exactly what happened thereafter is difficult due to the self-serving nature of most of the extant accounts, as well as their strong anti-Grand Duke bias. The most common version, based on a description by Iudenich's chief of operations, General E. V. Maslovskii, is that the Grand Duke opposed an assault on the fortress, due to its strong defenses and the negative political consequences of a failed attack. The Caucasus Army had exhausted most of its supplies during its offensive. To attack Erzerum, it would need to strip the Kars fortress of its ammunition. Should the operation go wrong, the Caucasus Front as a whole would be almost entirely without strategic reserves. According to Maslovskii, Palitsyn considered this too risky and advised the Grand Duke against it. As a result, the Grand Duke forbade Iudenich to take the ammunition from Kars or to storm Erzerum.[61]

Maslovskii's memoirs are the main source for stories about the Grand Duke's role in these events, but they must be read with a degree of caution because Maslovskii gave himself the dominant role in making the decision to attack the fortress and because, as Maslovskii admitted, his relations with the Grand Duke were not good. Maslovskii claimed that he carried out a reconnaissance and realized that the Ottoman defenses were much weaker than previously imagined. He therefore urged Iudenich to storm the fortress. Iudenich insisted that he could only do this with the Grand Duke's permission and telephoned Bolkhovitinov in order to get it. Eventually, after Iudenich insisted, the Grand Duke conceded, permitted the assault, and allowed the ammunition to be brought forward from Kars.[62]

Maslovskii claimed that even after the decision was taken, General Palitsyn came to Iudenich's headquarters to try to stop the operation, calling it "madness."[63] General Shatilov, who was also on Iudenich's staff, confirmed this in his memoirs, adding, "Even after permission had been given to storm the Turkish fortress, the Grand Duke and his entourage didn't stop trying to hinder the operation."[64]

In his diaries, however, Palitsyn makes no mention of either the Grand Duke's or his own opposition to the planned assault. He wrote only that he had agreed with the Grand Duke's original decision on 6 (19) January not to allow Lastochkin to assault Erzerum on the run, and that when he later broached the subject (storming Erzerum) with the Grand Duke, the latter told him that "this is the business of the Commander-in-Chief [i.e., Iudenich]. He knows, he leads, he prepares, and we will give him and do for him whatever he demands."[65]

According to Palitsyn, the Grand Duke visited Iudenich's headquarters in the town of Gasan Kala in the middle of January, and the decision to storm Erzerum was made either there and then or soon afterward, although on this Palitsyn was a little vague. On 19 January (1 February), he recorded, "the operation of the storm is decided, but I don't remember on what date and the telegram was prepared without me."[66]

Other records indicate that the Grand Duke did indeed visit Iudenich's headquarters on 19 January (1 February). A telegram from Bolkhovitinov to Iudenich on 16 (29) January noted that the Grand Duke, accompanied by Palitsyn, an adjutant, and Doctor Malama, would arrive in Karaurgan on 17 (30) January and then move on to Sarykamysh, reaching Gasan Kala on 19 January (1 February).[67] Other telegrams followed, stating that the Grand Duke wanted "no greetings, no honor guards, everybody should get on with their work."[68]

Putting this all together would suggest with near certainty that the Grand Duke did reject the original request to assault Erzerum on 6 (19) January, but this was not the same as rejecting the full-scale assault that Iudenich proposed a little later, and Maslovskii's description of events seems somewhat inaccurate. The Grand Duke does appear to have had severe doubts about the attack. According to Prince Roman Petrovich, Nikolai Nikolaevich felt that it would be better to wait for reinforcements, and he delayed a day before giving his consent to the operation.[69] But Maslovskii's claim that the Grand Duke outright rejected the plan (if only initially) is hardly substantiated, and it seems that by 19 January (1 February), after traveling to see Iudenich, the Grand Duke had given the plan his approval.

Iudenich undoubtedly deserves most of the credit for what was to follow;

the idea to storm Erzerum was Iudenich's, as was the execution. All that the Grand Duke did was to give his approval but his decision was important, and it proved to be the correct one. The result was one of the greatest Russian victories of the war.

Erzerum's defenses consisted of an inner core of 11 forts and batteries with two more forts on each flank. Field fortifications, including trenches and wire, covered the ground between the forts. Fully manning the defenses required about 75,000 men and 1,000 guns, but after their losses in previous weeks, the Ottomans had no more than 50,000 men and 300–400 guns. Still, the fortress's defenses were strong, and although Iudenich had an advantage in numbers (having about 80,000 men at his disposal), it was not so great as to make victory certain.[70]

Iudenich's plan was to avoid the main line of fortifications to the east of the city and instead to strike from the north over the Kargapazar ridge, which had been left undefended as the Ottomans considered it impassable, due to both the steep terrain and the winter weather. The attack on Erzerum started on 29 January (11 February) 1916. Hundreds of Russians froze to death trying to cross the Kargapazar Ridge, but others succeeded. By 1 (14) February, they had outflanked most of the fortress's defenses, and the next day the Ottoman troops began abandoning their positions. Early on the morning of 3 (16) February, the Russians entered the city. Erzerum had fallen.[71]

According to Prince Roman Petrovich, "When the news of the capture of Erzerum reached Tiflis ... a jubilant crowd gathered outside the palace.... Uncle Nikolasha opened the window. When the crowd saw him, a deafening cheer rang out." The Grand Duke ordered an adjutant to invite a delegation from the crowd into the palace, and representatives of the town council and social organizations came in. Mayor Khatisov made a patriotic speech, and "Uncle Nikolasha gave a short reply, praising the heroism of the Caucasus Army." A group of Georgians then presented the Grand Duke with some wine, which he drained in one go.[72] "The town and the palace were in some sort of daze," Palitsyn wrote. "It was the sort of joy which was capable of completely deranging both a man's body and his mind."[73] "The environment in which the Grand Duke is living is dragging him into raptures, and it is very difficult to free him from this," he wrote a little later. "The third, fourth and subsequent days of February were complete madness in terms of the degree of agitation and rapture." The ecstatic mood was bound to lead to mistakes, Palitsyn felt, adding, "I feel sorry for the Grand Duke. He feels this himself sometimes, but then he bends and agrees to things he should not agree to. This habitual manner of deciding operational matters has worked for the good in the past, but will bring harm in the future."[74]

On 7 (20) February, the Grand Duke left Tiflis to visit Erzerum in person. His train took him as far as Kars. From there he and his entourage went by car to Erzerum, spending the night at Iudenich's headquarters. The next morning, the Grand Duke received a delegation, which brought him symbolic keys to the town. He then inspected troops on the square outside the headquarters, gave out medals to soldiers who had fought in the assault of the fortress, and passed in review a line of soldiers bearing captured Ottoman flags. This done, he went by car with Iudenich to inspect the fortress. Photographs taken by Prince Roman Petrovich, who accompanied them, show the Grand Duke and Iudenich standing in their car, parked on tightly packed snow, saluting the troops. Roman Petrovich recorded that when they drove back to Kars at the end of the day, "My uncle was in the best of moods."[75]

The capture of Erzerum further enhanced the Grand Duke's reputation in Russia. On 17 February (1 March) 1916, the Imperial Court in Petrograd told the Grand Duke's personal office that the press was requesting pictures of the Grand Duke and permission to publish them. The Court asked the Grand Duke's staff to speak to him to get permission more quickly.[76] In the public eye, Grand Duke Nikolai Nikolaevich rather than General Iudenich was the man responsible for the victory at Erzerum. General Laguiche noted that, at Stavka, "The officers' attachment to their former Supreme Commander, a rare thing, almost unique, remains the same at Supreme Headquarters. The officers on learning the news accosted one another and congratulated each other that, 'At least the Grand Duke has had this satisfaction.' Nobody even mentions General Iudenich."[77]

The question now arose of how best to exploit the victory at Erzerum. According to Palitsyn, on 12 (25) February, Iudenich came to Tiflis to brief the Grand Duke on a proposal to allow the army to recover from its losses in the recent campaign and rebuild its supplies. He suggested leaving a small vanguard to cover the approaches to Erzerum and withdrawing the rest of the army to the rear to enable it to regain its strength. Listening to this, wrote Palitsyn, "The Grand Duke said nothing," limiting himself to asking Palitsyn, Ianushkevich, and Bolkhovitinov for their opinions. Palitsyn expressed the view that resting was "morally unacceptable," and that the army should advance rapidly to exploit its victory and smash the Ottoman army while it was on the run.[78] Palitsyn claimed that the Grand Duke agreed with him. The outcome was a compromise: the army would advance, but with fewer forces than Palitsyn had hoped.[79]

The renewed Russian offensive made good progress. On 17 February (1 March), Iudenich's army captured the town of Bitlis, south of Erzerum. Meanwhile, the expeditionary corps in Persia was also advancing. On 13

(26) February, Baratov's troops took Kermanshah, and on 6 (19) March they entered the main German stronghold in Isfahan.[80] With this, the campaign to secure Persia reached a successful conclusion.

The Russian victories created some difficulties of an administrative nature. A large part of the population of eastern Turkey fled in the wake of the Russian advance, while those who remained suffered from food shortages. On 17 February (1 March), the Grand Duke wrote to the Council of Ministers that it was necessary to do something about this "for political and health reasons, and to secure the rear of our army." He noted that in one region there were 35 Turkish villages whose inhabitants "urgently needed food aid." He requested that the Council of Ministers give him the necessary credits to provide it.[81] War Minister Polivanov replied, however, that the Caucasus Army should pay for the aid out of its own funds.[82]

A month later, the Grand Duke issued an order about the use of abandoned land, decreeing that local inhabitants could use such land as long as they left some untouched in case the owners returned. The Grand Duke also encouraged the return of Armenian refugees to their lands. Together, he hoped, these measures would serve "to decrease our supply of food aid to the local population to a minimum, and to provide for our forces from local resources."[83] The Grand Duke rejected, however, a proposal to settle refugees from Galicia on the conquered lands. This followed earlier proposals from Agriculture Minister Krivoshein and General Iudenich to settle Russian colonists there.[84] Responding specifically to the suggestion about resettling refugees from Galicia, the Grand Duke remarked that the permanent loss of Galicia was not certain and that the refugees might in due course be able to return there. More significantly, though, the proposal, in his view, was based on a misperception that the Muslims of the Caucasus were unreliable and that Russian rule in the Caucasus required the settlement of Orthodox Slavs. "I completely reject" this view, the Grand Duke wrote, adding:

> One must bear in mind not individual episodes from the life of small border Muslim tribes, but the activity of the entire multi-million population of the Caucasus, which is strongly united with the state organism of Russia. Events of the current war have proved without doubt that the historic tribes of the Caucasus are loyal en masse to Russia, and honestly stand on guard to protect its interests.... I believe that attempts to colonize the Caucasus ... would cause confusion and discontent among the diverse local nationalities.[85]

On 17 (30) March, the Grand Duke issued an order concerning the protection of cultural artifacts. Many of these had come under Russian control as a result of the advance, he wrote, but he had received news that "ancient monuments are being thoughtlessly spoiled and destroyed, or, on the pretext of preserving them for science, are becoming objects of trade. Considering such actions completely impermissible, I declare that all ancient monuments without exception come under the protection of the state." This was to include churches, monasteries, mosques, historic civil and religious buildings, cemeteries, archives, libraries, museums, and their contents. The Grand Duke ordered that all of these be strictly guarded, and he forbade the buying, selling, or collection of ancient books, manuscripts, and engraved stones for any reason.[86]

As Iudenich's army marched further into Turkey, an opportunity arose to seize another prize, the port of Trebizond on the Black Sea coast. At the beginning of March, the Grand Duke traveled to Batum to meet the commander of the Black Sea Fleet, Admiral A. A. Eberhardt, and to discuss with him a plan to take Trebizond by landing two brigades by sea. On 17 (30) March, Palitsyn described the Grand Duke as "agitated" and irritated by a feeling that an opportunity had been lost after the capture of Erzerum to deal the Ottoman army a fatal blow. (Supposedly Nikolai Nikolaevich had said, "The victory wasn't exploited.") Palitsyn also noted that he was nervous about the risk of a naval landing and "the continuous presence of Iudenich" in Tiflis. As Palitsyn wrote at the time, "The Grand Duke's nervous mood results in him beginning to get involved in trivia and he gets irritated with people."[87]

Despite his anxiety, the Grand Duke ordered the operation against Trebizond to go ahead. On 22 and 23 March (4 and 5 April) 1916, twelve transport ships carrying two brigades of infantry (about 5,000 men) left the port of Novorossiisk, protected by two cruisers and four destroyers. On 26 March (8 April), the troops landed on the Turkish coast just east of Trebizond. From there, they moved along the shoreline, reaching the front line two days later. On 31 March (13 April), they began their attack, supported by Russian naval guns. The Ottoman defenses soon collapsed, and on 5 (18) April, the Russian army entered Trebizond.[88]

By now, the Russians had advanced far from their home bases and lacked the ability to pursue their defeated enemy much further, while Ottoman reinforcements were arriving from Gallipoli. Furthermore, the British in Mesopotamia were about to suffer a humiliating reversal, allowing the initiative to slip back into Ottoman hands. The first six months of the Grand Duke's tenure as Viceroy had brought nothing but victory. In the summer of 1916, for a brief moment these victories would appear to be under threat.

CHAPTER 21

Governing the Caucasus, May 1916–February 1917

DESPITE ITS MANY DEFEATS, the Ottoman army was far from finished, and by spring 1916 it was on the verge of a spectacular victory against the British Empire. In late 1915, a British force under Major General Charles Townshend had advanced up the Tigris River from Basra, reaching a point just south of Baghdad before being forced to retreat to the town of Kut-al-Amara. There the British force of about 13,000 men dug in, only to find itself surrounded shortly afterward.

All attempts to relieve the garrison in Kut failed. By March 1916 the British had been cut off for nearly four months, supplies were running low, and it seemed certain that the garrison could not hold out much longer. In a desperate attempt to help his allies, on 19 March (1 April) Grand Duke Nikolai Nikolaevich ordered General Baratov to march out of Persia into Mesopotamia toward Baghdad, to try to pull Ottoman forces away from Kut.[1]

The operation was not a success. Baratov's initial objective was the town of Khanaqin (nowadays just on the Iraqi side of the Iran–Iraq border). Baratov reached it on 12 (25) April but confronted a large Ottoman force, which halted his advance. Four days later, he received news that the British at Kut had surrendered. Baratov ordered a retreat back to Persia.[2]

Perhaps bearing the Grand Duke's help to the British in mind, on 9 (22) April General Hanbury Williams telegraphed Lord Kitchener and recommended that Britain make the Grand Duke honorary colonel of a regiment of hussars. Hanbury Williams also noted that the Tsar retained a very positive view of Nikolai Nikolaevich. "He always speaks to me of his admiration of the G. D.," he wrote, "and told me 'in confidence' last night that later on he will make him a field marshal.... He is delighted at the idea of the G. D. being made an Hon. Col."[3]

The Grand Duke never got his field marshal's baton. Nor did he get his honorary colonelcy. On 3 (16) May, Kitchener replied, saying that it was impossible. "I saw the King last night," he wrote, "and he was much exercised at your proposal that the Grand Duke should be given a Cavalry Regiment.... The King pointed out that no British regiment had ever been given to anyone other than a sovereign or heir apparent and he did not like any alteration in this rule as it might lead to difficulties in the future."[4]

On 26 April (9 May), delegates from across the Caucasus assembled in Tiflis at the Grand Duke's invitation for a conference to discuss his proposal to establish zemstva in the region. Nikolai Nikolaevich hosted the delegates for lunch at his palace, where he proposed a toast to the Tsar and opened the conference with a short speech.[5] In this he told the delegates,

> Having assumed the post of Viceroy ... I reached the conclusion that to enhance the productive forces of this most wealthy part of the Russian State, we must develop as soon as possible its population's independence, so that, inspired by a love of the region, its labor should have a productive character.... Personally, I expect a lot for the Caucasus from the future zemstva, believing that only by the joint labors of government and zemstvo institutions can creative work be carried out in future years.[6]

The conference lasted several days, and the Grand Duke was pleased with its results.[7] On the final day of the conference, he addressed the delegates again, thanking them for their work and promising that legislation to create zemstva would now go forward.[8] The Grand Duke's talk of the "population's independence" and the "joint labors" of government and society indicated that, although he was still not a liberal, he had come to recognize that the state had to share some power with the people. He had acknowledged this back in 1905, when he had urged the Tsar to accept the October Manifesto, but then the acknowledgment had been forced. Now it rested on more positive conviction.

Nikolai Nikolaevich also endeavored to reform the administration of the Caucasus Army. "From the first days of my arrival in the Caucasus, it was clear to me that the army's rear and its supply were managed in a scandalous fashion," he told the Tsar. Part of the problem was the poor state of the roads and the railways. "I have done everything possible to improve the capacity of the Caucasus railway," he said. He had asked to be given control of the main line in the Caucasus, the Vladikavkaz Railway, but this had been denied to him, "and, as I predicted, chaos now reigns." The Grand Duke also cast some of the blame on General Iudenich who, he claimed, resisted change in the supply system and with whom "there had been conflict." Still, Nikolai Nikolaevich noted, "General Iudenich possesses many qualities which exceed his deficiencies, and so I keep him." "God's help is already clear. And that is *everything*," the Grand Duke concluded. He closed with the words, "Your loyal subject, who fervently loves you, Nikolasha."[9]

The war had put a severe strain on the Russian economy and in particular on the railway system, which proved incapable of supplying the needs of both the army and the civilian population. By early 1916, the Caucasus, along with the rest of the Russian Empire, was suffering from food shortages. Harvests in 1915 and 1916 were quite good, but transportation bottlenecks and a so-called "scissors crisis" (in which growers were unwilling to sell their produce because prices for food were low, whereas prices for manufactured goods were high) prevented much of the harvest from coming to market.[10] Grand Duke Nikolai Nikolaevich had little, if any, control over this situation and considered that the food shortages could have "serious consequences both for the army and for the Caucasus region."[11] Indeed, in February 1916, protests against food shortages led to riots in Baku and "the looting of 116 retail establishments and three million rubles of damage to local businesses." After the city governor ignored orders to tell troops to fire on the rioters, Nikolai Nikolaevich telegraphed him to obey his orders and to use "the most decisive means" in order to end the troubles. The governor obeyed, the troops fired on the rioters, and the troubles came to an end.[12]

The Grand Duke urged the population of the Caucasus to stay calm. After the victory at Erzerum, he thanked it for its contribution to the war effort, expressing his hope that the food situation would improve. "Not only the soldier, but also the civilian who remains behind him participates in a victory such as that at Erzerum," he said. "I am convinced that the inhabitants of Tiflis will quietly wait for the moment when it will be possible to acquire more food at a low price."[13]

The shortages affected the army as well as civilians. In February 1916, General Palitsyn wrote, "in my view, [the situation in the rear] is absolutely abnormal.... The Grand Duke also inclines to the view that it is abnormal."[14] "The Grand Duke ... understands this," Palitsyn wrote, "but because of some inexplicable property of his character does nothing about it."[15]

In May 1916, the Grand Duke did at last act, issuing an order instructing commanders to take "all available measures" to improve the situation. These were to include "immediate measures" to improve the roads and to reorganize transports.[16] This, however, did little more than urge commanders to do what they should have been doing anyway. A more comprehensive reform did not come until 19 June (2 July) 1916, when the Grand Duke finally issued an order reorganizing the management of the army's rear.

This order, which Palitsyn recorded that he drafted,[17] transferred responsibility for the army's supply from corps to army level. The Grand Duke ordered that the Army Chief of Supply take responsibility not merely for overseeing but also for commanding the army's rear services. A new Directorate of the Army Chief of Supply was created, which would control all transport resources.[18] In due course, the Grand Duke appointed General Ianushkevich as the Chief of Supply to take charge of this new system.[19] Palitsyn considered this a mistake but noted, the Grand Duke "believes in him [Ianushkevich]."[20]

It would not seem that the army's supply situation improved in any noticeable way as a result of these new measures. In October 1916, the Grand Duke wrote to the Tsar that "The Turks are weakened but so are we. The main cause of our weakness is that we don't eat enough."[21] A report by the head of the army reserve in the same month commented, "Allowances get worse every day. Part of the reserve does not receive a significant part of its ration every day.... Some days there is no hot food at all.... Hunger has given birth to criminality of unforeseen proportions.... There is no firewood closer than ten versts from the reserve bivouacs. People are badly dressed, some do not even have underwear."[22]

Nevertheless, the Russian army continued to perform well. Exploiting their victories at Gallipoli and Kut, in spring 1916 the Ottomans had reinforced their army facing Iudenich in eastern Turkey. On 14 (29) May, they began an offensive that succeeded in advancing a short way toward Erzerum before halting in early June. After a pause of about ten days, the Ottomans attacked again in mid-June.[23] They also commenced a counter-attack against Baratov's expeditionary corps, pursuing him into Persia.[24]

Facing this dual threat, the Grand Duke sent General Palitsyn to urge General Iudenich to start an offensive of his own. According to Palitsyn, Iudenich had previously refused to do this, but faced with the Grand Duke's insistence he now conceded, although the shortage of supplies delayed him from starting the attack until 19 June (2 July).[25] After nearly a week's hard fighting, by 25 June (8 July) the Russians had broken through the main Ottoman line, and the Ottoman troops were retreating rapidly to the east.[26] The Russian army had again won a significant victory.

Meanwhile, the issue had arisen of what to do with conquered Turkish territory after the war. On 14 (27) June, Foreign Minister Sergei Sazonov wrote to the Grand Duke about the future of the occupied lands. "The greatest difficulty with the issue at hand consists of resolving the Armenian question," he wrote. He was not, he said, in favor of creating an autonomous Armenia under Russia rule, or of favoring the Armenians over other groups, particularly Muslim ones.[27]

On 3 (16) July, the Grand Duke replied to Sazonov, "I fully agree with you," and he added,

> It is my firm opinion that the Armenian question is completely absent within the current boundaries of the Russian empire, and we should not even permit it to be mentioned, as Armenians who are Russian subjects in the Viceroyalty are Russian subjects with the same rights as Muslims, Georgians, and Russians. I consider that the authorities in the region entrusted to me must strive to treat all nationalities equally, without exception.... In essence the Armenian question exists only outside the pre-war boundaries of the empire, that is in the Turkish regions conquered by us.... Russia must consider the suffering inflicted during the course of the war on the Armenians as a result of Muslim oppression. There can be no doubt that in reconstructing the conquered regions of Turkey the principles of legality and justice and complete impartiality toward all nationalities inhabiting the region must be strictly observed.[28]

On 22 June (5 July), the Grand Duke wrote to the Tsar asking him for financial assistance for his chief civilian advisor, Prince Vladimir Orlov. At the Tsar's behest Orlov had invested a large sum of his own money into developing a railway in the Voronezh region of southern Russia. This had left him facing "complete ruin." The Grand Duke asked the Tsar to help Orlov. "We need well chosen people here," he wrote, "and the most important is the chief. I have it in the form of Vladi. If I lose him, I lose all."[29]

Back at the front, on 30 June (13 July) Baratov abandoned Kermanshah and withdrew deeper into Persia.[30] On the main front in eastern Turkey, however, Iudenich's army was continuing to advance. On 4 (17) July, it captured the town of Baiburt and on 12 (25) July, Erzindzhan. This was to mark almost the furthest extent of the Russian advance during the war.

In light of the good news, Nikolai Nikolaevich decided to visit the scenes of his army's victories. On 15 (28) July, he set out from Tiflis for Baiburt with a suite of 11 persons,[31] including General Laguiche, who was visiting from Stavka and reported that the Grand Duke "constantly underlined his feelings for our country [France]."[32]

From Baiburt, the Grand Duke and his party traveled on to Trebizond, where they were met on 18 (31) July by the town commandant General A. V. Shvarts. Both Shvarts and his wife, who was in Trebizond with him, left accounts of the Grand Duke's visit.

On arrival, according to the general, the Grand Duke went straight to the house of the town mayor, where he met the mayor and the local Greek orthodox priest, the latter of whom gave him a speech of greetings in Greek, to which the Grand Duke replied in French, thanking him for the welcome. The Grand Duke then rested until evening, when he received a report from the general about the state of the region's defenses.[33] The next day, the Grand Duke inspected the Bos-Tepe heights above the port, viewed the shore batteries, attended a service at the local Greek Orthodox Church, reviewed troops of the Kars Regiment, and had lunch on the side of a mountain overlooking the port. After lunch he visited the town's land defenses, before ending the tour with a trip to the local hospital.[34]

Mrs. Shvarts, in her account, reversed the order of events. In her version, the Grand Duke went first to the church for a short service, and then to the hospital, where he met his niece Princess Marina Petrovna, who was working there as a nurse. Seeing her, wrote Mrs. Shvarts, "The Grand Duke tenderly kissed her and stroked her cheek." The Grand Duke then drove up a newly constructed road to the top of the Bos-Tepe heights, where he inspected troops from the Kars Regiment and had lunch on the mountainside.[35] The lunch tent had a magnificent view of Trebizond and the sea beyond and, Mrs. Shvarts commented, was decorated "with greens, flowers, and flags.... The air was wonderful, with neither stuffiness nor dust."[36] "It's so nice that I don't want to leave," the Grand Duke said.[37] After lunch, Nikolai Nikolaevich continued his inspection of the local fortifications and ended his day with a visit to a mosque.[38]

Early the next morning, 20 July (2 August), the Grand Duke left Trebizond and visited Erzindzhan, where he reviewed some of the troops who had seized the town. Among those present was a junior Cossack officer, F. I. Eliseev, who recorded the scene in his memoirs several decades later. "The Grand Duke," wrote Eliseev, "was dressed in a gray *cherkeska*, a black *beshmet* [a quilted jacket worn under the *cherkeska*] and a tall gray astrakhan *papakha* [fur hat] cocked slightly backward. His right hand lay invariably on the handle of a Caucasian saber. He didn't smile at all and was very pensive. It seemed to me then that he felt very tired."[39]

From Erzindzhan, the Grand Duke headed back to Tiflis. Upon arrival, he had to deal with potential unrest among Muslims of the Caucasus. Recognizing the political difficulties that conscripting Muslims for military service might cause, the Russian Empire had refrained from doing so. Although some Muslims had volunteered to join the army and had formed an entire division, the so-called "Savage Division,"[40] most Muslims in the Empire were not directly engaged in war-related work, and by summer 1916 the Empire was in need of their services.

On 25 June (8 July) 1916, the Tsar issued a decree conscripting Muslims for non-military service in labor battalions. The move was immensely unpopular. Within weeks, armed uprisings began among the Muslims of Turkestan.[41]

Grand Duke Nikolai Nikolaevich considered himself a friend of the Caucasus's Muslims, and he wished to avoid the unrest that had broken out in Turkestan. On 24 July (6 August) 1916, he wrote to the Tsar to inform him that issues concerning the Muslims had to be dealt with very carefully. The decree on labor conscription had created "ferment," he said, adding, "Muslims consider themselves insulted by being conscripted for labor, which they consider shameful, especially those who think that they are capable of military service. Every measure concerning the Muslim population requires a lot of preparatory measures before being enacted, which in turn requires a lot of time. Unfortunately, I was not warned about this population's labor conscription and could not prepare for it." It would be best, the Grand Duke continued, to permit those Muslims willing to volunteer for military service to do so, to which end the army should form separate Muslim units, which would be used not against fellow Muslims on the Turkish front but only against Germany and Austria-Hungary. Those Muslims not willing to serve in the army could be used for labor, but "only in the form of a voluntary appeal to them with a call to work to help the army." Anything else could cause violent disturbances.[42]

On 30 July (12 August), the Grand Duke received replies from General Alekseev and the Deputy Minister of War, General P. A. Frolov. Alekseev rejected the Grand Duke's suggestion about forming Muslim military units. There were, he said, insufficient officers for such units, as well as "insufficient numbers of horses, weapons, and clothes."[43] Frolov, however, informed the Grand Duke that he could determine for himself how to implement the conscription decree.[44] The Grand Duke replied that he would act accordingly.[45]

Following this exchange, on 9 (22) August the Grand Duke issued an appeal to the people of the Caucasus. He worded the appeal carefully to avoid mention of any specific ethnic or religious groups:

> During two years of war, the nations living in the Caucasus have given several heroes to our incomparable and brilliant armed forces. History will never forget what has given even more glory to the already celebrated Caucasus.
>
> The Sovereign Emperor has ordered the recruitment of new warriors, so that after solid training, when the need becomes manifest, they can join the army and vanquish the enemy.
>
> .... It is the turn of the population of the Caucasus to make the sacrifice in the name of the general good.... I am convinced that all new recruits will fulfill their duty with respect for the Tsar and their country.... I will be delighted to report to the Sovereign Emperor that the inhabitants of the Caucasus will accomplish their duty with enthusiasm and pleasure.[46]

By now, the situation in Persia had deteriorated further. Baratov's corps suffered terribly during its retreat from Mesopotamia: "great numbers of horses died, and ... hundreds of men fell out, stricken with malaria, dysentery, and sun stroke." On 28 July (10 August), the Ottoman army captured Hamadan.[47] The Grand Duke dispatched one regiment of reinforcements to Persia, but more could not be spared. "Within the limits of the strength available to me, everything which can be done to strengthen our forces in Persia has been done," he informed the Ministry of Foreign Affairs.[48]

By now, Baratov had only about 7,000 men capable of fighting. The situation in Persia appeared critical. Fortunately for the Russians, the Ottoman troops were almost equally debilitated, and after seizing Hamadan they halted their advance.[49] Simultaneously, major operations stopped on the main Turkish front, both sides having exhausted themselves in the battles of the previous months. During the final months of 1916 the front was by and large quiet, but General Palitsyn recorded that the Grand Duke remained nervous. "Our dispositions are unsuited for defense and the Grand Duke knows this," he wrote on 2 (15) September. "With good reason he crosses himself every time a telegram announces 'all quiet.' But there is nothing he can do. He telegraphs Iudenich often, but the matter remains essentially untouched."[50]

September 1916 marked the Grand Duke's first anniversary as Viceroy of the Caucasus. On 23 September (6 October), he sent the Tsar a detailed report of his year's activities, rating his own achievements highly. "I allow myself to say that I have already achieved several positive results," he told the Tsar. Still, he had become aware of many problems. As he noted, "Even a superficial acquaintance with the Caucasus has convinced me that broad reforms are needed in the area of local life." In particular, land reform was necessary, as land was very unevenly distributed and large tracts of it lay unused. Trade and industry were weak, and the railway network needed further development. Government administration was poorly staffed; and civil servants were badly paid and lived in poverty, a situation the Grand Duke considered "impermissible."

The Grand Duke commented, "One of the most reliable means of raising the well-being of the Caucasus ... is, in my opinion, the development of the population's initiative." It was this idea that had propelled him to draw up the plan to establish zemstva.

The Grand Duke also wrote that he had taken measures to improve education; he had sent a proposal to the Duma for a law to create a polytechnic institute in Tiflis, had added studies in agriculture and forestry to the curricula at the institutes in Krasnodar and New Alexandria, and had opened a medical faculty for women in Tiflis. He was also stepping up railway construction, including building a line from Batum to Trebizond.

There were, he noted, serious tensions between different national and religious groups in the region, especially Muslims and Armenians. Reducing these tensions was extremely important in the Grand Duke's opinion, to which end the government needed to maintain one guiding principle—"to treat all nationalities in the Caucasus identically."

The Grand Duke then outlined his views on the main Caucasian nationalities. Georgians he considered "lazy." The Armenians were the most capable of the Caucasian peoples, he believed, but their national cohesiveness meant that they posed potential political problems for the Russian Empire. By contrast, he believed that "One [could not] doubt the firm bonds between the Caucasus's Muslims and Russia." The Grand Duke's main concern was the Muslim clergy. These were for the most part educated in the Ottoman Empire or Persia, from where they brought hostile political ideas into Russia. At present Muslim schools were in very poor condition, and this situation encouraged Muslims to go abroad to study. Catholics and Armenians in the Caucasus had their own religious schools, and the Grand Duke concluded, "It is my deep conviction that there is no basis for preventing the creation of similar schools for Russian Muslims, but, on the contrary, we should encourage their establishment, assigning the necessary resources from the treasury."[51]

The Grand Duke's report ignored one of the most immediate problems facing the Caucasus—the continuing shortages of food,[52] which continued to worsen. In January 1917, "the town of Kutaisi went without bread for a fortnight," while "hunger was rife in Tbilisi and other cities, and deaths from famine occurred in country districts."[53] Because of these conditions and because of his order to the governor of Baku to fire on rioters in February 1916, the Grand Duke has been denounced in a recent history as "indifferent to the local mood." "With his military-minded approach to administrative problems," Firouzeh Mostashari complains, Nikolai Nikolaevich "was unable to strike a balance between reform and repression" and instead "alienated the local population by opting for force."[54]

This charge is unfair. Certainly, in his report to the Tsar, the Grand Duke glossed over some serious problems and trumpeted his successes more than the situation justified. Nevertheless, good news outweighed bad. On the military side, recent reverses in Persia notwithstanding, Nikolai Nikolaevich's troops had won a succession of victories. And on the civilian side, he had proved himself an energetic Viceroy, pushing forward reform proposals and taking an even-handed stance on nationalities issues. His policies were more liberal than Mostashari makes out, involved much more than violent repression, and appear to have won over at least part of the Caucasian population. In May 1916, the Tsar received a report from the Caucasus, which, he told his wife, noted that "the native tribes have become much more loyal than they were before, and they attribute this to the influence of the august cousin [Nikolasha]."[55] Indeed, the Caucasus managed to avoid the armed uprisings that struck Turkestan in summer 1916. Nikolai Nikolaevich had good reason to be pleased with his first year in office.

He was rather more anxious about the state of the Empire as a whole. Although in June 1915, in an effort to reach out to liberal public opinion, the Tsar had agreed to change some ministers and recall the Duma, he had since reversed direction. Most notably in February 1916 he had replaced Prime Minister Goremykin with Boris Sturmer, a man whose reactionary views and German name did little to endear him to the Russian public. Discontent with the government was growing and the prospect of revolution appeared increasingly real.

On 5 (18) October, Chaplain Shavelskii came to Tiflis from Stavka to visit the Grand Duke. Arriving around midnight, Shavelskii expected to find that the Grand Duke had already gone to bed, but instead he found Nikolai Nikolaevich, Pyotr Nikolaevich, and their wives waiting for him in the lobby of the Viceroy's palace. Nikolai Nikolaevich gave Shavelskii an icon of Saint Nino, who brought Christianity to Georgia in the fourth century AD, and took him up to his room, asking him "How is the Emperor?" "His Majesty has ordered me to pass on his greetings," the chaplain replied. "The Emperor didn't say anything else?" the Grand Duke asked. "It seemed to me that I greatly offended him with my negative response," Shavelskii wrote later. "Evidently, the Grand Duke expected something more serious and warm than a simple sending of greetings."[56]

Shavelskii stayed in Tiflis for two days, spending a great deal of time talking with Nikolai Nikolaevich, who expressed his fears that the country was on the brink of collapse. The Grand Duke was not alone in these concerns. In the middle of October, General Alekseev drafted a letter to the Emperor warning him of impending disaster. "Your Imperial Majesty," the letter read, "I consider that the minute has come when I am obliged to report the true state of affairs to You. The whole rear of the army ... is in a state of ferment.... All this is leading slowly, but steadily, toward an inevitable outburst of stormy emotions among the people."[57]

Alekseev was not the only person warning the Emperor. Nikolasha's cousin Grand Duke Nikolai Mikhailovich visited the Emperor at the start of November and gave him two letters, which apparently contained accusations of some sort against the Empress.[58] Aleksandra Fedorovna was most indignant. She was "utterly disgusted" by Nikolai Mikhailovich's letters, she told her husband. "He and Nikolasha are my greatest enemies in the family, not counting the black women."[59]

On 17 (30) October, Nikolai Nikolaevich wrote to the Tsar. He thanked him for conceding to him on the issue of Muslim conscription. "Everyone is overjoyed," he wrote. "I hope to have about 80,000 Muslim volunteers for labor." He then asked for a personal audience at Stavka. "I will report to you personally," he wrote. "I repeat, a personal and direct report is required."[60]

The Emperor agreed to the audience, and the Grand Duke arrived in Mogilev on 7 (20) November. Various members of the staff met him at the train station, and having greeted them, Nikolai Nikolaevich invited Chaplain Shavelskii to speak to him in private in his wagon. Shavelskii recorded that he told the Grand Duke that he had recently warned the Emperor about Prime Minister Sturmer and Rasputin. "You did well to speak to the Emperor," the Grand Duke supposedly replied. "But the problem is not Sturmer, not [Interior Minister A. D.] Protopopov, and not even Rasputin, but her, only her. Take her away, put her in a monastery, and the Emperor will become a completely different person."[61]

After talking with Shavelskii, the Grand Duke visited Nicholas II himself. "N. has arrived with Petiusha today," the Emperor wrote to the Empress. "He has not changed, and looks well in his cherkeska."[62] Unfortunately, the Emperor did not reveal what he discussed with Nikolai Nikolaevich, who stayed at Stavka for two days. For the most part, it seems to have been matters related to the Caucasus. But shortly before leaving, the Grand Duke apparently broached the topic of Russia's internal politics. Grand Duke Andrei Vladimirovich wrote that Nikolai Nikolaevich later told him this:

> I spoke with Nicky in a very sharp manner.... He just said nothing and shrugged his shoulders. I told him straight: "It would be more pleasant if you swore at me, struck me, chased me out of here, rather than say nothing. Don't you see that you will lose your crown? Come to your senses before it's too late. Install a responsible ministry.... Are you not ashamed to have believed that I wanted to overthrow you? You have known all your life how devoted I am to you, I inherited this from my father and my forefathers, and you could suspect me! I am ashamed for you, Nicky!"[63]

Shavelskii claimed that just before he left, Nikolai Nikolaevich took him to one side and recounted his final meeting with the Emperor. "I told him: 'The situation is catastrophic. We all want to help you, but we are powerless if you won't help yourself,'" the Grand Duke supposedly said. Then, pointing to the room occupied by Tsarevich Aleksei, the heir to the throne, the Grand Duke ostensibly said, "If you won't take pity on yourself, take pity on him." "The Emperor cried, embraced, and kissed me," the Grand Duke told Shavelskii, but he concluded, "Nothing will come of it!... It's all her fault."[64] The Grand Duke then left Stavka. He and the Emperor would never meet again.

We have no way of knowing how reliable Shavelskii's and Grand Duke Andrei Vladimirovich's accounts are, but it seems certain that Nikolai Nikolaevich did indeed say something along the lines they claimed. On 9 (22) November, the Dowager Empress Mariia Fedorovna recorded in her diary that Grand Duke Georgii Mikhailovich had told her, "We are on the threshold of revolution.... Let us hope that Nicky's conversations with four different people will open his eyes and bear fruit. Alekseev, Shavelskii, Nikolai [Grand Duke Nikolai Mikhailovich], and, finally, Nikolasha, whom it was evidently hardest and most unpleasant to listen to, have all told him the truth."[65] The Tsar could not claim that he had not been warned of the threat of revolution.

En route back to Tiflis, on 10 (23) November, Nikolai Nikolaevich stopped at Kiev, where he visited the Dowager Empress. "It was terrible to hear everything that he [Nikolasha] told my poor Nicky," she wrote in her diary after her meeting with the Grand Duke.[66]

Back at Kiev station after seeing the Empress, the Grand Duke had another meeting, this time with General V. I. Gurko, a son of the Gurko under whom Nikolai Nikolaevich had fought in the Russo-Turkish war. Gurko was traveling in the opposite direction and had stopped in Kiev en route to Stavka, where he was due to take over as Chief of Staff from General Alekseev, who was ill. Gurko later recorded:

> Although I had had the opportunity of seeing the Grand Duke in an official capacity, I had never had an unrestrained conversation with him.... But here I met a man extremely affable and frank, fully approving of my selection as a successor to General Alekseev.... The Grand Duke touched upon the personality of the Emperor and told me that the opinion circulated by the crowd did not give a proper impression of the man. The Grand Duke advised me to be fully frank with the Tsar in all things, and not to hide the reality with an idea of sparing him grief.[67]

After parting with Gurko, Grand Duke Nikolai Nikolaevich returned to Tiflis. There it appears that he became an accessory to treason.

In the late 1920s, details emerged of a supposed conspiracy in late 1916 and early 1917 to overthrow Nicholas II and put Grand Duke Nikolai Nikolaevich on the throne. Supposedly, when asked, the Grand Duke considered accepting the crown and, even though he finally declined, did not inform the authorities of the plot, an act of remarkable disloyalty.[68] On the face of it, the story seems improbable. The former commander of the Guards Corps, General V. M. Bezobrazov, who visited the Grand Duke in Tiflis in October 1916, recorded that Nikolai Nikolaevich remained absolutely loyal to the Emperor. "At 12 noon the Viceroy Grand Duke Nikolai Nikolaevich received me," Bezobrazov wrote in his diary. "After lunch we had a talk.... He talked about his loyalty to the Sovereign. He said: 'Should the Sovereign order me to jump out of this window, I would do so without hesitation.'"[69] Equally, if Grand Duke Andrei Vladimirovich's account of Nikolai Nikolaevich's last meeting with the Tsar is to be believed, in November 1916 Nikolai Nikolaevich had still considered the suggestion that he might plot to overthrow the Tsar deeply insulting.

Nevertheless, General Danilov believed that the allegations were true, writing in 1930 that he had checked them with the participants.[70] Moreover, one of the key figures involved, Aleksandr Khatisov, the Mayor of Tiflis, confirmed the entire account in his memoirs. According to Khatisov, he visited Moscow in November 1916 to attend a conference of the Town and Zemstvo Union (Zemgor). After the police shut the conference down on the orders of the Minister of the Interior, the head of Zemgor, Prince G. E. Lvov, called a private meeting of five of the conference delegates at which he proposed overthrowing the Tsar in favor of Grand Duke Nikolai Nikolaevich. The delegates agreed and charged Khatisov with putting the proposal to the Grand Duke when he returned to Tiflis. This Khatisov did on 1 (14) January 1917, telling the Grand Duke, "The situation is critical.... It is the opinion of the city and provincial executives that Nicholas II should be deposed.... Only the High authority of Your Excellency at the head of the movement is in a position to make the transition to replace the Tsar. I shall communicate Your decision secretly to Prince Lvov who shall make the necessary preparations on the spot."[71]

Khatisov claims that the Grand Duke said that "he was not prepared to give me an answer. He asked me to give him three days to study the matter. Then he questioned me in detail in regard to the situation in Moscow and Saint Petersburg. He wanted to know from what sources Prince Lvov obtained his information about the mood of the army. He was interested in the story of the Moscow conference." Three days later, Khatisov received a summons to visit the Grand Duke, who told him,

> I have called you to give you my decision which I shall ask you to communicate to Prince Lvov. Knowing well the Russian Moujik and the Russian soldier, knowing that the Russian people is [sic] loyal to his Tsar, that he cannot comprehend the intricacies of political transformations, that he will never follow or recognize the man who raises his hand against the Tsar, I reject your proposal to head such a movement. I know that the army in its entirety will never follow our plans, and there must be no new stirrings nor conflicts in these grave days of Russia.[72]

Khatisov then telegraphed to Lvov the code words "The hospital must not be opened," and the proposed coup was canceled. A short while later Khatisov received word from the Grand Duke's palace that the Tsarist police were aware of the plot and that the Tsar planned to transfer Nikolai Nikolaevich to be Viceroy of the Far East and to send Khatisov with him.[73] Apparently, relations between the Grand Duke and Tsar, once extremely intimate, had broken beyond repair.

There is no good reason to doubt Khatisov's account. Despite his protestations to Bezobrazov, the Grand Duke was not as loyal as he once had been. Chaplain Shavelskii wrote of his own meeting with the Grand Duke in October 1916 that "under the influence of the disgrace he had suffered, and even more because of the worsening atmosphere in the country, for which he could not but find the Emperor guilty because of his blind subordination to his wife and Rasputin, the Grand Duke's worship of the Emperor had weakened. I felt that at this time he was going through a great spiritual struggle."[74]

The Grand Duke's political views had also evolved. This had been a gradual process, beginning with his acceptance of the October Manifesto in 1905. The war had accelerated the process, undermining Nikolai Nikolaevich's faith in the government's ability to provide the army with the supplies it needed and causing him to turn for help to members of the liberal opposition, particularly those associated with the zemstva, such as Prince Lvov. His plan to introduce zemstva in the Caucasus, coupled with his comments about developing the population's "independence," shows that his previous support for autocratic rule had been replaced by a somewhat more liberal perspective. His appeal to the Tsar during their final meeting to install a "responsible government" illustrated how far the Grand Duke had come. Meanwhile, his complaint that the Tsar had accused him of plotting against him perhaps suggests some lingering bitterness about his dismissal as Supreme Commander.

Within a few weeks, Nikolai Nikolaevich's loyalty would again be put to the test. On 23 February (8 March) 1917, revolution erupted in Russia.

CHAPTER 22

Revolution, March 1917

ON 23 FEBRUARY (8 March) 1917, female textile workers in Petrograd went on strike, protesting a bread shortage. What began as an economic protest rapidly turned into a massive political demonstration. By 25 February (10 March), hundreds of thousands of workers were out on the streets of Petrograd. The next day, the garrison commander, General S. S. Khabalov, sent soldiers into the streets with orders to disperse the crowds by force, but instead the troops mutinied and joined the demonstrators. Having lost control of the capital, the Council of Ministers resigned, and a group of Duma deputies, under the Duma chairman, M. V. Rodzianko, formed a Provisional Committee to take over the city and attempt to restore order. Meanwhile workers and soldiers formed councils ("soviets," in Russian), which they turned into alternative sources of authority. The Russian Revolution had begun.[1]

News of the trouble in Petrograd reached Grand Duke Nikolai Nikolaevich on 1 (14) March. He was in Batum meeting Admiral A. V. Kolchak, who in August 1916 had taken over command of the Black Sea Fleet. On hearing the news, the Grand Duke rushed back to Tiflis. At three o'clock that afternoon, he summoned Mayor Khatisov to the Viceroy's palace. According to Khatisov, the Grand Duke "asked me to divulge the news to the people of [the] Caucasus and the troops. At the same time he told me that his sympathies as Viceroy were wholly on the side of the rebels. To him, the events which had transpired were the logical result of a stupid policy, the same stupid policy which, thanks to the intrigues of Rasputin had exiled him … to the Caucasus."[2] In an announcement to the population of Tiflis the following day, Khatisov said that the Grand Duke told him,

> I am appealing to you as a representative of the population, believing that you are a genuine Russian patriot. I am speaking to you as Commander-in-Chief of the Caucasus Army. We are living through a moment of enormous historical significance at a time when our Caucasian troops are, with God's help, carrying out a victorious offensive which is so important for us and for

> our English allies. To achieve further success, we need above all calm in the rear. I appeal to you to do all you can to maintain this calm and I hope that the population of Tiflis will understand this and heed the call which I have made to it through you. The Motherland is precious to all of us. I understand that the population of Tiflis fervently wishes to create the conditions which will ensure victory. I am convinced that these conditions will be created. Given the population's trust in me, these words tell you a great deal. You can pass this on to the population. To achieve these conditions we must preserve calm in the Caucasus: these are the demands and conditions of this moment.[3]

On the following day, 2 (15) March, the political crisis reached its climax. The Duma leaders had by now decided that the only way to restore order was for the Tsar to abdicate. At Stavka, General Alekseev, who had recently returned to his post as Chief of Staff, shared this opinion. In order to persuade the Tsar to surrender his throne, Alekseev telegraphed the most senior commanders of Russia's armies asking them to send messages to the Tsar urging him to abdicate. Among those who received Alekseev's appeal was Grand Duke Nikolai Nikolaevich.

Nikolai Nikolaevich had devoted all his life to service of "Faith, Tsar, and Fatherland." Until recently, his personal devotion to Nicholas II had been beyond any doubt. But there was no guarantee that the Tsar would be able to cling to power. If the Tsar abdicated in favor of his son, the dynasty could perhaps survive and the war could continue to a successful conclusion. If he stayed, all might be swept away.

The Grand Duke's loyalty to Russia proved stronger than his personal loyalty to the Tsar, and he decided that Nicholas must abdicate. We have, unfortunately, only one account of how he reached this conclusion, and that comes from an unreliable and hostile source, General N. A. Epanchin, who claimed that he was told what happened by one of those present, General P. A. Tomilov, a member of General Iudenich's staff. According to Epanchin, Tomilov told him that on receiving Alekseev's telegram, the Grand Duke summoned him and Iudenich to Tiflis, where they discussed the matter together with General Ianushkevich. Iudenich declared that the Caucasus Army was completely loyal to the Tsar. On this basis, Ianushkevich drafted a message from the Grand Duke to the Tsar telling him this. On reading the message, however, the Grand Duke refused to sign it, and put it in his pocket. In its place he wrote a message of his own begging the Tsar to hand over the throne to his son.[4]

This story is second-hand and cannot be verified. We cannot know for sure what motivated the Grand Duke at this moment, although his growing dissatisfaction with the Tsar's rule must surely have played a major role in his decision, as possibly also did a sense that the revolution had been inevitable. If Khatisov is to be believed, the Grand Duke perhaps even regarded the Tsar's overthrow as a good thing. Furthermore, the fact that it was General Alekseev who was asking him to act may well have been important. Alekseev was the officer whose judgment the Grand Duke trusted above all others. If Alekseev felt that the Tsar's situation was irredeemable, then the Grand Duke, far removed from events, may well have felt that it was best to heed what he said. Whatever his reasons, later on 2 (15) March Nikolai Nikolaevich sent a telegram to the Tsar with the following message:

> Adjutant-General Alekseev has informed me of the unprecedented and fatal situation and has asked me to support his view that a victorious end to the war, so vital for the well-being and future of Russia, as well as the salvation of the dynasty, requires extraordinary measures. As a loyal subject, I feel it my necessary duty of allegiance, and in the spirit of my oath, to beg your Imperial Majesty on my knees to save Russia and your heir, being aware of your sacred feelings of love for Russia and for him. Make the sign of the cross and hand over to him your heritage. There is no other way. I ardently pray before God as never before in my life to sustain and guide you.[5]

How crucial this telegram was to the Tsar's subsequent decision cannot be determined. The Grand Duke was not the only person urging abdication. Still, Nikolasha's abandonment of him must have hurt the Tsar. With little support remaining, on the evening of 2 (15) March Nicholas II abdicated.

At the last moment, he changed his mind about his successor, and declared his heir to be not his son, but his brother Grand Duke Mikhail Aleksandrovich. He also made two final appointments, naming Prince G. E. Lvov Prime Minister and Grand Duke Nikolai Nikolaevich once again Supreme Commander of the army and fleet.

In light of subsequent events in 1917, ending with the coming to power of the Bolsheviks, who had campaigned on a promise to end the war, it is common to view the overthrow of Nicholas II as proof that Russians were weary of the war and eager for peace. This is an overly simplistic view of the true situation in February 1917. The political climate in Petrograd was unique, and more radical than in much of the rest of the country. Large numbers of Russians continued to want to carry the war through to a successful conclusion. The unpopularity of the Tsar and his government derived in part from a feeling that they were conducting the war incompetently and perhaps even deliberately sabotaging the war effort. For many, the change of regime was an opportunity not to end the war but to fight it more vigorously.

Once the public learned of the Grand Duke's reappointment as Supreme Commander, reaction was overwhelmingly positive. Telegrams of support streamed into Stavka[6] and Tiflis. On 3 (16) March, for instance, a telegram arrived from the town council of Sukhumi in Georgia. Referring to the Grand Duke's conversation with Khatisov, it read:

> Having learnt of your remarkable words to the population of the Caucasus, addressed to the Mayor of Tiflis, the Sukhumi town Duma has resolved to express to the valiant Caucasus Army and You, its glorious leader, its warm welcome, its complete trust and its sincere assurance that all efforts will be made to maintain order and calm, so that the Army can calmly and victoriously carry out its great task of defending the Fatherland.[7]

A message arrived the same day from the region of Karabakh. "All the nationalities of Karabakh," it said, "are ready to make all sacrifices for the success of our arms. Sustained by Your great trust, all nationalities are striving to maintain in the rear the peace and order required to achieve victory over the enemy."[8]

"I am happy to greet Your Imperial Highness on your high appointment. I pray to Allah for our complete victory over the enemy," wrote one Allahiarbek Ziulgadarov from Baku.[9] "On behalf of the merchants of Tiflis, I express to Your Imperial Highness our joy at your appointment to the high post of Supreme Commander," wrote Khachatur Afrikian.[10] "The workers of the Sluchanskii state stone and coal enterprise greet Your Highness and the glorious Army and do not doubt that under Your leadership the enemy will at last be smashed," wrote Engineer Egerov.[11]

The messages came from far and wide. From Taganrog on the far north- eastern corner of the Black Sea came a message that "The citizens of the town of Taganrog express to Your Highness their admiration of the selfless and valiant army and fleet ... and with all their soul wish that they quickly and completely overcome the enemy."[12] And much further to the north and east, beyond the Volga River, the following telegram came from Vyatka:

> Your Imperial Highness. The workers of the Vyatka-Volga steamship line on the Vyatka River welcome You on your appointment to the high post of Supreme Commander, and wish you good health for victory over the stubborn enemy. Our dream of seeing You at the head of our valiant forces to save our Motherland has come true, and our faith in final victory has been strengthened.... Glory to You, defenders of Russia.[13]

The Grand Duke sent his thanks to these greetings. In response to a message from the Zemgor committee of the Caucasus Front,[14] he replied, "I am very touched by the welcome of the Zemgor committee of the Caucasus Front. I believe that with God's help, if there is complete calm in the army's rear, our more than valiant forces, united with the entire people, will achieve final victory over the enemy."[15] "I was very happy to receive the welcome of the workers of the Suchanskii enterprise," the Grand Duke wrote to Engineer Egerov. "The victory of our armies over the enemy depends not only on the valiant troops, but also on the readiness of the workers of all defense enterprises to give their strength to the business of supplying the army with all it needs."[16]

To help preserve order, on 3 (16) March the Grand Duke met in Tiflis with representatives of the clergy, who promised to appeal for calm in their sermons. He also met members of the press, who, according to Prince Orlov, "promised to fully assist the authorities in their efforts."[17] The Grand Duke then published an appeal to the population of the Caucasus:

> The peoples of the Caucasus have already for several days reacted to political events with the virtue of patriots and with wise calm. I appeal to you to preserve this calm. Every honest son of Russia is obliged to give all his strength to support the government nominated by the State Duma. Only the concentration of complete power in its hands will save our army from rout and Russia from death.
>
> Everyone who struggles against this government commits a sin against Russia. Do not listen to revolutionary organizations, which call you to further disorders, and pay attention only to the voice of the Government....
>
> Addressing you, peoples of the Caucasus, I want you to know that I have ordered all officials, without exception, to obey the new Government with all the means at their disposal and that every attempt to oppose its orders will be punished with all the severity of the law.[18]

While making clear his loyalty to the new government, the Grand Duke wished to maintain his own prerogatives as Viceroy and Supreme Commander. In response to a demand that the Provisional Committee of the Duma be able to communicate directly with local authorities in the Caucasus,[19] he wrote to Rodzianko to insist that the existing chain of command be preserved, and that the government go through him.[20]

On 3 (16) March, the Grand Duke sent several telegrams to Prince Lvov. In one of these, he appealed to Lvov to keep him as Viceroy:

With satisfaction I can bear witness to the fact that from the day of my appointment as Viceroy the normal life of the Caucasus has in general passed peacefully, and in this time I have become convinced that the peoples of the region trust me. For the time being the population has reacted to the extremely important events of the past few days calmly, largely thanks to this trust, which makes me hope that we can preserve in the future the complete order which is necessary to develop the successes of the Caucasus army at the front, in particular the Persian front, and which more generally is necessary to achieve our most important task of bringing the war to a successful conclusion. The appointment of a new Viceroy in the current difficult conditions will inevitably mean the creation of a new regime, which will take a lot of time, so that the Viceroy can get to know all the questions concerning the region, but this will create a situation which in time of war is very dangerous.... I believe that it is highly desirable that for the common good the question of keeping me as Viceroy be raised, while giving me the right, with your agreement, to nominate a person who knows the region and who, remaining as my deputy in time of war, will continue to bring to life all the undertakings which the region needs.[21]

In another telegram to Lvov, the Grand Duke addressed the succession to the throne, telling the Prime Minister that "the abdication in favor of Grand Duke Mikhail Aleksandrovich as Emperor rather than the Heir Tsarevich will inevitably confuse the people," and that the failure to publish a manifesto confirming the accession of the new Emperor made the matter worse. The Grand Duke then continued,

I have received news about a supposed agreement being prepared between the government and the soviet of workers' deputies about calling a constituent assembly in six months' time. As Supreme Commander, responsible for the success of our armies, I consider it necessary to declare categorically that the conclusion of such an agreement would be a great mistake threatening Russia's destruction. I do not doubt for a minute that the Provisional Government, strengthened by the authority of the State Duma and the trust of society, will unite all patriotically minded Russians around itself. Considering the speediest resolution of the question of the Manifesto necessary, I have in mind that the Emperor's oath should follow the constitutional form of government. Such an act would put an end to the wavering about Russia's constitutional order and undoubtedly help calm people's minds.[22]

With this the Grand Duke declared himself a supporter of a constitutional monarchy in Russia. But although the Caucasus remained calm, Petrograd was still in turmoil and Grand Duke Mikhail Aleksandrovich did not feel that he could safely accept the crown. By the time that Nikolai Nikolaevich sent his telegram, Mikhail Aleksandrovich had already issued a declaration declining the throne. Romanov rule in Russia had come to an end.

On 4 (17) March, the Grand Duke sent his first order to the Russian army in his new term as Supreme Commander:

> By the monarch's will, according to the inscrutable ways of the Lord, I have been appointed Supreme Commander. Making the sign of the cross, I fervently pray to God to give me His assistance. I firmly believe that, for the good of the Motherland, He, the Most Powerful and All-Merciful One, will hear my prayer. I am deeply convinced that only with the all-powerful aid of God will I receive the strength and intellect to lead us to final victory.
>
> As far as you are concerned, you miraculous heroes, super-valiant knights of the Russian land, I know how much you are ready to give for the good of Russia and the Throne. All you need is God's help. Believe with me that God will help you. Know that Russia understands that the harmonious self-sacrificing labor of all its sons in the rear is needed to achieve final victory. With its dignity and calm it will show the whole world the greatness of the Russian soul and the steadfast strength of our Great Motherland.
>
> General-Adjutant Nikolai.[23]

Meanwhile, in a further effort to persuade influential people to help preserve order, on 4 (17) March, the Grand Duke met two Georgian socialists who represented the Menshevik branch of the Social Democratic Party (the other branch of the party being Lenin's Bolsheviks). The two in question were Noe Ramishvili and Noe Zhordania, who would in turn become prime ministers of a short-lived independent Georgian republic from 1918 to 1921. There was, the Grand Duke told them, "exemplary order" in the Caucasus. "This," he concluded, "is explained, in my opinion, by the fact that in the Caucasus social democracy has a great influence on the side of order. I hope that this will continue."[24] According to Khatisov, when the Grand Duke asked Zhordania and Ramishvili whether they trusted him, the answer was "Yes."[25] And according to Grand Duke Andrei Vladimirovich, Nikolai Nikolaevich told him that Zhordania and Ramishvili welcomed his words to them. "When they arrived, they excused themselves for their clothing and called me Your Imperial Highness. They both openly admitted that they had dreamed of a social revolution all their lives, but their dream was a constitutional monarchy, not the current anarchy. They didn't want this and would not allow a republican order of government."[26]

The Grand Duke's nephew Prince Roman Petrovich claimed, "My uncle was convinced that the Provisional Government would not challenge his appointment [as Supreme Commander]. He based this opinion on the grounds that Count Lvov had always had a good relationship with him."[27] However, the Provisional Government was under pressure from the radical groups controlling Petrograd to remove the Grand Duke. On 3 (16) March, the Petrograd Soviet ordered that Nikolai Nikolaevich be summoned to the capital where he could be arrested,[28] and a few days later the newspaper *Izvestiia* demanded that the government set the Grand Duke's appointment aside. "Should the Provisional Government leave him in charge of the army, it would be failing in its duty before the revolutionary people who have put it in power," the paper said.[29]

These sentiments were not fully representative of public opinion. On 5 (18) and 6 (19) March, yet more telegrams of support for the Grand Duke arrived in Tiflis. On 5 (18) March, for instance, the Grand Duke received a telegram from the town of Sevsk in Bryansk province, southwest of Moscow. "The townspeople of Sevsk," it read, "raise prayers before the Most High Throne for the victory of the Russian and allied armies over their stubborn enemy; may the Lord send you good health and strength for the good of our dear motherland."[30]

"The population of the town of Liven and the Liven region learned of your appointment as Supreme Commander with rapture and joy," said another telegram. "We firmly believe that together with all of Russia, with your experienced leadership, the valiant Russian army will smash the enemy."[31]

A third message read, "The townspeople of Kotelnich, having learnt the joyous news of the return of YOUR IMPERIAL HIGHNESS to the post of Supreme Commander, are deeply convinced of the full union of the front and the rear ... and of Your wise leadership. This is the guarantee of complete success over the enemy."[32]

And from Starobelsk in Ukraine came a fourth telegram, with the following: "The eyes of all patriotic sons, at this long awaited moment of renewal of the state order, are directed towards YOU, valiant leader of our steadfast army, in the hope of a speedy end to the stubborn struggle with the external enemy. All our heart is with YOU and our dear army. We wish it and its Leader complete success for the good fortune of our precious fatherland."[33]

More messages from other towns said similar things.[34] Again the Grand Duke sent his thanks. "I was very touched by the welcome of the united students of Odessa," he wrote in reply to one greeting. "God grant that Russian youth with its enthusiasm and burning love of its motherland will everywhere help in the calming of minds which is so necessary now for the correct work of the rear and for the victory of the army."[35]

The Provisional Government either was unaware of the support the Grand Duke enjoyed or did not care. It was a government in name only, lacking any authority, dependent on the goodwill of the radical mobs in Petrograd that had put it into power. Unable or unwilling to confront them, it decided to dismiss Grand Duke Nikolai Nikolaevich from his position as Supreme Commander. On 6 (19) March, Prince Lvov sent a message to General Alekseev at Stavka, warning him of this move.

Alekseev was aghast and immediately fired off a reply to Lvov firmly requesting that he change his mind and allow the Grand Duke to take up his post. Alekseev told the Prime Minister,

> The Grand Duke's character is such that once he has said that he recognizes and supports the new order he will not retreat one step from that position and will do what he has agreed to do. Without doubt I think that he is the chief which the Provisional Government desires and he has authority in the army, which already knows about his nomination and is receiving his orders. In general, he enjoys great favor and trust at many levels of the army, they believe in him. Reports we have received bear witness to the fact that the nomination of Grand Duke Nikolai Nikolaevich is being received with great joy and belief in success. In many units even enthusiastically! There is an understanding that the Grand Duke will provide a strong, firm power—the guarantee of the restoration of order.... I can only repeat that he will be a helper not a hindrance for the new government.[36]

Lvov did not heed Alekseev's request. Instead he sent a letter to the Grand Duke informing him that he was being removed from his post. However, the letter was slow to reach the Caucasus, and by the time the courier carrying it arrived in Tiflis, the Grand Duke was gone.

Not knowing of his dismissal, on 7 (20) March Nikolai Nikolaevich left Tiflis by train for Stavka in Mogilev. With him traveled his brother, Pyotr Nikolaevich, their wives, and Prince Roman Petrovich. The Grand Duke's route was to take him up through the Caucasus to Rostov-on-Don, then on to Kharkov, where Stana and Militsa would part ways with the men and go on to Kiev.

The journey turned into a triumphal procession. As the train passed through the Kuban and Terek Cossack regions, according to Prince Roman, "crowds stood in the stations and cheered uncle Nikolasha as he stood at the train window." It then stopped at Rostov-on-Don, where the Grand Duke invited Count A. N. Grabbe, the former commander of the Imperial Cossacks, onto the train for a long conversation. The next stop was at the town of Izium in eastern Ukraine. Here, wrote Prince Roman, the train "was surrounded by a huge crowd. There were shouts of hurrah, people waved the national flag, and wanted to see the Supreme Commander. My uncle was forced to get out. With a loud voice he answered the greetings and announced that he was convinced of a glorious end to the war."[37]

Next the train traveled to Kharkov. Prince Roman noted that "A crowd poured in front of my uncle's car and wanted to see him. When he appeared at the window, he was received with thunderous applause." According to another account, the local soviet of workers' deputies met the Grand Duke with the traditional Russian greeting of bread and salt and tried to persuade him not to go to Mogilev but to head straight to the front to take command of the army in person. The Grand Duke refused.[38]

Among the crowd at Kharkov station was Felix Iusupov Senior, who was en route to Petrograd with his family. He recorded:

> An amazing thing happened when the Grand Duke's train appeared. Despite the fact that the station was ringed with a battalion of sappers, the masses still managed to jump over [the barriers] and give the Grand Duke a grandiose ovation. I had not seen such a powerful demonstration for a long time. The "Hurrrahs" thundered in the air. The mood of the people was exalted and their faces radiated with some kind of brave hope and joy. They seemed to be saying, "Go, go, my dear, to save Russia from shame!" How many hands lifted and made the sign of the cross on the carriage, where the Commander in Chief calmly stood and bowed.[39]

Iusupov's son, who was with him in Kharkov, made similar observations, writing in his memoirs:

> We were told that the train in which the Grand Duke Nicolas Nicolaievitch was returning from the Caucasus had arrived in the station. To reach him, we had to make our way once more through the howling mob, which was now cheering the Grand Duke. He embraced me warmly, exclaiming: "At last we'll be able to triumph over Russia's enemies!" Our meeting was brief, as his train was leaving almost immediately.[40]

The Grand Duke's train arrived in Mogilev at four in the afternoon on 10 (23) March.[41] The next morning, the Grand Duke finally received the letter from Lvov dismissing him from the Supreme Command. "The Provisional Government ... has come to the conclusion that the situation which has arisen and exists at the present time renders necessary your resignation. The national feeling is decidedly and insistently against the employment of any members of the house of Romanov in any official position," Lvov wrote.[42]

Shortly after the Grand Duke received this message, General Alekseev and the Quartermaster General of the army, General A. S. Lukomskii, came to see him, intending to give him a briefing on the situation at the front. Instead, the Grand Duke informed them of the contents of Lvov's letter, and the two generals helped him to draft a reply.[43] This is what the reply said:

> I am happy once more to be able to prove my love for my country, which so far Russia has not doubted. In accordance with Paragraph 47 of the Regulations for Troops in the Field, which says that "In the event of the departure of the Supreme Commander, his duties shall temporarily devolve upon the Chief of Staff," I hand over this day to General Alekseev these duties until the appointment by the Provisional Government of the new Supreme Commander. At the same time I hereby beg the Minister of War to retire me from the army.[44]

Nikolai Nikolaevich also telegraphed the Minister of War. "I have relinquished the duties of Supreme Commander," he wrote. "I request you to retire me from the army with right to wear uniform, a right which I have according to law as a Knight of the Order of Saint George."[45]

This done, the Grand Duke ordered his brother, his nephew, and other members of his entourage to assemble in his carriage to sign an oath of allegiance to the Provisional Government. Once they had come, Nikolai Nikolaevich was the first to sign the oath. According to Prince Roman, his uncle pressed so hard on the paper that he broke his pen and spattered the page with ink.[46] Nikolai Nikolaevich next telegraphed Lvov once more. "Today I took the oath of loyalty to the fatherland and to the new state order," he wrote. "I will fulfill my duty to the end, as my conscience and the obligations I have accepted order me."[47]

The following day, the Grand Duke received an unexpected visit from a group of three railway workers, who had demanded to know whether it was true that he had resigned. On being told that it was, they insisted on seeing him. Nikolai Nikolaevich later described the incident himself as follows:

> The workers were led into my car. Their visit lasted for quite a long time, because I was obliged to explain everything in detail. The workers were an-

> gered by Prince Lvov's letter and told me not to give up the Supreme Command. They said that they wanted to stop the trains and drum up immediately all the workers in Mogilev to send a strong message. They said that they would immediately send a telegram to Petrograd. To avoid senseless bloodshed and to avoid worsening the prevailing chaos, I persuaded them to leave it alone.[48]

Hanbury Williams noted in his diary that the workers "said he was still the man they wanted" and threatened to stop his train from leaving Mogilev when it was time for him to depart. However, the general concluded, "one may rest assured that the G. D. will do nothing incorrect, or which may hamper the task of the Government."[49]

At three in the afternoon on 13 (26) March, the foreign military attachés visited Nikolai Nikolaevich to say farewell. Hanbury Williams recorded the event in his diary:

> We were all shown in together, and he was perfectly calm and collected, talking only about the war situation. He then bid us all a formal farewell, and the others left, I staying behind to talk to my old friend Galitzin.... While we were talking, the Grand Duke sent for me, and giving me his photograph, bid me a final goodbye.... What impressed one so much was his dignified and calm demeanour, not a word of reproach for anyone, only his steadfast love for his country, and determination not to hamper the already sufficiently difficult task of the Government.[50]

A short while later, the Grand Duke left Mogilev to travel to the Crimea, where he planned to spend his retirement. The departure was low key and unofficial. Alekseev entered the Grand Duke's carriage to say goodbye. Once he had left, the train began to move. Nikolai Nikolaevich "took off his epaulettes," wrote Hanbury Williams, "and slowly and sadly the train steamed out of the station on the way to the Crimea."[51]

After 45 years of service, Grand Duke Nikolai Nikolaevich's military career had finally come to an end. Soon his life would be in danger.

CHAPTER 23

Crimea, April 1917–April 1919

AFTER LEAVING MOGILEV, the 60-year-old Nikolai Nikolaevich went to live at Chaïr with Stana.[1] The Crimea provided a refuge for a number of other members of the Romanov family. Grand Duke Pyotr Nikolaevich, Militsa, and their children lived in Pyotr Nikolaevich's ornate palace, Diulber; the Dowager Empress Mariia Fedorovna and her daughters—Grand Duchesses Ksenia and Olga—along with their respective husbands, Grand Duke Aleksandr Mikhailovich and Nikolai Kulikovskii, lived at the nearby villa of Ai-Todor; and Ksenia and Aleksandr's daughter Irina and her husband, Felix Iusupov Junior, lived at Iusupov's palace, Koreiz.

On 10 (23) April, the Grand Duke attended the marriage of one of his nieces, Princess Nadezhda, to Vladimir Orlov's son Nikolai. Apart from that occasion, during April 1917 he stayed in seclusion at Chaïr. This was in part a political decision. "I took the firm decision," he wrote later, "not to intervene in politics, so as not to complicate the threatening and confused situation in Russia."[2]

On the night of 26/27 April (9/10 May), the Grand Duke's peace was rudely interrupted when a group of sailors arrived bearing letters from Justice Minister Aleksandr Kerenskii instructing them to search his house. The sailors took away the Grand Duke's pistol and his hunting weapons.[3] Shortly afterward, the Provisional Government posted guards outside the houses of the various Romanovs. From now on their movements were severely restricted.

The months immediately following the search were quiet. In July 1917, Grand Duchess Ksenia visited Nikolai Nikolaevich and reported that "He has got quite a lot older, and become emaciated, poor man."[4] Stories from those who met him at this time (reported by Julia Cantucuzen) seem to confirm the Grand Duchess's account, but these secondhand accounts may be unreliable. "He was more and more broken in health, often suffering from sciatica," Cantacuzen wrote, "and he had grown very thin and fragile looking. Occasionally someone was allowed to visit the old Chief ... and these brought back reports of the simple, restrained, and sad life of the villa."[5]

The political situation in Russia rapidly deteriorated throughout the summer and autumn of 1917. Then, on 25 October (7 November) 1917, Vladimir Lenin's Bolshevik Party seized power in Petrograd, theoretically on behalf of the soviets. Thereafter the Bolsheviks established a tenuous hold over most of the rest of Russia, including the Crimea. With this, the lives of the Romanovs changed decidedly for the worse.

In the Crimea, two different soviets competed for authority—that of Sevastopol and that of Yalta. The latter was far more radical than the former, but it was the former that took control of the Romanovs, putting them under house arrest. An armed force led by a boatswain of the Black Sea Fleet named Zadorozhnyi guarded them. The Yalta soviet appeared to want to execute the Romanovs, but the Sevastopol soviet was unwilling to countenance this unless it received specific orders from Lenin.[6] Zadorozhnyi thus perceived his task as being as much to protect the Romanovs from the Yalta soviet as to keep them imprisoned. Indeed, as time went on, a sort of reverse Stockholm syndrome came into play, with the prison guard falling under the sway of his prisoners.

At the end of February 1918, to make it easier to guard them, Zadorozhnyi ordered that all of the Romanovs (except for Grand Duchess Olga, who had married a commoner) move from their various homes into Diulber. There, Nikolai Nikolaevich slept in a large room on the ground floor that had previously been Pyotr Nikolaevich's study.[7] Felix Iusupov Junior wrote that the only person allowed to visit those in Diulber was his two-year-old daughter Irina, and he added:

> Through her, we managed to communicate with them. Her nurse took her to the gates of the park and the child entered it alone, with our letters pinned inside her coat. The answers reached us in the same way. Our little messenger never let us down. The conditions in Diulber were none too good; things were very uncomfortable and food was very scarce. Kornilov, the chef, who later kept a famous restaurant in Paris, did the best he could with the little he had; mostly buckwheat and pea soup. Once, for a treat, the prisoners of Diulber had donkey for lunch and billy-goat for dinner.[8]

On 20 February (3 March) 1918, Russia's Bolshevik government signed a treaty with Germany and Austria-Hungary in the city of Brest-Litovsk, ending Russia's involvement in the First World War. The Treaty of Brest-Litovsk brought peace between Russia, Germany, and Austria-Hungary, but at great cost to Russia: it ceded control of Poland, the Baltic region, Finland, Ukraine, and the land conquered from the Ottoman Empire. On learning of it, Grand Duke Nikolai Nikolaevich rejected it as illegitimate and held to the belief that the war had not ended and that Russia should resume it as soon as it could.[9]

Nevertheless, the treaty brought Nikolai Nikolaevich and his relatives help from an unexpected quarter—the German army. Under the terms of the treaty, the Bolsheviks had to withdraw from Ukraine. The Germans rapidly filled the gap, and by late April the German army was approaching the Crimea. The Bolsheviks prepared to flee.

At this point, the Yalta soviet decided to carry out one final act before the Germans arrived: the arrest and execution of the Romanovs. Fortunately for the Romanovs, Boatswain Zadorozhnyi had become, as the younger Felix Iusupov commented, "sincerely devoted to us." Forewarned that the Yalta soviet was sending an armed force to seize the Romanovs, Zadorozhnyi ordered his troops to defend Diulber and prevent them from being taken. He then summoned Grand Dukes Nikolai Nikolaevich, Pyotr Nikolaevich, and Aleksandr Mikhailovich, and Prince Roman Petrovich for a meeting. According to Prince Roman, "He walked over to Uncle Nikolasha and explained why he had come," telling him that part of his force had to go back to Sevastopol and that he lacked the strength to defend Diulber successfully in case of attack. He suggested that the Romanovs flee to the nearby town of Alupka and hide there.

The Grand Dukes rejected Zadorozhnyi's suggestion and told him that they would stay at Diulber and, Nikolai Nikolaevich said, "trust in God's grace and mercy." In response, Zadorozhnyi returned the weapons that had been confiscated the previous year, so that the Romanovs could have some means of defense. For the next few days, they mounted guard at Diulber, with Nikolai Nikolaevich personally guarding the Dowager Empress's bedroom. The troops of the Yalta soviet, on seeing that Diulber was defended, went away without attempting to attack. The crisis was averted. Then, suddenly, Zadorozhnyi's men disappeared, and from the palace towers the residents of Diulber saw German troops in the distance approaching Yalta. The Romanovs were free.[10]

On 1 (14) May, a German general knocked at the doors of Diulber. Prince Roman answered the knock and summoned his mother. The general said that he brought a message from Kaiser Wilhelm inviting the Dowager Empress and Nikolai Nikolaevich to Germany and that he would like to speak to them. Militsa replied that they would not be willing to receive him, but she would pass on his message and he should return to Yalta to await their response. The German left, and Militsa gave his message to Nikolai and Pyotr Nikolaevich. Both endorsed her response and sent one of their entourage, Baron A. I. Stahl, to Yalta to decline the invitation.[11] In the Grand Dukes' eyes, Germany was still the enemy.

The Bolsheviks having fled, Nikolai Nikolaevich returned to Chaïr, but he did not remain there long. Under Imperial rule, he had received a very generous annual stipend from the Tsar. This was no longer the case and he was short of money. In summer 1918, he sold Chaïr to a factory owner from the Urals named Ivanov. He then moved permanently into Diulber.[12]

Summer 1918 and the start of the autumn went peacefully. At the end of October, it became clear that Germany was losing the war, and the Germans began to prepare to leave the Crimea. They offered to take the Romanovs with them back to Germany, but the Dowager Empress rejected the offer. "Ksenia came to me before church and reassured me, telling me that Nikolasha and Stana share my point of view," she wrote in her diary on 28 October (10 November).[13] The next day, the armistice came into effect, and the First World War came to an end. A few days later the Germans abandoned the Crimea.

By now, civil war had broken out in Russia. A disparate group of anti-Bolshevik forces had gathered on the peripheries of the country and was attempting to advance toward Moscow to overthrow Lenin. Known as the Whites, in Siberia they were led by Admiral Kolchak and in southern Russia by Generals Alekseev and Kornilov (and later General A. I. Denikin), founders of the so-called "Volunteer Army." When the Germans left the Crimea, the Whites took control of it.

Many of the Whites viewed Nikolai Nikolaevich with great respect, and a group of White officers spontaneously formed a personal bodyguard of 80 men for him.[14] The Dowager Empress considered it ridiculous. "Officers are posted on all routes to Nikolasha, and are obliged to stop everybody they meet. A very stupid and idiotic undertaking, it's unpleasant even to think about it," she wrote in her diary.[15]

Freed from the Bolsheviks and the Germans, the Grand Duke began to receive visitors again. One of these was the former head chaplain of the army, Georgii Shavelskii, who arrived in the Crimea shortly after the Germans left. The Grand Duke, Shavelskii wrote later, "appeared cheerful.... Politically, he had grown up. The horrors he had lived through had not aroused any bitterness in him nor undermined his love of the people. He had become more liberal."[16]

Shavelskii also reported that the Grand Duke had fallen under the spell of a former naval captain, A. A. Svechin, who had become a mystic. Svechin went about preaching to all and sundry about the miracles and omens he had witnessed and about the prophecies of one Evgeniia, a priest's wife in Sevastopol who had prophesied that Grand Duke Nikolai Nikolaevich would be the savior of Russia. Shavelskii recorded that after dinner on his first evening at Diulber, the Grand Duke introduced him to Svechin and "with exultation began to tell me that the Lord had revealed His will through the amazing Evgeniia.... I listened to this gibberish, clenching my teeth, but eventually could not restrain myself and calmed them down, advising them not to tempt the Lord, not to demand signs and miracles, not to blindly believe every prophet.... My remarks did not please my interlocutors. The Grand Duke understood that he would not find me sympathetic, and quickly changed the subject." "I departed shocked by the Grand Duke," Shavelskii concluded.[17]

According to Shavelskii, the Grand Duke was expecting a visit from the former agriculture minister, A. V. Krivoshein, who was now representing the Volunteer Army at a conference of anti-Bolshevik forces at Jassy in Romania. The conference was meant to endorse a candidate to be leader of all the White armies. Shavelskii claimed that the Grand Duke believed that the conference would elect him as leader and Krivoshein would come to him with an invitation from the conference to take the post. He was willing to accept the position.[18] Krivoshein never came. The Jassy conference failed to endorse a leader, but General Denikin gathered the most support, not the Grand Duke. The Whites did not want to appear to be monarchists and did not want a Romanov at their head. Grand Duke Nikolai Nikolaevich would take no part in the Russian Civil War.

On 1 (14) January 1919, the Romanovs celebrated the start of the new year. Pyotr Nikolaevich, Stana, and Prince Roman visited the Dowager Empress, who was now living in a nearby villa, Kharaks, the former residence of Grand Duke Georgii Mikhailovich. The Dowager Empress noted in her diary, however, that "Nikolasha did not come. He *soi disant* simply can't go out without a guard, he has an officer escort—what stupidity!'[19]

The Romanovs' position in the Crimea was now again under threat. After the Germans withdrew from Ukraine, the Bolsheviks swarmed back in. By March 1919 they were nearing the Crimea. On 12 (25) March, Denikin sent a message to the Dowager Empress suggesting that she leave the Crimea and passing on an offer from the British to send a ship to enable her to do so.[20] Neither she nor Nikolai Nikolaevich wanted to depart. On 28 March (10 April), she recorded this in her diary:

> At two in the afternoon, Nikolasha arrived in an open car, which surprised me a lot, as he never leaves his house. He said that he had given his reply to Denikin through an English officer, telling him that at the present time he does not intend to leave here, but should the necessity arise, he would gladly accept the kind offer of the English. In other words, his opinion is exactly the

> same as mine. I used the opportunity to tell him that I greatly regretted that he was living the life of a recluse, which seems very strange. He replied that it was not worth his while leaving the house as his bodyguard surrounded him all the time, there were even guards in the garden. I remarked that I could not understand why he allowed all this, as there was no need for any guard.... Nikolasha insisted that there was nothing he could do about it, as he had no authority and did not want to interfere.... However, as always, he was very polite.[21]

Before long it became clear that staying in the Crimea was not an option if the Romanovs wanted to stay out of the Bolsheviks' clutches. On 24 March (6 April), the Dowager Empress received news that the Bolsheviks had captured the isthmus connecting the Crimea to the mainland. At this point, two British officers arrived bearing another invitation to the Dowager Empress to come to Britain, this time from her sister Queen Alexandra, the mother of King George V. The Empress replied, "I will do what Nikolasha does," and sent the officers on to the Grand Duke.[22]

The next afternoon, Nikolasha gave his reply: they should leave. A few hours later, the Romanovs, their servants and friends assembled on the quay at Diulber. Waiting offshore was a British battleship, HMS *Marlborough*. Two sloops transferred the Russians onto the ship. Altogether there were about 50 of them, including the Dowager Empress; Grand Duchess Ksenia and Grand Duke Aleksandr Mikhailovich and their children; Grand Duke Nikolai Nikolaevich and Stana; Stana's daughter, Elena, and her husband; Grand Duke Pyotr Nikolaevich and Militsa and their children; Felix Iusupov Senior and Junior and their wives; Doctor Malama; Baron Stahl and his wife; and about 30 servants.[23]

That evening, the *Marlborough* set off for Yalta, where on the morning of the following day, 26 March (8 April), it picked up more passengers, including Nikolai Nikolaevich's niece Nadezhda, with her husband and baby daughter. This brought the final tally of Russians onboard up to about 90. "That morning," wrote one of the British officers on the *Marlborough*, Lieutenant Francis Pridham,

> I witnessed the arrival on deck of the Grand Duke Nicholas and saw for the first time the little ceremony which he observed daily while he was onboard. With stately dignity, he approached the Empress, who was already seated on deck, presented himself to her with an immaculate military salute, and then paid her courtly and graceful homage by bending low and kissing her hand. The spectacle of this immensely tall man in his striking Cossack costume and

> the stately little old lady—his Empress—was indeed touching. Whenever we were able, those of us who could find an excuse for being in the vicinity made a point of watching his charming daily act of mediaeval chivalry.[24]

The Grand Duke made a great impression on Pridham, who described him as "a magnificent looking man ... dressed always while onboard HMS *Marlborough* in a splendid Cossack costume with the tall lambskin head-dress accentuating his great height, an awe-inspiring presence, a strong commanding personality tempered with great dignity and courtesy."[25] The Dowager Empress, who, despite the Grand Duke's courtesy, had never been a great admirer of his, was rather less impressed with him. For some inexplicable reason, she had convinced herself that he and his entourage would disembark at Yalta, but Nikolai Nikolaevich declined to leave the ship. "I told him that this was very unpleasant," the Empress wrote in her diary, "as I had invited Princess Bariatinskii and her family. He didn't want to listen and in reply only asked me to pass on to her that there were no places—what familiarity and what insolence!"[26]

At the Empress's insistence, the *Marlborough* stayed in Yalta for several days while refugees left the port on other vessels. According to Prince Roman, a group of officers who planned to go by ship to the Black Sea port of Novorossiisk to join the White Army asked Felix Iusupov Junior to pass on a request to Grand Duke Nikolai Nikolaevich that he come with them to take command of the Whites. "Felix was a little afraid of my uncle," wrote Prince Roman, and so he asked his mother to give the Grand Duke the message, which she did. "My father later told me that this conversation excited my uncle very much," Prince Roman concluded, "but because he realized that such a project was unrealistic without the consent of the Whites' leadership, he rejected the officers' proposal."[27]

On 29 March (11 April), the *Marlborough* left Yalta. As it passed out of the port, Nikolai Nikolaevich took the Empress aside and spoke to her by the ship's railings. At that point, a large ship full of White officers passed close by heading for Novorossiisk, and when the officers recognized the Empress, they sang the Imperial national anthem, "God Save the Tsar." Nikolai Nikolaevich saluted in response.[28] "I was touched to the depths of my soul," the Empress wrote.[29] The *Marlborough* headed out to the open sea. The Grand Duke would never set foot in Russia again.

That evening, the captain of the *Marlborough* invited the Grand Duke to dinner in the officers' wardroom, after which Nikolai Nikolaevich made a short speech in French to his British hosts. "Messieurs," he said,

> I thank you on behalf of my family for the hospitality which you have shown us onboard. This hospitality went straight to our hearts—believe me that our gratitude comes from the depths of our souls. Messieurs! Remember that these are not vain words, but those of an old soldier. I give you my word that as long as we live neither I nor my family will ever forget the manner in which we have been received. We sense the sincerity of your good feelings for us, and it is that which touches us the most. Permit me to raise my glass to the health of the commander of the *Marlborough* and all its officers—tell your comrades who are absent on duty that I drink to their health and how much I regret not having met them at this table.[30]

On 30 March (12 April), the *Marlborough* arrived off Constantinople, which had been occupied by British and French troops after the Ottoman Empire surrendered at the end of the First World War. The local British commander came onboard to give his greetings. Although it had rescued them from the Crimea, the British government was not willing to give refuge in Britain to the Grand Dukes, only to the Dowager Empress and Grand Duchess Ksenia, who were the sister and niece of Queen Alexandra. Learning of this, the Grand Dukes wished to disembark from the *Marlborough* at Constantinople, but the French and British would not agree to this either, and so they remained onboard for several days while alternative arrangements were made.

Stana and Militsa's sister, Elena, was Queen of Italy. Grand Duke Nikolai Nikolaevich therefore now applied to the Italian government for permission to go to Italy, while the British tried to find transport to take him and his family there in the event of a positive response.[31] In the meantime, on Palm Sunday, 31 March (13 April), the *Marlborough* anchored off the island of Halki in the Dodecanese island chain. The ship's chaplain, Reginald Churchill, led a service for the Russians in the captain's cabin using a portable altar, with a member of the crew playing a portable organ.[32]

The *Marlborough* remained at Halki for several days. Finally, the Grand Duke received a positive reply from Italy. The Italian government, in the name of the King and the Italian people, invited him and his family to come to Italy. On 3 (16) April, Nikolai Nikolaevich, his family, and their retinue transferred to another British vessel, HMS *Lord Nelson*. Before doing so, the Grand Duke gave the officers' mess a signed photograph of himself and showed the *Marlborough*'s officers the diamond-studded sword the Tsar had given him for the conquest of Galicia. As Pridham noted, the sword was "unobtrusively wrapped in a rather grimy piece of wash-leather."[33]

Next the Grand Duke crossed over to the *Lord Nelson*, which on 4 (17) April set sail for Genoa, where it arrived shortly afterward. The Grand Duke's life in exile now began. He and his brother agreed to use the surname Borisov, after the estate their father had owned in Belorussia. They planned to live incognito and to avoid any further involvement in Russian politics.[34] It was a resolution Nikolai Nikolaevich proved unable to abide by. Within a few years he would find himself being hailed once again as Russia's savior and dragged into playing a new and entirely unexpected role in the fractious politics of the Russian emigration.

CHAPTER 24

Exile, May 1919–December 1924

THE RUSSIAN CIVIL WAR continued for many months after the Romanovs fled the Crimea. At first, the main threat to Bolshevik rule came from Admiral Kolchak's army in Siberia, but in summer 1919 the Red Army defeated Kolchak's drive on Moscow and then relentlessly pursued him eastward. In February 1920, Bolshevik troops captured Kolchak and executed him. From that point on, the fighting in Siberia was largely over.

In southern Russia, Denikin's Volunteer Army swept through Ukraine and up toward Moscow in summer and autumn 1919, retaking the Crimea along the way. In late 1919, the Bolsheviks counter-attacked and drove the Whites back the way they had come. By March 1920, the Volunteer Army had lost all its territory except for the Crimea. Denikin resigned, and General P. N. Wrangel took over as the last major leader of the Whites.

Wrangel's army held on until November 1920, when a Bolshevik offensive forced him to abandon the Crimea. After this, no significant White forces remained in Russia to resist Bolshevik rule. Hundreds of thousands of Russians fled abroad. In general they avoided assimilating into their host communities and maintained the hope that the Soviet regime would fall and that they would be able to return home. In the meantime, they created a large number of political, economic, and cultural groups, which together formed a transnational Russian émigré society, commonly known as "Russia Abroad."[1]

The largest single group in this émigré society consisted of those remnants of Wrangel's army that managed in November 1920 to escape from the Crimea on ships and sail to Constantinople. The French army, which was occupying Constantinople, interned the Cossack units on the island of Lemnos and the rest of the troops in a valley just outside Gallipoli. The commander of the contingent at Gallipoli was General A. P. Kutepov, who as a captain had been one of the officers the Grand Duke had brought into the Imperial Guards. An extremely determined leader, Kutepov insisted that the demoralized soldiers under his command were still soldiers and as such were subject to military discipline and required to engage in military training. Over several months in 1921, he succeeded in restoring the morale of his troops and instilling in them a sense that the army must continue to survive. This "Gallipoli miracle," as it was known, had a significant impact on the future of the Russian emigration.[2]

In late 1921, the troops of Wrangel's army left Gallipoli and Lemnos and moved to Bulgaria and Yugoslavia. Eventually, as funding to maintain them in organized units dried up, the members of the army dispersed as individuals across Europe. This did not mean the end of the army. Its commanders kept in touch with their men so that the regiments could be re-created if the opportunity to restart the war against the Bolsheviks ever came. In effect, they became a shadow army with tens of thousands of soldiers.

In Constantinople, Wrangel attempted to unite the main political forces of the Russian emigration around his own person by forming a Russian Council containing representatives both of his army and of a broad array of Russian émigré organizations. The effort failed, in large part because of disputes between Wrangel and émigré monarchists. During the Civil War, the White armies had adopted the ideology of "non-predetermination," which meant that they would not campaign for either a monarchy or a republic but leave it to the Russian people to determine this issue once the Bolsheviks fell from power. Wrangel stuck firmly to this philosophy, believing that his army would split apart if it adopted a monarchist position. Relations between him and the monarchists soon became very bitter. Fearing that his Russian Council would fall under monarchist control, in 1922 Wrangel disbanded it.[3]

After his arrival in Italy in April 1919, these problems were not Grand Duke Nikolai Nikolaevich's concern. He had, after all, resolved to distance himself from politics. There is very little record of what he did in Italy during this nearly undocumented period of his life. Initially he lived in Genoa, but subsequently he moved to the nearby seaside resort of Santa Margherita, and at some point he also lived in Rome.[4]

In November 1921, the Grand Duke left Italy and settled in France, at Antibes near Cannes. At first, he and Stana lived in the Villa Taormina, which was owned by a former mayor of Antibes, Gustave Chancel. After a short while they moved to the Villa Thénard, which was originally built in the early 1850s for the chemist Louis Jacques Thénard, the discoverer of hydrogen peroxide.[5] Situated on high ground near the center of the peninsula known as the Cap d'Antibes, Villa Thénard enjoys a magnificent view of the sea from its back garden. In 1938, some years after the Grand Duke's death, an estate agent described it as, "An Italian villa, in very good condition, large rooms," with "a magnificent park, planted with palms, oranges, mimosas, and a vegetable garden." The basement contained a kitchen, office, wine cellar, and lodging for the villa guard; the ground floor consisted of a large hall, a large drawing room, a study, two master bedrooms, a bathroom, and a servant's room; the first floor had a smoking room, two large bedrooms, one of which had a balcony, two other bedrooms, and a bathroom; and the second floor had two more master bedrooms and five servants' bedrooms.[6]

The reason the Grand Duke left Italy appears to have been political. There were few Russian émigrés in Italy. Moving to France put the Grand Duke closer to the center of émigré politics. This mattered as he was by now being pressured to take a role in uniting the emigration. Wrangel's unity effort having failed, many émigrés then turned to Nikolai Nikolaevich as a possible leader who could bring them all together.

In March 1922, General Lukomskii, who in early 1917 had been Quartermaster General of the Russian army, suggested to General Wrangel that he should make a new effort to unite the Russian emigration around his army, but that the only person who had the authority to lead such a union was Grand Duke Nikolai Nikolaevich.[7] Lukomskii was not the only émigré putting forward the Grand Duke's name. In July 1922, the former head of the Don Cossacks, General P. N. Krasnov, and the journalist N. N. Chebyshev made similar proposals to Wrangel. In August 1922, therefore, Wrangel wrote to Nikolai Nikolaevich, telling him that many émigrés believed that his leadership would unite émigrés of different political persuasions. Wrangel asked the Grand Duke to let him know his wishes on the matter.[8] The Grand Duke did not reply. Wrangel's representative in Paris, General I. A. Kholmsen, informed Wrangel that he knew from someone close to the Grand Duke that Nikolai Nikolaevich never replied personally to letters and would not respond to Wrangel, as he feared that doing so would complicate an already difficult position. It was clear, Kholmsen wrote, that the Grand Duke believed that, while the great trust placed in him by émigrés was important, it was not enough. Before taking a leadership role, he would need to know that he had support inside Russia, and at present the mood there was unknown. In these circumstances, the Grand Duke believed that any declaration about becoming leader would be premature.[9]

In August 1922, the political situation was complicated by a declaration by Grand Duke Kirill Vladimirovich, who was living in exile in Germany, that he was "guardian of the Russian throne." A naval veteran, Kirill Vladimirovich had been aboard the battleship *Petropavlovsk* when it struck a Japanese mine outside Port Arthur on 31 March (13 April) 1904 and sank with the loss of almost 700 lives. Grand Duke Kirill Vladimirovich was one of only 53 members of the crew to survive.[10] Going strictly by the Romanov family tree, he was the closest surviving male relative of Tsar Nicholas II, his first cousin, and he had a good claim to the throne. There were problems with this, though. Most importantly, Kirill Vladimirovich's mother, Grand Duchess Mariia Pavlovna, was by birth a German princess, and on marrying her husband, Grand Duke Vladimir Aleksandrovich, she had refused to convert to Orthodoxy. Although later in life she did so, this was after the birth of her children, and strictly speaking, her Lutheran religion had rendered these children, including Kirill Vladimirovich, ineligible to become Tsar. Furthermore, Kirill Vladimirovich had appeared over-eager to support the new regime in February 1917, sporting a red band on his uniform when he marched his regiment of marines to swear allegiance to the Provisional Government. As a result, many émigrés disliked Kirill and regarded his claim to be the legal successor to the Tsar with disdain.

Still, most émigrés were monarchists and Kirill's announcement had some potential for rallying support to the monarchist cause. From Wrangel's point of view this was unacceptable: he feared that the rise of monarchism would tear apart what was left of his army. Something had to be done to counter Kirill Vladimirovich.

In November 1922 Wrangel met with his senior commanders to consider what to do. The majority felt that the best option was to find a new leader with sufficient authority to oppose Kirill's claim to the throne. The only person with such authority was Grand Duke Nikolai Nikolaevich. The meeting agreed that Nikolai Nikolaevich should step forward to unite the Russian emigration.[11]

In light of this decision, Wrangel sent his Chief of Staff, General E. K. Miller, to Antibes to see the Grand Duke. Nikolai Nikolaevich disappointed his visitor. He was not yet ready to take the leadership of the emigration, he told Miller.[12] The Grand Duke's reluctance to become involved in émigré politics did not deter his supporters. Generals Kutepov and Miller in particular were keen proponents of getting the Grand Duke to take command of the army in exile. According to Wrangel's former Chief of Staff, General Shatilov, the movement to unite around Nikolai Nikolaevich "undoubtedly arose spontaneously.... This movement began in the army, with Kutepov as the main participant."[13]

Faced with pressure from his generals to endorse the Grand Duke's leadership, Wrangel dispatched Generals Shatilov and Kutepov to Antibes to speak with the Grand Duke. They bore a letter asking Nikolai Nikolaevich to bring his influence to bear on monarchist officers whose actions Wrangel considered damaging to the army's interests.[14] Shatilov and Kutepov visited the Grand Duke in early March 1923. According to Shatilov, Kutepov explained to the Grand Duke that he had great support among émigrés, enjoying their "sincere sympathy and belief in his leadership." Shatilov told the Grand Duke that his silence was harming Wrangel, who was under attack from monarchists for not issuing a message of support for the Grand Duke's leadership but who could not issue such a message as long as the Grand Duke's own wishes were unknown. "It was clear that my insistence was not to the Grand Duke's liking, while he listened to Kutepov with noticeable satisfaction," Shatilov wrote later.[15]

Shatilov commented that the Grand Duke "had changed little" since he last saw him during the First World War and seemed full of strength, "but in conversation he did not display the same self-confidence as before."[16] Shatilov felt that Nikolai Nikolaevich was falling under the influence of those who were mounting a campaign of ever-increasing pressure on the Grand Duke to take an active role in émigré life. In April 1923, the Ataman of the Don Cossacks, General A. P. Bogaevskii, wrote to the Grand Duke after having met Kutepov. The White leaders had to step aside, Bogaevskii told the Grand Duke. "Only one name, honest and proud, is pronounced on both sides of the red boundary [i.e., inside and outside of communist Russia] ... that is the name of Your Imperial Highness." If the Grand Duke were to take the leadership of the Whites, he added, "all loyal children of Russia will joyfully subordinate themselves to your commands."[17]

In May 1923, Nikolai Nikolaevich moved from Antibes to the Château de Choigny in the village of Santeny just south of Paris. This was to be his home for the rest of his life. The cause of the move was again political. "I became aware," he wrote, "that my non-interference in politics and my refusal to receive people had begun to create the impression that I no longer cared for Russia's fate. I came to the conclusion that I had to personally verify how serious were the appeals to me to become active, and to satisfy myself who exactly wanted this and which political groups agreed.... Therefore ... I had to establish myself in the outskirts of Paris."[18]

Built between 1785 and 1810, the Château de Choigny was less a château than a large country house. A low brick wall, later made higher for the Grand Duke's security, surrounded the estate, with access through an iron gate protected by a small square guardhouse. The house lay just a short distance from the gate at the bottom of a paddock, which rose up from the back of the house to a wood. Described as "sober and simple,"[19] and as "a dear little country house, surrounded by a wood,"[20] the pale stone two-story building bore little decoration apart from an ornate veranda and reliefs between the large shuttered windows of the first and second floors.

Julia Cantacuzen, who came to Choigny for lunch in 1925, described the building as "clean, but very shabby,"[21] and a French journalist who visited in

1926 remarked that it was "falling into ruin."[22] In autumn 1926, the Grand Duke had to vacate it for several months for major repairs.[23] The rooms were small and, as one visitor wrote, "simply decorated."[24] The Grand Duke worked in the company of his dog Max at a desk in his study on the first floor. An old rug covered the floor, and portraits and pictures of Russia hung on the walls.[25]

When Stana first arrived at Choigny with her husband, she set up a chapel on a covered terrace outside, decorated with icons painted by Russian officers.[26] The Grand Duke later built a tiny octagonal chapel in the wood behind the house, with room inside for at most four or five worshippers. A priest from Paris came down on Sundays and religious holidays to lead services, and Cossacks who worked on the estate provided an improvised choir. On special occasions, such as Easter, a military choir came from Paris to provide more sophisticated music.[27]

In 1926 a French journalist described the Grand Duke's daily routine: he would get up around eight in the morning and work in his office until 12:30, at which point he would have lunch. After eating he would return to work, and before dinner at seven in the evening he would go out for a walk or a horse ride. After dinner, he would read and then go to bed.[28] He did not give parties, and as he told a 1927 interviewer, "I never visit Paris."[29] Those who wanted to speak to him had to come to Choigny.

Beginning in May 1923, a steady stream of guests set off from Paris by train and trekked the short distance from Santeny train station to Choigny. Among the first was General Miller, whom Wrangel dispatched to Choigny in May 1923 with instructions to tell Nikolai Nikolaevich that he was the only person capable of uniting the emigration, and that Wrangel wished to hand over to him responsibility for all matters, such as finance and politics, which were not directly connected to his army.[30] Wrangel also sent a telegram directly to the Grand Duke. He had, he wrote, been calling on Russians for three years to forget their quarrels and unite against the common foe, but he had been ignored. He now, therefore, appealed to the Grand Duke. "If your voice were heard," he told him, Russians would forget their quarrels and unite.[31]

This time the Grand Duke was more receptive. He told Miller that he was willing to start work, but he set the condition that all émigré organizations must recognize him as their leader.[32] This was an important condition. The Grand Duke was a reluctant politician; he was willing to become involved, but only if he was sure that people wanted him and that he had sufficient support to make his leadership meaningful. Émigrés would have to prove to him that this was the case.

In June 1923, the Grand Duke met Miller again. Miller persuaded Nikolai Nikolaevich to receive a number of prominent civilian visitors, including A. F. Trepov, Prime Minister of Russia between November 1916 and January 1917; S. N. Tretiakov, the leader of an émigré industrialists union named Torgprom; and A. V. Kartashev, a member of a centrist political organization called the National Committee.[33] The Grand Duke told Kartashev that he was indeed willing to lead a national movement, but only if not just the émigrés but also the people of Russia wanted him to.[34]

News that the Grand Duke was becoming involved in political activity spread rapidly across the Russian emigration, producing expressions of support from far-flung corners of Europe. The Grand Duke satisfied a desperate longing for strong leadership, which contrasted with what many remembered as the chaos of the Civil War era. A member of Wrangel's army working as a miner in Pernik in Bulgaria wrote to a fellow Gallipoli veteran, V. Kh. Davatz:

> After the example of iron Gallipoli with iron Kutepov, we dream of a new iron army and the merciless hand which will lead it. That is why, by the way, the dream of the Grand Duke—our former leader—lives on among officers and soldiers and probably the entire Russian people. Rumors of his severity as well as his justice—a severity in which the soldier and the general were equal—are not unimportant reasons why many, including we sinful residents of Pernik, await the moment when the Grand Duke will say his word. In our mines, when 5–10 Russians, regardless of rank, collect in a free minute, when they remember our former failures, and we begin to blame ourselves for our lawlessness, arbitrariness, intrigues, the way our commanders were concerned only with their own local interests, and so on and so forth, they remember the severe, glorious, Supreme Commander, who is dear and terrible to all. Many, many times I have heard people say, "It is time, time already to give him our word."[35]

From Sevlievo in Bulgaria, a report came that members of the Drozdovskii Regiment "await the union of the emigration around Grand Duke Nikolai Nikolaevich," and from Orkhanje in Bulgaria came another report that Gallipoli veterans "follow with hope all the work being carried out in Paris around Grand Duke Nikolai Nikolaevich."[36] A group of Cossacks in Bulgaria declared that they "call upon his Imperial Highness Grand Duke Nikolai Nikolaevich to take upon himself the leadership of Russia's salvation.... Cossacks abroad will all follow Grand Duke Nikolai Nikolaevich."[37] Similarly, another group of Cossacks in Bulgaria declared that "Only under Your Imperial Highness will

Russians in Russia and abroad unite into one harmonious, powerful family and save the one thing which is dear to us, our invaluable jewel, the Motherland. We impatiently await the happy moment when we will hear Your Imperial Highness's call as Supreme Leader of all Russia."[38]

Those who met the Grand Duke at Choigny generally came away with a positive opinion. One was a former Duma member, N. V. Savich. The Grand Duke had a legendary status, Savich told Wrangel, but until recently few Russians in exile had met him. Now that they had, they were impressed. He was physically strong, well informed, and a good judge of people. He could be a leader in truth as well as name, Savich concluded.[39]

Another visitor in summer 1923 was Ataman Bogaevskii. The Cossack leader spoke of the Cossacks' view of what needed to be done, in reply to which the Grand Duke asked whether the Cossacks would follow him if he called them. "With full sincerity I answered in the affirmative," Bogaevskii recorded.[40]

In September 1923, an "initiative group" of prominent émigrés began meeting to discuss how to form a committee that could unite the Russian emigration politically. S. N. Tretiakov told the group, "If we now have a chance of achieving some sort of union, it is solely because a new force of cohesion has appeared on the horizon—the Grand Duke." From his personal conversations with the Grand Duke, Tretiakov said, it had become clear to him that Nikolai Nikolaevich was disturbed by the different views his visitors had expressed about his role. This lack of unity among the émigré community meant that the Grand Duke "for now [did] not consider it possible to make an open declaration [of leadership]." "The Grand Duke," said Tretiakov, "considers such a step premature and wants society to come to a preliminary agreement and create a working unity organization which can support him in political work."[41]

In October 1923, the initiative group instructed its president, N. N. Shebeko, to visit the Grand Duke to convince him that he must lead the struggle to liberate Russia and to try to clarify his position on this matter. After seeing the Grand Duke, Shebeko reported back as follows: "He welcomes the creation of a unifying center. In addition, he definitively declared that he is willing to help the work of the new organization and will maintain full contact with it and its participants but considers that the fact of his collaboration must not be made public. As before, he leaves to himself the choice of the moment when he considers an open declaration possible."[42]

On 7 (20) November 1923, the Grand Duke outlined his position in a telegram to Russian monarchists in Nice:

> I thank you and your society from the bottom of my soul for the greetings, wishes, and feelings expressed on my [67th] birthday. I consider the great cause of saving the Motherland and restoring law and order in it, which people from every quarter are begging me to lead, to be my holy duty as a Russian, and if it suits God I will do my duty, giving all my strength and even my life to it. On that day, when circumstances show, and it is finally determined, that people in Russia are summoning me and waiting for me, I will not waste an hour and will help everyone for whom the fate of the Fatherland is dearer than their personal well-being.[43]

In mid-November 1923, several of those involved in the unity effort visited Nikolai Nikolaevich at Choigny. The Grand Duke asked to be kept informed of their activities and to receive minutes of their meetings. He also suggested the names of two more people who might join them—Generals Krasnov and Grabbe, who could represent the Cossacks.[44] The Grand Duke had particular confidence in Krasnov, whom he had invited to come to France and to whom he had offered a room at Choigny until he found a home of his own.[45]

"When I receive sufficient information that the time to act has come, I will not waste an hour and, with God's help, will carry out my holy duty to my Fatherland," the Grand Duke wrote to Ataman Bogaevskii at the beginning of December 1923.[46] In fact, the Grand Duke had already started acting. Since being forced into exile, Wrangel had run an intelligence department through General Kholmsen in Paris. In December 1923, he declared that henceforth he would focus entirely on his army, and that he would hand over responsibility for political matters, foreign policy, and intelligence to the Grand Duke.[47] The latter then created an Information Department under Prince S. E. Trubetskoi, to gather as much useful information about Soviet Russia as possible. Although Trubetskoi expressed doubts about sending agents into Russia, the Grand Duke, said Trubetskoi, "expressed the desire that I should nevertheless start work."[48]

In early 1924, the Grand Duke decided that General Kutepov should take over the leadership of the Information Department. In a letter a few weeks later, Kutepov claimed that he had refused the appointment, "reporting that I was unprepared for work here," but the Grand Duke insisted.[49] Kutepov therefore moved to Choigny and joined the Grand Duke's staff.

Nikolai Nikolaevich had by now moved far from his original non-involvement in émigré affairs. Nevertheless, he continued to refuse to accept invitations to publicly lead the unity effort. This effort was not going well.

The unity committee had failed to find common ground among its members, and in early 1924 its activity gradually fizzled out. The only legacy of the initiative was that it had managed to coax the Grand Duke into playing a more active role in émigré life.

In April 1924, the Grand Duke asked General Lukomskii to take responsibility for uniting émigré organizations in the United States, where Lukomskii had settled.[50] A short while later, he also asked Lukomskii to visit the Far East to determine the situation there.[51] Lukomskii, along with Kutepov, would eventually become one of the most important people in the Grand Duke's entourage.

At the start of May, the Grand Duke gave an interview to an American journalist, E. Roberts of the Associated Press. Nikolai Nikolaevich began by explaining his reasons for speaking to Roberts: "Until this time I have not received a single representative of the press. However, this time I am making an exception ... because there have been many mentions of my name, ascribing to me all sorts of views and thoughts which are entirely alien to me." He then laid out his opposition to the Bolshevik regime, which he characterized above all as godless. "Everything holy has been profaned," he said. "Many bishops, priests, and monks have been executed, in the most terrible ways.... The Bolsheviks are undermining the soul of the people, they want to tear up all its religious and moral foundations by the roots.... Russia lived by faith, and will live by faith, and this faith will save it.... The Bolsheviks are not only persecuting the Orthodox Church but all beliefs. The struggle is against God."

Having said this, the Grand Duke outlined his political beliefs, endorsing the White ideology of non-predetermination and trying to give reassurances that the collapse of Bolshevism would not mean a return of the old order:

> We must not here, abroad, predetermine for the Russian people questions of its state structure. They can be resolved only on Russian soil in accordance with the aspirations of the Russian people.... Now a party rules Russia in the name of class and international interests. It must be replaced by a national power, above classes and parties. This power must be firm and strong, but at the same time, just and enlightened. It must stand for the defense of law and order and of holy personal rights of private property.... The nationalities who make up the Russian state must have the right to freely develop their national life.... Land used by the peasants must not be taken from them. But the peasants will only be satisfied when the land is made their property.... Our industry ... can be restored only on the basis of an unshakeable right to private property.... The authorities must set themselves the task of improving the condition of workers.

Finally, the Grand Duke addressed the issue of his own leadership, telling Roberts, "I do not seek anything for myself, and as an old soldier I can only say that I am ready to give all my strength and my life in the service of the Motherland. But I consider it possible to stand at the head of a national movement only when I am convinced that the time and opportunity have come to make decisions in accordance with the aspirations of the Russian people."[52]

The Grand Duke's interview, which was translated into Russian and published in émigré newspapers, received a positive reception in the émigré community. But the attempt to unite the emigration was running into further problems, and far from everyone was willing to accept the Grand Duke's leadership. This was particularly true of certain elements of the Cossacks. Although Ataman Bogaevskii, who was notionally the political leader of the Don Cossacks, had said that the Cossacks would support the Grand Duke if he called on them, Bogaevskii was under pressure from the left-wing groups among the Cossacks who opposed unity efforts, believing that these were dominated by reactionaries.[53] Bogaevskii therefore always hedged his statements of support with a condition about speaking out only when the time was right. The Grand Duke had made it clear that he himself would not make a public declaration of leadership unless others first publicly declared their support for him, and Bogaevskii would not do this. Indeed, in March 1924 he wrote to the Grand Duke telling him that the promotion of his name among émigrés was "harmful for the common cause."[54]

Near the end of July 1924, Bogaevskii visited the Grand Duke at Choigny. "The Grand Duke received me coldly and drily," Bogaevskii wrote. "It was nothing like the reception last year—so tender and heartfelt." The Cossack leader tried to reassure Nikolai Nikolaevich that the Cossacks would follow him when the time was right, but the Grand Duke was not satisfied. "This is all very unclear and indefinite," he said. "I need full, unlimited trust, and I don't see it.... I don't understand what's going on with you Cossacks."[55]

Bogaevskii noted that the most influential person in the Grand Duke's entourage was Kutepov. Although Kutepov was unaware of this at the time, his intelligence activities for the Grand Duke had got off to a most unfortunate start. In an effort to find a means of placing agents inside Russia, Kutepov had made contact with one Aleksandr Iakushev, a man who claimed to represent an underground anti-Bolshevik organization called the Monarchist Organization of Central Russia and better known by its codename "The Trust." Supposedly the Trust had branches across Russia and connections with senior officers in the Soviet army. In fact it was a creation of the Soviet secret services, designed to deceive unsuspecting Russian émigrés. Iakushev was an agent provocateur.[56]

In August 1924, the Grand Duke met Iakushev.[57] Unfortunately, we do not have any record of his impressions, but it seems unlikely that he had any serious suspicions about him because Kutepov continued to work with Iakushev and used the Trust to send agents into Russia, where the Soviet secret services kept them under close surveillance. This set the scene for a later debacle, which in the eyes of some would thoroughly discredit Kutepov and his work.

On 18 (31) August 1924, Grand Duke Kirill Vladimirovich issued a manifesto declaring himself to be Emperor of Russia. A month later, on 21 September (4 October), the Dowager Empress published an open letter to Nikolai Nikolaevich. "I fear that this manifesto will create division ... worsening the situation," she said. Addressing Nikolai Nikolaevich, the Empress concluded, "I am sure that You, as the most senior member of the Romanov family, share my opinion."[58] On 7 (20) October, Nikolai Nikolaevich replied, telling the Empress:

> More than once I have stated my unflinching conviction that the future structure of the Russian state can be decided only on RUSSIAN SOIL, in accordance with the aspirations of the RUSSIAN PEOPLE. Viewing the declaration of Grand Duke Kirill Vladimirovich negatively, I call on all who share the opinion of HER MAJESTY and me to carry out our true duty to our motherland and tirelessly and uninterruptedly continue the holy task of liberating Russia.[59]

Wrangel, meanwhile, responded to the challenge from Kirill Vladimirovich with the creation in September 1924 of a new organization of his own—ROVS (*Russkii Obshche-Voinskii Soiuz*, the Russian General Military Union). Since the end of the Civil War, a multitude of military organizations had come into existence within the Russian emigration. Some were merely old comrades' associations of various regiments; others had a more serious purpose. ROVS united all of these with the remnants of Wrangel's army in a single federation under Wrangel's leadership. ROVS was the form the shadow army in exile would assume from now on.[60]

In early November the Grand Duke invited Generals Miller and Kholmsen to see him, and he asked them to pass on an invitation to Wrangel.[61] Wrangel then came to Choigny in the middle of the month. The Grand Duke told him that he agreed to take over the supreme command of all military organizations and units of the army in exile (Wrangel would remain "Commander-in-Chief"). In reply Wrangel told the Grand Duke that he would hand over to him all the funds at his disposal (including a million francs recently given to Wrangel by the Kolchak government's former representative in Japan, General M. P. Podtiagin).[62] Nikolai Nikolaevich confirmed the decision in a telegram to Wrangel on 16 (29) November 1924:

> Having received the letter of HER IMPERIAL MAJESTY THE EMPRESS MARIIA FEDOROVNA, on 7/20 October I appealed to all those who share her opinion and mine to unite and continue working for the cause of saving Russia. For the complete union of all military personnel in my name, I hereby assume, through the Commander-in-Chief, the leadership of the Army and of all military organizations. Orders to military units and military organizations will be given by me through the Commander-in-Chief. All commanders of individual units, military institutions, military establishments, military organizations, and also presidents of officers' unions and associations, will be appointed by me.[63]

For the third time in his life, Grand Duke Nikolai Nikolaevich assumed the title of Supreme Commander of the Russian army. Pressure now mounted for him to accept the political leadership of the Russian emigration as well.

CHAPTER 25

The Émigré Congress, January 1925–June 1926

IN RETROSPECT, the political squabbles of the Russian emigration seem rather pointless. Not only were émigrés remarkably fractious, but even if they had succeeded in uniting it is unlikely that they would have made any difference to the fate of Russia. By the mid-1920s Soviet power was firmly entrenched. As a result, some historians have accused Russian émigrés who hoped to overthrow the Bolsheviks of living in a "world of fantasy,"[1] and of pursuing lives "divorced from reality."[2]

The émigrés' political failure contrasts unfavorably with the vibrant cultural life of the interwar Russian emigration, associated with names such as Vladimir Nabokov, Sergei Rakhmaninov, and the Ballets Russes. Consequently, a common perception of the emigration is that of historian Robert Williams, who concludes that "The story of the political life of the Russian emigration ... is largely one of despair and ultimate defeat; the story of its cultural life is one of intellectual ferment and literary productivity."[3] Similarly, the author of one of the seminal histories of the Russian emigration, Marc Raeff, comments, "It is not very profitable to try to disentangle the complicated and sterile political factionalism of Russia Abroad," none of which "had anything but limited and passing interest." Furthermore, Raeff continues, "only the liberal and socialist publicists had anything of interest to say in their analyses of events in the Soviet Union. The conservative and reactionary monarchists thought only in terms of restoration."[4]

While these criticisms are not without some foundation, they go too far. Most émigrés, although conservative and in some "vague and sentimental way"[5] monarchist, were not reactionaries who "thought only in terms of restoration." Grand Duke Nikolai Nikolaevich's support of the philosophy of non-predetermination indicated an understanding that it was impossible simply to return to the past, an understanding which most shared. Furthermore, although the Soviet Union did not collapse in the 1920s and the émigrés' political efforts all came to naught, at the time émigrés could not know this. In the 1920s the Soviets experienced a series of political and economic crises that made it not unreasonable for people to believe that the regime might fall apart if given a hard enough push. Continuing the struggle against the Soviets was not a fantastic option.

The complex politics of the Russian emigration do require some untangling, if only because the emigration was fundamentally political in nature and politics provided the background to émigré life. Moreover, the efforts to unite the emigration did come to involve a substantial portion of the émigré community through the Émigré Congress, which assembled in Paris in 1926. The history of the Congress, which was closely associated with Grand Duke Nikolai Nikolaevich, is an important part of the history of the emigration as a whole.

At the beginning of 1925 a new unity group began meeting in the Paris apartment of former Prime Minister A. F. Trepov and agreed that it would be desirable to create a political committee that could provide a link between Grand Duke Nikolai Nikolaevich and the émigré community. On hearing this suggestion, the Grand Duke announced that the creation of such an organization was "premature." "Preparatory work is under way," he said, referring among other things to Kutepov's secret activities. "A lot is already being done. When I am convinced that the ground has been prepared, and this could be soon, I do not doubt that Russian patriots will follow the path that I indicate."[6]

The Grand Duke gave the same message to another visitor to Choigny, Pyotr Struve. One of Russia's leading political philosophers, Struve had served as Wrangel's foreign minister in the Crimea in 1920. The Grand Duke told him that he was already leading the army and in principle was also willing to lead a political unity organization, but only when the time was right. The creation of a formal political center was "premature and could even harm the cause," the Grand Duke concluded.[7]

By now, the Grand Duke had assembled a staff at Choigny to help him. The former head of civilian affairs at Stavka, Prince N. L. Obolenskii, became his personal assistant; General Kutepov ran the Information Department, responsible for intelligence matters, with the help of Prince S. E. Trubetskoi and three officers; General Lukomskii ran the Far Eastern and North American Departments; General P. K. Kondzerovskii controlled the Military Department, responsible for relations with émigré military organizations; and General M. N. Skalon acted as the Grand Duke's diplomatic courier.

Throughout 1925, the Grand Duke continued to receive a stream of visitors. One was émigré politician N. N. Lvov. Even in civilian clothes, the Grand Duke still gave the impression of a military man, Lvov wrote, adding,

> His voice sounds commanding and authoritative. There is something regal in his appearance, his voice, his manner.... The Grand Duke is extremely unpretentious; you do not feel awkward or constrained in his presence, the conversation immediately acquires a natural and sincere character, as if you had known each other for a hundred years.... I tell you: The Grand Duke is a Russian to the depths of his soul.... You and everyone can say, he is one of us.[8]

In June 1925 the latest unity committee resolved to summon a congress in Paris.[9] Officially, the organizers agreed, recognition of the Grand Duke as supreme leader of the emigration would not be the congress's express purpose. Unofficially this was in everybody's mind.[10] By the end of June 1925, a group chaired by Pyotr Struve had been set up to plan the congress. For the first time, a unity initiative moved beyond discussion into the realm of practical application.

In late June, the Grand Duke gave an interview to Struve for a new newspaper Struve had set up, *Vozrozhdenie* (*Rebirth*). "If you look at it from afar," the Grand Duke told Struve, "the situation in Russia seems unchanged, but if you look closer at what is happening there, then you feel that every year, every month brings us closer to the denouement." The lack of freedom in Russia had created a state of "extreme tension" and the impression that a crisis was imminent, the Grand Duke said. Fears that communism would be replaced by a reactionary government were a "chimera," and "Nobody should dream that it is possible to turn back the wheel of history. Our task is not to re-create the old order but to build a new Russia." Nikolai Nikolaevich then repeated much of what he had told the American press the year before, saying that "We must not here, abroad, determine for the Russian people the fundamental forms of its state structure."

The Grand Duke then added a comment that was no doubt designed to reassure Jewish émigrés that his leadership would not result in anti-Semitic policies. "I cannot hide the undoubted danger posed by the growth of anti-Semitic feelings," the Grand Duke said. "No national power ... can allow an explosion of elemental feelings in relation to Jews." The state must take decisive measures against pogroms, he concluded.[11] The Grand Duke laid out his opinions in more detail in a press statement:

> You ask me about my views on the Jewish question.... A healthy state order cannot be built on the dominance of any national minorities nor on the oppression of these minorities. Acts of force by one part of the population against others cannot be permitted by any Russian national authority worthy of the name. In particular, pogroms are completely impermissible. I person-

ally consider the most desirable order for Russia to be one in which all citizens without exception are equal before the law.[12]

The Grand Duke nevertheless issued a warning. The prominent role Jews played in the revolution and the communist party had contributed to the anti-Semitic mood, he said. If Jews continued to support the Soviets, anti-Semitism would continue to grow. Thus, the Grand Duke concluded, "the fate of Russian Jewry is in its own hands."[13]

The Grand Duke gave further press interviews in summer and autumn 1925. In September he spoke to Fernand Neuray, a journalist with *La Nation Belge*. According to Neuray, the Grand Duke repeated his belief that émigrés could not predetermine Russia's future state structure, adding, "I am neither a pretender nor an émigré in the sense that one used this word during the French revolution. I am a citizen and a soldier, concerned only with returning to his country to aid his motherland and his fellow citizens. When God has enabled our cause to triumph, the Russian people will decide for themselves what form of government they want to give themselves."[14]

By this point, the plan to summon an émigré congress in Paris had made some progress. On 1 (14) August, three members of the initiative group, Pyotr Struve, S. N. Tretiakov, and A. N. Krupenskii, visited the Grand Duke.[15] According to Krupenskii:

> He [the Grand Duke] expressed great pleasure in seeing representatives of different political tendencies before him, and said that this proved the desire for unity. He sees the Congress as having any use only in the event that it displays the unity of all state-minded Russian patriots, and if such unity is not achieved, it would be better not to have the Congress. The Grand Duke finished his speech by saying very categorically that his name should not be mentioned.[16]

Following this visit, on 13 (26) September the initiative group held a meeting with representatives of over 100 émigré organizations. The meeting elected a committee to organize the congress,[17] which immediately set about organizing elections of delegates and preparing an agenda. The congress was now definitely moving ahead.

Despite his initial skepticism about the congress and his reluctance to be publicly linked to it, by the end of 1925 the Grand Duke seemed to be modifying his attitude. "I am ready to make any sacrifice for the good of Russia," the Grand Duke told American journalist Ralph Heinzen. "That is why I finally agreed to stand at the head of the general Russian movement. People have been asking me to do this for three years. I hoped that they would find another leader, but now I am ready to take the burden on myself. I am willing if necessary, with pleasure, to give my life for the cause of liberating Russia."[18]

At the start of 1926, organizations across the Russian emigration held elections to appoint delegates to the congress. Not every organization participated: those on the political left refused to join in. Nevertheless, the delegates represented a broad spectrum of émigré society, a fact that meant that the congress would be the largest and most representative meeting of émigrés ever assembled. Two main blocs emerged. One believed that the congress must pledge "unconditional subordination to the Grand Duke" and declare him "National Leader." The other believed that the congress should merely coordinate its work with that of the Grand Duke and pledge allegiance to him only at the time when he himself made an open declaration of his leadership.[19]

Also dividing these blocs was the issue of what sort of permanent organization the congress should create, if any. Prince Obolenskii wrote to A. N. Krupenskii to outline the Grand Duke's view on this question. Any organization, he said, would be desirable "only in the event that its work corresponded to the views and intentions" of the Grand Duke.[20] "If an organization is *necessary*," General Lukomskii told Struve, "then we have no objections to its creation. But officially ... it cannot be linked with the Grand Duke's name."[21]

The organizers felt that the congress had to create some sort of permanent institution if it was to have any long-term meaning. However, while agreeing to this, they could not agree what form the permanent committee should take and what its relationship to the Grand Duke should be. On 20 March (2 April), therefore, Struve visited Grand Duke Nikolai Nikolaevich to show him the drafts of the congress's greeting to him and of its proposed resolution regarding a permanent committee. The Grand Duke did not like the drafts. In particular, he did not like the proposal to keep the creation of the proposed committee secret. "It is impossible to keep any secrets," he said.[22] The Grand Duke told Struve that he would not participate in the creation of the permanent committee, although if the congress felt it necessary to create it, he would not object. In those circumstances, it would be best that the resolution establishing the committee make it clear that "all its activity would be directed along the path which the Grand Duke was following" and that it would report all it did to him and "execute all His Imperial Highness's orders and instructions."[23]

The Émigré Congress opened at the Majestic Hotel in Paris two days later, on 22 March (4 April) 1926. The congress represented the culmination of all the efforts since 1921 to unite Russian émigrés. About 420 delegates attended, coming from émigré communities in 20 European countries, the United States, Turkey, the Far East, Egypt, and the Philippines.

Opening the congress, Struve proclaimed that it must be "ready without hesitation to follow the call of one Leader," a statement that caused the delegates to rise to their feet with "thunderous applause." Further references to the Grand Duke received equally enthusiastic receptions. "We must unite, and there is no need to mention who will lead us," declared Bishop Innokentii of the Old Believer Church. More "thunderous applause" followed. General Krasnov, according to the minutes of the Congress, told delegates outright:

> We believe in God's help and in Our Leader (Loud applause).... Our congress must turn us from a scattered and dispersed mass of Russian refugees who have no rights into a harmonious organization firmly united into one whole by a selfless love of our Great Motherland, and led by our Russian Leader, His Imperial Highness Grand Duke Nikolai Nikolaevich (Applause).... We await the signal: Advance! And we will follow our Grand Duke! (Loud applause.)[24]

Delegates devoted the second day of the congress to administrative matters, electing Struve as chairman and electing also a presidium and an organizational bureau. On 24 March (6 April), the third day of the congress, the organizational bureau prepared a greeting to Grand Duke Nikolaevich, endorsed by the congress as a whole:

> Your Imperial Highness,
>
> The Émigré Congress, having collected nationally minded Russians from all ends of the Russian diaspora, welcomes Your Imperial Highness as a firm bearer of the Russian state idea and as the glorious Supreme Commander of the Christ-loving Russian Military, a Leader summoned from the first days of the trials sent down on Russia from heaven to stand at the head of the Holy Cause of defending our Motherland.
>
> The Congress fully shares the great patriotic hopes laid on Your Imperial Highness's military valor and wisdom in statecraft by the broad masses both inside Russia and abroad. The Congress is sure that at Your call all Russians without hesitation will devote themselves to the great cause of liberating our Motherland.
>
> May God strengthen You in Your sacrificial labors to save and revive Russia![25]

The Presidium then traveled to Choigny and delivered the message to Nikolai Nikolaevich, returning that evening with his reply:

> I thank the Émigré Congress for its greetings and for everything expressed to me in it.
>
> The oppression of the Russian people, the humiliation and destruction of Russia, the persecution of Faith and the Orthodox Church and all type of theomachist persecution are unbearable.
>
> It would be unthinkable and shameful to remain indifferent to such disasters, and I value highly the readiness shown by the Congress of Russia's sons abroad to assist my undertakings to save the Motherland.
>
> Our thoughts should be directed not to predetermining its future destiny, but rather to the single and general aspiration of restoring law and order in Russia.
>
> May our people who are now without rights gain the freedom to freely establish the principles of their daily life and their organization for the good, glory, and greatness of Russia.
>
> This is my aim, and I will give it all my strength. With faith I put my trust in the Most High—may the day of the Motherland's salvation draw near.[26]

On the fourth day of the congress, delegates split into groups to discuss policy matters such as the economy, Cossacks, and youth. A report on the Soviet army by A. A. Maslennikov provided more opportunity for praising Grand Duke Nikolai Nikolaevich. The new Russian state power, Maslennikov stated, would stand above class and party interests and be led by the Grand Duke. "This leader is not elected," he continued. "He is not the fabrication of the Russian emigration. The emigration hears the sound of voices coming from our great Motherland. The Grand Duke is the leader appointed, religious people would say by God's Will, and non-religious people would say by the people's intuition. We must subordinate ourselves to such a leader as the voice of the suffering Motherland." Again, "thunderous applause" followed.[27]

On the next day, the fifth of the congress, delegates again worked in small groups and heard further reports. The day after, discussion began of a proposal put forward by the organizational bureau to create a permanent political organization known as the Russian Émigré Committee. This was to be authorized to act in the name of the Russian emigration on all matters affecting émigrés, but according to the resolution, "all the committee's activity must without fail be directed along the path followed by the Grand Duke Nikolai Nikolaevich," and the committee would have to keep the Grand

Duke informed of all its undertakings and follow his instructions. This followed the formula given by the Grand Duke to Struve several days earlier.

This was the most important matter the congress had to decide upon, and it soon became clear that there was no unity after all. The debate was fierce. Speaking in favor of the motion, Professor I. P. Aleksinskii told the congress, "We cannot conceive of an organization separated from the activity of our National Leader." Shouts of bravo rang out in support. N. N. Lvov, however, spoke out against the motion: "We are against dragging the Grand Duke into this undertaking," he said. "The Grand Duke is a national leader, not a refugee leader. This diminishes his name."[28]

On the seventh day, the debate continued, and the proposal to create the permanent committee went to a vote. The result was chaos. According to the rules of the congress, the proposal needed a majority of two-thirds of all votes cast to be passed. The final tally was 296 votes in favor, 146 against, and 14 abstentions. This was the worst possible result, as it was not even clear what the result was. If the abstentions did not count as votes cast, then there was, barely, a two-thirds majority in favor; if, however, the abstentions did count as votes cast, then there was not. This was an eventuality not covered by the rules. The presidium left to discuss the matter in private. Its members could not agree. The congress had reached a total impasse.

At this point, news of the problem reached Choigny, and a message came back to the Congress saying that the Grand Duke would only endorse a permanent committee that the delegates unanimously supported. In the event of disagreement, there should be none. Faced with this instruction, the proponents of the motion abandoned the fight, and the presidium declared the proposal defeated.[29]

On 29 March (11 April), the congress wrapped up its business. Before leaving, those who had supported the motion to create a permanent committee met and decided to create a new unity organization known as the Russian Patriotic Union, promising to subordinate themselves unconditionally to Grand Duke Nikolai Nikolaevich. Meanwhile, those who had opposed the motion created the Russian Central Union, which voted to recognize the Grand Duke as Russia's "National Leader."[30] The congress, which had been called to unite émigrés, thus ended up in the absurd position of creating not one, but two, unity organizations, dividing the emigration even further in the process.

A large part of the problem was that the entire movement to unite the emigration around the Grand Duke's person was undertaken not exactly against the Grand Duke's will but certainly not at his behest. He was always a reluctant political leader and, as such, evidently felt that it was up to others to prove their desire for him rather than for him to rally and recruit them. Just as when he had chaired the Council of State Defense, he was not a politician who maneuvered behind the scenes to get the result he desired but someone who left it to others to sort things out amongst themselves.

For some, the failure of the congress was proof of the Grand Duke's weakness as a leader. "The Grand Duke is like a powerless child who cannot walk and is afraid of every step in case he falls," wrote N. N. Lvov.[31] Certainly the Grand Duke did not provide firm leadership in this episode. Nevertheless, given the fractious nature of the Russian emigration, it is hard to see how anybody could have brought the main groups together. The expectations émigrés had of the Grand Duke as a unifying force were probably impossible to satisfy.

In the days immediately after the end of the Émigré Congress, Nikolai Nikolaevich invited all the delegates to visit him at Choigny in groups of about 50 at a time. "I ask you to pass on to those who elected you that I am completely satisfied with the results of the Congress, and in what was achieved by the Congress I see God's blessing," the Grand Duke told them. The congress, he said, "showed that we are all neither émigrés nor refugees, separated from Russia, but in our unity are part of Russia, a part of the Russian people.... Tell those who elected you that I firmly believe that with God's help Russia will be saved."[32]

In late May and early June 1925, the Grand Duke held a series of luncheons in the garden at Choigny for groups of prominent émigré leaders, to discuss the outcome of the congress and the way ahead. On 25 May (7 June) the guests included Wrangel, Struve, and former Prime Ministers Kokovtsov and Trepov. According to General Shatilov, Wrangel asked to be allowed to resign as Commander-in-Chief of the army in exile. The Grand Duke insisted that Wrangel remain in his position.[33]

On 2 (15) June, the Grand Duke lunched with 25 representatives of émigré organizations, including the Patriotic and Central Unions. Discussion followed the lines of debates before and during the Émigré Congress and was forthright and open. Some continued to argue that a permanent unity committee was needed, while others rejected this. There was no agreement.[34]

The third lunch, on 9 (22) June, was the smallest and most intimate of all, with many of the guests drawn from those who had attended the previous two events. The Grand Duke had prepared a statement entitled "Several Thoughts," which he delivered to the group. In this he commented that the creation of two organizations following the congress was an unwelcome outcome but, he added, this was not too significant. "I am inclined to consider that the formation of two disunited groupings is a temporary phenomenon, and that the common objective and goodwill of participants will lead them to cooperate." Having said this, the Grand Duke outlined his thoughts on what the practical "preparatory work" under his leadership should consist of. Above all, he said, it should consist of establishing relations with important actors in foreign states. This must be done in secret, he claimed, and only he as leader could be responsible for it. The second task should be maintaining contact with Russia. Again this work required secrecy and had to be concentrated in the hands of a single person. The third task was finding money. Finally, it was necessary to work to strengthen patriotic feeling among émigré youth.[35]

With this, Nikolai Nikolaevich laid out his priorities for the years to come. The attempt to unite the emigration had failed, but the Grand Duke did not take this as a sign that his work must cease. New challenges were about to appear. Of these the most important would be religious.

CHAPTER 26

Thoughts of God, July 1926–January 1929

IN THE SUMMER of 1926, the heads of the Russian Orthodox Church in Western Europe and North America, Metropolitans Evlogii and Platon, walked out of the body previously recognized as the supreme authority of the Church outside of Russia, the Holy Synod, and broke all ties with it. Many priests then followed suit and transferred their allegiance from the Synod and its chief Metropolitan, Antony, to Evlogii and Platon. Others remained loyal to the Synod. With this, the church formally split in two.

Complicated by political differences, the schism derived from confusion about where legitimate authority lay in the aftermath of the Russian Revolution. In December 1920, the overall head of the Orthodox Church, Patriarch Tikhon, had permitted the creation in Constantinople of a Temporary Higher Russian Church Administration Abroad to govern the affairs of the church outside Russia. In 1921, this administrative office moved to Yugoslavia. In May 1922, Tikhon issued a decree dissolving the Temporary Administration. In its place he put all parishes in Europe under the authority of Evlogii. The Temporary Administration refused to accept this decree, noting that Tikhon had been imprisoned by the Bolsheviks and claiming that the decree must have been forced upon him by his captors. Evlogii agreed with this decision, telling Metropolitan Antony that "the patriarch's order should not be obeyed, for the GPU [Soviet secret service] must have forced his hand."[1]

In September 1922, Antony replaced the Temporary Administration with a virtually identical body known as the Holy Synod. The Synod's supporters viewed it as the legitimate supreme authority in the church abroad. Evlogii's and Platon's supporters, however, maintained that they were the only two clergymen with legally valid appointments.

The death of Patriarch Tikhon in 1925 complicated matters even further, as for many years thereafter there was no official Patriarch. Instead there were several acting Patriarchal deputies, all of whom were under arrest except for Metropolitan Sergei of Nizhnii Novgorod. Theoretically, Sergei was head of the Church, but in reality his authority was questionable.

Initially, these were only technical matters of little significance, but over time they created conflicts between Evlogii and the Synod over who had authority over the Church in Europe, with Evlogii resenting the manner in which the Synod intervened to make appointments that in his view fell under his jurisdiction.

Politics complicated the matter. In 1919, Tikhon had ordered Orthodox clergy to remain politically neutral and neither support nor oppose the Soviet government. The Synod considered this an unacceptable position given the manner in which the Soviets oppressed the Church in Russia. Evlogii and others, however, felt that open opposition to the Soviet regime could intensify Soviet repression of the Church in Russia. To protect what remained of the Church there, they believed that it was essential to stay officially neutral.[2]

By 1926, the strain between Evlogii and the Synod had become too great, and the Synod voted to strip Evlogii of his autonomy as Bishop of Western Europe. At this point, Evlogii walked out.

Grand Duke Nikolai Nikolaevich was by instinct inclined to support the Synod. In a draft letter to Metropolitan Antony in 1925, the Grand Duke noted, "My mother, the nun Anastasiia, instilled in me from childhood a reverence for the Archbishops and their words. For me, the Russian Bishops' Synod has great force and significance."[3] Nikolai Nikolaevich subsequently rewrote the letter to eliminate the reference to the Synod, possibly to avoid seeming to take sides in the simmering dispute, but his original draft perhaps accurately reflects his belief in the Synod's authority.[4]

Despite this, the Grand Duke opted for neutrality in church affairs. In summer 1926 he received Evlogii at Choigny. After the Metropolitan explained his views on the Church situation, Nikolai Nikolaevich responded, "I do not consider that I have the right to judge the actions of our bishops." "I bowed before your knees," he reminded Evlogii later, "beseeching Your Excellency to strengthen peace in the Church."[5]

In the autumn of 1926, the Grand Duke moved out of Choigny as it underwent repairs and spent several months at the Château Maugarny in the town of Margency, just north of Paris. In October, in an effort to mend relations with the Cossack political leadership, he met the Atamans of the Don, Kuban, and Terek Cossacks, Generals Bogaevskii, Naumenko, and Vdovenko at the château. The meeting was not a success. The Atamans told the Grand Duke that they would be willing to follow him as national leader only if it became clear that this was the will of the Russian people, and that a declaration of support for him before then could cause bloody divisions among the Cossacks. The Grand Duke concluded that there was no possibility of any cooperation with the Atamans in the future and refused to receive them again.[6]

In November 1926, Nikolai Nikolaevich returned to Choigny, and on 25 December (7 January) he sent Christmas greetings to Metropolitan Antony with these words:

> I do not dare to judge questions of the holy canons of our Church and its organization abroad, but my heart is filled with grief at the sight of these disagreements. I brought up the question of peace in Church life with the Most Holy Metropolitan Evlogii when he visited me. On this day, which brings peace on earth and goodwill to all men, I bow to the ground before Your Excellency and beseech you and our Bishops abroad to establish peace in the Church.[7]

Antony was not forthcoming. In essence, he replied that the schism was all Evlogii's fault.[8] A month later, Antony wrote to the Grand Duke again. The Synod had stripped Evlogii of his position as Bishop of Western Europe and banned him from carrying out church services. "Metropolitan Evlogii has continually stirred up sedition in the church," Antony wrote.[9]

Prince Obolenskii replied to Antony on the Grand Duke's behalf. Many people were trying to drag the Grand Duke into the dispute, Obolenskii wrote, but the Grand Duke was firm in his position. These were not issues for laymen.[10] The implication was clear—the Grand Duke would not abandon his official neutrality.

This was not easy. Religious services required a priest, but all the priests accepted the authority of either Antony or Evlogii, and the wider public knew which Bishop each one supported. Should the Grand Duke attend any service, he ran the risk of appearing to endorse whichever side in the Church schism the priest in question supported. To avoid this, in February 1927 the Grand Duke stopped attending religious services.[11] "The days are very, very hard this year in light of the disorder in our Church Abroad," wrote Prince Obolenskii in March 1927. "The Grand Duke and Grand Duchess are very upset by this, and are taking it hard."[12]

On 29 April (12 May), the Grand Duke made another appeal to Metropolitan Evlogii. News that the Metropolitan was coming to Paris gave new hope of peace in the Church, the Grand Duke wrote. "I consider it once more my holy duty to appeal to you and to insistently beseech Your Excellency to restore peace and concord," he concluded.[13] Nikolai Nikolaevich had little influence in ecclesiastical circles, however. The schism continued unabated.

At the start of June 1927, the Grand Duke held a meeting at Choigny with Generals Wrangel, Kutepov, and Lukomskii, Prince Obolenskii, A. F. Trepov, former Finance Minister P. L. Bark, Professor I. P. Aleksinskii (representing the Patriotic Union), and A. O. Gukasov (representing the Central Union). The purpose of the meeting was to discuss the international situation, and particularly how to raise money. The United Kingdom had recently broken off diplomatic relations with the Soviet Union, and the Grand Duke was interested in knowing if there was any possibility of raising money there.

Bark said that it was impossible.[14] Few wealthy foreigners were willing to fund Russian émigré movements. According to General Lukomskii, at some point in the mid-1920s, Nikolai Nikolaevich received a visit from American newspaper magnate Robert Rutherford McCormick, who had visited him 11 years earlier at Stavka. McCormick brought with him his brother, Joseph, a US Senator from Illinois. The two McCormicks promised to form a group of powerful financial and industrial leaders in the United States and provide the Grand Duke with a large sum of money. A few months later, however, they announced that they had had to abandon the idea due to pressure from the US government.[15]

Lukomskii carried out several negotiations with other wealthy Americans on the Grand Duke's behalf, but with no results. The Grand Duke then wrote in person to General Hanbury Williams in England and to his former adjutant Mikhail Cantacuzen, who was now living in the United States, and through them acquired some money, but only "insignificant" amounts. The largest single donation was $10,000, received by Lukomskii from a wealthy merchant's widow, Elizaveta Nikolaevna Litvinova, when he was traveling through China at the Grand Duke's behest in 1926. Lukomskii also managed to send the Grand Duke the proceeds of the sale of two old steamers in Shanghai and eventually received 20,000 francs from Emmanuel Nobel, a cousin of Alfred Nobel, the inventor of dynamite. Apart from that, Lukomskii later wrote, "As far as I know, Grand Duke Nikolai Nikolaevich did not receive large sums from anybody."[16]

The shortage of money meant that the intelligence work conducted by the Grand Duke's Information Department was very constrained. At the meeting in early June, Kutepov noted that carrying out any activities in the Soviet Union was extremely difficult. In fact, it had proved more than difficult. By this time, Kutepov's activities had already suffered public exposure of a highly embarrassing sort. Kutepov had managed to plant several agents inside Soviet Russia through a contact in the Trust, Eduard Opperput. According to some stories, Opperput then became the lover of one of Kutepov's agents, Mariia Zakharchenko-Shultz. In April 1927, he revealed to her that he was in fact a Soviet agent and that the Trust was a Soviet provocation—and that he wished to defect. Opperput, Shultz, and Kutepov's other agents then fled to Finland, where Opperput issued a press statement revealing all about the Trust.[17]

The revelations were extremely embarrassing. Not only did the entire Russian emigration learn what Kutepov had been doing for the past few years, they learned also that he had been duped by a Soviet double agent. According to General Shatilov, Kutepov offered to resign. The Grand Duke insisted that he continue working.[18] Kutepov now resorted to terrorism, and in June 1927 sent a small group of agents led by a former officer in the White Army, Viktor Larionov, into Russia via Finland. Larionov and his team threw bombs into the communist party club in Leningrad and successfully made their way out of the city and back over the border into Finland. Inspired by this apparent success, Kutepov launched several more teams into Soviet Russia. This time, the Soviet secret services intercepted them, killing or capturing all of the agents. After this Kutepov determined that the risk was too great. His terrorist offensive came to an end almost as soon as it started.[19]

Grand Duke Nikolai Nikolaevich had once commanded an army of millions. Through Kutepov he was now the commander of a small group of unsuccessful international terrorists. The underground effort was meant to prepare the ground for eventual larger-scale efforts to overthrow the Soviet regime, but it was a dismal failure.

On his return home after the fundraising meeting in early June, General Wrangel reported to two close colleagues that the Grand Duke appeared unwell and that he was seeing fewer and fewer people.[20] In July, General Shatilov wrote to Wrangel that everyone in Paris was aware of the Grand Duke's failing health and had begun talking about his successor.[21] At one meeting in the middle of 1927, the Grand Duke had to abandon his guests. Shatilov claimed that "he suffered a stroke, lost consciousness, and fell from his chair."[22] Prince Obolenskii confirmed that the Grand Duke had been sick but said that it was merely a cold, not a stroke.[23]

In July, the Grand Duke received some religious consolation with the visit of Bishop Anastasii, who administered the Russian Ecclesiastical Mission in Jerusalem. In the hope that the Bishop could mediate in the Church schism, Nikolai Nikolaevich invited him to Paris and asked him to stay at Choigny.[24] Anastasii accepted the invitation, arriving on 22 June (5 July). The Grand Duke took the opportunity to start attending religious services again, taking communion with Anastasii in the Choigny chapel. From Choigny, the Bishop made regular visits into Paris, where he met Evlogii and some of his clergy. The mission ended in failure, and the split in the Church remained as wide as ever. After two weeks, Anastasii returned to Jerusalem.[25]

In early 1928, the Grand Duke was presented with an opportunity to help Bishop Anastasii and the Russian Church in Palestine. The Church was in severe financial difficulties, and the Palestinian courts had sequestered two of its properties on behalf of the creditors. On being informed of this, Nikolai Nikolaevich wrote to Winston Churchill, then Chancellor of the Exchequer in the British Government, asking him if the British (who controlled Palestine) could stop the sale of the properties. "It would be too cruel if the Russian people, who have fought and suffered and lost so much, were deprived even of their sanctuaries," he told Churchill.[26] A few weeks later, Churchill replied, saying that he had spoken to the Colonial Secretary who had sent a dispatch on the matter to the Governor of Palestine, General Herbert Plumer. He would, he said, send a further communication once he had Plumer's reply.[27]

Shortly afterward, the Grand Duke fell ill. On Easter Day 1928 he was too unwell to attend mass, and he had to receive holy communion in bed.[28] He was soon on his feet again, only to hear news that General Wrangel was seriously ill. The Grand Duke telegraphed Baroness Wrangel to give his sympathy. "We are deeply distressed by the news of your husband's illness," he told her. "We share your worries, and sincerely wish that his health is restored."[29] Wrangel's health continued to deteriorate, and on 12 (25) April 1928, he died, apparently of tuberculosis. On the same day, the Grand Duke issued an order to ROVS, informing its members of the general's death and telling them, "I deeply grieve with everybody for such a premature and heavy loss. May he rest in peace and be remembered forever."[30]

Wrangel's death left a void at the head of the army in exile. Four days later, Nikolai Nikolaevich filled it by appointing General Kutepov to replace Wrangel as head of ROVS. Aged only 45, Kutepov had a powerful following among younger White officers who admired him for his tough discipline and his restoration of the army's morale at Gallipoli in 1921. Even the failure of his underground operations in the Soviet Union had not dented his reputation. Indeed, in some quarters they had enhanced it, as many viewed him as the one leader who was actually trying to do something against the Soviets. He was to prove a popular choice as head of ROVS.

In June, the Grand Duke heard that the sale of the Russian properties in the Holy Land had been halted. "I do not know how," he wrote to Churchill in gratitude, "but I conjecture that such a solution was not reached without influence on your part, and I therefore consider it my duty to express my sincere and special thanks."[31] Churchill replied several weeks later. The British authorities had arranged a loan to the Russian Mission in Jerusalem through Barclay's Bank, he said, and the British government had agreed to guarantee it. They were now working on a more permanent solution.[32] In September 1928, Churchill then informed the Grand Duke that "a satisfactory settlement has been made of the difficulties of the Russian Orthodox Mission in Jerusalem."[33] "I was much rejoiced by your letter," the Grand Duke replied. "Please accept my sincerest thanks. Your name will for all time be connected with this affair and will never fade in the grateful memory of all Russians."[34]

On 31 September (13 October) 1928, the Dowager Empress Mariia Fedorovna died. Many émigrés wished to hold memorial services for her, but this created a problem—should such services be held in churches that pledged allegiance to the Synod or in ones that pledged allegiance to Evlogii? The head of the Union of Great War Veterans in Paris, General Arsenev, visited Grand Duke Nikolai Nikolaevich and raised this question. The Grand Duke responded, "military members' attitude to the quarrel in the emigration should be left entirely to the religious conscience of every military member," but he considered it "completely impermissible for military organizations and unions to hold requiems or prayers in churches subordinate to Evlogii."[35]

When word of this leaked out, rumors spread that the Grand Duke had endorsed Metropolitan Antony's side in the schism.[36] The problems in the Church had deeply divided ROVS members: some supported Evlogii, others Antony. Aware that taking either side could tear ROVS apart, Kutepov was keen to remain neutral and so moved quickly to dampen the rumors that the Grand Duke had demanded that members support Antony. After consulting Nikolai Nikolaevich, he issued a long circular to ROVS. The Grand Duke had told him the following, Kutepov said:

> Not predetermining the future structure of the Russian state, I do not consider myself Leader of any one group or party of Russian people who live abroad, but of all, including also those who live within Soviet Russia, regardless of whether they belong to this or that political party and even more whether they belong to this or that current within the life of the Orthodox Church abroad.... Personally, at present, I adhere to the so-called Synod Church, which, in my opinion, is completely correct in not considering Metropolitan Sergei, who has been placed under arrest by the Satanic authorities, to be its head, and I fully understand Metropolitan Antony's point of view that as long as the highest Bishops of the Church live under the yoke of the Third International, and cannot speak and write freely, any subordination to them is completely impermissible.
>
> This should be especially understandable to military people.
>
> A commander who is in prison is not a commander.
>
> Russians should pray in those Russian Orthodox Churches to which they

> are accustomed, provided that a holy fire of irreconcilability to Soviet power burns in their soul, and provided that their priests always summon them to struggle against the Satanic power which has seized our Fatherland and give their blessing to this struggle's Holy cause.[37]

The Grand Duke's message made his own personal allegiance to the Synod clear, but it also made it equally clear that others were free to worship as they saw fit. Thus, Kutepov told ROVS commanders, the Grand Duke's words left no doubt that ROVS members could visit any Russian church they wished.[38]

In the middle of October, Nikolai Nikolaevich had another clerical visitor—Bishop Serafim, a leader of the Russian Church in Bulgaria, who spent several days at Choigny. On 18 (31) October, the Grand Duke thanked Metropolitan Antony for sending Serafim to him and also for updating him on Church news. "I beg You to pray for me," he concluded.[39]

Four days later, on 22 October (4 November), Nikolasha and Stana left Choigny to stay at the Villa Thénard in Antibes.[40] The Grand Duke was now almost 72 years old and had suffered from a severe cold and bronchitis at some point during the autumn. He was feeling exhausted. He hoped that wintering in the south would be good for this heath.

This was not to be. On arriving in Antibes, the Grand Duke's condition worsened. On 30 November (13 December), he experienced severe heart abnormalities, which forced him to bed. By the following day, pneumonia had developed in his right lung, and he had a high temperature. Over the next few days, the Grand Duke's fever dropped and his condition appeared to be improving, but his doctors were concerned with the state of his heart.[41] On 5 (18) December, Prince Obolenskii informed Metropolitan Antony that "Today, the general picture is a little more favorable, but it remains threatening.... We pray for the help of the Almighty."[42]

By 10 (23) December, the Grand Duke's temperature was back to normal. Although he remained weak and in bed, there were grounds for thinking that the worst was past. On the morning of 23 December (5 January), he celebrated mass in bed. At three that afternoon he signed what would prove to be his final message to the Russian people:

> I greet everybody on Christmas.
>
> I pray to the LORD that we will see our Fatherland free, and see in it the triumph of faith and the reign of peace, love, and truth.
>
> I am touched to the soul and sincerely grateful for all the greetings sent to me during my illness.

Remember RUSSIA! And here in exile, devote all your thoughts, not reckoning your labors, strength, and resources, to the cause of its salvation, for the decisive hour of your unprecedentedly heavy sufferings is coming.

RUSSIAN people! Muster your strength, and go out again with the Cross on the path of your Great and Glorious existence.

Nikolai.[43]

At nine o'clock that evening, the Grand Duke suffered a heart attack. Within a few minutes he was dead.[44]

Epilogue

TWO HOURS AFTER Grand Duke Nikolai Nikolaevich died, a memorial service was held for him at the Villa Thénard. The next day, telegrams of condolence poured into the villa: from the Kings of Spain, Denmark, and Sweden; from the Queens of Britain and Italy; from the President and Prime Minister of France; from Marshals Foch and Joffre; and from many, many others.

Two days later, Nikolai Nikolaevich's body was laid out in a coffin draped with a Russian flag and a flag of the Imperial Russian Navy. In the central hall on the ground floor of Villa Thénard, according to the local newspaper, "a bier had been erected on which rested a monumental casket of polished oak, with gold handles, in which lay the Grand Duke's mortal remains. On the lid of the casket, beneath the large saber of a Cossack colonel which lay across it, one could read, 'Nikolai Nikolaevich, 1857–1928.'"[1] Officers and Cossacks of His Imperial Highness's Guard and the Life Guards Ataman Regiment stood guard. During the day visitors came to the villa to pay their respects.[2] Among them was the exiled Russian novelist Ivan Bunin, who four years later would win the Nobel Prize for literature. On learning of Nikolai Nikolaevich's death, Bunin was "very distressed and sad," his wife, Vera, recorded in her diary. "Little did I think," he told her, "when I saw him almost 40 years ago at Orel station, when he was walking on the platform while transporting his father's remains, and he was young and brilliant, with curly red hair, little did I think that our lives would cross again, and that I would greet his remains here in Antibes."[3] Some time later, Bunin described the scene at the Villa Thénard in his autobiographical novel *The Life of Arseniev*:

> In the hall is a crowd of silent people. With a particular resignation I make my way toward the second set of doors, and then raise my eyes—and instantly notice the large yellow-gray countenance reposing in an inordinately long coffin, in a yellow oaken sarcophagus, the high Romanov brow, the whole of that dead old man's head, no longer fair but gray, juts slightly forward, the finely carved nostrils look slightly contemptuous.... This head now looks large—so childishly thin and narrow have his shoulders become. He wears an old, quite plain, ruddy-gray cossack uniform, with no decorations except

> the Cross of Saint George on his breast, with loose, much too short sleeves, exposing, above his long flat hands, his yellowish arms, clumsily and heavily crossed; his hands are those of an old man, too, though still powerful, striking one by their woodenness and by the fact that in one of them he clasps in his fist, with menacing firmness, like a sword, an old cypress cross from Mount Athos, blackened with age.[4]

A local priest led a requiem service. "Ian [Ivan] was very agitated," wrote Vera Bunina, "tears ran in streams down his cheeks. There was a feeling that we were burying old Russia. You live on as if all your wounds have healed, and then you bump into something and the wounds are reopened, and it's painful, very painful." "After the requiem," she continued, "the relatives approached the coffin, first Pyotr Nikolaevich, then Militsa Nikolaevna. They got down on their knees and prayed, then kissed the cross, his forehead, and his hand. Militsa also kissed his medal, the Cross of St George. Then came the nephew, the niece, the nephew's wife, the stepson and stepdaughter, and then the rest.... Pyotr Nikolaevich and Militsa Nikolaevna made a deep bow to all and then left."[5]

The coffin was closed that evening. The next day, crowds filled the garden of Villa Thénard, while Cossacks in full dress uniform lined the road from the villa door to the street. Shortly before three o'clock in the afternoon, units of the local French garrison, the Ninth and Twentieth Battalions of Chasseurs Alpins, arrived under the command of the garrison commander. Marshal Pétain arrived a little later, accompanied by two generals. Other senior French civilian and local officials followed.

At three o'clock Bishop Serafim led prayers, and the Grand Duke's brother and other relatives carried the coffin to a hearse, which moved slowly off down the street between rows of French troops, followed by the Grand Duke's family, members of his entourage carrying his medals, and various dignitaries. Russians sang prayers, and the band of the Ninth Chasseurs Alpins played Chopin's *Funeral March*.

The cortege traveled to the Russian Orthodox Church in Cannes, a small but ornately decorated building capped by a small blue onion dome and a distinctly Russian bell tower. Inside, the coffin was covered once again with the flags of Russia and Saint Andrew and flanked by the standard of the Supreme Commander and the flag of France. The Grand Duke's medals were laid out in front. Wreaths decorated the entire church, and an honor guard of Russian officers stood by the coffin through the night.

The next day, 27 December (9 January), Bishop Serafim presided over the funeral service. Generals of the Russian army, beginning with Kutepov and

Iudenich, took turns to guard the coffin. Finally the funeral came to an end and the widowed Grand Duchess left the church. The coffin stayed in place for the rest of the day and through that night, guarded by more Russian officers. On the ninth day after the Grand Duke's death, after yet another service, the coffin was moved to a temporary resting place on the right side of the church.[6] Eventually the coffin was taken down to the crypt, where it remains to this day. The inscription on the Grand Duke's tomb gives only his name and dates and the title by which so many Russians knew him: *Verkhovnyi Glavnokomanduiushchii*, Supreme Commander.

Cast of Characters

Aleksandra Fedorovna, Empress — Wife of Nicholas II.

Aleksandra Petrovna, Grand Duchess — Wife of Grand Duke Nikolai Nikolaevich Senior; mother of Grand Dukes Nikolai Nikolaevich Junior and Pyotr Nikolaevich.

Alekseev, M. V., General — Chief of Staff of the South West Front, August 1914–March 1915; Commander of the North West Front, March 1915–August 1915; Chief of Staff of the Russian Army, August 1915–March 1917.

Anastasia Nikolaevna, Grand Duchess (Stana) — Wife of Grand Duke Nikolai Nikolaevich Junior; sister of Grand Duchess Militsa Nikolaevna.

Anastasii, Metropolitan — Head of the Russian Ecclesiastical Mission in Jerusalem.

Antony, Metropolitan — Metropolitan of Kiev and Galicia; head of the Russian Orthodox Church Outside Russia.

Baratov, N. N., General — Commander of the Persian Expeditionary Corps.

Bazili, N. — Representative of the Foreign Ministry at Stavka.

Birilev, A. A., Admiral — Naval Minister, 1905–1907.

Bobrinskii, G. A., Count — Governor General of Galicia.

Bogaevskii, A. P., General — Ataman of the Don Cossacks.

Bolkhovitinov, L. M., General — Chief of Staff of the Caucasus Army.

Brusilov, A. A., General — Commander of the Eighth Army.

Burenina, Sofia — Mistress of Grand Duke Nikolai Nikolaevich Junior.

Cantacuzen, Julia — Wife of Grand Duke Nikolai Nikolaevich Junior's adjutant Colonel Mikhail Cantacuzen.

Danilo, Prince — Heir to the Montenegrin throne; brother of Grand Duchesses Anastasia and Militsa Nikolaevna.

Danilov, Iu. N., General — Quartermaster General of the Russian Army, 1914–1915.

Dzhunkovskii, V. F., General — Deputy Minister of the Interior, 1913–1915.

Epanchin, N. A., General — Commander of the Third Army Corps, 1914–1915.

Evlogii, Metropolitan — Head of the Russian Orthodox Church in Western Europe.

Gazemkampf, M. A., General — Deputy Commander of the Petersburg Military District.

Goremykin, I. L. — Prime Minister of Russia, 1906 and 1914–1916.

Guchkov, A. I. — Leader of the Octobrist Party.

Gurko, I. V., General, later Field Marshal — Commander of the Advance Guard in the Russo-Turkish War; Commander of the Warsaw Military District.

Hanbury Williams, John, General — British military attaché.

Ianushkevich, N. N., General — Chief of Staff of the Russian Army, 1914–1915; Deputy Viceroy of the Caucasus, 1915–1917.

Iudenich, N. N., General — Commander of the Caucasus Army.

Ivanov, N. Iu., General — Commander of the South West Front.

Izvolskii, A. P. — Foreign Minister, 1906–1910.

Joffre, Joseph, General — Chief of Staff of the French Army.

Khatisov, A. I. — Mayor of Tiflis.

Kireev, A. A. — Slavophile philosopher and diarist.

Kirill Vladimirovich, Grand Duke — Pretender to the Russian throne.

Knox, Colonel Alfred — British military attaché.

Kondzerovskii, P. K., General — Chief personnel officer at Stavka.

Krivoshein, A. V. — Minister of Agriculture.

Ksenia, Grand Duchess — Sister of Nicholas II.

Kudashev, N. A., Prince — Representative of the Foreign Ministry at Stavka.

Kuropatkin, A. N., General — Minister of War, 1898–1904; Commander of the Russian armies in the Russo-Japanese War, 1904–1905.

Kutepov, A. P., General — Head of Grand Duke Nikolai Nikolaevich's Information Department in the 1920s.

de Laguiche, Pierre, General — French military attaché.

Langlois, Jacques, Commandant — French military officer; regular visitor to Stavka.

Lukomskii, A. S., General — Quartermaster General of the Russian Army, 1917; Assistant to Grand Duke Nikolai Nikolaevich during the 1920s.

Lvov, G. E., Prince — Head of Zemgor, and then of the Provisional Government.

Malama, B. Z., Doctor — Personal doctor of Grand Duke Nikolai Nikolaevich Junior.

Mariia Fedorovna, Empress — Wife of Emperor Alexander III; mother of Nicholas II.

McCormick, Robert Rutherford, "The Colonel" — Editor of the *Chicago Tribune*.

Miasoedov, S. A., Colonel — Gendarme officer, executed for treason.

Militsa Nikolaevna, Grand Duchess — Wife of Grand Duke Pyotr Nikolaevich; sister of Grand Duchess Anastasia Nikolaevna.

Miller, E. K., General — Chief of Staff of General Wrangel.

Moulin, Colonel — French military attaché.

Nicholas II — Emperor of Russia.

Nikola, Prince later King — Ruler of Montenegro; father of Grand Duchesses Anastasia and Militsa Nikolaevna.

Nikolai Nikolaevich Junior, Grand Duke (Nikolasha) — Inspector General of Cavalry, 1895–1905; President of the Council of State Defence, 1905–1908; Commander of the Guards and Petersburg Military District, 1905–1914; Supreme Commander of the Russian Army, 1914–1915 and March 1917; Viceroy of the Caucasus and Commander-in-Chief of the Caucasus Army, 1915–1917.

Nikolai Nikolaevich Senior, Grand Duke — Father of Grand Duke Nikolai Nikolaevich Junior.

Obolenskii, N. L., Prince — Head of the civil chancellery at Stavka; personal secretary of Grand Duke Nikolai Nikolaevich Junior in the 1920s.

Orlov, V., Prince — Head of the Military Chancellery of the Imperial Court; assistant to Grand Duke Nikolai Nikolaevich Junior in the Caucasus, 1915–1917.

Paléologue, Maurice — French ambassador.

Palitsyn, F. F., General — Chief of Staff to Grand Duke Nikolai Nikolaevich Junior while Inspector General of Cavalry; Chief of the General Staff, 1905–1908; military advisor to Grand Duke Nikolai Nikolaevich Junior, 1914–1916.

Poklevskii-Kozell, S. A. — Russian ambassador to Romania.

Pyotr Nikolaevich, Grand Duke — Brother of Grand Duke Nikolai Nikolaevich Junior.

Philippe, Monsieur — Holy man.

Polivanov, A. A., General — Deputy Minister of War, 1905–1912; Minister of War, 1915–1916.

Pototskaia, Mariia — Mistress of Grand Duke Nikolai Nikolaevich Junior.

Rasputin, Grigorii — Holy man.

Raukh, G. O. von, General — Quartermaster, then Chief of Staff of the Petersburg Military District, 1905–1908.

Rediger, A. F., General — Minister of War, 1905–1909.

Rennenkampf, P. K., General — Commander of the First Army, 1914–1915.

Rodzianko, M. V. — Chairman of the Duma.

Roman Petrovich, Prince — Son of Grand Duke Pyotr Nikolaevich.

Ruzskii, N. V., General — Commander of the Third Army, August 1914; Commander of the North West Front, September 1914–March 1915.

Sabler, V. K. — Procurator of the Holy Synod.

Sazonov, S. D. — Foreign Minister, 1910–1916.

de Sermet, Colonel — French military attaché.
Shatilov, P. N., General — Staff officer in the Caucasus Army; Chief of Staff to General Wrangel, 1920.
Shavelskii, Georgii — Head Chaplain of the Russian Army.
Stolypin, P. A. — Minister of the Interior, 1905–1906; Prime Minister, 1905–1911.
Struve, P. B. — Political philosopher; chairman of Émigré Congress, 1926.
Sukhomlinov, V. A., General — Minister of War, 1909–1915.
Valtsov, Dmitrii — Manager of the Pershino hunt.
von den Brinken, A. F., General — Chief of Staff of the Petersburg Military District.
Vorontsov-Dashkov, I. I., Count — Head of the Imperial Court, 1881–1897; Viceroy of the Caucasus, 1905–1916.
Witte, Sergei — Finance Minister, 1892–1903; Prime Minister, 1905–1906.
Wrangel, P. N., General — Commander of the White Army in the Crimea, 1920.
Zhilinskii, Ia. G. — Commander of the North West Front, 1914.

Notes

Introduction

1. A. K. Spiridovich, *Les dernières années de la cour de Tzarskoie-Selo*, vol. 1 (Paris: Payot, 1928), 5–96.

2. Boris Kolonitskii, *"Tragicheskaia erotika": obrazy imperatorskoi sem'i v gody pervoi mirovoi voiny* (St. Petersburg: Novoe Literaturnoe Obozrenie, 2010), 436.

3. A. A. Brusilov, *A Soldier's Notebook, 1914–1918* (London: Macmillan, 1930), 26.

4. Iu. N. Danilov, *Rossiia v mirovoi voine, 1914–1915 gg.* (Berlin: Slovo, 1924), 107.

5. Report, General Sir J. Hanbury Williams, 5 October 1915, National Archives of the United Kingdom (henceforth NAUK), PRO 30/57/67, 196–98.

6. Erich von Ludendorff, *Ludendorff's Own Story, August 1914–November 1918*, vol. 1 (Freeport: Books for Libraries Press, 1971), 142.

7. V. Sukhomlinov, *Velikii Kniaz' Nikolai Nikolaevich (mladshii)* (Berlin: Izdanie avtora, 1925), 104.

8. Memoirs, 482, Bakhmeteff Archive, Columbia University (henceforth BA), P. N. Shatilov Papers, Box 9, folder 12.

9. A. A. Kersnovskii, *Istoriia russkoi armii*, vol. 3 (Belgrade: Izdanie "Tsarskogo Vestnika," 1935), 671.

10. Ibid., 598.

11. Princess Cantacuzène, Countess Speransky, *Revolutionary Days: Recollections of Romanoffs and Bolsheviki, 1914–1917* (Boston: Small, Maynard, and Company, 1919), 391.

12. Ibid., 388.

13. Alfred Knox, "The Grand Duke Nicholas," *Slavonic and East European Review* 7, no. 21 (1929): 538.

14. "Epokha nashei pervoi revoliutsii, 1905–1907 gg.," tetrad' no. 3, Gosudarstvennyi Arkhiv Rossiiskoi Federatsii (henceforth GARF), f. R-6249, o. 1, d. 3, l. 11.

15. Sukhomlinov, *Velikii Kniaz'*, 105.

16. A. A. Kireev, *Dnevnik, 1905–1910* (Moscow: Rosspen, 2010), 279.

17. N. A. Epanchin, *Na sluzhbe trekh imperatorov* (Moscow: Nashe Nasledie, 1996), 355.

18. Sergei Witte, *The Memoirs of Count Witte*, trans. and ed. Sidney Harcave (Armonk: M. E. Sharpe, 1990), 518.

19. Iu. N. Danilov. *Velikii Kniaz' Nikolai Nikolaevich* (Paris: Imprimerie de Navarre, 1930).

1: Education of a Soldier, 1856–1873

1. E. A. Annenkova and Iu. P. Golikov, *Printsy Ol'denburskie v Peterburge* (St. Petersburg: Rostok, 2004), 289–90.

2. Spiridovich, *Les dernières années*, 396.

3. Posluzhnoi spisok Generala ot Kavalerii, Generala-Ad'iutanta Ego Imperatorskogo Vysochestva Velikogo Kniazia Nikolaia Nikolaevicha (henceforth Posluzhnoi spisok), Central State Historical Archives of Georgia, Tbilisi (henceforth CSHAG), f. 13, o.

25, d. 28.

4. David Chavchavadze, *The Grand Dukes* (New York: Atlantic International, 1990), 65.

5. N. M. Zatvornitskii, *Fel'dmarshal Velikii Kniaz' Nikolai Nikolaevich Starshii* (St. Petersburg: Tipografiia T-va M. O. Vol'fa, 1911), 4–7.

6. Epanchin, *Na sluzhbe*, 144.

7. Cited in Annenkova and Golikov, *Printsy Ol'denburgskie*, 290.

8. Archibald Forbes, *Czar and Sultan: The Adventures of a British Lad in the Russo-Turkish War of 1877–78* (New York: Charles Scribner's Sons, 1894), 133.

9. Inna Soboleva, *Velikie kniaz'ia doma Romanovykh* (St. Petersburg: Piter, 2010), 199–200.

10. Ibid., 189–92.

11. E. A. Annenkova and Iu. P. Golikov, *Russkie Ol'denburgskie i ikh dvortsy* (St. Petersburg: Almaz, 1997), 6.

12. Witte, *Memoirs*, 77–79; Danilov, *Velikii Kniaz'*, 20; A. A. Mosolov, *Pri dvore poslednego imperatora: zapiski nachal'nika kantseliarii ministra dvora* (St. Petersburg: Nauka, 1992), 145.

13. For details, see Christopher Warwick, *Ella: Princess, Saint and Martyr* (Chichester: Wiley, 2006), 236.

14. The causes of the paralysis are not known. Witte believed the cause to be a "nervous condition," whereas another story ascribes the paralysis to a riding accident and yet another to a spinal injury: Witte, *Memoirs*, 78; Soboleva, *Velikie kniaz'ia*, 193; Kolonitskii, "*Tragicheskaia erotika*," 380.

15. Soboleva, *Velikie Kniaz'ia*, 193.

16. Danilov, *Velikii Kniaz'*, 21–22. Nikolai Nikolaevich Junior's nephew, Prince Roman Petrovich, similarly stated that the younger Grand Duke took his mother's side: Prinz Roman Romanow, *Am Hof des letzten Zaren* (Munich: Piper, 1991), 29. For a contrasting view, from a highly biased source, of the Grand Duke's relationship with his mother, see: Sukhomlinov, *Velikii Kniaz'*, 49.

17. Kolonitskii, "*Tragicheskaia erotika*," 381.

18. Draft letter, Grand Duke Nikolai Nikolaevich to Metropolitan Antony, undated, 1928, Dom Russkogo Zarubezh'ia imeni A. I. Solzhenitsyna (henceforth DRZ), f. 2, o. 1, k. 5, ed. khr. 32, l. 5.

19. For a detailed analysis of the role of ceremony in Romanov Russia, see Richard S. Wortman, *Scenarios of Power: Myth and Ceremony in Russian Monarchy*, vols. 1 and 2 (Princeton University Press, 1995 and 2000).

20. *Vysochaishe utverzhdennyi tseremonial o sviatom kreshchenii ego imperatorskogo vysochestva gosudaria velikogo kniazia Nikolaia Nikolaevicha*, private collection, France.

21. Tetrad' s zamechaniiami o bolezni v. k. Nikolaia Nikolaevicha (mladshego), 1857, GARF, f. 646, o. 1, d. 317, ll. 1–9.

22. Raport vel. kn. Nikolaia Nikolaevicha (mladshego) Romanova vel. kn. Nikolaiu Nikolaevichu (starshemu) Romanovu, 22 April 1864, GARF, f. 646, o. 1, d. 29, l. 1.

23. Posluzhnoi spisok, CSHAG, f. 13, o. 25, d. 28.

24. Letter, Grand Duke Nikolai Nikolaevich Junior to Grand Duke Nikolai Nikolaevich Senior, 17 August 1865, GARF, f. 646, o. 1, d. 174, ll. 3–4.

25. Letter, Grand Duke Nikolai Nikolaevich Junior to Grand Duke Nikolai Nikolaevich Senior, 21 August 1865, GARF, f. 646, o. 1, d. 174, ll. 1–2.

26. Letter, Grand Duke Nikolai Nikolaevich Junior to Grand Duke Nikolai Nikolaevich Senior, 24 August 1865, GARF, f. 646, o. 1, d. 174, ll. 5–6.

27. Letter, Grand Duke Nikolai Nikolaevich Junior to Grand Duke Nikolai Nikolaevich Senior, 31 August 1865, GARF, f. 646, o. 1, d. 174, ll. 7–8.

28. Pozdravitel'noe stikhotvorenie vel. kn. Nikolaia Nikolaevicha (mladshego) otsu, 25 December 1865, GARF, f. 646. o. 1, d. 29, l. 1.

29. Soboleva, *Velikie Kniaz'ia*, 192–93.

30. V. F. Dzhunkovskii, *Vospominaniia*, vol. 1 (Moscow: Izdatel'stvo imeni Sabashnikovykh, 1997), 97.

31. Orlando Figes, *Natasha's Dance: A Cultural History of Russia* (London: Allen Lane, 2002), 120–23.

32. Letter, Grand Duke Nikolai Nikolaevich Junior to Grand Duke Nikolai Nikolaevich Senior, 18 September 1869, GARF, f. 646, o. 1, d. 174, ll. 19–21.

33. Warwick, *Ella*, 87–88. See also Wortman, *Scenarios of Power*, vol. 2, 312–15.

34. Sukhomlinov, *Velikii Kniaz'*, 42–43.

35. G. O. von Raukh, "Epokha nashei pervoi revoliutsii, 1905–1907," tetrad' no. 3, GARF, f. R-6249, o. 1, d. 3, l. 10.

36. Rapport sur les exercices du Camp de Krasnoe Selo: Avant-propos, no. 2564, 20 August 1906, 2-ème suite, Service Historique de la Défense, Château de Vincennes (henceforth SHD), 7 N 1477.

37. Cyrille Boulay, *La France des Romanov: De la villégiature à l'exil* (Saint-Amand-Montrond: Perrin, 2010), 18, 58.

38. Romanow, *Am Hof*, 85.

39. Letter Hanbury Williams to Kitchener, 2 March 1915, NAUK, PRO 30/57/67, 65.

40. Posluzhnoi spisok, CSHAG, f. 13, o. 25, d. 28.

41. A. Vorob'eva, *Rossiiskie iunkera, 1864–1917: Istoriia voennykh uchilishch* (Moscow: Astrel', 2002), 5.

42. John W. Steinberg, *All the Tsar's Men: Russia's General Staff and the Fate of the Empire, 1898–1914* (Washington, DC: Woodrow Wilson Center Press, 2010), 19.

43. Vorob'eva, *Rossiiskie iunkera*, 13–15.

44. Georgii Shavelskii, *Vospominaniia poslednego protopresvitera russkoi armii i flota*, vol. 1 (New York: Izdatel'stvo imeni Chekhova, 1954), 132–33.

45. Ibid., 134.

46. Danilov, *Velikii Kniaz'*, 354.

47. G. O. von Raukh, "Epokha nashei pervoi revoliutsii, 1905–1907," tetrad' no. 1, GARF, f. R-6249, o. 1, d. 1, l. 13.

48. Princess Cantacuzen, Countess Spéransky, née Grant, *My Life Here and There* (New York: Charles Scribner's Sons, 1921), 306.

49. G. O. von Raukh, "Epokha nashei pervoi revoliutsii, 1905–1907," tetrad' no. 1, GARF, f. R-6249, o. 1, d. 1, l. 14.

50. Oliver Ray, "The Imperial Russian Army Officer," *Political Science Quarterly* 76, no. 4 (1961): 592.

51. Peter Kenez, "A Profile of the Pre-Revolutionary Officer Corps," *California Slavic Studies* 7 (1973): 156.

52. Alexander, Grand Duke of Russia, *Once a Grand Duke* (New York: Cosmopolitan Book Corporation, 1932), 42.

53. Danilov, *Velikii Kniaz'*, 108.

54. Shavel'skii, *Vospominaniia*, vol. 1, 137–38.

55. Kersnovskii, *Istoriia*, 598.

56. Memoirs, 1364–65, BA, P. N. Shatilov papers, Box 12, folder 15.

57. Danilov, *Velikii Kniaz'*, 8.

58. Ibid., 365.

59. *Letters of the Tsaritsa to the Tsar, 1914–1916* (London: Duckworth, 1923), 100.

60. A. A. Ignat'ev, *50 let v stroiu* (Moscow: Sovetskii Pisatel', 1952), 121–22.

61. Sukhomlinov, *Velikii kniaz'*, 43.

62. Spiridovich, *Les dernières années*, vol. 1, 93.

63. A. F. Rediger, *Istoriia moei zhizni: vospominaniia voennogo ministra* (Moscow: Kanon-Press-Ts, 1999), 529.

64. Cantacuzen, *Revolutionary Days*, 391.

65. Shavel'skii, *Vospominaniia*, vol. 1, 131.

66. Ibid., 136.

67. Perevod stat'i, poiavivsheisia v gazete "New York Evening Post" (4 May 1925), BA, ROVS Collection, Box 162.

68. Romanow, *Am Hof*, 29.

69. Danilov, *Velikii Kniaz'*, 20.

70. Robert R. McCormick, "Two Grand Dukes Lead the Russians," *New York Times*, July 12, 1915.

71. A. V. Bogdanovich, *Tri poslednikh samoderzhtsa* (Moscow: Novosti, 1990), 467.

72. Kireev, *Dnevnik*, 53.

73. M. D. Bonch-Bruyevich, *From Tsarist General to Red Army Commander* (Moscow: Progress, 1966), 55–56.

74. Rediger, *Istoriia*, 529.

75. Shavel'skii, *Vospominaniia*, vol. 1, 136.

76. A. A. Polivanov, *Iz dnevnikov i vospominaniia po dolzhnosti voennogo ministra i ego pomoshchnika, 1907–1916 gg.* (Moscow: Vysshii voennyi redaktsionnyi sovet, 1924), 120.

77. "Dnevnik G. O. Raukha," *Krasnyi Arkhiv* 19 (1926): 91.

78. G. O. von Raukh, "Epokha nashei pervoi revoliutsii, 1905–1907," tetrad' no. 3, GARF, f. R-6249, o. 1, d. 3, l. 9.

79. Kenez, "Profile," 151.

80. Brusilov, *A Soldier's Notebook*, 26.

81. Shavel'skii, *Vospominaniia*, vol. 1, 136.

82. Rediger, *Istoriia*, 529.

83. Ibid., 531.

84. Ibid., 530.

2: First Shots, 1873–1878

1. Posluzhnoi spisok, CSHAG, f. 13, o. 25, d. 28.

2. Matitiahu Mayzel, "The Formation of the Russian General Staff, 1880–1917: A Social Study," *Cahiers du Monde Russe et Soviétique* 16 (1975): 311, 316.

3. Steinberg, *All the Tsar's Men*, 45–46.

4. Allan K. Wildman, *The End of the Russian Imperial Army: The Old Army and the Soldiers' Revolt (March–April 1917)* (Princeton University Press, 1980), 21–22.

5. Biograficheskie dannye o Velikom Kniaze Nikolae Nikolaeviche, GARF, f. 5826, o. 1, d. 166g, l. 236.

6. Rapport sur les exercices du Camp du Krasnoe Selo: Avant-propos, no. 2564, 20 August 1906, 2-ème suite, SHD, 7 N 1477.

7. Mayzel, "Formation," 303.

8. G. O. von Raukh, "Epokha nashei pervoi revoliutsii, 1905–1907," tetrad' no. 3, GARF, f. R-6249, o. 1, d. 3, l. 8.

9. N. P. Glinoetskii, *Istoricheskii ocherk Nikolaevskoi akademii general'nogo shtaba* (St. Petersburg: Tipografiia shtaba voisk gvardii i Peterburgskogo voennogo okruga, 1882), 248, 264, 268–74; *Otchet o zaniatiiakh nikolaevskoi akademii general'nogo shtaba za uchebnyi 1875–1876 god* (St. Petersburg: Tipografiia tovarishchestva "Obshchestvennaia Pol'za," 1876).

10. Glinoetskii, *Istoricheskii ocherk*, 285–86.

11. *Otchet o zaniatiiakh*.

12. Glinoetskii, *Istoricheskii ocherk*, 288.

13. *Otchet o zaniatiiakh*.

14. Glinoetskii, *Istoricheskii ocherk*, 171; Posluzhnoi spisok, CSHAG, f. 13, o. 25, d. 28.

15. Rediger, *Istoriia*, 79.

16. Posluzhnoi spisok, CSHAG, f. 13, o. 25, d. 28.

17. For the background to the war see: R. Grant Barnwell, *The Russo-Turkish War* (Philadelphia: John E. Potter, 1877), 414–41.

18. Letter, Grand Duke Nikolai Nikolaevich Junior to Grand Duke Pyotr Nikolaevich, 29 November 1876, GARF, f. 653, o. 2, d. 167, ll. 2–3.

19. Letter, Grand Duke Nikolai Nikolaevich Junior to Grand Duke Pyotr Nikolaevich, 12 December 1876, GARF, f. 653, o. 2, d. 167, l. 4.

20. Letter, Grand Duke Nikolai Nikolaevich Junior to Grand Duke Pyotr Nikolaevich, 18 December 1876, GARF, f. 653, o. 2, d. 167, l. 8.

21. Letter, Grand Duke Nikolai Nikolaevich Junior to Grand Duke Pyotr Nikolaevich, 26 December 1876, GARF, f. 653, o. 2, d. 167, l. 10.

22. Letter, Grand Duke Nikolai Nikolaevich Junior to Grand Duke Pyotr Nikolaevich, 2 January 1877, GARF, f. 653, o. 2, d. 168, l. 1.

23. Letter, Grand Duke Nikolai Nikolaevich Junior to Grand Duke Pyotr Nikolaevich, 22 January 1877, GARF, f. 653, o. 2, d. 168, l. 2.

24. Posluzhnoi spisok, CSHAG, f. 13, o. 25, d. 28.

25. V. V. Zherve, *General-Fel'dmarshal Velikii Kniaz' Nikolai Nikolaevich starshii: istoricheskii ocherk ego zhizni i deiatel'nosti* (St. Petersburg: Tipografiia postavshchikov dvora ego imperatorskogo velichestva t-va M. O. Vol'fa, 1911), 83.

26. Posluzhnoi spisok, CSHAG, f. 13, o. 25, d. 28.

27. Barnwell, *The Russo-Turkish War*, 454.

28. Forbes, *Czar and Sultan*, 30.

29. Barnwell, *The Russo-Turkish War*, 461.

30. Forbes, *Czar and Sultan*, 31.

31. Kolonitskii, "*Tragicheskaia erotika*," 382.

32. Francis Stanley, *St Petersburg to Plevna* (London: Richard Bentley and Son, 1878), 111.

33. Danilov, *Velikii kniaz'*, 24.

34. Zherve, *General-fel'dmarshal*, 96.

35. Alexander Jacob S[illegible]m, *The War in the East: An Illustrated History of the Conflict between Russia and Turkey [illegible] a Review of the Eastern Question* (New York: H.S. Goodspeed, 1878), 244.

36. Posluzhnoi spisok, CSHAG, f. 13, o. 25, d. 28.

37. Barnwell, *The Russo-Turkish War*, 483–85.

38. Colonel Epauchin, *Operations of General Gurko's Advance Guard in 1877* (London: Kegan Paul, Trench, Trübner and Company, 1900), 4.

39. Epanchin, *Na sluzhbe*, 100.

40. Epauchin, *Operations*, 99.

41. Ibid., 102.

42. Posluzhnoi spisok, CSHAG, f. 13, o. 25, d. 28.

43. Ibid.

44. Bruce W. Menning, *Bayonets before Bullets: The Imperial Russian Army, 1861–1914* (Bloomington: Indiana University Press, 1992), 69–70.

45. Posluzhnoi spisok, CSHAG, f. 13, o. 25, d. 28.

46. Barnwell, *The Russo-Turkish War*, 576.

47. Ibid., 598–99.

48. Telegram, Grand Duke Nikolai Nikolaevich Junior to Grand Duke Pyotr Nikolaevich, 9 January 1878, GARF, f. 653, o. 2, d. 168, l. 10.

49. Posluzhnoi spisok, CSHAG, f. 13, o. 25, d. 28.

50. Zherve, *General-fel'dmarsal*, 166.

51. Barnwell, *The Russo-Turkish War*, 626.

52. Richard Graf von Pfeil, *Experiences of a Prussian Officer in the Russian Service during the Turkish War of 1877–78* (London: Edward Stanford, 1893), 259.

53. Romanow, *Am Hof*, 24.

54. Zherve, *General-fel'dmarshal*, 194.

55. Ibid.

3: Hunting and Riding, 1878–1895

1. Posluzhnoi spisok, CSHAG, f. 13, o. 25, d. 28.

2. Danilov, *Velikii Kniaz'*, 31.

3. Posluzhnoi spisok, CSHAG, f. 13, o. 25, d. 28.

4. Telegram, Grand Duke Nikolai Nikolaevich Junior to Grand Duke Pyotr Nikolaevich, 22 February 1885, GARF, f. 653, o. 2, d. 169, l. 8.

5. Telegram, Grand Duke Nikolai Nikolaevich Junior to Grand Duke Pyotr Nikolaevich, 20 March 1885, GARF, f. 653, o. 2, d. 169, l. 9.

6. Letter, LTC de Sermet to the Minister of War, 28 August/9 September 1885, SHD, 7 N 1470.

7. Posluzhnoi spisok, CSHAG, f. 13, o. 25, d. 28.

8. Telegram, Grand Duke Nikolai Nikolaevich Junior to Grand Duke Nikolai Nikolaevich Senior, October 1885 [no precise date given], GARF, f. 646, o. 1, d. 174, l. 39.

9. Posluzhnoi spisok, CSHAG, f. 13, o. 25, d. 28.

10. Spisok velikikh kniazei i lits svity imp. Aleksandra III edushchikh na manevry v okrestakh Bresta i na okhotu v Spalu, 10 August 1886, GARF, f. 653, o. 2, d. 67, ll. 1–3.

11. Telegram, Grand Duke Nikolai Nikolaevich Junior to Grand Duke Pyotr Niko-

laevich, 12 November 1886, GARF, f. 652, o. 2, d. 169, l. 18.

12. Telegram, Grand Duke Nikolai Nikolaevich Junior to Grand Duke Nikolai Nikolaevich Senior, 1 December 1886, GARF, f. 646, o. 1, d. 174, l. 39.

13. Letter, Grand Duke Nikolai Nikolaevich Junior to Grand Duke Pyotr Nikolaevich, 7 January 1887, GARF, f. 653, o. 2, d. 170, ll. 2–3.

14. Letter, Grand Duke Nikolai Nikolaevich Junior to Grand Duke Pyotr Nikolaevich, 22 February 1887, GARF, f. 653, o. 2, d. 170, l. 13.

15. Letter, Grand Duke Nikolai Nikolaevich Junior to Grand Duke Pyotr Nikolaevich, 8 March 1887, GARF, f. 653, o. 2, d. 170, ll. 20–21.

16. Dmitrii Val'tsov, *Psovaia okhota ego imperatorskogo vysochestva velikogo kniazia Nikolaia Nikolaevicha v s. Pershino tul'skoi gub. 1887–1912* (St. Petersburg: Leshtukovskaia parovaia skoropechatnia P. O. Iablonskogo, 1913), 99.

17. Ibid., 15.

18. Telegrams, Grand Duke Nikolai Nikolaevich Junior to Grand Duke Pyotr Nikolaevich, 30 May and 6 June 1887, GARF, f. 653, o. 2, d. 170, ll, 37, 40.

19. Letter of Kaiser Wilhelm to Nicholas II, 18 November 1906, in Andrei Maylunas and Sergei Mironenko, eds., *A Lifelong Passion: Nicholas and Alexandra. Their Own Story* (London: Weidenfeld and Nicolson, 1996), 297.

20. Gordon Brook-Shepherd, *Archduke of Sarajevo: The Romance and Tragedy of Franz Ferdinand of Austria* (Boston: Little, Brown and Company, 1984), 97.

21. Antony Taylor, "'Pig-Sticking Princes': Royal Hunting, Moral Outrage, and the Republican Opposition to Animal Abuse in Nineteenth- and Early Twentieth-Century Britain," *History* 89, no. 293 (2004): 35.

22. Thomas T. Allsen, *The Royal Hunt in Eurasian History* (Philadelphia: University of Pennsylvania Press, 2006), 8–9.

23. Taylor, "Pig-Sticking Princes," 36.

24. Val'tsov, *Psovaia okhota*, 184.

25. Joseph B. Thomas, *Observations on Borzoi, Called in America Russian Wolfhounds* (Boston: Houghton Mifflin, 1912), 45.

26. Val'tsov, *Psovaia okhota*, 20–27.

27. Thomas, *Observations*, 46.

28. Val'tsov, *Psovaia okhota*, 31–36.

29. George Galitzine, "Charm of the Borzois," *Country Life*, November 16, 1989, 106. Reprinted in *The Princes Galitzine. Before 1917 ... and Afterwards* (Washington, DC: Galitzine Books, 2002), 514.

30. Lyn Snyder Hoflin, "Russkaia psovaia borzaia," available online at: <http://www.secrethavenkennel.com/resources/RussiaHoflin.pdf>. Accessed 23 April 2012.

31. Val'tsov, *Psovaia okhota*, 57–88.

32. Ibid., 109.

33. Ibid., 122, 126.

34. Ibid., 120.

35. Thomas, *Observations*, 46.

36. Val'tsov, *Psovaia okhota*, 135, 146.

37. Ibid., 137.

38. Ibid., 141.

39. Ibid., 166–67.

40. Ibid., 167–79.

41. N. Kravchenko, "Psovaia okhota," *Stolitsa i usad'ba* 2 (1914): 6–7.

42. Bogdanovich, *Tri poslednikh samoderzhtsa*, 78.

43. Ibid., 80.

44. G. O. von Raukh, "Epokha nashei pervoi revoliutsii, 1905–1907," tetrad' no. 3, GARF, f. R-6249, o. 1, d. 3, ll. 10–11.

45. G. O. von Raukh, "Epokha nashei pervoi revoliutsii, 1905–1907," tetrad' no. 3, GARF, f. R-6249, o. 1, d. 3, l. 11.

46. Mosolov, *Pri dvore*, 143–44.

47. Telegram, Grand Duke Nikolai Nikolaevich to Grand Duke Pyotr Nikolaevich, 3 September 1888, GARF, f. 653, o. 2, d. 171, l. 7.

48. Telegram, Grand Duke Nikolai Nikolaevich to Grand Duke Pyotr Nikolaevich, 5 January 1889, GARF, f. 653, o. 2, d. 172, l. 1.

49. Posluzhnoi spisok, CSHAG, f. 13, o. 25, d. 28.

50. Telegram, Grand Duke Nikolai Nikolaevich to Grand Duke Pyotr Nikolaevich, 20 March 1889, GARF, f. 653, o. 2, d. 172, l. 5.

51. See, for instance, Annenkova and Golikov, *Printsy Ol'denburgskie*, 296.

52. Danilov, *Velikii Kniaz'*, 36.

53. G. O. von Raukh, "Epokha nashei pervoi revoliutsii, 1905–1907," tetrad' no. 1, GARF, f. R-6249, o. 1, d. 1, l. 83.

54. Shavel'skii, *Vospominaniia*, vol. 1, 127.

55. Count Paul Vasili, *Behind the Veil at the Russian Court* (London: Cassell, 1914), 248.

56. Kireev, *Dnevnik*, 253.

57. Letter, Moulin to Minister of War, 5 February 1896, SHD, 7 N 1474.

58. Posluzhnoi spisok, CSHAG, f. 13, o. 25, d. 28.

59. *Dnevnik imperatora Nikolaia II, 1890–1906 gg.* (Berlin: Slovo, 1923), 20.

60. Posluzhnoi spisok, CSHAG, f. 13, o. 25, d. 28.

61. Rapport sur les manoeuvres de l'armée russe en Volhynie, 15 November 1890, SHD, 7 N 1472.

62. Ibid.

63. Posluzhnoi spisok, CSHAG, f. 13, o. 25, d. 28.

64. Ibid.

65. Letter, Moulin to Minister of War, 16 October 18, SHD, 7 N 1471; Greg King, *The Court of the Last Tsar: Pomp, Power, and Pageantry in the Reign of Nicholas II* (Hoboken: John Wiley and Sons, 2006), 90

66. King, *Court of the Last Tsar*, 90.

67. Ivan Bunin, *The Life of Arseniev: Youth* (Evanston: Northwestern University Press, 1994), 255.

68. Cantacuzène, *Revolutionary Days*, 387.

69. Witte, *Memoirs*, 204; Soboleva, *Velikie kniaz'ia*, 402.

70. Rapport sur les manoeuvres de Krasnoe Selo, 19 August 1891, SHD, 7 N 1472.

71. Letter, Moulin to Minister of War, no. 704, 19 August 1892, "Sur les manoeuvres de Krasnoe Selo," SHD, 7 N 1472.

72. Letter, Vorontsov to Alexander III, 4 August 1892, GARF, f. 671, o. 1, d. 2, l. 3.

73. Letter, Vorontsov to Grand Duke Nikolai Nikolaevich, 4 August 1892, GARF, f. 671, o. 1, d. 2, l. 1.

74. Wortman, *Scenarios of Power*, vol. 2, 118.

75. Ibid., 176.

76. Bogdanovich, *Tri poslednikh samoderzhtsa*, 179–80.

77. Posluzhnoi spisok, CSHAG, f. 13, o. 25, d. 28.

78. Letter, Grand Duke Nikolai Nikolaevich to Grand Duke Nikolai Aleksandrovich [future Emperor Nicholas II], 5 December 1892, GARF, f. 601, o. 1, d. 1311, ll. 1–2.

79. Letter, Moulin to Minister of War, no. 727, 11 January 1893, SHD, 7 N 1473.

80. Letter, Moulin to Minister of War, 6 March 1893, SHD, 7 N 1473.

81. Posluzhnoi spisok, CSHAG, f. 13, o. 25, d. 28.

4: Inspector General: Reforming the Cavalry, 1895–1904

1. Gudrun Persson, *Learning from Foreign Wars: Russian Military Thinking, 1859–73* (Solihull: Helion, 2010), 81.

2. Cited in Gervase Phillips, "'Who Shall Say That the Days of Cavalry Are Over?' The Revival of the Mounted Army in Europe, 1853–1914," *War in History* 18, no. 1 (2011): 5–6.

3. Menning, *Bayonets*, 145.

4. Persson, *Learning*, 82–84; Vladimir S. Littauer, *Russian Hussar: A Story of the Imperial Cavalry, 1911–1920* (Shipensburg: White Mane, 1993), 35.

5. For instance, Kersnovskii, *Istoriia*, 524.

6. Phillips, "Who Shall Say?" 8.

7. Stephen Badsey, *Doctrine and Reform in the British Cavalry, 1880–1918* (Aldershot: Ashgate, 2008), 64.

8. Gerard J. De Groot, "Educated Soldier or Cavalry Officer? Contradictions in the Pre-1914 Career of Douglas Haig," *War & Society* 4, no. 2 (1986): 52.

9. For a description of General P. N. Wrangel's use of such tactics, see: Alexis Wrangel, *General Wrangel, 1878–1929: Russia's White Crusader* (London: Leo Cooper, 1987), 72.

10. Stephen Brown, "The First Cavalry Army in the Russian Civil War, 1918–1920" (PhD diss., University of Wollongong, 1990), 35–36.

11. Steinberg, *All the Tsar's Men*, 93.

12. Particularly notable is Badsey, *Doctrine and Reform*.

13. Gervase Phillips, "Scapegoat Arm: Twentieth-Century Cavalry in Anglophone Historiography," *Journal of Military History* 71, no. 1 (2007): 37–38.

14. Alexis Wrangel, *The End of Chivalry: The Last Great Cavalry Battles, 1914–1918* (New York: Hippocrene, 1982), xviii.

15. Jean Bou, "Cavalry, Firepower, and Swords: The Australian Light Horse and the Tactical Lessons of Cavalry Operations in Palestine, 1916–1918," *Journal of Military History* 71, no. 1 (2007): 100.

16. Ibid., 114.

17. Ibid., 124.

18. Ibid., 116.

19. Phillips, "Scapegoat Arm," 40–48.

20. See, for instance, Phillips, "Who Shall Say?" 28.

21. Count Gustav Wrangel, *The Cavalry in the Russo-Japanese War: Lessons and Critical Considerations* (London: Hugh Rees, 1907), 55.

22. "Sur les manoeuvres de Krasnoe Selo," 25 August 1893, SHD, 7 N 1473.

23. Intelligence Division, War Office, *Foreign Manoeuvres, 1893: Extracts from the*

Reports of Various Officers on the Manoeuvres in Austria, France, Germany, Italy, Russia and Servia (London: War Office [Harrison and Sons], 1894), 52, NAUK, WO 33/54. This episode is also described in "Sur les manoeuvres de Krasnoe Selo," 25 August 1893, SHD, 7 N 1473.

24. Intelligence Division, War Office, *Foreign Manoeuvres, 1893: Extracts from the Reports of Various Officers on the Manoeuvres in Austria, France, Germany, Italy, Russia and Servia* (London: War Office [Harrison and Sons], 1894), 53, NAUK, WO 33/54.

25. Posluzhnoi spisok, CSHAG, f. 13, o. 25, d. 28.

26. Capitaine Deville, Comte-rendu d'un voyage en Russie, 10 August 1894, SHD, 7 N 1484.

27. Ibid.

28. Ibid.

29. Ibid.

30. *Dnevnik imperatora Nikolaia II*, 77.

31. Posluzhnoi spisok, CSHAG, f. 13, o. 25, d. 28.

32. Ibid.

33. Letter, Boyard to Minister of Foreign Affairs, 28 October 1895, SHD, 7 N 1480.

34. Ignat'ev, *50 let*, 101.

35. Ibid.

36. P. A. Polovtsoff, *Glory and Downfall: Reminiscences of a Russian General Staff Officer* (London: C. Bell and Sons, 1935), 39.

37. G. O. von Raukh, "Epokha nashei pervoi revoliutsii," tetrad' no. 3, GARF, f. R-6249, o. 1, d. 3, l. 11.

38. Polovtsoff, *Glory and Downfall*, 39–40.

39. See Irina Reyfman, *Ritualized Violence Russian Style: The Duel in Russian Culture and Literature* (Stanford University Press, 1999); Paul Robinson, "Courts of Honour in the Late Imperial Russian Army," *Slavonic and East European Review* 84, no. 4 (2006): 708–28.

40. Polovtsoff, *Glory and Downfall*, 41–44.

41. *Ustav stroevoi kavaleriiskoi sluzhby, 1896* (St. Petersburg: B. Berezovskii, 1905), 156, 158.

42. Rediger, *Istoriia*, 429.

43. Ibid., 530.

44. Ignat'ev, *50 let*, 100.

45. Epanchin, *Na sluzhbe*, 236–37.

46. Zhurnal Soveta gosudarstvennoi oborony po voprosu o general-inspektorakh, 28 November, and 3, 5, and 17 December 1907, RGVIA, f. 830, o. 1, d. 131, l. 10.

47. Ibid.

48. Order no. 12, 1898, in *Ustav stroevoi kavaleriiskoi sluzhbe*, 296.

49. Order no. 13, 1899, in *Ustav stroevoi kavaleriiskoi sluzhbe*, 298.

50. Order no. 12, 1903, in *Ustav stroevoi kavaleriiskoi sluzhbe*, 333.

51. Order no 13, 1899, in *Ustav stroevoi kavaleriiskoi sluzhbe*, 304, 299.

52. Ibid., 305–306.

53. Eliza Riedi, "Brains or Polo? Equestrian Sport, Army Reform and the Gentlemanly Officer Tradition, 1900–1914," *Journal of the Society for Army Historical Research* 84 (2006): 238.

54. Ignat'ev, *50 let*, 175.

55. Cited in Maksim Os'kin, *Krakh konnogo blitskriga: kavaleriia v pervoi mirovoi voine* (Moscow: Eksmo, 2009), 22.

56. Rapport sur les manoeuvres à Krasnoe Selo, 31 August 1896, SHD, 7 N 1474.

57. For details regarding the visits to France and Germany, see: Letter, Moulin to Minister of War, 5 February 1896, SHD, 7 N 1474; Telegrams to A. P. Izvol'skii, 6 and 18 August 1897, Arkhiv Vneshnei Politiki Rossiiskoi Imperii (henceforth AVPRI), f. 133, o. 1, d. 195, ll. 1–2.

58. Velikii Kniaz' Gavriil Konstantinovich, *V mramornom dvortse* (Moscow: Zakharov, 2001), 37–38.

59. Edward J. Bing, ed., *The Letters of Tsar Nicholas and Empress Marie* (London: Ivor Nicholas and Watson, 1937), 130.

60. Boulay, *La France des Romanov*, 116.

61. Iuliia Petrovna Rybakova, "In the Aleksandrinskii Theater," *Russian Studies in History* 31, no. 3 (1992–1993): 51.

62. Ibid., 52.

63. Velikii Kniaz' Gavriil Konstantinovich, *V mramornom dvortse*, 122.

64. Romanow, *Am Hof*, 223.

65. For information, see the website of the Music and Comedy Theatre, at: <http://rus-ballet.com/static-komediy-1.htm>. Accessed 15 May 2012.

66. Lydia Kyasht, *Romantic Recollections* (Binsted: Noverre, 2010), 126.

67. Warwick, *Ella*, 236.

68. Cantacuzène, *Revolutionary Days*, 384–87.

69. Posluzhnoi spisok, CSHAG, f. 13, o. 25, d. 28.

70. Danilov, *Velikii Kniaz'*, 46.

71. Zhurnal Soveta gosudarstvennoi oborony po voprosu ob ukreplenii osoboi komisii dlia razrabotki meropriiatii po razvitiiu otechestvennogo konevodstva, 16 December 1906, RGVIA, f. 830, o. 1, d. 105, ll. 2–9.

72. Danilov, *Velikii Kniaz'*, 74.

73. King, *Court of the Last Tsar*, 440.

74. Spiridovich, *Les dernières années*, vol. 1, 394.

75. Cited in Annenkova and Golikov, *Printsy Ol'denburgskie*, 298.

76. "Dnevnik A. N. Kuropatkina," *Krasnyi Arkhiv* 2 (1922): 9–10.

77. Letter, Grand Duke Nikolai Nikolaevich to Nicholas II, 10 March 1903, GARF, f. 543, o. 1, d. 20.

78. Ibid.

79. G. O. von Raukh, "Epokha nashei pervoi revoliutsii," tetrad' no. 1, GARF, f. R-6249, o. 1, d. 1, l. 76.

80. Spiridovich, *Les dernières années*, vol. 1, 126.

81. Baroness Sophie Buxhoeveden, *The Life and Tragedy of Alexandra Feodorovna Empress of Russia* (London: Longmans, Green and Company, 1930), 91–92, 134.

82. King, *Court of the Last Tsar*, 155.

83. G. O. von Raukh, "Epokha nashei pervoi revoliutsii," tetrad' no. 1, GARF, f. R-6249, o. 1, d. 1, l. 75.

84. For the case of Russia, see Julia Mannherz, *Modern Occultism in Late Imperial Russia* (DeKalb: Northern Illinois University Press, 2012).

85. Cited in Maylunas and Mironenko, *A Lifelong Passion*, 297.

86. Leonid Heretz, *Russia on the Eve of Modernity: Popular Religion and Traditional Culture under the Last Tsar* (Cambridge: Cambridge University Press, 2008), 22–39.

87. Wortman, *Scenarios of Power*, vol. 2, 386–88.

88. Cited in Maylunas and Mironenko, *A Lifelong Passion*, 229–30. For a fuller account of a miracle at Sarov, see: Paul Kulikovsky, Karen Roth-Nicholls, and Sue Woolmans, eds., *25 Chapters of My Life: Grand Duchess Olga Alexandrovna of Russia* (Kinloss: Librario, 2009), 65.

89. G. O. von Raukh, "Epokha nashei pervoi revoliutsii," tetrad' no. 1, GARF, f. R-6249, o. 1, d. 1, l. 75.

90. Report, Grand Duke Nikolai Nikolaevich to Nicholas II, 26 September 1903, GARF, f. 543, o. 1, d. 29, l. 8

91. "Dnevnik A. N. K[illegible]patkina," 78.

92. Rediger, *Istoriia*, 397.

93. Danilov, *Velikii Kniaz'*, 10. For other explanations of the Tsar's decision, see: Maylunas and Mironenko, *A Lifelong Passion*, 248; Epanchin, *Na sluzhbe*, 308.

94. "Asiaticus," *Reconnaissance in the Russo-Japanese War* (London: Hugh Rees, 1908), 35–36; Wrangel, *The Cavalry in the Russo-Japanese War*, 18.

95. Badsey, *Doctrine and Reform*, 192.

96. Kersnovskii, *Istoriia*, 525.

97. Sukhomlinov, *Vospominaniia*, 78.

98. Os'kin, *Krakh konnogo blitskriga*, 39.

99. Menning, *Bayonets*, 146; see also Steinberg, *All the Tsar's Men*, 88.

100. Sukhomlinov, *Velikii Kniaz'*, 46.

5: The October Manifesto, 1905

1. *Dnevnik imperatora Nikolaia II*, 130.

2. Ibid., 131.

3. Ibid.

4. Robert Massie, *Nicholas and Alexandra* (New York: Dell, 1967), 121.

5. Cantacuzène, *Revolutionary Days*, 35.

6. *Letters of the Tsaritsa to the Tsar*, 99.

7. *Dnevnik imperatora Nikolaia II*, 142–49.

8. Ibid., 160, 162.

9. Ibid., 166.

10. Abraham Ascher, *The Revolution of 1905: Russia in Disarray* (Stanford University Press, 1988), 26.

11. For general histories of the Russo-Japanese War, see: R. M. Connaughton, *The War of the Rising Sun and the Tumbling Bear: A Military History of the Russo-Japanese War 1904–5* (London: Routledge, 1991); Denis and Peggy Warner, *The Tide at Sunrise: A History of the Russo-Japanese War, 1904–1905* (New York: Charterhouse, 1974); J. N. Westwood, *Russia against Japan, 1904–05: A New Look at the Russo-Japanese War* (Houndmills: Macmillan, 1986).

12. Ascher, *Revolution*, 43.

13. Ibid., 58.

14. Ibid., 61–65; Sidney Harcave, *The Russian Revolution of 1905* (London: Collier, 1964), 48, 56.

15. Letter, Moulin to Minister of War, no. 2435, 25 March 1905, SHD, 7 N 1477.

16. I. I. Rostunov, *Russkii front pervoi mirovoi voiny* (Moscow: Nauka, 1976), 27.

17. Ibid., 28.

18. Posluzhnoi spisok, CSHAG, f. 13, o. 25, d. 28.

19. Letter, Grand Duke Nikolai Nikolaevich to Nicholas II, 18 March 1905, GARF, f. 543, o. 1, d. 158, ll. 36–37.

20. Rostunov, *Russkii front*, 27.

21. Ibid., 35.

22. Ibid., 36.

23. Sukhomlinov, *Vospominaniia*, 135–37.

24. Zhurnal osobogo Soveshchaniia pod predsedatel'stvom E. I. V. Velikogo Kniazia Nikolaia Nikolaevicha, 14, 16, 17, 18, 20, 21 May 1905, RGVIA, f. 830, o. 1, d. 3, l. 28.

25. Zhurnal no. 2 Osobogo Soveshchaniia dlia vyrabotki polozheniia o Sovete gosudarstvennoi oborony, 9 May 1905, RGVIA, f. 830, o. 1, d. 3.

26. Zhurnal no. 3 Osobogo Soveshchaniia dlia vyrabotki polozheniia o Sovete gosudarstvennoi oborony, 10 May 1905, RGVIA, f. 830, o. 1, d. 3, l. 13.

27. David MacLaren McDonald, *United Government and Foreign Policy in Russia, 1900–1914* (Cambridge, MA: Harvard University Press, 1992), 212.

28. For the history of the mutiny see Neal Bascomb, *Red Mutiny: Eleven Fateful Days on the Battleship Potemkin* (Boston: Houghton Mifflin, 2007).

29. John Bushnell, *Mutiny amid Repression: Russian Soldiers in the Revolution of 1905–1906* (Bloomington: Indiana University Press, 1985), 46.

30. Witte, *Memoirs*, 424.

31. Ibid., 464.

32. Zhurnal Soveta gosudarstvennoi oborony, 18 July 1905, RGVIA, f. 830, o. 1, d. 12, l. 3.

33. Zhurnal Soveta gosudarstvennoi oborony, 18 July 1905, RGVIA, f. 830, o. 1, d. 12, ll. 5–7.

34. Zhurnal Soveta gosudarstvennoi oborony, 1 September 1905, RGVIA, f. 830, o. 1, d. 21, l. 5.

35. Zhurnal zasedaniia Soveta gosudarstvennoi oborony, 22 September 1905, RGVIA, f. 830, o. 1, d. 24, ll. 2–4.

36. Zhurnal zasedaniia Soveta gosudarstvennoi oborony, 22 September 1905, RGVIA, f. 830, o. 1, d. 24, ll. 5–6.

37. Rediger, *Istoriia*, 535.

38. Ibid., 534.

39. Grand Duke Alexander, *Once a Grand Duke*, 267.

40. Bushnell, *Mutiny amid Repression*, 46.

41. Ascher, *Revolution*, 211.

42. Maurice Paléologue, *An Ambassador's Memoirs* (New York: George H. Doran, 1924), vol.1, 21.

43. Bushnell, *Mutiny amid Repression*, 70–71.

44. The Grand Duke refers to this telegram in a letter to the Emperor written on 3 September 1911: GARF, f. 601, o. 1, d. 1311, l. 2.

45. Dzhunkovskii, *Vospominaniia*, vol. 1, 83.

46. Witte, *Memoirs*, 483.

47. G. O. von Raukh, "Epokha nashei pervoi revoliutsii," tetrad' no. 1, GARF, f. R-6249, o. 1, d. 1, l. 13.

48. G. O. von Raukh, "Epokha nashei pervoi revoliutsii," tetrad' no. 1, GARF, f. R-6249, o. 1, d. 1, l. 14.

49. Kireev, *Dnevnik*, 107.

50. Howard D. Mehlinger and John M. Thompson, *Count Witte and the Tsarist Government in the 1905 Revolution* (Bloomington: Indiana University Press, 1972), 44.

51. Kireev, *Dnevnik*, 107–108.

52. Mosolov, *Pri Dvore*, 57. Witte repeated the same story: Witte, *Memoirs*, 486.

53. Diary, 17 October 1905, HIA, Nicholas II, Emperor of Russia.

54. "The Memorandum (Recollections) of Prince N. D. Obolenskii," in Witte, *Memoirs*, 617.

55. Danilov, *Velikii Kniaz'*, 355.

56. G. O. von Raukh, "Epokha nashei pervoi revoliutsii," tetrad' no. 1, GARF, f. R-6249, o. 1, d. 1, l. 15.

57. *Letters of the Tsaritsa to the Tsar*, 100.

6: Restoring Order, 1905–1906

1. Diary, 19 October 1905, HIA, Nicholas II, Emperor of Russia.

2. Edvard Radzinsky, *The Rasputin File* (New York: Anchor, 2000), 70.

3. Romanow, *Am Hof*, 198.

4. Bing, *Letters of Tsar Nicholas and Empress Marie*, 193–94.

5. Rediger, *Istoriia*, 532–33.

6. Ibid., 534.

7. Harcave, *The Russian Revolution of 1905*, 220; Bushnell, *Mutiny amid Repression*, 84–85.

8. G. O. von Raukh, "Epokha nashei pervoi revoliutsii," tetrad' no. 1, GARF, f. R-6249, o. 1, d. 1, ll. 19–20.

9. Prikaz po voiskam gvardii i Peterburgskogo voennogo okruga, no. 58, 16 November 1905, National Archives of Finland (henceforth NAF), Russian Military Documents (Venalaslet Sotilasasiakirjat, henceforth VESA), folder 5022.

10. "Dnevnik G. O. Raukha," 88.

11. Letter, Grand Duke Nikolai Nikolaevich to Raukh, 19 November 1905, Rossiiskii Gosudarstvennyi Istoricheskii Arkhiv (henceforth RGIA), f. 1656, o. 1, d. 61, ll. 6–7.

12. Zhurnal zasedaniia Soveta gosudarstvennoi oborony, 11 November 1905, RGVIA, f. 830, o. 1, d. 31, ll. 1–3.

13. Prikazanie po voiskam gvardii i peterburgskogo voennogo okruga, no. 267, 2 November 1906, NAF, VESA, folder 3453.

14. Letter, Grand Duke Nikolai Nikolaevich to Raukh, 19 November 1905, RGIA, f. 1656, o. 1, d. 61, l. 7.

15. G. O. von Raukh, "Epokha nashei pervoi revoliutsii," tetrad' no. 1, GARF, f. R-6249, o. 1, d. 1, ll. 30–31; "Dnevnik G. O. Raukha," 91.

16. Letter, Grand Duke Nikolai Nikolaevich to Nicholas II, 24 November 1905, GARF, f. 543, o. 1, d. 548, l. 3. See also: G. O. von Raukh, "Epokha nashei pervoi revoliutsii," tetrad' no. 1, GARF, f. R-6249, o. 1, d. 1, l. 25.

17. G. O. von Raukh, "Epokha nashei pervoi revoliutsii," tetrad' no. 1, GARF, f. R-6249, o. 1, d. 1, l. 21.

18. The painting is by Boris Mikhailovich Kustodiev. A print can be found in *Au service des Tsars: La garde impérial russe de Pierre le Grand à la révolution d'octobre* (Paris: Somogy, 2010), 182–83.

19. "Dnevnik G. O. Raukha," 93.

20. For some later references to these activities, see: letters, Grand Duke Nikolai Nikolaevich to Grand Duchess Anastasia Nikolaevna, 6 and 7 December 1908, GARF, f. 71, o. 1, d. 29, ll. 3 and 13.

21. G. O. von Raukh, "Epokha nashei pervoi revoliutsii," tetrad' no. 1, GARF, f. R-6249, o. 1, d. 1, l. 12.

22. Cantacuzène, *My Life*, 299.

23. Spiridovich, *Les dernières années*, vol. 1, 396.

24. Dzhunkovskii, *Vospominaniia*, 180–81.

25. G. O. von Raukh, "Epokha nashei pervoi revoliutsii," tetrad' no. 1, GARF, f. R-6249, o. 1, d. 1, l. 21.

26. "Dnevnik G. O. Raukha," 84.

27. G. O. von Raukh, "Epokha nashei pervoi revoliutsii," tetrad' no. 1, GARF, f. R-6249, o. 1, d. 1, l. 21.

28. Bing, *The Letters of Tsar Nicholas and Empress Marie*, 202.

29. Toivo U. Raun, "The Revolution of 1905 in the Baltic Provinces and Finland," *Slavic Review* 43, no. 3 (1984): 460. For more on the Baltic region in this period see: James D. White, "The 1905 Revolution in Russia's Baltic Provinces," in *The Russian Revolution of 1905: Centenary Perspectives* (Abingdon: Routledge, 2005), ed. Jonathan D. Smele and Anthony Heywood, 55–78.

30. Raun, "The Revolution of 1905," 462; White, "The 1905 Revolution," 60.

31. Bushnell, *Mutiny amid Repression*, 115.

32. Mehlinger and Thompson, *Count Witte*, 107.

33. G. O. von Raukh, "Epokha nashei pervoi revoliutsii," tetrad' no. 1, GARF, f. R-6249, o. 1, d. 1, l. 53.

34. "Dnevnik G. O. Raukha," 94; also, G. O. von Raukh, "Epokha nashei pervoi revoliutsii," tetrad' no. 1, GARF, f. R-6249, o. 1, d. 1, l. 54.

35. Ascher, *Revolution*, 333.

36. Ibid., 313–14.

37. "Dnevnik G. O. Raukha," 90.

38. Witte, *Memoirs*, 536.

39. Ibid.; "Dnevnik G. O. Raukha," 90.

40. Ascher, *Revolution*, 320.

41. Bushnell, *Mutiny amid Repression*, 130.

42. G. O. von Raukh, "Epokha nashei pervoi revoliutsii," tetrad' no. 1, GARF, f. R-6249, o. 1, d. 1, l. 36.

43. Witte, *Memoirs*, 493.

44. G. O. von Raukh, "Epokha nashei pervoi revoliutsii," tetrad' no. 1, GARF, f. R-6249, o. 1, d. 1, l. 37.

45. G. O. von Raukh, "Epokha nashei pervoi revoliutsii," tetrad' no. 1, GARF, f. R-6249, o. 1, d. 1, l. 39.

46. "Dnevnik G. O. Raukha," 89.

47. G. O. von Raukh, "Epokha nashei pervoi revoliutsii," tetrad' no. 1, GARF, f. R-6249, o. 1, d. 1, ll. 39–40.

48. G. O. von Raukh, "Epokha nashei pervoi revoliutsii," tetrad' no. 3, GARF, f. R-6249, o. 1, d. 3, ll. 5–6.

49. Bing, *The Letters of Tsar Nicholas and Empress Marie*, 211.

50. Ascher, *Revolution*, 332.

51. Mehlinger and Thompson, *Count Witte*, 110–11.

52. "Dnevnik G. O. Raukha," 97.

53. Zhurnal osobogo soveshchaniia, 28 January 1906, RGVIA, f. 830, o. 1, d. 31, ll. 3–6.

54. Zhurnal osobogo soveshchaniia, 28 January 1906, RGVIA, f. 830, o. 1, d. 31, ll. 7–11.

55. Zhurnal zasedaniia Soveta gosudarstvennoi oborony, 4 February 1906, RGVIA, f. 830, o. 1, d. 53, ll. 5–7.

56. Zhurnal zasedaniia Soveta gosudarstvennoi oborony, 4 February 1906, RGVIA, f. 830, o. 1, d. 53, ll. 7–8.

57. Zhurnal zasedaniia Soveta gosudarstvennoi oborony, 4 February 1906, RGVIA, f. 830, o. 1, d. 53, l. 8.

58. Zhurnal zasedaniia Soveta gosudarstvennoi oborony, 4 February 1906, RGVIA, f. 830, o. 1, d. 53, ll. 8–9.

59. Zhurnal Soveta gosudarstvennoi oborony, 9 February 1906, RGVIA, f. 830, o. 1, d. 50, ll. 10–11.

60. Ibid.

61. Zhurnal prodolzheniia zasedaniia Soveta gosudarstvennoi oborony, 15 February 1906, RGVIA, f. 830, o. 1, d. 48, ll. 1–7.

62. G. O. von Raukh, "Epokha nashei pervoi revoliutsii," tetrad' no. 2, GARF, f. R-6249, o. 1, d. 2, ll. 1–2.

63. G. O. von Raukh, "Epokha nashei pervoi revoliutsii," tetrad' no. 3, GARF, f. R-6249, o. 1, d. 3, ll. 7–8.

64. "Tsarskosel'skie soveshchaniia, neizdannye protokoly soveshchaniia v aprele 1906 goda, pod predsedatel'stvom byvshego imperatora po peresmotru osnovnykh zakonov s vvedeniem V. V. Vedovozova," *Byloe* 4 (October 1917): 196–97.

65. Ibid., 199.

66. Ibid., 208.

67. Ibid., 217–30.

68. Ibid., 234.

69. For an analysis of these events, see Abraham Ascher, *P. A. Stolypin: The Search for Stability in Late Imperial Russia* (Stanford University Press, 2001), 86–103.

70. Ibid., 110–12.

71. G. O. von Raukh, "Epokha nashei pervoi revoliutsii," tetrad' no. 2, GARF, f. R-6249, o. 1, d. 2, ll. 11–14.

72. Prikazanie po voiskam gvardii i peterburgskogo voennogo okruga, no. 90, 21 April 1906, NAF, VESA, folder 4518. Also, G. O. von Raukh, "Epokha nashei pervoi revoliutsii," tetrad' no. 2, GARF, f. R-6249, o. 1, d. 2, l. 49.

73. G. O. von Raukh, "Epokha nashei pervoi revoliutsii," tetrad' no. 2, GARF, f. R-6249, o. 1, d. 2, ll. 49–50.

74. Bushnell, *Mutiny amid Repression*, 194.

75. Spiridovich, *Les dernières années*, vol. 1, 79–83; Epanchin, *Na sluzhbe*, 352–53.

76. G. O. von Raukh, "Epokha nashei pervoi revoliutsii," tetrad' no. 2, GARF, f. R-6249, o. 1, d. 2, ll. 51–53.

77. G. O. von Raukh, "Epokha nashei pervoi revoliutsii," tetrad' no. 2, GARF, f. R-6249, o. 1, d. 2, ll. 52–53.

7: The Council of State Defense, 1906–1907

1. G. O. von Raukh, "Epokha nashei pervoi revoliutsii," tetrad' no. 2, GARF, f. R-6249, o. 1, d. 2, ll. 22–23.

2. G. O. von Raukh, "Epokha nashei pervoi revoliutsii," tetrad' no. 2, GARF, f. R-6249, o. 1, d. 2, ll. 24–26.

3. G. O. von Raukh, "Epokha nashei pervoi revoliutsii," tetrad' no. 2, GARF, f. R-6249, o. 1, d. 2, l. 27.

4. Zhurnal Soveta gosudarstvennoi oborony, 5 July 1906, RGVIA, f. 830, o. 1, d. 65, ll. 2–6.

5. Zhurnal Soveta gosudarstvennoi oborony, 5 July 1906, RGVIA, f. 830, o. 1, d. 65, ll. 7–17.

6. Letter, Rediger to Grand Duke Nikolai Nikolaevich, 22 June 1906, RGVIA, f. 830, o. 1, d. 25, ll. 8–10.

7. Zhurnal Soveta gosudarstvennoi oborony, 20 July 1906, RGVIA, f. 830, o. 1, d. 68, ll. 2–9.

8. Prikazanie po voiskam gvardii i peterburgskogo voennogo okruga, no. 190, 17 July 1906, NAF, VESA, folder 3453.

9. Steinberg, *All the Tsar's Men*, 235–37.

10. Rapport sur les exercices du Camp de Krasnoe Selo: Avant-propos, no. 2564, 20 August 1906, 2-ème suite, SHD, 7 N 1477.

11. Rapport sur les exercices du Camp de Krasnoe Selo: Avant-propos, no. 2564, 20 August 1906, SHD, 7 N 1477.

12. Ibid.

13. Diary, 8 October 1906, HIA, Nicholas II, Emperor of Russia.

14. Zhurnal Soveta gosudarstvennoi oborony, 19 October 1906, RGVIA, f. 830, o. 1, d. 79.

15. Zhurnal Soveta gosudarstvennoi oborony, 26 October and 10 November 1906, RGVIA, f. 830, o. 1, d. 81, ll. 2–3.

16. Zhurnal Soveta gosudarstvennoi oborony, 26 October and 10 November 1906, RGVIA, f. 830, o. 1, d. 81, ll. 4–5.

17. Zhurnal Soveta gosudarstvennoi oborony, 26 October and 10 November 1906, RGVIA, f. 830, o. 1, d. 81, ll. 7–11.

18. Zhurnal Soveta gosudarstvennoi oborony, 26 October and 10 November 1906, RGVIA, f. 830, o. 1, d. 81, ll. 12–24.

19. David Allan Rich, *The Tsar's Colonels: Professionalism, Strategy, and Subversion in Late Imperial Russia* (Cambridge, MA: Harvard University Press, 1998), 98; Bruce W. Menning, "War Planning and Initial Operations in the Russian Context," in *War Planning 1914*, ed. Richard F. Hamilton and Holger H. Herwig (Cambridge: Cambridge University Press, 2010), 86, 89.

20. Zapiska o poriadke razsmotreniia voprosov po ustroistvu i proektirovaniiu krepostei i ukreplennykh punktov, 29 September 1905, RGVIA, f. 830, o. 1, d. 26, ll. 3–5.

21. Letter, Grand Duke Nikolai Nikolaevich to Grand Duke Pyotr Nikolaevich, no. 197, 17 December 1905, RGVIA, f. 830, o. 1, d. 26, l. 7.

22. Letter, Palitsyn, no. 20, 29 May 1906, RGVIA, f. 830, o. 1, d. 26, ll. 28–33.

23. Letter, Grand Duke Nikolai Nikolaevich to Palitsyn, no. 164, 9 June 1906, RGVIA, f. 830, o. 1, d. 26, ll. 34–35.

24. Letter, Palitsyn, no. 97, 28 July 1906, RGVIA, f. 830, o. 1, d. 96, ll. 38–40.

25. Zhurnal Soveta gosudarstvennoi oborony, 18 November 1906, RGVIA, f. 830, o. 1, d. 92, ll. 2–6.

26. Zhurnal Soveta gosudarstvennoi oborony, 18 November 1906, RGVIA, f. 830, o. 1, d. 92, ll. 6–7.

27. Zhurnal Soveta gosudarstvennoi oborony, 18 November 1906, RGVIA, f. 830, o. 1, d. 92, ll. 7–8.

28. Zhurnal Soveta gosudarstvennoi oborony, 27 November 1906, RGVIA, f. 830, o. 1, d. 96, ll. 1–5.

29. Zhurnal Soveta gosudarstvennoi oborony, 27 November 1906, RGVIA, f. 830, o. 1, d. 99, ll. 2–3.

30. Zhurnal Soveta gosudarstvennoi oborony, 27 November 1906, RGVIA, f. 830, o. 1, d. 99, l. 8.

31. Ibid.

32. Zhurnal Soveta g arstvennoi oborony, 30 November 1906, RGVIA, f. 830, o. 1, d. 98, ll. 1–9.

33. Zhurnal Soveta gosudarstvennoi oborony, 30 November, and 2, 9, 11 December 1906, RGVIA, f. 830, o. 1, d. 97, ll. 1–41.

34. Witte, *Memoirs*, 721.

35. Bogdanovich, *Tri poslednikh samoderzhtsa*, 414.

36. G. O. von Raukh, "Epokha nashei pervoi revoliutsii," tetrad' no. 3, GARF, f. R-6249, o. 1, d. 3, l. 12.

37. Kyasht, *Romantic Recollections*, 245.

38. Bogdanovich, *Tri poslednikh samoderzhtsa*, 406.

39. Kireev, *Dnevnik*, 178.

40. Ibid., 179.

41. Maylunas and Mironenko, *A Lifelong Passion*, 297.

42. Ibid., 415.

43. Zhurnal soveta gosudarstvennoi oborony, 24 and 29 January, 2 and 7 April 1907, RGVIA, f. 830, o. 1, d. 173, ll. 45–47.

44. Stone, *The Eastern Front, 1914–1917* (London: Hodder and Stoughton, 1975), 31, 174–75.

45. William C. Fuller Jr., *Civil-Military Conflict in Imperial Russia, 1881–1914* (Princeton University Press 1985), 241.

46. Allan Wildman, *The End of the Russian Imperial Army*, 67, fn. 56.

47. Zhurnal soveta gosudarstvennoi oborony, 24 and 29 January, 2 and 7 April 1907, RGVIA, f. 830, o. 1, d. 173, ll. 6–7.

48. Yohanan Petrovsky-Shtern, *Jews in the Russian Army, 1827–1917: Drafted into Modernity* (Cambridge: Cambridge University Press, 2009), 184–91.

49. Zhurnal soveta gosudarstvennoi oborony, 24 and 29 January, 2 and 7 April, RGVIA, f. 830, o. 1, d. 173, l. 8.

50. Ibid.

51. Zhurnal Soveta gosudarstvennoi oborony, 10, 12, 21, 26 February, and 5, 8, 12 March 1907, RGVIA, f. 830, o. 1, d. 170, ll. 3–26.

52. Zhurnal Soveta gosudarstvennoi oborony, 10, 12, 21, 26 February, and 5, 8, 12 March 1907, RGVIA, f. 830, o. 1, d. 170, ll. 30–38.

53. Bing, *The Letters of Tsar Nicholas and Empress Marie*, 227.

54. Ibid., 228.

55. O. Iu. Danilov, *Prolog "Velikoi voiny" 1904–1914 gg. Kto i kak vtiagival Rossiiu v mirovoi konflikt* (Moscow: Pokolenie, 2010), 111.

56. Letter, Grand Duke Nikolai Nikolaevich to Olga Ivanovna Chertkova, 21 April 1907, RGIA, f. 696, o. 1, d. 824, ll. 1–3.

57. "Grand Duke Weds Divorced Princess," *New York Times*, May 13, 1907.

58. Maylunas and Mironenko, *A Lifelong Passion*, 301.

59. Ibid.

60. Cantacuzène, *Revolutionary Days*, 390.

8: Fall from Favor, 1907–1908

1. Rediger, *Istoriia*, vol. 2, 171–74.

2. K. F. Shatsillo, "Korni krizisa vooruzhenii russkoi armii v nachale pervoi mirovoi voiny," in, *Pervaia mirovaia voina: prolog XX veka*, ed. V. L. Mal'kov (Moscow: Nauka, 1998), 561.

3. Letter, Grand Duke Nikolai Nikolaevich to Nicholas II, no. 33, 24 August 1907, RGVIA, f. 830, o. 1, d. 115.

4. Shatsillo, "Korni," 561.

5. Rostunov, *Russkii front*, 42.

6. Zhurnal Soveta gosudarstvennoi oborony, 25 July 1907, RGVIA, f. 830, o. 1, d. 176, l. 2.

7. G. O. von Raukh, "Epokha nashei pervoi revoliutsii," tetrad' no. 2, GARF, f. R-6249, o. 1, d. 2, ll. 60–61.

8. M. Kritskii, "Aleksandr Pavlovich Kutepov: biograficheskii ocherk," in *General Kutepov: sbornik statei* (Paris: Izdanie komiteta imeni Generala Kutepova, 1934), 11–19.

9. This theory originates in Norman Stone, *Eastern Front*, 24–25.

10. Renseignement de l'attaché Mre, 20 March 1909, SHD, 7 N 1537.

11. For instance: Prikazanie po voiskam gvardii i Peterburgskogo voennogo okruga, no. 13, 17 January 1906; no. 62, 16 March 1906; no. 90, 21 April 1906; all in NAF, VESA, folder 4518. See also: Prikazanie po voiskam gvardii i Peterburgskogo voennogo okruga, no. 191, 18 July 1906, NAF, VESA, folder 3453.

12. Prikazanie po voiskam gvardii i Peterburgskogo voennogo okruga, no. 75, 26 April 1908, NAF, VESA, folder 4696.

13. Prikazanie po voiskam gvardii i Peterburgskogo voennogo okruga, no. 158, 25 August 1908, NAF, VESA, folder 4696.

14. G. O. von Raukh, "Epokha nashei pervoi revoliutsii," tetrad' no. 2, GARF, f. R-6249, o. 1, d. 2, l. 83.

15. For instance, Kersnovskii, *Istoriia russkoi armii*, 611–13.

16. Nicholas N. Golovine, *The Russian Campaign of 1914: The Beginning of the War and Operations in East Prussia* (Fort Leavenworth: The Command and General Staff School Press, 1933), 35.

17. Telegram, Bompard, no. 125, 3 August 1907, Ministère des affaires étrangères, archives diplomatiques, La Corneuve (henceforth MAe), Correspondance politique et commerciale 1897–1914, Russie, Box 83.

18. Zhurnal Soveta gosudarstvennoi oborony, 28 November, and 3, 5, 17 December 1907, RGVIA, f. 830, o. 1, d. 131, l. 8.

19. Zhurnal Soveta gosudarstvennoi oborony, 28 November, and 3, 5, 17 December

1907, RGVIA, f. 830, o. 1, d. 131, ll. 9–10.

20. Zhurnal Soveta gosudarstvennoi oborony, 28 November, and 3, 5, 17 December 1907, RGVIA, f. 830, o. 1, d. 131, ll. 11–59.

21. Menning, *Bayonets*, 220.

22. Memo, Grand Duke Nikolai Nikolaevich, 25 December 1907, GARF, f. 601, o. 1, d. 458, l. 3.

23. Menning, *Bayonets*, 227.

24. Memo, Grand Duke Nikolai Nikolaevich, 25 December 1907, GARF, f. 601, o. 1, d. 458, ll. 4–5.

25. Memo, Grand Duke Nikolai Nikolaevich, 25 December 1907, GARF, f. 601, o. 1, d. 458, l. 5.

26. Memo, Grand Duke Nikolai Nikolaevich, 25 December 1907, GARF, f. 601, o. 1, d. 458, ll. 5–6.

27. Rostunov, *Russkii front*, 43–44.

28. Menning, *Bayonets*, 227; William C. Fuller Jr., *Strategy and Power in Russia, 1600–1914* (New York: The Free Press, 1992), 426.

29. Radzinsky, *The Rasputin File*, 82.

30. For a description of the life of John of Kronstadt, see: Nadieszda Kizenko, *A Prodigal Saint: Father John of Kronstadt and the Russian People* (University Park: Pennsylvania State University Press, 2003).

31. Romanow, *Am Hof*, 200–201.

32. *Letters of the Tsaritsa to the Tsar*, 89.

33. Shavel'skii, *Vospominaniia*, vol. 1, 49.

34. Zhurnal Soveta gosudarstvennoi oborony, 25 February 1908, RGVIA, f. 830, o. 1, d. 181, l. 3.

35. Zhurnal Soveta gosudarstvennoi oborony, 25 February 1908, RGVIA, f. 830, o. 1, d. 181, l. 4.

36. Zhurnal Soveta gosudarstvennoi oborony, 25 February 1908, RGVIA, f. 830, o. 1, d. 181, ll. 6–16.

37. Zhurnal Soveta gosudarstvennoi oborony, 25 February 1908, RGVIA, f. 830, o. 1, d. 181, l. 16.

38. Rediger, *Istoriia*, vol. 2, 213.

39. Polivanov, *Iz dnevnikov*, 45; Danilov, *Prolog "Velikoi voiny,"* 126.

40. David Schimmelpenninck van der Oye, "Otnoshenie mezhdu voennymi i grazhdanskimi v III Dume," in *Posledniaia voina Imperatorskoi Rossii*, ed. O. R. Airapetov (Moscow: Tri Kvadrata, 2002), 27.

41. John David Walz, "State Defense and Russian Politics under the Last Tsar" (PhD diss., Syracuse University, 1967), 74.

42. Ibid., 74–75.

43. Rediger, *Istoriia*, vol. 2, 216.

44. *Lettres des Grand-Ducs à Nicolas II* (Paris: Payot, 1926), 9–10.

45. Ibid., 11–12.

46. Ibid., 13–14.

47. Steinberg, *All the Tsar's Men*, 272.

48. Chavchavadze, *The Grand Dukes*, 167.

49. Rediger, *Istoriia*, vol. 1, 535.

50. Ibid., 537.

51. A. S. Lukomskii, *Vospominaniia* (Berlin: Otto Kirchner, 1922), vol. 1, 43.

52. Menning, *Bayonets*, 219.

53. For an analysis of the causes of the Council's failure, see Michael Perrins, "The Council for State Defence, 1905–1909: A Study in Russian Bureaucratic Politics," *Slavonic and East European Review* 58, no. 3 (1980): 395–98.

9: The Calm before the Storm, 1908–1913

1. Yigal Sheffy, "A Model Not to Follow: The European Armies and the Lessons of the War," in *The Impact of the Russo-Japanese War*, ed. Rotem Kowner (London: Routledge, 2007), 260–64.

2. Prikaz po voiskam gvardii i peterburgskogo voennogo okruga, no. 16, 3 April 1908, NAF, VESA, folder 4696.

3. Colonel R. R. (Dicky) Davies, "Helmuth von Moltke and the Prussian-German Development of a Decentralised Style of Command: Metz and Sedan 1870," *Defence Studies* 5, no. 1 (2005): 85.

4. Prikaz po voiskam gvardii i peterburgskogo voennogo okruga, no. 16, 3 April 1908, NAF, VESA, folder 4696.

5. Ibid.

6. Ibid.

7. Prikaz po voiskam gvardii i peterburgskogo voennogo okruga, no. 43, 16 July 1908, NAF, VESA, folder 4696.

8. Prikaz po voiskam gvardii i peterburgskogo voennogo okruga, no. 46, 17 August 1908, NAF, VESA, folder 4696.

9. Polivanov, *Iz dnevnikov*, 48–50.

10. Letter, Touchard to Pichon, no. 228, 3 September 1908, MAe, Correspondance politique et commerciale 1897–1914, Russie, vol. 83.

11. Polivanov, *Iz dnevnikov*, 48.

12. Kireev, *Dnevnik*, 272.

13. Letter, Touchard to Pichon, no. 228, 3 September 1908, MAe, Correspondance politique et commerciale 1897–1914, Russie, vol. 83.

14. Raukh had not wanted to leave the staff to take a command position, but the Grand Duke insisted that he must. See: Letter, Grand Duke Nikolai Nikolaevich to Raukh, 1 June 1908, RGIA, f. 1656, o. 1, d. 61.

15. Prikaz po voiskam gvardii i peterburgskogo voennogo okruga, no. 48, 21 August 1908, NAF, VESA, folder 4696.

16. Ibid.

17. Prikaz po voiskam gvardii i peterburgskogo voennogo okruga, no. 64, 29 October 1908, NAF, VESA, folder 4696.

18. Svod zamechaniiam, Prilozhenie k prikazu no. 64, 29 October 1908, NAF, VESA, folder 4696.

19. Ibid.

20. Prikaz po voiskam gvardii i peterburgskogo voennogo okruga, no. 68, 9 December 1908, NAF, VESA, folder 4696.

21. Letter, Grand Duke Nikolai Nikolaevich to Grand Duchess Anastasia Nikolaevna, 6 December 1908, GARF, f. 671, o. 1, d. 24, ll. 3–6.

22. Letter, Grand Duke Nikolai Nikolaevich to Grand Duchess Anastasia Nikolae-

vna, 7 December 1908, GARF, f. 671, o. 1, d. 24, ll. 11–15.

23. Romanow, *Am Hof*, 222–23.

24. B. A. Nakhapetov, *Vrachebnye tainy doma Romanovykh* (Moscow: Veche, 2007), 286–88.

25. Sukhomlinov, *Velikii Kniaz'*, 47–48, 53.

26. Romanow, *Am Hof*, 321.

27. Ibid., 320–21.

28. Polivanov, *Iz dnevnikov*, 71.

29. Stone, *Eastern Front*, 13, 25–27.

30. Menning, *Bayonets*, 207.

31. Steinberg, *All the Tsar's Men*, 213.

32. Danilov, *Velikii Kniaz'*, 65.

33. A. I. Denikin, *Put' russkogo ofitsera* (Moscow: Vagrius, 2002), 107.

34. Spiridovich, *Les dernières années*, vol. 1, 327–29.

35. Ibid., 396.

36. Maylunas and Mironenko, *A Lifelong Passion*, 329.

37. Tost velikogo kniazia Nikolaia Nikolaevicha v Tsetin'e, AVPRI, f. 133, o. 470, d. 202, l. 1.

38. Letter, Grand Duke Nikolai Nikolaevich to Nicholas II, 2 September 1910, GARF, f. 601, o. 1, d. 13, l. 1.

39. Letter, Grand Duke Nikolai Nikolaevich to Grand Duchess Anastasia Nikolaevna, 13 November 1910, GARF, f. 671, o. 1, d. 30, ll. 1–3.

40. Letter Grand Duke Nikolai Nikolaevich to Grand Duchess Anastasia Nikolaevna, 17 November 1910, GARF, f. 671, o. 1, d. 30, ll. 12–13.

41. Letter Grand Duke Nikolai Nikolaevich to Grand Duchess Anastasia Nikolaevna, 18 November 1910, GARF, f. 671, o. 1, d. 30, ll. 14–15.

42. Sukhomlinov, *Vospominaniia*, 191.

43. Sukhomlinov, *Velikii Kniaz'*, 38–39.

44. Polivanov, *Iz dnevnikov*, 101.

45. Letter Grand Duke Nikolai Nikolaevich to Grand Duchess Anastasia Nikolaevna, 13 December 1910, GARF, f. 671, o. 1, d. 30, l. 16.

46. Letter Grand Duke Nikolai Nikolaevich to Grand Duchess Anastasia Nikolaevna, 14 December 1910, GARF, f. 671, o. 1, d. 30, l. 18.

47. Spiridovich, *Les dernières années*, vol. 2, 231–32.

48. Ibid., 73–74.

49. Posluzhnoi spisok, CSHAG, f. 13, o. 25, d. 28.

50. Letter, Grand Duke Nikolai Nikolaevich to Nicholas II, 3 September 1911, GARF, f. 601, o. 1, d. 1311, ll. 21–22.

51. Spiridovich, *Les dernières années*, vol. 2, 149.

52. Letter, Matton to Minister of War, no. 307, 14/27 February 1912, SHD, 7 N 1487.

53. Projet de programme pour la visite des 6e et 20e Corps d'Armée par S. A. I. le Grand-Duc Nicolas Nicolaevich, MAe, Correspondance politique et commerciale 1897–1914, Russie, vol. 41.

54. Telegram, Louis, no. 208, 23 April 1912, MAe, Correspondance politique et commerciale 1897–1914, Russie, vol. 41.

55. Telegram to Poincaré, 21 April 1912, MAe, Correspondance politique et commerciale 1897–1914, Russie, vol. 41.

56. Dzunkovskii, *Vospominaniia*, vol. 1, 682–83; Spiridovich, *Les dernières années*, vol. 2, 239–40.

57. Spiridovich, *Les dernières années*, vol. 2, 242–43.

58. Telegram, Colonel Matton to Minister of War, no. 376, 8 July 1912, MAe, Correspondance politique et commerciale 1897–1914, Russie, vol. 41.

59. Memoirs, 638, HIA, V. N. Kokovtsov Collection, Box 1.

60. Vladimir Sergeevich Trubetskoi, *A Russian Prince in the Soviet State: Hunting Stories, Letters from Exile, and Military Memoirs* (Evanston: Northwestern University Press, 2006), 256–57.

61. Telegram, Vieugué, no. 246, 23 May 1912, MAe, Correspondance politique et commerciale 1897–1914, Russie, vol. 41; Spiridovich, *Les dernières années*, vol. 2, 265.

62. Liste des officiers russes accompagnants Son Altesse Impériale le Grand Duc Nicolas Nicolaevitch, MAe, Correspondance politique et commerciale 1897–1914, Russie, vol, 41, 240–41.

63. Letter, Laguiche to the French Ambassador and the Minister of War, no. 10, 12/25 November 1912, SHD, 7 N 1478.

64. Telegram, Laguiche, 10 August 1916, MAe, Correspondance, politique étrangère, Avant Guerre 1914–18, vol. 754.

65. Friedrich Stieve, *Isvolsky and the World War*, translated by E. W. Dickes (Freeport: Books for Libraries Press, 1971), 100.

66. Sergei Sazonov, *Fateful Years 1909-1916: The Reminiscences of Sergei Sazonov* (London: Jonathan Cape, 1928), 68–74; Sean McMeekin, *The Russian Origins of the First World War* (Cambridge, MA: The Belknap Press, 2011), 23–24.

67. Letter, Laguiche, 10 November 1912, SHD, 7 N 1478.

68. Letter, Laguiche to the French Ambassador and the Minister of War, no. 10, 12/25 November 1912, SHD, 7 N 1478.

69. For comments to this effect, see: D. C. B. Lieven, *Russia and the Origins of the First World War* (London: Macmillan, 1983), 71–72; Danilov, *Prolog "Velikoi voiny,"* 223.

70. Christopher Clark, *The Sleepwalkers: How Europe Went to War in 1914* (New York: Harper Collins, 2013), 270, 448.

71. Letter, Laguiche, 30 March/12 April 1913, SHD, 7 N 1478.

72. Danilov, *Velikii Kniaz'*, 86.

73. Sazonov, *Fateful Years*, 88.

74. Ibid., 75.

75. Memoirs, Chapter II, 12, BA, P. L. Bark Papers, Box 1.

76. Letter, Laguiche to French Ambassador and Minister of War, no. 22, 1/14 December 1912, SHD, 7 N 1478.

77. Letter, 30 June 1913, SHD, 1 N 17.

78. Velikii Kniaz' Gavriil Konstantinovich, *Na mramornom dvortse*, 174.

79. J. Joffre, *Mémoires du Maréchal Joffre* (Paris: Plon, 1932), 133.

80. Ibid., 131–32.

81. Danilov, *Prolog "Velikoi voiny,"* 229.

82. V. N. Voeikov, *S tsarem i bez tsaria: Vospominaniia poslednego dvortsovogo komendanta gosudaria imperatora Nikolaia II* (Helsingfors: Details of publisher not given, 1936), 12.

10: Supreme Commander, Summer 1914

1. Andrew D. Kalmykow, *Memoirs of a Russian Diplomat: Outposts of the Empire, 1893–1917* (New Haven: Yale University Press, 1971), 196.

2. "Perepiska V. A. Sukhomlinova s N. N. Ianushkevichem," *Krasnyi Arkhiv* 3 (1923): 34, 57.

3. Letter, Laguiche to Dupont, 29 March/11 April 1914, SHD, 7 N 1478.

4. Romanow, *Am Hof*, 103.

5. Paléologue, *An Ambassador's Memoirs*, 22–23.

6. Ibid., 24.

7. Lieven, *Russia and the Origins*, 141.

8. Memoirs, Chapter VII, 8–9, BA, P. L. Bark Papers, Box 1.

9. Memoirs, Chapter, 16, BA, P. L. Bark Papers, Box 1.

10. Lieven, *Russia and the Origins*, 144.

11. Sukhomlinov, *Vospominaniia*, 233–34.

12. Danilov, *Velikii Kniaz'*, 365.

13. Cantacuzène, *Revolutionary Days*, 2–3.

14. Danilov, *Prolog "Velikoi voiny,"* 245.

15. Danilov, *Rossiia*, 13–15.

16. L. C. F. Turner, "[illegible] Russian Mobilization in 1914," *Journal of Contemporary History* 3, no. 1 (1968): 84.

17. Sazonov, *Fateful Years*, 199–205.

18. Memoirs, Chapter VII, 1–7, BA, P. L. Bark Papers, Box 1.

19. Maylunas and Mironenko, *A Lifelong Passion*, 294–95.

20. Cantacuzène, *Revolutionary Days*, 17–18; Knox, "Grand Duke Nicholas," 536; Shavel'skii, *Vospominaniia*, vol. 1, 85.

21. Romanow, *Am Hof*, 112.

22. Ibid., 113–14.

23. Memoirs, Chapter VII, 29, BA, P. L. Bark Papers, Box 1.

24. Cantacuzène, *Revolutionary Days*, 394–95.

25. Spiridovich, *Les dernières années*, vol. 2, 483.

26. Cantacuzène, *Revolutionary Days*, 17.

27. Paléologue, *An Ambassador's Memoirs*, 51.

28. Shavel'skii, *Vospominaniia*, vol. 1, 88.

29. Laura Engelstein, "'A Belgium of Our Own': The Sack of Russian Kalisz, August 1914," *Kritika: Explorations in Russian and Eurasian History* 10, no. 3 (2009): 144.

30. Alfred W. F. Knox, *With the Russian Army 1914–1917* (New York: Arno Press, 1971), 44.

31. Letter, Hanbury Williams to Kitchener, 6 February 1915, NAUK, PRO 30/57/67, 52–54.

32. Danilov, *Velikii Kniaz'*, 127–28.

33. Paléologue, *An Ambassador's Memoirs*, 61–62.

34. Ibid., 62–63.

35. Procès-verbal de l'entretien du 18/31 août 1911 entre les chefs d'État majeur des armées française et russe, MAe, Correspondance politique et commerciale 1897–1914, Russie, vol. 83.

36. Bruce Menning, "Fragmenty odnoi zagadki: Iu. N. Danilov i M. V. Alekseev v russkom voennom planirovanii v period predshestvuiushchii Pervoi mirovoi voine," in

Posledniaia voina imperatorskoi Rossii, ed. O. R. Airapetov (Moscow: Tri Kvadrata, 2002), 87.

37. Menning, "War Planning," 120–22.

38. Letter, Laguiche to Minister of War, no. 253, 13/26 October 1914, SHD, 7 N 757.

39. Telegram, Ianushkevich to Zhilinskii, 24 July 1914, HIA, Russia Shtab Verkhovnogo Glavnokomanduiushchego, Box 1.

40. Telegram, Ianushkevich to Zhilinskii, 25 July 1914, HIA, Russia Shtab Verkhovnogo Glavnokomanduiushchego, Box 1.

41. Danilov, *Rossiia*, 137–38.

42. Dokladnaia zapiska, Grand Duke Nikolai Nikolaevich to Nicholas II, 13 August 1914, GARF, f. 601, o. 1, d. 555, l. 1.

43. Telegram, Ianushkevich to Zhilinskii, no. 345, 28 July 1914, HIA, Russia Shtab Verkhovnogo Glavnokomanduiushchego, Box 1.

44. Ibid.

45. Telegram, Ianushkevich to Zhilinskii, 30 July 1914, HIA, Russia Shtab Verkhovnogo Glavnokomanduiushchego, Box 1.

46. Proclamation by the Russian Commander in Chief, 1 (14) August 1914, NAUK, FCO 371/2095, 34.

47. A. Iu. Bakhturina, *Okrainy rossiiskoi imperii: gosudarstvennaia i natsional'naia politika v gody pervoi mirovoi voiny (1914–1917 gg.)* (Moscow: Rosspen, 2004), 33–34.

48. Paléologue, *An Ambassador's Memoirs*, 81, 84.

49. For a detailed discussion of the Manifesto's origins, see: A. Iu. Bakhturina, "Vozzvanie k poliakam 1 avgusta 1914 g. i ego avtory," *Voprosy Istorii* 8 (1998): 132–36.

50. See, for instance, Bernard Pares, *The Fall of the Russian Monarchy: A Study of the Evidence* (London: Jonathan Cape, 1939), 190.

51. Bakhturina, *Okrainy rossiiskoi imperii*, 29.

52. Memorandum, H. Montgomery Grove, 12 December 1914, NAUK, FO 371/2445, 21.

53. Romanow, *Am Hof*, 124–25.

54. Danilov, *Rossiia*, 123.

55. Dzhunkovskii, *Vospominaniia*, vol. 2, 383–84.

11: Stavka

1. Shavel'skii, *Vospominaniia*, vol. 1, 109.

2. Knox, *With the Russian Army*, 43–45.

3. Henry Mélot, *La Mission du Général Pau aux Balkans et en Russie tzariste, 9 février–11 avril 1915* (Paris: Payot, 1931), 78.

4. Grand Duke Cyril, *My Life in Russia's Service—Then and Now* (London: Selwyn and Blount, 1939), 196.

5. Paléologue, *An Ambassador's Memoirs*, 302.

6. *The Letters of the Tsar to the Tsaritsa, 1914–1917* (London: John Lane the Bodley Head Limited, 1929), 2, 4.

7. Letter, 23 February 1915, Imperial War Museum (henceforth IWM), First World War Papers of Major the Lord Glyn, PP/MCR/67.

8. Mission du Général Pau, février–avril 1915, Rapport, SHD, 7 N 1548.

9. P. K. Kondzerovskii, *V stavke verkhovnogo* (Paris: Voennaia Byl', 1967), 23.

10. Ibid., 27.

11. Bernard Pares, *Day by Day with the Russian Army, 1914–15* (Boston: Houghton Mifflin, 1915), 17.

12. Paléologue, *An Ambassador's Memoirs*, 304–305.

13. *The Memoirs of General Prince Felix Felixovich Yusupov Count Sumarov-Elston*, unpublished translation by Christine H. Galitzine (private collection), 80.

14. Danilov, *Rossiia*, 192.

15. A. Bubnov, *V tsarskoi stavke. Vospominaniia admirala Bubnova* (New York: Izdatel'stvo imeni Chekhova, 1955), 28.

16. John Terraine, *Douglas Haig: The Educated Soldier* (London: Leo Cooper, 1963), 177.

17. Daniel William Graf, "The Reign of the Generals: Military Government in Western Russia, 1914–1915" (PhD diss., University of Nebraska, 1972), 115, fn. 65.

18. Danilov, *Rossiia*, 124.

19. Shavel'skii, *Vospominaniia*, vol. 1, 111.

20. Daniel W. Graf, "Military Rule behind the Russian Front, 1914–1917: The Political Ramifications," *Jahrbücher für Geschichte Osteuropas* 22, no. 3 (1974): 393.

21. For a map of the regions in question, see: Eric Lohr, *Nationalizing the Russian Empire: The Campaign against Enemy Aliens during World War I* (Cambridge, MA: Harvard University Press, 2003), 141.

22. For a photograph of these, in March 1915, see: *Letopis' Voiny, 1914–1915 gg.* 32 (1915): 507.

23. Memorandum, Hanbury Williams, 7 August 1915, NAUK, PRO 30/57/67, 209.

24. Letter, Hanbury Williams to Kitchener, 9 July 1915, NAUK, PRO 30/57/67, 128.

25. Kondzerovskii, *V stavke*, 25.

26. Shavel'skii, *Vospominaniia*, vol. 1, 119.

27. Kondzerovskii, *V stavke*, 25.

28. Letter, de Ryckel to the Belgian Minister of War, 24 November 1915, Musée Royal de l'Armée et d'Histoire Militaire, Brussels (henceforth MRA), Box 5001, 185/14/5579.

29. Kondzerovskii, *V stavke*, 25.

30. Stanley Washburn, *Field Notes from the Russian Front* (London: Andrew Melrose, 1915), 270.

31. Kondzerovskii, *V stavke*, 23.

32. Romanow, *Am Hof*, 287.

33. Kondzerovskii, *V stavke*, 24.

34. R. R. McCormick, "Two Grand Dukes."

35. Romanow, *Am Hof*, 289–90.

36. "Perepiska V. A. Sukhomlinova s N. N. Ianushkevichem," *Krasnyi Arkhiv* 3 (1923): 34.

37. Letter, Hanbury Williams to Kitchener, 5 June 1915, NAUK, PRO 30/57/67, 101.

38. "Stavka i Ministerstvo inostrannykh del," *Krasnyi Arkhiv* 26 (1928): 1–50.

39. Washburn, *Field Notes*, 44.

40. Knox, *With the Russian Army*, 42.

41. Robert R. McCormick, *With the Russian Army: Being the Experiences of a National Guardsman* (New York: Macmillan, 1915), 50.

42. Memoirs, Chapter XII, 9–11, BA, P. L. Bark Papers, Box 1.

43. Shavel'skii, *Vospominaniia*, vol. 1, 250.

44. Report, General Sir J. Hanbury Williams, 5 October 1915, NAUK, PRO 30/57/67, 197.

45. Danilov, *Rossiia*, 199.

46. *Voennyi dnevnik velikogo kniazia Andreia Vladimirovicha Romanova (1914–1917)* (Moscow: Izdatel'stvo im. Sabashnikovykh, 2008), 110–11.

47. Knox, *With the Russian Army*, 42.

48. Shavel'skii, *Vospominaniia*, vol. 1, 115.

49. Bubnov, *V tsarskoi stavke*, 45–46.

50. Kondzerovskii, *V stavke*, 22.

51. Telegram, Paléologue, no. 210, 7 February 1915, MAe, Correspondance politique et commerciale, Avant-Guerre, 1914–18, vol. 757.

52. Memorandum, Hanbury Williams, 7 August 1915, NAUK, PRO 30/57/67, 208.

53. The flag can be seen in a photograph of the Grand Duke and Cossack officers taken at Stavka in winter 1915: *Letopis' Voiny, 1914–15 gg.* 31 (1915), 490.

54. For a photograph of Shavelskii, see: *Letopis' Voiny, 1914–15 gg.* 34 (1915), 551.

55. Sir John Hanbury-Williams, *The Emperor Nicholas II as I Knew Him* (London: Arthur L. Humphreys, 1922), 244; Bubnov, *V tsarskoi stavke*, 29.

56. Mélot, *La Mission du Général Pau*, 80.

57. Mission du Général Pau, février–avril 1915, Rapport, SHD, 7 N 1548.

58. Letter Hanbury Williams to Kitchener, 3 January 1915, NAUK, PRO 30/57/67, 49.

59. Despatch no. X, Hanbury Williams to Buchanan, 22 December 1914, NAUK, FO 371/2446, 141.

60. Knox, "The Grand Duke Nicholas," 538.

61. McCormick, *With the Russian Army*, 56.

62. Ibid., 58–59.

63. Shavel'skii, *Vospominaniia*, vol. 1, 130; Danilov, *Velikii Kniaz'*, 115–16.

64. Shavel'skii, *Vospominaniia*, vol. 1, 131.

65. For a comparison with Joffre, see: O. R. Airapetov, *Generaly, liberaly, predprinimateli: rabota na front i na revoliutsiiu [1907–1917]* (Moscow: Tri Kvadrata, 2003), 49.

66. Shavel'skii, *Vospominaniia*, vol. 1, 120–21.

67. Iu. N. Danilov, *Rossiia*, 126.

68. Despatch no. Ji, Hanbury Williams to Buchanan, 17 January 1915, NAUK, FO 371/2446, 2–8.

69. Kondzerovskii, *V stavke*, 32.

70. Memoirs, Chapter XII, 12, BA, P. L. Bark Papers, Box 1.

71. Hanbury-Williams, *The Emperor Nicholas II*, 15.

72. Mélot, *La Mission du Général Pau*, 82.

73. McCormick, *With the Russian Army*, 55; Kondzerovskii, *V stavke*, 31.

74. McCormick, *With the Russian Army*, 56.

75. Bubnov, *V tsarskoi stavke*, 30.

76. Shavel'skii, *Vospominaniia*, vol. 1, 135.

77. Hanbury-Williams, *The Emperor Nicholas II*, 253–54.

78. Kondzerovskii, *V stavke*, 30.

79. Danilov, *Velikii Kniaz'*, 117.

80. Shavel'skii, *Vospominaniia*, vol. 1, 229–30.

81. Ibid., 297.

82. Letter, Hanbury Williams to Kitchener, 30 August 1915, NAUK PRO 30/57/67, 157.

83. Report, Laguiche to Minister of War, no. 26, 6/19 April 1916, SHD, 7 N 757.

84. Bubnov, *V tsarskoi stavke*, 12.

85. Shavel'skii, *Vospominaniia*, vol. 1, 233.

86. Rapport du Commandant Langlois sur sa Mission en Russie, 5 February 1915, Fasciscule 2, 1, SHD, 7 N 1547.

87. Danilov, *Rossiia*, 126.

88. Ibid., 208.

89. *Voennyi dnevnik velikogo kniazia Andreia Vladimirovicha*, 120.

90. Vladimir Mikhailovich Bezobrazov, *Diary of the Commander of the Russian Imperial Guard, 1914–1917* (Boynton Beach, FL: Dramco, 1994), D46.

91. Davies, "Helmuth von Moltke," 86.

92. Cited in Davies, "Helmuth von Moltke," 83.

93. Lawrence Sondhaus, *Franz Conrad von Hötzendorf: Architect of the Apocalypse* (Boston: Humanities Press, 2000), 163.

94. Terraine, *Douglas Haig*, 93. For a similar comment, see J. P. Harris, *Douglas Haig and the First World War* (Cambridge: Cambridge University Press, 2008), 192.

95. Elizabeth Greenhalgh, *Foch in Command: The Forging of a First World War General* (Cambridge: Cambridge University Press, 2011), 42, 337.

96. Stone, *Eastern Front*, 52.

97. Bubnov, *V tsarskoi stavke*, 27.

98. Telegram, Ianushkevich to Zhilinskii, 3 August 1914, in General'nyi Shtab RKKA, *Manevrennyi period 1914 goda: Vostochno-prusskaia operatsiia* (Moscow: Gosudarstvennoe Voennoe Izdatel'stvo Narodnogo Komissariata Oborony Soiuza SSR, 1939), 89.

99. A. A. Samoilo, *Dve zhizni* (Moscow: Voennoe Izdatel'stvo Ministerstva Oborony Soiuza SSR, 1958), 142.

12: Opening Salvoes, August 1914

1. W. Bruce Lincoln, *Passage through Armageddon: The Russians in War and Revolution, 1914–1918* (New York: Simon and Schuster, 1986), 55.

2. Menning, "War Planning," 129.

3. Ibid.

4. General'nyi Shtab RKKA, *Manevrennyi period 1914 goda: Vostochno-Prusskaia operatsiia*, 182.

5. Danilov, *Rossiia*, 156.

6. Knox, *With the Russian Army*, 49.

7. Proclamation by the Commander-in-Chief to the Peoples of Austria-Hungary, August 1914, NAUK, FCO 371/2096, 30–31.

8. Proclamation of the Commander-in-Chief to the Russian people, 5/18 August 1914, NAUK, FCO 371/2095, 41–42. For the original Russian text, see: Dzhunkovskii, *Vospominaniia*, vol. 2, 384; *Letopis' Voiny, 1914 goda* 1 (1914), 24.

9. "Perepiska V. A. Sukhomlinova s N. N. Ianushkevichem," *Krasnyi Arkhiv* 1 (1923): 217.

10. General'nyi Shtab RKKA, *Manevrennyi period 1914 goda: Vostochno-Prusskaia operatsiia*, 250–51.

11. Ibid., 256.

12. Telegram, Ianushkevich to Zhilinskii, 9 August 1914, HIA, Russia, Shtab Verkhovnogo Glavnokomanduiushchego, Box 1.

13. Rostunov, *Russkii front*, 118.

14. "Perepiska V. A. Sukhomlinova," 218.

15. Telegram, Grand Duke Nikolai Nikolaevich to Nicholas II, 10 August 1914, GARF, f. 601, o. 1, d. 592.

16. Telegram, Grand Duke Nikolai Nikolaevich to Nicholas II, 11 August 1914, GARF, f. 601, o. 1, d. 592.

17. Rostunov, *Russkii front*, 131–32.

18. Telegram, Ianushkevich to Ivanov, 10 August 1914, HIA, Russia, Shtab Verkhovnogo Glavnokomanduiushchego, Box 1.

19. Telegram, Ianushkevich to Ivanov, 11 August 1914, HIA, Russia, Shtab Verkhovnogo Glavnokomanduiushchego, Box 1.

20. Telegrams, Ianushkevich to Ivanov, 10 and 11 August 1914, HIA, Russia, Shtab Verkhovnogo Glavnokomanduiushchego, Box 1.

21. Kondzerovskii, *V stavke*, 35.

22. Danilov, *Rossiia*, 166.

23. Telegram, Grand Duke Nikolai Nikolaevich to Nicholas II, 12 August 1914, GARF, f. 601, o. 1, d. 592, l. 12.

24. Danilov, *Rossiia*, 149.

25. Telegram, Grand Duke Nikolai Nikolaevich to Nicholas II, 13 August 1914, GARF, f. 601, o. 1, d. 592, l. 15.

26. Telegram, Grand Duke Nikolai Nikolaevich to Nicholas II, 14 August 1914, GARF, f. 601, o. 1, d. 592, l. 17.

27. Stone, *Eastern Front*, 66.

28. Ibid., 88.

29. Danilov, *Rossiia*, 168–69.

30. Telegram, Ianushkevich to Ivanov, 17 August 1914, HIA, Russia, Shtab Verkhovnogo Glavnokomanduiushchego, Box 1; Golovin, "The Great Battle of Galicia," 40.

31. Telegram, Grand Duke Nikolai Nikolaevich to Nicholas II, 18 August 1914, GARF, f. 601, o. 1, d. 592, l. 23.

32. Telegram, Grand Duke Nikolai Nikolaevich to Nicholas II, 12 August 1914, GARF, f. 601, o. 1, d. 592, l. 24.

33. Knox, *With the Russian Army*, 90; Letter, Hanbury Williams to Buchanan, 10 October 1914, NAUK, FCO 371/2095, 255.

34. "Perepiska V. A. Sukhomlinova," 235.

35. Shavel'skii, *Vospominaniia*, vol. 1, 144–45.

36. Ibid., 145.

37. Telegram, Grand Duke Nikolai Nikolaevich to Nicholas II, 18 August 1914, GARF, f. 671, o. 1, d. 79, l. 1.

38. General'nyi Shtab RKKA, *Manevrennyi period 1914 goda: Vostochno-Prusskaia operatsiia*, 325.

39. Danilov, *Rossiia*, 184–85.

40. Dokladnaia zapiska, Grand Duke Nikolai Nikolaevich to Nicholas II, 30 August 1914, GARF, f. 601, o. 1, d. 556.

41. Telegram, Grand Duke Nikolai Nikolaevich to Nicholas II, 20 August 1914,

GARF, f. 601, o. 1, d. 592, l. 28.

42. Telegram, Grand Duke Nikolai Nikolaevich to Nicholas II, 21 August 1914, GARF, f. 601, o. 1, d. 592, l. 28.

43. Golovin, "The Great Battle of Galicia," 46.

44. Rostunov, *Russkii front*, 152.

45. Telegram, Ianushkevich to Oranovskii, 24 August 1914, HIA, Russia, Shtab Verkhovnogo Glavnokomanduiushchego.

46. General'nyi Shtab RKKA, *Manevrennyi period 1914 goda: Vostochno-Prusskaia operatsiia*, 334.

47. Ibid., 340.

48. Danilov, *Rossiia*, 44.

49. Telegram, Grand Duke Nikolai Nikolaevich to Nicholas II, 29 August 1914, GARF, f. 601, o. 1, d. 592, l. 44.

50. Telegram, Grand Duke Nikolai Nikolaevich to Nicholas II, 30 August 1914, GARF, f. 601, o. 1, d. 592, l. 47.

51. Order no. 32, 30 August 1914, RGVIA, f. 2003, o.1, d. 1, l. 40.

52. Shavel'skii, *Vospominaniia*, vol. 1, 159.

53. Ibid.

54. Kondzerovskii, *V stavke*, 43–44.

55. Dokladnaia zapiska, Grand Duke Nikolai Nikolaevich to Nicholas II, 30 August 1914, GARF, f. 601, o. 1, d. 556.

56. Telegram, Grand Duke Nikolai Nikolaevich to Nicholas II, 31 August 1914, GARF, f. 601, o. 1, d. 592, l. 48.

57. Telegram, Grand Duke Nikolai Nikolaevich to Nicholas II, 31 August 1914, GARF, f. 601, o. 1, d. 592, l. 5[illegible]

58. Telegram, Grand Duke Nikolai Nikolaevich to Nicholas II, 31 August 1914, GARF, f. 601, o. 1, d. 592, l. 49.

59. Dokladnaia zapiska, Grand Duke Nikolai Nikolaevich to Nicholas II, 7 September 1914, GARF, f. 601, o. 1, d. 556; Telegrams, Grand Duke Nikolai Nikolaevich to Nicholas II, 1 September 1914, GARF, f. 601, o. 1, d. 592, ll. 52–53.

60. Dokladnaia zapiska, Grand Duke Nikolai Nikolaevich to Nicholas II, 7 September 1914, GARF, f. 601, o. 1, d. 556, l. 6.

61. Telegram, Grand Duke Nikolai Nikolaevich to Nicholas II, 2 September 1914, GARF, f. 601, o. 1, d. 592, l. 56.

62. Rapport du Commandant Langlois sur sa Seconde Mission en Russie, 10 avril 1915, SHD, 7 N 1547.

63. Dokladnaia zapiska, Grand Duke Nikolai Nikolaevich to Nicholas II, 30 August 1914, GARF, f. 601, o. 1, d. 556, l. 1.

64. Letter, Laguiche to Minister of War, no. 253, 13/26 October 1914, SHD, 7 N 757.

65. Ludendorff, *Ludendorff's Own Story*, 81–82.

13: The Warsaw-Ivangorod Operation, September–October 1914

1. Telegram, Paléologue, no. 624, 17 September 1914, SHD 5 N 74.

2. General'nyi Shtab RKKA, *Manevrennyi period 1914 goda: Vostochno-Prusskaia operatsiia*, 459.

3. Dokladnaia Zapiska, Grand Duke Nikolai Nikolaevich to Nicholas II, 7 Septem-

ber 1914, GARF, f. 601, o. 1, d. 556, l. 4.

4. Dokladnaia Zapiska, Grand Duke Nikolai Nikolaevich to Nicholas II, 7 September 1914, GARF, f. 601, o. 1, d. 556, ll. 4–5.

5. Telegram, Grand Duke Nikolai Nikolaevich to Nicholas II, 8 September 1914, GARF, f. 601, o. 1, d. 592, l. 62.

6. Telegram, Grand Duke Nikolai Nikolaevich to Ivanov, 8 September 1914, HIA, Russia, Shtab Verkhovnogo Glavnokomanduiushchego, Box 1.

7. General'nyi Shtab RKKA, *Varshavsko-Ivangorodskaia operatsiia* (Moscow: Gosudarstvennoe Voennoe Izdatel'stvo Narodnogo Komissariata Oborony Soiuza SSR, 1938), 11–13.

8. Rostunov, *Russkii front*, 158.

9. General'nyi Shtab RKKA, *Varshavsko-Ivangorodskaia operatsiia*, 25–26.

10. Telegram, Ianushkevich to Ivanov, 12 September 1914, HIA, Russia, Shtab Verkhovnogo Glavnokomanduiushchego, Box 1.

11. General'nyi Shtab RKKA, *Varshavsko-Ivangorodskaia operatsiia*, 32.

12. Rostunov, *Russkii front*, 160.

13. Telegram, Ianushkevich to Ruzskii and Ivanov, 15 September 1914, HIA, Russia, Shtab Verkhovnogo Glavnokomanduiushchego, Box 1.

14. Ludendorff, *Ludendorff's Own Story*, vol. 1, 97.

15. Telegram, Ianushkevich to Ruzskii, 16 September 1914, HIA, Russia, Shtab Verkhovnogo Glavnokomanduiushchego, Box 1.

16. Kersnovskii, *Istoriia*, vol. 3, 672.

17. Telegram, Ianushkevich to Ivanov and Ruzskii, 18 September 1914, HIA, Russia, Shtab Verkhovnogo Glavnokomanduiushchego, Box 1.

18. Telegram, Grand Duke Nikolai Nikolaevich to Nicholas II, 18 September 1914, GARF, f. 601, o. 1, d. 592, l. 75.

19. See for instance: Telegram, Grand Duke Nikolai Nikolaevich to Nicholas II, 29 August 1914, GARF, f. 601, o. 1, d. 592, l. 44; Letters, Grand Duke Nikolai Nikolaevich to Nicholas II, 15 October 1914 and 19 February 1915, GARF, f. 601, o. 1, d. 1311, ll. 23, 28.

20. Cantacuzène, *Revolutionary Days*, 399.

21. Shavel'skii, *Vospominaniia*, vol. 1, 134.

22. Ibid.

23. Ibid., 187.

24. Order no. 75, 24 September 1914, RGVIA, f. 2003, o. 1, d. 1, l. 106.

25. Rostunov, *Russkii front*, 166–67.

26. Danilov, *Rossiia*, 218.

27. General'nyi Shtab RKKA, *Varshavsko-Ivangorodskaia operatsiia*, 159.

28. Ibid., 159.

29. Danilov, *Rossiia*, 218.

30. Telegram, Ianushkevich to Ivanov and Ruzskii, 30 September 1914, HIA, Russia, Shtab Verkhovnogo Glavnokomanduiushchego, Box 1.

31. Telegram, Ianushkevich to Ivanov and Ruzskii, 3 October 1914, HIA, Russia, Shtab Verkhovnogo Glavnokomanduiushchego, Box 1.

32. General'nyi Shtab RKKA, *Varshavsko-Ivangorodskaia operatsiia*, 257.

33. Telegram, Grand Duke Nikolai Nikolaevich to Nicholas II, 4 October 1914, GARF, f. 601, o. 1, d. 592, l. 91.

34. Message, Grand Duke Nikolai Nikolaevich to Kitchener, 17 October 1914,

NAUK, PRO 30/57/67, 4.

35. Telegram, Ianushkevich to Ivanov, 4 October 1914, HIA, Russia, Shtab Verkhovnogo Glavnokomanduiushchego, Box 1.

36. General'nyi Shtab RKKA, *Varshavsko-Ivangorodskaia operatsiia*, 263.

37. Telegram, Grand Duke Nikolai Nikolaevich to Nicholas II, 9 October 1914, GARF, f. 601, o. 1, d. 592, l. 96.

38. Telegram, Ianushkevich to Ivanov and Ruzskii, 9 October 1914, HIA, Russia, Shtab Verkhovnogo Glavnokomanduiushchego, Box 1.

39. General'nyi Shtab RKKA, *Lodzinskaia operatsiia* (Moscow: Gosudarstvennoe Voennoe Izdatel'stvo Narodnogo Komissariata Oborony Soiuza SSR, 1936), 31–32.

40. General'nyi Shtab RKKA, *Lodzinskaia operatsiia*, 32.

41. Ludendorff, *Ludendorff's Own Story*, vol. 1, 108, 110.

42. Letter, Grand Duke Nikolai Nikolaevich to Nicholas II, 15 October 1914, GARF, f. 601, o. 1, d. 1311, ll. 23–24.

43. Letter, Hanbury Williams to Kitchener, 21 October 1914, NAUK, PRO 30/57/67, 25.

44. Telegram, Grand Duke Nikolai Nikolaevich to Nicholas II, 16 October 1914, GARF, f. 601, o. 1, d. 592, l. 105.

45. General'nyi Shtab RKKA, *Varshavsko-Ivangorodksaia operatsiia*, 379.

46. General'nyi Shtab RKKA, *Lodzinskaia operatsiia*, 36.

47. Telegram, Ianushkevich to Ivanov, 19 October 1914, HIA, Russia, Shtab Verkhovnogo Glavnokomanduiushchego, Box 1.

48. General'nyi Shtab RKKA, *Lodzinskaia operatsiia*, 59.

49. Stone, *Eastern Front*, 101.

50. Telegram, Ianushkevich to Ivanov and Ruzskii, 20 October 1914, HIA, Russia, Shtab Verkhovnogo Glavnokomanduiushchego, Box 1.

51. Zapiski, vol. 1, 22, HIA, F. F. Palitsyn Collection, Box 1.

52. Zapiski, vol. 1, 64, HIA, F. F. Palitsyn Collection, Box 1.

53. Danilov, *Velikii Kniaz'*, 148.

54. Danilov, *Rossiia*, 222.

55. Danilov, *Velikii Kniaz'*, 150.

14: The Battle of Lodz, November 1914

1. "Iz istorii bor'by v verkhakh nakanune fevral'skoi revoliutsii," *Russkoe Proshloe* 6 (1996): 155.

2. Telegram, Grand Duke Nikolai Nikolaevich to Nicholas II, 26 October 1914, GARF, f. 601, o. 1, d. 592, l. 113.

3. Telegram, Ianushkevich to Ruzskii, 26 October 1914, HIA, Russia, Shtab Verkhovnogo Glavnokomanduiushchego, Box 1.

4. Telegram, Ianushkevich to Ruzskii, 28 October 1914, HIA, Russia, Shtab Verkhovnogo Glavnokomanduiushchego, Box 1.

5. Telegram, Ianushkevich to Ivanov and Ruzskii, 28 October 1914, HIA, Russia, Shtab Verkhovnogo Glavnokomanduiushchego, Box 1.

6. Zapiski, vol. 1, 52–53, HIA, F. F. Palitsyn Collection, Box 1.

7. Ibid., 63.

8. Telegram, Ivanov to Ianushkevich, 30 October 1914, HIA, Russia, Shtab Verk-

hovnogo Glavnokomanduiushchego, Box 1.

9. Telegram, Grand Duke Nikolai Nikolaevich to Ivanov, 30 October 1914, HIA, Russia, Shtab Verkhovnogo Glavnokomanduiushchego, Box 1.

10. Ludendorff, *Ludendorff's Own Story*, vol. 1, 118.

11. Danilov, *Rossiia*, 229.

12. General'nyi Shtab RKKA, *Lodzinskaia operatsiia*, 80.

13. Dispatch no. H, Hanbury Williams to Buchanan, 17 November 1914, NAUK, WO 106/1099, 1, 5.

14. General'nyi Shtab RKKA, *Lodzinskaia operatsiia*, 185.

15. Telegram, Ianushkevich to Ruzskii, 5 November 1914, HIA, Russia, Shtab Verkhovnogo Glavnokomanduiushchego, Box 1.

16. Telegram, Grand Duke Nikolai Nikolaevich to Nicholas II, 6 November 1914, GARF, f. 601, o. 1, d. 592, l. 122.

17. Telegram, Grand Duke Nikolai Nikolaevich to Nicholas II, 8 November 1914, GARF, f. 601, o. 1, d. 592, l. 126.

18. Telegram, Ianushkevich to Ivanov, 8 November 1914, HIA, Russia, Shtab Verkhovnogo Glavnokomanduiushchego, Box 1.

19. Telegram, Grand Duke Nikolai Nikolaevich to Nicholas II, 9 November 1914, GARF, f. 601, o. 1, d. 592, l. 128.

20. General'nyi Shtab RKKA, *Lodzinskaia operatsiia*, 257–59.

21. Danilov, *Rossiia*, 243.

22. Telegram, Ianushkevich to Ivanov, 10 November 1914, HIA, Russia, Shtab Verkhovnogo Glavnokomanduiushchego, Box 1.

23. "Stavka i Ministerstvo inostrannykh del," 25.

24. Telegram, Ianushkevich to Ivanov, 10 November 1914, HIA, Russia, Shtab Verkhovnogo Glavnokomanduiushchego, Box 1.

25. Telegram, Grand Duke Nikolai Nikolaevich to Nicholas II, 10 November 1914, GARF, f. 601, o. 1, d. 592, l. 129.

26. Bubnov, *V tsarskom stavke*, 97.

27. Telegram, Grand Duke Nikolai Nikolaevich to Nicholas II, 16 November 1914, GARF, f. 601, o. 1, d. 592, l. 136.

28. Telegram, Ianushkevich to Ivanov, 15 November 1914, HIA, Russia, Shtab Verkhovnogo Glavnokomanduiushchego, Box 1.

29. Zapiska o blizhaishikh meropriiatiiakh dlia obezpecheniia uspekha dal'neishikh voennykh operatsii, HIA, Russia, Shtab Verkhovnogo Glavnokomanduiushchego, Box 1.

30. General'nyi Shtab RKKA, *Lodzinskaia operatsiia*, 328–29.

31. Telegram, Grand Duke Nikolai Nikolaevich to Emperor Nicholas II, 5 February 1915, GARF, f. 601, o. 1, d. 592, l. 278.

32. General'nyi Shtab RKKA, *Lodzinskaia operatsiia*, 334.

33. Ibid., 335.

34. Telegram, Grand Duke Nikolai Nikolaevich to Nicholas II, 18 November 1914, GARF, f. 601, o. 1, d. 592, l. 161.

35. *The Letters of the Tsar to the Tsaritsa*, 14.

36. Telegram, Laguiche to Joffre, no. 1033, 5 December 1914, SHD, 5 N 74.

37. Telegram, Buchanan, no. 27, 5 December 1914, NAUK, FCO 371/2095, 315.

38. Telegram, Joffre to Ministers of War and Foreign Affairs, 21 December 1914, SHD, 5 N 74.

39. Telegram, Ianushkevich to Ruzskii, 22 November 1914, HIA, Russia, Shtab Verkhovnogo Glavnokomanduiushchego, Box 1.

40. "Perepiska V. A. Sukhomlinova s N. N. Ianushkevichem," *Krasnyi Arkhiv* 1 (1922): 142.

41. Bezobrazov, *Diary*, D24.

42. Graf, *The Reign of the Generals*, 72.

43. Rodzianko, *The Reign of Rasputin*, 118–19.

44. Ibid., 118.

45. Ibid.

46. Shavel'skii, *Vospominaniia*, vol. 1, 190.

47. Kolonitskii, *"Tragicheskaia erotika,"* 414.

48. Ibid., 413–14.

49. Telegram, Grand Duke Nikolai Nikolaevich to Nicholas II, 1 December 1914, GARF, f. 601, o. 1, d. 592, l. 168.

50. Zhurnal soveshchaniia sostoiavshevegosia v Breste 30 noiabria 1914 goda, HIA, Russia, Shtab Verkhovnogo Glavnokomanduiushchego, Box 1.

51. Telegram, Grand Duke Nikolai Nikolaevich to Nicholas II, 2 December 1914, GARF, f. 601, o. 1, d. 592, l. 171.

52. Stone, *Eastern Front*, 107.

15: Winter, December 1914–January 1915

1. Knox, *With the Russian Army*, 218.

2. General'nyi Shtab RKKA, *Lodzinskaia operatsiia*, 427.

3. Dispatches, no. V, Addendum, 19 December 1914, and no. W, 20 December 1914, NAUK, FCO371/2446, 136–38.

4. Knox, *With the Russian Army*, 223.

5. Order no. 203, 5 December 1914, RGVIA, f. 2003, o. 1, d. 1, ll. 353–54.

6. Kolonitskii, *"Tragicheskaia erotika,"* 432.

7. Ibid., 436.

8. Kersnovskii, *Istoriia*, 693–94.

9. Ibid., 693.

10. Buchanan, *My Mission*, vol. 2, 95.

11. Dispatch no. X, Hanbury Williams to Buchanan, 22 December 1914, NAUK, FCO 371/2446.

12. Dispatch no. Y, Hanbury Williams to Buchanan, 24 December 1914, NAUK, FCO 371/2446.

13. Dispatch no. Z, Hanbury Williams to Buchanan, 26 December 1914, NAUK, FCO 371/2446.

14. A. I. Spiridovich, *Velikaia voina i fevral'skaia revoliutsiia* (New York: Vseslavianskoe Izdatel'stvo, 1960), 80.

15. For various descriptions of the Grand Duke's talk with Hanbury Williams, see: Hanbury-Williams, *The Emperor Nicholas II*, 23–24, 248; "Stavka i Ministerstvo inostrannykh del," 34; Dispatch no. B1, Hanbury Williams to Buchanan, 30 December 1914, NAUK, FCO 371/2446, 166; Letter, Hanbury Williams to Kitchener, NAUK, PRO 30/57/67, 44; Telegram, Paléologue, no. 13, 3 January 1915, SHD, 5 N 74.

16. Roger Ford, *Eden to Armageddon: World War I in the Middle East* (New York:

Pegasus, 2010), 203–206.

17. Telegram, Grand Duke Nikolai Nikolaevich to Nicholas II, 20 December 1914, GARF, f. 601, o. 1, d. 592, l. 199.

18. Telegram, Grand Duke Nikolai Nikolaevich to Nicholas II, 23 December 1914, GARF, f. 601, o. 1, d. 592, l. 205.

19. Telegram, Grand Duke Nikolai Nikolaevich to Nicholas II, 23 December 1914, GARF, f. 601, o. 1, d. 592, l. 204.

20. Telegram, Ianushkevich to Ruzskii, 25 December 1914, HIA, Russia, Shtab Verkhovnogo Glavnokomanduiushchego, Box 1.

21. Telegram, Grand Duke Nikolai Nikolaevich to Nicholas II, 26 December 1914, GARF, f. 601, o. 1, d. 592, l. 208.

22. "Perepiska V. A. Sukhomlinova s N. N. Ianushkevichem," *Krasnyi Arkhiv* 2 (1922): 160–61.

23. Letter, Orlov to Grand Duke Nikolai Nikolaevich, 30 December 1914, RGVIA, f. 276, o. 1, d. 25, ll. 27–28.

24. Dispatch, no. F, Hanbury Williams to Buchanan, 14 January 1915, NAUK, FCO 371/2446, 199.

25. Telegram, Grand Duke Nikolai Nikolaevich to Nicholas II, 3 January 1915, GARF, f. 601, o. 1, d. 592, l. 219.

26. Rapport du Commandant Langlois sur sa Mission en Russie, 5 February 1915, Fasciscule 2, 2, SHD, 7 N 1547.

27. Telegram, Paléologue, 17 January 1915, MAe, Correspondence politique et commercial, 1896–1914, Guerre 1914–1918, Russie, vol. 641.

28. Order no. 1, 1 January 1915, RGVIA, f. 2003, o. 1, d. 2, ll. 1–2.

29. Letter, Kudashev to Sazonov, no. 272, 6 January 1915. HIA, N. de Basily Collection, Box 3, folder, General Headquarters, Correspondence 1914–1917.

30. Danilov, *Rossiia*, 282–83.

31. Ibid., 284–86.

32. General'nyi Shtab RKKA, *Lodzinskaia operatsiia*, 449.

33. Dispatch no. L1, Hanbury Williams to Buchanan, 21 January 1915, NAUK, FCO 371/2446, 216.

34. Hanbury-Williams, *The Emperor Nicholas II*, 38–39.

35. "Stavka i Ministerstvo inostrannykh del," 46.

36. Rostunov, *Russkii front*, 225.

37. For a description of the battles in the Carpathians, see: Graydon A. Tunstall, *Blood on the Snow: The Carpathian Winter War of 1915* (Lawrence: University of Kansas Press, 2010).

38. Telegram, Grand Duke Nikolai Nikolaevich to Nicholas II, 13 January 1915, GARF, f. 601, o. 1, d. 592, l. 238.

39. Telegram, Grand Duke Nikolai Nikolaevich to Nicholas II, 15 January 1915, GARF, f. 601, o. 1, d. 592, l. 241.

40. Telegram, Grand Duke Nikolai Nikolaevich to Nicholas II, 17 January 1915, GARF, f. 601, o. 1, d. 592, l. 244.

41. Telegram, Grand Duke Nikolai Nikolaevich to Nicholas II, 19 January 1915, GARF, f. 601, o. 1, d. 592, l. 247.

42. Spiridovich, *Velikaia voina*, 87.

43. *The Letters of the Tsar to the Tsaritsa*, 25.

44. Ibid., 26.

45. Bing, *The Letters of Tsar Nicholas and Empress Marie*, 292.

46. Danilov, *Rossiia*, 288–89.

47. GARF, f. 601, o. 1, d. 1311, l. 27, Letter, Grand Duke Nikolai Nikolaevich to Nicholas II, 19 February 1915.

48. Danilov, *Rossiia*, 289.

49. Dispatch, no. U1, 11 February 1915, NAUK, FCO 371/2446, 257.

50. Telegram, Grand Duke Nikolai Nikolaevich to Nicholas II, 28 January 1915, GARF, f. 601, o. 1, d. 592, l. 262.

51. Letter, Laguiche to Minister of War, no. 257, 30 January/12 February 1915, SHD, 7 N 757.

52. Telegram, Grand Duke Nikolai Nikolaevich to Nicholas II, 3 February 1915, GARF, f. 601, o. 1, d. 592, l. 274.

53. Telegram, Ianushkevich to Ruzskii, 2 February 1915, HIA, Russia, Shtab Verkhovnogo Glavnokomanuiushchego, Box 1.

54. Soveshchanie na Sedletse 4-go fevralia 1915 g., HIA, Russia, Shtab Verkhovnogo Glavnokomanduiushchego, Box 1.

55. Stone, *Eastern Front*, 118.

56. Telegram, Ianushkevich to Ivanov, 8 February 1915, HIA, Russia, Shtab Verkhovnogo Glavnokomanduiushchego, Box 1.

57. Telegram, Ianushkevich to Ivanov and Ruzskii, 10 February 1915, HIA, Russia, Shtab Verkhovnogo Glavnokomanduiushchego, Box 1.

16: Behind the Lines

1. Dispatch, no. U1, 11 February 1915, NAUK, FCO 371/2446, 257.

2. Shavel'skii, *Vospominaniia*, vol. 1, 234.

3. Ibid.

4. Lohr, *Nationalizing the Russian Empire*, 138.

5. Shavel'skii, *Vospominaniia*, vol. 1, 235.

6. Peter Gatrell, *A W[illegible] Empire Walking: Refugees in Russia during World War I* (Bloomington and Indianap[illegible] Indiana University Press, 1999).

7. Lohr, *Nationalizing the Russian Empire*.

8. Gatrell, *A Whole Empire Walking*, 21–22.

9. Lohr, *Nationalizing the Russian Empire*, 19–20.

10. Peter Holquist, "The Role of Personality in the First (1914–1915) Russian Occupation of Galicia and Bukovina," in *Anti-Jewish Violence: Rethinking the Pogrom in East European History*, ed. Jonathan Dekel-Chen et al. (Bloomington and Indianapolis: Indiana University Press, 2011), 52–73.

11. Letter, Kudashev to Sazonov, 31 August 1914, HIA, N. de Basily Collection, Box 3, folder, General Headquarters, Correspondence 1914–17.

12. Mark von Hagen, *War in a European Borderland: Occupations and Occupation Plans in Galicia and Ukraine, 1914–1918* (Seattle: University of Washington Press, 2007), 22.

13. Graf, *The Reign of the Generals*, 108–109.

14. Letter, Kudashev to Sazonov, 31 August 1914, HIA, N. de Basily Collection, Box 3, folder, General Headquarters, Correspondence 1914–1917.

15. Brusilov, *A Soldier's Notebook*, 59.

16. A. Iu. Bakhturina, *Politika Rossiiskoi imperii v vostochnoi Galitsii v gody pervoi mirovoi voiny* (Moscow: AIRO-XX, 2000), 160.

17. "Stavka i Ministerstvo inostrannykh del," 10–11; Shavel'skii, *Vospominaniia*, 167.

18. Bakhturina, *Politika*, 160.

19. Danilov, *Velikii Kniaz'*, 170.

20. Telegram, Nicholas II to Bobrinskii, no. 128, 15 September 1914, RGVIA, f. 2005, o. 1, d. 13, l. 475.

21. Shavel'skii, *Vospominaniia*, vol. 1, 170.

22. Letter, Sabler to Ianushkevich, 8 January 1915; telegrams, Ianushkevich to Sabler, 11 and 15 January 1915, RGVIA, f. 2005, o. 1, d. 13, ll. 547–51.

23. Shavel'skii, *Vospominaniia*, vol. 1, 171. Shavel'skii dates Sabler's visit as having taken place in late November, but unless Sabler made more than one visit, of which there is no record, Shavel'skii's memory must have been faulty.

24. Ibid., 175.

25. Danilov, *Velikii Kniaz'*, 170.

26. Letter, Ivanov to Grand Duke Nikolai Nikolaevich, 5 November 1914, RGVIA, f. 2005, o. 1, d. 13, ll. 328–29.

27. Order no. 189, 24 November 1914, RGVIA, f. 2005, o. 1, d. 13, l. 232.

28. Alexander Victor Prusin, *Nationalizing a Borderland: War, Ethnicity, and Anti-Jewish Violence in East Galicia, 1914–1920* (Tuscaloosa: University of Alabama Press, 2005), 38.

29. Ibid.

30. Joshua Sanborn, "Unsettling the Empire: Violent Migrations and Social Disaster in Russia during World War I," *Journal of Modern History* 77, no. 2 (2005): 305; Graf, "Military Rule," 398; Gattrell, *A Whole Empire Walking*, 17.

31. Holquist, "The Role of Personality," 53, 59.

32. Prusin, *Nationalizing*, 49.

33. Letter, Ianushkevich to Gesse, 16 April 1915, RGVIA, f. 2005, o. 1, d. 13, l. 438.

34. Letter, Ianushkevich to Bobrinskii, 16 April 1915, RGVIA, f. 2005, o. 1, d. 13, l. 439; see also ll. 441–42, letters, Gesse to Ianushkevich, 4 May 1915 and Ianushkevich to Gesse, 8 May 1915.

35. Telegram, Minister of Internal Affairs to all Governors and Town Mayors, 11 August 1914, RGVIA, f. 2005, o. 1, d. 24, l. 2.

36. Telegram, Grand Duke Nikolai Nikolaevich to Goremykin, 3 October 1914, RGVIA, f. 2005, o. 1, d. 24, l. 3.

37. Telegram, Ianushkevich to Goremykin, no. 70, 8 October 1914, RGVIA, f. 2005, o. 1, d. 24, l. 4.

38. "Iz istorii bor'by," 153.

39. Letter, Ianushkevich to Vladimir Fedorovich, no. 71, 8 October 1914, RGVIA, f. 2005, o. 1, d. 24, l. 5.

40. Telegram to Ianushkevich, 11 October 1914, RGVIA, f. 601, o. 1, d. 24, ll. 6–10.

41. Telegram, Ianushkevich to Goremykin, 14 October 1914, RGVIA, f. 601, o. 1, d. 24, l. 15.

42. Telegram, Ianushkevich to Ebelov, 12 October 1914, RGVIA, f. 601, o. 1, d. 24, l. 12.

43. Telegram, Ianushkevich to Goremykin, no. 304, 3 November 1914, RGVIA, f.

2005, o. 1, d. 24, ll. 50–59.

44. Letter, Ianushkevich to van der Flit, no. 1085, 20 December 1914, RGVIA, f. 2005, o. 1, d. 24, l. 133.

45. Telegram, Ianushkevich to Oranovskii, 26 December 1914, RGVIA, f. 2005, o. 1, d. 28, l. 78.

46. Letter, Ianushkevich to the Commander of the Kiev Military District, no. 4439, 12 June 1915, RGVIA, f. 2005, o. 1, d. 28, l. 132.

47. Ibid.

48. "Iz istorii bor'by," 154.

49. For explanations of this see: Lohr, *Nationalizing the Russian Empire*, 18; Sanborn, "Unsettling the Empire," 303; Heretz, *Russia on the Eve of Modernity*, 34–39, 153–54, 225.

50. Danilov, *Velikii Kniaz'*, 200.

51. G. O. von Raukh, "Epokha nashei pervoi revoliutsii," tetrad' no. 2, GARF, f. R-6249, o. 1, d. 2, l. 68.

52. Dzhunkovskii, *Vospominaniia*, vol. 2, 421.

53. *The Memoirs of General Felix Felixovich Yusupov*, 97; *The Diary of Princess Zenaida Nikolaevna Yusupov January 1–April 25 1919*, unpublished translation by Christine H. Galitzine (private collection), entry for 5 January 1919.

54. William C. Fuller Jr., *The Foe Within: Fantasies of Treason and the End of Imperial Russia* (Ithaca: Cornell University Press, 2006), 176.

55. Letter, Grand Duke Nikolai Nikolaevich to Nicholas II, 8 February 1915, GARF, f. 601, o. 1, d. 1311, ll. 25–26.

56. M. K. Lemke, *250 dnei v tsarskoi stavke (25 sent. 1915–2 iiulia 1916)* (Petersburg: Gosudarstvennoe Izdatel'stvo, 1920), 340–41.

57. *Voennyi dnevnik velikogo kniazia Andreia Vladimirovicha*, 128.

58. Fuller, *The Foe Within*, 133–48.

59. See for instance: Spiridovich, *Velikaia voina*, 110.

60. Fuller, *The Foe Within*, 162–65.

61. Gatrell, *A Whole Empire Walking*, 16.

62. Epanchin, *Na sluzhbe*, 33.

63. Telegram, Grand Duke Nikolai Nikolaevich to Nicholas II, 24 February 1915, GARF, f. 601, o. 1, d. 592, l. 324.

64. Telegram, Grand Duke Nikolai Nikolaevich to Nicholas II, 25 May 1915, GARF, f. 601, o. 1, d. 592, l. 445.

65. "Perepiska V. A. Sukhomlinova s N. N. Ianushkevichem," *Krasnyi Arkhiv* 3 (1923): 45.

17: The Carpathian Offensive, February–April 1915

1. Letter, Paget to Kitchener, 22 February 1915, NAUK, PRO 30/57/67, 5–7.

2. Letter, Paget to Kitchener, 25 February 1915, NAUK, PRO 30/57/67, 9–10.

3. Letter, 23 February 1915, IWM, First World War Papers of Major the Lord Glyn.

4. Ibid.

5. Telegram, Grand Duke Nikolai Nikolaevich to Nicholas II, 13 February 1915, GARF, f. 601, o. 1, d. 592, l. 296.

6. Tunstall, *Blood on the Snow*, 132.

7. Telegram, Grand Duke Nikolai Nikolaevich to Nicholas II, 17 February 1915,

GARF, f. 601, o. 1, d. 592, l. 306.

8. Telegram, Ianushkevich to Ruzskii, 16 February 1915, HIA, Russia, Shtab Verkhovnogo Glavnokomanduiushchego, Box 1.

9. Telegram, Ianushkevich to Ruzskii, 18 February 1915, HIA, Russia, Shtab Verkhovnogo Glavnokomanduiushchego, Box 1.

10. Ronald Park Bobroff, *Roads to Glory: Late Imperial Russia and the Turkish Straits* (London and New York: I. B. Tauris, 2006), 126–28.

11. Letter, Hanbury Williams to Kitchener, 2 March 1915, NAUK, PRO 30/57/67, 68.

12. Telegram, Grand Duke Nikolai Nikolaevich to Nicholas II, 17 February 1915, GARF, f. 601, o. 1, d. 592, l. 132.

13. Dispatch no. E, 4 March 1915, NAUK, FCO 371/2446, 289.

14. Letter, Grand Duke Nikolai Nikolaevich to Nicholas II, 19 February 1915, GARF, f. 601, o. 1, d. 1311.

15. Mélot, *La Mission du Général Pau*, 79–80.

16. Ibid., 88.

17. Rostunov, *Russkii front*, 222.

18. *Letters of the Tsar to the Tsaritsa*, 31.

19. For an example of Paléologue's habit of dissimulating in his dispatches, see: Clark, *The Sleepwalkers*, 436.

20. Telegram, Paléologue, no. 430, 18 March 1915, SHD, 5 N 74.

21. Paléologue, *An Ambassador's Memoirs*, vol. 1, 305.

22. Rapport du Commandant Langlois sur sa Seconde Mission en Russie, Fasciscule III, 5, 10 April 1915, SHD, 7 N 1547.

23. Telegram, Laguiche, no. 90, 25 March 1915, SHD, 5 N 74.

24. Rapport du Commandant Langlois sur sa Seconde Mission en Russie, Fasciscule I, 2–4, 10 April 1915, SHD, 7 N 1547.

25. Telegram, Ianushkevich to Ivanov and Ruzskii, 6 March 1915, HIA, Russia, Shtab Verkhovnogo Glavnokomanduiushchego, Box 1.

26. Danilov, *Rossiia*, 303.

27. Telegram, Ianushkevich to Ruzskii, 4 March 1915, HIA, Russia, Shtab Verkhovnogo Glavnokomanduiushchego, Box 1.

28. Danilov, *Rossiia*, 315.

29. *The Letters of the Tsar to the Tsaritsa*, 38.

30. Dzhunkovskii, *Vospominaniia*, vol. 2, 529.

31. Shavel'skii, *Vospominaniia*, vol. 1, 237.

32. Spiridovich, *Velikaia voina*, 142.

33. Order no. 166, 9 March 1915, RGVIA, f. 2003, o. 1, d. 3, l. 41.

34. Airapetov, *Generaly*, 52.

35. Whether ill health was really the reason for his resignation is disputed, but there is some evidence that it was: Telegram, Grand Duke Nikolai Nikolaevich to Nicholas II, 13 March 1915, GARF, f. 601, o. 1, d. 592, l. 344; Telegram, Laguiche to Minister of War, no. 126, 30 March 1915, SHD, 5 N 74; "Perepiska V. A. Sukhomlinova s N. N. Ianushkevichem," *Krasnyi Arkhiv* 3 (1923): 45.

36. Telegram, Grand Duke Nikolai Nikolaevich to Nicholas II, 15 March 1915, GARF, f. 601, o. 1, d. 592, l. 346.

37. Telegram, Grand Duke Nikolai Nikolaevich to Nicholas II, 19 March 1915, GARF, f. 601, o. 1, d. 592, l. 355.

38. "Stavka i Ministerstvo inostrannykh del: prodolzhenie," *Krasnyi Arkhiv* 27 (1928): 9, fn. 1, 4.

39. Telegram, Ianushkevich to Alekseev, 24 March 1915, HIA, Russia, Shtab Verkhovnogo Glavnokomanduiushchego, Box 1.

40. General'nyi Shtab Krasnoi Armii, *Gorlitskaia operatsiia* (Moscow: Voennoe Izdatel'stvo Narodnogo Komissariata Oborony Soiuza SSR, 1941), 29.

41. Ibid., 33.

42. Telegram, Grand Duke Nikolai Nikolaevich to Nicholas II, 25 March 1915, GARF, f. 601. o. 1, d. 592, l. 368.

43. Telegram, Grand Duke Nikolai Nikolaevich to Nicholas II, 26 March 1915, GARF, f. 601. o. 1, d. 592, l. 370.

44. Telegram, Grand Duke Nikolai Nikolaevich to Nicholas II, 29 March 1915, GARF, f. 601. o. 1, d. 592, l. 377.

45. Telegram, Grand Duke Nikolai Nikolaevich to Nicholas II, 30 March 1915, GARF, f. 601. o. 1, d. 592, l. 378.

46. Telegram, Ianushkevich to Alekseev, 30 March 1915, HIA, Russia, Shtab Verkhovnogo Glavnokomanduiushchego, Box 1.

47. McCormick, "Two Grand Dukes."

48. McCormick, *With the Russian Army*, 251.

49. Danilov, *Velikii Kniaz'*, 170; Shavel'skii, *Vospominaniia*, vol. 1, 239.

50. Voeikov, *S Tsarem*, 122.

51. See for instance, Dzhunkovskii, *Vospominaniia*, vol. 2, 535–36.

52. *The Letters of the Tsar to the Tsaritsa*, 40.

53. Danilov, *Velikii Kniaz'*, 172.

54. Shavel'skii, *Vospominaniia*, vol. 1, 175.

55. Spiridovich, *Velikaia voina*, 120.

56. Shavel'skii, *Vospominaniia*, vol. 1, 177.

57. Ibid., 240.

58. Order no. 321, 30 April 1915, RGVIA, f. 2003, o. 2, d. 3, l. 352.

18: The Battle of Gorlice-Tarnow, May–June 1915

1. Telegram, Grand Duke Nikolai Nikolaevich to Nicholas II, 15 April, GARF, f. 601, o. 1, d. 592, l. 393.

2. Telegram, Grand Duke Nikolai Nikolaevich to Nicholas II, 16 April, GARF, f. 601, o. 1, d. 592, l. 395.

3. Telegram, Grand Duke Nikolai Nikolaevich to Nicholas II, 17 April, GARF, f. 601, o. 1, d. 592, l. 397.

4. Richard L. DiNardo, *Breakthrough: The Gorlice-Tarnow Campaign, 1915* (Santa Barbara: Praeger, 2010), 48.

5. General'nyi Shtab Krasnoi Armii, *Gorlitskaia operatsiia*, 120.

6. Ibid., 121.

7. Telegram, Grand Duke Nikolai Nikolaevich to Nicholas II, 21 April 1915, GARF, f. 601, o. 1, d. 592, l. 402.

8. General'nyi Shtab Krasnoi Armii, *Gorlitskaia operatsiia*, 150–51.

9. Telegram, Ianushkevich to Ivanov, 23 April 1915, HIA, Russia, Shtab Verkhovnogo Glavnokomanduiushchego, Box 1.

10. Telegram, Ianushkevich to Ivanov, 24 April 1915, HIA, Shtab Verkhovnogo Glavnokomanduiushchego, Box 1.

11. General'nyi Shtab Krasnoi Armii, *Gorlitskaia operatsiia*, 208.

12. Telegram, Grand Duke Nikolai Nikolaevich to Ivanov, 26 April 1915, HIA, Shtab Verkhovnogo Glavnokomanduiushchego, Box 1.

13. Telegram, Grand Duke Nikolai Nikolaevich to Nicholas II, 28 April 1915, GARF, f. 601, o. 1, d. 592, l. 413.

14. General'nyi Shtab Krasnoi Armii, *Gorlitskaia operatsiia*, 323–24.

15. Telegram, Grand Duke Nikolai Nikolaevich to Nicholas II, 28 April 1915, GARF, f. 601, o. 1, d. 592, l. 414.

16. Telegram, Grand Duke Nikolai Nikolaevich to Ivanov and Alekseev, 27 April 1915, HIA, Shtab Verkhovnogo Glavnokomanuiushchego, Box 1.

17. General'nyi Shtab Krasnoi Armii, *Gorlitskaia operatsiia*, 300–301.

18. Stone, *Eastern Front*, 155; Knox, *With the Russian Army*, 273.

19. Letter, Hanbury Williams to Kitchener, 15 May 1915, NAUK, PRO 30/57/67, 74–81.

20. Letter, Hanbury Williams to Kitchener, 24 May 1915, NAUK, PRO 30/57/67, 91–96.

21. Letter, Kudashev to Sazonov, 5 July 1915, HIA, N. de Basily Collection, Box 3, folder "General Headquarters, Correspondence, 1914–1917."

22. Rodzianko, *The Reign of Rasputin*, 128.

23. Ibid., 129.

24. General'nyi Shtab Krasnoi Armii, *Gorlitskaia operatsiia*, 316.

25. Ibid., 314–15.

26. Telegram, Grand Duke Nikolai Nikolaevich to Nicholas II, 3 May 1915, GARF, f. 601, o. 1, d. 592, l. 422.

27. General'nyi Shtab Krasnoi Armii, *Gorlitskaia operatsiia*, 320.

28. Graf, *The Reign of the Generals*, 176.

29. Dzhunkovskii, *Vospominaniia*, vol. 2, 549.

30. *The Letters of the Tsar to the Tsaritsa*, 54–55.

31. Rodzianko, *The Reign of Rasputin*, 131–32.

32. Telegram, Ianushkevich to Alekseev, 6 May 1915, HIA, Russia, Shtab Verkhovnogo Glavnokomanduiushchego, Box 1.

33. Telegram, Grand Duke Nikolai Nikolaevich to Nicholas II, 21 May 1915, GARF, f. 601, op. 1, d. 592, l. 439.

34. Report, General Sir J. Hanbury Williams, 5 October 1915, NAUK, PRO 30/57/67, 183.

35. Telegram, Grand Duke Nikolai Nikolaevich to Nicholas II, 21 May 1915, GARF, f. 601, o. 1, d. 592, l. 439.

36. Telegram, Ianushkevich to Alekseev and Ivanov, 10 May 1915, HIA, Russia, Shtab Verkhovnogo Glavnokomanduiushchego, Box 1.

37. Telegram, Laguiche to Minister of War, no. 88, 23 May 1915, SHD, 5 N 74.

38. Telegram, Laguiche to Minister of War, no. 90, 25 May 1915, SHD, 5 N 74.

39. Shavel'skii, *Vospominaniia*, vol. 1, 251.

40. Ibid., 249–50.

41. Ibid., 252.

42. Ibid.

43. Telegram, Grand Duke Nikolai Nikolaevich to Nicholas II, 14 May 1915, GARF, f. 601, o. 1, d. 592, l. 424.

44. Telegram, Grand Duke Nikolai Nikolaevich to Nicholas II, 15 May 1915, GARF, f. 601, o. 1, d. 592, l. 426.

45. Telegram, Grand Duke Nikolai Nikolaevich to Nicholas II, 17 May 1915, GARF, f. 601, o. 1, d. 592, l. 430.

46. Telegram, Grand Duke Nikolai Nikolaevich to Nicholas II, 17 May 1915, GARF, f. 601, o. 1, d. 592, l. 432.

47. Telegram, Grand Duke Nikolai Nikolaevich to Nicholas II, 19 May 1915, GARF, f. 601, o. 1, d. 592, l. 436.

48. Michael T. Florinsky, "A Page of Diplomatic History: Russian Military Leaders and the Problem of Constantinople during the War," *Political Science Quarterly* 44, no. 1 (1929): 113–14.

49. Bubnov, *V tsarskoi stavke*, 139–40.

50. Shavel'skii, *Vospominaniia*, vol. 1, 253–54.

51. Telegram, Grand Duke Nikolai Nikolaevich to Nicholas II, 18 May 1915, GARF, f. 601, o. 1, d. 592, l. 433.

52. DiNardo, *Breakthrough*, 81–82.

53. Telegram, Grand Duke Nikolai Nikolaevich to Nicholas II, 21 May 1915, GARF, f. 601, o. 1, d. 592, l. 439.

54. Telegram, Ianushkevich to Ivanov, 21 May 1915, HIA, Russia, Shtab Verkhovnogo Glavnokomanduiushchego, Box 1.

55. Telegram, Grand Duke Nikolai Nikolaevich to Nicholas II, 23 May 1915, GARF, f. 601, o. 1, d. 592, l. 441.

56. Zapiski, vol. 1, 109–10, HIA, F. F. Palitsyn Collection, Box 1.

57. Telegram, Ianushkevich to Alekseev, 26 May 1915, HIA, Russia, Shtab Verkhovnogo Glavnokomanduiushchego, Box 1.

58. Dokladnaia zapiska, Grand Duke Nikolai Nikolaevich to Nicholas II, 25 May 1915, GARF, f. 601, o. 1, d. 611, ll. 1–2.

59. Telegram, Grand Duke Nikolai Nikolaevich to Nicholas II, 25 May 1915, GARF, f. 601, o. 1, d. 592, ll. 444–45.

60. Telegram, Grand Duke Nikolai Nikolaevich to Nicholas II, 26 May 1915, GARF, f. 601, o. 1, d. 592, l. 446.

61. Airapetov, *Generaly*, 79.

62. Radzinsky, *The Rasputin File*, 320.

63. Rapport du Commandant Langlois sur sa Quatrième Mission en Russie, 16 September 1915, part II, chapter 4, SHD, 7 N 1547.

64. Hubertus F. Jahn, *Patriotic Culture in Russia during World War I* (Ithaca and London: Cornell University Press, 1995), 173.

65. Rapport du Commandant Langlois sur sa Quatrième Mission en Russie, 16 September 1915, part II, chapter 3, 3, SHD, 7 N 1547.

66. Kolonitskii, "*Tragicheskaia erotika*," 513.

67. Rapport du Commandant Langlois sur sa Quatrième Mission en Russie, 16 September 1915, part I, chapter 1, 5, SHD, 7 N 1547.

68. Letter, Laguiche, 29 May/11 June 1915, SHD, 7 N 1545.

69. Letter, Hanbury Williams to Kitchener, 13 June 1915, NAUK, PRO 30/57/67, 109–13.

70. Rapport du Commandant Langlois sur sa Troisième Mission en Russie, 20 June 1915, fascicule III, 1, SHD, 7 N 1547.

71. Telegram, Grand Duke Nikolai Nikolaevich to Nicholas II, 5 June 1915, GARF, f. 601, o. 1, d. 614, l. 119.

72. Zapiski, vol. 1, 114, HIA, F. F. Palitsyn Collection, Box 1.

73. Postanovlenie soveshchaniia v Kholme, sostoiavshegosia 4 iiunia 1915 goda, HIA, Russia, Shtab Verkhovnogo Glavnokomanduiushchego, Box 1.

74. Danilov, *Rossiia*, 357.

75. Telegram, Ianushkevich to Alekseev and Ivanov, 7 June 1915, HIA, Russia, Shtab Verkhovnogo Glavnokomanduiushchego, Box 1.

19: The Great Retreat, July–August 1915

1. Letter, Orlov to Ianushkevich, 2 June 1915, RGVIA, f. 276, o. 1, d. 25, ll. 72–74.

2. Dzhunkovskii, *Vospominaniia*, vol. 2, 579.

3. *The Letters of the Tsar to the Tsaritsa*, 57.

4. Shavel'skii, *Vospominaniia*, vol. 1, 279.

5. Danilov, *Velikii Kniaz'*, 205–206.

6. Shavel'skii, *Vospominaniia*, vol. 1, 293–94.

7. Golovine, *The Russian Army*, 154.

8. *Letters of the Tsaritsa to the Tsar*, 100.

9. Ibid., 151.

10. Ibid., 154.

11. Telegram, Buchanan to Grey, no. 918, 28 June 1915, NAUK, FCO 371/2450.

12. *The Letters of the Tsar to the Tsaritsa*, 65.

13. Ibid., 66.

14. Zapiski, vol. 1, 143. HIA, F. F. Palitsyn Collection, Box 1.

15. Postanovlenie soveshchaniia v Sedletse, sostoiavshegosia 22-go iiunia 1915 goda, HIA, Russia, Shtab Verkhovnogo Glavnokomanduiushchego, Box 1.

16. Telegram, Grand Duke Nikolai Nikolaevich to Alekseev, 22 June 1915, HIA, Russia, Shtab Verkhovnogo Glavnokomanduiushchego, Box 1.

17. Shavel'skii, *Vospominaniia*, vol. 1, 257.

18. Postanovlenie soveshchaniia v Sedletse, sostoiavshegosia 22-go iiunia 1915 goda, HIA, Russia, Shtab Verkhovnogo Glavnokomanduiushchego, Box 1.

19. Zapiski, vol. 1, 146–47, HIA, F. F. Palitsyn Collection, Box 1.

20. Letter, Ianushkevich to Savvich, no. 2820, 26 June 1915, HIA, Russia, Shtab Verkhovnogo Glavnokomanduiushchego, Box 1.

21. Order no. 523, 26 June 1915, RGVIA, f. 2003, o. 1, d. 4, l. 155.

22. Order no. 524, 26 June 1915, RGVIA, f. 2003, o. 1, d. 4, l. 155.

23. Graf, "Military Rule," 401.

24. Telegram, Archbishop Aleksandr to Grand Duke Nikolai Nikolaevich, no. 6025, 6 July 1915, RGVIA, f. 2005, o. 1, d. 40, l. 85.

25. Telegram, Grand Duke Nikolai Nikolaevich to Archbishop Aleksandr, 10 July 1915, RGVIA, f. 2005, o. 1, d. 40, l. 86.

26. Telegram, Grand Duke Nikolai Nikolaevich to Nicholas II, 29 June 1915, GARF, f. 601, o. 1, d. 612, l. 7.

27. Telegram, Grand Duke Nikolai Nikolaevich to Nicholas II, 2 July 1915, GARF, f.

601, o. 1, d. 612, l. 22.

28. Telegram, Grand Duke Nikolai Nikolaevich to Nicholas II, 3 July 1915, GARF, f. 601, o. 1, d. 612, l. 21.

29. DiNardo, *Breakthrough*, 121.

30. Telegram, Grand Duke Nikolai Nikolaevich to Nicholas II, 4 July 1915, GARF, f. 601, o. 1, d. 614, l. 133.

31. Kratkii otchet o s"ezde v Sedletse, 6 July 1915, HIA, Russia, Shtab Verkhovnogo Glavnokomanduiushchego, Box 1.

32. Letter, Kudashev to Sazonov, 9 July 1915, HIA, N. de Basily Collection, Box 3, folder "General Headquarters, Correspondence 1914–17."

33. Zapiski, vol. 1, 163, HIA, F. F. Palitsyn Collection, Box 1.

34. Telegram, Grand Duke Nikolai Nikolaevich to Nicholas II, 6 July 1915, GARF, f. 601, o. 1, d. 614, l. 136.

35. Order no 183, 8 July 1915, RGVIA, f. 2003, o. 1, d. 4, l. 183.

36. Telegrams, Grand Duke Nikolai Nikolaevich to Nicholas II, 10 and 11 July 1915, GARF, f. 601, o. 1, d. 612, l. 29, and d. 614, l. 144.

37. Telegram, Grand Duke Nikolai Nikolaevich to Nicholas II, 12 July 1915, GARF, f. 601, o. 1, d. 614, l. 145.

38. Soveshchanie v Sedletse 15-go iiulia v prisutstvii ego Imperatorskogo Velichestva Verkhovnogo Glavnokomanduiushchego, HIA, Russia, Shtab Verkhovnogo Glavnokomanduiushchego, Box 1.

39. Telegram, Laguiche to Minister of War, nos. 155–56, 1 August 1915, SHD, 5 N 74.

40. Telegram, Grand Duke Nikolai Nikolaevich to Nicholas II, 16 July 1915, GARF, f. 601, o. 1, d. 614, l. 149.

41. Telegram, Grand Duke Nikolai Nikolaevich to Nicholas II, 17 July 1917, GARF, f. 601, o. 1, d. 614, l. 150.

42. DiNardo, *Breakthrough*, 125.

43. Telegram, Grand Duke Nikolai Nikolaevich to Nicholas II, 21 July 1917, GARF, f. 601, o. 1, d. 614, l. 154.

44. Hanbury-Williams, *The Emperor Nicholas II*, 47.

45. Soveshchanie v Rovno 24 iiulia 1915 goda v prisutstvii Ego Imperatorskogo Vysochestva Verkhovnogo Glavnokomanduiushchego, HIA, Russia, Shtab Verkhovnogo Glavnokomanduiushchego, Box 1.

46. Danilov, *Rossiia*, 368.

47. Telegram, Ianushkevich to Ivanov, 27 July 1915, HIA, Russia, Shtab Verkhovnogo Glavnokomanduiushchego, Box 1.

48. Telegram, Ianushkevich to Alekseev, 28 July 1915, HIA, Russia, Shtab Verkhovnogo Glavnokomanduiushchego, Box 1.

49. Telegram, Laguiche, no. 174, 11 August 1915, SHD, 7 N 1545.

50. Ibid.

51. Cantacuzène, *Revolutionary Days*, 66.

52. Shavel'skii, *Vospominaniia*, vol. 1, 299–300.

53. *The Letters of the Tsar to the Tsaritsa*, 61.

54. Michael Chernyavsky, ed., *Prologue to Revolution: Notes of A. N. Iakhontov on the Secret Meetings of the Council of Ministers, 1915* (Englewood Cliffs, NJ: Prentice-Hall, 1967), 25.

55. Transcript of message from Grand Duke Nikolai Nikolaevich to Krivoshein, 1 August 1915, RGIA, f. 1571, o. 1, d. 310, l. 4.

56. Zapiski, vol. 1, 178, HIA, F. F. Palitsyn Collection, Box 1.

57. Bonch-Bruyevich, *From Tsarist General*, 110.

58. Telegram, Grand Duke Nikolai Nikolaevich to Nicholas II, 4 August 1915, GARF, f. 601, o. 1, d. 614, l. 176.

59. Shavel'skii, *Vospominaniia*, vol. 1, 300.

60. A photograph of this letter can be found in Romanow, *Am Hof*, between pages 352 and 353. The original of the letter was sold in an auction in 2012 to an anonymous Russian purchaser. An earlier draft of the letter is in GARF, f. 601, o. 1, d. 1121, l. 1.

61. Polivanov, *Iz dnevnikov*, 208–10.

62. Chernyavsky, *Prologue to Revolution*, 106–107.

63. Shavel'skii, *Vospominaniia*, vol. 1, 313–14.

64. Chernyavsky, *Prologue to Revolution*, 80–82.

65. Telegrams, Laguiche to Minister of War, nos. 185, 187, 27 August 1915, SHD, 5 N 74.

66. Polivanov, *Iz dnevnikov*, 215.

67. Chernyavsky, *Prologue to Revolution*, 128, 137.

68. Ibid., 139–43.

69. Ibid., 165–66.

70. Shavel'skii, *Vospominaniia*, vol. 1, 314.

71. Bezobrazov, *Diary*, D60.

72. Zapiski, vol. 1, 194, HIA, F. F. Palitsyn Collection, Box 1.

73. A photograph of this letter can be found in Romanow, *Am Hof*, between pages 352 and 353.

74. Order no. 736, 23 August 1915, RGVIA, f. 2003, o. 1, d. 5, l. 128.

75. Hanbury-Williams, *The Emperor Nicholas II*, 49.

76. *The Letters of the Tsar to the Tsaritsa*, 70–71.

77. Letter, Hanbury Williams to Kitchener, 6 September 1915, NAUK, PRO, 30/57/67, 159.

78. Telegram, Laguiche, no. 207, 9 September 1915, SHD, 7 N 1545.

79. Kondzerovskii, *V stavke verkhovnogo*, 71.

80. Spiridovich, *Velikaia voina*, 197.

20: Victory in the Caucasus, September 1915–April 1916

1. Romanow, *Am Hof*, 324.

2. Ibid.

3. Ibid., 303–309.

4. Ibid., 310–11.

5. Ibid., 314.

6. Ibid., 316.

7. *Tanamedrové Azri*, September 24, 1915.

8. Letter, Stevens to Grey, 7 October 1915, NAUK, FCO 371/2444, 366.

9. Kolonitskii, "*Tragicheskaia erotika*," 498.

10. Romanow, *Am Hof*, 317–19; Letter, Stevens to Grey, 7 October 1915, NAUK, FCO 371/2444, 366.

11. Order, Offices of the Viceregalship of the Caucasus, no. 1, NAUK, FCO 371/2444, 368–69.

12. Kolonitskii, "*Tragicheskaia erotika,*" 498.

13. *Tanamedrové Azri*, September 24, 1915.

14. E. V. Maslovskii, *Mirovaia voina na Kavkazskom fronte 1914–1917 gg.* (Paris: Vozrozhdenie, 1933), 206; Memoirs, 20, BA, Nikolai Frantsevich Ern.

15. Danilov, *Velikii Kniaz'*, 281.

16. Memoirs, 435, BA, P. N. Shatilov Papers, 1921–1976, Box 9, folder 12.

17. Ibid., 478.

18. Zapiski, vol. 1, 233, HIA, F. F. Palitsyn Collection, Box 1.

19. Ibid., 219.

20. Ibid., 246–47.

21. Romanow, *Am Hof*, 330–33.

22. Opis' imushchestva Velikogo Kniazia Nikolaia Nikolaevicha i Velikoi Kniagini Anastasii Nikolaevny, nakhodiashchegosia vo dvortse, 10 April 1917, CSHAG, f. 1835, o. 1, d. 1.

23. Opis' veshchei Ikh Imperatorskikh Vysochestv Velikogo Kniazia Nikolaia Nikolaevicha i Velikoi Kniagini Anastasii Nikolaevny sdelannykh novykh i kuplennykh na dachu v Kodzhory, CSHAG, f. 1835, o. 1, d. 1.

24. A. G. Emel'ianov, *Persidskii front* (Berlin:Gamaiun, 1923), 38–39.

25. English-speaking historians have not to date paid much attention to the First World War in Persia, which remains understudied. Two recent publications on the subject are Mohammad Gholi Majd, *Persia in World War I and Its Conquest by Great Britain* (Lanham: University Press of America, 2003); Touraj Atabaki, ed., *Iran and the First World War: Battleground of the Great Powers* (New York: I. B. Tauris, 2006).

26. L. I. Miroshnikov, *Iran in World War I* (Moscow: Oriental Literature Publishing House, 1963), 41–43.

27. Ibid., 43–48.

28. Sean McMeekin, *The Berlin-Baghdad Express: The Ottoman Empire and Germany's Bid for World Power* (Cambridge, MA: The Belknap Press, 2010), 227.

29. Telegram, Grand Duke Nikolai Nikolaevich, 23 October 1915, AVPRI, f. 133, o. 470, d. 180, l. 112.

30. Letter, Grand Duke Nikolai Nikolaevich to Baratov, no. 2817, 23 October 1915, RGVIA, f. 2100, o. 1, d. 855, ll. 12–13.

31. Telegram, Grand Duke Nikolai Nikolaevich to Alekseev, 25 November 1915, RGVIA, f. 2100, o. 1, d. 560, l. 116.

32. Miroshnikov, *Iran in World War I*, 49.

33. Telegram, Bolkhovitinov to Baratov, 13 November 1915, RGVIA, f. 2100, o. 1, d. 560, l. 23.

34. Telegram, Bolkhovitinov to Baratov, 14 November 1915, RGVIA, f. 2100, o. 1, d. 560, l. 28.

35. Telegram, Grand Duke Nikolai Nikolaevich to Iudenich, 17 November 1915, RGVIA, f. 2100, o. 1, d. 560, ll. 58–59.

36. Telegram, Grand Duke Nikolai Nikolaevich to Sazonov, 24 November 1915, RGVIA, f. 2001, o. 1, d. 560, l. 95.

37. Telegram, Laguiche, 10 August 1916, MAe, Correspondance politique et commerciale, A-Guerre 1914–18, vol. 754, 67.

38. Telegram, Laguiche, no. 412, 9 December 1915, MAe, Correspondance politique et commerciale, A-Guerre 1914–18, vol. 754, 31.

39. Letter, Grand Duke Nikolai Nikolaevich to Krivoshein, 20 November 1915, RGIA, f. 1656, o. 1, d. 61, l. 14.

40. Andreas Kappeler, *The Russian Empire: A Multiethnic History* (Harlow: Pearson, 2001), 347.

41. Ronald Grigor Suny, *Looking toward Ararat: Armenia in Modern History* (Bloomington: Indiana University Press, 1993), 45.

42. Ibid., 47.

43. Ibid., 92.

44. Peter Holquist, "The Politics and Practice of the Russian Occupation of Armenia, 1915–February 1917," in *A Question of Genocide: Armenians and Turks at the End of the Ottoman Empire*, ed.Ronald Grigor Suny et al. (Oxford University Press, 2011), 155, 166–67.

45. Ronald Grigor Suny, *The Making of the Georgian Nation* (Bloomington: Indiana University Press, 1988), 171–72.

46. Michael A. Reynolds, *Shattering Empires: The Clash and Collapse of the Ottoman and Russian Empires, 1908–1918* (Cambridge: Cambridge University Press, 2011), 117.

47. Ibid., 145. See also: Alexander Khatissian [Khatisov], "The Memoirs of a Mayor (Part IV)," *The Armenian Review* 3, no. 2 (1950): 78–85.

48. Reynolds, *Shattering Empires*, 144.

49. Khatissian, "The Memoirs of a Mayor (Part IV)," 90.

50. Gatrell, *A Whole Empire Walking*, 152.

51. Reynolds, *Shattering Empires*, 156; McMeekin, *Russian Origins*, 211.

52. For a discussion of this, see Elena Campbell, "The Muslim Question in Late Imperial Russia," in *Russian Empire: Space, People, Power, 1700*–1930, ed. Jane Burbank et al. (Bloomington: Indiana University Press, 2007), 320–47.

53. Telegram, Grand Duke Nikolai Nikolaevich to Sazonov, 2 December 1915, RGVIA, f. 2100, o. 1, d. 560, l. 148.

54. Telegrams, Sazonov to Grand Duke Nikolai Nikolaevich, and Bolkhovitinov to Baratov, 5 December 1915, RGVIA, f. 2100, o. 1, d. 560, ll. 180–81.

55. Telegram, Iudenich to Grand Duke Nikolai Nikolaevich, 9 December 1915, RGVIA, f. 2100, o. 1, d. 855, ll. 21–22.

56. S. Macnaughtan, *My War Experiences in Two Continents* (London: John Murray, 1919), 215–16.

57. Maslovskii, *Mirovaia voina*, 243–44.

58. Zapiski, vol.1, 311–12, HIA, F. F. Palitsyn Collection, Box 1.

59. Ford, *Eden to Armaggedon*, 158.

60. Zapiski, vol.1, 227, HIA, F. F. Palitsyn Collection, Box 1.

61. Maslovskii, *Mirovaia voina*, 256–57.

62. Ibid., 259.

63. Ibid., 269.

64. Memoirs, 443, BA, P. N. Shatilov Papers, Box 9, folder 12.

65. Zapiski, vol. 1, 221, HIA. F. F. Palitsyn Collection Box 1.

66. Ibid., 228.

67. Telegram, Bolkhovitinov to Iudenich, 16 January 1916, RGVIA, f. 2100, o. 1, d. 421, l. 55.

68. Telegrams, Iudenich to Commandant Sarykamysh garrison, 16 January 1916;

Iudenich to Commander 1st Corps, 17 January 1916; and Bolkhovitinov to Commandant Karaurgan, 17 January 1916, RGVIA, f. 2100, o. 1, d. 421, ll. 50, 51, 54.

69. Romanow, *Am Hof*, 346.

70. W. E. D. Allen and Paul Muratoff, *Caucasian Battlefields: A History of the Wars on the Turco-Caucasian Border, 1828–1921* (Cambridge: Cambridge University Press, 1953), 350–54.

71. Ibid., 355–63.

72. Romanow, *Am Hof*, 347–48.

73. Zapiski, vol. 1, 233, HIA, F. F. Palitsyn Collection, Box 1.

74. Ibid., 248–49.

75. Romanow, *Am Hof*, 352.

76. Letter, Nachal'nik kantserliarii ministerstva Imperatorskogo Dvora to M. E. Krupenskii, 17 February 1917, GARF, f. 671, o. 1, d. 76, l. 342.

77. Letter, Laguiche to Minister of War, no. 26, 6/13 April 1916, SHD, 7 N 1473.

78. Zapiski, vol. 1, 236–38, HIA, F. F. Palitsyn, Box 1.

79. Ibid., 267.

80. P. N. Strelianov, *Korpus Generala Baratova* (Moscow: no details of publisher provided, 2002), 19–20.

81. Telegram, Grand Duke Nikolai Nikolaevich to State Secretary Nikolskii, 17 February 1916, RGIA, f. 1276, o. 19, d. 1230, l. 1.

82. Letter, Polivanov to Nikolskii, 19 February 1916, RGIA, f. 1276, o. 19, d. 1230, l. 2.

83. Holquist, "Politics and Practice," 168–69.

84. Reynolds, *Shattering Empires*, 160; Khatissian, "The Memoirs of a Mayor (Part IV)," 83.

85. Letter, Grand Duke Nikolai Nikolaevich to Minister of Internal Affairs, no. 31688, 9 December 1915, CSHAG, f. 13, o. 7, d. 2260.

86. Order no. 117, 17 March 1916, RGVIA, o. 2, d. 104, l. 89.

87. Zapiski, vol. 1, 269–70, HIA, F. F. Palitsyn Collection, Box 1.

88. Allen and Muratoff, *Caucasian Battlefields*, 379–83.

21: Governing the Caucasus, May 1916–February 1917

1. Strelianov, *Korpus Generala Baratova*, 23.

2. Emel'ianov, *Persidskii front*, 50–56.

3. Letter, Hanbury Williams to Kitchener, 23 April 1916, NAUK, PRO 30/57/67, 302–303.

4. Letter, Kitchener to Hanbury Williams, 16 May 1916, NAUK, PRO 30/57/67, 314.

5. Doklad v. k. Nikolai Nikolaevicha Nikolaiu II o podgotovke zemskoi reforme na Kavkaze, 7 May 1916, GARF, f. 601, o. 1, d. 995, l. 2.

6. Speech of Grand Duke Nikolai Nikolaevich at start of regional conference on zemstvo reform, GARF, f. 601, o. 1, d. 995, l. 4.

7. Doklad v. k. Nikolai Nikolaevicha Nikolaiu II o podgotovke zemskoi reforme na Kavkaze, 7 May 1916, GARF, f. 601, o. 1, d. 995, l. 2.

8. Speech of Grand Duke Nikolai Nikolaevich at end of regional conference on zemstvo reform, GARF, f. 601, o. 1, d. 995, l. 6.

9. Letter, Grand Duke Nikolai Nikolaevich to Nicholas II, 22 June 1916, GARF, f. 601, o. 1, d. 1311, ll. 29–31.

10. For an analysis of the causes of the food shortages, see Peter Holquist, *Making Wars, Forging Revolution: Russia's Continuum of Crisis, 1914–1921* (Cambridge, MA: Harvard University Press, 2002), 16–46.

11. E. A. Adamov, *Razdel Aziatskoi Turtsii: po sekretnym dokumentam b. Ministerstva inostrannykh del* (Moscow: Izdanie Litizdata HKID, 1924), 212.

12. Firouzeh Mostashari, *On the Religious Frontier: Tsarist Russia and Islam in the Caucasus* (London and New York: I. B. Tauris, 2006), 111.

13. *Tanamedrové Azri*, 27 February 27, 1916.

14. Zapiski, vol. 1, 242–44, HIA, F. F. Palitsyn Collection, Box 1.

15. Ibid., 271–76.

16. Order, 5 May 1916, HIA, Russia, Armiia, Kavkazskaia Armiia.

17. Zapiski, vol. 1, 328, HIA, F. F. Palitsyn Collection, Box 1.

18. Order no. 315, 19 June 1916, RGVIA, f. 2100, o. 1, d. 379, ll. 42–44.

19. Order no. 512, 9 September 1916, RGVIA, f. 2100, o. 2, d. 104.

20. Zapiski, vol. 1, 329, HIA, F. F. Palitsyn Collection, Box 1.

21. *Lettres des Grands-Ducs à Nicolas II*, 30.

22. Report, Chief of the Army Reserve of the Caucasus Army, no. 1687, 4 October 1916, RGVIA, f. 2100, o. 1, d. 1009, ll. 58–59.

23. Allen and Muratoff, *Caucasian Battlefields*, 395–99.

24. Strelianov, *Korpus Generala Baratova*, 44.

25. Zapiski, vol. 1, 313, HIA, F. F. Palitsyn, Box 1.

26. Allen and Muratoff, *Caucasian Battlefields*, 400–403.

27. Adamov, *Razdel Aziatskoi Turtsii*, 207–209.

28. Ibid., 211–12.

29. Letter, Grand Duke Nikolai Nikolaevich to Nicholas II, 24 June 1916, GARF, f. 601, o. 1, d. 1311, ll. 32–33.

30. Allen and Muratoff, *Caucasian Battlefields*, 432.

31. Telegram, Vyshinskii, 15 July 1916, RGVIA, f. 2100, o. 1, d. 421.

32. Telegram, Laguiche, 10 August 1916, MAe, Correspondance politique et commercial, A-Guerre 1914–18, vol. 754.

33. "Ot Ivangoroda do revoliutsii, chast' tretiaia," 38, HIA, Aleksei V. Shvarts Collection, Box 1.

34. Ibid., 39–41.

35. "Antoniia Vasil'evna Shvarts, 'Naznachenie v Trapezond,'" 26–27, HIA, Aleksei V. Shvarts Collection, Box 1.

36. Ibid., 28–29.

37. Ibid., 29.

38. Ibid., 30.

39. F. I. Eliseev, *Kazaki na kavkazskom fronte 1914–1917: zapiski polkovnika Kubanskogo kazach'ego voiska v trinadtsati broshiurakh-tetradiakh* (Moscow: Voennoe Izdatel'stvo, 2001), 223–24.

40. S. M. Iskhakov, "Pervaia mirovaia voina glazami rossiiskikh musul'man," in *Rossiia i pervaia mirovaia voina (materialy mezhdunarodnogo nauchnogo kollokviuma)*, ed. N. N. Smirnov (St. Petersburg: Izdatel'stvo "Dmitrii Bulanin," 1999), 423–24.

41. Ibid., 422–23; Sanborn, "Unsettling the Empire," 318–19.

42. Telegram, Grand Duke Nikolai Nikolaevich to Nicholas II, 24 July 1916, GARF, f. 601, o. 1, d. 592, l. 459.

43. Telegram, Alekseev to Grand Duke Nikolai Nikolaevich, 30 July 1916, RGVIA, f. 2100, o. 1, d. 383, l. 44.

44. Telegram, Frolov to Grand Duke Nikolai Nikolaevich, 30 July 1916, RGVIA, f. 2100, o. 1, d. 383, l. 41.

45. Telegram, Grand Duke Nikolai Nikolaevich to Frolov, 31 July 1916, RGVIA, f. 2100, o. 1, d. 383, l. 45.

46. *Tanamedrové Azri*, 9 August, 1916.

47. Allen and Muratoff, *Caucasian Battlefields*, 434.

48. Telegram, Grand Duke Nikolai Nikolaevich to Ministry of Foreign Affairs, 29 July 1916, AVPRI, f. 133, o. 470, d. 138, l. 31.

49. Allen and Muratoff, *Caucasian Battlefields*, 434.

50. Zapiski, vol. 1, 319, HIA, F. F. Palitsyn Collection, Box 1.

51. Doklad v. k. Nikolai Nikolaevicha Nikolaiu II o politicheskom polozhenii na Kavkaze, 23 September 1914, GARF, f. 601, o. 1, d. 997.

52. Kolonitskii, "*Tragicheskaia erotika*," 502.

53. David Marshall Lang, *A Modern History of Georgia* (London: Weidenfeld and Nicolson, 1962), 186.

54. Mostashari, *On the Religious Frontier*, 110.

55. *The Letters of the Tsar to the Tsaritsa*, 185.

56. Shavel'skii, *Vospominaniia*, vol. 2, 182–83.

57. "Iz istorii bor'by," 168.

58. *The Letters of the Tsar to the Tsaritsa*, 293.

59. *Letters of the Tsaritsa to the Tsar*, 433.

60. *Lettres des Grands-Ducs*, 30.

61. Shavel'skii, *Vospominaniia*, vol. 2, 222–23.

62. *The Letters of the Tsar to the Tsaritsa*, 294.

63. *Voennyi dnevnik velikogo kniazia Andreia Vladimirovicha*, 251–52.

64. Shavel'skii, *Vospominaniia*, vol. 2, 223–24.

65. *Dnevniki imperatritsy Marii Fedorovny*, 155.

66. Ibid., 156.

67. General Basil Gourko, *Memories and Impressions of War and Revolution in Russia, 1914–1917* (London: John Murray, 1918), 171–72.

68. Danilov, *Velikii Kniaz'*, 316–19; S. Mel'gunov, *Na putiakh k dvortsovomu perevorotu* (Paris: Rodnik, no date given), 105-112; see also E. E. Petrova and K. O. Bitiukov, *Velikokniazheskaia oppozitsiia v Rossii 1915–1917 gg.* (St. Petersburg: Asterion, 2009), 126–27.

69. Bezobrazov, *Diary*, D117.

70. Danilov, *Velikii Kniaz'*, 316.

71. Alexander Khatissian [Khatisov], "The Memoirs of a Mayor (Part V)," *The Armenian Review* 3, no. 3 (1950): 112.

72. Ibid., 112–13.

73. Ibid., 113.

74. Shavel'skii, *Vospominaniia*, vol. 1, 135.

22: Revolution, March 1917

1. Orlando Figes, *A People's Tragedy: The Russian Revolution, 1891–1924* (London: Jonathan Cape, 1996), 308–35.

2. Alexander Khatissian [Khatisov], "The Memoirs of a Mayor (Part VI)," *The Armenian Review* 3, no. 4 (1950): 108.

3. "Ot Tiflisskogo Gorodskogo Golovy k Naseleniiu gor. Tiflisa," 2 March 1917, CSHAG, f. 13, o. 2, d. 344, l. 29.

4. Epanchin, *Na sluzhbe*, 456.

5. Maylunas and Mironenko, *A Lifelong Passion*, 542.

6. Hanbury-Williams, *The Emperor Nicholas II*, 173–74.

7. Telegram, N. Ivanov to Grand Duke Nikolai Nikolaevich, 3 March 1917, CSHAG, f. 13, o. 22, d. 344, l. 31.

8. Telegram, Shakhnazarov to Grand Duke Nikolai Nikolaevich, 3 March 1917, CSHAG, f. 13, o. 22, d. 344, l. 39.

9. Telegram, Ziulgadarov to Grand Duke Nikolai Nikolaevich, 4 March 1917, CSHAG, f. 13, o. 22, d. 344, l. 59.

10. Telegram, Afrikian to Grand Duke Nikolai Nikolaevich, 4 March 1917, CSHAG, f. 13, o. 22, d. 344, l. 61.

11. Telegram, Egerov to Grand Duke Nikolai Nikolaevich, 4 March 1917, CSHAG, f. 13, o. 22, d. 344, l. 64.

12. Telegram, Bezchinskii and others to Grand Duke Nikolai Nikolaevich, 4 March 1917, CSHAG, f. 13, o. 22, d. 344, l. 67.

13. Telegram, workers of the Vyatka-Volga steamship line to Grand Duke Nikolai Nikolaevich, 4 March 1917, CSHAG, f. 13, o. 22, d. 344, l. 69.

14. Telegram, Khatisov and others to Grand Duke Nikolai Nikolaevich, 4 March 1917, CSHAG, f. 13, o. 22, d. 344, l. 112.

15. Telegram, Grand Duke Nikolai Nikolaevich to Khatisov, 4 March 1917, CSHAG, f. 13, o. 22, d. 344.

16. Telegram, Grand Duke Nikolai Nikolaevich to Egerov, 4 March 1917, CSHAG, f. 13, o. 22, d. 344, l. 63.

17. Telegram, Prince Orlov, 3 March 1917, CSHAG, f. 13, o. 22, d. 344, ll. 25–26.

18. "Ot Verkhovnogo Glavnokomanduiushchego k Naseleniiu Kavkaza," CSHAG, f. 13, o. 22, d. 344, ll. 18–19.

19. Telegram, Bublikov to Grand Duke Nikolai Nikolaevich, no. 4460, 2 March 1917, CSHAG, f. 13, o. 22, d. 344, l. 12.

20. Telegram, Grand Duke Nikolai Nikolaevich to Rodzianko, CSHAG, f. 13, o. 22, d. 344, ll. 1–2.

21. Telegram, Grand Duke Nikolai Nikolaevich to Lvov, 3 March 1917, CSHAG, f. 13, o. 22, d. 344, l. 24.

22. Telegram, Grand Duke Nikolai Nikolaevich to Lvov, 3 March 1917, CSHAG, f. 13, o. 22, d. 344, l. 35.

23. Epanchin, *Na sluzhbe*, 462; Ordre du Grand Duc Nicolas, MRA, Box 65, 185-3-94, 10.

24. *Tanamedrové Azri*, March 5, 1917.

25. Khatissian, "The Memoirs of a Mayor (Part VI)," 108.

26. *Voennyi dnevnik velikogo kniazia Andreia Vladimirovicha*, 252.

27. Romanow, *Am Hof*, 393–94.

28. Frank Alfred Golder, ed., *Documents of Russian History, 1914–1917* (Gloucester, MA: Peter Smith, 1964), 299.

29. Ibid., 301.

30. Telegram, Provorov to Grand Duke Nikolai Nikolaevich, 5 March 1917, CSHAG, f. 13, o. 22, d. 344, l. 100.

31. Telegram, Vasil'ev to Grand Duke Nikolai Nikolaevich, 4 March 1917, CSHAG, f. 13, o. 22, d. 344, l. 91.

32. Telegram, Shevelev to Grand Duke Nikolai Nikolaevich, 5 March 1917, CSHAG, f. 13, o. 22, d. 344, l. 93.

33. Telegram, Starobel'skai gorodskaia duma to Grand Duke Nikolai Nikolaevich, 5 March 1917, CSHAG, f. 13, o. 22, d. 344, l. 95.

34. These are to be found in CSHAG, f. 13, o. 22, d. 344.

35. Telegram, Grand Duke Nikolai Nikolaevich to the Presidium of the general meeting of the united students of Odessa, 5 March 1917, CSHAG, f. 13, o. 22, d. 233, l. 107.

36. Danilov, *Velikii Kniaz'*, 325.

37. Romanow, *Am Hof*, 393–94.

38. Danilov, *Velikii Kniaz'*, 327.

39. *The Memoirs of General Prince Felix Felixovich Yusupov*, 179–80.

40. Prince Felix Youssoupoff, *Lost Splendour: The Amazing Memoirs of the Man Who Killed Rasputin* (New York: Helen Marx, 2003), 275–76.

41. Telegram, no. 5a, de Ryckel, 25 March 1917, MRA, Box 65, 185-3-94, 14.

42. Hanbury-Williams, *The Emperor Nicholas II*, 180–81.

43. Lukomskii, *Vospominaniia*, vol. 1, 146.

44. Hanbury-Williams, *The Emperor Nicholas II*, 182–83.

45. Ibid., 183–84.

46. Romanow, *Am Hof*, 398.

47. Voeikov, *S Tsarem*, 285.

48. Romanow, *Am Hof*, 401–402.

49. Hanbury-Williams, *The Emperor Nicholas II*, 186.

50. Ibid.

51. Ibid., 256.

23: Crimea, April 1917–April 1919

1. Nakhapetov, *Vrachebnye tainy*, 289.

2. "Neskol'ko myslei," GARF, f. 5826, o. 1, d. 166b, l. 228.

3. Romanow, *Am Hof*, 412.

4. *Dnevniki imperatritsy Marii Fedorovny*, 199.

5. Cantacuzène, *Revolutionary Days*, 409.

6. Youssoupoff, *Lost Splendour*, 289; Grand Duke Alexander, *Once a Grand Duke*, 305.

7. Romanow, *Am Hof*, 419.

8. Youssoupoff, *Lost Splendour*, 290.

9. Romanow, *Am Hof*, 422.

10. Ibid., 426–30.

11. Ibid., 431.
12. Ibid., 435.
13. Ibid., 271.
14. Danilov, *Velikii Kniaz'*, 337–39.
15. *Dnevniki imperatritsy Marii Fedorovny*, 277–78.
16. Shavel'skii, *Vospominaniia*, vol. 2, 317.
17. Ibid., 317–18.
18. Ibid., 318–19.
19. *Dnevniki imperatritsy Marii Fedorovny*, 291.
20. Ibid., 314.
21. Ibid., 316.
22. Ibid., 320.
23. For a full list of passengers, see: Vice Admiral Sir Francis Pridham, *Close of a Dynasty* (London: Allan Wingate, 1956), Appendix VII.
24. Ibid., 70.
25. Ibid., 66.
26. *Dnevniki imperatritsy Marii Fedorovny*, 323.
27. Romanow, *Am Hof*, 452.
28. Ibid., 456; Pridham, *Close of a Dynasty*, 73.
29. *Dnevniki imperatritsy Marii Fedorovny*, 324.
30. Frances Welch, *The Russian Court at Sea. The Last Days of a Great Dynasty: The Romanovs' Voyage into Exile* (London: Short, 2011), 117–18.
31. Draft letters, 27 and 29 December 1926, DRZ, f. 2, o. 1, k. 1, ed. khr. 38. In these drafts, the Grand Duke mentions asking the Italian government for permission to travel there. Welch, *The Russian Court at Sea*, 147, cites a telegram from the British Commander-in-Chief Mediterranean of 1 (14) April, which states, "the Grand Dukes are now asking Italian government permission to reside in Italy." Prince Roman Petrovich, however, tells a different story: that the Grand Dukes received news of an invitation to Italy even before they left the Crimea and then received the invitation itself as soon as they reached Constantinople. See Romanow, *Am Hof*, 448, 457.
32. Typescript, Experiences in South Russia and Turkey 1919, IWM, 76/8, W. Roberts.
33. Pridham, *Close of a Dynasty*, 91.
34. Romanow, *Am Hof*, 453.

24: Exile, May 1919–December 1924

1. For general histories of Russia Abroad, see: Marc Raeff, *Russia Abroad: A Cultural History of the Russian Emigration, 1919–1939* (New York and Oxford: Oxford University Press, 1990); John Glad, *Russia Abroad: Writers, History, Politics* (Washington, DC, and Tenafly: Hermitage and Birchbark Press, 1999); L. K. Shkarenkov, *Agoniia beloi emigratsii* (Moscow: Mysl', 1986); M. V. Nazarov, *Missiia russkoi emigratsii* (Stavropol: Kavkazskii Krai, 1992).
2. Paul Robinson, *The White Russian Army in Exile, 1920–1941* (Oxford: Clarendon Press, 2002), 31–50.
3. Ibid., 51–64.
4. Proekt N. L. Obolenskogo, 27 March 1926, DRZ, f. 2, o. 1, k. 1, ed. khr. 38.

5. For histories of Villa Thénard and Villa Taormina, see Didier Gayraud, *Belles demeures en Riviera, 1835–1930* (Nice: Gilleta. Nice-matin, 2005), 98–101.

6. Agence Lefievre, Villa Thénard, Propriété à vendre au Cap d'Antibes, 7 September 1938, Archives municipales, Cannes, Cote 2S1193, Villa Thénard.

7. Letter, Lukomskii to Wrangel, 23 March 1922, HIA, P. N. Vrangel' Archive (henceforth WA), Box 143, File 23, 2–4.

8. Letter, Wrangel to Grand Duke Nikolai Nikolaevich, 5 August 1922, BA, ROVS, Box 161, File "Officers Unions and Monarchist Movements (1923–1924)."

9. Letter, Khol'msen to Wrangel, no. 35/s, 24 August 1922, HIA, WA, Box 143, File 23, 57–60.

10. John Curtis Perry and Constantine Pleshakov, *The Flight of the Romanovs: A Family Saga* (New York: Basic Books, 1999), 84–85.

11. Minutes of meeting of senior commanders with the Commander-in-Chief, 22 November 1922, HIA, WA, Box 143, File 22, 228–29.

12. Memoirs, vol. 7, 1330, BA, P. N. Shatilov Papers.

13. Memoirs, 1358, BA, P. N. Shatilov Papers, Box 12, folder 15.

14. Letter, Wrangel to Shatilov and Kutepov, 1 March 1923, HIA, WA, Box 143, File 23, 116.

15. Memoirs, 1343–44, BA, P. N. Shatilov Papers, Box 12.

16. Ibid., 1344.

17. Letter, Bogaevskii to Grand Duke Nikolai Nikolaevich, 22 April 1923, BA, Afrikan P. Bogaevskii Collection, Box 2, folder "Relations of Émigré Cossacks with Grand Duke Nikolai Nikolaevich."

18. "Neskol'ko myslei [Velikogo Kniazia Nikolaia Nikolaevicha]," in *Rossiiskii Zarubezhnyi S"ezd 1926: Dokumenty i materialy* (Moscow: Russkii Put', 2006), 721.

19. Boulay, *La France des Romanov*, 271.

20. Ralph Heinzen, "V tishi izgnaniia Velikii Kniaz' Nikolai Nikolaevich obdumyvaet sverzhenie bol'shevistskogo rezhima," in *Rossiiskii Zarubezhnyi S"ezd*, 372.

21. Press clipping of article by Julia Cantacuzen, December 1925, HIA, WA, Box 147, File 35.

22. Adrien Lefranc, "Chez un grand-duc en exil," 7 October 1926, DRZ, f. 2, o. 1, k. 1, ed. khr. 6.

23. Soobshchenie no. 1, 15 November 1926, HIA, WA, Box 147, File 35.

24. N. N. Lvov, "U Velikogo Kniazia Nikolaia Nikolaevicha v Shuan'i," 8 June 1925, in *Rossiiski Zarubezhnyi S"ezd*, 251.

25. Danilov, *Velikii Kniaz'*, 345.

26. P. N. Krasnov, *Otkrytoe pis'mo kazakam*, 6/19 November 1923.

27. Danilov, *Velikii Kniaz'*, 347.

28. Adrien Lefranc, "Chez un grand-duc en exil," 7 October 1926, DRZ, f. 2, o. 1, k. 1, ed. khr. 6.

29. Proekt interv'iu Velikogo Kniazia Nikolaia Nikolaevicha parizhskoi presse, January 1927, DRZ, f. 2, o. 1, d. 1, ed. khr. 41.

30. Letter, Wrangel to Miller, no. 03145, 15 May 1923, BA, ROVS, Box 3, folder "Wrangel."

31. Telegram, Wrangel to Grand Duke Nikolai Nikolaevich, 12 May 1923, BA, ROVS, Box 161, folder "Officers' Unions and Monarchist Movements (1923–1924) (2)."

32. Letter, Shatilov to Wrangel, 30 May 1923, HIA, WA, Box 143, File 23, 273–76.

33. Memoirs, folder 15, 1355, BA, P. N. Shatilov Papers, Box 12; Letter, Shatilov to Wrangel, 6 June 1923, HIA, WA, Box 143, File 23, 318–20.

34. Letter, Shatilov to Wrangel, 9 June 1923, HIA, WA, Box 143, File 23, 323–26.

35. Letter, unknown officer in Pernik to V. Kh. Davatz, 2/15 April 1923, HIA, E. K. Miller Collection, Box 16, folder 22.

36. Svodka o zhizni chastei gallipoliiskoi gruppy v Bolgarii za avgust mesiats 1923 goda, BA, ROVS, Box 166, "Russian Army in 1923–1924."

37. Prigovor, 2-go avgusta 1923, Colonel Turoverov, BA, Afrikan P. Bogaevskii Collection, Box 2, folder "Relations of Émigré Cossacks with Grand Duke Nikolai Nikolaevich."

38. Prigovor Stanichnogo Sbora Plovdivskoi Stanitsy, 1 January 1924, BA, Afrikan P. Bogaevskii Collection, Box 2, folder "Relations of Émigré Cossacks with Grand Duke Nikolai Nikolaevich."

39. Letter, Savich to Wrangel, 8 August 1923, HIA, WA, Box 146, File 30, 651–55.

40. "Ot Donskogo Atamana," BA, Afrikan P. Bogaevskii Collection, Box 2, folder "Relations of Émigré Cossacks with Grand Duke Nikolai Nikolaevich."

41. *Rossiiskii Zarubezhnyi S"ezd*, 19.

42. Ibid., 53.

43. Reply to Russian monarchists in Nice, 7/20 November 1923, DRZ, f. 2, o. 1, k. 1, ed. khr. 1, l. 12.

44. *Rossiiskii Zarubezhnyi S"ezd*, 77–79.

45. Memoirs, folder 15, 1389, BA, P. N. Shatilov Papers, Box 12.

46. "Ot Donskogo Atamana," BA, Afrikan P. Bogaevskii Collection, Box 2, folder "Relations of Émigré Cossacks with Grand Duke Nikolai Nikolaevich."

47. V. G. Bortnevskii, *Zagadki smerti generala Vrangelia* (St. Petersburg: Biblioteka zhurnala "Novyi Chasovoi," 1996), 37.

48. *Rossiiskii Zarubezhnyi S"ezd*, 101–102.

49. Letter, Kutepov to Lukomskii, 7 April 1924, HIA, A. S. Lukomskii Collection, Box 1, Correspondence, Kutepov A.

50. Letter, Kutepov to Lukomskii, 24 April 1924, HIA, A. S. Lukomskii Collection, Box 1, Correspondence, Kutepov A.

51. Letter, Kutepov to Lukomskii, 15 (28) July 1924, HIA, A. S. Lukomskii Collection, Box 1, Correspondence, Kutepov A.

52. Beseda b. verkhovnogo glavnokomanduiushchego E. I. V. Velikogo Kniazia Nikolaia Nikolaevicha s predstavitelem amerikanskoi pechati na Paskhe 1924 g., DRZ, f. 2, o. 1, k. 1, ed. khr. 19.

53. See, for instance, Protokol chastnogo soveshchaniia chlenov ob"edineniia soveta Dona, Kubana i Tereka, 26 June 1924, BA, Afrikan P. Bogaevskii Collection, folder "Relations of Émigré Cossacks with Grand Duke Nikolai Nikolaevich," Box 2.

54. See, for instance, Letter, Bogaevskii to Grand Duke Nikolai Nikolaevich, 7 March 1924, BA, Afrikan P. Bogaevskii Collection, folder "Relations of Émigré Cossacks with Grand Duke Nikolai Nikolaevich," Box 2.

55. See, for instance, Priem Velikim Kniazem Nikolaem Nikolaevichem Donskogo Atamana, 24 July 1924, BA, Afrikan P. Bogaevskii Collection, folder "Relations of Émigré Cossacks with Grand Duke Nikolai Nikolaevich," Box 2.

56. Unfortunately, many accounts of the Trust are full of inaccuracies. Perhaps the best study is S. L. Voitsekhovskii, *Trest: vospominaniia i dokumenty* (London, Ontario: Zaria, 1974).

57. It is almost certain that the Grand Duke and his staff were entirely taken in by Iakushev, but for an alternative viewpoint see: N. Vinogradov, "Pravda o svidanii bol'shevitskogo agenta Iakusheva-Fedorova s Velikim Kniazem Nikolaem Nikolaevichem," *Vozrozhdenie* 48 (1955): 109–18.

58. Letter, Empress Mariia Fedorovna to Grand Duke Nikolai Nikolaevich, 21 September (4 October) 1924, BA, Afrikan P. Bogaevskii Collection, folder "Relations of Émigré Cossacks with Grand Duke Nikolai Nikolaevich," Box 2.

59. Letter, Grand Duke Nikolai Nikolaevich to Empress Mariia Fedorovna, 7 (20) October 1924, BA, Afrikan P. Bogaevskii Collection, folder "Relations of Émigré Cossacks with Grand Duke Nikolai Nikolaevich," Box 2.

60. Robinson, *The White Russian Army in Exile*, 97–112.

61. Memoirs, folder 16, 1464, BA, P. N. Shatilov Papers, Box 12.

62. Ibid., 1471–74.

63. Telegram, Grand Duke Nikolai Nikolaevich to Wrangel, 16 November 1924, HIA, WA, Box 147, File 35.

25: The Émigré Congress, January 1925–June 1926

1. R. C. Williams, *Culture in Exile: Russian Émigrés in Germany, 1881–1941* (Ithaca: Cornell University Press, 1971), 290.

2. O. L. Polivanov, "Psikhologiia russkoi emigratsii," in *Iz istorii rossiiskoi emigratsii: sbornik nauchnykh statei* (St. Petersburg: Tret'iaia Rossiia, 1992), 23.

3. Williams, *Culture in Exile*, 290.

4. Raeff, *Russia Abroad*, 9–10.

5. Ibid., 8.

6. *Rossiiskii Zarubezhnyi S"ezd*, 216.

7. Nabrosom politicheskoi deklaratsii dlia rukovostva Sablina E. V., DRZ, f. 2, o. 1, k. 1, ed. khr. 13, ll. 1–3; Pis'mo Velikogo Kniazia Nikolaia Nikolaevicha kniaziu N. L. Obolenskomu, DRZ, f. 2, o. 1, k. 1, ed. khr. 15, l. 1.

8. *Rossiiskii Zarubezhyi S"ezd*, 252–54.

9. Ibid., 260.

10. Ibid., 275–78.

11. Conversation of the editor of *Vozrozhdenie* with Grand Duke Nikolai Nikolaevich, BA, ROVS, Box 162, folder, "Officers' Unions and Monarchist Movements (1924–1929)."

12. Proekt publichnogo zaiavleniia Vel. Kn. Nikolaia Nikolaevicha, DRZ, f. 2, o. 1, k. 4, ed. khr. 60, l. 5.

13. Ibid.

14. "Les Russes en exil: un entretien avec le Grand-Duc Nicolas," *La Nation Belge*, September 11, 1925, copy in HIA, WA, Box 147, File 35.

15. *Rossiiskii Zarubezhnyi S"ezd*, 293.

16. Ibid., 297–98.

17. Ibid., 322–33.

18. Ibid., 370.

19. Ibid., 680.

20. Letter, Obolenskii to Krupenskii, GARF, f. 5826, o. 1, d. 166d, ll. 6–7.

21. Comments by Lukomskii on a draft declaration by Struve, 27 January 1926, GARF, f. 5826, o. 1, d. 166d, ll. 6–7.

22. Slova Velikogo Kniazia Nikolaia Nikolaevicha Akademiku P. B. Struve, 2-go aprelia 1926 goda, GARF, f. 5826, o. 1, d. 166d, l. 126.

23. *Rossiiskii Zarubezhnyi S"ezd*, 679.

24. Ibid., 467–76.

25. Ibid., 496.

26. Ibid., 511.

27. Ibid., 530.

28. Ibid., 593–620.

29. Ibid., 627–51.

30. Ibid., 683–84.

31. Letter, Lvov to Wrangel, 1925, HIA, WA, Box 150, File 41, 66–67.

32. Slova Velikogo Kniazia Nikolaia Nikolaevicha, skazannye pri prieme chlenov Zarubezhnogo S"ezda 12-go i 13-go aprelia 1926 godam, BA, Sviatopolk-Mirskii Collection; *Rossiiskii Zarubezhnyi S"ezd*, 687.

33. Memoirs, folder 17, 1544–47, BA, P. N. Shatilov Papers, Box 12.

34. Konspekt vystuplenii gostei na prieme u Vel. Kn. Nikolaia Nikolaevicha 15.06. 1926 g., DRZ, f. 2, o. 1, k. 5, ed. khr. 2, ll. 11–14.

35. Proekt vystupleniia Vel. Kn. Nikolaia Nikolaevicha, DRZ, f. 2, o. 1, k. 5, ed. khr. 2, l. 24; "Neskol'sko myslei," GARF, f. 5826, o. 1, d. 166g, ll. 228–34.

26: Thoughts of God, July 1926–January 1929

1. Dimitry Pospielovsky, *The Russian Church under the Soviet Regime, 1917–1982*, vol. 1 (Crestwood: St. Vladimir's Seminary Press, 1984), 114–20.

2. Ibid., 121–36.

3. Draft letter, Grand Duke Nikolai Nikolaevich to Metropolitan Antony, DRZ, f. 2, o. 1, k. 5, ed. khr. 12, l. 3.

4. For comments by contemporaries reflecting the belief that the Grand Duke supported Antony, see: Letter, von Lampe to Father Vasilii, 10 July 1928, GARF, f. 5853, o. 1, d. 31, ll. 15646–47; ll. 15641–42, Letter, von Lampe to Abramov, 28 June 1928; Memoirs, folder 1, 1575, BA, P. N. Shatilov Papers, Box 13.

5. Letter, Grand Duke Nikolai Nikolaevich to Evlogii, 29 April/12 May 1927, DRZ, f. 2, o. 1, k. 5, ed. khr. 44, l. 13.

6. Exactly what the Grand Duke and Bogaevskii said to each other became a matter of bitter dispute between Bogaevskii and General Lukomskii. Copies of the exchange between Lukomskii and Bogaevskii about this meeting are in BA, P. V. Kartashev Collection, folder "Lukomskii, Aleksandr Sergeevich"; GARF, f. 5826, o. 1, d. 166e; GARF, f. 5826, o. 1, d. 61; DRZ, f. 2, o. 1, k. 4, ed. khr. 58.

7. Letter, Grand Duke Nikolai Nikolaevich to Metropolitan Antony, 25 December 1926, DRZ, f. 2, o. 1, k. 5, ed. khr. 35, ll. 2–3.

8. Letter, Metropolitan Antony to Grand Duke Nikolai Nikolaevich, 30 December 1926, DRZ, f. 2, o. 1, k. 5, ed. khr. 5, l. 8.

9. Letter, Metropolitan Antony to Grand Duke Nikolai Nikolaevich, no. 187, 2/15 February 1927, DRZ, f. 2, o. 1, k. 5, ed. khr. 38, l. 1.

10. Letter, Obolenskii to Metropolitan Antony, 11/24 February 1927, DRZ, f. 2, o. 1, k. 5, ed.khr. 38, l. 14.

11. Letter, Obolenskii to Father Denasii, 29 July 1927, DRZ, f. 2, o. 1, k. 5, ed. khr. 21, l. 6.

12. Letter, Obolenskii to Father Denasii, 8/21 March 1927, DRZ, f. 2, o. 1, k. 5, ed. khr. 21.

13. Letter, Grand Duke Nikolai Nikolaevich to Metropolitan Evlogii, 29 April/12 May 1927, DRZ, f. 2, o. 1, k. 5, ed. khr. 44, l. 13.

14. Zasedanie 2-go iiunia 1927 goda u Ego Imperatorskogo Velichestva Velikogo Kniazia Nikolaia Nikolaevicha v Shuan'i, DRZ, f. 2, o. 1, k. 1, ed. khr. 43, ll. 11–21.

15. General Lukomskii, "Bor'ba s bol'shevikami," HIA, A. P. Arkhangel'skii Collection, Box 2.

16. Ibid.

17. Robinson, *The White Russian Army in Exile*, 140.

18. Memoirs, folder 1, 1571, BA, P. N. Shatilov Papers, Box 13.

19. Robinson, *The White Russian Army in Exile*, 141–42.

20. Letter, Wrangel to Abramov and Barbovich, 9 June 1927, HIA, WA, Box 147, File 33, 199–203.

21. Letter, Shatilov to Wrangel, 11 July 1927, HIA, WA, Box 147, File 33, 272–73.

22. Memoirs, folder 1, 1573, BA, P. N. Shatilov, Box 13.

23. Letter, Obolenskii to Bishop Serafim, 4 July 1927, DRZ, f. 2, o. 1, k. 6, ed. khr. 102, l. 21.

24. Letter, Grand Duke Nikolai Nikolaevich to Bishop Anastasii, 4/17 May 1927, DRZ, f. 2, o. 1, k. 5, ed. khr. 45, ll. 18–19.

25. Letter, Obolenskii to Father Denasii, 29 July 1927, DRZ, f. 2, o. 1, k. 5, ed. khr. 21, ll. 5–6.

26. Draft of letter, Grand Duke Nikolai Nikolaevich to Churchill, 16 February 1928, DRZ, f. 2, o. 1, k. 6, ed. khr. 62, ll. 7–9.

27. Letter, Churchill to Grand Duke Nikolai Nikolaevich, 6 March 1928, DRZ, f. 2, o. 1, k. 6, ed. khr. 63, ll. 1–2.

28. Danilov, *Velikii Kniaz'*, 350.

29. Telegram, Grand Duke Nikolai Nikolaevich to Baroness Wrangel, no date, HIA, WA, Box 147, File 35.

30. Order no. 1, 25 April 1928, GARF, f. 5826, o. 1, d. 84, l. 1.

31. Letter, Grand Duke Nikolai Nikolaevich to Churchill, 30 June 1928, DRZ, f. 2, o. 1, k. 6, ed. khr. 65, l. 4.

32. Letter, Churchill to Grand Duke Nikolai Nikolaevich, 10 July 1928, DRZ, f. 2, o. 1, d. 6, ed. khr. 65, ll. 6–7.

33. Letter, Churchill to Grand Duke Nikolai Nikolaevich, 24 September 1928, DRZ, f. 2, o. 1, k. 6, ed. khr. 67, l. 1.

34. Letter, Grand Duke Nikolai Nikolaevich to Churchill, September 1928, DRZ, f. 2, o. 1, k. 6, ed. khr. 67.

35. Vypisk iz protokola zasedaniia Pravleniia Soiuza Ofits. Uchast. Vel. Voiny v Parizhe, 7 October 1928, GARF, f. 5826, o. 1, d. 99, l. 125.

36. Report, General Shatilov, 19 October 1928, GARF, f. 5826, o. 1, d. 99, l. 111.

37. Circular to heads of ROVS departments, GARF, f. 5826, f. 2, o. 1, d. 99, ll. 129–31.

38. Ibid.

39. Letter, Grand Duke Nikolai Nikolaevich to Metropolitan Antony, 18/31 October 1928, DRZ, f. 2, o. 1, k. 6, ed. khr. 36.

40. Soobshchenie no. 17, 27 October/9 November 1928, HIA, Mariia Wrangel Collection, Box 7, Leadership of White Movement, Grand Duke Nikolai Nikolaevich.

41. For details of the Grand Duke's final illness, see: Soobshchenie no. 19, HIA, Mariia Wrangel Collection, Box 7, Leadership of White Movement, Grand Duke Nikolai Nikolaevich.

42. Letter, Obolenskii to Metropolitan Antony, 18 December 1928, DRZ, f. 2, o. 1, k. 5, ed. khr. 36.

43. Danilov, *Velikii Kniaz'*, 352.

44. The death certificate in the Archives municipales, Antibes, gives the time of death as 2100 hrs.

Epilogue

1. *Le Réveil Antibes*, January 12, 1929.

2. Danilov, *Velikii Kniaz'*, 350.

3. Diary of Vera Bunina, 6 January 1929, Leeds Russian Archive (LRA), MS 1067–395. I am very grateful to Richard Davies for assisting me in tracking down this reference.

4. Bunin, *The Life of Arseniev*, 156–57.

5. Diary of Vera Bunina, 7 January 1929, LRA, MS 1067–395.

6. *Le Réveil Antibes*, January 12, 1929.

Bibliography

Archives

Archives municipales, Antibes
Death certificate, Grand Duc Nicolas Nicolaevitch Romanoff

Archives municipales, Cannes
2S1193—Villa Thénard

Arkhiv vneshnei politiki Rossii (AVPRI)
Fond 133—Kantseliariia ministra inostrannykh del

Bakhmeteff Archive, Columbia University (BA)
Bark, Pyotr Lvovich
Bogaevskii, Afrikan P.
Ern, Nikolai Frantsevich
Kartashev, Pyotr Vasilevich
ROVS
Rozen, Konstantin N.
Shatilov, Pavel Nikolaevich
Sviatopolk-Mirskii, N. V.

Central State Historical Archive of Georgia, Tbilisi (CSHAG)
Fond 13—Kantseliariia namestnika na Kavkaze

Dom Russkogo Zarubezh'ia imeni A. I. Solzhenitsyna (DRZ)
Fond 2—Obolenskii, N. L.

Gosudarstvennyi Arkhiv Rossiiskoi Federatsii (GARF)
Fond 543—Kollektsiia rukopisei tsarskosel'skogo dvortsa, 1863–1916
Fond 601—Imperator Nikolai II
Fond 646—Romanov Nikolai Nikolaevich (starshii)
Fond 653—Velikii Kniaz' Pyotr Nikolaevich
Fond 671—Velikii Kniaz' Nikolai Nikolaevich mladshii
Fond 5826—Russkii Obshche-Voinskii Soiuz
Fond 5853—von Lampe, A. A.
Fond R-6249—von Raukh, G. O.
Fond 6460—Abramov, F. F.

Hoover Institution Archives (HIA)
Arkhangel'skii, Aleksei P.
Baratov, Nikolai N.
de Basily, N.

Golovin, Nikolai N.
Kokovtsov, Vladimir Nikolaevich
Kussonskii, P. A.
Lukomskii, Aleksandr
Maslovskii, Evgenii V.
Miller, Evgenii Karlovich
Nicholas II, Emperor of Russia
Palitsyn, Fedor Fedorovich
Russia: Army. Kavkazskaia Armiia
Russia: Shtab Verkhovnogo Glavnokomanduiushchego
Shvarts, Aleksei V.
Struve, Pyotr
Vrangel', Mariia
Vrangel', P. N.

Imperial War Museum, London (IWM)
PP/MCR/67—First World War Papers of Major the Lord Glyn
PP/MCR/98—W. G. Roberts

Leeds Russian Archive (LRA)
Diary of Vera Bunina, MS 1067-395

Ministère des affaires étrangères, archives diplomatiques, La Corneuve (MAe)
Correspondance politique et commerciale, 1896–1914:
Guerre 1914–1918, Russie, vols. 14, 41, 83, 641
Correspondance politique et commerciale, A-Guerre 1914, vols. 754, 757

Musée Royal de l'Armée et d'Histoire Militaire, Brussels (MRA)
Box 65, 185/3/94
Box 5001, 185/14/5579
Box 5494, 185/14a/7090

National Archives, Finland (NAF)
Russian Military Documents (Venalasiet Sotilasasiakirjat, VESA), folders 1628, 3299, 3453, 4518, 4696, 5022—Prikazy i prikazaniia po voiskam gvardii i Peterburgskogo voennogo okruga, 1905, 1906, 1908, 1914.

National Archives, United Kingdom (NAUK)
CAB 37/124/54
FCO 371/2095-96
FCO 371/2444-52
PRO 30/57/67
PRO 30/57/84
WO 106/1099
Intelligence Division, War Office. *Foreign Manœuvres, 1893: Extracts from the Reports of Various Officers on the Manœuvres in Austria, France, Germany, Italy, Russia and Servia*. London: War Office, 1894—WO 33/54.

Intelligence Division, War Office. *Foreign Manœuvres, 1898: Extracts from the Reports of Various Officers on the Manœuvres in Austria-Hungary, Bulgaria, France, Germany, Holland, Rumania, Russia, Servia and Switzerland.* London: War Office, 1899—WO 33/2819.

Intelligence Division, War Office. *Foreign Manœuvres, 1899: Extracts from the Reports of Various Officers on the Manœuvres in Austria-Hungary, Denmark, Germany, Holland, Italy, Russia and Switzerland.* London: War Office, 1900—WO 33/2821

Intelligence Division, War Office. *Foreign Manœuvres, 1900: Extracts from the Reports of Various Officers on the Manœuvres in Austria-Hungary, Belgium, France, Germany, Holland, Italy, Russia and Switzerland.* London: War Office, 1901—WO 33/2822

Intelligence Division, War Office. *Extracts from the Reports of Various Officers on the Manœuvres in Austria-Hungary, France, Germany, Holland, Roumania, Russia, Servia and Switerland, 1901.* London: War Office, 1902—WO 106/6165.

Rossiiskii Gosudarstvennyi Istoricheskii Arkhiv (RGIA)

Fond 696—Tolstoy, D. I.
Fond 1276—Sovet Ministrov
Fond 1571—Krivoshein, A. V.
Fond 1614—Adleburg, A. V.
Fond R-1656—von Raukh, G. O.

Rossiiskii Gosudarstvennyi Voenno-Istoricheskii Arkhiv (RGVIA)

Fond 276—Orlov, V. N.
Fond 549—Imperatorskaia nikolaevskaia voennaia akademiia
Fond 830—Sovet gosudarstvennoi oboronoi
Fond 2003—Stavka
Fond 2005—Grazhdanskaia kantseliariia shtaba Verkhovnogo Glavnokomanduiushchego
Fond 2100—Shtab glavnokomanduiushchego voiskami kavkazskogo fronta.

Service Historique de la Défense, Château de Vincennes (SHD)

1 N 17
5 N 74
7 N 757
7 N 1470–74, 1477, 1478, 1480, 1484, 1485, 1487, 1537, 1545, 1547, 1548

Newspapers/Magazines

Letopis' Voiny
New York Times
Novoe Vremia
Poslednie Novosti
Le Réveil Antibes
Tanamedrové Azri
Vozrozhdenie

Diaries and Memoirs

Alexander, Grand Duke of Russia. *Once a Grand Duke.* New York: Cosmopolitan Book Corporation, 1932.

Bezobrazov, Vladimir Mikhailovich. *Diary of the Commander of the Russian Imperial Guard, 1914*–1917. Boynton Beach, FL: Dramco, 1994.

Bogdanovich, A. V. *Tri poslednikh samoderzhtsa.* Moscow: Novosti, 1990.

Bonch-Bruyevich, M. D. *From Tsarist General to Red Army Commander.* Moscow: Progress, 1966.

Brusilov, A. A. *A Soldier's Notebook 1914–1918.* London: Macmillan, 1930.

Bubnov, A. *V tsarskoi stavke. Vospominaniia admirala Bubnova.* New York: Izdatel'stvo imeni Chekhova, 1955.

Buchanan, Sir George. *My Mission to Russia and Other Diplomatic Memories.* Vols. 1 and II. London: Cassell, 1923.

Cantacuzène, Princess, Countess Spéransky, née Grant. *My Life Here and There.* New York: Charles Scribner's Sons, 1921.

———. *Revolutionary Days: Recollections of Romanoffs and Bolsheviki, 1914–1917.* Boston: Small, Maynard and Company, 1919.

Cyril, Grand Duke. *My Life in Russia's Service—Then and Now.* London: Selwyn and Blount, 1939.

Denikin, A. I. *Put' russkogo ofitsera.* Moscow: Vagrius, 2002.

The Diary of Princess Zenaida Nikolaevna Yusupov, January 1–April 25, 1919. Unpublished translation by Christine H. Galitzine. Private collection.

"Dnevnik A. N. Kuropatkina." *Krasnyi Arkhiv* 2 (1922): 5–112.

"Dnevnik G. O. Raukha." *Krasnyi Arkhiv* 19 (1926): 83–109.

Dnevnik imperatora Nikolaia II, 1890–1906 gg. Berlin: Slovo, 1923.

Dnevniki imperatritsy Marii Fedorovny (1914–1920, 1923 goda). Moscow: Vagrius, 2005.

Dzhunkovskii, V. F. *Vospominaniia*, 2 vols. Moscow: Izdatel'stvo imeni Sabashnikovykh, 1997.

Eliseev, F. I. *Kazaki na kavkazskom fronte, 1914–1917: zapiski polkovnika Kubanskogo kazach'ego voiska v trinadtsati broshiurakh-tetradiakh.* Moscow: Voennoe Izdatel'stvo, 2001.

Emel'ianov, A. G. *Persidskii front.* Berlin: Gamaiun, 1923.

Epanchin, N. A. *Na sluzhbe trekh imperatorov.* Moscow: Nashe Nasledie, 1996.

Gavriil Konstantinovich, Velikii Kniaz'. *V mramornom dvortse.* Moscow: Zakharov, 2001.

Gourko, General Basil. *Memories and Impressions of War and Revolution in Russia, 1914–1917.* London: John Murray, 1918.

Hanbury-Williams, Sir John. *The Emperor Nicholas II as I Knew Him.* London: Arthur L. Humphreys, 1922.

Ignat'ev, A. A. *50 let v stroiu.* Moscow: Sovetskii Pisatel', 1952.

Joffre, J. *Mémoires du Maréchal Joffre.* Paris: Plon, 1932.

Kalmykow, Andrew D. *Memoirs of a Russian Diplomat: Outposts of the Empire, 1893–1917.* New Haven and London: Yale University Press, 1971.

Khatissian [Khatisov], Alexander. "The Memoirs of a Mayor." *Armenian Review* 2, no. 3 (1949): 40–47; 2, no. 4 (1949): 104–16; 3, no. 1 (1950): 87–106; 3, no. 2 (1950): 78–92; 3, no. 3 (1950): 97–115; 3, no. 4 (1950): 106–13.

Kireev, A. A. *Dnevnik, 1905–1910.* Moscow: Rosspen, 2010.

Knox, Alfred W. F. *With the Russian Army, 1914–1917.* New York: Arno Press, 1971.

Kondzerovskii, P. K. *V stavke verkhovnogo*. Paris: Voennaia Byl', 1967.

Kulikovsky, Paul, Karen Roth-Nicholls, and Sue Woolmans, eds. *25 Chapters of My Life: Grand Duchess Olga Alexandrovna of Russia*. Kinloss: Librario, 2009.

Kurlov, P. G. *Gibel' imperatorskoi Rossii: vospominaniia*. Moscow: Zakharov, 2002.

Kyasht, Lydia. *Romantic Recollections*. Binsted: Noverre Press, 2010.

Lemke, M. K. *250 dnei v tsarskoi stavke (25 sent. 1915–2 iiulia 1916)*. Petersburg: Gosudarstvennoe Izdatel'stvo, 1920.

Littauer, Vladimir S. *Russian Hussar: A Story of the Imperial Cavalry, 1911–1920*. Shippensburg, PA: White Mane, 1993.

Ludendorff, Erich von. *Ludendorff's Own Story, August 1914–November 1918*. Vol. 1. Freeport, NY: Books for Libraries Press, 1971.

Lukomskii, A. S. *Vospominaniia*. Berlin: Otto Kirchner, 1922.

Macnaughtan, S. *My War Experiences in Two Continents*. London: John Murray, 1919.

Maylunas, Andrei, and Sergei Mironenko, eds. *A Lifelong Passion: Nicholas and Alexandra: Their Own Story*. London: Weidenfeld and Nicolson, 1996.

McCormick, Robert R. *With the Russian Army: Being the Experiences of a National Guardsman*. New York: Macmillan, 1915.

The Memoirs of General Prince Felix Felixovich Yusupov Count Sumarov-Elston. Unpublished translation by Christine H. Galitzine. Private collection.

Miliukov, Paul. *Political Memoirs, 1915–1917*. Ann Arbor: University of Michigan Press, 1967.

Mosolov, A. A. *Pri dvore poslednego imperatora: zapiski nachal'nika kantseliarii ministra dvora*. Saint Petersburg: Nauka, 1992.

Nadejda. *Once I Had a Home: The Diary and Narrative of Nadejda Lady of Honour to the Imperial Majesties the Late Empress Alexandra Feodorovna and the Empress Maria Feodorovna of Russia*. London: Duckworth, 1926.

Paléologue, Maurice. *An Ambassador's Memoirs*. Vols. 1, 2. New York: George H. Doran, 1924.

Pares, Bernard. *Day by Day with the Russian Army, 1914–1915*. Boston and New York: Houghton Mifflin, 1915.

Pfeil, Richard Graf von. *Experiences of a Prussian Officer in the Russian Service during the Turkish War of 1877–78*. London: Edward Stanford, 1893.

Polivanov, A. A. *Iz dnevnikov i vospominanii po dolzhnosti voennogo ministra i ego pomoshchika, 1907–1916 g*. Moscow: Vysshii Voennyi Redaktsionnyi Sovet, 1924.

Polovtsoff, P. A. *Glory and Downfall: Reminiscences of a Russian General Staff Officer*. London: G. Bell and Sons, 1935.

Pridham, Vice-Admiral Sir Francis. *Close of a Dynasty*. London: Allan Wingate, 1956.

Rediger, A. F. *Istoriia moei zhizni: vospominaniia voennogo ministra*. 2 vols. Moscow: Kanon-Press-Ts, 1999.

Rodzianko, M. V. *The Reign of Rasputin: An Empire's Collapse*. Gulf Breeze, FL: Academic International Press, 1973.

Romanow, Prinz Roman. *Am Hof des letzten Zaren*. Munich: Piper, 1991.

Samoilo, A. A. *Dve zhizni*. Moscow: Voennoe Izdatel'stvo Ministerstva Oborony Soiuza SSR, 1958.

Sazonov, Sergei. *Fateful Years, 1909–1916: The Reminiscences of Sergei Sazonov*. London: Jonathan Cape, 1928.

Shavel'skii, Georgii. *Vospominaniia poslednego protopresvitera russkoi armii i flota*. 2 vols.

New York: Izdatel'stvo imeni Chekhova, 1954.
Spiridovich, A. K. *Les dernières années de la cour de Tzarskoie-Selo.* 2 vols. Paris: Payot, 1928.
———. *Velikaia voina i fevral'skaia revoliutsiia.* New York: Vseslavianskoe Izdatel'stvo, 1960.
Sukhomlinov, V. *Vospominaniia.* Moscow: Gosudarstvennoe Izdatel'stvo, 1926.
Trubetskoi, Vladimir Sergeevich. *A Russian Prince in the Soviet State: Hunting Stories, Letters from Exile, and Military Memoirs.* Evanston: Northwestern University Press, 2006.
Vasili, Count Paul. *Behind the Veil at the Russian Court.* London: Cassell, 1914.
Voeikov, V. N. *S tsarem i bez tsaria: Vospominaniia poslednego dvortsovogo komendanta gosudaria imperatora Nikolaia II.* Helsingfors: N.p., 1936.
Voennyi dnevnik velikogo kniazia Andreia Vladimirovicha Romanova (1914–1917). Moscow: Izdatel'stvo im. Sabashnikovykh, 2008.
Washburn, Stanley. *Field Notes from the Russian Front.* London: Andrew Melrose, 1915.
Witte, Sergei. *The Memoirs of Count Witte.* Translated and edited by Sidney Harcave. Armonk: M. E. Sharpe, 1990.
Youssoupoff, Prince Felix. *Lost Splendour: The Amazing Memoirs of the Man Who Killed Rasputin.* New York: Helen Marx, 2003.

Collections of Documents

Adamova, E. A., ed. *Razdel Aziatskoi Turtsii: po sekretnym dokumentam b. Ministerstva inostrannykh del.* Moscow: Izdanie Litizdata NKID, 1924.
Bing, Edward J., ed. *The Letters of Tsar Nicholas and Empress Marie.* London: Ivor Nicholas and Watson, 1937.
Bortnevskii, V. G. "'Stavia Rodinu vyshe lits' (Iz arkhiva generala I.G. Barbovicha)." *Russkoe Proshloe* 6 (1994): 112–47.
Chernyavsky, Michael, ed. *Prologue to Revolution: Notes of A. N. Iakhontov on the Secret Meetings of the Council of Ministers, 1915.* Englewood Cliffs, NJ: Prentice-Hall, 1967.
General'nyi shtab Krasnoi Armii. *Manevrennyi period 1915 goda: Gorlitskaia operatsiia.* Moscow: Gosudarstvennoe voennoe izdatel'stvo, 1941.
General'nyi shtab RKKA. *Manevrennyi period 1914 goda: Lodzinskaia operatsiia.* Moscow: Gosudarstvennoe voennoe izdatel'stvo, 1936.
———. *Manevrennyi period 1914 goda: Varshavsko-Ivangorodskaia operatsiia.* Moscow: Gosudarstvennoe voennoe izdatel'stvo, 1938.
———. *Manevrennyi period 1914 goda: Vostochno-prusskaia operatsiia.* Moscow: Gosudarstvennoe voennoe izdatel'stvo, 1939.
Golder, Frank Alfred, ed. *Documents of Russian History, 1914–1917.* Gloucester, MA: Peter Smith, 1964.
"Iz istorii bor'by v verkhakh nakanune fevral'skoi revoliutsii." *Russkoe Proshloe* 6 (1996): 148–80.
Krasnov, P. *Otrkytoe pis'mo kazakam.* No. 4, 6/19 November 1923. Paris: Imprimerie Presse Franco-Russe, 1923.
The Letters of the Tsar to the Tsaritsa, 1914–1917. London: John Lane the Bodley Head Ltd., 1929.
Letters of the Tsaritsa to the Tsar, 1914–1916. London: Duckworth, 1923.
Lettres des Grands-Ducs à Nicolas II. Paris: Payot, 1926.

Nicolas Mikhailovitch, Grand Duc. *La fin du tsarisme: lettres inédites à Frédéric Masson (1914–1918)*. Paris: Payot, 1968.
"Perepiska V. A. Sukhomlinova s N. N. Ianushkevichem." *Krasnyi Arkhiv* 1 (1922): 209–22; 2 (1922): 130–75; 3 (1923): 29–74.
Rossiiskii Zarubezhnyi S"ezd 1926: dokumenty i materialy. Moscow: Russkii Put', 2006.
"Stavka i ministerstvo inostrannykh del." *Krasnyi Arkhiv* 26 (1928): 1–50.
"Stavka i ministerstvo inostrannykh del: prodolzhenie." *Krasnyi Arkhiv* 27 (1928): 3–57.
"Tsarskosel'skie soveshchaniia, neizdannye protokoly soveshchaniia v aprele 1906 goda, pod predsedatel'stvom byvshego imperatora po peresmotru osnovnykh zakonov, s vvedeniem V. V. Vedovozova." *Byloe* 4 (1917): 183-245.
"Tsarskosel'skie soveshchaniia. Protokoly sekretnogo soveshchaniia po voprosu o rasshireniia izbiratel'nogo prava." *Byloe* 3 (1917): 217-65.
Ustav stroevykh kavaleriiskoi sluzhboi, 1896. St. Petersburg: B. Berezovsky, 1905.
Vysochaishe utverzhdennyi tseremonial o sviatom kreshchenii ego imperatorskogo vysochestva gosudaria velikogo kniazia Nikolaia Nikolaevicha. Private collection, France.

Unpublished Dissertations

Brown, Stephen. "The First Cavalry Army in the Russian Civil War, 1918–1920." PhD diss., University of Wollongong, 1990.
Graf, Daniel W. "The Rule of the Generals: Military Government in Western Russia, 1914–1915." PhD diss., University of Nebraska, 1972.
Walz, John David. "State Defense and Russian Politics under the Last Tsar." PhD diss., Syracuse University, 1967.

Books and Articles

Airapetov, O. R. *Generaly, liberaly i predprinimateli: rabota na front i na revoliutsiiu [1907–1917]*. Moscow: Tri Kvadrata, 2003.
Airapetov, O. R., ed. *Posledniaia voina imperatorskoi Rossii*. Moscow: Tri Kvadrata, 2002.
Allen, W. E. D., and Paul Muratoff. *Caucasian Battlefields: A History of the Wars on the Turco-Caucasian Border, 1828–1921*. Cambridge: Cambridge University Press, 1953.
Allsen, Thomas T. *The Royal Hunt in Eurasian History*. Philadelphia: University of Pennsylvania Press, 2006.
Anastasii, Arkhiepiskop. *Nravstvennyi oblik v Boze pochivshego Velikogo Kniazia Nikolaia Nikolaevicha*. Paris: Rapid—Imprimerie, 1929.
Annenkova, E. A., and Iu. P. Golikov. *Printsy Ol'denburgskie v Peterburge*. Saint Petersburg: Rostok, 2004.
———. *Russkie Ol'denburgskie i ikh dvortsy*. Saint Petersburg: Almaz, 1997.
Aratiunian, A. O. *Kavkazskii front, 1914–1917*. Yerevan: Aiastan, 1971.
Ascher, Abraham. P. A. *The Revolution of 1905: Russia in Disarray*. Stanford University Press, 1988.
———. *Stolypin: The Search for Stability in Late Imperial Russia*. Stanford University Press, 2001.
"Asiaticus." *Reconnaissance in the Russo-Japanese War*. London: Hugh Rees, 1908.
Atabaki, Touraj, ed. *Iran and the First World War: Battleground of the Great Powers*. New York: I. B. Tauris, 2006.

Badsey, Stephen. *Doctrine and Reform in the British Cavalry, 1880–1918*. Aldershot: Ashgate, 2008.
Bakhturina, A. Iu. *Okrainy rossiiskoi imperii: gosudarstvennaia i natsional'naia politika v gody pervoi mirovoi voiny (1914–1917 gg.)*. Moscow: Rosspen, 2004.
———. *Politika Rossiiskoi imperii v vostochnoi Galitsii v gody pervoi mirovoi voiny*. Moscow: AIRO-XX, 2000.
———. "Vozzvanie k poliakam 1 avgusta 1914 g. i ego avtory." *Voprosy Istorii* 8 (1998): 132–36.
Barnwell, R. Grant. *The Russo-Turkish War*. Philadelphia: John E. Potter, 1877.
Bascomb, Neal. *Red Mutiny: Eleven Fateful Days on the Battleship Potemkin*. Boston: Houghton Mifflin, 2007.
Bobroff, Ronald Park. *Roads to Glory: Late Imperial Russia and the Turkish Straits*. London and New York: I. B. Tauris, 2006.
Bortnevskii, V. G. *Zagadki smerti generala Vrangelia*. St. Petersburg: Biblioteka zhurnala "Novyi Chasovoi," 1996.
Bou, Jean. "Cavalry, Firepower, and Swords: The Australian Light Horse and the Tactical Lessons of Cavalry Operations in Palestine, 1916–1918." *Journal of Military History* 71, no. 1 (2007): 99–125.
Boulay, Cyrille. *La France des Romanov: De la villégiature à l'exil*. Saint-Amand-Montrand: Perrin, 2010.
Brook-Shepherd, Gordon. *Archduke of Sarajevo: The Romance and Tragedy of Franz Ferdinand of Austria*. Boston: Little, Brown and Company, 1984.
Bunin, Ivan. *The Life of Arseniev: Youth*. Evanston: Northwestern University Press, 1994.
Burbank, Jane, Mark von Hagen, and Anatolyi Remnev, eds. *Russian Empire: Space, People, Power, 1700–1930*. Bloomington: Indiana University Press, 2007.
Bushnell, John. *Mutiny amid Repression: Russian Soldiers in the Revolution of 1905–1906*. Bloomington: Indiana University Press, 1985.
Buxhoeveden, Baroness Sophie. *The Life and Tragedy of Alexandra Feodorovna Empress of Russia*. London: Longmans, Green and Company, 1930.
Chavchavadze, David. *The Grand Dukes*. New York: Atlantic International, 1990.
Clark, Christopher. *The Sleepwalkers: How Europe Went to War in 1914*. New York: Harper Collins, 2013.
Cockfield, Jamie H. *White Crow: The Life and Times of the Grand Duke Nicholas Mikhailovich Romanov, 1859–1919*. Westport, CT: Praeger, 2002.
Connaughton, R. M. *The War of the Rising Sun and the Tumbling Bear: A Military History of the Russo-Japanese War 1904–5*. London: Routledge, 1991.
Crawford, Rosemary, and Donald Crawford. *Michael and Natasha: The Life and Love of the Last Tsar of Russia*. London: Weidenfeld and Nicolson, 1997.
Danilov, Iu. N. *Rossiia v mirovoi voine 1914–1915 gg*. Berlin: Slovo, 1924.
———. *Velikii Kniaz' Nikolai Nikolaevich*. Paris: Imprimerie de Navarre, 1930.
Danilov, O. Iu. *Prolog "Velikoi voiny," 1904–1914 gg. Kto i kak vtiagival Rossiiu v mirovoi konflikt*. Moscow: Pokolenie, 2010.
Davatz, V. Kh. *Fünf Sturmjahre mit General Wrangel*. Berlin: Verlag für Kulturpolitik, 1927.
Davies, Colonel R. R. (Dicky). "Helmuth von Moltke and the Prussian-German Development of a Decentralised Style of Command: Metz and Sedan 1870." *Defence Studies* 5, no. 1 (2005): 83–95.

De Groot, Gerard J. "Educated Soldier or Cavalry Officer? Contradictions in the Pre-1914 Career of Douglas Haig." *War & Society* 4, no. 2 (1986): 51–69.

DiNardo, Richard L. *Breakthrough: The Gorlice-Tarnow Campaign, 1915*. Santa Barbara: Praeger, 2010.

Engelstein, Laura. "'A Belgium of Our Own': The Sack of Russian Kalisz, August 1914." *Kritika: Explorations in Russian and Eurasian History* 10, no. 3 (2009): 441–73.

Epauchin, Colonel. *Operations of General Gurko's Advance Guard in 1877*. London: Kegan Paul, Trench, Trübner and Company, 1900.

Figes, Orlando. *Natasha's Dance: A Cultural History of Russia*. London: Allen Lane, 2002.

———. *A People's Tragedy: The Russian Revolution 1891–1924*. London: Jonathan Cape, 1996.

Florinsky, Michael T. "A Page of Diplomatic History: Russian Military Leaders and the Problem of Constantinople during the War." *Political Science Quarterly* 44, no. 1 (1929): 108–15.

Forbes, Archibald. *Czar and Sultan: The Adventures of a British Lad in the Russo-Turkish War of 1877–78*. New York: Charles Scribner's Sons, 1894.

Ford, Roger. *Eden to Armageddon: World War I in the Middle East*. New York: Pegasus, 2010.

Fuller, William C. *Civil-Military Conflict in Imperial Russia, 1881–1914*. Princeton University Press, 1985.

———. *The Foe Within: Fantasies of Treason and the End of Imperial Russia*. Ithaca: Cornell University Press, 2006.

———. *Strategy and Power in Russia, 1600–1914*. New York: The Free Press, 1992.

Galitzine, George. "Charm of the Borzois." *Country Life*, November 16, 1989, 106. Reprinted in *The Princes Galitzine. Before 1917 … and Afterwards*, 514. Washington, DC: Galitzine Books, 2002.

Gatrell, Peter. *A Whole Empire Walking: Refugees in Russia during World War I*. Bloomington and Indianapolis: Indiana University Press, 1999.

Gayraud, Didier. *Belles demeures en Riviera, 1835–1930*. Nice: Gilleta. Nice-matin, 2005.

General Kutepov: sbornik statei. Paris: Izdanie komiteta imeni Generala Kutepova, 1934.

Glad, John. *Russia Abroad: Writers, History, Politics*. Washington, DC and Tenafly: Hermitage and Birchbark Press, 1999.

Glinoetskii, N. P. *Istoricheskii ocherk Nikolaevskoi Akademii General'nogo Shtaba*. St. Petersburg: Tipografiia shtaba voisk gvardii i Peterburgskogo voennogo okruga, 1882.

Golovin, N. "The Great Battle of Galicia (1914): A Study in Strategy." *Slavonic Review* 5, no. 13 (1926): 25–47.

Golovine, Nicholas N. *The Russian Army in the World War*. New Haven: Yale University Press, 1931.

———. *The Russian Campaign of 1914: The Beginning of the War and Operations in East Prussia*. Fort Leavenworth: The Command and General Staff School Press, 1933.

Graf, Daniel W. "Military Rule behind the Russian Front, 1914–1917: The Political Ramifications." *Jahrbücher für Geschichte Osteuropas* 22, no. 3 (1974): 390–411.

Greenhalgh, Elizabeth. *Foch in Command: The Forging of a First World War General*. Cambridge: Cambridge University Press, 2011.

Gurko, V. I. *Features and Figures of the Past: Government and Opinion in the Reign of Nicholas II*. Stanford University Press, 1939.

Hagen, Mark von. *War in a European Borderland: Occupations and Occupation Plans in*

Galicia and Ukraine, 1914–1918. Seattle: University of Washington Press, 2007.

Harcave, Sidney. *The Russian Revolution of 1905*. London: Collier, 1964.

Harris, J. P. *Douglas Haig and the First World War*. Cambridge: Cambridge University Press, 2008.

Heretz, Leonid. *Russia on the Eve of Modernity: Popular Religion and Traditional Culture under the Last Tsar*. Cambridge: Cambridge University Press, 2008.

Hoflin, Lyn Snyder. "Russkaia psovaia borzaia." <http://www.secrethavenkennel.com/resources/RussiaHoflin.pdf>.

Holquist, Peter. *Making Wars, Forging Revolution: Russia's Continuum of Crisis, 1914–1921*. Cambridge, MA: Harvard University Press, 2002.

———. "The Politics and Practice of the Russian Occupation of Armenia, 1915–February 1917." In *A Question of Genocide: Armenians and Turks at the End of the Ottoman Empire*, ed. Ronald Grigor Suny et al., 151–74. Oxford University Press, 2011.

———. "The Role of Personality in the First (1914–1915) Russian Occupation of Galicia and Bukovina." In *Anti-Jewish Violence: Rethinking the Pogrom in East European History*, ed. Jonathan Dekel-Chen et al., 52–73. Bloomington and Indianapolis: Indiana University Press, 2011.

Iz istorii rossiiskoi emigratsii: sbornik nauchnykh statei. St. Petersburg: Tret'iaia Rossiia, 1992.

Jahn, Hubertus F. *Patriotic Culture in Russia during World War I*. Ithaca and London: Cornell University Press, 1995.

Johnson, Douglas W. "Geographic Notes on the War. Part I." *Bulletin of the American Geographical Society* 47, no. 5 (1915): 358–61.

Kappeler, Andreas. *The Russian Empire: A Multiethnic History*. Harlow: Pearson, 2001.

Kenez, Peter. "A Profile of the Pre-Revolutionary Officer Corps." *California Slavic Studies* 7 (1973): 121–58.

Kersnovskii, A. A. *Istoriia russkoi armii*. Belgrade: Izdanie "Tsarskogo Vestnika," 1935.

King, Greg. *The Court of the Last Tsar: Pomp, Power, and Pageantry in the Reign of Nicholas II*. Hoboken: John Wiley and Sons, 2006.

Kiste, John van der, and Coryne Hall. *Once a Grand Duchess: Xenia, Sister of Nicholas II*. Stroud: Sutton, 2002.

Kizenko, Nadieszda. *A Prodigal Saint: Father John of Kronstadt and the Russian People*. University Park: Pennsylvania State University Press, 2003.

Knox, Alfred. "The Grand Duke Nicholas." *Slavonic and East European Review* 7, no. 21 (1929): 535–39.

Kolonitskii, Boris. *"Tragicheskaia erotika:" obrazy imperatorskoi sem'i v gody pervoi mirovoi voiny*. St. Petersburg: Novoe Literaturnoe Obozrenie, 2010.

Kravchenko, N. "Psovaia okhota." *Stolitsa i usad'ba* 2 (1914): 3–7.

Lang, David Marshall. *A Modern History of Georgia*. London: Weidenfeld and Nicolson, 1962.

Lieven, D. C. B. *Russia and the Origins of the First World War*. London: Macmillan, 1983.

Lieven, Dominic, ed. *The Cambridge History of Russia, Volume II 1689–1917*. Cambridge: Cambridge University Press, 2006.

Lincoln, W. Bruce. *Passage through Armageddon: The Russians in War and Revolution, 1914–1918*. New York: Simon and Schuster, 1986.

Lohr, Eric. *Nationalizing the Russian Empire: The Campaign against Enemy Aliens during World War I*. Cambridge, MA: Harvard University Press, 2003.

Majd, Mohammad Gholi. *Persia in World War I and Its Conquest by Great Britain*. Lanham: University Press of America, 2003.

Mal'kov, V. L., ed. *Pervaia mirovaia voina: prolog XX veka*. Moscow: Nauka, 1998.

Mannherz, Julia. *Modern Occultism in Late Imperial Russia*. DeKalb: Northern Illinois University Press, 2012.

Marshall, Alex. *The Russian General Staff and Asia, 1800–1917*. London: Routledge, 2006.

Maslovskii, E. V. *Mirovaia voina na Kavkazskom fronte, 1914–1917 gg.* Paris: Vozrozhdenie, 1933.

Massie, Robert K. *Nicholas and Alexandra*. New York: Dell, 1967.

Mayzel, Matitiahu. "The Formation of the Russian General Staff, 1880–1917: A Social Study." *Cahiers du Monde Russe et Soviétique* 16 (1975): 297–321.

McDonald, David MacLaren. *United Government and Foreign Policy in Russia, 1900–1914*. Cambridge, MA: Harvard University Press, 1992.

McMeekin, Sean. *The Berlin-Baghdad Express: The Ottoman Empire and Germany's Bid for World Power*. Cambridge, MA: The Belknap Press, 2010.

———. *The Russian Origins of the First World War*. Cambridge, MA: The Belknap Press, 2011.

Mehlinger, Howard D., and John M. Thompson. *Count Witte and the Tsarist Government in the 1905 Revolution*. Bloomington: Indiana University Press, 1972.

Mel'gunov, S. *Na putiakh k dvortsovomu perevorotu*. Paris: Rodnik, n.d..

Mélot, Henry. *La Mission du Général Pau aux Balkans et en Russie tzariste, 9 février–11 avril 1915*. Paris: Payot, 1931.

Menning, Bruce W. *Bayonets before Bullets: The Imperial Russian Army, 1861–1914*. Bloomington and Indianapolis: Indiana University Press, 1992.

———. "War Planning and Initial Operations in the Russian Context." In *War Planning 1914*, ed. Richard F. Hamilton and Holger H. Herwig, 80–142. Cambridge: Cambridge University Press, 2010.

Miroshnikov, L. I. *Iran in World War I*. Moscow: Oriental Literature Publishing House, 1963.

Mostashari, Firouzeh. *On the Religious Frontier: Tsarist Russia and Islam in the Caucasus*. London and New York: I. B. Tauris, 2006.

Nakhapetov, B. A. *Vrachebnye tainy doma Romanovykh*. Moscow: Veche, 2007.

Nazarov, M. V. *Missiia russkoi emigratsii*. Stavropol: Kavkazskii Krai, 1992.

Os'kin, Maksim. *Krakh konnogo blitskriga: kavaleriia v pervoi mirovoi voine*. Moscow: Eksmo, 2009.

Otchet o zaniatiiakh nikolaevskoi akademii general'nogo shtaba za uchebnyi, 1875–1876 god. St. Petersburg: Tipografiia tovarishchestva "Obshchestvennaia Pol'za," 1876.

Pares, Bernard. *The Fall of the Russian Monarchy: A Study of the Evidence*. London: Jonathan Cape, 1939.

Perrins, Michael. "The Council for State Defence, 1905–1909: A Study in Russian Bureaucratic Politics." *Slavonic and East European Review* 58, no. 3 (1980): 370–98.

Perry, John Curtis, and Constantine Pleshakov. *The Flight of the Romanovs: A Family Saga*. New York: Basic Books, 1999.

Persson, Gudrun. *Learning from Foreign Wars: Russian Military Thinking, 1859–1873*. Solihull: Helion, 2010.

Petrova, E. E., and K. O. Bitiukov. *Velikokniazheskaia oppozitsiia v Rossii, 1915–1917 gg.* St. Petersburg: Asterion, 2009.

Petrovsky-Shtern, Yohanan. *Jews in the Russian Army, 1827–1917: Drafted into Modernity.* Cambridge: Cambridge University Press, 2009.

Phillips, Gervase. "Scapegoat Arm: Twentieth-Century Cavalry in Anglophone Historiography." *Journal of Military History* 71, no. 1 (2007): 37–74.

———. "'Who Shall Say That the Days of Cavalry Are Over?' The Revival of the Mounted Army in Europe, 1853–1914." *War in History* 18, no. 1 (2011): 5–32.

Pipes, Richard. *Struve: Liberal on the Right, 1905–1944.* Cambridge, MA: Harvard University Press, 1980.

Pospielovsky, Dimitry. *The Russian Church under the Soviet Regime, 1917–1982.* Vol. 1. Crestwood: St. Vladimir's Seminary Press, 1984.

Prusin, Alexander Victor. *Nationalizing a Borderland: War, Ethnicity, and Anti-Jewish Violence in East Galicia, 1914–1920.* Tuscaloosa: University of Alabama Press, 2005.

Radzinsky, Edvard. *The Rasputin File.* New York: Anchor, 2000.

Raeff, Marc. *Russia Abroad: A Cultural History of the Russian Emigration, 1919–1941.* New York and Oxford University Press, 1990.

Raun, Toivo U. "The Revolution of 1905 in the Baltic Provinces and Finland." *Slavic Review* 43, no. 3 (1984): 453–67.

Ray, Oliver. "The Imperial Russian Army Officer." *Political Science Quarterly* 76, no. 4 (1961): 576–92.

Reyfman, Irina. *Ritualized Violence Russian Style: The Duel in Russian Culture and Literature.* Stanford University Press, 1999.

Reynolds, Michael A. *Shattering Empires: The Clash and Collapse of the Ottoman and Russian Empires, 1908–1918.* Cambridge: Cambridge University Press, 2011.

Rich, David Allan. *The Tsar's Colonels: Professionalism, Strategy, and Subversion in Late Imperial Russia.* Cambridge, MA: Harvard University Press, 1998.

Riedi, Eliza. "Brains or Polo? Equestrian Sport, Army Reform and the Gentlemanly Officer Tradition, 1900–1914." *Journal of the Society for Army Historical Research* 84 (2006): 236–53.

Robinson, Paul. "Courts of Honour in the Late Imperial Russian Army." *Slavonic and East European Review* 84, no. 4 (2006): 708–28.

———. *The White Russian Army in Exile, 1920–1941.* Oxford: Clarendon Press, 2002.

Rostunov, I. I. *Russkii front pervoi mirovoi voiny.* Moscow: Nauka, 1976.

Rutherford, Ward. *The Ally: The Russian Army in World War I.* London: Gordon and Cremonesi, 1977.

Rybakova, Iuliia Petrovna. "In the Aleksandrinskii Theater." *Russian Studies in History* 31, no. 3 (1992–1993): 50–86.

Sanborn, Joshua A. *Drafting the Russian Nation: Military Conscription, Total War, and Mass Politics, 1905–1925.* DeKalb: Northern Illinois University Press, 2003.

———. "Unsettling the Empire: Violent Migrations and Social Disaster in Russia during World War I." *Journal of Modern History* 77, no. 2 (2005): 290–324.

Schem, Alexander Jacob. *The War in the East: An Illustrated History of the Conflict between Russia and Turkey with a Review of the Eastern Question.* New York: H. S. Goodspeed, 1878.

Schimmelpenninck van der Oye, David, and Bruce W. Menning, eds. *Reforming the Tsar's Army: Military Innovation in Imperial Russia from Peter the Great to the Revolution.* Cambridge: Cambridge University Press, 2004.

Sheffy, Yigal. "A Model Not to Follow: The European Armies and the Lessons of the War."

In *The Impact of the Russo-Japanese War*, ed. Rotem Kowner, 253–68. London: Routledge, 2007.
Shkarenkov, L. K. *Agoniia beloi emigratsii*. Moscow: Mysl', 1986.
Smele, Jonathan D., and Anthony Heywood, eds. *The Russian Revolution of 1905: Centenary Perspectives*. Abingdon: Routledge, 2005.
Smirnov, N. N., ed. *Rossiia i pervaia mirovaia voina (materialy mezhdunarodnogo nauchnogo kollokviuma)*. St. Petersburg: Izdatel'stvo "Dmitrii Bulanin," 1999.
Soboleva, Inna. *Velikie Knaz'ia doma Romanovykh*. St. Petersburg: Piter, 2010.
Sondhaus, Lawrence. *Franz Conrad von Hötzendorf: Architect of the Apocalypse*. Boston: Humanities Press, 2000.
Stanley, Francis. *St Petersburg to Plevna, Containing Interviews with Leading Russian Statesmen & Generals*. London: R. Bentley, 1878.
Steinberg, John W. *All the Tsar's Men: Russia's General Staff and the Fate of the Empire, 1898–1914*. Washington, DC: Woodrow Wilson Center Press, 2010.
Stieve, Friedrich. *Isvolsky and the World War*. Translated by E. W. Dickes. Freeport, NY: Books for Libraries Press, 1971.
Stone, Norman. *The Eastern Front, 1914–1917*. London: Hodder and Stoughton, 1975.
Strelianov, P. N. *Korpus Generala Baratova*. Moscow: N.p., 2002.
Sukhomlinov, V. *Velikii Kniaz' Nikolai Nikolaevich (mladshii)*. Berlin: Izdanie Avtora, 1925.
Suny, Ronald Grigor. *Looking toward Ararat: Armenia in Modern History*. Bloomington: Indiana University Press, 1993.
———. *The Making of the Georgian Nation*. Bloomington: Indiana University Press, 1988.
Taylor, Antony. "'Pig-Sticking Princes': Royal Hunting, Moral Outrage, and the Republican Opposition to Animal Abuse in Nineteenth- and Early Twentieth-Century Britain." *History* 89, no. 293 (2004): 30–48.
Terraine, John. *Douglas Haig: The Educated Soldier*. London: Leo Cooper, 1963.
Thomas, Joseph B. *Observations on Borzoi, Called in America Russian Wolfhounds*. Boston: Houghton Mifflin, 1912.
Tunstall, Graydon A. *Blood on the Snow: The Carpathian Winter War of 1915*. Lawrence: University of Kansas Press, 2010.
Turner, L. C. F. "The Russian Mobilization in 1914." *Journal of Contemporary History* 3, no. 1 (1968): 65–88.
Val'tsov, Dmitrii. *Psovaia okhota ego imperatorskogo vysochestva velikogo kniazia Nikolaia Nikolaevicha v s. Pershine tul'skoi gub., 1887–1912*. Saint Petersburg: Leshtukovskaia parovaia skoropechatnia P. O. Iablonskogo, 1913.
Vinogradov, N. "Pravda o svidanii bol'shevitskogo agenta Iakusheva-Fedorova s Velikim Kniazem Nikolaem Nikolaevichem." *Vozrozhdenie* 48 (December 1955): 109–18.
Voitsekhovskii, S. L. *Trest: vospominaniia i dokumenty*. London, Ontario: Zaria, 1974.
Vorob'eva, A. *Rossiiskie iunkera, 1864–1917: Istoriia voennykh uchilshch*. Moscow: Astrel', 2002.
Vorres, Ian. *The Last Grand-Duchess: Her Imperial Highness Grand-Duchess Olga Alexandrovna*. London: Finedawn, 1964.
Warner, Denis, and Peggy Warner. *The Tide at Sunrise: A History of the Russo-Japanese War, 1904–1905*. New York: Charterhouse, 1974.
Warwick, Christopher. *Ella: Princess, Saint and Martyr*. Chichester: Wiley, 2006.
Welch, Frances. *The Russian Court at Sea. The Last Days of a Great Dynasty: The Romanovs' Voyage into Exile*. London: Short, 2011.

Westwood, J. N. *Russia against Japan, 1904–05: A New Look at the Russo-Japanese War.* Houndmills: Macmillan, 1986.

White, James D. "The 1905 Revolution in Russia's Baltic Provinces." In *The Russian Revolution of 1905: Centenary Perspectives*, ed. Jonathan D. Smele and Anthony Heywood, 55–78. Abingdon: Routledge, 2005.

Wildman, Allan K. *The End of the Imperial Army: The Old Army and the Soldiers' Revolt (March–April 1917).* Princeton University Press, 1980.

Williams, R. C. *Culture in Exile: Russian Émigrés in Germany, 1881–1941.* Ithaca: Cornell University Press, 1971.

Wortman, Richard S. *Scenarios of Power: Myth and Ceremony in Russian Monarchy: From Alexander II to the Abdication of Nicholas II.* Princeton University Press, 2000.

Wrangel, Alexis. *The End of Chivalry: The Last Great Cavalry Battles, 1914–1918.* New York: Hippocrene, 1982.

———. *General Wrangel, 1878–1929: Russia's White Crusader.* London: Leo Cooper, 1987.

Wrangel, Count Gustav. *The Cavalry in the Russo-Japanese War: Lessons and Critical Considerations.* London: Hugh Rees, 1907.

Zaionchkovskii, A. M. *Pervaia mirovaia voina.* Saint Petersburg: Poligon, 2000.

Zaionchkovskii, P. A. *Samoderzhavie i russkaia armiia na rubezhe XIX–XX stoletii, 1881–1903.* Moscow: Mysl', 1973.

Zatvornitskii, N. M. *Fel'dmarshal Velikii Kniaz' Nikolai Nikolaevich Starshii.* St. Petersburg: Tipografiia T-va M. O. Vol'fa, 1911.

Zherve, V. V. *General-Fel'dmarshal Velikii Kniaz' Nikolai Nikolaevich starshii: istoricheskii ocherk ego zhizni i deiatel'nosti.* St. Petersburg: Tipografiia postavshchikov dvora ego imperatorskogo velichestva t-va M. O. Vol'fa, 1911.

Index